Madras
Rediscovered

A Historical Guide to Looking Around
(Supplemented with Tales of 'Once Upon a City')

S Muthiah

First published as *Madras Discovered* by EastWest, an imprint of Westland Publications Private Limited, in 1981

Published by EastWest, an imprint of Westland Books, a division of Nasadiya Technologies Private Limited, in 2023

No. 269/2B, First Floor, 'Irai Arul', Vimalraj Street, Nethaji Nagar, Alapakkam Main Road, Maduravoyal, Chennai 600095

ISBN: 9789357765855

10 9 8 7 6 5 4 3 2 1

Typeset by Mot Juste Communication Services Private Limited
Printed at Nutech Print Services, India

Contents

Preface

Totally revised and added to substantially

This is the eighth edition of *Madras Discovered/Madras Rediscovered* – and still it keeps growing. I have no doubt that if there are ninth and tenth editions, it will grow even more, for every day I learn something new about this city with a fascinating history.

In this edition, I have added a prologue at the request of many that I should be a little more specific about what there was in this part of the South, Tondaimandalam, before Fort St George was established and the Madras of today grew. That prologue, while recognising – as has been done over the years throughout the book - that many parts of Madras are hundreds of years older than the 1639 Madraspatnam, nevertheless stresses the point that the Madras/Chennai of today owes its growth to Fort St. George and that every single institution of today's Madras – except its temples – has its roots in the contributions made by the Establishment in Fort St. George.

In going through every word of the Seventh Edition, I found a few errors of fact, a few typos, and a few statements that needed updating. All that has been corrected in this edition, but more significant are the substantial additions. These owe much to my colleague Sriram V, my own findings for my weekly column in *The Hindu* – which in turn owes not a little to its readers – and the writings of many who've written about the people, places and institutions of the city for the Press or in commemorative books. Truly, this ever-growing historical guide to Madras/Chennai would not be what it is without the contributions just mentioned. May they too keep growing. And ensure Madras's contribution to Modern India is not forgotten.

S MUTHIAH

Chennai
May 2018

Preface to a completely revised, expanded and updated edition

This is the seventh edition of what began as *Madras Discovered* and grew into *Madras Rediscovered*. It has been nearly six years since the previous edition and in that period there have been two reprints with no changes, necessitated because I hadn't found the time to go through earlier editions with a fine-toothed comb, correct what was necessary, elaborate on much that had received only passing mention in the previous editions, add new material from what had kept piling up in my scrapbooks, and bring everything as up-to-date as possible. The first six months of 2013 gave me this opportunity, but what contributed greatly, thanks to a considerable degree to Sriram V, a friend, colleague and fellow-chronicler particularly clued in on what happened in 20th Century Madras and what exists in it today, agreeing to go through my first revision and then doing so meticulously, resulting in an even more comprehensive look at Madras, 'The First City of Modern India'. He has also made the Index a considerably more detailed, and more useful, one.

This is an edition that has also benefited much from my Monday column, *Madras Miscellany*, in *The Hindu*'s Madras and web edition MetroPlus supplements, the fortnightly I edit, *Madras Musings,* several books on Madras written by me and others during this period, and several correspondents in India and abroad who provide me with a wealth of material on Madras, reflecting the fact than not a few find the story of the city fascinating. This enthusiastic support led to a Tamil translation by Karthik Narayanan being published by Kizhakku in 2009 which did well enough to persuade the publishers to follow it up in 2014 with one of this revised, expanded and updated version.

That Tamil edition, however, led to a former Chief Minister of Tamil Nadu expressing displeasure with this chronicler, and the claim that this book was a 'history of Chennai', because his political record had not been highlighted. It is in this context that I emphasise here that this is NOT a history of the city; the subtitle to *Madras Rediscovered* makes it amply clear that it is "a historical guide to looking around", in other words, a guide looking at, in the historical context, those buildings and places that are memorials to the significant contributions Madras has made (to India) over what is now nearly 375 years. If anyone wants a history of the city, he should refer to the three volumes I have edited on *Madras that is Chennai: A 400-year record of the First City of Modern India.* In *Madras Rediscovered* the reader will find only stories about landmarks past and present. In fact, this Chief Minister will find himself and his mentor mentioned over half a dozen times each in it, NOT for their political leadership but for their talent and artistic contributions to Madras. Yes, there might be some history in these pages, but that is purely incidental to the focus on historical buildings and places.

With this comprehensive revision and expansion, I hope the next edition will not warrant much addition. But as I've always said, people like Sriram and I every day find something new in a city full of stories.

S MUTHIAH

Chennai
December 2013

Preface to a further revised and expanded edition

What you hold in your hands, a bulkier than ever look at Madras that is now Chennai, is in effect the sixth edition of *Madras Discovered*. What I find significant about this edition is that in the 26 years since the book was first published, this edition has been necessitated in the quickest time, ever, just three years. To me that's a happy sign that more and more people are getting involved with the story of Madras and the wealth of history the city is heir to. Perhaps my years of telling the story of this 'First City of Modern India' is at last having some effect.

This time, I've been able to go through the text of the previous edition with a fine-toothed comb and eliminate several factual errors as well as the mistakes a printer's devil in a hurry had made. No prizes, however, if you spot an error, particularly in a date; just give me the chance to correct it in the next edition.

I have also added considerably to the edition that came out in 2004 – and that in no small measure has been due to inputs of two others who have emerged as recorders of Madras History in recent years, Sriram V(enkatakrishnan) and K R A Narasiah. Then there has been all that information readers have been sending me for my column 'Madras Miscellany' in *The Hindu* and to *Madras Musings*. There have also been contributions made by several books on Madras that have been written in the intervening years, not the least being my own books on which primary research has been done, namely the stories of the Connemara Hotel (manuscript), the University of Madras and its *Senate House*, the Madras Port, Rm Alagappa Chettiar (manuscript) and Lt. Gen. Inderjit S Gill, PVSM, MC. The book has also benefitted from numerous souvenirs various people have sent me. Madras during the last three years has also boomed even more than when the boom began c 2000. Bits and pieces of that story too have been included. All this additional information will make this a rediscovery of the city for readers who have read any of the earlier editions of the book.

Meanwhile, the battle for heritage continues in the city. At moments there are heartening signs that heritage and history are being paid attention to, at other times they are treated callously. We, my readers and I, can only live in hope. But while we do so, let us remember that this book is only scratching the surface of the story of Madras's great contribution to modern India; there's much more to be unearthed and retailed and I hope my readers will contribute to that over the next few years as I continue my search.

S MUTHIAH

Chennai
December 2007

Preface to the Revised Edition of *Madras Rediscovered*

In effect the fifth edition of *Madras Discovered*, which first appeared in 1981, this edition has grown still more in the five years since the last edition. Much of that growth has been entirely due to other books I've written in the intervening years.

Looking Back From Moulmein, the biography of the late A M M Arunachalam of the Murugappa Group, and *The Ace Of Clubs*, the story of the Madras Club, have both provided considerable additional information besides what was mined while helping with two other books, *The Unfinished Journey*, the biography of M Ct M Chidambaram Chettyar, and *60 Landmark Years*, the story of E C C, the construction and engineering contracts division of Larsen & Toubro. Another book I played a small role in – *Madras – The Architectural Heritage* – also provided many new insights. But the greatest part of the new inputs derived from two columns I did for *The Hindu*, 'Madras Miscellany', still going strong as I write these lines, and 'Madrascapes', which after a first innings awaits starting its second. Both these columns have received a considerable response and it has been that feedback, as well as the response to Chennai Heritage's *Madras Musings* that I edit, that have provided much information about the old families of Madras and their homes.

With the previous edition of *Madras Rediscovered* out of stock for some months before I got down to updating the book and faced with repeated requests for a new edition of it, I haven't had the time to do full justice to the wealth of information that came my way while writing those columns. So a still more complete edition awaits another day; meanwhile, I've found enough material to swell this book by another 10,000 words or so. With revisions and corrections to parts of the fourth edition having been carried out, what you have before you is a version of *Madras Rediscovered* that could well be a rediscovery for readers too.

I must also note that in the past five years, Madras has been enjoying an economic boom that has led to highrise taking over much of the core of the city, large business complexes coming up on the periphery, and an explosion of consumerism that has seen shops, restaurants and entertainment facilities mushroom. Coupled with the city becoming the Automobile Capital and Medicare Capital of India, congestion has become the greatest threat to a city once known for its spaciousness and graciousness. Though the Madras of the pages that follow might not be recognisable in ground reality, the past still survives in the city, precariously though it might be, to remind those that will listen that the prosperity of today is entirely rooted in the history of Madras, the first city of Modern India. To protect that history, the conservationists continue to cry themselves hoarse seeking a Heritage Act or, at least, Heritage Regulations. But there's little response. The heartening signs however are the restoration of *Senate House, Raj Bhavan* and *Rajaji Hall* getting underway, the renewal and readaptation of several old houses for commercial use as shops and restaurants, the formation of Heritage Clubs in several schools, and Madras – with the help of *Madras Rediscovered* – being taught as a subject in half a dozen colleges. That's what makes me feel optimistic that the Madras of this book will one day receive the recognition that is its due.

S MUTHIAH

Chennai
November 2004

Preface to the First Edition of the retitled book

This should in fact be the fourth edition of *Madras Discovered*. But with *Madras Discovered's* publisher now in new robes and the book having grown by at least 10,000 words besides being considerably revised, we have together decided to issue it as a new book under a new title, *Madras Rediscovered*.

Madras Rediscovered has the benefit of much that has happened in the six years since the last edition of *Madras Discovered*. Of the corporate histories I have written in this period, three have revealed much of Madras. *Getting India on the Move*, the story of Simpson & Co and the Amalgamations Group that grew from it, *The Spencer Legend*, the story of that giant department store, and *The Spirit of Chepauk,* the story of the Madras Cricket Club and the beginnings of sport in South India, have all provided much material, directly or indirectly, for this edition. Then there was the coffee-table book I did, *Madras – Its Past and Its Present.* For this book, and the other three, much research was done from primary sources by Rajind N Christy, my dedicated researcher, and this has yielded far more valuable information than what I had garnered reading a wealth of material, for that material could best be termed only as secondary and tertiary sources. Rajind Christy's primary research, for those books as well as for this edition, has, therefore, led to many revisions in the present book as well as a fair amount of addition and some deletion. Thus, *Madras Rediscovered* is not only a substantially expanded book, but it has brought a greater degree of accuracy and precision to what had earlier been generalities or deductions in specific cases.

It must be noted as this edition goes to press that, in the intervening years since the third edition of *Madras Discovered,* the city has grown significantly – upwards, closer together and in population. It is today indeed a bustling metropolis with its quality of life significantly affected for the worse, but it remains a city that is still green and much more open to the skies than most other cities in India. Unfortunately, growth has in many ways destroyed several bits and pieces of its manmade heritage and has in more recent years begun to affect its natural heritage. Despite these changes, I have retained the original text as it was, as though nothing has happened, but have added a supplementary comment or two to bring readers up-to-date. Significantly, some awareness of heritage and the necessity to preserve it has been creeping into both official and non-official thinking and, as these lines are written, one major conservation project, the restoration of the Police Headquarters, has been completed, there is talk of restoring half a dozen other important public buildings in the next couple of years, and a Heritage Act has been recommended to Government by an official committee.

One important question that arose during this revision and expansion was whether to go along with the Government view of History. Government had in 1996 changed the name of Madras to Chennai. It is a change I disagreed with on historical grounds – and so did many others. But while I accept for official use the now-gazetted name for the city, I decided to stick to Madras in this book. After all, this book is a quest for the past in this city – and that past belongs to Madras and not Chennai. I have clarified that point of view further in the appropriate place.

And, as I have said in three previous prefaces, there's much to be still discovered about Madras. *Madras Rediscovered,* even in its present more comprehensive form, is not the last word on the subject. But to be able to put down that word, there's still much to be sought in Madras's past. Help from anyone interested in making *Madras Rediscovered* still more complete would be welcome.

S MUTHIAH

Chennai
January 1999

Preface to the Third Edition

In the six years since the second edition of *Madras Discovered,* I've read Love very much more carefully, there has been 'discovery' of several old classics about the city and I've sadly watched several of the city's landmarks vanish, even if they encouraged a further search for their antecedents. There also occurred a significant anniversary, the city's 350th birthday.

Regrettably, it was not celebrated on the same scale as Calcutta celebrated its 300th anniversary about the same time. But there was more interest shown in the city than in the last forty years and this manifested itself in several others writing about it. To all of them, too many to single out individually, I'm indebted for more information about Madras.

But even if all this had not necessitated a considerably revised and enlarged third edition, there was one serendipitous happening that just had to be included. And that was discovery, purely by chance, that the Thimmappa connection still remains in the city and that his descendants still call Madras 'home'. To discover that the family of one of the founders is still going strong in the city is a happy fact that needed to be recorded. All the rest that's expanded this edition substantially pales beside the discovery that Alavandar Naidu and others of the Thimmappa family are very much a part of today's Madras scene. They are, indeed, the 'First Family of Madras'.

If and when there is a fourth edition of *Madras Discovered*, I hope there will be additional information about other early families, Indian as well as British; perhaps I might even find a Madra or a Day or a Cogan somewhere. I appeal once more, as in years past, not only for such information but for more about Madras the City, how it began and grew. Because there is such information somewhere out there, *Madras Discovered* remains not the last word on this city.

S MUTHIAH

Madras
December 1992

Preface to the Second Edition

The first edition of *Madras Discovered*, I was happy to find, was well received. Besides the favourable comment it got locally, several persons abroad acknowledged its use as a reference book on the early British period in India.

Philip Davies, who wrote the monumental *Splendours of the Raj – British Architecture in India 1660-1947*, acknowledged it as an aid and source book. Then Louise Nicholson, who provided "the Discerning Traveller" with "a Practical Guide" in her splendid *India in Luxury,* referred to *Madras Discovered* as the best guidebook to the city.

It was all very heart-warming, but though *Madras Discovered* was planned as a historical guide to the city, I had always felt the historical – and the conservation of it – should take precedence over its character as a guidebook. The location and sites were merely standing memorials to the history and legends of Madras.

And to emphasise the stuff of history Madras abounds in, I have planned this second edition slightly differently. The first edition has naturally been considerably revised, updated, expanded – and indexed. But in addition to this, I have added an anecdotal elaboration of some part of each chapter. Called 'Once Upon a City', these tales tell the stories (and histories) of different aspects of life in Our Towne of Madraspatnam during the centuries. I hope these tales of 'Once Upon a City' will help to bring brick and mortar alive and help readers recognise the ghosts who walk through the corridors of much of Madras, City of Legends.

For several of the additions of this volume and the 'Once Upon a City' tales, I must acknowledge the kind permission given by several publications for use here of material I had first written for them: *Aside*, that magazine of Madras which cares for the city, *Swagat*, Indian Airlines' in-flight journal, and *Namaste*, the Welcomgroup publication. I must also thank T P Janakiram for the pains he took to get just the right pictures to illustrate several points made in these pages. And the Madras Chamber of Commerce for their kind permission to reproduce one of their prints of Old Madras on the cover.

Once again, I look forward to more material from readers that will enable this volume to expand further. And once again I hope some of the words within will strike a sympathetic chord somewhere and help conserve a little bit of the historical in Our Town, Madras.

S MUTHIAH

Madras
December 1987

Preface to the First Edition

After years abroad – punctuated by occasional visits to a Madras remembered as a leisurely but gracious town of conservative people and large houses with larger 'gardens' – I came 'home' to a metropolis in 1968-69, but found it essentially unchanged. True, the town I had known had grown bigger, become more populous and acquired an industrial base. But at heart it had remained the charming overgrown village of the 30s and 40s and 50s; a leisurely, gracious town with quaint old-world values, that had spread itself out comfortably in its quest to retain the spaciousness of the past.

My first assignment on my return here was to prepare 'copy' to accompany a street guide to Madras. A brief history of an old British company followed. And out of those quests for information was born my interest in the history of Madras and a need to do my bit to conserve its relics. This slim volume, therefore, is as much a historical guide for those who wish to look around Madras, or wish to find out more about their city, as it is a plea to conserve not only its spacious environment but also its cultural and historic relics, be they Indian or European.

Most of the material included here was discovered in the course of a search that is part of a bigger project. Some of it has already been published in *Aside*, that magazine of Madras which indeed cares for the city's past, present and future. To its editor, Abraham Eraly, I am particularly grateful for permission to use material first published in his magazine. I must also thank Suresh Bhimsingh for all the trouble he took to get just the right photographs for this book.

The occasional error and omission could well crop up in such a compilation as this. I will be very grateful if they are pointed out or if additional information is provided, so that they may be included in subsequent editions. There might also be some readers who feel there is a Western bias to this book. This is perhaps inevitable, since most of the records on the subject are by Western writers or Indians using those same sources. Indian sources appear non-existent. I would, therefore, particularly appreciate receiving further material about those mentioned in these pages and especially authentic information about the great Indian families of Old Madras, which would enable me to straighten the records.

S MUTHIAH

Madras
December 1981

Illustrations

METROPOLITAN MADRAS

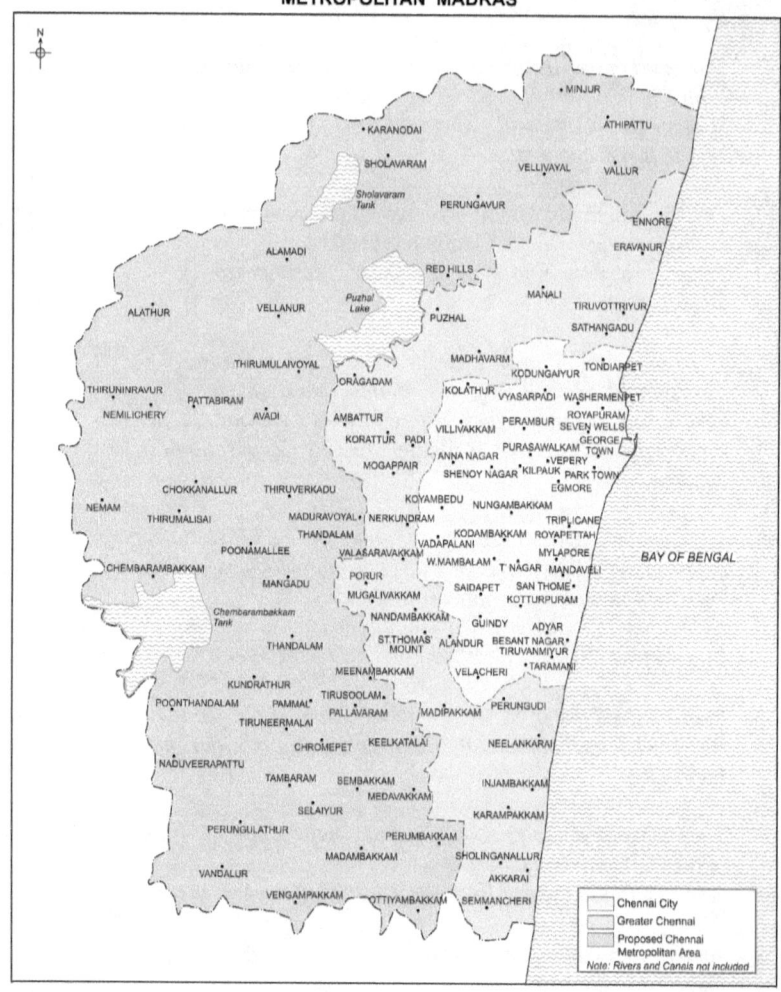

Prologue

A headline during one recent Madras Week read 'Madras is 50,000 years old'. Or did it say that it is 500,000 years old? I forget, but what I do remember is that tools from the Paleolithic Age were found for the first time in India in a southern suburb of Madras and that in more recent times relics from the Iron Age were found in the Kilpauk-Egmore area of the city. The former discovery places life in the Madras region between 500,000 years ago and 15,000 CE and the latter between 1200 and 200 BCE. Certainly no one disputes that humans lived in the Madras hinterland for eons. Nor is there any dispute that they lived in the area during the numerous later times it changed hands from one ancient empire to another.

Madras that is Chennai today is an agglomeration of towns and villages dating to historic times, places mentioned in ancient manuscripts and the ballads of the sages, the Vaishnavite Alwars of the 5th and 6th Centuries CE and the Saivite Nayanmars of the 7th and 8th Centuries CE. Ancient inscriptions too have been found chiseled in granite – usually in temples – referring to places that are a part of Madras today. But most of them date to the Pallava period (276-897 CE and its peak 571-633 CE) and to the later Chola period, the 12th and 13th Centuries CE; in fact, none have been found dating to before the 7th Century CE. Of the earliest legendary names associated with the region, there are no contemporary inscriptions, only later writing and the oral history of the ages.

Tradition has it that the great philosopher-poet of the Tamils, Thiruvalluvar was born in ancient Mylapore some time between the 4th Century BCE and the 1st Century CE (31 BCE according to the Tamil Nadu Government). St. Thomas, the Apostle of India, is believed to have lived in Mylapore between 60 CE and 72 CE. And Mylapore has been referred to as a great port by Ptolemy the Greek geographer (100-170 CE). It is centuries later that you get any kind of documentation that Mylapore was one of the two great Pallava ports from which the culture of India travelled to the lands of the East. That kind of legendary past is why, when Government wanted to change the name of Madras to Chennai, I had suggested Mylapore as being more appropriate. But the antipathy of that Government to the Mylapore of the day is another story.

Triplicane – Tiruallikeni – has long been sung of by the ancient sages as being part of Mylapore. In this Vaishnavite township's famed temple is an inscription dating to 807 CE describing Pallava king Dantivarman. Of him, the saintly Vaishnavite sages have sung that he built the entire town and temple.

Earlier than the Triplicane inscription are several that refer to what is now the industrial suburb of Manali. In neighbouring Tiruvottriyur's main temple have been found inscriptions describing the local administration system of the Pallavas. Sages, saints, scholars and poets have over the centuries (8th-15th CE) recorded their visits to what was once a sacred town.

At the other end from Tiruvottriyur is another religious centre, Tiruvanmiyur. Its Saivite temple is rich in inscriptions from the Rajendra Chola period (1014-1044 CE), but, for a temple said to date to at least the Pallava period, it strangely lacks Pallava inscriptions. Not lacking in them are the suburban towns of Pallavaram and neighbouring Tirusoolam, both near the Airport. Pallavaram's periphery also hosts a rock-cut monolithic cave typical of 7th Century Pallava craftsmanship.

Indeed, many of the other old villages that are a part of Madras today are also part of the pallava territory of Tondaimandalam - if you are not being fanciful and claiming a heritage hundreds of thousands of years old. According to Prof. P Rajaraman, the natural boundaries of Tondaimandalam were the River Swarnamukhi in the Nellore District in the north, the River Pennar in the South Arcot District in the south, the eastern Ghats in the west, and the Bay of Bengal in the east. Kanchipuram was its capital. Present-day Chennai is at the eastern end of these boundaries.

Going by ancient manuscripts and the balladic hymns of the sages, Tondaimandalam has a history going back to Asokan times (3rd Century BCE). Among the famed Mackenzie Manuscripts are palm-leaf ones describing a tribal people called the Kurumbas living in what was called Tondainadu. They were conquered by Ashoka, it is stated, when he stretched his kingdom south, the area becoming the southernmost boundary. But as the powers of his successors waned, the First Cholas of Karikalan took over Tondaimandalam and a kinsman, Tondaiman Ilam Tiraiyan, governed the territory in the 2nd Century CE.

What happens after that is not very clear, as are periods during the next 1300 years, when kingdoms north of Tondaimandalam invaded it and ruled it for brief intervening periods. But both hymns and inscriptions give almost entirely uninterrupted Pallava rule from the 3rd Century to the 9th Century CE, divided only into four dynastic periods. The Pallavas were succeeded by the Second Cholas from the 9th Century to the 13th Century CE. Then follows 100 years and more of rule by various kingdoms from north of the border before Vijayanagar establishes its rule in the 14th Century. But after Emperor Krishnadevaraya dies in 1529, that rule is weakened by several Governors of Vijayanagar territory establishing themselves as overlords rarely answerable to an 'Emperor', who was little more than nominal. It was on this scene that there arrived the Portuguese, the Dutch and the British – the Madras that is the Chennai of today developing in the hands of the commercial representatives of the last-named.

What is significant, in the context of this prologue, is that in all the hymns sung and in all those inscriptions found in Tondaimandalam in the area where Madras is today – and there were others found in Velachery, Padi, Poonamallee and San Thomé, all in Madras or just outside it – there is no mention of Madraspatnam or Chennapatnam. Pages of detailed history summarised above, have been written by eminent historians about Tondaimandalam and its hinterland, but in none of them is a place called Madraspatnam or Chennapatnam mentioned.

The first mention of Madraspatnam is in the "Firman granted by Demela Vintatedro unto Mr. Francis Day, Chiefe for the English In Armagon, in behalf of the Honble company for their tradeing and fortifieng at Medraspatam..." This document dated 1639 mentions "the port of Medraspatam,, several times but there is not one mention of a Chennapatnam. What the document, however, makes clear is that a place, "a port" already existed. But no mention of this port is found in any inscription or document other than in English East India Company correspondence, one letter mentioning "a place Called Madraspatam, neere St Thomay."

The first mention of Chennapatnam is when a genealogical list of the Damarla family (at the time the Rajah of Kalahasti's) with no dates to them was obtained by the company in 1800. Fifth on the list, from the time of the first person who "held in Enaum (gift) the village of Daumel in the Conjeevaram Province", is Daumel Comar Chinapa Nairdu (who) "founded the Village of China(k)upom, now called Chinapatam or Madras." The first mention of the name Chennapatnam is in a land grant dated 1646 to the Chenna Kesava perumal Temple. And the first mention of the name in the official records is in 1652. So Chenapatam also existed, as the same or a nearby village. Thus, it would seem two villages, or possibly two names for one village, did exist before the English established Fort St George in one of them in 1639-40, but were not significant enough to warrant a place in any temple inscription or earlier literature or the songs of the sages.

Midst pages more of such confusion, that authoritative historian of Madras Col H D Love says that what is "definitely established" is the fact that "a village called Madraspatam existed prior to the settlement by the East India Company's factors" and that within a few years of the founding of Fort St George, "the new town which had grown up around the Fort was commonly known to the natives as Chinapatam, either in deference to the Naik's wishes, or because the site had originally borne that name." Love adds a third fact, "While the official centre of the settlement was designated Fort St. George, the British applied the name Madraspatam to the combined towns."

And that is the Madras of the pages that follow:

What seems clear to me from the above is that though the villages of Madraspatam and Chinapatam may have existed before the British turned a sod in their vicinity, they were not important enough places to warrant notice in ancient times. They derived their significance only after the raising of Fort St George by 1640 in one or the other of them. And that Fort St George called the area of its location and its immediate surroundings Madraspatam. With Fort St George in due course absorbing all the ancient villages and more neighbouring them, it called the town that developed Madraspatam. And that is the Madras we know – and recall in this book. We are not recalling Tondaimandalam of the Pallavas and the Cholas and of others, where there may have existed a less than noteworthy place called Madraspatam or Chinapatam, but a Madraspatam that the East India company men, their employees of several races, and the Indians who settled as their neighbours created and helped grow into a metropolis over 375 years and more.

How many of today's residents of Madras that is Chennai – including claimants of the city's ancient lineage can date to family roots beings sunk here from before 375-year benchmark? I can think of only one. There may be a few others, whom I'd be delighted to hear from. But to me the substantial majority of the people who live in the city today and call it home are unlikely to have connections with it for more than five generations! We are all migrants to a city we have helped create on some foundations laid by a few British and a few thousand Indians. Recognition of their contribution to the development of Madras that is Chennai is what the pages that follow are about.

1

What's in a Name?

Memories of a childhood long past are of grandparents, in mofussil districts that are still the back of beyond in South India, talking in awe of a wondrous place called 'Patnam'. Or was it 'Pattanam'? In later years, catching up with Tamil purists, I also caught up with other names like 'Chennai' and 'Chennaipattinam' and found they still meant the same place. But to most people in India, the historic city on Coromandel's famed shores is Madras, be it pronounced as 'Ma-draas' or 'Mad-dras' or 'Madharaas' or 'Medras'.

Madras, the first city of South India, indeed of modern India, and capital of Tamil Nadu, that historic land of ancient culture, is, surprisingly, a comparatively new city. It owes its genesis to Andrew Cogan and Francis Day of John Company, rather, the Honourable East India Company, two determined men who, despite their superiors' pessimism, gratefully accepted in the 17th Century a grant of land from the local Nayaks (governors of the Telugu-speaking Vijayanagar Kingdom) at Wandiwash and Poonamallee, Venkatappa and his brother Aiyappa, respectively. They established on it a 'factory' (a trading post that was in effect a warehouse-cum-residence with some fortification) that was to grow into the seat of British power on the Coromandel coast. That grant is dated July 22, 1639, but since Day reached Madraspatam – the name mentioned in the grant – only on July 27th, the chances are that 'July' is an error and August 22, 1639, is more likely the date the East India Company acquired the land to found their settlement. Certainly, a few heritage buffs in Madras have since 2004 been celebrating Madras Day every year on August 22nd, with a Madras Week built around it.

The settlement founded over three and a half centuries ago was known in its early years by such names as Medraspatnam, Madrapatam and Maddaraspatan (1639), Madrazpatam (1640), Madrespatnam (1641), Maddaras (1642), Madras (for the first time, in 1653), Madrespatan (1654), Madrasapatan (1656), Madrispatnam (1658) and Maderas and Madirass (1673), depending on whether it was Nayak, British East Indiaman or Frenchman, Dutch burgher or 'Portuguee' talking about what appears from all descriptions to have been a God-forsaken place in those early years. But always there was the variation on the same theme, 'Madras'. So, naturally, "Why Madras?" Especially when the word has little or no association with the two major languages of the region, Tamil and Telugu, yet seems to have had Nayak recognition in that grant to the English.

No satisfactory answer has ever been given to the question "Why Madras?". Whether the question refers to the reasons for the founding of the settlement or to the name itself, the answers have, over the years, remained singularly unconvincing. There is little doubt that Madras, the place, was the idea of Day, described as a hard-drinking, enthusiastic gambler and lusty womaniser, who was the factor (agent in charge) of John Company's dilapidated 'shop' at Armagon (Durga Raya Patnam), some way to the north of that desolate sandy strip of land he chose for his new 'factory'. It was his idea, his choice, this surf-lashed exposed spit, rounded on two sides by rivers and washed by the sea on the third, making it, in effect, a narrow protected peninsula, but a site without a safe landing place. It was also Day who, with the help of his *dubash*[1] Beri Thimmappa of Palacole, near Maddepollam (in present-day Andhra Pradesh), finalised terms with the local powers and got the grant. To Day's slightly more correct chief at Machilipatnam, Cogan, goes the credit for encouraging the boisterous Day, making the first official landing, building the first fortified factory which was to grow into the Fort St George we know, and colonising the place. The result of which industry is Madras today. The supreme irony is that neither founding father, Day or Cogan, nor their Indian aides, Thimmappa, the *dubash* from Palacole who became Chief Merchant, and Nagabattan, the gunpowder-maker of the Company (both of whom were on the first official voyage), are remembered anywhere in the city.

---

[1] Interpreter-middleman ... from *dvi bhasha* – two languages. But in practice a middle-man.

Day's own explanation for choosing this barren, sandy site was that its hinterland offered "excellent long Cloath and better cheape by 20 per cent than anywhere else"! A noted gossip of the time, however, had it that the choice was determined by Day having a mistress in Portuguese San Thomé; the nearby settlement-to-be would ensure "their Interviews might be the more frequent and uninterrupted"! Whether this was indeed the case is a matter for conjecture, but that there was a mistress appears to have been gossip with some substance; a friend and successor to the charge of Madras, Henry Greenhill, is reported as having succeeded to the willing gentlewoman!

Whatever Day's reason for his choice of the site for the Company's new factory, when he got down to brass tacks he needed someone to negotiate on his behalf the initial grant of even such an unprepossessing place. There is little doubt that Thimmappa was that intermediary. And from available information it would seem that it is to the wily Thimmappa we owe the most intriguing answer to "Why Madras?" the name.

Between the two main gates of Fort St George today is a walled-up portion where once was the main Sea Gate and only entrance to the Fort from the east. From there to water's edge was, in those days, all beach. To the west of the gate was the settlement Day and company founded. This site, a mere strip of land, was granted just south of a tiny village where lived a few fisher-families who were visited from time to time by two French Capuchin priests. Some sources say this village was called Madraspatnam, (Medraspatam) the Madraspatam of the Nayak's grant. Legend has it that its headman was a Roman Catholic named Madarasan (Mada Raja – *Madham* = Faith, or *Maatha* = (Holy) Mother?). Legend also has it that Day did not have much luck with this rather independent headman, whose banana grove was the chosen site for the fort. It was then that Thimmappa stepped in and promised to get the factory called Madarasanpatnam if the headman would agree to his *thope*[2] being taken over. Madarasan was no doubt thrilled by the idea of being remembered by posterity, but the official grant had to be made by the Damarla brothers, the local Nayaks of the Rajah of Chandragiri (the last remnants of Vijayanagar) – and they wanted the new settlement named Chennapatnam after their father Chennappa (Chennappa – *chenna*

---

[2] Garden, orchard.

= pleasing) Nayak. So there was, possibly, a *kuppam*[3] called Madras-patam, a fort possibly called Madarasanpatnam and its Indian settlement (colonised, before long, mainly by 'imported' weavers) called Chenna-patnam (this name being found in the records as early as 1646). In time, all merged and grew into the city known as Madras to most of the world and as Chennai to Tamil purists, despite its Telugu origins.

It should, however, be recorded that when Sriranga Raya ascended the Vijayanagar throne in 1642 he dismissed Damarla Venkatappa and issued a new grant to the British, the first royal grant, in November 1645. The grant refers to Madras as "Sriranga Rayapatanam my town". The name has survived nowhere but in the Raya's *cowle*[4], and Madras or Chennai – and versions of them – are the only names by which the City of today has ever been known. Indeed, from the time of the first settlement, the city's name in official documents has been Madras in English and Chennai in Tamil, both names happily co-existing for 375 years and more. What need was there then for the great name change in 1996 that made Madras Chennai?!

Name change or not, Madras survives in everyday use and the explanation for Madraspatnam or the Madarasan name remains a question. Two more likely answers are, however, offered. One, that the *kuppam* had been established by fisherfolk who were parishioners of the Madre de Deus Church at San Thomé, 5 km to the south, and they had adapted the Church's name for their village, just as their headman had made an adaptation his. The second explanation, and, in many ways, a more likely one, is that both took their names from a family of wealthy Portuguese benefactors – the Madra or Madera or Madeiros family of San Thomé, a family also associated with the Madre de Deus Church. Wealthy families in those days were certainly the squires of whole villages – in this case fishing villages.

There is, indeed, evidence to indicate that the Madra family were the most prominent members of early San Thomé[5] and, later, Madras. When the foundation of a new chapel of St Lazarus was being excavated in

---

[3] Tiny village, generally poverty-stricken.

[4] Order of grant.

[5] A Portuguese settlement established in the 1520s to the south of where Madras was to be founded.

the 1920s in San Thomé, an engraved tombstone was found with a coat-of-arms (indicating, undoubtedly, family eminence) and words to the effect that the stone honoured Manuel Madra and his mother Lucy Brague, widow of Vincente Madra, who together built a church there in 1637. The family is said to have lived near Assumption Church, which was built in 1640 in Mylapore.

Another Madera (or Madra) of San Thomé was Cosmo Lourenco, who in 1681 held a militia command in Fort St George. He married the daughter of a wealthy Portuguese free merchant in Madras, John Pereira, whose "gardens" are, today, in northwest George Town, and the Madera family became one of the richest in 17th Century Madras. It was Cosmo Madera who built Descanco Church in Mylapore (its site a part of the 'Trail of St Thomas' in Madras). On his death in 1703, he was buried there. Cosmo Madera's son Luis was a seafarer and free merchant of note who lent money frequently to the Government of Madras as did, in later years, his widow, the famous Mrs Madeiros. It was Mrs Madeiros who sold one of their houses to the Government when they sought a 'garden house' for the Governor. The Madra (or Madeiros) family flourished in the San Thomé area from at least the last decades of the 16th Century – and there are no records of any place called Madras before that! Couldn't the name have derived from this undoubtedly distinguished family of the time, who were 'landlords' of several fishing *kuppams* on this coast? It seems very plausible.

Other theories associated with the City's name include one that it is derived from the Persian word *madrasa,* a term describing a Muslim school and indicating in this case the possible existence of a Muslim educational institution nearby. But the Muslim settlement in the present Triplicane-Royapettah area and its schools and colleges date only from the latter half of the 18th Century. There are, however, records of Muslim traders residing in this area from earliest East India Company times. And it is significant that a domed Muslim style of architecture was a notable feature of the very first Governor's house built in the 17th Century in the Company's fort. There has also been at least one writer who explained the village name of 'Makhraskuppam', found in a Persian chronicle of the Nawabs of the Carnatic, as being derived from Marakkayar-kuppam – a village of seafaring Muslims (*Marakkayar* – from Arab *markab* = Tamil *marakkalam* = ship).

Whatever, then, be the explanation for the name Madras, India, there is no doubt at all in the case of Madras, Oregon (USA).[6] This century-and-more-old small town got its 'accidental name' from 'the imprint on a bolt of cloth made in 'Madras, India', according to an American dictionary of place names. Madras's eminence has been entirely due to such trade. But its growth, though linked with commerce, is altogether another story.

It is the story of mergers of the settlement successive John Company councillors made with ancient villages, such as Triplicane, Mylapore, Egmore and Nungambakkam, that had a much older historical past. (see *Prologue*). It is the story of British Madras from which modern India grew. But that's a story that dates only from the time of Day, and the city itself, still expanding, has only to look back a couple of centuries to discover the first years of its present shape.

That irregular, semi-circular shape, which today occupies 426 sq. km (about 165 sq. miles), is the core city administered by the Greater Chennai Corporation. To the 176 sq. km (about 65 sq. miles) it was, 250 sq.km were added in 2011 to make what is the Madras city of today. It runs about 45 km along the seacoast – much of it wide, sandy beach – and is about 20 km at the widest. The elongated city lies near the 13th North Parallel and parallel to 80° longitude. It is horizontally trisected by the Cooum River in the centre and the Adyar River in the South, and is vertically divided by the Buckingham Canal, which runs parallel to the coast almost through the entire length of the city). The city falls within the 1189 sq.km (459 sq.miles) that became the Greater/Chennai Metropolitan Area in 1975, having within its limits eight municipalities, 11 town panchayats, 179 village panchayats and 10 panchayat unions.

Until Independence, Madras was the capital of what, in British times, was called the Madras Presidency, then Province, which included Tamil-, Telugu-, Malayalam- and Kannada-speaking areas – comprising virtually the whole of South India. In 1956, the post-Independence Madras State was divided into Madras State and the Telugu state of Andhra Pradesh as a result of the reorganisation of states on a linguistic basis. Parts of Madras State were also added that year to Mysore State which became

---

[6] There is also a tiny village called Madras in Texas and a slightly bigger one in Australia.

Karnataka and to Travancore-Cochin State that became Kerala. In 1968, Madras State became Tamil Nadu. Today, Madras, the fourth largest urban agglomeration in India (population in the 2011 Census: 5 million appx. within the pre-2011 Corporation city limits and approximately 4 million more in the rest of the urban agglomeration) is the capital of this sole Tamil-speaking State of the Union.

Though it might not have the eminence today of the other three metropolises, and a couple of other major cities in the country claim greater progress, there is little doubt that all of them, not to mention the rest of the subcontinent, owe much to the seeds of modern progress first sown in Madras. The first major settlement established by the British, and then the only major Western settlement in India, Madras, till the 1760s, laid the foundations on which modern India has grown. It is a proud heritage whose story is told in the following pages.

A Search for Roots

I had promised to show him Robert Clive's watering-holes in and around Madras. Little did I realise he'd turn up at my house in the best Clive manner, complete with coach and escort. His outrider that morning roared up on an iron steed, quickly dismounted at my gate and threw a smart salute. Moments later the carriage chugged up behind the police inspector and ensconced in the auto-rickshaw was a short, tubby, safari-suited Stanley Clives[7] peering owlishly through heavy glasses to make sure he'd got right an address no Clive had ever known. Once sure, he broke into a broad, most unClive-like grin and proceeded to explain the comedy of errors that had earned him a police escort and which had raised in his esteem more than a notch the Madras police force whose sense of duty encompassed helping harassed strangers.

Escortless, we set out in the steps of Robert Clive – only to wish later on, while trapped for an hour in a traffic jam in Mannady Street in the middle of erstwhile 'Black Town', that we had kept our friendly inspector. But before the jam, we did get around to some of Robert Clive's haunts. In 'White Town' – Fort St George, to you – there was Clive Corner in what was once Admiralty House, a home for a while of Clive; there was Fort Museum, once a 'business centre', now with relics of the Clive era; and there was St Mary's Church where Clive married Margaret Maskelyne.

"Ah," said the genealogist in search of ancestors and descendants, "but this was not the first time they got married. I give it to you exclusively – and you can tell the world," Stanley Clives[8] generously offered, "this was their second marriage!" All that business of love at first sight or Robert falling in love with her picture and getting her to

---

[7] How Clive became Clives is another story altogether. An illiterate ancestor who could only say "my thumb's my mark" had his name written in a Church marriage register by the Vicar. Now that Vicar wrote a fine copperplate with all the flourishes and one of the flourishes was a squiggle at the end of the name. That squiggle was ever after read as an 'S' and so Clive became Clives!

*come out to marry him is so much balderdash, according to Cousin
Stanley. "This was an arranged marriage if ever there was one and they
were married by proxy a full nine months before Margaret set out for
Madras. I've found the records in Shropshire. The wedding in St Mary's
only sanctified what had already been registered in Shifton!"*

'Old Black Town' – the High Court Campus – and 'New Black Town',
*which is still called George Town and which still has many low-doored
houses that remain as they were in Clive's day, were all we could do
before lunch. Cuddalore and Fort St David, Tiruchchirappalli and
Samayavaram, Arcot and Pondicherry would have to await Stanley
Clives' next visit. But since he was searching not only for Robert's
'foreign' roots but for those of other kin as well, Stanley Clives made
sure he visited* Banqueting Hall – *now* Rajaji Hall – *built by the second
Lord Clive, Robert's son Edward[8]; Clive Battery, also built by him at
the end of North Beach Road; and the Museum. "You don't know the
treasures you have in Madras," moaned Stanley Clives. "That Museum
of yours, for instance, has the finest collection of arms of the age of
Clive to be found anywhere in the world. But no attention at all is paid
to this treasure. I must write to Mrs Gandhi about it. She seems to be
interested in the national heritage."*

*Stanley Clives, electrical engineer, engineering consultant, genea-
logist and strictly amateur historian now turning author, was in Madras
to add to his information on the Clive family. "I've traced over
4,000 Clive kin, before and after Robert and going back to Lady
Godiva," he told me, "but there's very little information about so many."
Which was why he was in Madras, trying to trace the stories of several
with Madras connections. But Stanley Clives' most earnest quest – though
he doesn't emphasise it – must be for Cousin George, a direct ancestor
of Stanley Clives, who came out with Robert on his second tour. He made
a fortune in India before going back and very likely formed a banking
consortium in England that sent back money to India for 'investment'.
One of those 'investments' might well have been the infamous Paul
Benfield, who got the Nawab of Arcot into debt, by generously lending
to him. Benfield's subsequent claims and what followed certainly led to
the Nawab ceding the Carnatic (virtually Tamil Nadu) to the British.*

---

[8] All the locations in Madras that popular legend associates with Clive, are Edward
Clive sites, NOT Robert Clive's. The latter, in his time, was, like his contemporaries,
virtually confined to the Fort; the move to live outside the Fort was still 30-40 years
away.

2

Day's 'No-Man's-Sand'

India's Coromandel coast had, for centuries, been sought by traders from Rome and Greece, Araby and Cathay. And after the great 'Age of Exploration', the Dutch and the Danes, the French and the English followed the Portuguese. Even the Americans, Belgians, and Swedes made short stays.

This much sought after coast is the Choramandala of the Portuguese, the Choromandal of the Dutch and the Cholamandalam, the fifth province, of the Vijayanagar Empire. Its name could have derived from the village Karimanal (black sand) near once-Dutch Pulicat. Or it could be from the Telugu Kharamandalam (*khara* = hot) or the legendary village of Khara. Or it could derive from the great Chola dynasties whose kingdoms at various periods hugged this coast.

Whatever the reasons for the name, it was a five-shilling price-rise on a pound of pepper by the Dutch that led to Britain's grandest age, the Age of Empire, having its beginnings on this legendary coast. That price hike caused a group of 24 merchant-importers of London to form, in December 1600, the East India Company, to seek for itself the bounties of the East. The Company got down to business on January 1,1601.

In the early decades of the 17th Century, the East India Company operated from Surat on India's west coast (to which William Hawkins and his men of the galleon *Hector* had come in 1600) as well as on what today is the Andhra (North Coromandel) coast in the east, where the Masulipatam (Machilipatnam) factory was established in 1611. But with trading conditions being made more difficult for them by their better-entrenched neighbours and rivals, the Portuguese and the Dutch, the Johnny-come-latelys at Masulipatam were looking for a more propitious place to set up permanent shop. And, as already mentioned, when Day discovered a strip of 'no-man's-sand' and persuaded the local chieftains to grant him the land to establish a trading post, the Madras of today was conceived.

This sandy strip – about 5 km in length, 2 km in width, from about today's Royapuram in the north (which, with its heritage of fishing, may have been Madarasan's *kuppam)* to the Cooum mouth in the south and the Buckingham Canal in the west – was what was deeded to the East India Company on August 22, 1639. Damarla (Damal is a village near Kanchipuram on the Bangalore road) Ayyappa Nayak of Poonamallee, a friend of Day's *dubash* Thimmappa, was instrumental in arranging this gift. He persuaded his brother, Damarla Venkatadri (or Venkatappa) of Wandiwash, who was, at the time, the Vijayanagar Empire's 'Governor' of the coast from Pulicat to San Thomé, to make the grant which Day gratefully accepted. Venkatadri Nayak anticipated trade, Persian horses and military protection as being benefits that would derive from the grant.

Day had unwisely established the Armagon factory in 1626 a little north of Pulicat (Tamil: Palaverkadu) – the first Dutch settlement on the Coromandel coast, established in 1609, and where they, in 1615, built *Castle Geldria.* Pulicat was to remain the headquarters of the Dutch possessions in the East till the late 17th Century. It was to be 1781 before Fort Geldria was taken over by the British. Its vegetation-overrun remains and the tombstones in its cemetery may still be seen. But in the early 17th Century, Armagon was having constant trouble with the powerful Dutch at Pulicat. Day was, therefore, on the look out for a new factory site. It is officially recorded – whatever the gossip might say – that he accepted the Madras site because: (1) it had a hinterland where the cloths he sought were 20 per cent cheaper; (2) the strip of land was reasonably well protected on the south and west by rivers – the Cooum and Elambore[1], respectively – and on the east by the sea; and (3) the rulers were friendly and offered all help for trade and settlement. The authorities in Surat were not convinced. But Day and

---

[1] Also known in various records as the North or Triplicane River and which later became a part of the Buckingham Canal.

his superior at Machilipatnam, Cogan, together with their Indian assistants and a few writers (clerks), 25 European soldiers, led by Lt Jermyn and Sgt Jeffery Bradford[2] (all of them ancients picked up from the taverns of London, so to speak), and local artificers eventually arrived at Madraspatnam in the *Eagle, Unity* and a third ship on February 20, 1640, to start work on the settlement, despite getting little or no encouragement from their superiors either in Surat or Bantam (Banten, Java). Construction began on March 1st. Yet, for all their inestimable contribution to the founding of this metropolis, Day and Cogan were hounded by John Company for the expenditure they had incurred. But before they bowed out, not on the best terms with each other, consequent to the reprimands, they had established Fort St George as the main bastion of the Company's power in India. That it did not remain so was not their fault.

The new English 'factory' in the early 1640s was little more than a small wall-enclosed and fortified enclosure within which were a main Fort House, all raised without foundations and completed in a rudimentary form, it would seem, on April 23, 1640, St George's Day (thus explaining the name of the Fort) and 15 or so thatched huts. This 'factory' was to grow into the Madras of today. Cogan himself contributed to that by moving to Madras on September 24, 1641, thereby establishing it as the seat of British power on the Coromandel coast. By 1652, Bengal and even Bantam were put under Fort St George. Cogan's move came while Day was in England answering – successfully – charges for being "the first projectour of the fort of St George".

With houses of settlers coming up to the north and south of the Fort and a surrounding wall being built to protect them, 'White Town' came into existence. To the north of it, on what is the High Court campus today, then had developed from the 1640s an Indian settlement called 'Black Town' by the English from 1676, but in the early days called 'Out Town' or 'Gentu (Telugu) Town'. This 'Black Town', in the shadow of the Fort and stretching to today's NSC Bose Road and south Broadway areas, came to be known as Chennapatnam. In time, it grew into the George Town we know today.

---

[2] Some accounts spell the name 'Broadford'.

In 'Black Town', three Indian officials supervised the settlement. They were: the *Adhikari*, the headman, who maintained order, collected revenue and exercised magisterial functions; the *Kanakkapulle*, or *Adhikari's* accountant; and the *Pedda Nayak*, the chief watchman, who maintained law and order and brought offenders to trial before the *Adhikari* at the Choultry (the Town House = Town Hall). Besides these officials, the leaders of the Indian town were the Company's Merchants headed by the Chief Merchant. John Company advanced money to these merchants who commissioned the weavers and dyers brought from the Andhra districts to manufacture cloth for the Company's export trade. The other citizens of eminence in the Indian town were the *dubashes*, who did the same for the free merchants and Company-men indulging in private trade. Seshadri Nayak and Konneri Chetty were the first Company Merchants, designated so in the 1650s. Manali Muthukrishna Mudaliar was the last Chief Merchant, the office of Company Merchant being abolished in 1770 by Export Warehouse-Keeper Warren Hastings. The Company, for its part, established in 1675 different grades for its civil servants, comprising apprentices, writers, factors, merchants, Senior Merchants (who were also Councillors) and the Governor.

The 'urban agglomeration' of the Fort, with 'White Town' within and 'Black Town' without, was the genesis of today's metropolis. Nurtured by the English, the tiny settlement grew into a moderately large town, adding to its size by swallowing many of the neighbouring villages. Triplicane was the first to be obtained, in 1676, on rent from the Sultan of Golconda. Boston-born Governor Elihu Yale (whose modest gifts resulted in the famous American university being named after him) was responsible for negotiating the lease of Egmore, Purasawalkam, and Tondiarpet from the Emperor Aurangazeb, the villages being granted only in 1693 after Yale's departure. In 1720, the Company acquired these four villages (the four 'Old Towns') which until then had been only on annual lease. In 1708, five new villages were added to the fold: Tiruvottriyur, Nungambakkam, Vyasarpady, Ennore and Sathangadu (the five 'New Villages'), all granted by Nawab Daud Khan. The Nawab of the Carnatic celebrated his accession to the *ghadi* by granting the English, in 1742, Vepery (Vippore), Perambur, Pudupakkam, Ernavore and Sadayankuppam. San Thomé and Mylapore were occupied in 1749 by the English in the name of their alliance with Golconda against France. And, so, tiny settlement grew into large town, town into city and city into metropolis.

By the end of the 17th Century, Madras was the chief English settlement in India. But by 1774 Calcutta was the capital of Britain's Indian empire and, in the 19th Century, Kipling described Madras as that "withered beldame brooding on ancient fame". The British may have forsaken Madras – but not the generations of immigrant Madrasis. They ensured that Day's settlement prospered and grew into a cosmopolitan metropolis. Today, in the early 2000s, it is one of India's boom cities.

The Mystery of the Woman in the North River

Soon after Francis Day of Armagon had founded Madras, and his boss, Andrew Cogan, Chief of Agency at Masulipatam, had moved the seat of the Agency to Madras, Cogan was confronted with 'The Mystery of the Woman in the North River'. It provided Madras its first recorded murder.

One day, when something like a log was spotted in the river that (once) flowed past the western walls of Fort St George and entered the sea to its north, several persons volunteered to swim out to verify what this object floating out to sea was. The log turned out to be the decomposed body of a 'native woman' who had been missing from her house for several days past. The body was soon hauled ashore. Since no wounds were visible, it was presumed the woman had drowned herself and orders were issued for the disposal of the body. One of the 'rescuers', however, was not content to leave well enough alone; he demanded that he be paid something for his efforts. Whereupon a bystander tartly retorted that "he had no reason, of all men, to require any such thing, for that she had mainteyned him and his consort for a long time together."

All eyes now turned on the "rescuer", and a pair sharper than the rest spotted blood on his cloth. A part of his cloth was also found to be a part of what was wrapped around the woman's body. But he vehemently denied all accusations of murder, until his house was searched, and all the clothes and jewellery of the victim were found. He now confessed that he'd committed the crime, together with his "male consort". But this accomplice, it was found, had fled the town two or three days earlier.

Agent Cogan, however, was more concerned with the legal aspects of murder in his 'territory' than with the crime itself. He wrote to the Nayak

*who governed the hinterland, and to whom, theoretically, the newly
founded Madras belonged, enquiring what action he should take in this
matter. The Nayak replied that Cogan should mete out justice according
to English law, failing which justice by country law would be done.
The Nayak pertinently asked Cogan, "If justice be not done, who would
come and trade here, especially when it shall be reported it was a place
of theeves and Murtherers?" Cogan thereafter acted speedily, especially
with the capture of the "Second Murtherer", and then reported,
"...unwilling to give away our (authority) to those who are too readie to
take it, wee did justice on them and hanged them on a Gybbet, where
they hung till the 11th of Xber (1641)...," being then cut down only
because the Nayak came on a visit!*

*A second murder some months later complicated life even further for
Cogan – this time because it was an all-White affair, involving persons
of different European nationalities. In this case, three Portuguese soldiers
from San Thomé came, on the evening of August 11, 1642, to
Madraspatnam and got into a drunken brawl with a Dane in a "base
Arrack house". Setting upon their drinking companion with rapiers,
they wounded him in seven places! A two-man British patrol was sent to
part the combatants, but was set on by the three Portuguese, one of
whom, Antonio Myrando by name, "ran one of our two soldiers into the
right Pappe, that instantly he dyed without speaking a word"!*

*The three brawlers immediately fled, but were captured within the
hour. The killer was soon identified and the others sent back to San Thomé
from where a stream of official correspondence now ensued, requesting
the release of the "phydalgo". The Nayak, however, demanded justice,
and enforced his demand by sending 500 soldiers into Madraspatnam
in case of a Portuguese attempt at rescue! In the circumstances, Cogan,
who could not reprieve the fidalgo without orders from Surat, was "forced
to excecute him the 13th do morning. And because he pretended to be a
Gentleman as aforesaid, wee shott him to death before our Corps du
Guard."*

*Myrando was one of 270 soldiers who had come aboard 11 frigates
the previous May to relieve San Thomé, and till the Fleet departed on
August 20th the soldiers ran riot, getting away not only with murder but
other heinous crimes as well. Myrando himself had killed a man in
San Thomé on August 1st and sought sanctuary in Fort St George.
When this was refused, he "vou'd... to be the death of some Englishe*

man ere he left the Coast". And having kept his word, he confessed proudly, before going to face the firing squad, that "this was the 7th Murther he had committed"! No wonder Cogan's Council claimed, "All the Citizens rejoice at what wee did"! The execution apparently also had a salutary effect on the Portuguese of San Thomé, for the Council reported, "Since then wee have byn wonderful at ease in respect of the Portugalls, for till then wee were dayly troubled with one or other."

Day, who succeeded Cogan as Agent in August 1643, was, on the 8th of January, 1644, called on to resolve another tricky situation, this one resulting from "a most unfortunate accident made soe by the Success and not the Intent". The "court's" final judgement in this case was delivered on the basis of "probabilities and likelyhood", as "all other proofs sleep".

This particular situation was created by Sgt Jeffery Bradford of the Garrison, who had permission to live outside the Fort. On the night of the 7th, he entered his darkened house after duty and found, at this "most unseasonable tyme, hid there," an unexpected visitor. In the ensuing struggle to hold the intruder, who was determined on flight, the swordless Sergeant drew a knife and cut him "soe for to give him a Marke for to Discover and Knowe him the next day"!

Finding the man the next day was not difficult, for he "proved a Corpse"! But when a worried Day sent his surgeon to examine the body, there was none. The Sergeant's victim, the surgeon learned, had bled to death because he had been afraid to get assistance to stanch the bleeding. Thereafter, "his Parents had intered him early in the morning, being ashamed of the act," the surgeon reported. A town meeting of Europeans and Indian elders thereupon decided that, under local law, the deceased had met with his just deserts and the Sergeant was not really at fault. Nevertheless they felt it necessary to advise the deportation of the Sergeant, but this could not be complied with as there was no substitute available. On the Gunner guaranteeing that Bradford would not escape, it was agreed to let him go about his duties in Madras until a replacement came out from England, when he could be sent back. Bradford, an Armagon factory man ever since he came out to India as a Corporal in 1632, was with Day at the founding of Madras.

Three separate crimes, three different ways of meting out justice. That was earliest Madras. And the situation did not improve much until Agent George Foxcroft (himself in prison at the time of the receipt of the Royal Commission and put there by his predecessor Sir Edward Winter – all of which is another tale of boisterous Olde Madras!) was appointed "Governor of Our Towne", with full powers to try all those accused of capital crimes.

There being no clear cut legal procedure to deal with crime in the first quarter-century of "Our Towne's" existence, Foxcroft was forced to write to the Court of Directors for instructions when Mrs Ascentia Dawes, wife of a Councillor, killed her slave girl Chequa, alias Francisca. The Company replied on March 3, 1666, that it was very sorry for the "inhumane Act Perpetrated by Mrs Dawes in Murthering of her Servant" but they needed time to consider the whole situation and give advice not only on how to proceed "with her and others (if any) that were assisting to her in the Murther" but also how to prosecute in future "persons that shall committ the like horrid actions within the Lymitts (of) our Forte and Towne of Madras."

A week later, the Court of Directors despatched the momentous letter by which, under the Company's Charter of 1661, Madras got a Governor. Foxcroft was behind bars when this letter reached Madras "constituting" him "Governour of Our Towne and Fort... as well as Agent" and appointing him "a Councell under our Seale." Instructions were also given on how to proceed with the trial of Mrs Dawes. This trial, the first by jury in Madras, indeed India, commenced after Foxcroft was reinstated in 1669.

As the first step in "Rex vs Ascentia Dawes", 24 persons were summoned for a Grand Jury and returned the indictment previously made. Still following London's instructions, 36 prospective jurors for a jury of 12 were summoned, the indictment was read and Mrs Dawes informed that she could discharge any 20 of the prospective jurors without showing cause. She objected to three, including Winter, and then six Englishmen and six Portuguese were sworn in. Once again the indictment was read, the witnesses examined, and then the Jury retired to consider its verdict. Two hours later they were back, finding her guilty of "the Murther" but "not in manner and forme", and therefore in need of "directions from the Court." The Court thundered back that the Jury could only say "Guilty" or "Not Guilty" – "without exception or Lymitation." Out went the Jury again, returning in minutes for Foreman Edward Reade to deliver a verdict of "Not Guilty"!

Even the Court was shocked. Since the verdict was "contrary to all expectation," the Court, "supposing it to be a mistake," asked Reade again what the verdict was. "Not Guilty," he repeated. Then the Court asked each Juror in turn what his verdict was, and each replied "Not Guilty." And, as Foxcroft anticlimactically adds in his report of the proceedings, "Whereupon she was quit."

Detailed reports of the whole case were sent back to England by Foxcroft with a request that clearer guidance and trained assistance be sent out to help out in future cases, for "Wee found ourselves at a loss in several things for want of Instructions, having no man understanding the Laws and formalityes to instruct us, as... whether anything more had to be said to the Jury when they brought in such an unexpected verdict."

So ended 'The Case of the Slave Girl and the Councillor's Wife'. The unfortunate girl may not have got justice, but Madras, more fortunately, got a Governor and "the beginning of modern judicial Administration."

3

To Metropolitan Limits

With trigonometrical and topographical surveys of India having had their origins in Madras in 1800 – the original base line for "The Great Indian Trigonometrical Survey" was a 7-mile-long straight line along Mount Road, between Fort St George and St Thomas' Mount – the city has always been map-conscious and so it is no difficult task to cartographically discover its growth. But long before the surveyors got down to theodolites there were two maps of the beginnings of the city – Fryer's map of 1673 and Langlé's map of 1688.

The fort of Cogan and Day was planned more or less as a square enclosure with bastions at each corner and connecting walls, its centre 190 yards from the sea and 110 from the river on the west. Within the approximately 110 by 100 yards enclosure, it had been planned to situate the 'factory' diagonal to the square. When East India Company surgeon Dr John Fryer visited Madras in 1673 and drew what amounted to the first map of British Madras, he showed the 'Factory House' – which he called the *Governor's House* and others *Fort House* – situated right in the middle of the Inner Fort, indeed diagonal to the walled square and resembling a Muslim edifice with its domed roof. Also domed was the Guard House set in the west wall. This foundationless fort survived till 1714, when it was levelled and the 'Fort Square'[1] created.

By the end of 1640, only the southeast bastion to protect 'Factory House' had been built. It was 1653 before the other three bastions were built, joined with connecting walls and the Inner Fort completed, at a

---

[1] Later the Parade Ground, now usually a parking lot.

cost of 9,250 pagodas[2] (most of the money coming out of Day's pocket!).
Meanwhile, rude dwellings of European settlers – many of them
Portuguese from San Thomé – sprang up about the Fort, which soon
came to be called the 'Castle'. To the north of the 'Castle' a Catholic
chapel was built in 1642 by the Capuchin missionary, Father Ephraim
de Nevers, a man of saintly nature. To protect these new civilian
constructions, an 'Outer Fort' was built, with four bastions and
connecting walls on three sides, the western side being protected by the
Elambore River. Work on this started in the mid-1640s and gathered
pace only in 1653, after the completion of the Inner Fort, and finished
in 1666. This complex in its entirety was the nucleus of the present Fort
St.George. Gates in the northern wall of the Outer Fort led to a growing
Indian town of merchants, weavers and dyers and their retinue. This
Indian settlement, 'Black Town', had sunk roots in 1640-41.

In effect, Madras at this time was the 'Castle' (or 'Inner Fort')
enclosing within its walls and four bastions the 'Factory House' and the
official European quarter; the 'Outer Fort' enclosing this 'Castle', other
European homes and the Capuchin St Andrew's chapel – all protected
by four bastions, three walls and two gates, the Middle and Choultry
Gates, in the north wall leading to 'BlackTown'; 'Black Town', to the
north of the 'Outer Fort', was protected by mud walls. Between the
'Outer Fort' and 'Black Town' was a wide parade, the market place or
'Buzzar'. All this is shown in Dr.John Fryer's sketch of 1673. Curiously,
though, it shows neither the Sea Gate nor the Great Bastion Governor
Langhorne built to the south of the Sea Gate c.1673, but shows on the
southeast bastion of the Inner Fort the Cross of St.George which
Governor Yale raised only in 1687!

By the autumn of 1640, there were 300 or 400 families of weavers
from the Telugu country (now Andhra settled outside 'White Town'
and about 70 houses inside. The only Englishman living outside the Fort
at this time was the country-born Thomas Clarke who built himself a
house in 1640/1 just outside the fort and to the northwest of it – at a
place where the Caldera Point bastion was developed, which was about
where the railway lines now curve into the Fort's station. He has been
described as "the first Inhabitant" and came from Armagon. He later
built himself a house to the east of the Popham's Broadway-NSC Bose

---

[2] 1 pagoda = appx. Rs 10 when the Pound Sterling was about the same value.

Road junction. Clarke died in 1683 and his tombstone is part of St Mary's courtyard. This house was later inherited by Nicholas Manucci, who arrived in Madras in 1686 and about whom more anon. He had married Clarke's widow Elizabeth in Pondicherry.

In 1674, there were 118 houses within Fort St George and 75 houses in 'Black Town', about half the houses in the Fort being Portuguese-owned. Fryer says that there were about 300 English and about 3,000 Portuguese in Madras at the time. Langlé's map in 1688 shows just how fast the English (White) and Indian (Black) Towns grew from Fryer's time. Row upon row of houses are marked, each separated by straight roads, the entire planning in chequer-board style, a possible plan for the long blocks of latter-day New York City!

The earliest reliable map of modern Madras, however, was drawn sometime between 1707 and 1709 after a survey ordered by Governor Thomas Pitt. In it, the city limits appear to be a *kuppam* just south of the Fort, the Elambore River to the west, and, in the north, a line about 500 yards beyond what is now called Elephant Gate Street in George Town. The Governor's castle is centred to the east in a walled square. To the south of this Inner Fort's neighbour, St. Mary's Church, and near the eastern walls is the Town Hall, clearly shown as a domed building. Just north of the Fort is Black Town with the Town Temple in its centre. Across from Black Town's North Wall is 'Muthial Peta' and to its west, separated by a drain, is 'Peddanaigue Pete'. South of the 'Peddanaigue Pete' and sandwiched between it and The Island is the 'Company's garden', Pitt's rest-and-recreation 'country seat' – with a mansion in a walled enclosure and a small fort to the south. It's a map that presents a magnificent picture of 70-year-old Madras.

In 1693, *Fort House* was pulled down and moved eastwards, to where what became the second Governor's House, built by 1695, is today part of the central portion of the Secretariat. The Pitt Map shows the new position of *Governor's House* – a flat-roofed building, parallel to the walls, and 110 feet by 55 feet in extent – names roads within the Fort and indicates a mint, a hospital, a storehouse, the Town Hall, and a carpentry yard in addition to the earlier buildings. The Town Hall, now occupied by the Army, was built next to St Mary's in 1680 and enlarged at a cost of 4,000 pagodas to its present dimensions in 1692. Its cupola no longer survives. Significantly, the second Black Town, 'Muthial Peta', to which 'Black Town' residents moved after their first settlement was razed by the Company, and neighbouring 'Peddanaigue Pete' are clearly depicted in the map as settlements developed on a gridiron pattern. Obviously, there was a population here too, before the first Black Town was razed in the middle of the 18th Century, much of it probably migrant.

In 1711, Governor Harrison demolished the 'Inner Fort' and, with the rubble, raised a 'Fort Square' – Parade Ground – opposite *Governor's House*. At its western end was the Fort's main gate to the rest of the town. He also rebuilt the hospital, the mint and many of the barracks in the Fort.

After the 1746 French occupation of Madras and San Thomé ended in 1749, work on strengthening the Fort began and after Lally's siege in 1758-59, the last great reconstruction of the Fort took place under Governor Pigot (1755-63). Robins, Brohier, Scott, Call, Benfield ... an honoured roll-call of engineers ... were responsible for the rebuilding of the Fort from 1750. After a short period of inactivity in the 1760s, work on strengthening the Fort was renewed in 1771 and continued until 1783 when the last major work was completed.

A map of Madras in 1733, reproduced by Talboys Wheeler and therefore called by his name, sheds more light on the boundaries of the surrounding villages, but indicates a shift of only 1,500 yards on the northern boundary, extending Peddanaickenpet and Muthialpet. Six block houses built in the early 18th Century to protect the northern boundary, from near the Elambore River to the beach, were named after the six most important Company Merchants of the period. They may well have financed these constructions, which were linked by a 'Bound Hedge' of aloes and thorny plants. 'Bondage' (a variation of 'Bound Hedge') survives in the name of a lane in Royapuram!

Conradi's map, after a new survey in 1755, "marks the transition from ancient to modern Madras." The southern boundary here is arbitrary, merely a line about a distance of 1,000 yards south of the Cooum mouth, including Chintadripet and a part of Triplicane. The Elambore River is still the western boundary of north Madras. But the northern boundary is definite, a few yards further north than shown in the 1733 map. In 'Black Town' alone there were more than 8,700 houses, according to 1750 statistics. In the 1760s, the British razed 'Black Town' after the second French siege, created an esplanade in its place and encouraged the development of a 'New Black Town' north of the Esplanade, incorporating Peddanaickenpet and Muthialpet.

In 1772, a survey of the city fixed the northern limit of the Esplanade with six boundary stones. Only one of these 15-foot tall masonry obelisks remains – at Second Line Beach, near *Dare House*, cared for by Parry & Co, announcing in granite the Esplanade's boundary as of January 1, 1773. A second was discovered in 1996, being treated as a cornerstone of a shop-house on the Badrian Chetty Street corner. It was spotted when the building was being pulled down for new development and met with the same fate despite several pleas to the developers. The other boundary pillars were at the junctions of Popham's Broadway, Kondi Chetty Street, Stringer Street and, probably, Linghi Chetty Street with what was China Bazaar Road, later Esplanade Road, and is now NSC Bose Road.

In 1775, there was a proposal to plant a hedge along the limits of Madras. The proposal was dropped, but a perusal of the survey indicates the Madras limits at the time: the Adyar River in the south, up to a point near the present Mount Road-Chamier's Road junction, then along Mount Road and Nungambakkam Tank Road, then around Chetput and Vepery and so to the sea at a point a mile from Black Town's northern wall. A northern boundary stone was found on Monegar Choultry Street in more recent times.

The last time, in John Company's day, that the limits of Madras were fixed, was on November 2, 1798, when they were formally announced by the Governor-in-Council and a new map was drawn. The limits to the south and west were as in 1775, but the western limits now moved further out, past Chetput to take in Kilpauk and Perambur. From north of Perambur, the northern boundary ran to the sea, incorporating Tondiarpet. Thus, by the beginning of the 19th Century, Madras City had almost taken its pre-2011 shape.

When Madras celebrated its tercentenary in 1939, the only major change in the City's extent from the 1798 limits was the inclusion of Mambalam, in 1923, making the railway line the western boundary.

The first organised census of the City was taken in 1871 and a population of 397,552 was recorded for the eight municipal divisions of the City, which covered an area of 27 sq miles. The census of 1931, following the inclusion of Mambalam (which is now Theagaroyanagar), recorded a population of 647,232 – the population not even doubling and the city area increasing by just about 3 sq miles.

But then came the War years – and Madras has not stopped growing since. Adyar, Guindy and Saidapet were first added in the south, West Mambalam, Kodambakkam, Aminjikkarai and Ayyanavaram in the west. Twentyeight towns and villages, amounting to 19 sq miles, were incorporated between 1941 and 1951, adding nearly 65 per cent to the City's earlier expanse. Only the northern boundaries did not really change. Over that decade, the population increased from 777,481 to 1,416,056, mainly due not so much to the new villages as to migration as the city industrialised for War and sought a new workforce. With industrialisation being Nehru's answer to independent India's self-sufficiency, both industry and the migrants needed for it kept growing. By 1971, the population of the City alone – not counting Greater Madras into which Francis Day's coastal strip had really expanded – was 2,469,449, a six-fold increase in a hundred years, whereas the city's area, now amounting to about 51 sq miles, almost the same as in 1951, was not even double what it was a century earlier. Ten years later, with the addition of almost 16 sq miles, the City had at last more than doubled its 1871 area, but its population (3.3 million) was now over eight times what it had been then. New developments in the West – Anna Nagar (the old Naduvakkarai) and K K Nagar – the ancient villages of Velacheri and Tiruvanmiyur in the south and Erukkancheri in the north had contributed to this rather more rapid expansion in the quarter century after 1951.

And still Madras grows. As the Millennium dawned, it was not the city alone. The city and suburbs had from 1975 become one – the Chennai Metropolitan Area – from Minjur in the north to Vandalur and Semmancheri in the south, and Nemam and Thiruninravur in the west, an urban agglomeration 1, 189 sq.km (459 sq.miles) in extent and with a population of a little over 10 million in 2017, nearly 9 million of it within Chennai Corporation limits.[3] As 2018 began, it was announced that this thriving modern metropolis with flourishing industrial suburbs would be expanded into an urban agglomeration of 8878 sq. km (3428 sq. miles) whose planning would be in the hands of the Chennai Metropolitan Development Authority (CMDA).

But for all its modern growth, metropolitan Madras still remains true to much of its fascinating historic past. And vestiges of that fascinating past may be seen in many places of interest in and around the city.

---

[3] It is estimated that the 2011 additions under the Corporation of Madras will make the population within the new Corporation limits a little over 8.5 million.

Pushing the Map Ever Forward

The Survey of India, one of the world's oldest, biggest and best survey institutions, has the closest links with Madras – almost all its founding officers being Madras hands.

The Government Survey School, the first modern technical institution to be established in Asia, was founded in Madras in 1794 and developed into a civil engineering college. But long before surveying became a subject of education, maps were being prepared in Madras.

Dr John Fryer's plan of Madras, dated by some to 1673 and by others to 1691, vies with Langlé's plan of 1688 to be considered the earliest map of British Madras. They are amongst the first maps prepared in India after the Age of Exploration, but both lack accuracy. Perhaps the earliest reliable map of Madras, the result of the first accurate survey of the City, is the Pitt Map of 1711-12, that was prepared on the orders of the Governor, Thomas Pitt. A map of 1733, named after Talboys Wheeler who first published it many years later, was the result of the second survey, this one ordered by another Governor Pitt, Cousin Morton. A survey in 1755 produced F L Conradi's map, then 1798 saw another survey and another map, W Ravenshaw produced the map of 1822 and Lawford the map of 1861. By then, Madras was in modern times and the Company had given way to the sarkar.

It was long after mapping had been encouraged by the Pitts, Saunders and Pigot that the foundation of the Survey of India was laid – also with the closest possible Madras connections. James Rennell, a 23-year-old ship's captain, was the man Robert Clive ordered to "start at once on a general survey of Bengal", thus beginning the Survey of India story in 1765. But Rennell's surveying career had begun on the

Coromandel Coast, the southern reaches of which he had mapped in 1763 while skippering a coastal trader that plied between Tondi and Point Calimere. All Clive had wanted from Rennell was a plan of Bengal, instead he got a topographical survey, compelling him to appoint "Captain Rennell, a young man of distinguished merit in this branch, to be Surveyor-General" (of Bengal). Rennell was directed "to form one general chart from those already made". The result was the celebrated Bengal Atlas. By the time he was 35, Rennell was as frustrated by his failure to overcome Nature in his push into Bhutan and the Himalaya as he was sick. He returned to England, where the 'Father of Indian Geography' lived on for another fifty years, much of it spent in supervising for the Company the work of the splendid surveyors who succeeded him and opened out India to unification.

The dour Scot, Colin Mackenzie, better remembered for his scholarliness and the superb collection that constitutes the nucleus of the Oriental Manuscripts Library that is housed behind the Madras University library in Chepauk, and William Lambton, a mild and patient Yorkshireman, were the first of these great pioneers. And both began their surveying careers in Madras. Mackenzie arrived in Madras in 1783 as an Ensign in the Engineers. Lambton arrived there in 1798 with Arthur Wellesley's 33rd Regiment that he had joined in 1796. Mackenzie joined Wellesley's regiment on the march to Seringapatam, where the man the world remembers as Wellington won his first spurs. Together, the two men who were to delineate the face of India, played a notable role in breaching the defences of Tippu. But it was in peace that the two were to make their name, together with a third little-remembered name, Dr Francis Buchanan, to whom the Indian Botanical and Zoological Surveys owe much. To this trio, India also owes much for the "re-discovery" of its ancient monuments, the sculpted wonders of the past.

Mackenzie had already carried out a survey of the Deccan, before the final Mysore War began. Now he embarked on a survey of Mysore. Lambton, meanwhile, was working on a survey to link the Coromandel Coast with the Malabar Coast, a project whose cost perturbed a Council that felt any traveller wishing to reach Seringapatam had "only to say so to his head palanquin bearer and he'll get there without recourse to Lambton's map"! This project was the beginning of the Great Trigonometrical Survey of India, of which he was made Superintendent in 1818. Lambton and his Great Theodolite marched from Cape Comorin to Central India, establishing the great Survey of India tradition that the map must go only forward, no matter what hazards and obstacles its servants may encounter. In 1823, Lambton died in a survey tent and his assistant, George Everest, took over as Superintendent of the great push forward and flogged the Great Arc ever northwards. Everest's reward was the christening with his name of Peak XV, discovered by calculation in 1852 to be the highest mountain in the world. The calculations and drawings based on the work of both was done by another Madras hand – Joshua de Penning, who was educated in what became St George's School and went on to head the back office of the Great Trigonometrical Survey in Calcutta.

The surveyor most intimately connected with Madras, however, was Mackenzie. All his life was dedicated to the Presidency of which he was appointed the first Surveyor-General in 1810. Five years later, he was appointed the first Surveyor-General of all India and moved to Calcutta. There he died in 1821, as much of a broken heart over having to leave his beloved Madras as of age and illness. But in those last years in Calcutta, he was as much concerned with the Great Trigonometrical Survey as he had been in Madras, for in 1818 the Government took it over from Madras. The work of the GTS is, however, better remembered today than the supervision of Mackenzie or the brilliant maps he did of Mysore and the Deccan. It is for his Indological hobby that Mackenzie is remembered, not his work, yet he was perhaps the greatest of those early surveyors who believed that if you could move you could work.

A later contribution to surveying was Governor Robert Palk who in 1765 got Lt William Stevens to survey Adam's Bridge and, as a consequence of his enthusiasm, has both the Bay and Strait named after him: Palk Bay and Palk Strait.

4

The Fort Where It All Began

1. Of Clive and Wellington

Fort St George, which today houses the Government of Tamil Nadu, is still much as it must have been when it was an 18th Century British bastion. Its flagstaff was still recently, the tallest in the land. Here, in *'Clive House'* and *Wellesley House*, in St Mary's Church and the Museum, there is still much of earliest Madras.

From time to time, *'Clive House'* has a corner of it opened to the public. And at such times, remembered in *Clive Corner* is Empire-founding Robert Clive who arrived in India on May 31, 1744, as a 19-year-old Company Writer on a salary of £5 per annum. When the French took Fort St George in 1746, Clive was among those who escaped – and found his true vocation on the battlefield. He and Dupleix first crossed swords at the battle for Fort St David, Cuddalore, where he had re-joined the Company's forces after his escape and where he received his military training and commission.

Major Stringer Lawrence, generally considered the founder of the Indian Army, was his mentor. It was Lawrence who in 1747 organised the Indian *peons,* employed for guard duties by John Company from its earliest days, into a formal militia, though Governor Yale had taken the first steps towards this in 1689. This militia was made a regular sepoy military formation comprising two battalions by Lawrence in 1758, in anticipation of the second French siege. Growing to eighteen battalions over the next few years, and comprising the Carnatic and Circars[1] Infantry

---

[1] There were five battalions of Circars Infantry, mainly Telugus, and 13 battalions of Carnatic Infantry, mainly Tamils.

stationed in four centres, this was the nucleus of the Madras Army that grew into the Indian Army.

Clive's first victories were his campaigns in the Arcot and 'Trichinopoly' districts, where, sallying forth from Fort St David, he harassed the enemy lines. His first great military feat followed: the 'Arcot diversion' and the defence of that besieged town. When Fort St George was rendered to the British in 1749, Clive was among the first to enter Madras. He was raised to the rank of Captain, given the Stewardship of Fort St George and honoured with the title Bahadur. Peace, marriage and a trip home followed. Then came undying fame.

He was only 32 when he set forth with the expedition to Bengal – and Plassey (Palashi, today) – after Calcutta had fallen to Siraj-ud-Dowlah. He was recommended to lead the land forces, mainly comprising topasses and troops of the Carnatic Infantry (later, together with the Circars Infantry, the Madras Native Infantry and still later the Madras Regiment, the oldest regiment in the Indian Army), "as the person in all respects best qualified for the undertaking of the Calcutta expedition," by his friend Robert Orme, later famous for his epic *A History of the British Nation in Industan from 1745,* but, at the time, because of his literary ability, confidant of many of the unlettered powers-that-were in the Madras Presidency.

Clive had returned to Cuddalore from England only four months earlier, in June 1756; in September he was requested to forsake the comfort of a Deputy Governorship and proceed from Fort St David to Bengal to 'chastise' Nawab Siraj-ud-Dowlah. After securing eastern India, Clive returned to England only to come back for a third and last time, in 1765, this time as Governor of Bengal and Commander-in-Chief of British Forces in India. In 1772, he left India for good, as usual triumphant but nevertheless with a reputation besmirched.

Twice, in his earlier Madras days, Clive had attempted suicide while living in *Writers' Building,* then located between what were later known as *Wellesley House* and *'Clive House'.* On this site, there later came up the 'Grand Arsenal', still used by the military but not as an arsenal. When he exchanged the quill for the sword, Clive gave up his attempts at courting death, seeking the self-inflicted variety thereafter only whenever he relinquished arms. It was during one such period of depression, after attaining his greatest success, that he, on November

Fort St. George in the 18th Century

OVERNOR'S HOUSE & COUNCIL CHAMBER, *Assembly Hall, Secretariat* and *Ministerial* ces. B. TOWN HALL, now **Army's Fort Offices.** C. *Mary's Church.* D. GUARD ROOM now **Defence** ces. E. ADMIRALTY HOUSE (CLIVE HOUSE), now **Pay and Accounts Office** and the **Office of the** *haeological Survey of India, Southern Circle.* F. *LESLEY HOUSE,* now **Defence Offices.** G. THE

ARSENAL, now **Defence Offices.** H. **King's Barracks,** then as now. J. **Barracks,** then as now. *K. OFFICERS' MESS,* and before that the *PUBLIC EXCHANGE HALL* and *LIGHTHOUSE,* now the **Fort Museum.** L. **Flagstaff,** the tallest in the land. *M. Parade Ground (CORNWALLIS SQUARE). N. Fort House. P. Bank. Q.* **New Secretariat Multistorey Building.** *R. Cornwallis Cupola. S. Police Station. T. Hospital. U. Post Office*

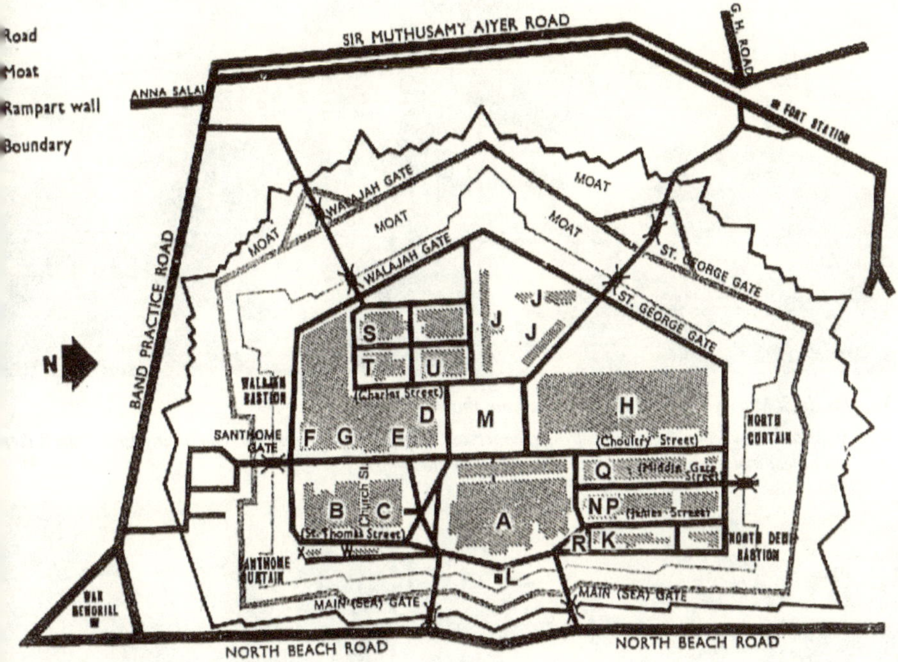

A plan of Fort St. George... where the past still lingers.
St. George's Gate and moat...now open for the wheels of Government.

3. *Inside St Mary's Church...its altarpiece not the only relic of history.*

4. *Steps to a Governor's worship...from a courtyard flagged with tombstones (including Elizabeth Baker the oldest inscription in British India – seen in close-up)*

22, 1774, finally succeeded in fulfilling his death-wish. But theories of murder are also bandied about.

During his later Madras days, Clive and his wife lived in a house rented from an Armenian merchant, the 'Great House on Charles Street'. It served as the Governor's house immediately after the rendition. It later served as his town house for a while. The Courts of Admiralty – established in 1687 as a Court of Appeal – sat in this building from 1755, thus being responsible for its official name, *Admiralty House*. This building, now popularly called *Clive House*, is on the southern side of the Fort. Today, it is the regional office of the Archaeological Survey of India, which has restored a part of it in 2006. A 'museum' corner, set apart here in memory of the man who, it may be argued with some justification, laid the foundation for today's Indian Union and yesterday's British Empire, has been kept opening and closing from 1990. It has had to contend with military security, lack of maintenance and just plain lack of bureaucratic interest. But when resurrected from time to time, the most recent being in 2009, it does warrant attention. As does the restored first floor ballroom which serves from time to time as an exhibition hall.

The Grand Arsenal was designed by Col Patrick Ross and was opened for use in 1772. Ross' architectural style, with its many sculptured embellishments, has been described as "florid". The Arsenal was built on inverted arches by contractor John Sullivan for 28,000 pagodas. It remained in use as an arsenal till 1931.

There was yet another formidable soldier who learnt his trade within the solid walls of Fort St George. In what came to be called *Wellesley House,* between *Clive House* and the San Thomé Gate, there had lived in 1798 Col. the Hon Arthur Wellesley. At about the same time, his elder brother, Richard Wellesley, Lord Mornington, Governor-General of India and first of the true Imperial expansionists, had come down from Calcutta and lived in the Fort, supervising the operations against Tippu Sultan that were to lead to the final subjugation of all South India. The younger Wellesley, his 33rd Regiment on attachment to the Madras Army, was in residence in Fort St. George for many months, helping with the arrangements for the Mysore campaign. From here he rode falteringly against Tippu Sultan – on one occasion saved by Colin Mackenzie when he lost his way – but then performed great deeds with the Madras Army against the Marathas, particularly at Assaye, before returning Home to

those legendary triumphs he is best remembered by – against Napoleon.
Arthur Wellesley was the man who became the first Duke of Wellington,
hero of Waterloo.

Wellesley House, over 200 years old, alas, fell victim to inter-
departmental rivalry over its maintenance, and a portion of it collapsed
in November 1980. Little or nothing has been done since to preserve
this historical building built in 1796 and one of the 16 protected
monuments among the 30 or so buildings in the Fort. But it precariously
survives adjacent to the Grand Arsenal and is accessible through it.

2.The bells of St Mary's

Whenever the bells of St Mary's toll, they ring in a historic church
from where, time and time again in centuries past, there had gone forth
humble worshippers to perform deeds of derring-do and to achieve fame,
fortune – and, in some cases, notoriety. It was in St Mary's, the Company
Church in Fort St George, that Elihu Yale had worshipped, as had, 'Pirate'
Pitt and Robert Clive, Stringer Lawrence and Robert Palk the Chaplain
who became Governor, Warren Hastings and Eyre Coote, 'Nabob'
Rumbold and Andrew Bell who gave England the Madras monitorial
system of education, Cornwallis and Wellesley who became Wellington,
'Boy' Malcolm and Tom Munro. The stories of most of them are the
very stuff of the legend of Dick Whittington who heard another peal of
bells. Whether the contemporary view of imperialism assigns these early
parishioners of St Mary's niches of fame or notoriety, there is no denying
them their place in history – even if, in the case of some, it is only the
history of Madras – and the first steps they took from there to achieve it.

All this would make St Mary's a rather special church even if it was
not the first church purpose-built by the Anglicans east of Suez. Sadly,
no more does it enjoy all the pomp and circumstance it had seen in more
regal days when it was, first, the church of the first congregation, then
that of the Governor's Congregation, later the Garrison Church, before
becoming what it is today – an ancient monument, the oldest British
building in Madras, in which a church has been resuscitated by a small
but enthusiastic congregation, the Church of South India and the
Archaeological Survey of India.

It was on March 25, 1678, that excavation work began for the church
Governor Streynsham Master was determined to build to make good the
lack of an Anglican church in Madras. Since the foundation work

commenced on the Annunciation Day of the Blessed Virgin, the church was named St Mary's in Her honour. Master, an India hand from the time he was 16, might have been "blunt and imperious in bearing... (caring) little to conciliate those around him," but he did "bring order out of chaos" in most of the British settlements in 17th Century India by his accomplished book-keeping and auditing abilities. Regulations for better administration, rules for the conduct of Company officials, and the first spirited attempts at introducing the rudiments of civic and judicial organisation were Master's contributions to early Madras. But he also seems to have been one of the founders of red tape – which perhaps remains in Fort St George as a monument to him! The more concrete memorial to him, however, is St Mary's, the church the Company had not wanted.

John Company, from its earliest times, did little to encourage Anglican Britain's religious faith in India, fearing the challenge to the Company's writ, and the authority of its officials, the clergy might pose. The earliest British in Fort St George, Anglicans for the majority, often worshipped at the Catholic chapel Cogan permitted the Capuchin priest Ephraim de Nevers, skilful arbitrator, scholar and remarkable linguist, to build in the Fort. St. Andrew's was built in 1642, looking like a wood shed, then developed as a permanent structure in 1675. This was the first Church built in British India. Father de Nevers had been invited by Agent Andren Cogan as early as 1640 to settle in the Fort. Father de Nevers also conducted in the church what might be considered India's first English school. It was not till 1647 that Madras got an Anglican chaplain, who used a room in 'Fort House' as a chapel – a practice followed by his successors for the next three decades or so.

Pomp-loving Streynsham Master, finding worship in these surroundings cramped, and noting that the Capuchins had been permitted to rebuild their chapel as a fine new church, St Andrew's, in the Fort in 1675, not only persuaded his Council that it was time Madras had an Anglican church of its own but also convinced them that they should not wait for the reluctant Company to change its mind and build it, but should raise the funds for it themselves. The Governor himself showed the way by contributing 100 of the 805 pagodas eventually subscribed by 38 donors. Yale, later to be Governor but at that time a lowly Writer, contributed 20 pagodas, three-fifths of his annual salary! Master and Yale, as London 'Nabobs' over three decades later, were appropriately associated with another church-building effort – the Church of St George the Martyr in Queen's Square, London, honouring England's patron saint whose name had been bestowed on the Fort they had both once served in.

With the Catholic church located to the northwest of 'Fort House', Master decided his church should be to the southeast and there Master Gunner and bastion designer William Dixon built a solid construction not only to be able to withstand sieges and cyclones but also the ravages of time itself. And, so, St Mary's stands today in one of the tree-shaded corners of the Fort, much as most of it must have been when Dixon built it and his successor Edward Fowle embellished it. The sanctuary, steeple (early 18th Century and used as an observation post during Lally's siege of 1758-59), tower and vestry were later additions or extensions to the brick-and-polished-*chunam* (lime) church Dixon built. The original building was a rectangular box, about 60 feet by 90 feet, with outer walls four feet thick and a bomb-proof curved roof, two feet thick! Wood was used only for the doors, windows and the ornate embellishments of the West Gallery, now abbreviated but which once ran across the church and seated Governor and Council. Its carved teakwood balustrade dates to 1680. The tower, detached from the church, was built in 1701 and a steeple was added to it in 1710. The tower was linked to the church in 1760; the curved flight of steps outside was part of these extensions. The obelisk-like spire, designed by Colonel Gent, was added in 1795 after a proposal to make the tower a lighthouse was turned down. The Thwaites and Reed clock from Hastings, Sussex, was added to the tower in 1902. Above the large open windows are lovely stained glass arches that filter a multicoloured glow into the church when the windows are closed.

Work on the church was completed in 1679 and Master and Council applied to the Bishop of London for authority to consecrate it. Permission arrived in October 1680, and, on Thursday the 28th, with Governor and Council attending in state and all other English residents of the settlement present, the Rev Richard Portman took the oaths, consecrated the church and became the first chaplain of St Mary's.

Master, and the first congregation, set conventions that were to be followed for many years – full wigs, the most constricting of European clothes, the Governor in periwig and laced coat walking in state from *Fort House* to the church between 200 soldiers drawn up in two lines all along the short walk, the residents awaiting his arrival, then following him into the church while the organ pealed the voluntary with which, as Ensign Thomas Salmon (1699) would have it, "they salute God and the Governor"! The first organ was bought by the church in 1687. The present organ, the fifth, dates to 1894. The City's first grand concert of sacred music was held in the church in 1794 with Michael Topping, a name better associated with the Observatory, the organist, and Lady Oakeley, the Governor's wife, among those who sang parts of the Messiah.

For the first 150 years the Company Church in the Fort was to remain the Presidency Church. However, with a working class group of Anglicans settled in Black Town, the Rev R H Kerr built with the community St. Mark's, off North Broadway, in 1800. This church was rebuilt in 1888 and is on an intriguingly named road, Chapel Church Road, possibly, indicative of growthfrom chapel to church. This was the first Anglican Church to be built outside the Fort. In it is buried the Rev Kerr and to him there has been raised a monument. But with the spread of 'garden houses' over the Choultry Plain and into Egmore and Vepery, new churches were built, St George's, to grow into the Cathedral, in 1816, and St Matthias' at Vepery in 1823, the earliest ones. And with them began the slow decline of St Mary's. It became a garrison church, serving the British regiments stationed in the Fort. But when the 1st Essex marched out on August 15, 1947 and the 3rd Sikh Light Infantry took over, this association too came to an end.

In March 1948, the church was transferred to Indian trustees. On April 1, it became the responsibility of the Church of India (now South India) – the State maintaining it only as a monument. The committee which runs the church has ever since tried to live up to the promises in the original petition of the private donors who founded St Mary's: "... we ... do promise hereafter to refuse and renounce to put this Church or any part of it to any profane or common use whatsoever, and desire it may be dedicated wholly and only to Religious uses ... promising that ... We and our successors in this place will ... see it conveniently repaired and decently furnished..."

During the 1985 restoration, the famed marble-like Madras 'mirror-finish' of the walls was meticulously refurbished by artisans from Karaikudi in Chettinad where it is most seen, using the ancient formula of pure eggshell lime (or was it the inferior seashell lime?), special river sand, milk and fermented *kadukka (myrobalan)*-and-jaggery water. But conventional painting elsewhere rather diminished the antique appearance of the church. By 2000, however, restoration appeared needed again[2] and was begun in time for a celebration of the church's 325th anniversary.

***

Generations of worshippers and clergy have left behind in St Mary's mementoes that would be the envy of any museum. In many of these memorials are the last vestiges of remembrance of times past and of the men and women who helped to make Madras history. But no memento is more poignant than the weathered but elaborately scribed tombstones that pave the narrow northern yard bound by the 19th Century railings. Many of these tombstones tell the stories of persons who had lived and worked and died in Madras from the first days of its founding, forty years before St Mary's. These silent slabs are also a moving sidelight of the Anglo-French wars for the wealth of Coromandel.

When the Catholic French occupied Fort St George from 1746, they had at first used St Mary's as a military dormitory, then as a store. But of physical desecration to relics holy or revered there had been little. When Lally besieged Madras in 1758-59, however, the Fort's cemetery (a part of the 'Guava Garden' where Law College now is) was a battleground, the French making use of many of the obelisks and tombs and memorials there to provide their infantry cover and their guns foundations. As a consequence of the siege, the British razed 'Old Black Town' and the adjacent cemetery to provide a clear field of fire. As part of this post-war operation they moved the inscribed tombstones to St Mary's yard in 1763. A few stones in the yard are also from the old Capuchin Church of St Andrew's. When Hyder Ali threatened the Fort in 1782, the tombstones were dug up again and used to mount guns on the ramparts. But many broke, and when they were restored in 1807 – not quite where they had once been – only 104 had survived.

Still to be seen amongst these 104 is the tombstone of Elizabeth Baker, wife of Aaron Baker, first President of Madras. Mrs Baker died at sea after childbirth, when still three weeks away from Madras, but was brought here for burial. Her tombstone, with its 1652 date, is the oldest

---

[2] A reflection of the quality of modern understanding of ancient techniques is the deterioration this had suffered in the late 1990s and the difficulty restorers had in reviving it when they began another restoration effort in 2001.

British inscription in India! Another early tombstone in the yard is that of Nathaniel Foxcroft, son of the first victim of a 'coup' in Madras. The younger Foxcroft, who had also been imprisoned with his father (see 'A Winter's Tale'), died in 1670. The only Tamil tombstone among the lot is one from St Andrew's Church. It remembers Thaniappa Mudaliar aka Lazarus Timothy, "one of the founders of Pondicherry". He was probably the dubash of Francois Martin; certainly his descendants were *dubashes* of important personages in the French East India Company. This tombstone, dating to 1691, is the oldest Tamil tombstone in Madras and may be found at the eastern end of the courtyard.

A fragmented stone let into the curved staircase is all that is left of the memory of Agent Henry Greenhill (d. 1658), who had been around from the founding of Madras and had negotiated several times with the country powers the extent of the settlement's site. But the first Governor to have been buried in the Church precincts, beneath where the tower was later built, was Francis Hastings (d. 1721). Hastings was ousted from the gubernatorial seat after just a year and a half of power, then, while ill, charged with embezzlement, the accusation leading to shock, illness and death. George Pigot, twice Governor of Madras, died in rather similar circumstances in 1777, after the Council had confined him at St Thomas' Mount. He was the first Governor to be buried in the church proper, his tombstone bearing no name but only a cross and the words *'In Memoriam'*. Other intra-mural interments – the last was in 1875 – included Governor Henry Ward, better known for his achievements in Ceylon; the well-loved Thomas Munro, who sits saddleless, hence stirrupless, astride his steed on the Island Grounds; and John Doveton, friend of Tippu Sultan. Magaretta Baroness Hobart and her infant son John are also interred here. She was the first wife of the first Lord Hobart to be Governor of Madras. This Lord Hobart (Gov: 1794-98) gave his name to Hobart, Tasmania. The second Lord Hobart (Gov: 1872-75) is interred in the church.

Besides the tombs, there are several monuments inside the church as well as numerous memorial tablets on the six detached pillars. Most of them the work of John Flaxman and James Bacon, they were shipped out from England. Amongst those so remembered is Schwartz (1726-98), that Lutheran Missionary better known in Thanjavur where he was close to the Maratha rulers and where he founded in 1784 St Peter's School, whose first 40 boys and girls were perhaps the first Indians to be taught

English in school in the Mofussil. And then there's John Burgoyne, who brought out the first European cavalry to India, the 23rd Light Dragoons, but who is better known for leading the opposition to Robert Clive in Britain; he did little of note in India before his death and burial inside St Mary's, the position of the grave not being now known. And there's a plaque or two that asserts that 'coup du soleil'[3] was responsible for the remembered's death!

Adorning the church's walls in a rather tattered state until 1984 were the Regimental colours of British regiments that served in Madras, the most interesting of which belonged to Neill's Blue Caps, founded in 1688, later the first British regiment formed by Stringer Lawrence in India. This regiment came to be known as the 102nd Royal Madras Infantry and, later, as the Dublin Fusiliers. The oldest regiment of the Indian Army of today, the Madras Regiment, now headquartered in the Wellesley Barracks in Wellington, near Coonoor, was first raised in 1758 by Stringer Lawrence; this regiment was the heir of the Indian militia he had raised in Fort St David in 1747/48. The first two battalions were raised in Madras on December 4th to defend Fort St George against Lally's anticipated onslaught. Lally's 40-day siege began on January 2, 1759.

Some of the flags are now in the Fort Museum, preserved as well as can be. But the tombstones and memorial tablets remain, a significant part of St Mary's historical wealth. Browsers walk with history everywhere in this church. Many a tablet has a moving story to tell of those who passed on and the times they had lived in. No wonder the Church has been described as the 'Westminster Abbey of the East'.

The font of black Pallavaram granite has been in use since 1680, but its wooden cover was carved only in 1885. Baptised in it were the children of Job Charnock, founder of Fort William and Calcutta in 1690 and whose name has been given to this granite (Charnockite). Charnock, legend has it, had, in Bihar, rescued by force a Hindu widow who was about to be consumed by the flaming pyre of her late husband. She lived with Charnock for the rest of her life and it was their three daughters – Mary, Elizabeth and Catherine – who were baptised in St Mary's in 1689 when Charnock, Agent in Hoogli, arrived in Madras, fleeing his station in the face of Mughal power. When he returned to Bengal, funded and equipped by Madras, he founded Calcutta. Also baptised here was

---

[3] Sunstroke!

David Yale, Elihu's son. David Yale was four when he died and a memorial commemorating him, but forgotten by most today, is still to be found in the Law College grounds; another memorial is the remains of Fort St David, Cuddalore, that his father built and named as much after him as the patron saint of Wales.

The first marriage to be celebrated in St Mary's was that of Elihu Yale and Catherine Hynmer (the widow of his friend and 2nd in Council, Joseph Hynmer) on November 4, 1680, the bride being given away by Governor Master. It was also here that, on February 18, 1753, Clive was married to Margaret Maskelyne by that famous Lutheran missionary Rev Fabricius, who, at the time, was acting chaplain of St Mary's. And standing witness to a marriage here on December 2, 1798 was Arthur Wellesley, Waterloo still many years ahead. The church records, from consecration to the present era – except for the period of French occupation – are still preserved, some in the church, some in the Fort Museum. But the earliest Register of Baptisms, Marriages and Burials, from October 28, 1680 to December 31, 1786, dates in the original only from 1739, the records before that date having been painstakingly recopied in this parchment volume from the original – to ensure preservation – by Alexander Wynch, later to become Governor. Wynch, it is reported, was paid 50 pagodas for his labour.

Some of the Registers are on exhibition in the church. So is a visitor's book, dating from 1903 to 1947, replete with the signatures of visiting royalty and nobility. Other records may be seen in the Fort Museum.

Amongst the church's valued possessions is the altar piece, a huge painting of *The Last Supper* in the Raphael manner. There is a dubious tradition that suggests that it was brought from Pondicherry as part of the loot of 1761. Better recorded is the fact that it does not find mention in the church property listed in 1756 but is listed in the Vestry records of 1782. Some Art authorities attribute it to George Willison, who was in Madras from 1772 to 1780 trying to make his fortune, like many another European artist, painting portraits of the rich in Madras. Willison appears to have been the court painter for the Nawab of the Carnatic and is believed to have painted this picture for his patron who presented it to the Governor's Church c. 1780. The painting, reputedly the oldest representation in India of the great Biblical scene, was moved to a position above the altar in 1902, it is reported. The altar rails were a present from the Princess of Tanjore in 1877.

Other treasures the church owns are Streynsham Master's *Bible* (printed in 1660), presented in 1881 to the church by a latter-day Master, an Indian Civilian, and the church's silver plate. This plate includes an arms-embossed alms-dish presented by Yale in 1687, an arms-embossed, inscribed basin and flagon bought with the proceeds of a legacy left to the church in 1698 by Mary Lady Goldsborough, wife of one of the Company's directors who had accompanied her husband to Madras when he came out to head an inquiry commission, a large communion cup and cover that might have been made from a part of the Pondicherry booty, and several silver pieces of Danish workmanship presented by the Danish Tranquebar Mission when it closed down. All of it is on loan from the church to the Fort Museum. The organ in the church was imported in 1894 from Hill & Co., England, and cost Rs. 300. It replaced an organ gifted in 1859 which itself replaced another gift made in 1760. Between 1760 organ and the first, the 1687 organ, there had been another one, of which little is known.

It was here that Dr Daniel Corrie was enthroned in 1835 as the first Bishop of Madras. Until then, the chaplains of St Mary's – a distinguished line that included Robert Palk, who became Governor, Andrew Bell and Dr Richard Kerr – supervised all matters of the Protestant church in the Presidency.

Tombstones and memorials, registers, paintings and silver plate – material for a museum, some might say – are all that survive within St Mary's bomb-proof building. But in truth it is the history of Madras and Empire that live on here, for here one walks with the ghosts of Fort St George, men and women who went on to found an Empire that was almost two hundred years of world history, who went on to provide Madras with its first library, first school (a schoolmaster, Ralph Ord, was first hired by the Company in 1677, but St Mary's Charity School, which has grown into St George's, was founded in 1715), first orphanage, first poor relief (the beginnings of the Monegar Choultry), first hospital (which was the nucleus of today's General Hospital), and first Government Press! They also left India a legacy on which modern India was built.

South of the church, separated from it by Church Street and houses on it, was Madras's first Town Hall (now domeless), with a debtor's prison below the main hall. Until newer buildings were built on The Island to meet the Army's growing needs, it was Army headquarters for

Tamil Nadu and Kerala and during the Indian Peace-Keeping Force's unhappy stay in Sri Lanka, in the late 1980s, it was the nerve-centre of operations. Today, it serves as the Fort commandant's offices. East of the Church is St. Thomas' Street, nicknamed Snobs' Alley and once lined with 18th Century houses of councillors and, later senior officers. A derelict three-storied house stands at the end of it, believed to be from the first construction in this street and, if so, possibly, the second or third oldest building in the Fort.

3. The portals of power

The last great historic period of construction in the Fort began soon after the French were ousted in 1749; Benjamin Robins, FRS, distinguished mathematician and the Company's Chief Engineer for the Eastern Settlements, drew up the original plan in 1750, but died of exhaustion the next year. Frederic Scott continued the planning for the reconstruction, and John Brohier, who had completed Robins' work on Fort St David, Cuddalore, did the engineering, but left in 1757 to plan Calcutta's Fort William. John Call then took over, and almost promptly had his work doubled by Lally's siege which left almost every building in the Fort damaged, 'Black Town' plundered (the English burial ground not spared) and Chepauk village and the 'garden houses' in the suburbs and at the Mount razed to the ground. Call and his assistant Benfield were responsible for considerable reconstruction, until Call retired in 1770. Patrick Ross then took over and gave the Fort its final form – including providing it with cisterns to hold water for 6,000 men for four months! Ross' completed fort, very much what today's fort is, was 100 acres in extent to the glacis, 42 of these acres (620 yards north to south, 330 yards east to west) enclosed within the fortifications. Between 1756 and the completion of the work in 1783, 7.5 million rupees were spent on construction. This was the fourth and final development of the Fort which had begun as a wall-enclosed warehouse-cum-residence. Almost the entire west front, looking formidable and impenetrable to this day, was the work of the controversial building contractor, Paul Benfield, in the 1770s. Benfield resigned as a Company engineer to take up building contracts. He built well – but he also made a fortune in the process.

Much of historic interest in the Fort's buildings is decades older than its final shape. All barracks were concentrated in one rectangular block, which was built to the west of what was the Portuguese Square (where the new tower block, Namakkal Kavignar Maligai, is). The barracks comprised two long blocks of rooms linked at the ends by two short blocks of rooms, thereby leaving a long courtyard in the middle. When completed in 1756, these massive two-storied barracks were called the King's Barracks, and housed a King's regiment, Government ensuring there was always one in station often the French occupation. They were extended in 1962 to provide in all more than 110,000 square feet space – enough for the whole battalion in residence. Many other barracks came up subsequently, but northwest of these was, until the middle of the 20th Century, Garrison Theatre, its dressing rooms part of the 1735 building, though its stage was of 1944 vintage. The Capuchin chapel was sited approximately between what is now called *Fort House* by the Army (and now occupied by the Chief Garrison Engineer) and the towering new block in Portuguese Square. This was the site Cogan had granted Father Ephraim de Nevers in 1642. This Catholic church, St Andrew's, which served the Fort as a centre of inter-denominational worship until St Mary's was built for the Anglicans, was pulled down in 1752, when the English became suspicious of the role the Catholic priests played during the wars with the French.

The handsomest building in the Fort today, dominating the architectural landscape and vying with St Mary's beauty, is the classical Secretariat Building, the front portion housing the State Legislative Assembly, and the 1910 second storey, the offices of the Ministers and Secretaries of the State Government. An impressive portico and a short flight of steps lead to the Assembly, but the most striking feature of the building is its towering pillars, twenty of them, in jet black.

These pillars of Pallavaram *gneiss* – Charnockite – are the best of a 32-pillar colonnade that was constructed in 1732 from *Fort House* to the Sea Gate and were used as a kind of meeting place and storage space (called the Pillared Godam) for the merchants and traders. It was also used from time to time as a granary, the home of the first government printing press, and the first-ever Government Records Office (which grew into the Archives). The pillars were eventually dismantled and used to embellish the Legislature building being built in 1910.

The colonnade was built by Governor Morton Pitt, who was born and bred in Fort St George. Morton Pitt's cousin Thomas was Governor in 1698 and made the Pitt family fortune with his acquisition of the famous 410-carat Pitt (Regent) Diamond (136 carats cut). Thomas Pitt was the grandfather of 'The Great Commoner' and at one time he and his three sons sat simultaneously in the House of Commons.

Pitt is said to have paid £ 24,000 to an Indian dealer, Jamchund, for the diamond – though the many scandalous stories said different – and later sold it to the Regent of France for £ 135,000. Many associate Pope's lines in his *Moral Essays* with Pitt. The lines read:

Asleep and naked, as an Indian lay,

An honest factor stole a gem away;

He pledged it to a Knight; the Knight had wit,

So kept the diamond and the rogue was bit.

(*"So robbed the robber and was rich as P* _____*,"* became a snide but popular concluding alternative.)

As for the black Pallavaram granite pillars, they were carried away to Pondicherry in 1746 by the French conquerors and returned to Madras only in 1762, when they were re-erected on their original site. In the 19th Century, the colonnade was converted into a closed building, a hall for official entertaining. When Edward Clive's *Banqueting Hall* was built, the old pillared hall was used for the Government Press and, later, as a record room. But this 'pillar godown' was demolished in 1910 and the pillars incorporated in the renovation of the main building that was undertaken that year. The new Legislative Council Chamber – as it was called then – with this facade was built on the site of this pillared old banqueting hall. Alas, the Charnockite pillars no longer reflect the shine of polished black; they have been painted!

The main gates to the Secretariat – striking in wrought iron – are of 1930s vintage, the main sea wall being battered down for them and the old, main 'Sea Gate' – which, its site now centred between them, was once the only gate that could be entered from the landing place on the beach – being walled up. The main gate was the Chief Customer's Post in the early days of the Fort and goods used to be landed on the beach not 50 feet away from it! On this beach, on land reclaimed, stand park and Port Trust buildings today.

On the land (western) side are clearly visible today the Fort's solid double walls and the deep moats protecting each of them. Two sets of massive wooden double gates, each fitted with huge iron bolts and each set duplicated in the two walls, provide entry into the Fort from this side. Well into the 1930s, soldiers in the Fort's barracks used to fish in the moats. In the 1990s, an intricate system of escape tunnels leading out of the fort was found near St George's Gate. It is believed similar systems exist by the Wallajah and San Thomé Gates to the south.

John Company's first Council Rooms used to be in what was called *Fort House*. This 'house' was demolished in 1693 and a new three-storeyed one built in its place, the Governor using the second floor for his residence and private office. This new house, to the east of the old one, was the nucleus of the present Secretariat Building, to which the wings were added in 1825. Amongst the surviving British buildings in Madras, this 'core', built by Governor Nathaniel Higginson, one of the least controversial early governors, is the second oldest, being just 15 years 'younger' than St Mary's Church.

The new three-storey building was built closer to the Fort's east wall and faced westwards. Work on it was completed in 1717. This was left in a sad state after the French had marched out of the Fort in 1749 after their three-year occupation of it. The building was then repaired and extended, but leaving its core intact. Work on this restoration was completed c.1785. Further improvements were made to the building in the early 1800s, by when it was only Council Chamber and Secretariat with no residential accommodation for the Governor who had moved to Chepauk. When completed with a curved frontage, half pillars, balustrades, and windows it looked rather like the facade of America's *White House*. The *White House* was built between 1792 and 1800. Did it inspire the architects and engineers in Madras 25 years later?

To the east of this 'core', and an intrinsic part of it, is the State's noble Assembly Hall on which work started in 1910 and received the finishing touches by 1919 – magnificent woodwork and black-and-white stone paving enhancing its beauty. This chamber hosted the Madras Legislative Council from 1921 to 1937, when the Council became the Legislative Assembly. While work was underway from 1937 to transform the hall to meet the changed situation, the Assembly met in the University of Madras's *Senate House* (July 1937 to December 1938) and in *Government House's Banqueting Hall* (January 1938 to October 1939). The Assembly was suspended during World War II and in 1946 moved back into its chamber in Fort St George that had remained unused from the time of the 1937 renovation when seats had been provided for a 260-member House. Much of the wood-work in these premises was by T Battacharry who had set up his woodwork business in 1894. In it are handsome busts of those who once adorned the Council, as visitors or as members: Edwin Montague of Reforms fame; Sir P Rajagopalachari, the first President (Speaker) of the Madras Legislative Council which was inaugurated on January 12, 1921 by the Duke of Connaught; and Dewan Bahadur L D Swamikannu Pillai, the second elected President (1924), who was responsible for establishing the Legislature Library (1921). The impressive President's Chair was presented to the Council on March 6, 1922 by Lord and Lady Willingdon. Lord Willingdon was then the Governor of the Madras Presidency. The first Prime Minister (the designation changing to 'Chief Minister' in 1952) was A Subbarayulu Reddiar.

The first legislature of any kind to be established in the Madras Presidency was the Madras Legislative Council in 1861. It was a non-representative advisory body that saw the introduction of elected members only in 1892. The Minto-Morley Reforms of 1909 introduced indirect election of members to the Council. In 1919, direct elections were introduced. 'Province' replaced 'Presidency' after the Reforms, when locally elected voices were heard. Between 1920 and 1937, the Legislative Council was a unicameral legislature for Madras Province.

The Government of India in 1935 created a bicameral legislature in Madras Province, consisting of the Governor, a Legislative Assembly (the lower house) and a Legislative Council. The lower house consisted of 215 members, further classified as general members and reserved members representing special communities and interests. The new legislature was to come into being in 1937.

The election for the Assembly was held in February 1937 and the Indian National Congress obtained a majority. C Rajagopalachari became the first elected Prime Minister/Premier[4] under the provincial autonomy system guaranteed by the Government of India Act of 1935. The first Assembly was constituted in July 1937 and met in *Senate House*. Bulusu Sambamurthi and A. Rukmani Lakshmipathi were elected as the Speaker and Deputy Speaker respectively. Then came the War and no sittings of the Assembly.

On August 15, 1947, India became independent and the new Indian Constitution came into effect on January 26, 1950, with Provinces

---

[4] Terms used till 1952, when "Chief Minister" came into practice.

becoming States. The then-existing Assemblies and the Government were permitted to function after the War till new elections on the basis of universal adult suffrage were held in January 1952. Under a Delimitation of Constituencies Presidential Order in 1951, the new Madras Assembly's strength was 375 members elected from 309 constituencies, including 66 two-member constituencies each with more than 100,000 voters.

An arch commemorating the diamond jubilee of the Tamil Nadu Legislative Assembly (which came into being as the Madras Legislative Assembly in 1952 after the Republic of India was constituted in 1950) was inaugurated in 2013 a little south of the Legislature on the main road leading from it. The arch, a rectangular structure 16m tall and 33m wide, features architecture inspired by both South Indian and Western Classical. The legend 'Tamil Nadu Legislative Assembly Diamond Jubilee Commemorative Arch' is inscribed in English and Tamil, in addition to the words '60 years'.

One of the earliest significant events of those sixty years occurred on October 1, 1953. A separate Andhra State, consisting of the Telugu-speaking areas of the composite Madras Province, was formed and the Kannada-speaking area of Bellary District was merged with the then Mysore (now Karnataka) State. Malabar District was merged with Travancore-Cochin (Kerala from 1956) State. All this reduced the strength of the Legislative Assembly to 190. When the Tamil-speaking area of Kerala (present-day Kanniyakumari District) and Shencottah taluk were added to Madras State in 1956, the strength of the Assembly was increased to 205, and then, in 1959, to 206 when a constituency from Andhra Pradesh was allotted to Madras. In 1965, the elected strength of the Assembly was increased to 234 under another Delimitation of Constituencies. And, so, today, with one nominated member representing the Anglo-Indian community, a practice from Independence, the number of members is 235.

In 1969, Madras State, which was Madras Province till 1950, was renamed Tamil Nadu and, subsequently, the Assembly came to be known as the Tamil Nadu Legislative Assembly. The Legislative Council was abolished with effect from November 1, 1986. With the abolition of the Council, the legislature became a unicameral body again.

The Legislative Assembly today sits in Fort St. George, which has historically been the seat of power from the founding of Madraspatnam in 1640. But as already related, it has, from time to time, moved out of the Fort over the years. But when it met after World War II, and immediately after Independence, it did so in the Fort.

In March 1952, however, when the strength of the Assembly had risen to 375 under the new constitutional guidelines, it was briefly moved into temporary premises behind *Government House* in *Government Estate* for a couple of months, while the finishing touches were being put to a new Assembly building in a southwestern corner of *Government Estate*. This was necessitated because the existing Assembly chamber in the Fort had a seating capacity of only 260. On May 3, 1952, the members moved into this newly constructed Assembly building. The Assembly functioned from this building till the end of 1956 when its strength came down to 190 in January 1957. It then moved back to Fort St. George, where it remained till January 2010. The building it left was converted into a performance hall, more of which anon.

During the 13th Assembly, the then Government announced a decision to shift the Assembly and the Secretariat to a new building in *Government Estate*. Construction of this building began in 2008 and was completed in 2010. The Assembly started functioning in it from March 2010. After the 2011 elections, however, the successor Government shifted the Assembly back to the chamber in Fort St. George, where it sits as these lines are written.

The Teutonic-looking - some say rock-fortress-like - 2010 Assembly building, designed by German architects for a Chief Minister passionate about Tamil culture, is from 2014 a multispecialty hospital. To its south in the same campus has come up government-style high-rise for a medical college and hostels. This has ensured that there is no chance at all of this Assembly building seating the Tamil Nadu Assembly again, killing the hopes of a Chief Minister who had laid the foundation stone for it in 2008 to mark his 50th year as a member of the Assembly.

This hallowed chamber in Fort St. George has echoed to some of the most silver-tongued speeches in English ever made by Indians, who received a place in it for the first time in 1861. Amongst those who so graced it were V S Srinivasa Sastri and S Satyamurti, C Rajagopalachari and C P Ramaswami Aiyar, those twin giants Lakshmanaswami and

---

[5] The present Madras Collectorate is sited on this building's remains and the huge Cornwallis cupola stands in front of it.

Ramaswami Mudaliar, P T Rajan and T S S Rajan, S Varadachari and P Subbaroyan, P Theyagaroya Chetty and P V Rajamannar and Muthulakshmi Reddy, pioneering woman doctor, doughty warrior against the *devadasi* system and, perhaps, the first woman to preside over a legislative body anywhere in the world. Indeed, she was the first woman to be nominated (1927-28) to any legislature in India and became its first Deputy President. Rukmini Lakshmipathy was the first elected woman representative in the Madras Legislature (1937). She too became its Deputy Speaker and went on to become, in 1946, the first woman Minister in Madras. The first woman Chief Minister of the State, Janaki Ramachandran (widow of popular Chief Minister M G Ramachandran) took her oath here in 1988, but had the shortest incumbency ever, quitting office within 24 days after failing to demonstrate her majority.

To the rear of this stately building is the Parade Ground, first developed as a part of 'Fort Square' by Governor Harrison around 1715. These grounds, in more recent times, have been witness to a couple of the largest crowds ever seen in Madras – when T Prakasam, Chief Minister of Madras, welcomed Independence Day, and the second when C N Annadurai, first DMK Chief Minister, who ushered in a new era of Tamil consciousness in the State, spoke to the people after his Dravida Munnetra Kazhagam (Dravidian Progressive Party) came into power in 1967.

The Parade Ground has, in the past, been known by a couple of other names as well; 'Barracks Square' pinpointed the barracks around it and 'Cornwallis Square' the location of the 14.5 feet tall Cornwallis statue by Thomas Banks. The statue, the first monument exported to India for public viewing, arrived in Madras in 1800 and was erected under a conventional circular cupola, a dome crowning the pillars, at the eastern end of Parade Square with its back to *Governor's House*. Parade Square was ceremonially renamed Cornwallis Square.

Cornwallis saw the statue himself in 1805, when he stopped in Madras en route to Calcutta. He died shortly after arriving in Bengal and Madras decided to erect a cenotaph to commemorate him. A large octagonal cupola topped by a central base for a dome over it and a tall, crowning obelisk was erected in Teynampet, at the Mount Road junction with the road that led to Adyar. The latter became Cenotaph Road. But the statue never moved there. The cenotaph itself was, however, shifted to First Line Beach in 1806, opposite what was *Bentinck's Building*. With the

Banqueting Hall *(now* Rajaji Hall)*...built by a son to honour his father's victories.*

Till not so long ago, entrance to Gandhi Illam *(now no more) in* Government (House) Estate. *The oil press here, V.O. Chidambaram's burden, has been moved midst the Park of Memorials in Guindy.*

7. *Fort Museum...now memorial to Fort Exchange (business centre), bank and lighthouse.*
8. *Painted memories of an imperial past...in what was the Fort Exchange's coffee room.*

Secretariat expanding, the Cornwallis statue was moved in 1925 from Cornwallis Square to the Cenotaph on First Line Beach. Its towering superstructure was replaced by a roof sloping gently towards a point. The statue stayed there for just three years, moving in 1928 to the Connemara Library as the salt and moisture-laden air of the sea at First Line Beach began attacking the marble, particularly the frieze at the bottom, showing the triumphant but tasteless acceptance of Tippu's sons as hostages. Then, in 1950, it made its last journey to the Fort Museum. The cupola in Parade Square remained there till 1935 when it was shifted to where it stands now, just outside, and to the south of Fort Museum. The Cenotaph on First Line Beach remains where it was, an empty shell now doubling up as a convenient urinal. In its day, however, it was a landmark.

In 1810, the evening outing to the Cenotaph, on Mount Road, 'four miles' from the Fort, was thus described: "...and on the sweep round this monument they slowly circle as in the gay ring in Hyde Park at home." A few years later, writers speak of "an oval form; and...enclosed space...laid out with paths and planted with a few evergreen" where "it is the fashion for all the gentlemen and ladies of Madras to repair, in their gayest equipages...(and) later round and round the cenotaph for an hour, partly for exercise, and partly for opportunity of flirting and displaying their fine cloths..."

4. The Yale fortune

To the north of the Secretariat is the Fort Museum, until the 1940s the Fort Officers' Mess. On this site once stood a house belonging to a free merchant, Robert Hughes, but this was acquired by a company promoted in 1787 by Peter Massey Cassin, a free merchant, to develop a meeting place where free merchants could conduct their transactions in comfort. The present building was ready for use in 1795, its construction facilitated by the profits of a lottery. Part of it, however, was opened in 1790 and the Exchange Coffee Tavern opened in 1792. Downstairs were housed warehouses, offices and a bank which was the forerunner of the City's banking system. This was the Bank of Madras, more of which anon.

The 'Long Room' upstairs was the Public Exchange Hall (a meeting place for merchants, brokers and ship's commanders) with more offices on either side of it. In time, a library and a coffee tavern were established on the premises, Madeira, tradition has it, also being served and the preferred drink. On the roof was built Madras' first lighthouse by the owners of the Exchange. It started working from November 22, 1796 with Cassin, one of the proprietors, as its first Superintendent. The lighthouse was an octagonal, wooden structure, rather like a flat-roofed tepee and was topped by a glass-enclosed 'light room' which housed 12 lamps burning coconut oil that had to be replenished through the night. The lights 90 feet above sea level – but not always operational – could be seen from ships' decks 17 miles out at sea and 25 miles from mastheads. This lighthouse, reconstructed in 1818, then looking like having four metal legs forming a tepee holding up a cylindrical container with the lamps, was as intriguing looking lighthouse as you can ever see. It functioned until January 1,1844, when a lighthouse in the High Court compound – atop a 125 ft tall Doric column – became functional. From the roof of the Exchange, messages would be exchanged with ships entering or anchored in the Roads and most transactions were completed in this way.

This congenial set-up, however, did not last very long. Governor Edward Clive (Robert's son) wanted the free merchants out of the Fort and, in 1826, the John Company government rented the building for offices. In 1861, it became the Officers' Mess of whichever British regiment was quartered in the Fort. Making the occupation permanent, the government in 1882 acquired the building for Rs 61,000 from the shareholders, by now many of them Indians. When the last British regiment marched out, it was decided to develop a museum in the building. The driving force behind establishing a 'British era' museum here was Col. D M Reid of W A Beardsell's, a 'boxwallah' with many interests. He mooted the idea in 1944, as a Member of the Legislative Council, and substantially funded it himself.

The Fort Museum, which was formally opened in February 1948, has a fine collection of the original writings of the men who made Madras. Paintings of past Governors and Nawabs adorn the walls of the parqueted ballroom, overlooked by the ornate Governor's Gallery. The oldest British portraits still in Madras – those of King George III and Queen Charlotte – dating to 1761, are to be seen here. In the Hall of Arms, medieval weapons and guides to their handling are displayed. Early coins, silverware, porcelain, manuscripts, engravings and aquatints of early Madras are also on display. So is a cage with a story all its own to tell. Not to mention the peregrinating 14½-foot Thomas Banks statue of

Cornwallis with the bas relief round its base of Tippu Sultan handing over his two young sons as hostages to Cornwallis.

On the bastion in front of the main entrance to the legislature is a stainless steel flagstaff raised in 1994. Atop it flutters proudly the Indian Tricolour. This flagstaff[6] replaced a towering 150-foot teakwood flagstaff – the tallest flagmast in India till recently – which had first been raised on the southeast bastion of the Inner Fort by Governor Yale in 1687. On it he had hoisted England's Cross of St George for the first time over Fort St George. The flagpole was made from the mast of an East Indiaman[7] that had foundered in Madras Roads after a storm. This flagstaff was later moved to the southeast bastion of the Outer Fort. But when it got to its present location, the central bastion on the east, in unclear. This central bastion, erroneously called by many 'The Great Bulwark', was built by Governor Langhorne c.1675 between the Sea Gate and the southeast bastion of the Outer Fort. When the Sea Gate was walled in – a date uncertain – this huge bastion became the central feature of the east wall of the Fort. And on this was raised the Yale flagpole, possibly during the final reconstruction of the Fort in the 1770's. But when did the Sea Gate give way to the two gates of today and, if the Great Bastion became the centre point of the east face, when were all the outer walls rebuilt to make that happen? The full story of the construction of the Fort awaits telling one day.

Elihu Yale, who contributed the flagpole, was born in the colony of Massachusetts and was brought back as an infant to England, and raised there. He came out to Madras in 1672 as a 24-year-old Company Writer. In 15 years he had risen to Governor! Serving as Governor from 1687 to 1692, he contributed much towards the development of Madras, where he was forced to live for a while after retirement, settling accounts that were being queried, even as he continued to accumulate a fortune.

Out of this fortune, Yale in 1718 contributed textiles, books and pictures to the Collegiate School in Connecticut – his father had first settled in New Haven, in the colony of Connecticut, where the school had been founded. The textiles realised £ 562 12s. The books and paintings were valued at about £ 600 – and for these gifts the university the school grew into was named after him! Yale, on his return to London,

---

[6] Height 110 feet, but much heavier than its predecessor.
[7] Very likely the *Loyall Adventure* which had been battered by the cyclone of October 4-7, 1687.

allocated his fortune to develop in his house one of the largest art and artefacts collections of the time.

It was Yale who, in January 1682, had negotiated with the Marathas and obtained, for the Company, settlement and trading rights in Porto Novo (Mahmud Bander), Cuddalore (Islamabad) and Kunimedu, Coromandel ports all. Near Old Cuddalore (Tegnapatnam), he renovated an old Indian fort and renamed it Fort St David. This Fort was to ensure the Company's toe-hold in India when the French threw the English out of Fort St George. Fort St David served as seat of the Presidency from 1746 to 1752, as many as three years after the rendition of Madras to the English after the French occupation.

Yale, a strong personality who is alleged to have hanged his groom for being absent without leave, got on well with Europeans and Indians alike. His tenure was a high point in early Madras history, though his last years in Madras were trouble-ridden ones. He secured from the Mughals confirmation of Company rights over other Coromandel ports, including Masulipatam and Vizagapatam; obtained rights to mint Mughal rupees; organised the first Indian militia (1689); and sought the outright grant of what became known, together with Triplicane, as the 'Four Old Towns'. It was also in his time that the Corporation of Madras, suggested by Company Chairman Sir Josiah Child, was established. And it was in similar circumstances that Yale established a Company insurance office in Madras in 1687. Despite all this achievement, he left Madras under a cloud, but the famed University in America assured him remembrance by posterity.

The Fort's Great Romance

The romance of the shy, retiring, studious Warren Hastings and Maid Marian, a bright but extravagant blonde, is the very stuff that makes true love an eternal bestseller. What they could have had in common no one has ever been able to explain, but through the decades their love held true, first daring a scandalised society, then weathering all the cruel buffetings of fate.

Hastings first came out to India in 1750, a 17-year-old Writer on the Calcutta roster of John Company. When he sailed back to England, he returned with a modest fortune, a good reputation and the eminence of almost having reached First in the Bay before he was thirty. But a spending spree in London almost ruined him and, two years later, Hastings was looking to the Company for a job. But Clive, who was then in charge of Bengal, did not want Hastings in Calcutta, so he was posted to Madras and sailed for India in March 1769.

Also aboard The Duke of Grafton *on this voyage was a young couple, the Baron and Baroness Karl von Imhoff. The Baron, an impecunious member of the Nürnberg aristocracy, had traded the sword for the paint brush, but could not make ends meet either in Germany or London. Patronage in London, however, got him a cadetship in the Madras Army, and Imhoff was quick to accept the offer as there was the chance of 'moonlighting' in Madras where the prospects of painting the portraits of Nawabs and 'Nabobs' held out hope of considerable reward. And so he sailed with his strikingly attractive 22-year-old wife, Maria Chapuset, a Huguenot from Stuttgart, whose most engaging characteristics were her gaiety and vivacity. But she was also a woman of wit and intelligence and the combination was just what was necessary to appeal to the retiring widower Hastings.*

A poor sailor, Hastings became progressively ill during the long nine-month voyage. Maria, who initially no doubt must have had her eye on the main chance of what the influential Hastings could do for her husband in Madras, nursed him through it all. But nursing changed to intelligent conversation, and a meeting of minds led to Maria Imhoff becoming Warren Hastings' official hostess aboard the ship.

Once in Madras, it seemed almost inevitable that Hastings would not only set up house for the Imhoffs but would also move in with them, a ménage à trois that Madras society strangely accepted without too much public murmur. After ten months in Madras and painting half the settlement, Imhoff wanted to try his luck in Calcutta – and the Council agreed. But Imhoff left his wife and son behind and so, very properly, Hastings moved into a Fort house on Church Street (Lane) next to St Mary's, though he remained the most regular visitor of the 'fair female' till she sailed for Calcutta to join her husband in October 1771. Hastings stayed on in Madras as Second in Council and waited for the promised Governorship. His affair with Maria might have died a natural death through the separation, but, out of the blue, just three months later, there came the news that was to change his whole life. He was appointed Governor of Bengal – and hastened there.

By February 1772 Hastings was installed in Council House, Calcutta, to begin the most glorious years of his career, but regularly visiting his small property in Alipore, near which the Imhoffs lived. It wasn't long before the Imhoffs were once again supported by Hastings and all Calcutta was not only agog at the goings-on but was also rife with rumours of bargains the Baron and Governor were trying to strike.

Whatever the truth behind the rumours, the fact was that the Company ordered the Council to ship back the Baron if he continued to decline military service. And so the Baron sailed to England, where, towards the end of 1773, he received £ 1,000 in two instalments from a relative of Hastings, to whom was handed over a portrait of the Governor. Meanwhile, in Alipur, the Governor began building a splendid mansion on his property, the work supervised by the Baroness, who lived in the house he had leased for her nearby. He had also settled a considerable sum of money on her, for the education of the Imhoff children. Calcutta had no doubt about the relationship between the now-designated Governor-General, India's first, and the fashionable Baroness whose quaint English was so charming. But the Proconsul, who did not wear his heart on his sleeve, had other ideas.

He waited patiently – as was his wont – till official news finally reached Calcutta in 1777 that the Baron had been granted a divorce in June 1775 on grounds of incompatibility and being "an abandoned conjugal mate". Then Warren Hastings surprised all Calcutta by marrying, on August 8, 1777, Anna Maria Appolonia Chapuset, the bride being given away by his former schoolmate and then Chief Justice, Sir Elijah Impey. With no time wasted on a honeymoon, the Governor-General presented to Calcutta society, at a reception on the 11th, Britain's first First Lady of India, whom all Calcutta thereafter called his 'Governess'. It was a perfect marriage of total love and understanding that was to last till Hastings' death 41 years later. He was the adoring, indulgent husband who never looked at another woman and could not bear to be separated from his 'Marian', the devoted wife who was "his paradise and his refuge".

Of Hastings' great love it has been said: "When they were separated, his professions of love pursued her.... he worshipped her bodily beauty.... but most of all he loved her spirit.... and, in her.... he found the sanction of all he lived for." No wonder it was that "beloved Marian" not only held his heart in thrall, but also had a "fixed ascendancy over his mind"! And all India knew it. To please Marian was to gain the favour of the Governor-General. But the expression of favour on several occasions bordered on the gross misuse of office.

Calcutta was humming with rumours about all this, but only behind closed doors. And there, behind closed doors, the rumours would have remained, but for the crusading zeal of a man who may be considered modern India's first journalist – James Augustus Hickey, the founder of India's first newspaper, the Bengal Gazette, *in 1780. Hickey was not a man to mince his words. And when he declared that the way to a good Company post was "to pay your constant devoirs to Marian Alipur", the Government declared war on him and the very first battle in India between the Government and the Press began.*

Hickey's Bengal Gazette *was a four-page weekly that depended for the most part on the painfully slow East Indiamen for news from newspapers from 'Home' and newsletters and correspondence from the various coastal factories. In addition, it published whatever news and gossip about the British in Calcutta Hickey himself could gather. Much of this gossip truly entertained all of English-speaking Calcutta except perhaps the victims. But Hickey also delighted in heckling officialdom in his columns. Officialdom's wrath, however, did not become public until the* Gazette *was ten months old.*

A November issue of the paper for the first time overstepped the bounds of wisdom when it made a personal attack on Marian Hastings. On November 14th, the Governor-General acted! He ordered that "…. as a weekly newspaper called Bengal Gazette…. *has lately been found to contain several improper paragraphs tending to vilify private characters and to disturb the peace of the settlement, it is no longer permitted to be circulated through the channel of the General Post Office."*

Hastings' action, however, was insufficient to gag Hickey who proclaimed that such action was "the strongest proof of the arbitrary power and influence that can be given." Thundered Hickey, defending his attacks on Hastings and Impey, "I consider the liberty of the Press to be essential to the very existence of an Englishman and a free Government. The subject should have full liberty to declare his principles and opinions and every act which tends to coerce that liberty is tyrannical and injurious to the community…." Having stated this he proceeded to increase the scandalous gossip content of his paper.

One particularly libellous allegation landed him in further trouble in June 1781. On the orders of the Government, he was arrested, tried on several counts of defamation, found guilty and sentenced to imprisonment and fines. But this was not to stop Hickey. While in gaol, he continued to edit his paper, neither toning down his language nor hushing his accusations. Now followed action after action against his tirades. The Court ordered that his press be seized. And with the seizure, the Gazette *ceased publication. The man who was unable to take care of his wife and children while he was in gaol, yet who managed to bring out his paper regularly, was at last beaten. Hickey never published the* Gazette *again.*

Little is known of what happened to him after his press was confiscated. Many years later, in 1800, when Hastings had retired to England, Hickey wrote to the former Governor-General asking him to recommend him (Hickey) for a job in Calcutta. Hastings obliged, it is believed, but there is scant record of Hickey thereafter. He died in obscurity, unsung, unremembered. But in his day he had led Hastings and his beloved Maid Marian a pretty dance.

5

The Mall to the Mount

1. The Mount Road Press

All the City's thoroughfares lead, quite logically, out from the Fort. The best known of them, running southwest from the Fort, is now officially Anna Salai, named after the late Chief Minister, C N Annadurai. But despite official decrees, this wide thoroughfare, widened in 1796, will forever be known by its centuries-old name, Mount Road, so called because it leads in a southwesterly direction through the city to St Thomas' Mount. Today, this broad highway that leads on past St Thomas' Mount and heads south to the end of India, Cape Comorin (Kanniyakumari), 450 miles to the south, is part of a busy commercial sector in the city. During early British times, however, it was a mall for the British to enjoy their leisure. Earlier still, it was a historic road linking the villages of the coast to Kanchipuram.

Mount Road emerges from the southwest gate of the Fort – 'Wallajah Gate' – and crosses what was the Elambore River over a bridge built on the site of the Wallajah Bridge of 1756. The road, once banyan-tree lined on both sides, then runs across The Island – right in the middle of this stretch is the Munro Statue (possibly on the very spot where Governor Pigot was arrested in a 1776 coup) – and crosses the Cooum over the Periyar Bridge that was called St George's Bridge officially and Triplicane Bridge unofficially (since, in the days before South Beach Road, this was the main road to Triplicane) from when its 1715 avatar was rebuilt in 1805 by Lt. Thomas Frager. It became the Lord Willingdon Bridge in the 1920s after it was again re-developed. At the southern end of the bridge, there is a statue of, in seated pose, E.V.Ramaswamy

Naicker, popularly known as 'Periyar' (The Wise Elder), 'Father of the Dravidian Movement' and a pioneering preacher of its Dravidian philosophy and radical rationalism. Opposite the splendid gates of *Government Estate*, used to be a well-maintained statue of Edward VII. The statue by George Wade was a gift to the city from Lodd Krishnadoss Balamukundadoss Lodd Govindoss. This statue has been removed and put in hibernation like much else as the Metro work interminably progresses. What happened to a fountain that was raised as a cenotaph to Col John Cumming Anderson, an engineer responsible for much irrigation and other waterworks in 1869/70, is not known. Anderson was appointed the Presidency's first Chief Engineer (Irrigation) in 1867 and was responsible for the Red Hills Waterworks scheme that was implemented by an assistant of his, William Fraser, in 1869-70. From the junction where the Anderson Cenotaph stood, till it made way for traffic signals sometime in the first half of the 20th Century, there begins two miles of commercial Madras at its busiest and best. Virtually starting if off are, on one side, *Government Estate* with what was intended to be a new Assembly-Secretariat complex but is now, as already mentioned, a hospital and, on the other, the home of *The Hindu* and *The Mail* building – buildings associated with what used to be called "The Mount Road Press".

The man who fathered the Press in India, James Augustus Hickey, was a scandalous character who liked nothing better than malicious gossip-mongering. But when he started his *Bengal Gazette* on January 29, 1780, he described his Calcutta weekly as a paper "open to all parties, influenced by none ... (considering) the liberty of the Press to be essential to ... a free Government". And so he took on Governor-General Warren Hastings as well as Chief Justice Elijah Impey. For his libellous pains, Hickey went to jail. Eventually, in 1782, bereft of money, Hickey had to wind up the first attempt at journalism in India and resign himself to a life of poverty. Ever since then, newspaper history in India has been littered with the carcasses of newspapers that shone briefly and faded into oblivion. But most of the Mount Road dailies were of stronger stock.

On this historic stretch of road, however, only one paper still publishes in English. In 1981 *The Mail*, with links going back almost to the beginnings of journalism in Madras, faded from the scene. *The Hindu*, now circulation-proud, in its fledgling days – in fact, till the end of World War II – struggled to keep up with *The Mail*, though the two papers fought some epic battles in the first 70 years of *The Hindu's* existence. *The Indian Express*, of later vintage than both, was the third English daily publishing from Mount Road, but today it has moved its offices and press to the western suburbs.

Madras's earliest newspaper was the *Madras Courier*, first published on October 12, 1785 by the East India Company's Printer, Richard Johnston. Earlier the same year, London had seen the launching of Johnston's inspiration, *The Daily Universal Register*, forerunner of *The Times*, London. *The Courier*, right through the 36 years of its existence, remained a four-to-six-page weekly of tabloid size, containing Government notifications, a couple of pages of 'news' 'cribbed' from papers from 'Home', a page or so of local news and, in what space there was left, a few 'Letters to the Editor', contributions (mainly poetry of sorts) and advertisements. The price for this fare was one rupee (postage free) – paper being a commodity that was scarce.

The Courier did not face any competition till Hugh Boyd, friend of Goldsmith, Garrick and Nawab Wallajah (!), and its Editor from 1788 to 1791 in between being Master Attendant (Harbour Chief), found time again in 1793 to devote some of his energies to journalism. Both the *Hircarrah* and Boyd, its founder, died a year later – the latter in a state "so very insolvent". Soon afterwards, the *Courier*, which published from Stringer Street in Black Town, found new rivals, Government sponsored, setting up shop. *The Madras Gazette*, run by the Company's Solicitor Robert Williams, and the *Government Gazette*, edited by John Goldingham, Company Astronomer and Engineer, were both started in 1795. The latter was printed at the first Government Press, established in 1800 by enlarging the Male Orphan Asylum printing press. In 1836 was born *The Spectator*, first published by D Ouchterlony, then by C Sooboo Moodely and C M Pereira from the Spectator Press. The weekly, which became a tri-weekly in 1846 and the first English daily in 1850, was eventually swallowed by the *Madras Times* which in turn was taken over by *The Madras Mail*!

The strong journalistic tradition established in Madras by *The Spectator* was built on by the *Madras Times*. In 1835-36, there was a bi-weekly of the same name and it appears to have changed hands in 1859, when it was taken over by Justinian Gantz, who ran Gantz & Son, booksellers and printers.

John Gantz (1772-1853), an Austrian, who had worked for the East India Company as a draughtsman, architect, lithographer and topographical artist, had founded the company with his son Justinian (1802-1862). A view of the new bridge near the Government Estate, Madras, that appeared in the *Indian Magazine*, made John Gantz's reputation. Justinian Gantz practised as an architect and was described in the *East India Gazette* as a 'miniature painter'. He appears to have specialised in making drawings of European houses in Madras. He helped his father run their lithographic press in Vyasarpadi, and a Gantz Road exists in North Chennai. Gantz established his paper in Popham's Broadway in 1859. This was the year income tax was introduced in India – Governor Charles Trevelyan of Madras dissenting. So the *Madras Times* got off to a good start, with a stick with which to beat the Government and a dedicated effort to bring the Indians and British closer after the horrors of 1857. Under Charles Lawson and Henry Cornish, the *Madras Times* thrived and put Madras journalism on a sound footing. But when a proprietor-editor disagreement broke out into the open, the proprietor being a successor to the Gantz family, Lawson and Cornish promptly quit – and the first issue of their *Madras Mail* came out on December 15, 1868.

The first offices of *The Madras Mail* were on Second Line Beach (later Moor Street and now Dr Burhanudeen Street). The paper then moved into a first floor built for it over A D'Rozario & Co, Auctioneers, on First Line Beach (later North Beach Road and now Rajaji Salai). This road at the time abutted the beach and the surf and was often awash. It was no wonder that one of the first campaigns of the paper was for a proper harbour, safe for ships and passengers – and, no doubt, soothing to the churning innards of *Mail* journalists forced to watch from the windows of their office the wallowing ships and surf-tossed *masula* boats in the open roadstead! There also now commenced an intense rivalry between the two papers: *The Madras Mail* the voice of the Establishment – the Government and the British Merchant Princes; the *Times* a humbler but stormier paper, the voice of the European trader, planter and employee. The *Times*, under the editorship of the much respected William Digby in the 1870s and 1880s, was also more sympathetic to its Indian readers. *The Madras Mail* at the time was very pukka sahib.

It was in the early years of the 20th Century that Indian capital, as anticipated, found its way into the *Madras Times* and it moved to Mount

Road in 1910. By 1911, the paper began appointing Indians to its staff and, two years later, was fully Indian-owned by The Madras Times Printing and Publishing Co. On January 1, 1921, after having been taken over by John Oakshott Robinson of Spencer's, perhaps the first takeover king in India, the company changed its name to Associated Printers. That was also the year *The Madras Mail* sold what had by then become its property to the Bank of Madras's successors, the Imperial Bank, and moved to its new premises in Mount Road where its name and logo may still be seen as this edition goes to press but is unlikely to remain very much longer. The Madras Chamber of Commerce (1856) functioned for over 50 years from the first floor of *The Madras Mail*'s First Line Beach building and moved out only with the sale of these premises to the Bank – which was located to the south of what is now the State Bank of India's Main Branch. The State Bank of India's Zonal Headquarters came up on this site in recent years.

During its latter years, the *Madras Times* was never quite sure whether it was fish or fowl, white or brown. There was, however, little scope for a centrist paper and so the *Madras Times*, by now being published from a Mount Road address – where Associated Printers still functions as a jobbing house behind Higginbotham's – was doomed.

The *Times-Mail* merger took place later in 1921 when Robinson and friends formed Associated Publishers after taking over *The Madras Mail* and Higginbotham's, the booksellers, and added to it Associated Printers with which had come the *Times*. Associated Printers developed as the premier job printing house in Madras, Higginbotham's began growing into the biggest bookshop in the country, and *The Madras Mail* was the paper to read in South India. Arthur Hayles, who had joined the *Times* in 1912, came with it to *The Madras Mail* when the papers merged and in 1928 he became its Editor. On assumption of an office he was to hold till 1955, he dropped the 'Madras' from the masthead and *The Mail*, which he thought of as a national and not Presidency paper, was born. *The Mail* took on much of the character of the *Madras Times* and under Hayles, who not only became its best known editor but also a legend in Madras journalism, grew, in the 1930s and 1940s, to be the city's most popular paper. In 1931, Hayles' push to modernise *The Mail's* equipment succeeded and it became, with linotype and rotary printing, the leading newspaper press in India, indeed in British Asia.

In 1945, an overheard conversation in a restaurant led to the legendary Anantharamakrishnan of the Amalgamations Group taking over Associated Publishers and giving *The Mail* a more Indian direction. Addison's, another Amalgamations' company, contributed its printing unit to strengthen Associated Printers, which had already been expanded by adding Higginbotham's printing unit – all this making it the biggest printing press in Madras in the 1950s and 60s. Today, it no longer is what it was.

Long before the British Press in Madras really got established, there were the first glimmerings of a 'native' press, responsible for it Gazulu Lakshminarasu Chetty, described as a 'publicist', but, in fact, a personage of eminence who, instead of hiding his light under a bushel, made his views public as loudly as possible in a Tamil journal he had founded. Lakshminarasu Chetty started in October 1844 an English bi-weekly he called *The Madras Crescent*, meant as a 'counterblast' to *The Record*, a missionary journal. But *The Crescent* soon took on a political tinge when it became the voice of the Madras Native Association, perhaps the earliest Indian political association in the country.

The Crescent, unfortunately, died with Lakshminarasu in 1868, but was succeeded by *Native Public Opinion*, which had one 'native' Dewan, one 'native' Minister and one 'native' Professor as its founders. But when *The Madrasee* was founded soon after, it was found that Madras had no room for two 'native' papers in English and they were merged under *The Madrasee* banner. *The Madrasee*, however, in 1877 sided with the Anglo-Indian[1] Press in criticising the appointment of Muthuswami Aiyer as the first Indian judge of the Madras High Court, thereby offending its readership, and, shortly afterwards, had to fold. Out of its ruins – and to champion the cause *The Madrasee* had attacked – rose *The Hindu*.

The Mail and the *Times* provided G Subramania Aiyer, one of the founders of *The Hindu*, not only exemplary stylistic models to follow but also gave him a *raison d'etre* during his first quarter century of journalistic activity. Their unwillingness to condemn the despotism of bureaucrats, reluctance to expose the abuse of power, and rather ostrich-like views of "fairness and justice" were the gauntlet waiting to be picked up by a Subramania Aiyer willing to dare.

---

[1] The term used till 1911 for the British living in India. It was thereafter used to describe the community of mixed European and Indian descent.

It was in 1878 that the 23-year-old Subramania Aiyer and a fellow schoolmaster and friend, M Veeraraghavachariar, together with four other angry young men, law students all, started *The Hindu*, printing 80 copies in a Black Town press, Srinidhi, in Mint Street, and promising a four-anna weekly every Wednesday. The rest of *The Hindu* saga is told elsewhere.

Between the birth of the *Madras Times* and the era of *The Hindu-Mail* rivalry, Madras readers were offered a number of other papers, but few lasted long. The earliest among them was the *Madras Standard*, an Anglo-Indian paper founded in 1877. When the *Standard* Indianised, it acquired in 1892 a 21-year-old Editor, G Parameswaran Pillai, who made the tri-weekly a daily and thundered against the Establishment, both Indian and British. Both the *Standard* and Pillai died young.

Madras's first telephone exchange – 1881 – and a Government exam for shorthand – 1886 – made journalism easier for its practitioners. News agencies soon followed, and other newspapers, and magazines too. Kamala Sathianathan, the first woman BA and MA of the Madras University, started *The Indian Ladies' Magazine* in 1901, the first women's magazine in India. And in 1905, C Karunakara Menon, one of the pioneering staff of the *The Hindu*, started the *Indian Patriot* that struggled on till 1924. Lack of money and Annie Besant's *New India* (the old *Standard*), which so vigorously campaigned for Home Rule, hurt it. But *New India's* failure to back Gandhi saw that paper too wane.

In 1921 was born Madras's first morning paper, the *Daily Express*, a lively daily started by R W Brock, the editor of the *Madras Times* at the time it was taken over by Robinson. Unperturbed by the Establishment, Brock founded a paper to entertain. The paper featured a women's page, a children's corner, a magazine section. Brock did not stay long with the paper, and his successors could not make a go of it, so the *Daily Express* folded six years later.

The exit of the Englishman's *Express* enabled the *Indian Express* to be started in 1931/32 by a fearless, irascible Ayurvedic doctor, Varadarajulu Naidu, who has been described as the 'Tilak of South India' and who had founded *Tamil Nadu*, an outspoken Tamil weekly that had grown into a daily by 1927. Within a year, the *Express* was taken over by Sadanand of the *Free Press Journal*, Bombay, who left it to S V Swami (his manager from Bombay) and K Santhanam (Editor) to run. They borrowed from a financier, Ramnath Goenka, to modernise the press and start the *Dinamani*, their Tamil daily. Unable to sustain both papers, they allowed Goenka to take them over in 1939/40. He proceeded to build a newspaper empire that today (2012) is *The Indian Express* in the North and *The New Indian Express* in the South, the latter being published from 25 cities in the four southern states and Odisha. Indeed, the paper has come a long way from its Mookkar Nallamuthu Street days.

When the *Express* premises were gutted in 1940, *The Hindu* rented it its old offices at 100 Mount Road, where the *Express* remained till after the War, when it acquired the beautiful buildings and gardens of the Madras Club further down the roads – and allowed them to deteriorate. Even the *Ananda Vikatan* occupied 100 Mount Road for a while, till it acquired its own premises further up Mount Road. 100 Mount Road, pulled down in 1996 to make way for highrise, is where Mount Road curves into Wallajah Road and is all but hidden from view by a subway entrance and hawkers' stalls. For decades 100 Mount Road had survived as a shuttered derelict topped by a hoarding for *Frontline*, *The Hindu's* response to the magazine boom of the 1980s. The highrise that replaced it then became home for a few years to the Asian College of Journalism in which *The Hindu* had some interest, but when the College moved into its own home in Taramani in 2010, the building began to acquire an air of uncertainty about it, till in 2013. *The Hindu*, after decades of doubt started a Tamil newspaper here, *THE Indhu*, that has proved a success.

Apart from the Big Three of the Mount Road Press, there rose and fell from time to time several smaller English dailies and weeklies. *Swarajya* was started in 1922 by T Prakasam to highlight the non-cooperation movement. The successful lawyer gave up his practice, even returning his clients' fees in unfinished suits, and threw himself into journalism. For 12 years, *Swarajya* ran as a daily, but then failed because of bad management. It was revived as a weekly in 1956 by Khasa Subba Rao and survived till 1980, its distinguished editors including Subba Rao, C Rajagopalachari, Pothan Joseph and K Santhanam. In January 2015, it was restarted in Coimbatore, and is making a name for itself. Others that tried, but failed, in the 1940s and 1950s to make an impact on the Madras journalistic scene included the *Indian Republic*, the *Sunday Times*, the *Sunday Observer* and the *Free Press*. Then, in 1983, *News Today*, an evening daily, arrived. Though it filled the gap left by *The Mail*, it offered readers none of the Establishment-oriented, solid dowdiness *The Mail* had; instead, it concentrated on the Tamil Nadu political scene, enthusiastically partisan on all issues. After rather quiet beginnings, it brought to English journalism in Madras some of the parochialism and rumbustiousness that has enabled Tamil journalism to flourish since Independence. It was followed in 2005 by the *Deccan Chronicle*, a Hyderabad daily spreading its wings and setting the stage for newspapers from other States to start up here. The first to follow that lead was *The Times of India* which arrived in Chennai in 2008 to challenge *The Hindu* with considerable success.

The earliest Tamil papers were the *Rajavritti Bodhini* and the *Dina Varthamani*, both first appearing in 1855 and carrying general articles and translations from the English language Press. The first politically conscious Tamil journals were Salem Pagadala Narasimhalu Naidu's fortnightlies, *Salem Desabhimani*, started in 1878, and *Coimbatore Kalanidhi*, started in 1880. But it was Subramania Aiyer who decided that it was necessary to start a journal that would help educate the largest number of Tamil-speaking people in modern politics and self-government. And so, while still at *The Hindu*, he started the *Swadesamitran* in 1882 as a weekly. It has been said that through its columns he became "Tamil Nadu's foremost teacher in politics".

When Subramania Aiyer parted company with *The Hindu* in 1898 in sheer disillusionment, feeling that he was so fettered there by a business-conscious partner, that he could not freely wage his campaigns for social reform, he made the *Swadesamitran* his full-time business and a thrice-weekly paper. The next year he made it a daily, the first in Tamil. From 1899, for 17 years, the *Swadesamitran* was to remain the only Tamil daily – till the pro-British, anti-Congress *Dravidian* was started in 1916. Meanwhile, S Kasturiranga Iyengar from Coimbatore took over *The Hindu* and in his family the paper has remained, growing from strength to strength.

Narasimhalu Naidu, describing Subramania Aiyer's unaided, courageous Tamil venture, said, "G Subramania Aiyer was conscious that those with a knowledge of English are a small number and those with a knowledge of Indian languages the vast majority. He felt that unless our people were told about the objectives of British rule and its merits and defects in the Indian languages, our political knowledge would never develop. It was because of this conviction that he founded the *Swadesamitran*." It was a paper in those early days that not only "decorate(d) the drawing rooms of the rich and the palaces of zamindars, it also (was) seen in the hands of Sanga Boyan and Rama Boyan as well as women of all shades. It also (went) to Africa, America, Europe, Burma and other places..."

Subramania Aiyer, an Anglophile in his early years who saw himself as a bridge of understanding between ruler and ruled, was not as familiar with Tamil as he was with English. But it was left to him to create a whole new Tamil political vocabulary. One of his senior subeditors, Kurumalai Sundaram Pillai, defending Subramania Aiyer's style, explained that if the *Mitran's* style was not beautiful, "it is not right to hold Aiyer responsible for it, because the shortcoming is in the language. Our Tamil language has been mainly used for expressing religious ideas and for poetry. It does not have the wealth of vocabulary in political matters. Had Tamil been mainly used as a State language anywhere, it would have overcome this defect. Further, prose as such is not common in Tamil. It is a newcomer to the language... Under the circumstances, it is more difficult to write a faultless prose piece than a poetical one." Describing Subramania Aiyer's pugnacious style, Sundaram Pillai remembered that "Aiyer would say that one should write pungently with words 'dipped in a paste of the extra pungent thin green chillies'. He would never tolerate qualifying words which softened the sharp tenor of a sentence."

During its heyday, the *Swadesamitran* enjoyed a lusty circulation. That it was a period of national as well as international significance helped. It was the period of the Boer War, the Russo-Japanese War and the beginning of the Great War; of the partition of Bengal and the Swadeshi Movement; of V O Chidambaram Pillai's shipping company, his arrest and the Tirunelveli riots; of Subramania Aiyer's own arrest, the poet Bharati's flight to Pondicherry and Aurobindo Ghosh's arrival in the French settlement. It was the time of South India's awakening to national political activity.

The poet Subramania Bharati joined the *Swadesamitran* as a subeditor in 1904, and though he did very little editing he did a considerable amount of provocative writing. But with two positive personalities – Bharati and Subramania Aiyer – writing broadsides for the *Swadesamitran* at one time, something had to give – and Bharati left in 1906 to edit the newly started weekly *India*. It was in *India* that Bharati introduced, for the first time in South India, political cartoons. It was his cartoon and verse in support of VOC that led to Bharati having to flee to Pondicherry in 1908. Ten years later, he returned to Madras from exile and re-joined the *Swadesamitran* as a sub-editor. By the time Bharati returned to the *Swadesamitran*, G Subramania Aiyer, disappointed with the British, disillusioned with politics, and a sick man with failing eyesight, had sold his second paper.

Subramania Aiyer, a rigid disciplinarian who spoke little, letting his writing and his beliefs, which he would never compromise, speak for him, had in his early years of journalism been critical of the British bureaucracy, but nevertheless felt the British presence was necessary until India and its people could develop a Western-style political consciousness. His crusades against Hindu social evils and on behalf of a Western materialist philosophy irked the Hindu orthodoxy. In learning from the West – and especially from the British – Subramania Aiyer saw India's salvation. But when in May 1907 Lala Lajpat Rai was deported, following the Punjab agitation and arrests, Subramanya Aiyer became a changed man.

In a sweeping and sudden change, he became convinced that the British would not play fair with India and that a struggle would have to ensue before freedom was won. He was an angry, bitter man whose entire attitude towards the British became one of antagonism overnight. He went on a lecture tour of the South and repeated over and over again his new Anglophobic views. But his worst diatribes against the paramount power were reserved for the columns of the *Swadesamitran*.

The result of these vitriolic articles was that Subramania Aiyer was arrested on August 21, 1908, in Courtallam where he was convalescing. The same day, the offices of the *Swadesamitran* in Armenian Street and Subramania Aiyer's house in Triplicane were searched. Charged with sedition and refused bail, he spent a few days in jail and was then released on an undertaking never again to speak in public or write anything which might be interpreted as inciting class hatred or promoting sedition or disloyalty to the government. His justification for accepting these conditions, which he called "humiliating", was that "If Sir Arthur Lawley's Government could have guaranteed that hanging would be the punishment, I would have faced the trial with great cheer and a sense of great relief. (But) at this age and with this physical constitution, how could I endure the discipline of hard labour?" Subramania Aiyer continued to edit the *Swadesamitran*, but he was a beaten man now. The fire had gone out, his indomitable spirit was broken. It was now only a matter of time before he would throw in his hand altogether.

But even in this sad twilight Subramania Aiyer was a man admired throughout the country. Wrote Bharati from Pondicherry in 1914: "There is hope for Madras for she has still some veteran leaders of the calibre of Mr Subramania Aiyer... Unaided he has made Tamil Journalism a fact of the world in spite of his very imperfect early training in Tamil Literature... In Mr Subramania Aiyer's youth he had wholly neglected his mother tongue like most people in this country who claimed to have been 'educated' in English schools, but his mature patriotism had to realise later on that for the elevation of the Tamil race the Tamil language would be not only the most rational but the indispensable medium. They win who dare; Mr Aiyer dared and he has succeeded in establishing a Tamil daily journal which with all its faults is the most useful newspaper in the Tamil country. His whole political gospel can be summed up in these words: 'Peaceful but tireless and unceasing effort.' Let us sweat ourselves into Swaraj, he would seem to say."

By early 1915, Subramania Aiyer was seriously ill, and could no longer run the *Swadesamitran*. So he got the best possible man to take it over. On November 1, 1915, A Rangaswami Iyengar, Kasturi Ranga Iyengar's nephew and right-hand man at *The Hindu,* became editor (and proprietor) of the *Swadesamitran.* An able advocate before he became an even more able newspaper administrator and journalist, Rangaswami Iyengar was just the man the *Swadesamitran* needed at the time. There was to be no more extremism of Subramania Aiyer's Anglophobic days. Instead, the *Swadesamitran* got a constitutional expert and a political scientist who used an incisive scalpel in his editorials, analysing the pros and cons of the political happenings of the day – which is really what Subramania Aiyer had started the *Swadesamitran* for: to explain to the Tamil-speaking public the significance of political happenings. As able a speaker and writer in Tamil as he was in English, Rangaswami Iyengar made the *Swadesamitran* "a new force, potent and pervasive ... (which) invaded the placid atmosphere of vernacular journalism."

When Rangaswami Iyengar took over the *Swadesamitran,* he brought in his kin C R Srinivasan to manage the paper. Bharati too rejoined the paper in 1920. And the three were to make the *Swadesamitran* a literary masterpiece of political analysis. When Rangaswami Iyengar left in 1928 to become a memorable editor of *The Hindu*, Srinivasan became editor and manager – and, in time, proprietor – of the *Swadesamitran*. Then began perhaps the finest era of the paper, Srinivasan's trenchant writing being masterpieces of Tamil prose as well as well-informed and soundly-argued persuasive literary efforts. Ably assisting him was A Krishnamachariar – who could never keep it short nor write in popular style. But at the drop of a turban he could write columns of the most informative prose, on any subject, to fill up space. With this formidable combination to contend with, not one of the new Tamil dailies that kept cropping up could oust the *Swadesamitran* from its position as the premier Tamil daily – not *Tamil Nadu* in 1927 and not *Dinamani* in 1934.

With the death of Srinivasan there came the deluge. A son who did not quite measure up to his father's tremendous abilities, constant labour problems, a rash of politically articulate journals which spoke the Tamil of the common man, and the inability to cope with the powerful backing the *Dinamani*, its only quality rival, got from the parent Goenka organisation, all led to the sorry state the *Swadesamitran* found itself in, in its last decades. In the end, it couldn't even find a proper buyer – and the end was inevitable; it was bought for its real estate.

It was the end of an era. Tamil Journalism began to change. It began to see the electorate not merely as an educated elite, benevolent to the less fortunate, but as every Tamil-speaking adult, literate, barely literate and illiterate. Every one of them needed to be informed and it felt its contributions should, therefore, be comprehensible to the barely literate who, in turn, could enlighten the illiterate.

Despite these changing times and attitudes, the *Dinamani* has survived successfully as a quality Tamil newspaper, though in the 1990s it began to modify its style a bit to suit popular taste. That taste is catered to by papers like the tremendously successful *Dina Thanthi* – headquartered in Rundall's Road but founded in Madurai in 1942 by the venerable C P Adithanar, considered an elder statesman of Tamil politics, who at different times backed Congress, rural Tamil, and Dravidian interests – and a host of imitators who rule the roost of Tamil daily journalism. Their tone might be strident, but they, more than anything else, have made the masses of Tamil Nadu politically conscious and knowledgeable about the world around. Treading a middle path in style and presentation has been *Dinamalar*, founded in 1951 in Trivandrum, and putting down roots in Tirunelveli in 1956 and settling in Madras in 1979. But

Dinakaran and *Malai Murasu* are more politically committed. The former, founded in 1977, is in the fold of regional TV leader 'Sun' and now challenges *Dina Thanthi* for the lead, while *Malai Murasu*, which was spun off from the house of *Dina Thanthi,* is content reaching out to supporters of the DMK. And there's *THE Indhu (The Hindu's* rather separate Tamil daily) being classily different.

2. Coffee and Cinema at Round Tana

Mount Road is a broad, bustling modern thoroughfare, but here and there you find landmarks of an earlier, more elegant age. The entire commercial stretch of Mount Road is, in fact, a curious amalgam of buildings, modern highrise and plate-glass rubbing beams with Indo-Saracenic towers of elegance and Colonial Baroque of other ages.

Somewhere in between in architectural style is the first important commercial complex on Mount Road. Just where the Periyar Bridge's southern end joins Mount Road, and overlooking the busy junction where Periyar sits in handsome sculpture, are the off-white and white buildings, in Art Deco style, of Simpson & Co, flagship of the Amalgamations Group. The early 20th Century art deco commercial architecture of these buildings is complemented in corporate offices within which reflect an age of greater spaciousness and comfort when the epitome of taste decreed discreet embellishment and polished leather-and-wood interiors.

It was in 1840 that a wheelwright named A M Simpson arrived in Madras, very likely from Edinburgh. Soon he was into harness-, boot- and palanquin-making. By 1845, he had done well enough to move from Poonamallee High Road into his own premises on Mount Road, where now the Cosmopolitan Club stands. In Simpson's main hall, there still stands a bell labelled "1845, Original Works Bell". Here, he established a coach-building business soon to be known throughout India and even beyond the seas; Simpson's, starting from 1851, regularly exhibited in London and booked orders for coaches.

When the Railway affected the business of hiring coaches of all description for road travel, one of Madras's largest posting establishments, Burghall's Stables, closed down. And in 1877, these extensive acres by the Cooum were acquired by Simpson's. Here, Simpson's expanded its coach-building works, established its body-building works, when the age of motoring dawned in Madras in 1903 and even attempted to build the first Indian-made (steam-driven) car. In the 1930s and 1940s, it built the handsome buildings that are now the Group's headquarters (after acquiring the neighbouring premises from Spencer's in 1938/9).

The premises Simpson's acquired were 200 Mount Road, which together with 199 Mount Road which *The Hindu* bought in 1936 to develop its new building, were once the motor car showrooms and workshops of Oakes & Co, in an earlier age Madras's leading department store but at the time of these transactions a Spencer property, having been one of J O Robinson's first takeovers. In its workshops behind the handsome frontage, Simpson's, moving from trade to industry, founded in 1952 its first factory, to manufacture diesel engines. By moving from importing Perkins engines to assembling them and then manufacturing them, Simpson's pioneered a revolution in momentum in India and got the country moving on motorised wheels.

In time, Simpson's was to acquire several other British business houses, many of them Mount Road 'names', and became the Amalgamations Group. Responsible for this growth was S Anantharamakrishnan, popularly called 'J', who joined Simpson's as Secretary in 1930. One of the few Indians to reach eminence in British commercial institutions in the heyday of Empire, the transfer of Simpson's into J's hands before Independence was a model of goodwill that few other British business houses emulated in that era of passionate and heated nationalism.

As already mentioned, among the companies to come within the Amalgamations' fold were Associated Publishers and *The Mail*. To the south of Simpson's is *The Hindu* and its neighbours are *The Mail* building and, a part of *The Mail's* campus, the quaint, Chisholm-designed home of P Orr and Sons, once Madras's leading jewellers. 'J', given the opportunity to acquire this company too, took it over for a short time, but then sold it off while retaining the real estate. P Orr's clock tower was once connected with the Madras Observatory and signalled Standard Time to this busy quarter.

Peter Orr, the founder of the firm in 1849, was a talented engineer and is credited with having invented a mechanical process to work the city's *punkahs* (old, hand-pulled fans) by steam. His son Robert moved the business into the present premises in 1873, after Chisholm had created a 60 feet by 30 showroom that still retains vestiges of what it was: the showroom as art. Shining tiles for the flooring, embellished walls, gleaming ornamental rosewood showcases for the silver and watches and jewellery, ornate chandeliers and an array of coats of arms of British and Indian royalty that once made this " a veritable art gallery"; till recently a ghost of that glorious past, it was tastefully renovated in 2011. P.Orr's in its heyday was famous for its 'Swami Silver' (silverware decorated with Indian themes) bearing its famed Lion hallmark. It also ran an armoury, sold scientific instruments and bicycles, and manufactured under licence 'Swan' brand fountain pens renamed 'Blackbird'.

Behind the showroom were developed in 1893/94 the firm's horological workshops whose architecture and vestiges of the past long fascinated building-watchers. In 2011, however, the Metro rail under construction received permission from the High Court to pull the workshops down to make way for one of its facilities. The 55 km long underground (55 per cent) and elevated (45 per cent) first phase of the Metro, running in two corridors, is scheduled to be completed in two stages, end-2017(elevated) and end 2019 (underground). The eastern line will run from Washermenpet via Central to Alandur and the Airport via Mount Road/Anna Salai. The western loop line will run from Central via Poonamallee High Road, Koyambedu and Alandur to St.Thomas' Mount where it will connect with the suburban line and the Mass Rapid Transit System (MRTS) when the latter's final extension from Velachery to The Mount is completed. (As these lines are written, the 21-stop MRTS runs between Beach and Velachery.) Plans have been drawn up with a 2024 target for three more corridors, totalling about 115 km of track, linking Marina with Poonamallee, Madhavaram with Siruseri, and Madhavaram with Sholinganallur.

Madras's other leading dealer in clocks and watches is Gani and Sons, started by Gani Namazi from Persia in 1906 as the South India Watch Company. In 1909, it became Gani & Sons and in 1914 the firm moved into the three-storey building in Park Town that it still occupies. It looks after stand-alone clock towers in Royapettah, Mint, Doveton and Pulianthope.

A little beyond POrr's is India Silk House, which occupies a Jaipuri-styled building raised by the Anjuman Trust, established in 1885, to run an Industrial Training Institute in it from 1904. Round the corner was the Viscountess Goschen Hostel where the ITI now functions. India Silk

House moved into the Mount Road building in 1947 and on the first floor there flourished, till the 1960s, one of the best 'tiffin rooms' of the India Coffee House chain, its coffee, *dosais* and omelettes served by handsomely clad, beturbanned waiters in immaculate surroundings being something special. A few buildings down the road was the New Elphinstone Theatre, demolished in the early 1980s for commercial highrise, but once among the City's finest. The theatre and a neighbouring dance hall and bar used to be favourite haunts of the 'Tommies' in the years between the Wars. Nearby here, it is said, Stringer Lawrence, little remembered 'Father of the Indian Army', had a garden house in the 1760s.

Most of Madras's cinema theatres started in this area. But the first one, the Bioscope, was started in Popham's Broadway by a Mrs Klug in 1911; it closed in a few months. Electric was the first one to be established in the Mount Road area. Warwick Major and his partner Reginald Eyre began screening silent films in 1913 in what they named the Electric, "a large corrugated iron shell with a brick facade" in what is now the Mount Road Post Office campus. The shed developed into a more ornate building which still survives, though no longer as a theatre. The Posts and Telegraphs Department, which bought the theatre in 1915 to house the Mount Road Post Office, built its Main Post Office and other highrises all around it, and in neighbouring Taylor's Yard but, thankfully, appears to have had a soft corner for this bit of historic incongruity in today's bustling Mount Road and has preserved it, in 1998 developing it as its Philatelic Bureau and Philatelic Exhibition Hall and renovating it in 2017. Its exhibits include the Penny Black, the first stamp in the world (1848), the first stamp in Asia (1852), the first stamp in India featuring Queen Victoria, the first stamp in independent India, and several pieces of post office equipment. In the Electric's heyday, it had leading caterer d'Angelis run an open-air bar and café in its garden.

Across Mount Road from where the New Elphinstone was, fronting at the Ellis Road-Wallajah Road junction, a man called Cohen started the Lyric in 1907 as a hall for entertainment. Its location was the first floor of the business he had acquired, (Wallace) Misquith & Co, which sold imported musical instruments, its best business being in pianos and church organs. An organ assembled by Misquith's around 1900, with much of it made in Madras, is in Zion Church, Chintadripet. The Lyric's hall, where once were Misquith's chambers for instrumental music practice, was used for cinema screenings for a short time in 1913 and was called the Empire Cinema. It had to close down because of a fire in March 1914. Later that year, J F Madan of Calcutta, at the time running the largest cinema chain in India, took over the Empire and changed it to his organisation's trade name, Elphinstone. In 1915, Madan's bought the Misquith Building and made the Elphinstone a permanent cinema theatre, the first in Madras with a balcony.

Misquith's, founded in 1842, in time became today's Musee Musicals, whose connections with the Trinity College of Music were bequeathed to it by Misquith's which was an examination centre from 1901. Musee Musicals' location from the 1950s further down Mount Road in the old Dinroze estate, and for decades in the same compound as the city's oldest Chinese restaurant, Chungking, which survived till 2012, when Musee Musicals took away that space too. Misquith's used to have music salons on the first floor first hired by those wanting to practise. This music shop was started by a Wallace Misquith. Nothing is known about him, but there is a better record of a William Misquith who played the organ, piano, violin, concertina and several other instruments. William Misquith also taught music, tuned pianos and repaired musical instruments. He was the organist at St Stephen's Church in Ooty, where Misquith's had a branch, and at St Matthias' Church, Vepery. He was also choirmaster at St Matthias' and St Thomas' Church, San Thomé. He died young in 1888, when he was only 37 and was probably Wallace Misquith's son.

To the rear of Misquith's is Ellis Road offering service and sale for a wide range of photographic equipment. Starting the road off is the rear of the once-famous 110 Mount Road, once *The Hindu*'s office and press and now, entering from Ellis Road, the home of its Tamily daily, *THE Indhu*.

The Gaiety, in Blacker's Road, and behind and kitty corner from the Electric was Madras's third cinema theatre and the first Madrasi-owned one, built in 1914 by film pioneer RaghupathyVenkaiah. He followed this up with the Crown in Mint Street in 1915/1916 and with, around the same time, the Globe, a Purasawalkam landmark and perhaps the most architecturally striking cinema construction in the city, which became Roxy with new ownership. All three have fallen to the wreckers' hammers between 2010 and 2012. The Wellington[2] was built further down Mount Road by R.Dorabjee in 1918 and in time became a cinema hall associated with S S Vasan's films. And then there was a lull. When Hollywood films demanded better theatres, the Sohrab Modi-owned New Elphinstone Theatre[2] was built across the way from the erstwhile Elphinstone Theatre in 1932, providing Madras with its poshest theatre, vaudeville being offered during the intervals. With it, the cinema habit was firmly established in Madras.

The New Elphinstone came up on the site of the Lycaeum, a theatre, dance hall and 'indoor stadium' for boxing. A part of this entertainment tradition here was Jafar's Ice-cream Parlour in the New Elphinstone campus. It was as the Elphinstone Soda Fountain run by 'Barney Dorai' that Jafar's started around 1910. When 'Barney Dorai' left for England after Independence, Jafar, who had worked with him, took over and the business continued in the family till the Millennium. With its 23 varieties of ice-creams, its innumerable varieties of sundaes and other made-on-the-spot concoctions, its huge jars of sweets and marshmallows, and the range of jellies it offered, Jafar's was from the 1930s to the 1960s synonymous with 'goodies'. And so it was here that the young men and women about town in Madras used to gather to perch on its tall bar-stools facing the imported soda fountain and while away their evenings and holidays. But when the New Elphinstone went under, Jafar's had to move. And it did, to narrow Waller's Road, round the corner from India Silk House, where the vast Jafar ice-cream- and jelly menu, the large glass jars of sweets, the unused soda fountain and the caring service all survived till the 1990s. By then no one had the time for painstakingly made ice-cream confections and, so, custom dropped and a legend faded.

None of these early theatres exists any more. The oldest surviving theatre in Madras is, however, in Davidson Street, George Town, today called Batcha, after its present owner. First established around 1916 as N.H. Murch's National Theatre, which offered films shows and stage performances, it was taken over in 1936 by the Dandekar family, who named this theatre on the first floor of a building 'Minerva' and dedicated it to cinema. It became one of the most popular names in the city for the best of Hollywood. It was also the first cinema theatre in Madras to be air-conditioned. Batcha took it over sometime around the new Millennium and offers indifferent fare.

---

[2] Both no more, making way for shopping plazas after the economy opened up in the 1970s.

Just past New Elphinstone, and of an earlier age, were other landmarks of 19th Century Madras, most of them now no more. R Maclure's was a leading pharmacy from 1894. Maclure's soda water was also a well-known name of the period. A neighbour was E C Barnes, leading opticians; Barnes, it is said, committed suicide by walking into the sea when business slumped after Independence. A couple, however, survive. Beyond was Allbutt's, another firm of pharmacists, dating from 1881, beginnings on Broadway at the present location from the 1930s, as is J.F.Letoille's (1928), also pharmacists, but which prides itself on its rosewood furniture being still in place. Between them was Klein and Wiele, the photographers.

By these shops was a rickety old building that bore the nameboard of its owner, the Madras Mahajana Sabha. This early headquarters building of the Sabha was pulled down in 1997/98 and rebuilt. A neighbour was *G Venkatapathi Naidu Building*, more about which anon.

The Mahajana Sabha, founded in 1884, two years before Congress, is perhaps the country's oldest Indian political institution and was born of the Theosophical convention of that year. During its first few years, this vocal voice of public opinion functioned from *The Hindu's* 100 Mount Road offices and then moved into its own spartan premises across the way. After Independence, the Sabha reduced its political links with Congress and became more a cultural body. Its own premises were rented out and it began functioning in an old building behind the LIC's tower block on Mount Road. In this first home of the Madras's first Masonic Lodge, an upper floor housed the Sabha's offices, reading room and fine library till its own building was rebuilt and occupied in the new millennium.

As Mount Road gently curves further southwest from the New Elphinstone site, it falls into Round Tana, the spacious junction it makes with Wallajah Road, the road from Nawab Wallajah's Chepauk Palace. At the junction, the late C N Annadurai looks down upon the City from his pedestal on the site where there had once been an intriguing, 40-foot square, ornately arched pavilion, splendidly domed and with an ornamental drinking water fountain of a slightly earlier age within. This pillared, open *mandapam* was named after the Maharajah of Vizianagaram, who had gifted it to the City as a place of rest, but it was better known as 'Round Tana', the 'round' deriving from the roundabout surrounding the pavilion and the 'tana' from the police post that once existed here. During the War years an underground air-raid shelter was built on the site. In 1945, Corporation Commissioner J P L Shenoy, noticing that the domed water-fountain attracted a large crowd of idlers every day who also used the area as a latrine, decided to do away with the fountain and develop a large underground public convenience beneath it and a parking facility above. The fountain was dismantled stone by stone, reassembled in a nearby park, and named the Vizianagaram Fountain. The underground conveniences were built ensuring adequate water and cleaning space. The bonus was the greater parking space above ground. Now it's an underground pedestrian facility surmounted by the statue and called Anna Circle.

To the Circle's west, occupying a triangular plot, is a large Bata showroom. Once there was in this triangle, formed by Blacker's Road and Mount Road, Madras's finest hotel, Hotel d'Angelis. Giacomo d'Angelis, a confectioner from Messina in Sicily who had trained in France, arrived in Madras in 1880. The same year, he opened what he called his 'Maison Francaise' here and described himself as a "manufacturing confectioner, glacie, &c., general purveyor and mess contractor." His 'Kitchen Department' was stated to be "the first of its kind... Superintended by a First Class French Chef." This catering service, in time, became a favourite of *Government House,* across the way from it. Governor Lord Ampthill (1900-06), in particular, insisted that d'Angelis cater to all his parties.

In 1906, d'Angelis announced the opening of "a small hotel on the premises, Mount Road, for our customers from up-country." By 1908, he had developed it as the property he had long dreamed of, Hotel d'Angelis. It had a Parisian garden and all its wrought iron fixtures (like the decorative railings of its streetfront first storey verandah) were imported. In it were installed Madras's first electrical hotel lift, hot water on tap, electric fans, floors of imported tiles, an ice-making plant and cold storage, and a three-table billiard room. Its French and Italian cuisine was renowned throughout India. A flavour of it was also available in Ooty, where d'Angelis ran Sylk's Hotel (owned by C Sylks from 1868) from the 1880s till 1925, when a new management changed its name to Savoy Hotel but continued to let d'Angelis run it. In 1943, what had been started as Dawson's Hotel in 1842/3 and was finally branded the Savoy, was taken over by Spencer's and is today managed as the Taj Savoy.

Bosotto's, another leading firm of confectioners, also with Italian connections, took over Hotel d'Angelis in 1928 and continued to maintain it as one of Madras's best hotels, Jardine's English cricket team staying in it in 1934. And Sassoon's of Bombay had a showroom in the hotel. But with World War II looming, Bosotto, who had in 1928 lent his name for a bakery started by his milk-suppliers, sold the hotel to the bakery owner, whose family still keeps the name alive in the bakery business though they sold off the hotel. In more recent times, the legendary hotel became Airlines Hotel, then a restaurant, and finally a rundown office complex. In 1986, the building was damaged by fire and that put paid to any thoughts of resurrection. But it survived unnoticed as a dilapidated office complex with hotel room numbers still visible on the walls, a rabbits' warren of rooms and toilet space, a central courtyard and surrounding verandahs-cum-corridors, till it was demolished in early 2018.

Across the road from here was the gracious old South Indian Co-operative Insurance Building, which housed Indian Airlines local offices from the start of the airline in 1953 until the building was pulled down in 1980. This Indo-Saracenic Henry Irwin-building was originally built in the 1890s by contractor T Manavala Chetty as the showrooms of the famous firm of Gujarati jewellers, T R Tawker and Sons, a family whose philanthropy in Madras is legendary. It was then called the *Tawker Building*. Next door is stately *Victory House*, home of the *Swadesamitran* till 1975. It now is a shopping mall developed by the business house founded by V G Panneerdas, the man who made it from rags to riches, introducing along the way Madras to consumer product hire purchase. This building was Whiteaway Laidlaw's ('General Drapers') in the 1890s. Whiteaway's was one of the biggest stores for a wide range of moderately priced household products.

The building was built in the Indo-Saracenic style in the 1890's by Robert Laidlaw as a branch of the main department store established by him in Calcutta in 1882. Though no one knows very much about Whiteaway, 'the Selfridge's of the East' was always called 'Whiteaway's', even if it was Laidlaw who developed it as an empire. The store had branches in 20 cities in India as well branches in Colombo, Singapore, Penang, Kuala Lumpur and Shanghai and specialised in furnishings, haberdashery and tailoring as well as imported household items.It was shortly after Independence, that Whiteaway's closed shop in India and sold off the wealth of property it had in the country.

Robert Laidlaw, a Scot, arrived as a 21-year-old in Calcutta in 1877 and started life there as an importer and exporter, dealing in everything from textiles to diamonds. After starting Whiteaway's as a small drapery store and growing it, he built a bigger fortune with tea estates in India, rubber estates in Malaya and a wide range of other businesses in South and Southeast Asia. But he was an investor from Britain whose profits did not all return there. He contributed hugely to charities in India, particularly to developing St.George's Homes' buildings in Ketti (Ooty) in 1914 and to the building of a school on the same campus which is today called the Laidlaw Memorial School.

Next door to Whiteaway Laidlaw's in Madras used to be Longman and Green, publishers, then Wrenn, Bennett's ('General goods'), established in 1889, where 8 annas bought many a toy. Wrenn, Bennett's, Indian-owned since 1938, then began to concentrate on furniture. The firm now occupies premises on General Patter's Road (where the name survives but as auctioneers.) near the Wellington Theatre, which itself in the 1990s was replaced by a high rise office-cum-shopping complex. Also on General Patter's Road is V.K. and Sons, monument and stone engravers, established in 1910 and still engraving inscriptions by hand.

Before reaching these two erstwhile Mount Road landmarks, there were, round the corner, almost in Wallajah Road, a couple of other Madras landmarks of another age, near where the Lyric was. Past '100 Mount Road' were the Coronation Durbar restaurant and Udipi Sri Krishna Vilas, the first Udipi-style restaurant to be established on what was considered the mall of the pukka sahibs. Its founder, K Krishna Rao, another rags-to-riches hero, moved from a dingy George Town establishment to these premises in 1926 and began what has now become an international 'Udipi Vegetarian' tradition synonymous with the name 'Woodlands'. Coronation Durbar, famed for its *biriyani* and *kormas*, was established in 1911 to mark the Delhi Durbar. Both restaurants, which got on most amiably despite their totally different characteristics, were pulled down in the mid-1990s to make way for highrise.

It was in the early 1920s that Krishna Rao, then a sturdy, hardworking youth employed in a George Town 'hotel'[3], was offered his boss's second

---

[3] A 'hotel' or a 'mess' in Indian English is a restaurant. A 'military hotel' is a non-vegetarian restaurant.

'hotel' for Rs 700, to be paid in monthly instalments of Rs 50. The thrifty but ambitious young man mulled over the proposition, then made up his mind to invest in the Acharappan Street restaurant in George Town, not far from where he was slogging as a junior cook on Rs 20 a month. With that decision he was on his way, not merely to becoming a *restaurateur extraordinaire*, but to establishing the first international restaurant chain serving Indian food. He inspired Woodlands-type restaurants throughout urban India and from New York to Tokyo. A number of them were Krishna Rao's, but the majority were not even franchised by him. The free use of the Woodlands' name never bothered him; he was happy so long as South Indian vegetarian cuisine, especially of the Udipi variety, was making its mark nationally and internationally.

The knowhow of *cordon bleu* Udipi cuisine Krishna Rao learned the hard way in and around Kadandale (a corruption of *kadanda kallu* = grinding stone), a sylvan little village in the Udipi area of South Kanara, Karnataka. Here, a priest of the Subrahmanya Temple eked out a modest living offering prayers, practising ayurvedic medicine, tending a much-partitioned plot of land and providing advice. To this much-respected *archaka* was born a son on October 21, 1898. His early years were to prove no bed of roses for the boy who was named Krishna after his grandfather. He was underfed, he was practically illiterate, being taken out of school to help around the house and farm, and he was ill-clothed, but he thrived physically, developing a mental fortitude that helped him to make the best use of circumstances.

Fed up with the atmosphere at home, Krishna Rao left it and found work in one of the eight *mutts* in the Udipi area. The new job did much for his religious education, but little for his health. A severe bout of malaria sent him home and left him without a job. When better, he found work as a 'helper' in a village 'hotel' – and so began the drudgery that was to mark the early years of his working life, drawing water, dishwashing, tending the fires and, above all, grinding the flour daily for *idlis*[4] and *dosais*[5]. Grinding flour in stone mortars seemed to be his destiny – and it seemed a most appropriate destiny for one from the Village of Grinding Stones!

---

[4] Steamed rice-and-lentils cakes.
[5] Thin rice-and-lentils pancakes.

It was while working at this Rs 3-a-month job that his sister got married to a 'hotel' owner from Madras. Ranganna, his brother-in-law, painted Madras as the promised land and, for once, Krishna Rao asserted himself – and had his way. He arrived in Madras, an awe-struck boy from the back of beyond but with all of Dick Whittington's hopes.

Those hopes seemed a long way away when he began as a house servant in George Town on Rs 5-a-month – washing, sweeping and grinding. Three months later he was a kitchen boy on Rs 8-a-month in a Thambu Chetty Street 'hotel' and his work was more of the same from 5 in the morning till late at night. Six months later, a brief interlude in a suburban restaurant followed. And then it was back to a restaurant in Post Office Street, off Thambu Chetty Street. The salary of Rs 20-a-month seemed handsome, but the work was more of the same, even as he progressed from 'cleaner', 'helper' and 'server' to junior cook. The grinding stone seemed his destiny, but while Krishna Rao slept on the pavement after work he kept dreaming of when he'd become "a big man", rid of the millstone.

His dreams began coming true in an unexpected fashion – even though it was to take years for them to mature. The owner of the Post Office Street restaurant, struck by the energy and application of young Krishna Rao, made his junior cook a tempting offer for his second 'hotel'. This second venture, not far away, in Acharappan Street, was not doing as well as the first as it lacked personal attention. Krishna Rao decided to give it the attention it needed and became a 'self-employed professional', though his work and lifestyle remained the same.

At Acharappan Street, a 'full cup' of coffee was 1¼ annas, two *idlis* were an anna, lunch was four annas – a mere quarter of a rupee – and fruit salad and ice cream were two annas each. Even at those prices, it was not long before Krishna Rao was making a daily profit of over Rs 100, "a magic number in those days". But, for all his success, his "soul longed for something different".

The answer was to move. "If the George Town area was the nerve-centre of finance and commerce, it was Mount Road that had grown to be the home of fashionable business, newspaper offices and cinema theatres," his biography states. And so to Mount Road he moved, to the arterial road of modern Madras where there existed "not a single, decent vegetarian restaurant". Closing down the Acharappan Street 'hotel' – where a vague reminder of the past remains in the form of a wholesale provision store in a new multistorey block – he set up shop at Round Tana, establishing with Udipi Sri Krishna Vilas the first modern vegetarian restaurant in Madras – well-lit, comfortably finished and boasting marble-topped tables. There were special sections for Brahmins, non-Brahmins and even Muslims – and they all flocked there for the vegetarian specialities of Udipi.

Credit from his suppliers and low prices that ensured large turnovers and greater profits enabled Krishna Rao to make a success of the restaurant he started in *Belloc* on a rent of Rs 90 a month. The boom necessitated a partner – and a second and bigger restaurant a little further down Mount Road, Udipi Hotel. When the partners amicably parted in 1933, Krishna Rao retained Udipi Hotel, his partners Krishna Vilas. Seven years later, Krishna Rao was offered back USKV – and till the mid-1990s it contentedly shared its buildings with Coronation Durbar Restaurant, not one whit put out by the excellence of its neighbour's chicken *biriyani*.

With the restaurants thriving and Madras growing, Krishna Rao's thoughts now turned to "a real hotel" – not another 'hotel'. When a building contractor named Munivenkatappa bought the Raja of Ramnad's town house – opposite Wesley School in Royapettah – for Rs 80,000, he planned on converting it into a hotel. But the only one who came forward to run it was Krishna Rao. He took the building on a 10-year lease at a rent of Rs 500-a-month and, acknowledging the accuracy of the house's name, which it took from its setting in what appeared to be a lush green park, christened it Woodlands Hotel. The Woodlands legend had begun.

It was 1938 and the 45 rooms in this "royal palace in miniature, set in spacious and colourful gardens" did a roaring business at Rs 2.50 a day for a single room with all meals and Rs 5 to Rs 10 for a double room – again with all meals. Soon, Woodlands was to become more popular than Modern Hindu Hotel on General Patter's Road, the only other 'Indian residential hotel' in the city.

When his lease expired and was not renewed, Krishna Rao began looking around for a new property. A 4-acre property on Edward Elliot's Road became available when the A M M Murugappa Chettiar family bought the Mysore Palace in San Thomé and planned on moving from their Elliot's Road mansion. Investing heavily in the property – Rs 2.5 lakh was a large sum in 1952 – Krishna Rao commenced transforming the mansion and grounds into New Woodlands. A *kalyana mandapam* (wedding hall) and an adjoining temple were two of his innovations; cottages for families was another; and a covered stage for concerts and meetings was a fourth. These, together with air-conditioned rooms, a swimming pool – the first in a vegetarian hotel – the finest in vegetarian cuisine and impeccable service made New Woodlands "the finest vegetarian hotel in Madras". The traditions and standards it set are now being followed by scores of others in India, some with the Woodlands links, others benefiting from Krishna Rao's experience.

With New Woodlands established, it's been one success after another. Woodlands Drive-in – one part of the Madras Agri-Horticultural Society's gardens – opened in April 1962, the first vegetarian drive-in restaurant. Other restaurants and hotels followed in urban India. New York's Madras Woodlands opened in 1974. Singapore Woodlands followed. It's been a long way from thatched hut to Woodlands Hotel. But a sad note to that journey was struck in 2010 when Woodlands Drive-In had to close after Government refused to renew its lease of this part of its gardens to the Agri-Horticultural Society. In its place, Government developed an imaginatively planned botanical park that's proved popular with visitors even with minimal facilities for refreshments. Initially called *Tholkappiam Poonga*, it is, after a change of government, nameless but referred to by many still as 'Woodlands Poonga'.

Not far from the Poonga, a bit to the east of it, is where Stella Maris College, moving from San Thomé settled in, in 256 grounds of spaciousness in 1960. The property, believed to be called *The Cloisters* and owned by John de Monte, was one of the many properties he left to the Mylapore Diocese.

3. Commerce in Clubland

Mount Road begins to move out from Round Tana past that stretch on its eastern side of once-famous British colonial commercial names, such as Whiteaway, Laidlaw and Wrenn, Bennett and reaches Christ Church and its towering steeple, which was built for the large Eurasian[6] population that lived and worked in the area (the villages of Narasinghapuram, Chintadripet, Pudupet and Royapettah) and who had,

---

[6] A footnote in a history of the church says, "At the beginning of the nineteenth century they were called Indo-Britons; in the second and third quarters of the century they were known as East Indians; in the fourth quarter they were known as Eurasians; they are now (early twentieth century) called Anglo-Indians. These changes were made at their own request."

from 1842, sought a church and school close by. The church, designed by John Law, was built on land donated by Thomas Parker Waller whose livery stables adjoined the property. The building, developing the compound and the making of the solid wooden furniture (by Deschamps, a well-known cabinet maker of the time) cost Rs 37,000. Waller's land and building contribution was estimated at Rs 12,200. Work on the church began in 1850 and the church was consecrated in December 1852. The congregation, however, had met in a Waller building from 1842 (which it called the Mount Road Chapel) and a school was also established on the premises; this school now has its own buildings in the church campus. Next door to the school is Devi Theatre complex, one of the first multiplexes in the city, designed by K.V. Srinivasan and built by ECC of the Larsen & Toubro group. It opened in 1970, but was pulled down for commercial development in 2016. Next door, till 2014, was an even older theatre, Shanti, which opened in 1961. Originally owned by G. Umapathy but bought in 1962 by the Sivaji Ganesan family, it became an iconic venue, screening every Sivaji Ganesan films.

Cheek by jowl with Christ Church was the Plaza Theatre, which opened in 1945 as New Theatre, home stage for a renowned Madras theatre company founded in 1891. Suguna Vilas Sabha – with whose legendary offerings Pammal Sambanda Mudaliar will always be remembered – began in a small room in a house in George Town. From 1902 onwards, it functioned from the Victoria Public Hall and staged most of its plays there despite the poor acoustics. In 1936, it acquired 36 grounds in Mount Road and in them built its own theatre, New Theatre. But the post-war cinema boom put paid to the stage, the theatre was leased out as a cinema hall and, in 1974, the Sabha moved into the first floor of a dingy neighbouring building where it survived as a social club. It was in 1910 that billiards, cards and refreshments were introduced into an organisation founded for stagecraft – and it is those pastimes that now dominate its activities. When the Plaza Theatre lease came to an end in 1997, work began on developing the property as a modern social club. The new building is named after M A M Ramaswamy of the Chettinad family, who in the 1980s and 1990s enthusiastically took to giving new life to old clubs.

Adjoining it is a club with an even older lineage and a more significant history. An imposing, tall-columned, high-ceilinged colonial edifice, well hidden behind tall trees, is the home of the Cosmopolitan Club, the premier Indian club in British times, when it was considered "the best Indian Association in the whole of India". The Cosmopolitan Club was founded in 1873 "to (introduce) Europeans... to the principal residents and thereby (afford them) some insight into Indian Society." Originally located in *Club House*, Moore's Garden, Nungambakkam, the Club built its present building on the 13-ground site of Simpson's first carriage works and moved into it in 1882. Once, meeting place of the Indian elite of Madras where many a decision was taken that influenced British policy in the Province, it is today much more of a family club whose excellent South Indian cuisine keeps a burgeoning membership happy. A little past the Club are the quaint yesteryear premises, now refurbished, of Lawrence and Mayo and what were once The Madras Stables, but is now the goods yard of Sri Rama Vilas Service, once lorry transporters and now clearing agents. SRVS is another Amalgamations unit and is the first on this stretch of Mount Road on either side of which is much property belonging to the Group. Beyond SRVS is a striking Indo-Saracenic construction, *Bharat Building* of insurance fame, one of the City's pioneer attempts at highrise and now a derelict, about which anon.

Bharat Building, with its dome and spires and towers, with arches in a variety of styles, is striking for its styling run riot. Sadly, its splendid front facade is hidden from view by the 'genuine' and tastelessly built *Bharat Building* of post-Independence vintage. Work on the main building, designed by J H Stephens of the Madras PWD, started in March 1894 and it opened in 1897 as *Kardyl Building*, when W E Smith's became W E Smith & Co. Ltd. It was described at the time as "a palatial structure... one of the sights of the city... ten times the size of those which were occupied originally"! With its three facades and several 100-foot towers, it made "a far greater show than any other commercial building on Mount Road."

W E Smith, who arrived in India in 1868 and came to Madras from Ootacamund ten years later, started as a pharmacist, then built up his own business which grew into "wholesale and manufacturing druggists... opticians, dealers in surgical... instruments and makers of aerated waters." In its day, *Kardyl Building* had a magnificent showroom 60 feet by 40, rooms for doctors and dentists on the first floor along Mount Road, quarters for Smith & Co's assistants along Gen Patter's Road, and even a cafe and beer bar. In the rear compound was the aerated water factory.

The W E Smith business was bought by Spencer's in 1925 and incorporated in Spencer's pharma business. *Kardyl Building* was offered for sale separately and was bought by Bharat Insurance in 1934. The building now belongs to the Life Insurance Corporation of India as a consequence of the nationalisation of life insurance in 1957. The Corporation, intent on pulling it down, had its tenants move out of the building in 2006 and pulled a part of it down before a court order stopped further wrecking. But with the damage done, what next? The courts have ruled it should be restored to what it was before the wreckers' hammers battered parts of it and renovated, but as these lines are written, the LIC does not seem in any hurry to do anything with the building which precariously remains without a roof under open skies.

The regional headquarters of the LIC is just a few doors south, built on the site of a printing and publishing organisation, the Madras Publishing House, that the Rajah of Bobbili had taken over in 1943 and sold as real estate to the United India Insurance Company in 1951. The LIC building was till the 21st Century one of the country's tallest buildings, Madras's first modern highrise, and one of the first in the country. Work on this landmark had originally been started in 1953, by M Ct M Chidambaram Chettyar, who had planned it as the headquarters of his United India and other businesses. When Government nationalised insurance, it took over the partly completed construction and, after a delay, continued with the work, opening for business in 1959 with 12 floors. As technology to build such highrise was not available in India at the time, British architectural consultants and engineers, Brown and Moulin, did the job working with contractors Coromandel Engineering, a unit of the Murugappa Group, its owners kinsmen of Chettyar. In 1975, a fire badly damaged the building. Subsequent refurbishment added two more storeys.

Associated with the design of the LIC tower block was Laxman Mahadeo Chitale who in 1924 became one of the first Indian Associates of the Royal Institute of British Architects, if not the first. Nine years later he became a Fellow of this prestigious institution. He was the first Indian architect in South India with British qualifications after working in the UK with Henry V Lanchester, renowned British town planner and architect. The 1930s to the early 1950s was the age of Art Deco in Madras and Chitale, establishing his own practice in 1932, was to establish an enviable reputation, raising many of the most striking buildings of the time, some of them still landmarks.

Among them are the Oriental Building (1935) at a corner of Armenian Street in George Town, where it is the LIC's City Branch office now, Pachaiyappa's College (1938), A.C. College of Technology, the Central Leather Research Institute (1947), and Rajah Annamalai Hall (1950).

M Ct M Chidambaram Chettyar's sons Muthiah and Pethachi raised the second major modern Mount Road highrise building, the Indian Overseas Bank's headquarters, in 1964. The Bank was founded by Chidambaram Chettyar in 1937 and functioned from the first United India building, built across from Law College in 1940, by building contractor Kaval Lal Mehta, till it moved into its own multistorey building in January 1964. The latter came up in the front garden of palatial *Amir Bagh*, a property Chidambaram Chettyar's son Muthiah bought in an auction. *Amir Bagh* itself was used as the Bank's training school, but was pulled down in 1987/88 and a multistorey Annexe to IOB's headquarters was built on the site, opening in 1993.

The roots of United India were sunk in 1906 by the Lingam Brothers and Vijendra Rao, their United India Life Insurance Company established in a spirit of Swadeshism: To be "owned, controlled and managed exclusively by Indians". In 1924, Sir M.Ct.Muthiah Chettiar took over the Company and in 1927-28 reconstituted it to expand its boundaries beyond the Madras Presidency. When he died in 1929, his son, M.Ct.M. Chidambaram Chettyar (MCt), took up the reins and grew it into one of the leaders in the Indian insurance business before nationalisation in 1956. Under his leadership, United India established branches from Karachi to Hong Kong. And to befit a company with such a spread MCt began building impressive offices – in the art deco-style – in many of the major cities. To crown it all, he and his favourite builder, Kaval Lal Mehta, got down to raising the *United India Building* as the Group's headquarters on Esplanade Road. MCt wanted a landmark building – and when the building was inaugurated it was certainly one of the handsomest in the Madras of the time. A particularly noteworthy feature was the pyramidal echo topping the tall central façade, a design with overtones of the traditional Tamil temple *gopuram*. Then followed several other buildings in similar style in different parts of India and abroad, all architecturally noticed in the 1940s and all of whose construction was personally supervised by MCt.

But the way his businesses were growing, that success needed to be reflected still more in the buildings they were housed. In July 1953 MCt told the United India Life shareholders at the 47th AGM, "Plans are getting ready for the construction of our building in Mount Road, Madras, to be jointly owned by the New Guardian of India Life Insurance Company and ourselves, This will be a unique construction in 14 floors… I expect this building will be ready in time for the celebrations of our Golden Jubilee, early in 1956." It was planned as Madras's first tower block, the tallest building in the city. MCt had wanted it to be 18 stories, but officialdom cut it down to 14.

Behind the LIC building, in a lot owned by it – and which was part of the Lodd Govindoss estate in an earlier period – are two old buildings, one of which had been the Masonic Lodge already referred to and which till recently housed a dry-cleaner who draped his work over the Masonic emblems. The Pioneer Laundry was established here in 1918, succeeding Garratt's, a tailoring establishment. The Laundry shared rented space with Murray & Co., the auctioneers, who moved out in more recent years. On the first floor, till its return to its own premises post-Millennium, was the Mahajana Sabha's library, one of the numerous small libraries in the city with a wealth of earlier Indian publishing. Perhaps the most famous of this ilk is the Maraimalai Adigal Library in Linghi Chetty Street in George Town established in 1958 with a strong collection of Saiva Siddhantha books. In 2008, it donated its collection to the Connemera Library. Another is the Ranade Library in Mylapore, founded by R Raghunatha Rao, V Krishnaswami Aiyar and P R Sundara Aiyar in 1904. The library opened to the public in 1905, its home on Brodie's Road. Gokhale laid the foundation stone for the library to the rear of the present Mylapore MRTS Station. The library moved into its present building in 1928. Above it, the library built the Srinivsasa Sastri Hall in 1955. In 1966 it added the Gokhale-Sastri Institute and Shanmugasundaram Hall across the road from it. The Ranade Library's 8000-book collection is particularly strong in history. Sharing a birthday with the Library is the South Indian National Association, a discussion group that has long considered the Library its home.

The newest of these libraries is the Roja Muthiah Research Library established in Mogappair (West Anna Nagar Extension) in 1996 and moved to the Taramani Campus area in 2005. Roja Muthiah Chettiar's eclectic collection of 1,00,000 books and magazines in Tamil and sundry other printed material, like notices, posters and invitation cards, as well as stamps, coins etc., from wherever the Nattukottai

Chettiars had done business in South and Southeast Asia, had been housed by him in his house in Kottaiyur, Chettinad. Threatened with fragmentation or even destruction when he died, the collection was fortunately rescued by the University of Chicago which collaborated with a Madras trust, Mozhi, to establish the Madras research centre and microfilm all Roja Muthiah's material. With cataloguing and microfilming of Tamil material in other libraries under way, the institution, now managed by another Trust, is fast evolving as a major research library for Tamil Studies.

In the other building behind the LIC tower block were the city's best-known auctioneers, Murray & Co, founded in the early 1920s and in these premises from 1927. A wholly Indian firm from the first, who auctioned much on Court's orders, it took its name from a judge of the High Court, Murray Coutts-Trotter (from 1915 and Chief Justice 1924-29), to give it the British image that, it was felt, was needed for business in the pre-Independence era. Murray's Sunday auctions are very much part of life in Madras even today, but from 2013 they are in Mandaveli.

Just past the LIC building is a striking white colonial-style edifice, of early 20th Century vintage, from where the State Bank of India operates its Mount Road office. Its Ionic pillars echo St Andrew's Kirk's. And on its doors are carved the Bank of Madras's coat of arms.

On this stretch were also two photographic studios with a long history. G K Vale's, which was near the LIC building, is one of the oldest Indian-owned studios in the South and had its beginnings in Bangalore. It moved in 1995 to Pycroft Gardens Road in Nungambakkam. But even older is Klein and Peyerl, near *Gove Building*, long a shell after a fire in 1987 but more recently a site for development. A Mr.Wiele – a British citizen of German descent – started a studio sometime after the middle of the 20th Century, then invited Theodor Klein, born of German parents in Madras in the 1870s, to join him as a partner. Wiele and Klein's Photographic Studio was the original name and it was located at 11 Mount Road, facing Round Tana where the stretch from the Fort curved into the main stretch leading to the Mount. The earliest records of it are mention of the firm in 1890 as prize-winners at the Madras Fine Arts Exhibition. Photographs taken by it in 1892 still survive. Klein and his young wife Valeska lived on the premises after they were married in England in 1909.

The partners added studios in Ooty and Coonoor before long. But after World War 1, Klein bought out his partner and took another German, Michael Peyerl, as an employee. He also moved to the later Mount Road location after selling the No 11 Mount Road building which was redeveloped in 1919 as the *G Venkatapathi Naidu Building*, which itself was pulled down in 2012 for new development. Around 1920, the firm became Klein and Peyerl. Klein died in the Nilgiris while interned during World War II, and his wife inherited the business which she decided to run in partnership with Peyerl. After the War, they decided to leave India and the firm passed into Indian hands. With changing times and technology, the firm began to wane and, after the fire, the new owner's interest in photography and block-making came to an end. The building long remained a shell till it was in more recent times redeveloped as a commercial complex.

In its heyday, however, besides taking studio portraits, Wiele, Klein, Peyerl and Klein's brother-in-law Erwin Drinneberg – holidaying with his wife Elizabeth in Madras in 1929-30 – took hundreds of pictures of Madras and Presidency scenes from the 1890s to the 1930s. Many of these photographs found their way to Germany and over 500 of them were gifted by Elizabeth Drinneberg to the J & E Von Partheim Stiftung (Endowment) in Heidelberg in the 1970s. Almost all of them, states a German researcher, were taken by Klein or Peyerl; Drinneberg was no photographer.

A large collection of large and small glass plate negatives featuring Madras, other parts of South India and a few major North Indian destinations was found by pure chance in the 1980s and, after passing through a few hands, this provenance-less collection, but almost certainly the work of Klein and Peyerl, is now owned by Vintage Vignettes, a five-man partnership in Madras. Sadly, there is no record, not even a diary, dating the pictures or the photographer. Many of the Madras pictures from this collection appear in the writer's *Madras – its Past and its Present* (1995, 2011), but in most cases his dating is guesswork based on the internal evidence.

Before Wiele's studio there was the one opened by John Perratt Nicholas in 1857, on his arrival in Madras. The very next year, he was exhibiting at the Madras Photographic Society's exhibition. James, his brother, joined him four years later. By 1865, there was a studio in Ootacamund too and, for two years, one in England which James and his wife Ellen established, when they took a break there. They recruited 15-year-old Albert Penn and sent him out to the Madras studio in 1864. In 1865, Penn was asked to run the studio in Ooty, where he was to live for almost half a century. In 1875, he acquired the Ootacamund branch of Nicholas & Company, as Nicholas Brothers had become, and ran it under his own name.

In May 1895, James' wife died and two months later he was also dead. They had no children. James and his wife were running the studio at the time, John having left the business to freelance till he left India sometime in the 1890s.The Madras studio continued in business till at least 1905, little known about its last decade or so.

Beyond Klein and Peyerl's, there is striking Indo-Saracenic again in *Gove Building* – a 1916 construction now housing a motor showroom. Next door is *Agurchand Mansions*, once *Khaleeli Mansions*, Mount Road's first 100-foot-high building. Both the Agurchand and Khaleeli names are part of Madras's commercial history from the 1840s. Mohammed Khaleel Shirazi migrated from Persia to India and made a fortune in indigo. He built for the family a mansion in Pantheon Road where one of the city's first shopping malls, single-storey though it be, *Fountain Plaza*, and one of the city's first highrise office complexes, *Shirazi Mansion,* came up in the 1970s.

Gove Building was originally *Cuddon Building*, built as a showroom fit for Simpson's many motor car agencies. George Cuddon, who joined Simpson's in 1890 and headed it from 1898 till his death in 1916, had started work on the showroom in 1914 with the intention of making it the finest motorcar showroom in the South. Completed after his death, the showroom remained a Simpson's showplace till its refurbishing on the present site was completed in 1943, when *Cuddon Building* was sold to V S T Motors and became *Gove Building. Cuddon Building,* when built, had a 90-foot frontage, of green and white granite, and a floor of Italian marble. It was a showroom fit for Maharajahs and belted knights – who were frequent visitors – and has been restored to that class again in 2016, to showcase Mercedes Benzes.

Behind *Agurchand Mansions* there were, until the 1990s, several of Madras's old 'garden houses', palatial structures run to seed and occupied by Government and commercial offices. One mansion even had stables for elephants! Col Patrick Ross, the engineer responsible for the last great reconstruction of the Fort, built and owned one of these garden houses. All these later became Khaleeli property. They have all now given way to gardenless modern highrise.

One of the six garden properties Her Highness Azim un Nissa Begum, *"nikah* wife of the late Nawab of the Carnatic" (Ghulam Mohammed Ghouse – 1825-55 – the last titular Nawab of the Carnatic) owned in the 1850s was *Rushkairam* or *Wood's Garden* on Mount Road, where *Agurchand Mansions* stands fronting the post-Millennium Taj Club House hotel., Originally a garden bungalow, *Rushkairam* is believed to be Col Patrick Ross' house. The Begum herself never lived in it, leasing it repeatedly to several of the Company servants and once even for the Castle Hotel. It was known as *Wood's Garden* (Wood's Road runs alongside) after Edward Wood, who in 1811 was Registrar of the Sudder Court and later Chief Secretary. It was in 1910 bought by Khaleeli Shirazi who built in front of it on Mount Road, between 1923 and 1925, *Khaleeli Mansions,* the city's tallest building at the time. When Khaleeli Shirazi settled the properties on his sons, Abbas Khaleeli got *Khaleeli Mansions* and Khasim Khaleeli *Rushkairam.* The two sons married the daughters of Sir Mirza Ismail, Dewan of Mysore. Abbas Khaleeli, an Oxonian, was a brilliant ICS officer who opted for Pakistan "which needed experienced administrators". *Khaleeli Mansions* was declared evacuee property, and put up for auction. Sah Agurchand Manmull bid for it successfully and it became *Agurchand Mansions. Rushkairam* remained with the Khaleeli family till the 1990s when it was bought and demolished to make way for the hotel now managed by the Taj.

Right opposite *Agurchund Mansions* was *Umda Bagh (MacLean's Garden,)* a second property of the Begum. It is Quaid-e-Millat Government Arts College for women today. In 1816, Colah Singanna Chetty, a *dubash,* owned it. It was later acquired by the Armenian merchant Edward Samuel Moorat. In the second half of the 19th Century, it was owned by the Begum, but was rented by the principal wife of the then Prince of Arcot, Khair un Nissa Begum, and became the social centre of the Muslim aristocracy in Madras.

In the late 19th Century, the senior Begum, or her descendants, sold the property to the family of Lodd Krishnadoss Balamukundoss. In 1901, the All India Muslim Educational Conference was held in Madras and a request was made that the Madrasa-i-Azam, founded in 1849 and functioning till then at Chepauk, be given the property. Government acquired *Umda Bagh* from the Lodd family for the *madrasa* and the Madrasa-i-Azam came to be housed in the original *Umda Bagh* palace, which is now in a serious state of disrepair. The Diwan Khana of Firuz Hussain Khan Bahadur, principal agent of the senior Begum, became the residence of the Principal of the school. In the same compound was set up the Government Mohammedan College in 1919, which acquired its handsome buildings within the compound in 1934. This institution became the Government Arts College for Men in 1948. When the College moved to Nandanam in the early 1970s, a women's arts college was founded here in 1974 and subsequently included Quaid-e-Millat in its name, in honour of Muhammad Ismail Sahib, leader of the Indian Union Muslim League. It is not clear as to who the MacLean was whose name is referred to in the legal papers in connection with this property.

The senior Begum's other four properties were *Mahbub Bagh* or *Turnbull's Garden* in Adyar, including a parcel of land on Mowbray's Road, *Ghaus Bagh* in Nungambakkam, *Farah Bagh* or *Dare's House* in Ennore, and *Ahmed Bagh* or *Farren's House* in Red Hills.

Adjacent to them is a spacious estate occupied till early 2007 by the *Indian Express* and reached by Club House Road. Once called Lord Pigot's Road, it possibly changed because his controversial second sojourn as Governor of *Olde* Madras was better forgotten.

To the rear of *Express Estate* is General Patter's Road, on either side of which the Lodd Govindoss family – one of the three Gujarati families who were major players in the city's commerce and public life in the 19th Century – had their mansions, including the main family mansion, *Govind Palace,* that is now a school. The erstwhile Midland Theatre, once the West End and latterly the Jayaprada, complex was built in this campus, once known as *Patter's Gardens* when it was parcelled out. The theatre, a landmark in its West End days, is no more.

Lodd Govindoss was the son of Lodd Krishnadoss Balamukundadoss who arrived in Madras in 1840 and got involved in the Gujarati textile trade. Among the other acts of munificence by the richly ringed, earringed and turbanned Lodd Govindoss were the gifting of land, in his General Patter's acreage, to the Congress Party to build its local headquarters *Satyamurti Bhavan*, and helping build the nurses' quarters in the Gosha Hospital. He also sold *Umda Bagh* to the Government at half the valued price of Rs. 3 lakh.

Even before the Lodd family's arrival in Madras, Chatoorbhoojadoss Kushaldoss had established a banking and textile business, C K & Sons, in Mint Street in 1828. His grandson Chathoorbhoojadoss Govindoss was a legendary figure in the Madras of the early 20th Century. Among his contributions to Madras are the statue by Joseph Mclure of King George V in George Town – at a cost of Rs 45,000 in 1914 – and the land for the Madras Pinjrapole, that asylum for sick, infirm and abandoned animals which still survives in Ayanavaram, in the city's northwest. It was he who built *Kushaldoss Gardens* on Poonamallee High Road at a cost of Rs. 12 lakh "for use by the public".

The third of the major Gujarati families of Madras was that of Gocooldoss Jumnadoss who founded his business in China Bazaar in 1883. What was significant about this family is that as early as the first decade of the 20th Century, the founder's nephew, who was in charge of the family's business, was a Director of Binny's two mills – a unique position for an Indian in those times. In fact, in 1906-07, when Binny's became Binny & Co. Ltd. from a partnership firm, he presided over the Board meetings during the changeover. A member of the family was always on the Binny Board for several years thereafter.

Where General Patter's Road falls into Royapettah High Road is the original Woodlands Hotel, alas in woodlands no more, its garden space occupied by a huge cinema complex. Modern Hindu Hotel, which succeeded Brind's Hotel, was originally where the Odeon was on General Patter's Road, a popular cinema theatre for many years and then a lingering failure. It was succeeded by the Melody Theatre for some years, till the latter too closed down, in the new Millennium.

Express Estate was once the home of the Madras Club, founded in 1832 as a residential European Club and described in an earlier age as "the finest in India... the Headquarters... the Ace of Clubs", Indians, women and dogs not admitted. J D White of White's Road, who was granted ground by Government here in 1809, built the original 'garden house' that was bought by the Club from its then owner, a Mr Webster, in May 1832 to be the Club's home after additions were made to it. The need for more space led to Waller's 'compound' being added in 1852 and Devenish's in 1853. These two purchases extended the property to Patullo's Road. In 1855, the swimming 'bath' – the city's first and, when with the *Indian Express* later, covered and used as a repository for old newspapers – was completed in what had been Devenish's compound.

The statue near where the Road to the Mount begins... stirrupless majesty, memorial to 'Munrolappa'. Round Tana is Anna Circle today... and C N Annadurai's statue, of the 1970s, commemorates the Father of Tamil Resurgence.

11. *This was till early 2004 all that was left of "The Ace of Clubs"... a relic of splendour in* Express Es▮
Now that too is no more.

12. *One of the last surviving 'garden houses' in Madras –* Lushington Gardens, *Saidapet.*

Restoration could have made it a Roman Bath! Between 1865 and 1867, the Club was further expanded to a Robert Chisholm design and got its pillared and pedimented Pantheonic handsomeness. And in 1876 the first tennis court in South India was laid in its gardens.

The splendid building with Pantheonic overtones survived till 2004 in a dreadful, dilapidated state in *Express Estate* together with its derelict octagonal 'smoking room', a Gothic, timbered pavilion with stained glass windows that Chisholm also designed. The 'Diwan', as the pavilion was called, and its later additions, a billiards room and a cards room, were to the rear of the main building and were linked to it by a covered way. West of this complex was another old house that was incorporated into the campus in 1898, *Hick's Bungalow*, bought from Hick in 1822 by Capt Archibald Patullo who commanded the Governor's Bodyguard. *Hick's Bungalow* was tastefully restored by Ramnath Goenka, the owner of the *Indian Express*, and he made it his family home. The Club's Ladies' Pavilion – necessary because the club would not allow women into the main buildings – was completed in 1898, slightly in front of the main buildings and to their north. The 'Hen House', where the ladies would await their husbands, was later remodelled and used as the *Express Estate* offices after a spell of Max Muller Bhavan occupation.

All this, except *Hick's Bungalow* at the southern end of the property, has now vanished; *Express Estate* now houses one of the biggest shopping malls in the country, a multiplex cinema and a hotel. As these lines are written, further modern development is planned here. Curiously, on a site where once stood a symbol of old Western culture, what has risen on it reflects today's Western culture.

The Club also maintained the kennels of the Madras Hunt which could well have pre-dated the Club itself, given the beginnings of mounted sporting activity in Madras in a formal manner in the 1770s. In the Madras Club of today there hangs a coloured lithograph featuring the members of 'The Madras Hunt: 1865' getting ready to ride out. In the background are, it is stated, the handsome buildings of *Government House*, Guindy (*Raj Bhavan* today) – but they look more like the Assembly Rooms, more of which anon, or even the Club. The hounds used by the Hunt were imported every year, many a ship's captain bringing them out free! The lithograph is believed to have been presented to the Club in 1865.

The Madras Club, the second oldest in India, is still the premier club in Madras, but it no longer is the preserve of the European Establishment that it was, when it opened its doors on May 15, 1832 after a founders' meeting in February. The first President was H Chamier, a senior Civilian. Within a few months of its founding it had over 1,250 members. Fifty years later, it had a membership in India of 2,400, a staff of 175 and property valued at about Rs 165,000.

Today, the Club has merged with, and occupies the lovely garden – almost park-like – premises of the Adyar Club, on the banks of the river at the end of Moubray's (TTK) Road. Once this 'garden house' was historic *Moubray House*, or *Moubray's Cupola*, and a magnificent tree-shaded avenue led to it all the way from the beginning of Moubray's Road.

The splendid cupola of this building is a thing of beauty and engineering ingenuity. George Moubray, who arrived in Madras in 1771 as Government Accountant, acquired 105 acres of the river bank on an annual rent of 80 pagodas! Here he built the core of the mansion that survives as the Madras Club today. This was the first building to be built on the banks of the Adyar. Built in the Classical style with an European-style dome surmounting it, the building could well have been the work of Paul Benfield, a building contractor who would have been a contemporary of Moubray who tended the finances of the Governing Council of Madras.

Moubray left India in 1792, but what happened to his *Cupola* is unclear till 1802 when it seems to have passed into the hands of Francis Latour & Co. John de Monte, a Portuguese businessman, and a Papal Knight, acquired the property in 1810, probably when Latour's was absorbed by the firm Arbuthnot, de Monte's that year. The cart-track leading to the house was converted into a splendid avenue in 1816. Several Justices of the High Court occupied the house after the 1820s. The Adyar Club leased the property soon after it was formed in 1890 "to escape the austerities of the Madras Club", which permitted no women or mixed social activities at the time.

John de Monte died in 1821 without an heir; his wife Mary was of unsound mind and their son Christopher had died in 1816 while on his way back to India from Germany. The three are buried in the church at Covelong which, together with several other institutions there, are benefactions by the business magnate. Mary de Monte was the sister of Christopher Bilderbeck whose eponymous business house was once one of the largest exporters of Madras cottons, such a Madras Handkerchiefs.

When Chevalier de Monte died, he left all his vast property in trust to the Archdiocese of Mylapore. It was from the Church that the Adyar Club leased the property which at the time stretched from the river to Chamier's Road, Kotturpuram (Gandhi Mandapam) Road to Pugh's Road.

After World War II, both clubs faced straitened circumstances. The Madras Club sold its Club House Road property for Rs 1.3 million to Ramnath Goenka in 1947[7] and built manorial 123 Mount Road across from Church Park School, a century-old Roman Catholic institution. As *Branson Bagh*, this new 5-acre site had been owned by the Rajah of Bobbili, who sold it to the Club for Rs 254,000. When the Club, which moved in April 1948 into the purpose-built clubhouse it raised here to echo its first home, sold the building to Khivraj Chordia in 1961, the value had appreciated to Rs 2.7 million. The building, hidden by the Safire Theatre, India's first multiplex cinema, opening in 1964 with three theatres and which has now been pulled down to make way for modern highrise office space after the property was bought and sold by a political party, was an Income Tax Office till the 1980s. Adjacent to it was one of the buildings put up for family quarters and this too survived as office space. But in the new Millennium the entire *Branson Bagh* complex has given way to new constructions.

By the late 1950s, the two clubs were struggling to survive, even in abbreviated circumstances. In the end, the task was too much for both; they merged as the Madras Club, which, in April 1963, acquired *Moubray's Cupola* from the Archibishop. Mount Road was left to commerce – and historical oblivion. The "abbreviated circumstances" refer not only to the Madras Club's smaller property at *Branson Bagh*, but also to the Adyar Club losing much of its acreage in the post-Independence period.

The trustees of the Moubray estate too had kept selling off acres of *Moubray's Gardens* from the early 1950s. The Adyar Club lost much of its 12-hole golf course in these sales, but steadfastly refused to buy any of the property, though it kept improving the premises it occupied and the garden it retained. Except for the porch. Moubray's octagonal central reception hall and cupola, and two halls on either side of it which were

---

[7] Goenka for a while rented it to the P&T Department to serve as the Post Master General's office till the building of the Mount Road Post Office was completed.

the drawing room and dining room (to later become the Ballroom and Bar & Billiards Room), all the rest of Madras Club till 2017 is Adyar Club handiwork. The entire main building has been beautifully restored in 2011/2012.

With the Adyar Club admitting Indians in restricted numbers to membership from 1960, in a last ditch effort to save itself, but failing, it was inevitable that the Indian membership would have to be accepted by the Madras Club when the Clubs merged. And when that happened the Madras Club slowly began adding to its membership. But despite its cosmopolitan membership, the Madras Club did not get its first Indian President till 1973, A K Sivaramakrishnan. That was almost 100 years after it had dispensed with British and French chefs and accepted Indian cooks as best for 'Butler Cuisine' – Western dishes with an Indian touch.

A noteworthy move with the Club wherever it went was a memorial plaque remembering all the members who gave their lives during the Great War. With the Club wanting only the best, it approached Edward Lutyens for a design. The renowned architect accepted this minor commission – and promptly forgot about it. Several reminders later, he wrote to the Club towards the end of 1922 that he had lost his original drawings but would do them again. It was to be six months later before he sent the Club drawings for the plaque and got its approval. He then placed an order with E.P.Broadbent of London in June 1923 to do the modelling and with M/s. H.J.Jenkins & Sons Ltd of Torquay to do the work in marble. The memorial tablet eventually arrived in Madras in January 1924. The modelling had cost £75, the tablet and shipping charges £215 and Lutyens' professional charges were £30. In May 1924, Fenn & Co. of Madras erected the tablet in the Club's handsome Reading Room in its first home. Now it graces an outer wall of the Club's residential quarters.

Some of the *Moubray's Gardens* property was sold to the US Consulate-General in the early 1950s and three pre-fabricated houses duly arrived from America to occupy most of this land. The Consul-General's house itself was purpose-built and is said to be the biggest Government-owned American house in India if you don't count the Ambassador's in Delhi!

The first American representation in India was in 1792, when Benjamin Joy, "first American Consul to the East Indies", was appointed in Calcutta. In 1794, he made William Abbott Consular Agent in Madras. Abbott, a

British merchant and Arcot creditor, became Mayor of Madras in 1798. He and Joy were business associates too. With John Company not recognising the consulate, the representation died out in 1802 and did not become formalised till 1852 in Bombay and very much later elsewhere. This despite the first presence of an "East Indian" in the US being recorded in December 1790 when "a dark man from Madras" was sighted in the Salem, Massachusetts, streets. He was brought to the US by his employer, John Gibaut, a ship's captain, according to the Peabody Museum, Salem. As a footnote it might be added that the *United States*, out of Philadelphia, was the first American vessel to voyage to India, arriving in French Pondicherry in December 1784. Its captain, Thomas Bell, was reported to have negotiated with the Nawab of the Carnatic for a settlement on the Coromandel Coast to help fulfil the dreams Thomas Willing, the owner of the ship, had of an American East India Company. But the British soon put paid to those notions.

***

Madras got a regular US Consular Agent in 1867 (Joseph Thompson) and a Consul in Nathaniel Stewart in 1908. The Consulate became a Consulate-General in 1947. Roy E B Bower was appointed the first Consul-General for South India and the Consulate-General moved in the 1950s from First Line Beach to a new building on Mount Road where the Bank of America is now. On First Line Beach, the Consulate had occupied premises in the old Lawyers' Building of Parry & Co from the time of the first Consul and continued in Parry's new building, *Dare House*, till the move to Mount Road. In 1969, the Consulate-General moved to its own building at Gemini Circle, built on land leased from the Church of South India next to St George's Cathedral. The building, built around a South Indian style courtyard, was designed by a New Orleans firm, Burt, Lebreton and Lamantia, the last-named – who derived his name from Don Quixote's village – doing most of the conceptualisation after travels through much of Tamil Nadu's deep south.

It was an American Consul-General who, in 1969, got the American Oil Company, working on developing Madras Refineries and Madras Fertilisers, to build the Madras Club its swimming pool in return for temporary membership (confined to the swimming pool area except in the case of the seniormost executives) to AMOCO's American engineers and technicians.

***

Going back to where Gen Patter's Road starts from the *Bharat Building* and doing Mount Road's western edge, the stretch to Gemini Circle begins with the *dargah* of Hazarath Syed Moosa Sha Khaderi, across the road from *Bharat Building* and popularly known as the 'Mount Road Dargah'. At this ancient tomb-shrine, people of all faiths seek favours and blessings every Thursday. Legend has it that when a British engineer in olden times ordered it demolished for road-widening, workmen at the erstwhile burial site refused to work when blood spurted from the soil. When the engineer persisted, he was, it is related, struck dead! An opulent new mosque with splendid facilities for the faithful has now come up by the *dargah* of the saint Syed Moosa Sha Khaderi who arrived from Baghdad in the early 17th Century. The holy man, who lived in a house next to where he was buried, was renowned as a great healer. His descendants now maintain the shrine. The five-storeyed Makkah Masjid is one of the largest mosques in South India and has a 100-foot-tall minaret. Its five halls offer 5,000 sq ft of space to accommodate 5,000 worshippers at a time, with facilities for women worshippers too.

Just a short walk from the *dargah* is a place of worship that's truer to the village than to Madras. The huge stone Ayyanar in front of the Pachaiyamman Temple here is a true village deity and guardian come to town.

West of the *dargah* is that part of Government Press once known as the Lawrence Asylum Press. The press opened for business in 1798 and its *Almanac*, a comprehensive database of Madras first published in 1800, was one of the earliest publications in Madras; the origins of the Press in Madras are not incorrectly associated with it. The Indo-Saracenic frontage of the Press now houses the Handicrafts Corporation's Poompuhar showrooms. Almost next door is Higginbotham's, till the Millennium the largest bookshop in the country, floor-spacewise, and the oldest, being founded by the side of its present Mount Road site in 1844 by Librarian Abel Joshua Higginbotham of the Wesleyan Book Depository. The shop moved into new stained-glass-windowed, marble-floored, high-ceilinged premises, still its home, in 1904 to celebrate its diamond jubilee. Behind the shop are two acres of godowns and Associated Printers, once the *Madras Times'* Press and buildings here provide a living picture of 19th Century and early 20th Century industrial spaciousness. A bit further south, the Amalgamations Group's showrooms hide from view the acres that the Group's Addison & Co has occupied for decades.

These acres have a few stories of their own. Two *Castlets,* mini-castles with crenellated towers, were built facing each other here by, and as his home, Major Fiott de Havilland, in the first quarter of the 19th Century. Old maps of the area show them well off Mount Road, not far from the Cooum. De Havilland, the Company's engineer, is best remembered for adapting the plans of junior engineers and creating St. George's Cathedral and St Andrew's Kirk in the form we now know them today. Sadly, between the two consecrations, his wife Elizabath, passed away and was, in 1818, the first burial in St. George's Cemetery.

One of the earliest engineers of the city whose works can be identified with any certainty, de Havilland 'built Mount Road', which probably means he laid out the northern half of the road. He then constructed the Great Bulwark, to protect Fort St George from a threatening sea. The wall, built between 1820 and 1828, was of length 10,000 feet and was completed "well within its estimate".

The Madras Bulwark was clearly noteworthy, for it was studied when the Great North Holland Canal was being thought of in 1849 to prevent the sea from entering the Low Countries. It was recorded that prior to the Bulwark, inroads "of up to 100 yards in extent had been made in the beach" by the sea. And the Dutch report on the great Madras wall added: "A protecting bulwark was constructed, of about a mile and three quarters in length, along the ordinary line of the beach, just beyond the point where the surf waves broke and in hurricanes it was subject to the full action of the waves. It was composed simply of rough stones, resting against a retaining wall of brick and *chunam*. The stones have been allowed to take their natural slope... and although the bulwark was not carried above the ordinary level of the coast, which was 18 feet above high water, it might be said that scarcely a stone had been displaced since it was first erected in 1821."

The Bulwark extended from the southeast angle of the glacis of the Fort and ran parallel to the Esplanade, ending just off Clive Battery on First Line Beach. In later years, the structure, known to all as de Havilland's Bulwark, formed the foundation on which the Beach Road, fronting the Fort, runs. When a subway was built to connect North Beach and South Beach Roads in 1967, excavations revealed remains of the Bulwark. More of it surfaced in 1978 when the area near the Beach Station was dug up.

After building all these landmarks, including his home, de Havilland sold the *Castlets* in 1825 and returned to Britain and retirement. Tom Luker, who acquired Addison & Co, a printing press at the time in *Eastern Castlet,* is thought to have bought the entire eastern half in 1886 for the multifarious activities he was planning (printing, vehicle dealerships and repairs etc.). The successor Addison & Co., pulled down the *Eastern Castlet,* that had been used as the Company's offices well into the 20th Century, to raise new showrooms.

Meanwhile, the *Western Castlet* was having a life of its own. It was acquired in 1931 by the South India Nursing Association as its headquarters and to run a European nursing home. The Association, founded in 1920 by European, Anglo-Indian nurses, had absorbed into it that year the Lady Ampthill Nursing Service and Institute, a European nurses' association founded in 1904. The acquisition of *Western Castlet* and its new avatar was under the patronage of Lady Willingdon, the Governor's wife, and the property became known as the Lady Willingdon Nursing Home. The nursing home remained there till it built a more hospital-like property on Pycroft's Garden Road and moved there in 1953.

While the nursing home was planning to move out, it began looking for a buyer for its property and found one in Attilio Bosotto, who ran the hotel and confectionery business of the same name on Mount Road, near Round Tana. He was thinking of establishing a second hotel in Madras (he had one in Ooty). But when he began to feel the post-Independence Indian climate was not right for foreign investment, he decided to dispose of the property. His friend, M R Rajagopala Naidu, teaming with the Raja of Bobbili had, in 1942, formed Rayala (deriving from Rayalaseema) Corporation to distribute Swedish Halda typewriters in India and, eventually, manufacture them. Naidu was also attracted by real estate. And so the *Western Castlet* passed into his hands. It was renamed *Rayala Towers*.

It was here, in a shed behind the building, that the first Halda typewriter assembled in India saw the light of day on March 13, 1956. Eventually, it was to have its own factory in Guindy, where Ashok Leyland is now headquartered. The *Towers* were put to commercial use in due course and in the early 1980s were pulled down to raise a modern *Rayala Towers*. That has, overcoming a host of problems, come to pass only from 2000 onwards.

Nicholas Brothers, the leading photographers of the time, and Gantz and Son were occupants of *Western Castlet* in the 1860s, which would make the building some sort of office complex of the time. Gantz, booksellers and publishers, sold, among other items, photographic prints from many photographers from India and abroad. And that included pictures from the Nicholas Brothers. But when James Nicholas married Ellen, the daughter of Abel Joshua Higginbotham, the founder of Higginbotham's, also booksellers and publishers, James wanted to supply pictures only to Higginbotham's. John, the elder brother and the person who had negotiated the arrangement with the Gantzes when he had started Nicholas Brothers, objected and the brothers parted ways. In fact, John Nicholas withdrew from the business side of photography and kept his links with the business only as a freelance photographer. Ellen Nicholas took his place and could well have been Madras's first woman professional photographer.

A well-known picture of the two *Castlets,* thought to be a water colour by John Gantz dating to the 1850s, shows a huge expanse of empty space between the two buildings. Havilland was at the time building St Andrew's Kirk on Poonamallee High Road and had planned a dome resting on 16 Corinthian pillars to shelter its nave. Though domes had been built on buildings all over North India and, in the past, in a few places in South India, the skill seemed to have vanished in the South. de Havilland therefore wondered whether it could be done for St Andrew's. And it was in that empty expanse between his homes that he experimented with the dome for St. Andrew's. But why the good Major needed to build two *Castlets* as homes, remains an intriguing question. The answer to these could have vanished with the twin buildings, one of which became Addison's home.

Addison's, established as a small printing and publishing house in 1873 by a Garratt, took its name, 'The Addison Press', from that prolific essayist and critic, Joseph Addison, of the *The Tatler* and *Spectator,* and not his younger brother Gulston, Governor of Madras in 1709. The press was taken over in 1886 by a Scottish journalist from Ceylon, Tom Luker. Luker came to *The Madras Mail* in 1882 on a stopgap six-month assignment with glowing testimonials, including one from the Hon P Ramanathan of the Ceylon Legislative Council, which read, "I have much pleasure in stating that the *Ceylon Observer* never had a better Reporter on its staff than yourself." While at the *Observer*, Luker became a proficient printer too, and took charge of its printing press. Seeing opportunity in Madras, Luker decided to stay and, in 1885, was hoping to be appointed Superintendent of the Lawrence Asylum Press. But when this did not materialise, he began looking around for a press of his own – and there was The Addison Press. Joined by his brother Frank, also a printer, they developed the press but added other lines of business, like watches, stationery, and fancy goods. Then, in 1891, Tom Luker pioneered bicycles in Madras – and, keen cyclist himself, set the example for a cycling craze. He also introduced the rickshaw in the city. And he pioneered Pitman Shorthand in South India by running classes for stenographers and journalists.

In 1904, Addison's became the first formal agents in the city for cars (Alldays and Humbers) and motorcycles (Triumphs). This warranted the 120 feet by 42 showroom that came up in 1909 to hide the Addison workshops from Mount Road. Today, that long and impressive frontage, added to in 1913, is part of an Amalgamations group showroom and, in a walled-in portion, is also home of a bank. The additional Addison's premises opposite Spencer's were acquired in 1918 to meet the growing needs of the motor repairs workshop. A neighbour was Noel's Hotel which was owned by M D Soundararajan whose multifarious interests included the Madras Publishing House which he bought in 1939 and sold to the Rajah of Bobbili in 1946. During the War years, Noel's dance floor and bar were the favourite haunt of British and American troops. It later became the Savoy, then took a vegetarian avatar as Hotel Indian and Hotel Gokul before closing down in the 1960s.

Though Addison's became the city's premier automobile dealers, Simpson's body-building activities made it bigger. In the early 1940s, Tom Luker's sons decided to sell up and Simpson's made its first major acquisition. It was in the fitness of things that when the Amalgamations group decided to test the waters of car manufacture in India, it was Addison's that, on November 15, 1950, turned out the first Indian-assembled car, a Morris Minor. Legal problems with a rival manufacturer put an end to this pioneering venture and turned Addison's to other business. It is today a leading manufacturer and exporter of cutting tools.

Between Higginbotham's and Addison's, the old and the new blended till the second decade of the 21st Century – the old, striking in the midst of modernity and seen in the buildings housing a reptile-skin store, what was the oldest record-shop in the city – Saraswathi Stores – and, till the

1990s, when it was pulled down, the Electricity Board's old buildings, once the Army Clothing Factory. Saraswathi's recording studio used to draw large street crowds whenever the famous came to record their talent for HMV, Odeon and Columbia. When tapes began taking the place of records, Saraswathi's was leased by a restaurateur who demonstrated that a 'mod' vegetarian 'Udipi' restaurant could draw a crowd – even if it was a different clientele. Imaginative conservation, a demonstration of how a striking old building could be transformed, helped in making 'Dasa' popular. But the lessee's own circumstances brought a bright idea to an end. And the building was pulled down to make way for an ultra modern office block. The neighbouring Vummudiar shopping complex used to be a well-known bar and billiards saloon. And by it, in a restored old house of uncertain heritage was Annalakshmi, a high end vegetarian restaurant manned by volunteers from a Swamiji's following. This building too has fallen to the developers, but the restaurant has moved to posher surroundings and professional management, where you pay the bill and not as you feel like as in its older avatar.

South of Addison's are the buildings housing a college for women - to be referred to further on – and, then, across Commander-in Chief Road are the home of Spencer & Co and the hotel it owns, the Connemara, one of three, the other two, the West End in Bangalore and the Savoy in Ooty, all now managed on long lease by Bombay's famed Taj Group of Hotels.

Spencer's, a once-famed department store, was housed in a building that for ninety years was a landmark in Madras. A fire in 1981 devastated one of Madras's handsomest Gothicised Indo-Saracenic buildings and a new highrise replaced it in 1991. Even though the entire façade and shell of the old building survived the fire, it was pulled down by the developers to raise one of the biggest shopping complexes in India at the time, in fact, its first major mall, *Spencer Plaza*, where Spencer's, its new retail stores, and scores of other retail outlets have space but no character. It was to be another 15 years and a bit before Madras began to get other giant malls, Chennai City Centre in 2006, Ampa-Skywalk in 2007/8, Express Avenue in 2010 and Phoenix in 2013, with a luxury mall, Palladium, added to in 2018. Across from *Spencer Plaza* is the Mount Road Police Station. Its century-and-more-old building that was the model for police stations in the city, was pulled down and in a bit of quirkishness, a new one built to recall the old Spencer's landmark.

The once giant store had its beginnings in a small business described as "wine and general merchants". Charles Durrant had started his store in 1863 and had added auctioneering to its activities. Durrant's was, it is stated, located on the site where Hotel d'Angelis came up. J W Spencer joined Durrant as a partner in 1864 and Durrant and Spencer's survived till the founder's retirement in 1867. The two had been assistants in Oakes & Co on Broadway, then the largest department store in Madras. Taking over from Durrant, Spencer then called the company J W Spencer & Co. In 1871, Eugene Oakshott joined him and they were a team till Spencer retired in 1882. Oakshott took over not only Spencer's but also Johnny Dimante's store – founded in 1868 – near where Curzon's is today, enlarged the business by moving Spencer's to the premises of his new acquisition and gave the combined business the Spencer name.

Spencer & Co moved to the present location on December 2, 1895, establishing itself in its new home as a major department store in India; indeed, in time, it was to become the biggest in Asia! In 1897, a limited liability company was formed. There was always an Oakshott as a director or senior manager from then until 1974. The first sale in the new shop was, naturally, a bottle of champagne – to a Mr Sowden, General Manager of T A Taylor's, who being in the wholesale liquor business, had probably supplied the stock in the first place! In its heyday, Spencer's had 80 departments in its showroom, 60 branches throughout the country and operated 300 and more railway restaurants from Peshawar to Trivandrum, Guwahati to Karachi besides several hotels! A railway meal was a memorable one in those days. As was a Spencer's cigar – its famous 'Light of Asia' brand, made in its Dindigul factory which was started in 1889, Winston Churchill's favourite. Spencer's – its first two hotels, store and godowns – occupied an area that stretched from where the Local Library Authority building now is to Commander-in-Chief Road, from Mount Road to the Cooum River, a truly vast area Oakshott had foresightedly bought in the 1890s.

The landmark building of Spencer's was an Indianised Gothic masterpiece created by W N Pogson. The famous *Spencer Hall* had a unique ceiling with carved, arched teak beams and used stained glass for decoration. Spencer's huge godowns were worthy of note at the time – but in 1985 were pulled down to make way for *Spencer Plaza's* requirements. In the new shopping mall, the facade of Spencer's old building finds memorial space in an abbreviated atrium.

Spencer's growth owed much to J O Robinson, Oakshott's nephew, who built an Indian commercial empire in the 1920s. It was he who teamed Spencer's with Oakes & Co, founded in 1843 in Popham's Broadway, and made the combination the country's biggest department store. Oakes, known for its wines, hardware, furnishings, furniture, dressmaking, millinery, and even cars and cycles, also functioned next to Simpson's from 1895. It was as Spencer's motor car showroom that Simpson's took over this property. Oakes' Broadway premises had on its campus. Beehive foundry, manufacturing a variety of hardware. In 1892, Oakes also established a cigar factory in Guindy in what used to be the house of the Collector of Chingleput.

The name Beehive Foundry and its original home still survive on Popham's Broadway, now called Prakasam Salai. The foundry came into the fold of the family-owned Indian Commerce & Industries Co. P. Ltd (ICI) c.1920. ICI was founded in 1907 by Kowtha Suryanarayan Row. The foundry is today called the Beehive Foundry Engineering Works and proclaims its specialties as steel structures and fabricated steel products. It still operates from *Beehive Buildings*, Prakasam Salai.

Popham's Broadway in New Black Town is where Oakes, Dalgairns & Co put down roots in 1843 as an importer of what we would now call consumer goods. In 1848 it became known as Oakes, Partridge & Co., 7 Broadway, to which address the original firm had moved in 1845. Here it built an ornate showroom for a variety of products and called it *The Madras Exchange Hall*. This building was gutted by fire in 1852 and rebuilt in a less ornate style. By 1857, it had become Oakes & Co., a department store, the biggest in South India, if not the country. With many of its customers residents of the Great Choultry Plain post-1857, Oakes decided to move its retailing operations, including, in time, motor car sales and service, to Mount Road (referred to elsewhere). *Exchange Hall* became Oakes' auction hall and hardware store, with the foundry established behind the *Hall*. The foundry, founded in 1893, specialised in making ships' castings.

By this time, Spencer's had not only begun to catch up with Oakes but also overtaken it and spread itself throughout India. In 1923 John Oakshott Robinson, a man considered by many as the first takeover king in British India, personally acquired all Oakes' retail operations, and its cigar factory in Guindy, later selling all this to Spencer's. Only the Beehive Foundry and the Broadway property were not taken over by Robinson. The foundry as well as Oakes' premises at 93-95 Broadway passed into ICI hands sometime around then.

In 1914, Madras contributed to the Great War effort a hospital ship that was named, in thanks for the contribution, H.S. *Madras*. It was built in Britain as a passenger-cum-cargo ship for service in the Bay of Bengal but was converted into a hospital ship at the request of Lord Pentland, then the Governor of Madras. All the iron, steel and brass work used in that refitting in Madras came from the Beehive Foundry. Madras also contributed six squadrons to the Royal Flying Corps and the Royal Air Force during the two World Wars. The 35, 79, 98, 99, 234 and 264 are still called 'Madras Presidency Squadrons' in memory of the aircraft Madras once funded for them.

Beyond Spencer's is the IOB (Indian Overseas Bank)[8] building, designed and built by ECC of the Larsen & Toubro Group the third major highrise in the city at a time when multistorey buildings were few and far between. Between them is the new home, from 1956, of the Victoria Technical Institute, a Government-sponsored non-profit organisation that, from its conception in 1887 as a Jubilee celebration for Queen Victoria, and its birth in 1889, has done much to promote indigenous handicrafts. It offers visitors a fascinating variety of South Indian handicrafts. Next door is the home of the *Ananda Vikatan* (Happy Humorist).

4. Trendsetting with a smile

The *Ananda Vikatan* – amongst Madras's earliest Tamil magazines and the trendsetter for so many Tamil magazines which have followed in its footsteps – owes its genesis to *Ananda Bodhini*, a monthly that was successfully published for 15 years, from July 1915. Its publisher was a successful mail order businessman, Nagavedu Munnuswami Mudaliar. Mail order purchasing was very popular in those days and Mudaliar's intention in starting this magazine with a 'readable mix' was purely to increase his business.

The *Vikatan* was Poothoor Vaidyanatha Iyer's challenge to *Ananda Bodhini*. A journalist with nearly 30 years' experience when he started the *Vikatan* in 1925, Vaidyanatha Iyer's basic formula for the magazine – as

---

[8] Indian Overseas Bank

well as the several publications he started and folded after selling the *Vikatan* to S S Vasan in 1928 – was twice-told vintage jokes and humorous verse. But it wasn't a formula that clicked. Vasan, however, improved on the formula and created a success. It was only in the post-War era that the *Ananda Vikatan* was seriously challenged – and even overtaken – but, it must be remembered, only by magazines sticking broadly to Vasan's basic formula.

At the time Vasan took over the *Ananda Vikatan* he was running Vasan's Advertising Service as well as a mail order business. He was also doing some hack writing, translating popular English fiction for Tamil publishers. But he was best at putting publicity to good use and judging popular taste. The best example of Vasan's dramatic use of publicity was the full-page advertisement – an unheard of gimmick in those days! – he persuaded the staid *Swadesamitran* to accept in his pre-*Ananda Vikatan* days. The advertisement, for his pop work *Ilvaazhkkaiyin Irahasiyangal* (*Secrets of Wedded Life*), was the first full-page one to be carried by the venerable paper. Vasan, who was not exactly rolling in wealth at the time, even persuaded the *Swadesamitran* to accept the ad on payment of only a token advance! "When people see my advertisement," he is reported to have told the paper's Advertising Manager, "they will rush with their money orders for my book and I will then be able to pay you." Vasan was right. Just as he was right when he advertised his first Prize Competition – *Sor Pudhir* (Word Puzzle) – in the *Ananda Vikatan* he took over. This and most of his subsequent competitions ensured not only a circulation boom but also substantial growth of his mail order business.

In the early Vasan days, the *Ananda Vikatan* was housed at the north end of Mint Street. As the monthly grew into a fortnightly and then planned to become a weekly, it needed more space not only for itself but also for Vasan's several mail order addresses. And so the magazine shifted to Broadway, near Mannady, in 1933, the year Vasan started The *Merry Magazine*, a humorous English magazine that ran such serials as 'Bala the Bad Woman', 'Devi the Dancer' and 'Private Joyful in Madras'! In November that year, the *Vikatan* became a weekly and set the pattern for the popular Tamil magazines of today.

When Vasan took over the *Vikatan*, he also became its Editor. One of his first contributions to it was a serial, *Indra Kumari*, later published in book-form. But Vasan was basically an ideas man; not for him the day-to-day drudgery of writing or editing. So he began to recruit one of the most talented editorial staffs ever to grace a Tamil publication.

Vasan was an inveterate racegoer, a successful punter and, later, racehorse-owner. But one day, Vasan, on the spur of the moment, decided to give up racing – and that was it: such instantaneous contrary action was typical of Vasan. Crossword puzzles were one of the most popular features he introduced in the *Vikatan*. But when intellectual journalists attacked such contests on moral grounds, Vasan did not give up the puzzles. Instead, in 1934, he started another weekly, *Naradhar*, dealing purely with the arts, matters intellectual, society and no competitions – and made a success of it. As soon as criticisms of his policies had died down and he had made his point, he suddenly decided to stop all competitions in the *Ananda Vikatan* as well. Then he wound up *Naradhar* too!

When 'Mali' Mahalingam, the man who did as much for the *Vikatan* with his strokes as 'Kalki' (R Krishnamurthy) did with his pen, joined the magazine soon after it moved to Broadway, sketches of famous persons began to appear on the cover. From Indian ink caricatures the cover illustrations moved to colour cartoons. Inside the magazine were short stories, serials, several rehashes of material from British and American magazines, but always plenty of humorous skits, biting satire, delightful cartoons and light-hearted jokes. *Anandham*, joy and happiness, was its aim. R A Padmanabhan, then new to Broadway, recalls that humour in the Tamil Press at the time "revolved around a few established themes. The miseries of the Thanjavur mirasdar, the eternal quarrel between mother-in-law and daughter-in-law, the love of jewellery of the womenfolk, the affluent in search of pleasure, the tricky public women, the miserly zamindar and the foibles of new-fangled fashion...The jokes...were earthy, broad and uninhibited. Neither castes and communities nor individual professions were touchy, and one could joke freely without being worried about offending anyone." No wonder a magazine whose 'logo' was (and is) that of a happy brahminical-looking character – created by C V Margabandhu, who signed as C V Morgan, and embellished by Mali, the first caricaturist of the Tamil Press – could joke about sacred threads and Brahmin rituals.

Typical of *Vikatan* humour in those days was the tale of the Muslim who laid hands on a Komatti Chetty. Shouted the Chetty, "Arre Sayabu, for holding me by my tuft I excuse you. But if you had touched my sacred thread I don't know what I would have done." The aggressor changed his grip to the thread and challenged, "Now let us see what you will do." Whereupon the Chetty wriggled out of the thread and fled! Then there was the occasion Kittu's father did not notice the boy performing the daily prayer ritual of the Brahmin, *sandhya vandanam*. When asked about it, Kittu swore he had done it at the nearby pond. "But there is no water there!" exclaimed the father, at which a flabbergasted Kittu burst out: "Really! that idiot Ramu told me there is!" On another occasion there was the widow with the shaven head who, complaining about barbers not attending to her regularly, moaned, "If only my influential husband were alive he'd have got me a dozen barbers in no time!" Even Gandhiji was not sacrosanct. His fast had one husband telling his novel-reading wife, "If you don't intend to serve me food, I will go on hunger strike!" And it also had one beggar telling another, "Not a morsel since morning! At this rate we too will have to announce that we are going on a fast!"

Vasan and Kalki between them took the *Vikatan* to new heights of circulation, which inevitably brought in advertising. Advertising Manager T Sadasivam even enticed the British product manager by taking, in 1934, full-page advertisements in the London *Advertiser's Review* and *Advertiser's* Weekly, asking them: "Is your advertisement being carried by the *Vikatan*?" Such enterprise kept the *Vikatan* the magazine-leader in the South till the 1940s. Then Kalki and Sadasivam, with C Rajagopalachari's support and M S Subbulakshmi (Sadasivam's wife) singing her way to fame and fortune in films, challenged its pre-eminence with their weekly they called *Kalki*. But both were overtaken by a brash newcomer in the 1950s, *Kumudam*, which made the *Vikatan* formula more "pop" and created a new formula that not only all the Tamil magazines of the 1970s and 1980s magazine boom follow, but which even the *Vikatan* has begun to adopt as it fell behind the circulation leader. But its heyday was an era no Tamil reader will forget.

5. Sahibs in Nawabland

Beyond the *Ananda Vikatan* offices is Thousand Lights. From Spencer's to Thousand Lights, on either side of the road, there once used to be the 'garden houses' of rajahs and zamindars. Bobbili, Kirlampudi and Jatprole, from north to south, occupied homes that are now huge automobile showrooms and workshops. The 5-acre TVS motor

workshops is, for instance, in *Gopala Bagh*, bought from the Rajah of
Bobbili in 1945 at Rs.1 lakh an acre. Further south, by Church Park,
was Jeypore property, which was rehabilitated as 'Amethyst', one of
21st Century Madras's places to be seen in. Part-fashion boutique, part-
restaurant, part-exhibition and performing space, it splendidly
demonstrated how old buildings could be put to profitable use. Sadly,
the owner thought highrise[9] would be more profitable and the tenant
moved out to create another garden-rich 'Amethyst' in an old warehouse
and the space around it near the rear gate of the TVS workshops. In the
Rajah of Venkatagiri's property nearby came up in 1974 the K N
Srinivasan-designed Sathyam multiplex, since 2006 recreated as a
modern film complex with five theatres in it, besides high end snacking,
dining and childcare facilities.

In Thousands Lights is another venerable Madras commercial name,
J Fenn & Co, undertakers and sculptors. Established in 1854 on Mount
Road by John Fenn, it passed into the hands of one of his employees,
Vembuli Naicker, in 1892 and has remained in the family since. It was his
grandson, Govinda Naicker, who introduced the motorised hearse to
Madras with an 'Essex' in 1931. Naicker, a talented sculptor, once headed
a team of 20 sculptors.

Marking the end of Thousand Lights are St George's Cathedral, the
contrasting, modernistic US Consul-General's office with the traditional
South Indian courtyard and stone work, and the impressive Anna flyover
that leads into the Teynampet stretch where Mount Road runs a more
southerly course and officially retains its original name. The Anna
flyover, inaugurated on July 1, 1973, was the longest (1600 feet) in the
country at the time. The 48-ft wide flyover was the first in the South and
the third in the country. It was built by East Coast Construction &
Industries. On either side of a roundabout beneath the flyover are identical
statues of a rearing horse being led by a syce. They commemorate a ban
on racing in the 1970s which was in 1985 rescinded and the sport was
run by the Government till it handed it back to the Madras Race Club in
1995 by which time many patrons of the sport had lost interest in racing
as a sport in Madras, though it still survives. Teynampet, once all 'garden
houses' between Adyar River and the Long Tank, was the hub of the

---

[9] Highrise is on hold because a Heritage Conservation Committee, which on Court orders
came into existence in 2010, has 'listed' *Jeypore House*.

Great Choultry Plain. A few of these houses of the past survive hidden behind new Government highrise in a tree-shaded stretch opposite the Congress Grounds. Some of them are Railway bungalows, but the first of them after the Gemini flyover is a house with a story. Taken over to house the offices of the Directorate of Medical Services, who remodelled its portico, *Minor Bungalow*, over a hundred years old, once was home to Newington College, an exclusive educational institution, run for the sons of rajahs and zamindars. Such male youth have long been described as 'minors' in Madras English, so, the name of the bungalow.

Its Vice Principal was Clement de la Hey, who appeared to be more interested in cricket than his wife. Dorrie Hey, it is alleged, was a lively young woman who seduced several of the handsomer students. The cuckolded husband was what today might be called 'a bit of a racist'. The link between the two characterisations is not very clear, but apparently some of the boys hatched a plot and killed de la Hey. The legal battle that followed the murder in the early 1920s was a *cause celebré* of early 20th Century Madras. It remains one of Madras's most famous unsolved murders. But the once-infamous building no longer remains, it was pulled down not long ago and replaced by a new one for the DMS.

Almost opposite *Minor Bungalow* is the new Kamaraj Memorial Hall, its handsome flight of steps, the striking traditional polished black granite pillars and long foyer a splendid architectural example to modern builders in Madras. This construction and the neighbouring Congress Grounds were all once known as *Blacker's Garden*. Some way past it, on the *Minor Bungalow* side of the road, is the Rs 15-million building raised as headquarters of the Dravida Munnetra Kazhagam, *Anna Arivalayam*. Built in 1987 in five acres of spaciousness, this modern building, with echoes of Chola towers, is one more modern building in Madras with traditional Tamil architectural overtones that party leader Muthuvel Karunanidhi has lent a helping hand in designing. The Anna Memorial, the Rajaji Memorial and *ValluvarKottam* elsewhere in the city, all have something of his ideas. The Party's Youth Wing has moved further down the road to a new building, but this reflects European Classical. *Anna Arivalayam* also houses Kalaignar TV's studios, a splendid research library focussed on the growth of the Dravidian movement, and a huge wedding hall. To the east of *Anna Arivalayam* was *Abbotsbury*, originally a bungalow and replaced by C S Loganatha Mudaliar in the 1950s with what was perhaps Madras's first purpose-built wedding hall. It later became the property of his partner J H Tarapore. After passing through a couple of hands, *Abbotsbury* was pulled down for a luxury hotel, but what came up remained a shell for years before it opened as the Hyatt Regency in 2012. The hotel remembers *Abbotsbury* in the name of its main hall.

From where the Plain ended at Cenotaph Road begins Nandanam, with its YMCA College of Physical Education, the first of its kind in the East and for ever associated with Harry Crowe Buck, the American from Springfield College, Massachusetts, who introduced here, for the first time in India his *alma mater*'s contribution to international sport, basketball.

The College's beginnings were in the YMCA Training School of Physical Education founded in the YMCA's Esplanade buildings in 1920, after Buck had arrived in 1919. Buck's dynamism and the School's training record led to Sir Dorabjee Tata inviting him to train the first-ever Indian team to the Olympics – the Paris Games of 1924. Out of Buck's and Tata's efforts was born the All India Olympic Association that year.

In 1928, Buck moved the School to the more spacious grounds of Wesley School in Royapettah. Then the 'Y' acquired 53 acres of land in Saidapet, followed by 12 more acres, and Buck's dreams of a College of Physical Education not dissimilar to his alma mater, the world's first college of physical education, came true in 1932. The next year work began on the College's main building, *Massey Hall*. The city's first sport-focused swimming pool and boxing ring are still used here. And on the campus are the house Buck built for himself and his wife Marie and a small mausoleum over the tomb where he was buried in 1943.

Neighbouring the College's grounds are the Cosmopolitan Club's golf links. The golf course was laid in the 1930s on the site of a cattle pen and slaughter house (of the Government Cattle Farm) and gave Indians their first opportunity of freely participating in the sport. Boating facilities were added at the riverside end of the course, but these no longer exist. The pavilion recalls the contribution of the Maharaja of Travancore.

Across the road from these grounds, and extending to Nungambakkam, is where the Long (Mylapore) Tank was. In the early days of rowing as a sport in Madras and then of the Madras Boat Club (founded in 1867), the Long Tank in front of *Blacker's Garden* (close to the Gemini Flyover) was frequently used for regattas.

Beyond Nandanam is Saidapet, Syed Khan's *pettai* ('domain'), a gift by the Nawab of Arcot, in 1730, to Syed Shah, one of his retinue. To develop the area as a weaving settlement, Syed Shah divided in into four quarters, kept one for himself, another for weavers, a third for traders and a fourth for artisans. Once, all Nandanam and Saidapet west of Mount Road and the land across the Adyar River now known as Kotturpuram belonged to the Nawab and was called the *Nawab's Gardens*. This vast, tree-shaded park was the Nawab's country retreat and his palace was where another, more modern, palatial home, *Adyar House*, was built in 1958 by M A Chidambaram of the Rajah of Chettinad's family, to a design by Kiffin-Peterson of Prynne, Abbott and Davis. It is said that *Adyar House* in Kotturpuram was built on a mound formed by the debris of the Arcot palace. The Nawab's gardens around the palace are now no more, the area fast-developing as one of the city's better residential localities, but the name 'Nawab's Gardens' still remains here as a reminder of things past. A name that has, however, lost currency here is Mortimer's Bottom. Once a part of the scrub forest that was much of Kotturpuram, Mortimer's Bottom owes its name, legend has it, to a Mr Mortimer of the Madras Hunt who fell off his horse during the chase after jackal and landed in a patch of prickly pear (a cactus) with painful results. Posterity claimed him, it is said, when the Hunt returned and found him being relieved of the thorns in public!

Nandanam itself, across the river from Kotturpuram, appears to have been partly owned by the Rajah of Ramnad and the Maharajah of Pithapuram who bought it from an Englishman called Gambier, the area indicated on an early 20th Century map as *Gambier's Gardens*, presumably once property of Edward John Gambier, Chief Justice, 1836-50. This part of Saidapet owes its name to C Rajagopalachari when he was Chief Minister in the early 1950s. He named it after the Tamil Year it was inaugurated in. In it, the Madras Housing Board's City Improvement Trust did much housing development in what it called Nandanam Extension, yet another part of the old Government Cattle Farm, the lay-out, buildings and greenery owing much to Capt D Gnanolivu and May George, the State Housing Board Chairman and Chief Engineer. One of the buildings they raised here was Madras's first highrise apartment block, a CIT nine-storey building with 48 apartments at a cost of Rs. 30 lakh for senior Government Servants. When it came up in 1966 it was the tallest residential building in the city and it still towers over the rest of the Extension – it was 1968 before Southern Investments built in Egmore *Montieth Court*, the city's first highrise apartment block (five stories) developed by a private sector builder. One of the neighbouring buildings that the Housing Board's highrise towers over was in the 1970s called *Denver House*, named after Denver, Colorado, whose seventh sister city Madras was. American Fulbright scholars and students and visiting Denver residents used to stay in this guest house at a time when Madras had few facilities for Americans on a budget. But that is a thing of the past.

As for the Kotturpuram gardens, they passed into the ownership of Justice Sir S. Subramania (Mani) Aiyer, but his son had to sell them after running up debts. At the court auction, in 1928, the Rajah of Chettinad bought the property and later shared it with Dewan Bahadur A M Murugappa Chettiar. The division ensured each family the property on one side of the road and this each developed. The names of the roads in the Murugappa half commemorate members of the family.

The two halves of the former Nawabi domain are divided by the usually water-short Adyar River that once every few years springs a surprise by flooding the area. The river is forded in Saidapet and Kotturpuram by handsome new bridges, the former replacing the historical Marmalong Bridge in 1966 and the latter a link between Kotturpuram and Nandanam forged in 1980-81.

Just before the Saidapet bridge there are, on the left of the road, the original buildings of the first modern teachers' training college in British territories in Asia (an institution whose doors first opened in 1856 as a Normal School in Vepery and which moved to the defunct Model Farm in Saidapet in 1889 as the Government College of Education, which had been so named in 1887). Tamil teacher training started in 1949. The College is now called the Institute of Advanced Studies in Education. It is an institution which will ever be associated with the name of Charles Todhunter who is remembered in the name of the housing colony here – but which owes its genesis to Alexander Arbuthnot, the Presidency's first Director of Public Instruction.

The main tower-embellished block, inaugurated in 1889 but with a part of it now derelict, and the twin buildings with curved frontages which housed a school – that enabled the teacher-trainees to get better experience – were striking features of the Teachers' Training College campus, which has two other heritage buildings but all in sad shape. The strikingly designed School building was pulled down in 2013, another victim of the Metro.

The College's first Principal was J.T. Flower and it awarded the Licentiate of Teaching (L.T.) till the Bachelor of Education degree began to be conferred from 1940. The L.T. was awarded only to graduates and the first two to receive the Licentiate (in 1888) were Joseph Daniel (First Class) and Abraham Gnanakkan Nadar (Second Class). Among its most famous L.Ts. were the Rt. Hon Srinivasa Sastri, S. Radhakrishnan, the former President, and Anathasayanam Iyengar, Speaker of the first Lok Sabha.

The Model Farm and the cattle farm earlier mentioned were both part of the Saidapet Experimental Farm set up by Government in 350 acres in 1865. William Robertson, an Agriculture graduate, came out from England to manage it in 1868 and started a Farm School in it with six 'apprentices' on stipends. The School grew into an Agricultural College, India's first, in 1896 with Robertson as its first Principal. When the farm did not produce noteworthy results, Government shut it down, put all the land, except for 20 acres given to the College, to other use, including providing 40 acres for the Teachers' Training College and a golf course. In 1906, the Agricultural College moved to happier surroundings when it got 500 acres in Coimbatore. There it became the Agricultural College and Research Institute and, in 1971, the Tamil Nadu Agricultural University, one of India's premier institutions.

Across the road from these buildings was handsome *Panagal*[10] *Building* with stained-glass windows. This was once the office of the Collector of Chingleput and, until the building was pulled down in 1990, was used by him for some of his work. Its 'court room', dating to when Collectors were also Magistrates, was particularly impressive, ornately embellished in wood and stained glass, yet conveying the sombre atmosphere of jurisprudence of another age. A new government tower block has now taken its place – and another bit of Madras history has vanished.

A little way before these buildings (opposite a government veterinary hospital) stands a massive house just off the main road, now completely

---

[10] Pronounced Paanagal, 'gal' as in 'regal'.

surrounded by scores of smaller houses occupying its once magnificent gardens and almost cutting its splendour off from the public view (which its few proud occupants might not mind at all). Though gardens there are none today, occupied as they are by a maze of houses and lanes, this is a splendid example of a 'garden house' of the 1830s and is the former *Lushington Gardens*, next door to which was the Nicholas Morse-Dubash Mootia choultry. Once, the site of these houses was a famous cactus garden called the Nopalry (nopal = a cochineal[11]-nourishing cactus), cultivated in 1789 by Dr James Anderson of natural science fame. Most of the plants were removed to Bangalore's Lal Bagh in 1800, though from 1837 a botanical garden continued to flourish here for a short while. Lushington's mansion in these gardens was later used as the residence of the Collector of Chingleput.

A little way to the rear of *Lushington Gardens*, just west of the railway station, is a splendid temple tank and by it the 300-year-old Karaneeswarar Temple with its magnificent *gopuram*.

In a small garden on Mount Road, by the lane leading to *Lushington Gardens*, is a pillar commemorating the munificence of Madras merchant Adrian Fourbeck who left a legacy for a small bridge to be built here. The bridge across what was the Long Tank Drainage Channel that cuts Mount Road was opened in 1786. It was raised by the executors of his will and built by Col. Patrick Ross, the builder of the Fort. Further on, where Mount Road now leads out of the City across the new Maraimalai Adigal Bridge over the Adyar River in Saidapet, there was commemorated in a plaque that was retained in the new bridge, wealthy Armenian Coja Petrus Uscan, whose name is associated with many a historic occasion in 18th Century Madras. Work on the Metro has seen the plaque partially hidden, hopefully only till restored and made visible in the future.

Between Fourbeck's Bridge and the Maraimalai Adigal Bridge, to the west of Mount Road are the red Indo-Saracenic buildings of the King Institute, believed to have been designed by Henry Irwin and occupied in 1905. The Institute, founded as a small pox vaccine depot in 1899, began its growth to a 16-department organisation in 1903 when the Bacteriology Department was added. An old 'cottage' in the campus was the original vaccine depot. Today, the Institute manufactures five different vaccines and specialises in disease prevention and public health.

---

[11] A South American winged insect.

MaraimalaiAdigal Bridge in Uscan's day was Marmalong Bridge, a name that is but one version of the name of the nearby village of Mambalam (once Europeanised as 'Mamlan'). An ancient causeway of uncertain date, it was redeveloped as a bridge at a cost of 30,000[12] pagodas by Uscan in 1726 as part of his contribution to making access easy to Little Mount, on the south bank of the river near the Bridge, and St. Thomas' Mount. Uscan's bridge, improved from time to time, was rebuilt as the MaraimalaiAdigal Bridge, work starting on it in the 1950s and ending in 1966, the first step in a major rebuilding programme necessitated by growing traffic, a programme still continuing and changing the silhouettes of the City's bridges. But now, as a hundred years ago, when the poet Edwin Arnold crossed it and noted it, the Adyar River generally runs dry in parts and its bed has long been used by all the dhobis "of the capital... the air filled with the thunder of a thousand wet clothes slapped upon the flat stones." Only, the thunder has been diminishing nowadays, modern traffic drowning it. And the clothes' drying, one of the more offbeat attractions of Madras, is even less to be seen with the Metro – and laundries – elbowing them out of the river bank/bed.

---

[12] About Rs 1,00,000 at the time.

'The Hindu' Experience

You might like The Hindu *or you may not, but no one interested in the public word can ignore it. Its record has been enviable. One of the first major Opposition papers in Imperial times,* The Hindu*'s involvement in the struggle for Independence was considerable. For the past seventy years, it has been one of the country's biggest and more successful newspapers. Technologically,* The Hindu *led where others followed.*

My own involvement with The Hindu *is nearly 80 years old, the last 50 years of them a part of a daily ritual, during which the paper has always reminded me of a one-time neighbour abroad. A middle-aged wisp of a woman in a nine-yard saree, chattering away in impeccable but strongly accented English, she organised the neighbourhood's best coffee parties and bridge sessions in the mornings, drove herself through snarled traffic for sareed tennis in the afternoons, and with supreme aplomb threw boisterously successful cocktail parties or staid sit-down dinners, replete with her best silver and traditional vegetarian cuisine, in the evenings. Yet she remained true to Olde Madras in all those years, in dress and makeup, in habits and customs, above all in the practice of rituals of faith and worship. She was, bless her daunting soul, the finest example I knew of that rather overpowering but slowly vanishing personality, the Modern Orthodox Madras Conservative. And* The Hindu *has tended to be that over the years.*

Jawaharlal Nehru felicitated 'The Old Lady of Mount Road' once with a similar but perhaps better stated expression of his thoughts: "...The Hindu *... always reminds me of an old maiden lady, very prim and proper, who is shocked if a naughty word is used in her presence. It is eminently the paper of the bourgeois, comfortably settled in life. Not for it the shady side of existence, the rough and tumble and conflict of public life. Several newspapers of moderate views have also this 'old maiden lady'* standard. They achieve it but without the distinction of The Hindu and, as a result, they become astonishingly dull in every respect."

But The Hindu was not always like that. And in those early years, as well as in its heyday, it never shunned "the rough and tumble of public life". In its infancy and youth it regularly tilted at Conservatism and Orthodoxy. Only it was never strident, though on occasion it could be quite sensational. It was only in the 1960s that The Hindu really settled down to the complacency and dullness of prosperity.

The Hindu was in fact born in ire. Six angry young men, all barely out of their teens, felt the Anglo-Indian Press (newspapers owned and edited by the British) campaign against the appointment of T Muthuswami Aiyer as the first Indian Judge of the Madras High Court was blatantly unfair and should be rebutted forcefully. So they borrowed a Rupee and twelve annas and founded The Hindu, printing 80 copies and promising a 4-anna weekly (every Wednesday at first, then Thursday). The early issues were of eight pages and a quarter of today's page size.

In that first issue of September 20, 1878, while elsewhere welcoming the appointment of the new judge and condemning the Anglo-Indian press' attitude, 'The Triplicane Six' justified their venture editorially so: "...it is not so much the alleged born ways of thinking and speaking imputed to the educated Hindus that has occasioned the absence of public opinion as the want of a well conducted native press to which the public may look to regulate their opinion. The Press does not only give expression to public opinion, but also modifies and moulds it according to circumstances. It is this want that we have made bold to attempt to supply. It is the duty of the section of the native community that claims to be educated to fill up as far as it is possible and practicable the gap separating the governors from the governed. We feel this and we attempt to do justice to our feeling... The principles that we propose to be guided by are simply those of fairness and justice. It will always be our aim to promote harmony and union among our fellow countrymen and to interpret correctly the feelings of the natives and to create mutual confidence between the governed and the governors...."

These would-be moulders of public opinion were two schoolmasters, the 23-year-old G Subramania Aiyer of Tiruvaiyyar, and his 21-year-old fellow-tutor and friend at Pachaiyappa's College, M Veeraraghavachariar of Chingleput, and four law students,

T T Rangachariar, P V Rangachariar, D Kesava Rao Pantulu and N Subba Rao Pantulu. It wasn't long before the students became lawyers and prudently parted company with their fiery editor Subramania Aiyer and his strongest supporter, Managing Director Veeraraghavachariar. The erstwhile schoolmasters now settled down to filling a long-felt need for "a native organ in the metropolis of Southern India", treading boldly where others had failed.

That The Hindu *founded by unknown youths – its Editor's only claim to fame a few feature articles on the German Sanskrit scholar Max Müller that he wrote for* The Madras Mail *– survived where earlier the publications of the Presidency's most eminent Indians had failed was undoubtedly due to the undaunted hard line Subramania Aiyer and Veeraraghavachariar took, "(thinking) for the people and (giving) shape to the nebulous ideas of leaders who were willing to strike but reluctant to wound the foreign rulers."*

Yet the Founding Fathers of The Hindu *were Anglophiles to a great extent. They were convinced that the world was "destined to be guided by Europe", especially Britain, accepted to a considerable degree "the superiority of a Western rule", and recognised themselves as "natives" who needed guidance. "How enormously the Indian people are indebted to British rule for everything that makes human life worth living, that imparts to it happiness, dignity and the quality of progress,...,"* The Hindu *wrote in 1894 of what it considered, together with Gokhale and others, "divine ordained" rule. But* The Hindu *was equally convinced that the Anglo-Indian Press should be challenged, despotic bureaucrats condemned, and the abuse of power exposed.*

The paper was convinced that the discontent of the people was the result of "oppressive taxation and the insolence of the ruling class". It condemned the constant efforts to strengthen the hands of the Executive. And pointed out that "millions of money... are carried to a distant foreign country...The frightful drain has gone on since that first establishment of British supremacy...and has even been a source of the keenest embarrassment to the rulers. This drain continues to increase and the sore and bent back of the taxpayer continues to be loaded with further burdens."

And so, almost from its birth, The Hindu *collided head-on with the Administration. "No harsher words," it has been said, were ever used in* The Hindu *than when it took on Governor Mountstuart Grant-Duff.*

Lashing out at the Governor and the judiciary, following the Salem Riots of 1884, The Hindu *thundered, "...the prosecution of the so called Salem Rioters and their convictions were ...executed in a vindictive spirit, not very honourably and utterly unworthy of a civilised Government." On the Chingleput Ryots' case in 1881*, The Hindu *charged Grant-Duff with allowing the affair "to cast dirt on the fair face of British Justice." And the paper summed up its* béte noire *on a couple of occasions so: "Oh! Lucifer! How art thou fallen? Oh! Mr Grant-Duff, how you stand like an extinct volcano in the midst of the ruins of your abortive reputation as an administrator! Erudite you may be, but a statesman you are not"; and again, "if Mr Grant-Duff's Indian career has exemplified one fact more than another, it is the little value mere mental endowments possess among the qualifications for successful statesmanship. Sympathy, felicity, tolerance... are far more necessary and useful than retentive memory and accomplished quotations... Mr Grant-Duff has failed as Governor of Madras..."; and yet again, "...by conniving at the administrative scandals that have brought the Government of Madras into such odium... he has made himself unpopular to all classes of people".*

But if Subramania Aiyer could be eloquently violent, he could also be equally gallant. Of Mrs Grant-Duff he wrote that she had been making "amends for the gruff, unpopular and cynical manner her husband had been holding forth... the ring of earnestness that always characterises her utterances has half redeemed the unpopularity of her husband."

The Hindu *in those years also did not hesitate to criticise legal tribunals. When a Mylapore temple trustee who pushed a policeman was sentenced*, The Hindu, *unafraid, asked the Chief Justice, "Would an English judge sentence a respectable citizen of London...for causing the hat of a police constable to fall from his head? Why should a serious view be taken in this country of an offence which in England would be dismissed with a warning to the offender?" When some British soldiers chased two women in Guntakal and shot the man who tried to protect them, Ashford the accused was acquitted. Commented* The Hindu, *"...the Ashford case affords another example of the almost sure miscarriage of justice where a European is the offender and a native the victim." Two days later it wrote, "Is there any safety for the natives of the country from the ravages of European soldiers? This is the question which naturally occurs to anyone who hears of the verdict in the Guntakal murder case. We do not hesitate to say it is decidedly a perverse verdict."*

Commenting on the arrest of Tilak in Poona in 1897, The Hindu *answered Anglo-Indian support of Government's measures so:* "The Indian Press would not do its duty if it fails to write strongly and with indignation on the mad doings of the Bombay Government and so long as it has the freedom which the law gives it, it would write frankly and freely and would recognise no vocation in a constant singing of hallelujas to the European service..." *After Tilak was sentenced,* The Hindu *wrote,* "The British Government in India would appear to have taken leave of its old traditions of freedom, benevolence and popular sympathy and have fallen entirely into the ways of irresponsible reactionaries..."

The Hindu's *views at this time in history, it is patent, were unambiguous. It idolised 'Father' Ripon, who succeeded Lytton, the Viceroy* "the people of India can never think of without a curse... (who) left the country without a single soul being sorry for it." *The paper repeatedly affirmed its belief in the bonds with Britain, but* "conceived a just aversion" *to the bureaucracy which was* "the object of our hatred and contempt." *It felt that Britain would produce better results in India with greater* "sympathy for the indigenous institutions of the conquered country" *than by introducing* "principles of scientific government ... neither understood nor liked... in a spirit of reckless haste and high-handedness."

These Delphic pronouncements of The Hindu *that ran into columns and its enthusiastic encouragement of letters from its readers – both not a little due to the early financial constraints and limited staff, which made news secondary, much of it being 'lifted' from other papers published at home and abroad – were to be the hallmark of 'The Oracle of Mount Road' for decades to come. But catering as the paper did to an erudite micro-minority at the time, the formula worked and the paper went from success to success. Yet, even as English journalism began to change in India from 1990s,* The Hindu *did not quite succeed in shaking off its partiality for its own opinions, as well as those of many of its readers, in preference to more hard-core journalism involving investigative and more colourful reporting. But its occasional investigative successes in more recent times tended to be overwhelmed by verbosity and opinionatedness.*

In 1883, The Hindu *became a tri-weekly, retaining its original format, but coming out every Monday, Wednesday and Friday evening. The same year, with the help of prominent well-wishers, it acquired its own press and premises. This new address, 100 Mount Road, was to remain The*

Hindu's home till 1939. From here issued the paper with a front-page full of advertising and its three back pages also at the service of the advertiser (a practice that came to an end only in 1958 when it followed the lead of its idol, The pre-Thompson / Murdoch Times, London). In between there were more views than news, but from the beginning there was a London Letter and a considerable amount of Indian news from the Imperial capital. It was this emphasis on London and Delhi as well as the news from other Presidency towns and even such faraway places as Cuba and the Sudan, that made The Hindu *claim to be, despite its South Indian circulation base, a national newspaper from its inception. Nevertheless, the paper had room to spare for comment on such mundane matters as the lighting up of Grant-Duff's Marina as well as* Banqueting Hall. *And its reports of the tragic fire at the People's Park Christmas Fair in 1887 would shame those reporters who covered the LIC building inferno ninety years later.*

The Hindu's *national image was enhanced when it announced the birth of the Indian National Congress on December 12, 1885, stating, "The object of the Congress... is to bring to a focus our scattered political energy and to give solidity and organisation to native opinion... (on such) topics in which... all parts of the country are interested..." The status of* The Hindu *was made even more secure when its Editor moved the first-ever resolution of the Congress at the inaugural sessions on December 28, 1885.*

From the very beginning of Congress, The Hindu *kept emphasising the secular nature of the Party.* The Hindu *itself in its early years owed much of its editorial panache to its friend, philosopher and guide, Surgeon-Major Nicholson of St Thomas' Mount, and much of its later prosperity to the Maharajah of Vizianagaram and Nawab Humayun Jah Bahadur, a descendant of Tippu Sultan. All of which made the decision of 'The Triplicane Six' to call the paper what they did rather curious. Their reason why has never really been explained, but* The Hindu *by no stretch of imagination could be called a denominational paper, though Kasturi Gopalan, lover of racing and astrology and father of the paper's Sports Page, which made its debut in 1925, introduced in 1964 the still-continuing daily Religious Discourse; that, however, is more an expression of a theocentric view of life rather than a serious attempt to propagate Hinduism, leave alone the Vaishnavism of the Hindu's proprietors.*

The Religious Discourse, however, is a far cry from what Subramania Aiyer thought fit for his newspaper. Shortly after The Hindu *became an evening daily, on April 1, 1889, Subramania Aiyer launched the paper's first columnist, 'Sentinel', whose 'Olla Podrida' took sly digs at the foibles of the upper class, British as well as Indian. A few months later, 'A Native Observer' launched another column, intended to act as a brake on educated Indians imitating the West. Both columns were to pose the first major problems for* The Hindu. *The 'Native Observer's conservative views on Hinduism started a major controversy in the columns of the paper which ended only when* The Hindu *revealed the identity of the columnist as Sir T Madhava Rao and chastised him: "Within the short period of three years, Raja Sir T Madhava Rao has changed his opinions on political and social questions and the change has been decidedly for the worse... We believe our aims...must be...not of a civilisation which, however venerable its antiquity, is for practical purposes more or less antiquated and useless." Those words of Subramania Aiyer the reformist were almost the first words in the rift that was to break up* The Hindu *ownership.*

When the Rani died in 1895, The Hindu *felt that since the late Sir Madhava Rao had left about Rs 10 lakh and since two of his three sons held "respectable appointments in the public service", a lakh should be set apart "to do some charity to commemorate the names of their distinguished parents." And, not prepared to leave well enough alone, it added: "These remarks apply to the case of the late Sir T Muthuswami Aiyer also, in whose case, his son, Mr Swaminatha Aiyer, holding a place in the civil service, there is a greater obligation for something being done to recognise the claims of the public on the savings of those that grow rich at their expense."*

'Sentinel's' problems with The Hindu, *on the other hand, were mostly as a result of his ambitions. 'Sentinel' was none other than Eardley Norton, the eminent British criminal lawyer, who, when he had been Coroner of Madras, had sued the paper for its comments against him, the first defamation case against the paper. But after* The Hindu *had apologised, Norton and Subramania Aiyer became friends and 'Olla Podrida', with its biting humour and parody, was the result, though a short-lived one, the column running only from May to December 1889.* The Hindu's *support of Norton, however, continued for years.*

When Norton's election to the Imperial Legislative Council in 1894 was threatened, The Hindu *came out strongly in support of him. It then opened its columns to acrimonious correspondence when Norton, within a month of his election, resigned his seat, in consequence of an adultery suit being filed against him. Subramania Aiyer's partiality for Norton continued despite the lawyer's personal tirades at the Madras Congress Sessions in 1894 against those who disagreed with him. These attitudes of Norton turned Veeraghavachariar against him and when, in 1898, the lawyer contested a Corporation seat in Triplicane, Veeraraghavachariar wrote a 'Letter to the Editor' that* The Hindu *published under his name. Editorially, however, the paper, though keeping a neutral attitude, made no secret of its admiration for Norton. And when the Englishman won, congratulated him warmly.*

The Norton incident added fuel to the flickering flames of discord between the two proprietors of the paper that had grown to 12 pages, become a daily and claimed the second largest readership in South India. That discord grew out of the differences of opinion the proprietors had over social reform. Subramania Aiyer was a dedicated crusader against the social evils of Hindu society. He sought to raise the age of marriage, he advocated widow remarriage, he wished a better place for the Untouchables, he demanded the abolition of child marriages, caste and nautch parties.

Subramania Aiyer was not a man to preach what he would not practise. He remarried his eldest daughter Sivapriyammal, who had been made a virgin widow at 13, to a boy in Bombay during the 1889 Congress session. When a child died in a Triplicane home where there had been a widow remarriage and the community would not help at the funeral, Subramania Aiyer sent his own purohit *to officiate. On another occasion, in 1893,* The Hindu *carried a display advertisement with the heading "Wanted Virgin Widows to Marry".*

The paper did not tread softly when attacking orthodoxy: "The Hindu that offends the orthodoxy is not argued with but is persecuted and denied all the pleasure of association and the solace of religion. It is the intolerance that has killed individuality in this country. The arbitrary power exercised by a section of the Hindu society has so far demoralised the whole...To exercise this arbitrary power...to see its own capricious and fossilised regulations implicitly obeyed without regard to change and changing conditions, has become the end it is ever conscious of; it will even calmly face its own destruction rather than admit itself to be wrong in any respect and adopt change. It is otherwise inconceivable that any community with an intelligent self-consciousness should set its face as the Hindu community does, against its best material and educational interests being advanced by foreign travel and against the physical and moral stamina of its youths being improved by a more humane and more rational set of marriage customs. The Hindu nation cannot produce a great man, a man that can stand comparison with any of the glorious group of heroes, men of great originalities and moral power, of undaunted enterprise, who have made Europe the mistress of the globe, until it emerges from its present condition of constraint all round and arrives at a condition of greater freedom to individuals."

Subramania Aiyer thundered away: "The degraded condition of the Pariah and other kindred classes is notorious and the peculiarities of the Hindu social system are such that from this system no hope whatever of their amelioration can be entertained...It seems to us to be hopeless for the Pariahs...to expect redemption from anything that the Hindu might do...No amount of admiration for our religion will bring social salvation to these poor people. It is Christian missionaries alone that will and can educate them and advance their worldly well-being in all ways. If we cannot do this service to our low caste countrymen...let us not grudge these countrymen of ours the service of foreign beneficence..."

The Hindu *was Subramania Aiyer's vehicle for his crusades. But in a conservative society such crusading zeal was destined inevitably to be faced with a hostile backlash. And Veeraraghavachariar, in charge of the business side, found the repercussions hurting the paper's finances. The fallout was predictable, the partnership being dissolved in October 1898, Norton presiding over the formalities which saw Subramania Aiyer quitting – taking over full-time the Tamil language* Swadesamitran *he had founded as a weekly in 1882 and which in 1899 he would convert into a daily. Veeraraghavachaiar took over the struggling* Hindu.

In Subramania Aiyer's day, The Hindu *fought some epic battles with* The Madras Mail *and the* Madras Times, *Reuter's (which it accused of "tendentious" reports of India) and* The Times, *London (The Hindu being "thunderstruck" by 'The Thunderer's' "mendacity" and willingness to publish "trash from ...India"). But the times were not ripe for the entire Subramania Formula and, after the great Editor's return from England in 1897, he held himself anguishedly in check, responding to the loquacious organisation man Veeraraghavachariar, "the custodian of Congress prestige in Madras" and the brains behind every Congress session held there in his time. But literary silence was foreign to that disciplinarian and man of few spoken words, Subramania Aiyer, even to protect a losing investment, and soon the bickering began again, fundamentally over the issues of social legislation, for which, Veeraraghavachariar contended, their readership was not ready. Veeraraghavachariar felt that, with Subramania Aiyer's policies, neither would circulation increase nor would they be able to raise outside financial help. So they came to the parting of the ways. But the bad blood never quite diminished.* The Swadesamitran *and* Veeraraghavachariar's *Tamil bi-weekly* Hindu Nesan *went at each other hammer and tongs over* The Hindu's *new policies. One reply of Veeraraghavachariar's led to Subramania Aiyer suing for defamation, a published apology, however, settling the case.*

Subramania Aiyer, called the greatest journalist of his generation, a product of Western education and culture, felt there was no hope for an India living with the traditions of the past. In Western training and attitudes to society alone did he see hope for India. Even as late as 1903, at the Silver Jubilee celebrations of The Hindu, *he was speaking out for "change, reforms and progress...(they are) the life of a nation, whereas blind and thoughtless conservatism lead to stagnation and eventual ruin." Long before Women's Lib he felt that what was offensive in Hindu society was its treatment of women. Today, the ideals he fought for are enshrined in the Constitution.*

While he was at The Hindu, *Subramania Aiyer never once felt that* de mortuis nil nisi bonum *should be a matter of policy. In unsparingly reviewing the work of the dead, he felt: "When a man dies we can review his work fully. The dead do not care what we write. Let the living take a lesson from our policy... Let all feel that even when they die their defects – if they injure the national cause and national self-respect – will not be forgiven..." He himself lived up to this code – to a point.*

In 1907, there came upon him a total metamorphosis, following the Punjab arrests and the deportation of Lala Lajpat Rai. He now was convinced the British had to be ousted forcibly. He wrote to The Hindu, *"The boasted freedom of British rule in India now stands exposed in its horrid nakedness"! His sudden change almost made an extremist of him. Boycott British goods, give up titles and honorary offices, he urged. The new radical – now beyond even* The Hindu's *changed stand – was arrested in 1908 for sedition and refused bail. A sick man, stricken by leprosy, the thought of jail was now too much for him – and he agreed to furnish sureties for his silence. He was never quite the same man again. He died in 1916. But he had lived to see the seed he had planted grow into a thriving tree.*

For a while after Subramania Aiyer left The Hindu, *however, it seemed the growing tree might wither. The 12 pages contained far less news, much more views and six pages of advertising. But despite a Sunday supplement – introduced late in 1898 – attempts to rent out a portion of the building, and a willingness to undertake commercial printing, the paper barely managed to survive. In 1901, Veeraraghavachariar attempted to make* The Hindu *a limited company with a capital of Rs 1,20,000. But the scheme failed, with less than half the offered 1,200 shares being subscribed – possibly because much of the educated elite were government servants prohibited from taking shares in joint stock companies. Two years later, the indomitable paper celebrated its Silver Jubilee, note being made by Veeraraghavachariar that the paper had defended four libel suits in the period, losing three of them heavily and settling one.*

As The Hindu's *adventurousness began to decline, so did its circulation, which was down to 800 copies when the sole proprietor decided to sell out. The new purchaser was* The Hindu's *Legal Adviser, S Kasturi Ranga Iyengar, a politically ambitious lawyer who had migrated from a Kumbakonam village to practise in Coimbatore and thence to Madras. Kasturi Ranga Iyengar's ancestors had served the Courts of Vijayanagar and Mahratta Tanjore. An earlier Kasturi Ranga Iyengar of Innambur village had served as Paymaster of the Raja Serfoji's forces. His third son, Sesha Iyengar, served as the Tanjore Collectorate's chief translator of Marathi documents. It was Sesha Iyengar's third and last son who traded the Law for Journalism, pursuing his penchant for politics honed in Coimbatore and by his association with the 'Egmore Group' led by C Sankara Nair and Dr T M Nair.*

Kasturi Ranga Iyengar was past forty when he decided to buy The National Press and its major publication, The Hindu, *much against the advice of friends and relatives who termed it "a mad venture." On April 1, 1905 he took over the paper for Rs 75,000.*

From the first, Kasturi Ranga Iyengar treated The Hindu *as a business proposition, a tradition continued to this day, when its owners say "it's the family's ONLY business". He took over a 12-page tabloid-sized (half the present size) newspaper and soon made it a 16-page paper with a good advertising revenue. Subscribers in arrears just did not get the paper.* The Hindu *only wanted fully paid-up subscriptions. But Kasturi Ranga Iyengar also ensured that subscribers got their money's worth – a newspaper with much more up-to-date news. He subscribed to Reuter's telegraphic news service; published court cases* in extenso *(a practice continued until the 1950s but now sadly discontinued; it used to provide columns of sensational reading, as in such cases as the Bawla murder case involving the Indore Royal Family and the Lakshmikanthan Case involving leading Madras cine artists and musicians); and provided space for a weather report, shipping and commercial information, and 'Sporting News', continuing with this a tradition Subramania Aiyer had started of reporting County Cricket and beginning a new tradition of reporting Racing.*

The formula worked and Kasturi Ranga Iyengar ended his first year with a small profit of Rs 150! He had also inaugurated a new editorial policy for the paper. In July 1905 the paper wrote of "A Pauperised India" in these terms: "Is there now a single intelligent Indian who still cherishes a hope that the British Parliament will ultimately save India from ruin?...India's hope does not lie in British statesmanship; it lies solely and entirely in her own exertions." A month later the paper wrote: "The only wise, beneficial and permanent arrangement is to transfer the chief control over the Government of India...to...the people who alone are the rightful and competent guardians of the country's interests." This was a radical break with the Subramania Aiyer past. The Hindu *was saying 'Quit India' long before Congress!*

But it was not this policy that was to establish The Hindu *as the South Indian's adjunct to his steaming morning coffee. It was, among other things, the paper's unrelenting attitude towards Messrs Arbuthnot and Co, a great Madras bank that crashed in 1906. The Bank's insolvency affected thousands, from Governor Lawley and Maharajas to those investors of "the earning classes".* The Hindu, *which called the Arbuthnot business "a swindle of the vilest description... decoying innumerable innocent men and women in its rapacious maw...," campaigned for over a year seeking justice for the investors, but whereas it may have been instrumental in getting Sir George Arbuthnot, a major Anglo-Indian personality, convicted of misappropriation, it failed to get adequate compensation for those hit hardest by the crash. Nevertheless,* The Hindu *established its reputation as a newspaper concerned for the man in the South Indian sun.*

By 1912, The Hindu *was a 16-page tabloid-sized newspaper and was devoting a considerable amount of space to tilting with Annie Besant, whose contentions were first questioned by Subramania Aiyer in 1894. In the next quarter of a century* The Hindu *crossed words interminably with Mrs Besant and her* New India, *clashing over Theosophy, J Krishnamurthi and Gandhi and agreeing only on her Home Rule movement. The highly personalised, bitter attacks and counter-attacks would come as a surprise – nay, shock – to readers of today's paper.* The Hindu, *for instance, informing its readers in 1912 that "the law courts will form the theatre where an interesting page of theosophical history will be unfolded to the public," commented that "only fools or mad men could believe in this 20th Century that the boy Krishnamurthi is an incarnation of the divinity. Mrs Annie Besant and Leadbeater have made up a story ..." Defamation suits by Mrs Besant were successfully defended by* The Hindu.

In 1920, The Hindu *was again doing what today would be considered uncharacteristic. It reported the proposed marriage of Theosophist G S Arundale to a Hindu girl, who, it claimed, was a minor.* The Hindu *warned Arundale and Besant – described as guardians of many Hindu families – "that their responsibilities will be terrible and that the reaction of such a step on their political and educational activities will be intense." Nevertheless, the 40-year-old Arundale married the 16-year-old Rukmini Sastri in a civil ceremony in Bombay and* The Hindu *was left gnashing its teeth.*

On such local "pet aversions", and in its continuing campaign against the bureaucracy and racial discrimination, did The Hindu *continue to get hot under its collar. On the national issue, the paper was more restrained, though its stand was unmistakable. Initially continuing to affirm its loyalty to the British throne and counting among its "blessings" British rule, it gradually shifted its stand from Moderatism to Gandhian opposition, the change beginning in 1918 with the publication of the Montagu-Chelmsford Reforms. This was* The Hindu's *finest hour, when its cause became the independence of India and its story was inextricably intertwined with the Indian Nationalist movement.*

As much responsible for this glorious age of vociferous opposition as
its Proprietor-Editor were his two nephews and Assistant Editors,
A Rangaswami Iyengar and S Rangaswami Iyengar, both to be famous
Editors and to die in office in the decade after Kasturi Ranga Iyengar's
death in 1923. A politician-journalist, a close friend of Motilal Nehru, a
man who took a legalistic view of affairs, A Rangaswami constantly
strived from 1928 to bring the official and unofficial worlds closer
together, using his remarkable political insight to make The Hindu a
vehicle of political thought. But with him also began an era of moderation
not always in line with Congress or Gandhian decisions, ending the
more firebrand eras of Kasturi Ranga Iyengar and S Rangaswami. To
A Rangaswami, "unjust", if used with indisputable facts, was as effective
a word as "damned unjust", a view The Hindu has rather stuck to ever
since.

S Rangaswami was of a different mould. A non-political wielder of a
brilliant, caustic and critical pen, he was the man for Kasturi Ranga
Iyengar's campaigns of moral indignation. An avid reader of everything
from penny dreadfuls to World Literature, a perennial protester against
the social and moral conventions of society, especially Brahmin society,
his trenchant writings were masterpieces of satire and irony and his
exchanges with that eloquent dandy, Srinivasa Sastri, epic.

It was S Rangaswami who described the Moderates as "Moderates
only in their patriotism" and Moderatism as "not a policy but a disease."
After the Punjab disturbances and the Amritsar tragedy he asked, "How
can there be peace when we do not know whether we have won or lost?
If we have won let that be made clear by deeds and not by words which
might mean anything or nothing. If we have lost then obviously there
can be no cessation, no halting by the wayside till India's honour and
self-respect are vindicated." He advised Moderates afraid that the
Reforms would be withdrawn that "there are occasions on which it is
wiser to let go the bird in the hand and pin our hopes on those in the
bush." Of British rule he said that "we do not think the British connection
is sacrosanct...There is no divine right about the British connection."
The Hindu had come a long way from the days of the Founding Fathers.

But if it did not hesitate to chastise the British, it was no less ready to
take on Gandhiji. S Rangaswami, writing in 1920, said: "It is perhaps
India's misfortune than Mr Gandhi's fault that he should be possessed
of a mind so mercilessly logical. Prepared himself for the greatest of

sacrifices, it is open to question whether he does not impose on his following conditions the rigour of which is greater than it can bear." He added, "The strength of a chain is not in its strongest but its weakest link...Does Mr Gandhi seriously think the (non-co-operation) movement will retain its outstanding characteristic of non-violence concurrently with chaos, anarchy and disorder?"

It was, however, for Srinivasa Sastri that S Rangaswami reserved his choicest language. Describing "the official apologist" as "the pet lamb of the British government," The Hindu *wrote, "It was said of the Austrians that they had a genius for defeat. It may be said with equal justice of Mr Sastri that he had a genius for surrender and this is the man who is nowhere less honoured than in his own Presidency..." When Mr Sastri took with him a white valet to Australia,* The Hindu *bitingly commented: "It is a stroke of Mr Sastri's shrewdness. It is in fact a practical demonstration of Mr Sastri's belief in a white Australia policy. Had he taken a brown valet, who knows whether Australian labour would not have struck work as an infringement of its trade union rules and thus made it impossible for Mr Sastri even to land? Knowing as he did that white Australia was dead against competition of coloured labour and approving of the white's ideal, Mr Sastri had no option but to refuse to be a party to importing coloured labour into Australia. That perhaps explains at once the selection of a white valet and Australian labour's silence."*

But it was on the question of the freedom of the Press that The Hindu *of Kasturi Ranga Iyengar's day – and to a somewhat lesser extent during his son Srinivasan's stewardship – waxed most eloquent.* The Hindu *first strongly asserted its views on this subject in the wake of its comments on the Punjab turmoil, when the Government sought security deposits. The paper answered: "We feel no doubt that the action of the Madras Government ... is a violent stretch of the arbitrary power conferred by the Act. It is a gross and dangerous infringement of the liberty of the Press and if the present policy is continued it must lead to the extinguishment of honest and independent journalism in this country. So far as* The Hindu *is concerned the contemplation of a perverted application of the Press Act and the involving of it into further pains and penalties will not have the result of inducing it to swerve from its past traditions and the path of journalistic independence and rectitude which it has always maintained. It may have to close down on account of bureaucratic intolerance and the harsh misapplication of an unjust law..."*

During the Moplah riots of 1921 – its climax being the death of 66 out of 100 prisoners who were confined overnight in a closed iron wagon that was part of the Calicut-Madras train – The Hindu *unmistakably reiterated its stand when it was asked to publish only official reports. "We may be wrong," the paper said, "but we feel that an attempt is being made to put the Press in blinkers and we do not propose to submit ourselves to that operation. Putting it bluntly, the public have no confidence in official accounts and to ask us to refuse publication to others unless they have the imprimatur of departmentalised truth is asking us to betray our responsibility to the public."*

An ardent Congressman, an admirer of Tilak and direct action, but above all a man who sought a new and free India, Kasturi Ranga Iyengar made the voice of The Hindu *"a clarion call that might annoy but could not be ignored." Throughout his editorship his policy was "that no leader is above criticism because he is well meaning, that no policy is sacrosanct as such..." And Tilak himself learnt this by experience.*

When Kasturi Ranga Iyengar died in December 1923, he left a paper with a circulation of 17,000 and considerable advertising support, a paper recognised by officialdom as well as the citizenry as a major communication force. To make all this technically possible he had, between 1921 and 1923, installed the first rotary printing press in Madras and modern type composing machines, setting the trend the paper follows to this day of being first with modern newspaper technology in India. He arranged for an efficient news-by-telegram service and ensured quick delivery of the paper to the remotest areas. He had taken over a paper with "a high political reputation and as low a financial outlook as possible," a paper in which Subramania Aiyer had made "righteousness readable," and made it into a paying proposition. He made "readable righteousness" remunerative, but not at the expense of human interest – often at its most interesting in the extensive readers' column – leavening humour, and comprehensive coverage of meetings down to those of even sanitary inspectors.

On Kasturi Ranga Iyengar's death, there was a kindred soul in S Rangaswami ready to step into his editorial shoes while Kasturi Srinivasan tended the management. It was a natural and successful partnership that lasted until Rangaswami's untimely death in 1926.

Srinivasan, for his part, encouraged brightening up the paper. In the mid and late 1920s there commenced numerous entertaining features – cartoons, a full picture page, a weekly women's page, short stories and humorous skits aplenty. The paper published wedding photographs, pictures of arrivals and departures (this exposure becoming a status symbol), of social functions and entertainments, of successful persons and new appointees. It was a paper as game to publish a whole page of pictures of Governor Lord Goschen's daughter's Madras wedding as it was to publish pictures of the ex-Maharaja of Indore and his American fiancee as well as columns of reports on their international romance. This was a liveliness that was to gradually die down when A Rangaswami came in as Editor in 1928, fading out almost completely in the 1930s. The sports page, the weekly women's page, the pictorial page and the erudite Weekly Literary Supplement (another instance of following where The Times, *London, led) survived till World War II, but only the first-named came through the restrictive rigours of that holocaust intact. There has, however, been some revival of the literary supplement and women's and pictorial features since the 1990s. In fact, since the new Millennium it has added a Metro supplement that offers a wealth of material for the mod young reader, male and female. But back to the past....*

During the two decades before War's end, The Hindu *made significant innovative strides. By 1925, it had attained broadsheet size, publishing at least 12 pages daily. In 1928 it started an illustrated weekly that was to become the Sunday Magazine Section in 1941. In 1930 was started the first 'morgue' in an Indian newspaper – a library with a scientific system of indexing and cross-referencing, which is now completely digitised. In the mid-1930s, a cinema page and a gardening page were introduced. In 1938 it became the first newspaper in the country to have a teleprinter connection from the Central Telegraph Office to receive the news. And at War's end it luxuriated in a circulation of over 45,000!*

During the first quarter of this period – from 1928 till his death in 1934 – A Rangaswami was Editor, and it was inevitable that The Hindu's *hard line policy would undergo a change. Its attitude now was one of conciliation; the Gandhian change of creed to "Swaraj meaning complete Independence" did not receive* The Hindu's *whole-hearted backing. But when Sardar Vallabhbhai Patel was arrested even before the civil disobedience campaign,* The Hindu *asked in an echo of its old voice,*

"How can we measure the perversity of a Government that has forced into imprisonment -a man...so anxious for a peaceful and just settlement of the great issue upon which Mahatma Gandhi has launched his great campaign?" By 1933, however, there came the parting of the ways with Gandhi. The issue was Satyagraha, The Hindu *asserting that Civil Disobedience "has outlived its usefulness as a method." It no longer saw a future in non-violence. This was almost the last influence on* The Hindu *– but an abiding one ever since – of A Rangaswami Iyengar who had once acted as Gandhi's secretary at a London Round Table Conference. With his death, Srinivasan became Managing Editor, the post he held till his death in 1959, assisted by his younger brother Gopalan, co-proprietor, printer and publisher.*

When Srinivasan took over The Hindu *is attitude mellowed further; no matter that he was almost as ardent a Congressman as his Tilak-admiring, battle-welcoming father, he preferred to tread softly. When Devadas Gandhi of the* Hindustan Times *was arrested during the 1942 'Quit India' troubles, all* The Hindu *would say was, "This is an order that simply takes our breath away...the Chief Commissioner makes it impossible for them (the Press) to fulfil their duty to the public which is to give it all the news which in their judgement is fit to print." But Srinivasan, presiding over the All-India Newspaper Editors' Conference, did say, "There is no question of our willing submission to any proposal which in our opinion is derogatory to the profession or in any way prevents us from functioning as responsible newspapers." These views he demonstrated in action when, late in 1942, Government banned news on the fast of a Prof Bhansali. The Srinivasan-led AINEC retaliated by blacking out Government circulars, Honours Lists and speeches not affecting the public interest,* The Hindu *leading the way. When the Government retaliated by withdrawing facilities to the paper's reporters,* The Hindu *commented, "No popular Government would dream of brushing aside the public's right so lightly as the Madras Government has shown itself ready to do since it would clearly see that such action as that of the Madras Government would really amount to cutting off the nose to spite the face," and suspended publication on January 6, 1943. On resumption of publication, the paper loftily declared that "those who little mindful of the great question of principle involved have criticised the Press for a decision which inevitably meant some little inconvenience to the public should have known that it could be no pleasure to the newspapers to place such voluntary restrictions on their own usefulness and that only a paramount sense of duty to the public could have sustained them in this effort to vindicate the right of the public to be kept informed even during the war..."*

Even as late as April 1951, discussing proposed amendments to the Constitution, The Hindu *was arguing at length with Pandit Nehru to leave the Press alone, pointing out "that quite a large number of galling restrictions on the freedom of the Press, which were an unblest legacy of British rule, but which the courts have held to be repugnant to the Constitution and void, will be revived and become effective for mischief if the amendment should be adopted."* The Hindu *wrote, "(Government) looks upon the Press more or less as a kind of permanent opposition... Mr Nehru should free himself from the obsession that the Press...is...incapable of taking an unbiased or rational view of Government's policies..."*

The Srinivasan Age was an era during which The Hindu *adopted a conciliatory attitude, convinced that freedom would come with negotiation. The paper and its leadership played no little role in Congress accepting office in the States, in the process forging stronger links than Kasturi Ranga Iyengar had first established with C Rajagopalachariar. No less was* The Hindu's *concern for the national economic future – and it published possibly the first five-year plan dreamed up for India by an Indian, M Visweswarayya, the great Mysore planner. It also changed its attitude to Imperial honours, seeking the abolition of these "anachronisms". But all was not unrelieved seriousness. David Low and his cartoons commenced their long association with* The Hindu *in January 1938. And soon after, the paper lost a High School subscription when the school's teachers disagreed with a light* Hindu *editorial applauding a magisterial dismissal of a plaint by a Calcutta school-teacher who had felt aggrieved when he had unwittingly sat on a prickly cactus placed on his chair by a student-prankster, the master's dignity suffering further indignity when the chair collapsed under his uncomfortable, squirming weight!*

Settled in its new Mount Road home, No 200, on November 24, 1939, the paper celebrated its Diamond Jubilee, affirming its faith in democracy, "free discussion that is the life breath of democracy," and belief in its own unquestionable educative role. It felt that, abroad, the masses were "educated enough to read greedily but not to read seriously," thus "swamping the discriminating few." This view has changed to an extent in the new Millennium, but at that time felt that this should not happen in India. "It is not by bludgeoning the reader's mind but by reasoning with it that the soundest and most lasting results can be achieved," the paper contended. Stating that the pros and cons must be fairly set out and that it was incumbent on the Press "to maintain steadily this appeal to higher instincts," The Hindu *eschewed being a popular paper – "a tabloid". It felt news should not be sensationalised, that it must be presented "in a well ordered manner... each item in its appointed place." But though it slightingly spoke in the same breath of "so called human interest stories and similar shop window devices," the paper, while carrying extensive coverage of Sport, especially of Cricket and Racing, neither considered pastimes of the masses, even had a correspondent writing regularly on the fashions at the races! And it once devoted columns of space for two months to a controversy that posed the question "Did Sita, Rama's consort, lie and if so was it pardonable?", the issue first cropping up when Srinivasa Sastri challenged an allusion by S Satyamurti referring to his contention that there were occasions when the Gandhian truth would do more harm than good.*

Some of The Hindu's *most newsworthy achievements during this period came as much by good organisation as by chance.* The Hindu *(which became a morning paper only in November 1940) carried the news of the Japanese surrender, when most of the country's other morning dailies (including* The Times of India*) missed the story, because a subeditor was posted to monitor radio bulletins every night during the War and he tuned into the BBC, for a last check, at 4.30 a.m, before going home, the last edition already being under print. Similarly, the paper scooped Lal Bahadur Shastri's death, carrying the story in the same issue as which it led with the Tashkent Accord. In this instance, all subeditors had gone home after the paper had gone to press, but a teleprinter mechanic, who spotted the news, and a proof-reader informed Srinivasan, who got the machines stopped and the 'flash' carried. Or there was the case of Kennedy's assassination, the news breaking in India minutes after the first edition of* The Hindu *was airborne. The air fleet was recalled and a new edition was hurriedly printed and airlifted.*

The magnificent organisation that could convert even a half-chance into an "exclusive", however, had another side to its nature too in those days. Like its guru, The Times, London, *it did not believe, as it does today, in personalising news by such popular devices as bylines and pictures of correspondents. Such were the ways of* The Hindu *from its inception – the emphasis on views rather than news – that it had Assistant Editors and subeditors, but no Chief Reporter till 1905 and a News Editor only after World War II broke out. The attitude of these men and those who followed them was that news must be presented comprehensively and as unsensationally as possible, no matter how much space was required, provided all the facts were included.*

It is splendid organisation, guided by rare business acumen, that has been demonstrated in every generation of the Kasturi family – not usually found among Press barons, leave alone journalists – that has taken The Hindu *from strength to strength, especially in the post-Independence years when it did not have the 'nationalist' label any longer to help boost its sales. The paper grew from a 50,000 circulation in 1955 to over 500,000 in 35 years and to a million just 15 years later, soon after it celebrated its 125th anniversary. This phenomenal growth is testimonial to the organisational skills of Srinivasan, Gopalan and their descendants, particularly Gopalan's son Kasturi.*

Srinivasan helped create the Press Trust of India in the early 1940s, the first Indian news agency. In 1947, The Hindu *started India's first sports weekly. In 1962,* The Hindu *was the first Indian paper to charter planes to distribute copies; in 1963 it acquired its own planes for distribution, the only paper in the country to have ever done this and one of the few in the world. In 1969 it commenced electronic facsimile reproduction for the first time in India. In the 1970s it was the first newspaper to use photocomposition. In 1977 its Sunday paper introduced the Indian newspaper-reading public to colour features and colour advertisements for the first time. And in 1986, it started a Delhi issue by using satellite transmission and also began to use facsimile transmission for news photographs, again leading the Indian newspaper field. In 2017* The Hindu *was publishing from 18 centres in the South and in U.P., the Punjab, Bengal and Maharashtra, with a virtually different paper being seen in Delhi and in Mumbai in particular.*

All this technological pioneering began with G. Kasturi who combined it with editorial sobriety and sound management. He joined the paper immediately after college, took over as Editor in 1965 and remained at the helm till 1991, making The Hindu *the success it is And with success has grown the determination to adhere closely to the formula established by Srinivasan: comprehensive coverage of all news that has official confirmation; didactic editorials that offer high priest advice to all and sundry; and a blunt refusal to "dig up private lives of public men with an eye on sensation and circulation," reputations of public personalities thus being "perfectly safe in its hands".*

And so The Hindu *goes on. Like Old Man River...just rolling along. But as already stated gathering new steam from the 1990s .when it began to offer several supplements looking at a heap of softer subjects on which the young Indians of a new, more Westernised India were becoming more focussed. And in keeping with this trend, the family stepped out of editorial roles in 2012 and professional journalists were appointed Editors of all its publications, which post-1978 included the country's leading sports magazine,* Sportstar *(1978),and a serious general magazine,* Frontline, *both shepherded in by N.Ram who succeeded Kasturi. In 1994, it launched a business newspaper,* Business Line, *and in 2013, in a break with tradition, it began publishing in Tamil, a daily broadsheet with its own outlook on men and matters even if it bears the same name 'Tamilised' –* THE Indhu [The Hindu (*Tamil*)]. *Shortly after that, professional management followed with a professional CEO-cum-Managing Director, and two Independent Directors on the Board and a restructuring of the Companies.*

6

The Thoman Tradition

Beyond Saidapet and Maraimalai Bridge is Guindy and City limits. Then begins St Thomas' Mount, once a favourite rest and recreation resort of Company servants and, as early as 1685, a Company sanatorium. Even earlier, in 1654, the records of President Aaron Baker speak of it as a place to go "a hauking". And in 1678 Streynsham Master used "to take the fresh aire" there. The Company's *Mount House*, a forgotten location, was the first garden house here and it was followed by Captain George Heron's. By 1750, there were a number of other British 'garden houses' at the Mount as well as mansions of Indians, Portuguese and Armenians. In fact, quite "a large and agreeable town" had grown here. In later Imperial times, this salubrious town became a Cantonment. The military connection still remains, many a famed regiment getting the opportunity of an easy posting after a stint on India's borders. A centuries' older tradition here, however, is the Thoman tradition.

To most Indians, and certainly to almost all Western influenced Christians, Christianity came to India following the flags of the Portuguese and the French, the Dutch, the Danes and the British. Which is anywhere between 1,300 and 1,600 years away from the truth! That truth is that the Indian Christian is almost certainly over 1,900 years old today and quite possibly is almost as old as Jesus Christ!! That is how old the Thoman tradition in India is – certainly in South India. Whichever school of Thoman thought the believers belong to – and there are several, with the adherents usually at loggerheads with one another – there is one thing they all agree on. And that is the ancient lineage of the Syrian Christian, dating back to at least the Second Century of Christianity.

The more romantic Thoman tradition, especially in Madras, has it that Thomas Dydimus, the Doubting Apostle, sailed with the merchant Habban, envoy of King Gondophares of Parthia (northwest India), and came to Musiris (Cranganore in Kerala)[1] in 52 C E. There he made his first conversions – of Hindus as well as long-settled Jews – at Palayoor. Thereafter he travelled down the Malabar Coast, making conversions in several areas and establishing at least seven churches in eight years, before crossing to the Coromandel Coast. He eventually reached Mylapore, where he spent the last years of his life.

The legends narrate that he used to preach on the beach that is now part of San Thomé and in a shrine atop what is now called St Thomas' Mount. They tell of how he lived in a cave in a hill, now called Little Mount – a point between the two major locations associated with him – and how, when he used to walk to and from the beach, he would rest and preach at where Luz Church was built in Mylapore and at the spot where the Madeiros family built Descanco (Rest) Church some years later. It is also said that he was killed in 72 C E on St Thomas' Mount, and buried in his beach at Mylapore, from whence his remains were centuries later moved to the crypt of the church that has now become the Basilica of St. Thomas. From there his remains were taken to a shrine in Edessa in Iraq where every July a great festival is held to commemorate his reburial and at which is sung the 4th Century hymn: "Thou the great lamp, one among the Twelve, with oil from thy cross replenished India's night, floodest with light...." From Edessa the remains of St Thomas are said to have been moved to the Greek island of Chios, then to Ortona on Italy's Adriatic Coast where they remain to this day. But each resting place still has some relics of Thomas – Madras has a small hand bone and the head of a lance in the Basilica crypt. Whether you believe, with Marco Polo, that Thomas was martyred atop the 91.5 metres (300 feet) high mount, speared to death or accidentally killed by a hunter's arrow while in the area, the hill called St Thomas' Mount or Parangi Malai (*parangi = feringhi* = European/foreigner – and *malai* = hill, in Tamil) has, for centuries, been a hallowed place of pilgrimage. It must be also recorded that there is a tradition that he was martyred at Little Mount and that St. Thomas' Mount was only another place where he regularly preached.

---

[1] Recent excavation locate Musiris in Pattanam, a little south of Cranganore.

The Portuguese, however, believed that it was on the Big Mount that he was martyred. And, so, in 1514 (or was it 1523?, as believed by some), on the orders of King Emanuel, they rebuilt the chapel of the Nestorian Monastery that was on this site when Marco Polo visited it in 1292. A few years later, Portuguese settlers from the village of San Thomé, led by Father Gaspar Coelho, Vicar of the Mylapore Church, discovered, during 1547 excavations at the Mount, a 'Bleeding Cross' with old Sassanian Pehlevi inscriptions on it (it also had spots that looked like blood-stains and which reappeared after being scrubbed away). This cross they built into the wall behind the altar of the church which stands to this day, dedicated to the Madonna of the Mount, 'Our Lady of Expectations', and where the ancient Indian tradition of entering a place of worship barefooted is still followed. In Portuguese times, a bonfire used to be lit nightly on the Mount to guide mariners, who in turn offered prayers of thanksgiving for a safe voyage and fired their guns in salute.

The 'Bleeding Cross', tradition has it, was chiselled from the rock by the Apostle himself. Tradition also has it that it first publicly bled on December 18, 1558, during Mass, and that it has 'bled' periodically ever since, the last occasion recorded being in 1704. Also above the altar is an oil painting of the Madonna painted on wood and mentioned in writing as early as 1559. This picture of the Holy Virgin and Child is popularly believed to have been one of seven painted by St Luke and brought to India by Doubting Thomas, who, it is said, carried it with him everywhere during his wanderings. The annual festival of the church is held in December and the faithful flock here to fulfil their vows, many of these taking various forms of penance, including some penitents ascending the steps on their knees.

At the northern foot of the Mount is a gateway of four big arches surmounted by a cross with the year 1547 inscribed on it. Inside are several gravestones of the Portuguese era. Beyond is the balustrade-flanked flight of 135 steps to the Mount that owes its existence to Coja Petrus Uscan's philanthropy. The Stations of the Cross alongside the steps are a 20th Century contribution. The oldest Armenian inscription here is on a tombstone in the church and reads "Gregorio Parao (Gregory Sarkies of Erevan, a pearl merchant), Armenio, 1707". Evidence in the church, in the embellishments of its altar and pulpit, indicate much Armenian contribution. The 14 paintings of the Saints on the wall are said to be Armenian gifts; certainly their inscriptions are in Armenian.

Teachers taught in architectural elaboration...a school on the campus of Teachers' Training College, Saidapet. Alas, pulled down in 2013.

At the head of the new Marmalong (Maraimalai Adigalar) Bridge, Armenian benefactor Petrus Uscan, who built the first bridge here, was remembered in this commemorative stone. But what has the Metro done to it as this edition goes to press?

15. *The Mount of Thomas...and the steps leading to the Church the Portuguese built.*
16. *Inside the Church on the Mount...where the Bleeding Cross (centre) is only one of several relics.*

Was Gregory Sarkies one of the benefactors? As late as the first quarter of this century, the Armenian connection with this church was very close; in fact, it was thought of as "belonging to the Armenian Community".

At the foot of the steps, surrounded by trees, is the English Wesley Church, dating to 1829. And on the plain to the east of it are St Thomas' Garrison Church completed in 1827 at a cost of about Rs. 45,000 (consecrated in 1830), other architectural relics of Britain's finest military era and sites of ancient Anglo-French battles. The Garrison Church, established for the cantonment of Madras, a military reservation that stretches from St Thomas' Mount to Pallavaram, is by the great trunk road from which branches led to French Pondicherry, Danish Tranquebar and Dutch Nagapattinam. Protestant chaplains had visited the area from 1795, but it was 1805 before they sought a church and another 20 years before they got it, built along the lines of St Clement's in The Strand, London. Within the handsomely furnished church – the handiwork of British artillery officers at the Mount Cantonment over the years – is a large painting of the appearance of Jesus before Thomas and the other disciples. Major J B Richardson, who is said to have painted it, commanded one of the batteries at the Mount. The tall steeple the church possessed was, in recent times, abbreviated its 12 feet at the request of pilots landing at Madras Airport.

The Thoman tradition is also strong in Saidapet at Little Mount (*Chinna Malai* in Tamil), just three kilometres before St Thomas' Mount (which the Portuguese called 'El Grande Monti'). Developed into religious prominence by the Portuguese in the 16th Century, Little Mount now has two churches associated with legends of the Apostle of India. One is a new circular church of Our Lady of Health, as much out of aesthetic integration with the older church and atmosphere as are the even newer, cinematic style Stations of the Cross. This Church was built to commemorate the 19th Century of St Thomas' martyrdom and was consecrated in 1971. It was built on the site of an existing shrine said to have been first built in 1711 as an addition to the original shrine built by the Portuguese in 1551. This old chapel, the Blessed Sacrament Chapel, still stands, and is connected to the new church to its front.

In the old church is the entrance to a cave in which St Thomas is believed to have lived a life of prayer and penance, coming forth only to preach the gospel to the thousands who flocked to hear him. High in the eastern portion of the cave is an opening (now barred) and by it a palmprint. Tradition has it that it was through this 'window' the Apostle escaped to St Thomas' Mount, fleeing his persecutors. The hand-print, clearly visible, is traditionally said to be the saint's, as is said of the footprint at the foot of the hillock. In the cave is an altar on which the faithful light their candles.

A cross cut into the rock at the rear of the cave is believed to be one before which Thomas prayed and offered Mass. Also to the rear of the small Portuguese Church of the Resurrection is a spring said to have been caused by Thomas striking the rock with his stick to draw water from it to quench the thirst of those who came to arid Saidapet to hear him preach. The water from this spring is believed to have curative powers.

The Little Mount Festival of Our Lady of Health, on the fourth Saturday and Sunday after Easter every year, is a noteworthy event in the Madras calendar, resembling as it does in its fun and fervour a medieval religious fair.

The Missing Merchantmen

The missing merchantmen of Madras are many. The Portuguese are almost forgotten, the British remain in the names of business houses and streets, and the various Chetties have got lost in a drive to bring about a casteless society by erasing caste names from road signs. Amongst the earliest of the merchantmen of John Company's Madraspatnam, who thrived in and around Fort St George solely as a business community, were the Armenians and the Jews. Of the Jews there is scant record; the Armenians are better remembered because of street name and church in George Town and the contributions – now little recognised – Coja Petrus Uscan (Woskan) and a few others made to Madras.

The first Armenian settlement in Madras dates back to at least the 1660s. The oldest tombstone of an Armenian, 'Khoja David', found in Madras is dated 1663. The stone was found, understandably, near Little Mount and was inscribed with the name Coja David Margar. Early Armenian settlers, having no church of the Orthodoxy, worshipped in the Catholic chapel of the Capuchin Fathers in the Fort – and so, perhaps, grew the affinity of the Madras Armenians to the Roman Church[2]. The Company, pleased with the "sober, frugal and wise" ways of the Armenians, extended to them in 1688 the same rights as the English. When the Armenian settlers increased to 40, the Company sanctioned them a plot of ground (somewhere on what is the High Court campus now), offered to build them a church of timber for their own use and allowed them a grant of £ 50 a year for the maintenance of a priest. The Armenians accepted all these gladly and persuaded still more Armenians to settle in old Madras. On this site they later built, in 1712, a more permanent church – which, like everything else in that area, was demolished after the French sieges.

---

[2] A few became Roman Catholics too, having long lived in India and points east where there were no Armenian churches when they settled there.

It was with Petrus (Peter) Uscan, who later bore the title 'Coja', that the community gained eminence. Coja Petrus was the wealthy Armenian who defied Dupleix. When the French took Madras in 1746 they seized all his possessions and carried them off to Pondicherry. Coja Petrus, however, escaped from the French in a Danish ship and sought refuge in Tranquebar where Dupleix reached him with an offer: Come under French protection in Pondicherry and have restored to you the confiscated property. The appeal also had religious overtones, being made in the name of the Madras Capuchin chapel where he worshipped. Coja Petrus replied in biting verse that the Armenian tradition was to remain loyal to a person's benefactors, in this instance the British on whose territory he'd earned his wealth. As for his property, the French were welcome to it, but it would be nice if they would sell it all and distribute the proceeds amongst the poor; after all, "the renowned French Treasury" could not be so badly off as to need his wealth to meet its deficits!

On the rendition of Madras in 1749, Mrs Madeiros (whom we've met before in these pages) and Petrus Uscan were the only two Catholics allowed to remain in permanent residence in the Fort, the Coja continuing to enjoy the large 'Company House on Choultry Gate Street' (near the Fort's old northern entrance, where the new multi-storey block has come up) that had been given to him in 1728 by the Company on a 99-year lease. But the Capuchin chapel in the Fort was destroyed by the British, who believed Padre Severini and his fellows had spied for the French. The Chapel of Our Lady of Miracles in Vepery would have met the same fate if it had not been the chapel Coja Petrus had built for his own use. The British were determined to take over this chapel and hand it over to the representatives of the SPCK, at that time members of the Danish Protestant Mission from Tranquebar, but Coja Petrus managed to ward off these threats. When he died, however, the SPCK again claimed the chapel, mission houses and gardens – and received the lot in November 1752! Years later, the Capuchins were paid Rs 50,000 compensation for the two churches, but the Protestants stayed on in Vepery.

In 1823, on the Hunter's Road site of Uscan's chapel, St Matthias' Anglican Church was consecrated, and there, to this day, may be seen the tombstone of Coja Petrus, the ardent Catholic whose munificence is still to be seen in many parts of Madras. "After I expire let my body be buried in the Chapel Nossa Senhora de Milagres, which I got erected at Vippore. Let 1,500 Pagodas be placed in the hands of the Superior, padre

Severini, to finish the remainder of the work of the Chapel ... ornamenting the Same ... Let 1,500 Pagodas more be placed in the hands of the said Superior to let them at interest, and with the interest thereof a dayly Mass to say for my soul...." had read the will, in part, of *Coja Petrus Uscan.* His tombstone in St Matthias' churchyard reads in Latin and Armenian, *"Raised on high by his renown, his head hidden in the clouds, here lies, sunk beneath the sod, one who reconciled discord and appeased strife, the strong support and pillar of the Armenians, the protector and warm defender of the poor, a man generous and liberal in repairing the loss and damage suffered by the public, one who spent his money lavishly and without stint to promote the worship of God and sacred buildings, Petrus Uscan, grandson of Coja Pogus (Paul), an Armenian, whose heart is in Julfa. Aged 70, he departed this life on January 15, 1751."*

Tradition has it that his heart was indeed taken in a golden box to Julfa, near Isphahan in Persia, and buried there in the yard of All Saviour's Cathedral, wherein hangs a life-size portrait of Uscan painted in Madras in 1737. In the portrait, pen in hand, he writes in Armenian, "The fear of the Lord is the beginning of Wisdom." And on one side of the picture is painted a heart beneath which is an Armenian verse by him, translating as, "My heart longs for home, where, should it not be able to go, then I desire that, when my last day comes, my heart be sent to my native town, so that I, Petrus Uscan, shall have a grave there." And so Coja Petrus went home, leaving behind in Madras Rs 7 lakh in cash alone – despite all the losses he had suffered! When his wife died a few years later, she, being childless, left all their wealth to charity.

Coja Petrus was heir to a family that had traded with the East for generations. Though no stranger to Madras himself, Petrus Uscan did not settle here until 1723 when he arrived from Manila. Trade between India and this Spanish bastion was an Armenian monopoly at the time. The Armenians also handled the bulk of the Madras trade to other eastern markets as well as to West Asia.

Soon after his arrival in Madras, the local Nawab visited the town and Coja Petrus received him in manner regal. A pleased Nawab offered Coja Petrus a boon in return and the Coja prayed for the sole monopoly of Madras's import trade as well as onward trade into the interior of these imported items. Petrus Uscan's wish was granted and he proceeded to amass immense wealth ... only to lose much of it as already described.

Pious, upright and humble, Petrus Uscan used much of his wealth to benefit religious institutions. He liberally contributed to the Armenian-built St Rita's Church (1729-40) in San Thomé, where a slab on the east wall has inscribed on it in Armenian, "In memory of the Armenian nation, 1729." That was the year when, in April, the San Thomé grave of St Thomas was opened for veneration by the faithful, Petrus Uscan being one of the Witnesses at the opening. Coja Petrus's contributions to keep alive the Thoman tradition were numerous. He built the first bridge across the Adyar at Saidapet, pro bono publico, *in 1726 at a cost of Rs 1 lakh (30,000 pagodas). He also left in perpetuity with the Administrator-General 1,500 pagodas for the upkeep of this bridge on the road to the two Mounts, and a further 1,500 pagodas for the maintenance of the broad stone-steps flanked by walls (and the whitewashing of the church's walls and portico) that he had had constructed in 1728 at St Thomas' Mount, to make access to the summit easier for pilgrims.*

Coja Petrus was a Company Councillor and a trusted envoy of the British, especially of Governor Benyon. When General Raghuji Bhonsle of the Nagpur kingdom invaded the Carnatic in 1740 and overran most of it, Coja Petrus was sent by Benyon with rich presents to mediate – and succeeded so well that he came back with peace, as well as authorisations for the British possessions of Trichinopoly, Madras and Fort St David (Cuddalore)! On another occasion, he secured from the Nizam rights for the British to mint coins in Madras.

Succeeding Coja Petrus as Armenian leader in Madras was another personality almost as colourful, Aga Shawmier Sultan (Soothanoomian), son of Coja Sultan David. On Aga Shawmier's chapel grounds in George Town, partly, the site of the Armenian cemetery which gave the street its name, was built the present Armenian Church, consecrated in 1772, and in it is a room, 'Shawmier's Room', built to the memory of his wife who died in 1765. Shawmier, who made a fortune from pearls, dried fruit and rose water, lent prodigiously to that perpetually impecunious Nawab, Muhammad Ali Wallajah. The Nawab's debts were one of the 'Great Scandals of Our Towne'. It so happened that, when the scandal was at its worst and the English were pressing the Nawab hardest for repayment, Aga Shawmier happened to call on Muhammad Ali, who asked whether Shawmier, afraid of Wallajah's financial position, had come "to demand your just claims from me." The abashed visitor promptly renounced his debt, taking out from his robes the relevant promissory notes and tearing them up, saying, as he scattered the pieces,

"Not so, my Lord...My claim against you is but a little dust from your shoes." Moved by this flamboyancy, Muhammad Ali reciprocated by presenting the title deeds of Noomblee village as an outright, tax-free gift in perpetuity to the Armenian and his heirs!

Aga Shawmier inherited from his father a house famous in Madras history, the 'Great House in Charles Street', now partially occupied by the Archaeological Survey of India's regional office, which has restored a part of it. This house had belonged to the phenomenally successful Coja Nazar Jacob Jan who lived in Madras from 1702 and is the first Armenian settler in the city to be identified with a history. There certainly were earlier Armenian settlers in Madras, but being not as prominent or as successful as Coja Nazar Jan, their contributions have been lost in the mists of time. On Coja Nazar's death in 1740, the house, and much property in Julfa, passed on, through bequest, to Coja Sultan David, Shawmier's father, in whose time it first came to be known as the 'Great House'. Aga Shawmier in turn inherited the house which was coveted by the British on their return to Madras. The house in 1750 became the official residence of the Deputy-Governor of Madras[3] on a rent of 30 pagodas a month! Robert Clive also lived here for some time – so the better known name, Clive House. Eventually, Shawmier sold it to a Portuguese, de Castro, who in turn sold it for 6,000 pagodas to the Company in 1755. And they bought it to accommodate visitors. Admiral Watson came to stay and hold Court here in 1758, a precedent leading to the Courts of Admiralty sitting here and the name, Admiralty House. This house was later developed as the Governor's Town House and subsequently served as venue for State functions till Banqueting Hall was built.

Coja Nazar's property in Persia caused a lot of heart-burn and suffering to many. When Sultan David sent his wife Anem and son Shawmier to claim what had been willed to him, the Mayor of Julfa seized them and had them "inhumanly beaten" until they renounced Jacob Jan's will. Anem David was also forced to draw large bills on her husband and give the Madras Government the power to enforce acceptance! Sultan David's protests and the Council's support of his claim led to action in Isphahan which resulted in the Mayor being hauled before the Magistrate, having his ears lopped off and "dying a miserable

---

[3] Madras had only a Deputy Governor immediately after the rendition in 1749, the Governor continuing to live in Fort St. David, till he moved back in 1752.

death," Shawmier and mother returning thereafter to Madras! In time, Shawmier, who moved with his family to Negapatam after the sale of the house in Charles Street, became a millionaire who sent King Heraclius II of Georgia gifts and received from him in 1786 the town of Loree in Tiflis. When Georgia became part of Russia, Aga Shawmier was given ten years to come over, or to send his male heirs there, to take over the town. But he chose Madras and the whole family died here.

Aga Shawmier died in 1797 and was buried beside his wife in the Armenian churchyard, their ancestral property. The leadership of the Armenian community in Madras thereafter passed on to Aga Samuel Moorat, property owner extraordinary and founder of a trust which enabled Armenian youth in Europe to enjoy the finest education. This philanthropist died in 1816 and was buried in the Roman Catholic Cathedral in Armenian Street, where, in Moorat Chapel, lie buried his wife (1828) and son Edward (1837) as well. Edward Samuel Moorat, who lived a life of great luxury, inherited from his father all the area to the west of the Cooum, including Moorat Gardens *(today's* Moore's Garden?*) and what became the College of Fort St. George campus (the DPI campus), which he sold to Government in 1827. In 1821, he bought* The Pantheon, *the buildings and 22 acres that have now grown into the Museum complex and to which Connemara Library and the Art Gallery have been added. Edward Moorat sold this property to Government for Rs 28,000 in 1830 and, soon after, became owner of what was later to be known as* Umda Bagh. Umda Bagh *is now part of the Quaid-E-Millat Women's Arts College campus on Mount Road and got its name when the property was acquired, on Moorat's death, by the Wallajah family.*

Around this period too, John Arathoon, who was in the gemstones business, got married into another leading Armenian family, the Babooms, who were in the textiles business. In Royapuram is Arathoon Road, another Armenian marker in the city. Whether it was named after John or one of his descendants is not known, but it is believed that an Arathoon was responsible for maintaining the Tiruvattore Gate that led into the city through the road from the North and this became Arathoon Road. More significantly, a road parallel to its east, West Madha Church Road, could well be called the 'Road of Perfect Harmony' for on it are a Catholic and a Protestant Church, a Parsi Fire Temple, a Hindu shrine and a Muslim dargah.

Of the same era was the last great Madras-Armenian, the Rev Harathun Shimavonian, who was born in Shiraz in 1724 but who lived almost all his life in Madras, where he died in 1824 and was buried in the Armenian churchyard. The Rev Shimavonian set up a press and publishing house in Madras in 1789 to print and issue books in the classical Armenian language. He was Editor-Founder of Azdarar, first published in Madras in 1794 and claimed to be "the first Armenian Journal in the World"! The journal, sad to say, did not last long – and the few attempts to revive it also failed! Before Shimavonian's press, there was Shawmier's press (1772) and after it there were Satur Agavillian's (1809) and a Shawmier press again. All these made Madras a major centre of Armenian publishing, but by 1850 it all came to an end.

Not long after, there faded from the Madras scene a community who, for over a century, were the foremost traders in the south of India, operating from Negapatam, Seringapatam and Madraspatam, using their own ships and Danish shipping to trade with Europe, Persia and Manila in precious stones and costly fabrics. The community was so rich that two of them offered Catherine II of Russia millions to liberate the Armenians from the Persian yoke and take them under her wing, but the plan failed. And many an Armenian remained a wanderer.

Where are they now, the Armenians and Jews of Madras who once controlled so much of the City's trade? The Jewish exodus was so long ago that they are no longer remembered in Madras.

The Jewish tradition in the south of India, however, goes back to almost the first years of the Christian Era, the old records of the Kerala Jews indicating settlements being established around 5 CE by Jews fleeing West Asia. Most of the Jews who settled in Madras soon after it was founded were, however, Jews from England with Portuguese antecedents or from Italy (Leghorn) and had such names as James de Paivia, Isaac de Porto and Moses de Castro. Shortly before Paivia's death in 1687, he established with Antonio de Porto, Pedro Pereira and Fernando Mendes Henriques, 'The Colony of Jewish Traders of Madraspatam'.

The Jews were considered such good citizens that the charter of the first town Corporation, inaugurated in 1688, nominated three of them to serve as Aldermen, awarded equal representation with the English themselves, the Portuguese and the 'Hindus'. They were also permitted to live in 'White Town' – unlike the Armenians in the early days – and in 1687 at least six Jewish diamond merchants were living there. The Armenians were also prominent in Madras trade of the period, but it was not till 1692 that they were treated more equally by the English and it was well into the 18th Century before they superseded the Jews as the leading non-English trading community.

The Jews of early Madras had from 1680 a lucrative trade in exporting diamonds to London and importing in exchange, from their fellow Hebrew merchants there, silver, rough coral and polished coral beads and pearls. So it was that the quarters of these coral-dealers in north Muthialpet came to be known as Pavalakkarar Theru or Coral Merchants' Street (pavalam (T) = coral). Curiously, the Jews were succeeded, nearly two centuries later, on this street by the Nagarathar, the money-lending and gem-dealing Nattukkottai Chettiars who to this day maintain a business presence, though a much diminished one, and three choultries in this affluent, but crowded and dirty street. The Rangoon mudam houses businesses, but the Chettiar Mudam and Chinna Mudam offer accommodation. Nearby is a 'garage' for the theru (chariot) which is taken in procession from here to the temple in Tiruvottriyur every year.

The Jews had a burial ground in Peddanaickenpet and until a municipal school came up in recent years on its site at the north end of Mint Street, a portion of the cemetery, long out of use, could be seen. But while the school was being raised in 1983, the tombstones in the cemetery were removed first to the Royapuram cemetery and then to the Lloyd's Road cemetery near the Marina and there, approached through filthy surroundings, they have a well-kept corner to themselves.

The tomb of Jaques (James) de Paivia, the first of the Jewish diamond merchants[4], was one of the four that remained in the Mint Street cemetery. It is no longer found at Lloyd's Road, but at the new site have been relocated the tombstones of two other Hebrew diamond merchants, Solomon Franco (1763) and Isaac Sardo (1709). The old site was last used in 1964, Esther Cohen's tombstone at the new site attesting to this date. That the Jewish Cemetery is still occasionally used is indicated by Eileen Joshua's tombstone, dated 1997. The Joshua family, originally from Kerala, now looks after the cemetry.

---

[4] Moses de Castro, who left Madras in 1786, was the last of the Anglo-Jewish diamond merchants to live in the city.

While this edition was being revised, a Davvid Levi got in touch with me and said he was in the merchant navy, but home was Madras. And it had been for generations going back to the early Sephardic Jewish settlers. His ancestor was a great grandfather, Rabbi Saloman Halevi, who came to Madras in the early 1900s. Issac Street, where the Madras Paradesi (Foreigner) Synagogue and Cemetry was till the 1930s, was named after his maternal great grandfather, Issac Henriques de Castro, a businessman from Amsterdam, The Netherlands. Our family is the last of the Paradesi Jews in Madras, says Levi.

One who was not buried in the Jewish Cemetery was Bartolomeo Rodrigues, one of the first Aldermen and who succeeded to the leadership of the community, the others being de Paivia and Domingo de Porto. When Rodrigues died in 1693, he was buried virtually with State honours in the vast gardens of his mansion in Muthialpet. It has been said that his tomb had a tall and handsome marker and was "somewhere" near Old Jail Road, between Broadway and Thambu Chetty Street, presumably in Mannady.

7

The Road South

Just before St.Thomas' Mount – to be developed in the next few years as a major urban railway junction where the Metro, MRTS, Suburban **and regular** rail services will meet in South Madras – is striking Kathipara Junction with its huge, sweeping flyovers that link Mount Road, GST Road, the 100-ft road to Vadapalani and Anna Nagar, and to St.Thomas' Mount and beyond to the highway to Bangalore. Just outside St.Thomas' Mount, on the road to Bangalore, is the serene War Graves Cemetery established in 1952 by the Commonwealth War Graves Commission. Designed by British architect Henry Brown, here, amidst immaculately manicured lawns, are 850 graves of British and other Allied soldiers who died in South and East India during World War II. At the back of the Cemetery is a large granite plaque with over 1000 names of those who died in the two regions during World War I inscribed on it. At the entrance of the Cemetery is the Stone of Remembrance – "Their names liveth for ever more" – and in the midst of the Cemetery, rising high above the row on row of neat white headstones is the Cross of Sacrifice. Each headstone bears, besides name and regiment, a symbol of the faith of the person buried. The cemetery is looked after by the British Association of Cemeteries in South Asia (BACSA), an NGO founded in Britain in 1977.

A little past the cemetery is the Chennai Trade Centre, a huge, well-equipped complex intended for trade and industrial exhibitions as well as conferences. Then there's the Larsen and Toubro industrial and construction conglomerate with its architecturally striking modern buildings, and two of the major private multispecialty hospitals in the city, MIOT and Sri Ramachandra. All around, once farmland and water bodies, is now new residential and commercial development.

Past Kathipara Junction are Alandur to the east of the highway and St Thomas' Mount to the west. Fed by them is the CSI St Thomas Higher Secondary School, a name given in 1962 but whose roots are in an 1864 primary school started there. The area south of them, on both sides of the highway and up to Pallavaram, is today,as it was in late British times, an expansive military cantonment and honoured regimental station. The first barracks and officers' bungalows were built here in 1775-6 and Major Matthew Horne became the first Commandant of the station. Today, the Officers' Training Academy (OTA) here is one of the finest military institutions in the country, entered through an imposing new Charnockite archway and past a captured Pakistani tank. The cantonment was till recent years a major polo-playing centre and its Mohite Stadium, once a battlefield, has a splendid expanse of turf, now used for mini-golf.

The cantonment gets off to a start from a tall, generally neglected cupola in the middle of the Great Southern Trunk Road. The memorial is to Lt Col Sam Dalrymple of the Madras Artillery and was raised in 1821-2; what "valuable services" the Colonel rendered to warrant this honour is not known, but the cantonment was for long the headquarters of the Artillery in the old Madras Presidency. Several of the handsome cantonment buildings date to the early 19th Century; a plaque on a wall in the Officers' Mess of the OTA commemorates the erection of the building in 1815 and the use of it for over a century as the Officers' Mess of the Madras Artillery.

The Officers' Training Academy, Madras, began as the Officers' Training School in 1962/1963, established to train men and women (from 1991) for short-term commissions in the Indian Army. Every batch also included a few trainees from neighbouring countries intending to join their respective armies. The OTS put down firm roots in Madras as the Academy in 1999. It has several heritage buildings in its 670-acre campus, about which little is known. These include The White House, the headquarters of the OTA, a well-maintained vision out of the past like a neighbour, Flagstaff House, the Commandant's residence built in 1928 as, it is stated, the home of the Garrison Commander of 'the Madras Presidency Army', and the Old Theatre. Then there's the Stone Quarry Lake that's been developed as a perennial lake at the base of a quarried hill "for leisure and watermanship" and a bridge across the Adyar that looks as though it could date from Petrus Uscan's day.

Atop the Mount, looking down on this scene, is the church built on the site where St Thomas is said to have been martyred. It is tended by nuns of the Franciscan Order who established, in 1901, their convent just a few steps below the ancient shrine. Their immaculate cemetery, with every tombstone alike and lined with military precision, is on the other side of the Church. The oldest tombstone in it dates to 1918. Not far from it, on the mountain slope, are two memorials, one a free standing Charnockite plaque, gleaming black, the other an obelisk. The former is the Geological Survey of India's (GSI) National Geological Monument to the name Charnockite, coined for the granite found in the region by a former GSI head, Thomas Holland, and named after its use for the tombstone of Job Charnock of Calcutta, the city he is considered the founder of in 1689. It was erected in 1975. The obelisk was erected through subscription by the entire Horse Artillery Regiment to a beloved commanding officer, Col John Noble, who is remembered in nearby Noble Street and whose erstwhile garden (later called *Maanthoppu* – 'Mango Garden') – is now the premises of Rane Engine Valves Ltd., and The Trident Hotel, originally a Rane initiative. A newer memorial at the Mount, unveiled in 2003 but well hidden under a banyan tree, commemorates the start here of the Great Trigonometrical Survey of India by William Lambton in 1802.

Church, convent, tombstones and memorials look down upon Madras's international and domestic airports at Tirusoolam, located about four kilometres south of Mohite Stadium and across the road from the Tirusoolam suburban railway station. Within the parking campus of the airport, surrounded by official buildings, is a small but ancient Hindu shrine that the faithful would not allow to be pulled down when the new airport buildings were being raised in 1984. The airport has now been considerably expanded and totally redesigned, work commencing in 2008 and the new terminals opening in 2013. Passenger capacity is expected to increase from 9 million a year to 14 million and, aside expansion, a second airport for the city is being looked into.

Madras's first airport was a mile south, at Meenambakkam, near St Thomas' Mount. This area, before it was taken for airport use, was the Mount Golf Club links. The Madras Flying Club came to Meenam-bakkam long before passenger traffic, Avadaiappan, SAA Annamalai and Solaiappan, three Nattukkottai Chettiars, among the first members of this private club. Avadaiappa Chettiar was the fifth person and the first Indian to get a private pilot's licence (1931). The second Indian and 6th on the list was Annamalai Chettiar (a little later in 1931) and 21st was Solaiappan. They all had their own aircraft and later took aviation to the mofussil by starting a flying club in their 'homeland', Chettinad, in the village of Kanadukathan, 250 miles south of Madras. The skeleton of Avadaiappa Chettiar's aircraft is being brought to life again by an antique collector as these lines are written. The first Indian to get a commercial pilot's licence was Captain V Sundaram (1937).

The Club, the oldest in India, was founded in October 1929 by G. Vlasto, a pilot, and was incorporated on March 4, 1930. Governor Sir George Stanley was the first Patron of the Club and formally inaugurated it on August 20, 1930. The first instructional flight took off on July 21, 1930, under the command of Flt Lt H. N. Hawker, the Club's first pilot instructor. The first indian instructor was Mohammed Ismail Khan, who served with the Club from 1942. The first international flight from Madras was flown to Colombo by the Club's Chief Flying Instructor, Tyndale-Biscoe, in 1935. The next year, Tata's chief pilot, Neville Vintcent, flew the first Madras-Colombo airmail service.

The Madras airstrip was then called St Thomas' Mount, but became Meenambakkam in 1948 when Madras got the first post-Independence air terminal in the country. When it was first opened, there was a village in the triangle formed by the runways and it was years before it could be dislodged. The subsequent development of the aerodrome into an airport owed much to Chief Minister Kamaraj. The first Madras-based airline was Rm Alagappa Chettiar's Jupiter Airways that operated a Madras-Delhi service from June 1948. Alagappa Chettiar was the fourth Chettiar to get a pilot's licence.

There was once another sporting activity associated with this airstrip, motor racing. When Rex Strong and K.Varugis raced each other in MGs on the streets of Madras, motor racing was born in the city, the Madras Motor Sports Club being founded through the efforts of M.A.Chidambaram and others in 1953. Its early competitions were on the Meenambakkam runway, but with civil aviation growing apace the Club shifted its activities in 1955 to a World War II airstrip in Sholavaram, a northwest Madras suburb. In 1990 the Club inaugurated a splendid race track in 200 acres of space at Irungattukottai, near the new auto hub of Madras, Sriperumbudur.

Long before the Club, d'Angelis the hotelier, inspired by Bleriot, had got Simpson's, the city's leading coach builders, to build him an aeroplane. He tested this made-in-Madras machine in Pallavaram and, then, arranged a public demonstration – charging entrance fees – on the Island Grounds in March 1910, just seven years after the Wright brothers. He even took up a passenger from the crowd on one of his several flights that day! This was the first flight seen in Madras. Addison's, pioneer motor car and motorcycle agents, are also said to have built an aeroplane about this time – and there is, as a consequence, some debate about who built d'Angelis' aircraft. But the *India Weekly* is categorical – it was Simpson's.

This aeroplane, manufactured and flown in India, was designed by D'Angelis and built by Samuel John Green, who came out as a "motor engineer" to Simpson's in 1902 and later became a partner. He was to be, in time, responsible for the first built-in-India car, a steam car he unveiled in Madras and which the Press prophetically greeted with the headline "New Industry for Madras". Simpson's was to later, during World War II, pioneer coal burners to fuel motor vehicles.

Addison's, Simpson's and Oakes – all now part of the Amalgamations group, the last-named through its spin-off George Oakes – were well-entrenched as agents for imported cars by the time World War I started. The first car to be exhibited in Madras made a run on Mount Road in 1894, but it was 1901 before the city got its first car. A J Yorke, a Director of Parry & Co, brought his car out from England and used it to drive daily from *Ben's Gardens*, Adyar, to Parry's Corner. Sir Francis Spring's car, a more visible presence on the roads in 1903, was the South's first registered car, bearing the number MC-1. The first Indian-owned car was building contractor T Namberumal Chetty's, MC-3, imported from France. From these beginnings, motorised traffic has grown several fold in the City, as befits a city with the reputation of being the auto industry capital of India, clogging all the roads.

When the auto industry developed in Madras in the early post-World War II years it was in the City's industrial north and west, Tiruvottriyur, Ennore, Sembiam, Avadi and Ambattur, except for Standard Motors, which chose a southern suburb. It was in Tiruvottriyur that motor-cycle manufacture began with the Enfield Bullet in 1955. Ashok Leyland heavy vehicles, and Standard and Enfield triggered the auto ancillary industry, which has made Madras its hub in India. Leyland roots were in 1948, when Ashok Motors started assembling Austin cars in Ennore. In 1954, Leyland (UK) teamed with it and heavy vehicle manufature began. Enfield Bullets, imported by K R Sundaram Iyer and K Easwaran of Madras Motors, began to be assembled by them from 1953, inspired by the Army's and Police interest in the vehicle. Now owned by Delhi's Eicher Group and with three factories in Madras, it is a major player in the two-wheeler market.

When the auto boom began, c.2000, except for Ford and BMW in the south, it concentrated on Sriperumbudur in the southwest which has, with Hyundai and several auto ancillaries, become a boom town. But even that is now being overtaken from c.2010 by Oragadam, a little to the west of Ford's and further south of Sriperumbudur, hosting three major auto factories (Daimler Benz trucks, Nissan and Renault cars) and numerous ancillaries.

Some of the heaviest concentration of traffic is on Mount Road, the road to the Mount, and its extension, the GST Road, National Highway No 45. This road, which leads to NH 7 and Cape Comorin, moves out of city limits at St Thomas' Mount and for the next 20 kilometres runs through ancient villages that are part of Metropolitan Madras. Just beyond the Mount, Meenambakkam and Tirusoolam is one of them, Pallavaram.

Pallavaram, a site of major archaeological finds, is better known for its association with the great Pallava King, Mahendra Varman (7th Century), and the temples he built in this region. A cave shrine excavated by him on the slope of Pallavaram Hill – and now a *dargah* sacred to the Muslims of the area – is considered the most ancient of the historic antiquities of the Madras region, the pillared hall here the forerunner of the Mamallapuram shrines. But predating these by centuries are the several prehistoric finds made in the Pallavaram area, discoveries of men like Robert Bruce Foote[1], who, pioneered the study of prehistoric archaeology in India by his work in this region. Earthenware tombs with undecorated pottery in them and sepulchral monuments are some of the Pallavaram finds now in the Madras Museum, the search for them having been triggered by Foote's discovery in 1863 of a palaeolithic stone

---

[1] Foote, described as the 'Father of Prehistory in India', is said to have discovered 459 prehistoric sites in India, mainly in the Madras Presidency. Foote offered to sell his collection of prehistoric finds from South India to the Madras Museum in 1898. These were finally purchased in 1904, Rs. 33,000 being paid for 4,000 pieces! Amongst them is that very first 1863 find.

implement in a ballast pit at Pallavaram's Brigade Grounds. The area not only yielded evidence of Stone Age man but later finds here and near the Adyar and in Kilpauk provided evidence of the Iron Age and Megalithic Man.

Nearby Tirusoolam has a Chola temple, with 11th-12th Century inscriptions. The temple is located amidst four hills. Tirusoolam derives its name from Tiruchuram, the family of chieftains who once controlled the greater part of the present Madras region. The Tirupurasundari Tirusoolanathar Temple is believed to have been built by Kulothunga Cholan II. The hill shrine of Tiruneermalai, also nearby, was once a forest shrine about which the Alwars (saints) sang. Called the Neervanna Perumal Temple, this ancient Vaishnavite shrine has some invaluable bronzes. The adjacent village of Kunrathur is the birthplace of the classical poet Sekkilar who is said to have built the Nageswarar Temple there and conducted its first prayers about the beginning of the 12th Century. Nearby is the ancient hill temple of 'Kunrathur Kumaran', associated with the saint Arunagirinathar. Several other ancient temples in various states of disrepair are to be found in and around Kunrathur. Mangadu is another village that has temples of Pallava times, the Kamakshiamman Temple particularly well-preserved. It is here that there is a Sri Chakra which, it is said, was installed by Adi Shankara.

Pallavaram and neighbouring Chromepet (together Pallavapuram) are major centres of Madras's historic and famed hides-and-skins industry. Chromepet got its name from the Chrome Leather Company G A Chambers established in 1912, setting up a tanning and leather goods manufacturing operation on a 25-acre site in southern Pallavaram. Chambers, an English leather-worker, arrived in Madras in 1894 and, after a stint in leather exports, started a tannery in 1903, where he eventually implemented the technique[2] of chrome tanning. After various business vicissitudes, Chambers founded the company that gave a township its name. By 1916, a modern tannery and chrome leather factory were established and the beginnings of Tamil Nadu's now-famed leather industry established. Chambers' daughter Ida, a figure of stature in Madras well into the 1960s, later brought enlightened management to what was one of the major industrial units in pre-Independence Madras.

---

[2] Alfred Chatterton, a dynamic Director of Industries, Madras, in the first decade of the 20th Century, pioneered the technique and several others in the Province.

Principal William Meston (1921-30) and Alexander Moffat, charged with the responsibility of finding a site, zeroed in on Tambaram. The deciding factors were that the South Indian Railway was proposing an electrified suburban train service and that the Forest Department was planning to consider the Selaiyur Forest as no longer Reserve Forest. The Tambaram Scheme was approved by the Board in January 1927. Then began the campaign to get the Government of Madras to grant the college 400 acres of the forest and funds for the first buildings. Eventually, it was October 1930 when the College took possession of the land.

Pallavaram, like St. Thomas' Mount, Royapuram and Perambur, remains home to an Anglo-Indian population, though a diminishing one. Noteworthy in Pallavaram is Veteran Lines, with its old Anglo-Indian 'cottages' featuring tiled roofs and trellised verandahs. St. Stephen's Church here still has a substantial Anglo-Indian congregation.

Veteran Lines got its name from the homes built here for retired Royal Artillery NCO's and Other Ranks and their families, the wives generally Anglo-Indian. The Anglo-Indian community here had grown to serve the Cantonment. St.Stephen's Church was built, following a successful subscriptions drive by four Anglo-Indian women, on the site of an earlier church raised in 1847 "in the Main Guard of the Presidency Cantonment of Pallavaram." The first church, raised on the initiative of Rev. Walter Powell, for "pensioners, veterans and troops at Pallavaram" was a two-storied building, with a large room above furnished as a church and rooms below for a school. In 1901, the Main Guard building was demolished, being declared "unsafe", and the church moved into Barracks No.4. When the bomb-proof barracks building started developing cracks, plans for a new church surfaced in 1933. On completion, it was consecrated in 1935. The many gifts the new church received included pews from St. Mary Magdalene's Church in Poonamallee and the pulpit from St. Stephen's Church, Ooty.

Beyond Chromepet is Tambaram with its T B Sanatorium, one of the oldest in this part of the world, an upgraded Siddha Medicine Institute developed anew, a Free Trade Zone, the suburban electric train service's workshops, and the splendid, tree-shaded campus to which Madras Christian College (MCC) formally moved on January 30, 1937. The Tambaram Sanatorium was started as a private venture in 1929 by Dr. David Chowry-Muthu (originally Saverimuthu) who lived and practised in England but regularly visited his family in Madras. Government granted him 250 acres of land for his venture and he built a 12-bed hospital. In 1937, he handed it over to Government and it is today called the Government Hospital of Thoracic Medicine.

Principal William Meston (1921-30) and Alexander Moffat, charged with the responsibility of finding a site for MCC, once it was decided that the growing college needed more space than it had in its George Town location, near the Fort, zeroed in on Tambaram. The deciding factors were that the South Indian Railway was proposing an electrified suburban train service and that the Forest Department was planning to consider the Selaiyur Forest no longer Reserve Forest. The Tambaram Scheme was approved by the Board in January 1927. Then began the campaign to get the Government of Madras to grant the college 400 acres of the forest and funds for the first buildings. Eventually, it was October 1930 when the College took possession of the land.

Meston's successor, the Rev. Dr. Alfred Hogg (1930-38), implemented the scheme, overseeing the actual transfer of the College. It took nearly 18 years before the transfer was completed. The first sod was cut in January 5, 1932 and a cottage to be later known as *Barnes Villa* (still surviving) was built. And into it, at the end of March 1932, Prof. Edward (Ted) Barnes and Alice Barnes moved. The first 'settlers', they were to supervise the development of the whole campus, watching buildings designed by the Swiss architect Henri Schaetti come up, offering suggestions to make them more student-friendly, and adding to the degraded scrub forest several rare plant species.

Hundreds of species of plants and trees, many of them exotics, were introduced in the campus by them, several supplied by other members of the faculty as well as alumni. The couple nurtured the seedlings in their home and supervised their transplantation. Barnes not only documented all the species in the campus but he wrote profusely about them to international journals. But perhaps his most valuable written contribution was *The New Environment: Detailed Description of the Tambaram Site* (1937) which detailed "the physical boundaries, nature of water and soil, the kinds of tests done on them, the climatic conditions, the meteorological descriptions, and the wild life of the campus."

Today, the College's 365 acres host 150 species of trees, 450 species of plants, 150 species of birds, 75 species of butterflies and several species of small fauna and numerous species of reptiles. Much of the tree growth today is about 75 years old. The total building cost of the campus when it was finally completed c.1955 was about Rs. 33 lakh. A second phase of building expansion began in 1959, with the introduction of postgraduate studies, and goes on to this day. The College's Bishop Heber Church has an 1841-vintage pipe organ gifted to it in 2014.

MCC's sylvan campus, rich in flora and fauna, includes what is called the Selaiyur Forest and has been declared a bird and wild life sanctuary.

The MCC School, which together with the College had been in George Town, moved into 25 acres in Chetput on October 21, 1950. Land for the school was purchased here in 1946 for Rs. 2.5 lakh – possibly a garden house called *Claycroft* on Harrington Road – and Rs. 11 lakh was spent on buildings. Responsible for this was the third Indian principal, the legendary Kuruvilla Jacob who headed the School from 1931 to 1963 and developed it into one of the leading schools in South India.

From the Selaiyur Forest, National Highway 45, the extension of Mount Road, begins its long run south, past where one of the first cars to be made in India, the Standard, used to be manufactured in a factory on what is now a site of highrise commercial development, splendid Vandalur Zoo, the huge Ford factory and the smaller BMW factory, and the first integrated modern township, Mahindra City. Beyond the new limits of Greater Madras it heads to Tiruchchirappalli, around which the Carnatic Wars raged, to Madurai, heartland of the Tamils, and then, as NH-7 to the parched Deep South and Land's End. Off it is the road to Pondicherry, now Puducheri, whence the great Tamil poet Subramania Bharati fled from Madras.

The Tormented Genius

There are few enough parts of the world that can boast of even one hero associated with a national struggle. To be able to boast of THREE must be unique indeed. Yet, that is exactly what a 25-kilometre stretch between Kovilpatti and Tuticorin in Madras Province's Tinnevelly (now Tirunelveli) District can claim. On this stretch of road are the villages of Ettaiyapuram, Panchalankurichi and Ottapidaram, whose contribution to the history of India's freedom struggle and to the Tamil challenge of British power is the stuff of legends.

The first of these legendary heroes was Veerapandiya Kattabomman – Getti Bomma Naik – the poligar of Panchalankurichi, and it was he who inspired the Swadeshi steamship hero, V O Chidambaram Pillai of Ottapidaram, (VOC), the poet-patriot Subramania Bharati of Ettaiyapuram, and Bharati's friend, the scholar-revolutionary V V S Aiyar, in the early years of the 20th Century. Each may have done his own thing, but they were united in their love of freedom and devotion to the Tamil language and Tamil culture. And for that love they suffered – leaving behind a host of indelible legends.

Kattabomman was betrayed to the British by his own people, the very poligar of Ettaiyapuram whom he was trying to protect. But when he died, hanged summarily from a tamarind tree near Kayattar, a legend was born. As though to compensate for that great betrayal, Ettaiyapuram produced Tamil Nadu's great poet-patriot Subramania Bharati, who was born there on December 11, 1882.

Bharati died in 1921, at the age of 39, and S Satyamurti wrote of him: "Had he been born in England, he would have been the poet laureate... Had he been born in any free country, he would have risen to such heights of eminence... Had he been born even in Bengal, he would have been a Rabindranath Tagore... So long, however, as the Tamil language lives and there is a spark of patriotism in Tamil Nadu, Subramania Bharati's songs will live."

Bharati was born into a middle class family that lost its money in business, his father being a better Tamil scholar than a businessman. Bharati was therefore compelled to find employment early. He worked for a couple of years in the service of the Raja of Ettaiyapuram, then for six months as a school teacher in Madurai. It was during these years that it became obvious that he had inherited his father's love for Tamil. But his first published poem, which appeared in the Madurai literary monthly Viveka Bhanu, *was described as a verse in "jaw-breaking Tamil"! This sonnet was called 'Thanimai Irakkam' and its author was bylined as 'Ettaiyapuram C Subramani Bharati'. The 14-line poem used so many words the ordinary reader could not follow that the editors had to provide footnotes to explain some of them. This pedantic style of Bharati's early days was quite in contrast to his later, more communicative style. A critic writes that this "stylistic transformation took place after he came to Madras in 1904 and became a working journalist." From 1905 his style became simpler, and by 1908 he was in "the forefront of the new stylists." This metamorphosis took place during Bharati's association with the* Swadesamitran. *It was not only his style that changed when he began this association. To his poetic fervour he added patriotism. And so began his long years of political and personal travail.*

Journalism made Bharati a national hero, the Swadesamitran *made him a journalist. It might well be said that they were made for each other, for they were both born in the same year. During the two years that he was a subeditor with the* Swadesamitran, *Bharati not only was trained as a journalist by Subramania Aiyer but also acquired his fire. The bouquet of heady wine made Bharati want to burst into patriotic verbal extravagance. This was not for Subramania Aiyer, his Editor. When S N Tirumalachari started the weekly* India *in May 1906, he gave Bharati the free hand the poet sought. Then began his finest era.*

India *was a product of the Swadeshi movement, whose first stirrings against the British had been exhibited in 1905, in the protest against the partition of Bengal. Freedom was what* India *sought – and it made no bones about it, its motto on Page One saying what the French Revolution*

was all about, in French as well as in Tamil: Swatantiram, Samattuvam,
Sahodaratvam (Liberté, Egalité, Fraternité). India *took on a host of
Swadeshi causes in the years that followed. But the first that got* India
*into hot water was when the Government objected to a Bharati cartoon
(in those days artists drew the cartoons editors dreamed up). This cartoon
showed ships taking away grain from India while the people of the country
were starving. Government also found objectionable this 'exhortation'
to Lord Krishna by Bharati:*

> When will our thirst for
>   liberty be quenched?
> When will our love for
>   slavery die out?
>
> When will the fetters on the
>   hands of our Mother be removed?
> When will our troubles cease
>   and become things of the past?
>
> O, Krishna, hero of the
>   *Mahabharata* and protector of the Aryas!
> Is it not your grace that helps
>   one to victory?
>
> Does it look well that we,
>   your adorers, should suffer?
> Are famine and disease the
>   lot of your devotees?
>
> If so, for whom are all the good things
>   of the earth?

*Government filed plaint against the editor of the paper and obtained
a conviction. M Srinivasan was sentenced to five years R I despite his
plea that he was not the real editor of the paper, that he did not know
how to write a news story, that he was a poor relative of the proprietor
and had only lent his name for the masthead at Rs 30 a month! The
Government then began considering whether a warrant could be issued
against Bharati. On advice said to have been given by various local
elders, Bharati fled south to Pondicherry in French India. It was
September 1908. Within a few weeks, the printing equipment of* India

was smuggled into Pondicherry and the weekly began publication again – the banned paper, smuggled into the Madras Presidency, being more in demand than before it had to re-locate. But late in 1909, Bharati had problems with his management, which was having trouble making both ends meet, what with the ban on the paper in Madras affecting its advertising revenues. Bharati quit.

India's *loss was Tamil literature's gain, for Bharati during the next few years concentrated on poetry, several of his major works being composed in 1912. Man cannot, however, live by poetry alone – and so Bharati continued his meanderings in the world of Pondicherry journalism. But every journal he worked for soon folded – British bans proving too much for them. Fortunately for literature, Bharati was now persuaded to forget journalism for the nonce and concentrate on the poetic talent he had revealed in* Karma Yogi.

Bharati, in exile and deprived of a journalistic career, undoubtedly turned softer. The same thing had happened to VOC, who had come out of jail a crushed man, and, earlier, Subramania Aiyer, who had been shattered by the very threat of imprisonment. Aurobindo Ghosh, a fellow exile in Pondicherry, turned to spiritualism and V V S Aiyar, another fiery revolutionary in exile, turned to the world of letters, writing the first Tamil short story in 1917, Kulathangarai Arasamaram, *after an initial spell of training gunmen. In this atmosphere of broken dreams and literary timewhiling, Bharati attempted to retain his interest in politics by writing sedate letters to the editors of Madras journals. As his prose became less fiery, his verse became more lyrical. He became the supreme poet. He also gave up his rural indifference to appearance and opted for a buttoned-up frock coat, loose turban to hide his baldness, and a pampered moustache to go with his clean shave.*

V V S Aiyar and Aurobindo Ghosh, in this epochal period, adapted themselves to the quiet of Pondicherry and found peace in non-violence. But Bharati found only a great restlessness in his creativity. It was as though his head was on fire, remarks a biographer. He rarely stayed at home; he would wander restlessly along the beaches or through the groves night and day; no one knew what he was looking for, but that he was in the throes of a spiritual and personal crisis was apparent. It was then that he met Kulla Sami, an unkempt samiyar *(guru/sadhu), who gave him peace – and also introduced him to opium. Bharati could not do without it for the rest of his life.*

Within days of the end of World War I, Bharati received news that the British would take a lenient view if he re-entered the Presidency, provided he did not take an active part in politics. Bharati, who had found Pondicherry a "large prison", leapt at the chance. He straightaway went to his wife's home in Kadayam, western Tinnevelly, and there, betwixt communing with nature and God, worked on plans to publish a 40-volume illustrated collection of his works. In a circular to friends he appealed: "Please send whatever you can as loan towards the printing expenses. I expect from you at least Rs 100. Kindly induce at least twenty more of your friends to lend me similar and much larger sums, if possible. I shall give stamped 'pro-notes'.... (and) pay the generous interest of 2% per month in view of my large profits. Expecting, very eagerly, your kind reply and scores of money orders...." As further inducement, he added a postscript: "All Government restrictions against me have been removed and all accusations withdrawn and so Government officials may also be asked to subscribe...." Few came to his help. He followed the English circular with a similar one in Tamil that expressed his conviction that his books would "sell more commonly and faster than kerosene oil and matchboxes."

Failing to get the financial response he wanted, he went to his hometown to seek the Raja of Ettaiyapuram's patronage. He sang before the Raja: "By your presence, the slur that there is no Tamil King who patronises Tamil letters is gone; by my presence, the slur that there is no great poet in present-day Tamil Nadu is gone. Will you not come forward to shower your patronage on me with palanquin honours and bags of gold?" The Raja certainly loved Tamil, but he loved his position better. Afraid of how the British might react if he patronised a rebel, the Raja ignored the pleas.

The tone of the circular and the song in Ettaiyapuram are typical of the Bharati of this period, the last three or four years of his life. He was as obsessed with a premonition of death as he was with the belief that he was immortal. He posed for a photograph with his walking stick held like a sceptre. On a visit to the Trivandrum Zoo, he persuaded a keeper to let him pat a lion, which he did, reportedly, while informing the lion: "O, Lion King, here I am, the Poet King." It is probably even more apocryphal that the lion roared three times! And then there is that famous incident of his only meeting with Gandhiji.

Bharati made a flying visit to Madras in 1919, his first in eleven years, to address a public meeting on Triplicane Beach, just as he had done several times before he had fled the city. Hearing that Gandhiji was in town, he burst in on him one afternoon with a typical "Enna Oi!" (What, man!), and, seating himself next to the leader on his cot, without any preliminaries asked "Mr Gandhi" to preside over the Triplicane meeting that evening. "I am sorry I cannot come today. Can you have your meeting tomorrow?" asked Gandhiji. "No, I cannot. I take leave, Mr Gandhi. I bless the movement you are about to launch," replied Bharati and left the room as abruptly as he had entered it. A startled Gandhi wanted to know who that was and Rajaji replied that "he is our Tamil nationalist poet." Gandhi expressed concern and advised, "He must be properly taken care of. Is there none in Madras to do this?" The Swadesamitran, *to which Bharati had been contributing (for Rs 30 a month, sent to his wife) contemporary features and pen pictures ever since he left it, now volunteered an even more permanent arrangement.*

Bharati rejoined the Swadesamitran *as a privileged subeditor in November 1920, on a salary of Rs 75 a month. When Rajaji had seen him a year earlier at that meeting with Gandhiji he had been shocked by Bharati's appearance: "When I had seen him last, his face was like a full moon, luminous. But now it had lost its liveliness and was shrunk and dried up. What a pity he has become like this, I sorrowed." It is a description echoed in the memory C R Srinivasan had of his first meeting with Bharati. Srinivasan, the manager of the* Swadesamitran *at the time Bharati returned to the paper, remembered a shout on the road that slowed down a* jutka, *out of which leapt a man whose coat tangled with the vehicle's safety bar and tore. Unmindful of the damage, the man bounded up the stairs and peeped into Srinivasan's room. They introduced themselves. Srinivasan later recalled: "The Bharati I saw that day is indelibly imprinted on my mind's eye. Middling height. Thin build. Shining, light brown complexion. Layer after layer of a turban wound round the head. A broad forehead. A dot of kum kum of a quarter anna size in its middle. Thick brows that stood guard over the roving eyes. The upturned nose highlighting the sunken cheeks. Though an aggressive moustache hid the upper lip, the lower lip revealed a listless life. A shirt without buttons to cover the body and an alpaca black coat over it. That too torn while jumping from the cart. He sat on the chair. Tongue-tied, the eyes rolled around, sizing everything. They alighted on me also, moving up and down. Rebellious eyes; sorrowful eyes; eyes that exuded peace; eyes that captivated. They stole my heart."*

Bharati was given a free hand to write what he wanted. He wrote daily, on political topics, social developments, national progress... He also wrote an occasional creative piece. But the fire had almost gone out. His last article, in August 1921, was on Rabindranath Tagore's successful trip overseas. It was at about this time he sang for the last time in public. It was at a meeting on Triplicane Beach and the song was his famous Bharata Samudayam Vaazhkhavey. *It was a song inspired by the fate of a former colleague and fellow-nationalist who could no longer afford a square meal a day. For a few moments the old revolutionary spirit stirred again as Bharati sang:*

> Let us make a new law
> and observe it for ever:
> If even one among us has to starve,
> let us raze the whole world!

When Bharati moved to Madras with his wife Chellamma and two daughters, he had first lived near the Swadesamitran's *first offices on Errabalu Chetty Street. But a doctor-friend and patron persuaded Bharati to move from George Town to Triplicane so that he and his family would be nearer medical attention if it became necessary. And so Bharati moved to Triplicane.*

Bharati was not a fit man when he returned to Madras; opium had taken its toll. He now turned more and more to religion, and, morning and evening, would visit the Parthasarathy Temple to pray. He would help carry the idol around the temple streets during festival times. He would lead bhajan *singers in procession through the streets of Triplicane. And he would feed the temple elephant daily with the plantains and coconut of the* prasadam. *His devotion was so great that he was considered more an eccentric than a genius in Triplicane.*

One morning in July 1921, Bharati took his usual offering to the elephant and called out to it, "Here I am, Mitra, offering you fruit." The elephant was in rut and restless. It was facing away from Bharati when he called out to it. Turning towards the sound, it swung its trunk and Bharati took the full force of the blow and fell, almost under the elephant's feet. But the animal did nothing more to the poet – nor to his friend who pulled the bleeding Bharati out of danger several minutes later. Bharati's daughter found her father some hours afterwards at home with "a cut in the upper lip caused by the elephant's tusk ... and ... an abrasion on the head ... Fortunately the wounds were not serious. Father's turban saved him." Bharati, who had gone back to feeding the elephant once he was up and about, wrote: "Had the elephant wanted to hurt me, it could have trampled me to death after I fell down, but it did nothing." It also had nothing to do with the poet's death a few weeks later. That was a result of a week-long bout of dysentery and Bharati's generally weakened condition.

On September 12, 1921, Bharati's emaciated body, weighing less than a hundred pounds, was consigned to the flames at the Triplicane cremation grounds. Less than twenty people accompanied the bier on that last journey. A few years after his death, his songs were proscribed once again by the Madras Government. After that, the poet-patriot was almost forgotten. Till the Bharati revival in 1982.

8
A Tale of Two Islands

Of Madras City's three other main thoroughfares running out of the Fort, two, South Beach Road (now renamed Kamarajar Salai in memory of that great Tamil leader of the masses who passed away in 1975) and North (or First Line) Beach Road (now Rajaji Salai, commemorating C Rajagopalachari, the ablest politician Madras has produced and the first Indian Governor-General), run true to their names, while Poonamallee High Road (now E V R Periyar Salai, honouring the great rationalist and Dravidian leader) runs west. Almost in the imaginary angle Poonamallee High Road and South Beach Road might form and just south-west of Fort St. George is a major 'lung' of the city known as The Island. How this island came to be formed is part of Madras's geographical history.

Madras is today trisected by two rivers, whose courses meander from west to east, and is bisected by a canal that runs north-south. But once upon this city's time, the area covered by Madras today was divided in four by three rivers – and of canal there was none. The years between have been spanned by a tale of two islands which narrates how Man has changed the geography of the territory that is Madras today.

Come Tourist Fair time, January to March every year, reference to its Island Grounds location becomes more frequent (though *Fairlands* is the name – of the corner where the Fair is held and where the Tourism Department offers a couple of other facilities – that Government has been trying to popularise). Few, however, realise that the terrain they refer to is indeed an island, and an island of not insignificant size at that.

This island, somewhat diamond in shape and now about 1,500 yards by 1,000 yards across diagonally, is a geographical feature that was manmade in almost the first years of Madras. The original land grant for Madras, as already narrated, was for a narrow spit of land locked in by the sea to the east, the Triplicane or Poonamallee (now the Cooum) River, where it entered the sea, to the south, and by a shallow river to the west. This river, described as lagoon-like by some geographical authorities, and totally useless for navigational purposes, was what tempted man to tamper with the geography of the region.

Today, this river is part of the Buckingham Canal. Once, however, this river's very name was in doubt. The British settlers called it the North River – presumably because it flowed down from the north. The local inhabitants called it the Elambore (Elumbur) River – yet it was nowhere near ancient Elambore, or what is called Egmore today, though it was close enough to Purasawalkam and Veppore (Vepery), tributary villages of Elambore from the earliest days. In fact, the course of the river was, almost throughout its passage, parallel to the sea – that is, to the west of the Fort and about two kilometres from the coast. But in its last stages it changed course; at the southwest corner of the present General Hospital grounds it bent back sharply on itself, then travelled northeast for about 800 yards before sharply turning south at the Fort's walls and flowing about a further 800 yards to join the silted mouth of the Triplicane River.

Between the lower curve of the Elambore's 'S' and the north bank of the final reaches of the Cooum was a shady expanse of land – now The Island, but in those early days a peninsula almost 1½ times the present extent and as early as 1643 (when it was first called an 'island') coveted as a potential economic gain by the settlers. A letter of that year states that this ground is "situated in the river under the command of the castle, whereon is likely to be made a great quantity of salt yearly, which is one of the constantest commodities in all eastern parts, and much monies are got thereby everywhere." This peninsula was linked to the mainland at a point opposite where Park Station now is, and is quite likely the 'Meleput' of the original grant, where salt pans were located.

The present Andhra, Tamil Nadu, Kerala and Karnataka Area Army Headquarters is on land reclaimed from the river course and filled with the soil of *Nari Medu* (Fox Hill, but for some curious reason called Hog Hill by some early recorders) when it was flattened, first as part of the river-diversion plan, then on General Eyre Coote's order during the Second Mysore War in 1769.

Who decided to convert peninsula into island has not been recorded, but Yale is certainly on record as having been most concerned with the North River and the peninsula. Even before becoming Governor in 1687, he had suggested that the course of the North River be diverted more westwards to enable expansion of 'White Town'. Later, in 1690, he suggested a bridge be built across the North River, from Fort to peninsula. Though these projects of Yale's were never carried forward in his day, his successors appear to have built on his plans.

Governor Nathaniel Higginson, who had been the first Mayor of Madras, succeeded Yale as Governor and in his six years of impeccable governance developed Madras considerably. It was during his tenure that, the record states, "orders were issued in 1696 that the cutt river be cleared," obviously reference to an artificial channel. It would seem that someone during this period felt that the two rivers – only about 350 yards apart at the North River's first bend, which encompassed the Company's Garden and the Governor's new 'garden house' that existed on what is now the General Hospital campus in Park Town – should be joined. It has been stated that the channel was cut "with the object probably of equalising flood levels." But whatever the reason, the trench-digging gave Madras its 'Island'.

'Pirate' Pitt, an 'Interloper' who later decided to go 'straight' by serving John Company faithfully, succeeded Higginson in 1698. Thomas Pitt is remembered for his dubious acquisition of the Pitt Diamond. But many feel he should be better remembered for his 11 years as Governor, "a period which proved to be the Golden Age of Madras in respect of the development of trade and increasing of wealth." Pitt was an outdoorsman who enjoyed living in the two 'garden houses' – apart from the Park Town house, another had been acquired in Guindy by then – where he could indulge himself in his passion for gardening. This interest he diverted in 1705 to the marshy 'island', dredging it, hedging it all round, embanking it and improving it. He created a magnificent diagonal avenue of double trees across The Island, facing his 'garden house', and planted ornamental groves near this 'Great Walk'. He provided fine pasture for cattle and built here timber-yards and hog-pens, a slaughter-house and a powder-house! There were bowling greens and spacious walks, teal ponds and "other curiosities" created for the relaxation of the Madras gentry. But after Pitt, interest in this 'lung' waned, though money was spent on making a thoroughfare through it.

In 1715 was built the first permanent bridge linking island and mainland – the Island Bridge, which was to evolve into Wallajah Bridge, built in 1756 and widened to its present extent in 1820. Triplicane Bridge, subsequently Willingdon Bridge and now Periyar Bridge, came up shortly afterwards, and was followed in 1718 by Garden Bridge (later General Hospital Bridge, and still later Stanley Viaduct, which now leads to Central Station in recently altered form). In 1725, Governor Macrae built a new powder factory on The Island and the space began to be put to greater military use, something that continues to this day.

In the second quarter of the 18th Century, the French threats to British interests were growing and once again there was talk of diverting the North River westwards – this time to extend the fortifications further southwest. Concrete plans were drawn up for this during Governor Benyon's time (1735-44), but nothing came of them. And, as was later accepted, the French, as a consequence, had no problem in marching in, in 1746, and then demonstrating during their stay that The Island could indeed be converted into a defensive fortification.

Lessons learnt, the Company got down to planning in earnest what Yale had suggested in the 1680s, seven decades earlier! Garrison Engineer Benjamin Robins drew up plans for diverting the North River and extending the fortifications. But Robins died before he could put into practice his plans, and so did his successor Scott. Their assistant, Brohier, then had the task of carving up The Island and this he did in 1755 by diverting the "Elambore River into a passage across the island, which had been cut by a flood five years before." The old course of the river became a protective 2.3 km long moat in the 1760s – still to be seen – and the outworks of the fortifications were built on a third of The Island, the northeast corner, reclaimed by the mainland. And so The Island achieved the shape it retains today.

These second thoughts on re-fortification were what enabled Madras to withstand the second French siege in 1758-59. But immediately after that siege was lifted, Col Call, then Garrison Engineer, made further plans for The Island. He first cleared 'Old Black Town' and the 'Guava Garden' cemetery. Then he ensured that a northwest portion of The Island was given for the cemetery of St Mary's Church. This cemetery, created in 1763 and in use till 1954, was the first of the modern encroachments on The Island that is divided in two by the thoroughfare to the Mount. Across from it is the later Armenian cemetery.

The Island's southeastern half became a parade ground for troops – and has officially, if not in fact, become so again, to judge by a board which made its appearance in the 1970s. In the western half were once ordinance store and the Governor's Bodyguard Lines – and, once again, the military are busy here, the Andhra, Tamil Nadu, Kerala and Karnataka Army headquarters, (an area command established in 1980) offices and the Officers' Mess now occupying the area. Across from the military campus and on the banks of the Cooum is the headquarters of the city's bus transport system, Metropolitan Transport, one of the best in the country. Next to it is St.Mary's Cemetery, with a well-maintained corner for the War Graves Commission and a bigger, but less well-kept one for Roman Catholics, but the greatest space, and the least maintained, is that for the Anglicans and other Protestants for whom it was first developed after the 'Guava Garden' cemetery gave way for Law College.

In a southeastern corner of the island is the Madras Gymkhana Club, no longer for military pukka sahibs alone, though the military foundations are recognised in its patrons and the automatic memberships to Garrison officers. Founded in 1885, it had, till around 1920, a membership restricted to Garrison officers. Here miniature golf continues where once were golf links, and a sporting link is retained with a past where racing began in the subcontinent two centuries ago and polo followed not long after. The Club's golf and racing heritage are curiously linked today, the Gymkhana's golf course being smack in the middle of the Madras Race Club's racecourse, having moved there in 1870, golf is the most competitive sporting activity of the Club today.

The Gymkhana's grounds are Defence property – as is the entire island. And on these grounds were played most of the sports introduced in India by the British. It was the Club that first gave Madras both codes of football in any organised format, the E K Chetty Cup tournament for soccer dating to 1895-6, when ten teams participated, and the Madras Gymkhana Rugby Football Challenge Cup tournament to 1900. Both sports, however, date to at least 1860s' beginnings in the city. The earliest record of a football match in Madras, in which the Gymkhana played a regimental team, is on January 9, 1894. The Gymkhana and the Madras United Club teamed together with the YMCA to found the Madras Football Association in January 1934. Both codes are not even a memory today in the Club. Tennis and Swimming have taken their place, though neither is particularly competitive. But even more popular is Bridge.

It was in this part of the island that the City's first Western theatre, the *Playhouse,* was built – it is first mentioned in 1778 – and amateur players regularly staged plays and other entertainments. When The Island had to be vacated for military reasons, the theatre was pulled down in 1786. It was originally proposed to shift the theatre to the north end of Broadway, on which site St Mark's Church was built in 1800 by John Goldingham, but in fact it opened in 1791 on the Great Choultry Plain, probably somewhere near Graeme's Road, and flourished there under the aegises of The Madras Theatrical Society till the Museum Theatre was built – and used by the Madras Dramatic Society, predecessors of the Madras Players of today founded *c.* 1955.

In the middle of Mount Road and The Island is the 1839-work of Sir Francis Chantrey which appropriately places Governor Sir Thomas Munro on a lofty pedestal. The pedestal was started by John Law and was completed by a local craftsman, Ostheider. The £ 12,500 cost of statue and pedestal was contributed by the public. Both, historians hope, will be allowed to remain here for ever, for, over a century before Independence, Munro was one of the first to present the Indian case to the rulers. "With what grace," he once wrote, "can we talk of paternal government if we exclude the natives from every important office, and say, as we did till very lately, that in a country containing fifteen million inhabitants no man but a European shall be entrusted with as much authority as to order the punishment of a single stroke of a rattan?..." More prophetically, in advice to the Company's Court of Directors on the ideal of colonial government, he said: "Your rule is alien, and it can never be popular. You have much to bring to your subjects, but you cannot turn India into England or Scotland. Work through, not in spite of, native systems and native ways, with a prejudice in their favour rather than against them; and when in the fullness of time your subjects can frame and maintain a worthy Government for themselves, get out and take the glory of the achievement and the sense of having done your duty as the chief reward for your exertions."

That great Indian statesman C.Rajagopalachari considered Thomas Munro "the ideal administrator". He wrote in 1961, "Whenever any young Civil Servant came to me for blessings or when I spoke to them in their training school, I advised them to read about Munro, who spent

47 of his 65 years in the Madras Presidency ... and left a record of service of which anyone may be proud... (He) was unpopular with his fellow officials and other British residents because of his sympathy with the people of the land and his admiration of some of their qualities...He was the great initiator of the peasant-wise settlement of land in India... It was his work in this direction... and his just and wise administration that have made his name a legend in South India."

Few from Britain who worked in India were more worthy of a monument than Munro. Subscriptions poured in for a statue when it was decided to commission one. £ 8000 of it was appropriated from this for commissioning the statue and Francis Chantrey in England was chosen as the sculptor for an "Equestrian Statue in Bronze of Sir Thomas Munro – place of Erection – Madras, dimensions not less than 10 feet high." Chantrey was not comfortable sculpting animals. Of his three equestrian statues, those of Munro, the Duke of Wellington and King George IV, it was later stated that Munro's figure was the finest while that of the horse was the worst; it was the reverse in the case of Wellington!

Tradition dictated that Munro being a fine horseman, who had died of natural causes, he had to be depicted on a horse that had all its feet on the ground. To sculpt Munro the only reference Chantrey had was a portrait by Sir Martin Archer Shee and that presented only one point of view while a sculpture needed to be seen from all sides. He considered his task complete when "not one objection was raised to the fidelity with which he caught the likeness of a man he never saw" when the 6-ton statue was displayed for public viewing by 1837 and Chantrey had made sure that everyone who was someone viewed it.

By early 1838, it was ready to journey to Madras on *The Asia*. With it came the plan for the base of the statue and what was to be between it and Chantrey's pedestal. The work on both was entrusted to the local firm of Ostheider's which was in existence till 1897.

The Asia docked two miles out in Madras Roads, and awaited the *masula* boats to come and offload its cargo. It proved to be a three-day operation . The horse was brought on shore one day, the figure on the next and the granite Chantrey pedestal on the third day. It was the single heaviest consignment received in Madras till then.

The statue was stored in Madras for the one year that it took before it was finally erected at the chosen spot. Eventually, it was opened to public view on the evening of October 23, 1839 with a salute of 17 guns. And the subscribers to the statue were entertained by the Governor.

Munro died of cholera, in Pattikonda, near Gooty, on the eve of his departure to England. His saddle-less statue on The Island remains a proud memorial to a just administrator, after whom children in Rayalaseema used to be named Munrolappa, and a horseman whom local legend maintained was a daring bareback rider. Chantrey appears to have dampened the legend somewhat with a saddlecloth.

Also on The Island used to be St Mary's Charity School – the first English-founded educational institution in Madras, started here in 1716 after beginnings in St. Mary's Church the previous year. The juxtaposition of Munro's statue and the site of St Mary's Charity School is apt, for it was Munro who, about a century after St Mary's, laid the foundation of modern education in Madras. He ordered a survey in 1822 that found that the city possessed, in most disorganised manner, 305 ordinary schools and 17 charity schools, a school for every 1,000 population, attended by 5,523 boys and 276 girls out of a population of 79,992 boys and 81,597 girls.

Education really took off only after this when Munro established a School Book Society, and set up a Directorate of Public Instruction to establish a school in every Collectorate and Taluk headquarters. The DPI began its work by establishing a training school for teachers in what is now the DPI office and which was then the College of Fort St. George campus.

This military-cum-sport-oriented island found itself in the 19th Century abutting yet another man-made island, though this second island is appreciated even less by the public as a water-locked territory. Which is not hard to understand, because the waterway that made it an island appears nowadays to be almost perennially dry. That narrow strip of land comprising Chepauk, San Thomé-Mylapore and the southern bulge of Mandaveli is indeed an island, surrounded as it is by the sea, the Adyar and Cooum Rivers AND the Buckingham Canal! Indeed there are 88 km of waterways in the main city, apart from the last named three. There are the ill-maintained Mambalam Drain, the Captain Cotton Canal and Otteri Canal.

The Buckingham Canal in Madras is just two parts of a four-part canal that is one of the longest in the country. The northern half of the Canal within the City was built at the turn of the 19th Century by Basil Cochrane who excavated what was left of the North River to create a navigable canal up to Durga Raya Patnam (Armagon of Francis Day's revered memory), near Nellore. Cochrane's feat involved the realigning and deepening of the North River, a considerable achievement that was not recognised till many years later. In fact, the second Clive derived all the initial recognition, the work in the initial stages being deemed work on the 'Clive Canal'! Cochrane eventually got his due, when the canal was opened in 1806, and, in the years that followed, Cochrane Canal was gradually extended up to Pedda Ganjam where it linked up with the canals of the Krishna and Godavari deltas. Meanwhile, a canal had been constructed in the south, from Papanchavadi in Chingleput District to the mouth of the Palar, near Sadras. This was, in time, extended to Markkanam in South Arcot and called the South Coast Canal.

This was the picture in 1875 when the Duke of Buckingham and Chandos took over as Governor and almost immediately was faced with one of South India's worst famines that lasted from 1876 to 1878. North Arcot and Chingleput were among the worse-affected districts, though stock-piling of grain in Madras enabled the City to escape the brunt of the disaster. To help the people during this crisis, the Duke put them to work – on relief projects. And the result was an eight-kilometre stretch of island-creating canal that linked the Adyar River with the Cooum near its mouth, just behind the present University buildings. Nearly Rs 30 lakh (over two-thirds of it on labour alone) were spent on this famine relief work during 1877-78. The total Buckingham Canal length in the core city is 31 km.

By 1882, this canal was extended to link with the South Coast Canal and the East Coast Canal, in effect linking Markkanam in the south, via the Cochrane Canal, with Kakinada in Andhra, a distance of 420 km (about 163 km in Tamil Nadu, the rest in Andhra Pradesh). The 30 km urban stretch of this waterway was, fittingly, called the Buckingham Canal, but, inevitably, the entire system, from the southernmost point to the link with the Andhra deltaic system at Pedda Ganjam, 300 km from Madras, was bestowed with the name of the Duke, Cochrane forgotten again.

The entire canal, 9-11 yards in width, and with 28 locks throughout the system, was a cheap means of transportation. There was regular traffic to Mamallapuram by boat from Mylapore!!

An 1898 history of the Canal records that by 1882 the Canal stretched "420 km from Pedda-Ganjam to Mercanum" and was a "principal means of communication, both for passengers and goods." In 1895-6, about 325,000 tons of goods valued at a bit over Rs. 25 million were carried on the Canal in about 1600 boats of around 22,000 tonnage! As late as 1960-61, after the separation of Andhra, 190,000 tons of goods valued at Rs.18.5 million were carried in 1200 or so boats in Madras State alone. Passenger traffic declined from a little over 26,000 persons to 19,000 between 1956-57 and 1960-61, still noteworthy numbers. It was the cyclone of 1965-66 that finally decided the fate of the Canal, many feel.

Firewood-laden boats used to ply the canal in the southern part of the city until just after World War II. Today, a few boats may still be seen using it to sail between Ennore, a northern suburb of the city, and the Andhra rice bowl town of Nellore. But the high cost nowadays of keeping it suitable for year-round navigation by desilting (especially in the dry season) has resulted in canal navigation not being looked at seriously. Worse, this attitude has resulted in allowing whole stretches of the canal in the city being used for the pillars of the new elevated rapid transit-rail service! To all intents and purposes, the urban stretch of canal has been lost for ever, no matter the lip service being paid to new promises of another look being taken at the canal in the light of ever rising fuel prices.

Just north of Ennore, near where Cochrane first started work on the canal, government has put up a new thermal power station, with the tallest chimney in the South, on an island created by canal, the sea and two inlets of the backwaters. Used by the power station as an office is an old house once called *Clive House*. Whether Clive the Second (c. 1800) used this as a holiday retreat is not known, but it is believed to have been one of the three holiday bungalows Binny & Co owned here from at least 1850. In the 1880s, the two smaller bungalows fell victim to erosion when a sand bar was opened and the big one was bought by the Salt Department. This was probably *Clive House*. Another house recorded is *Stone House*, a play on the name of its owner, Timothy Stonehouse, a Civilian.

An informal Ennore Club – I've also heard the name Union Club mentioned – long a European enclave, was started in the vicinity in 1787, some years before Binny & Co was founded. Its Clubhouse was built by private subscription, one of the Binnys pre-dating the business house, probably Charles, Secretary to the Nawab Wallajah, taking the lead. There appear to have been several holiday homes of Europeans in this area from the 1780s, fishing, rowing, and sailing, being the favoured pastimes. In the backwaters here, Ennore Creek, were held Madras's first rowing and yachting regattas predating the Madras Boat Club (1867) and the Royal Madras Yacht Club (1911).

The twin villages of Kattiwakkam and Ernavore, today's Ennore, came into East India Company hands in 1708. With them came backwaters and a beautiful stretch of beach – ideal for recreational purposes. And that's what the East India Company men began to put to good use after the Carnatic Wars with the French ended (1760's) and peace reigned. Weekending became a regular feature.

The earliest records of sailing in Madras are in the 1850s. The Ennore backwaters was a popular weekend retreat for the sahibs many of whom had cottages there. Lord Clive's house, which like many others kept changing hands, *Pottinger House*, *Douglas Castle*, *Thornhill House*, *Binny Lodge*, *Cox's Little Rocks*, *Dobbin's Bungalow* were a few of them. *Pottinger's House* was Governor Henry Pottinger's, but had been Edward Clive's. Pottinger preferred Ennore to Ooty to relax in.

The Madras Boat Club and the Ennore Club met every March and December for several years in a 'regatta' which was part rowing, part sailing, part land games and part shooting competition. An invitation for the two-day 1879 'regatta', including a survey map of the rowing course in the area lay-out, exists. The best part of that detailed document is instructions on how to do the 10 ½ mile journey from Madras. It suggests doing it by road or by boat, sailing on the Junction and Cochrane Canals. One of the boat options suggested is getting a boat which provides sleeping accommodation, thereby making a slow journey possible by night. When are we ever going to see the Buckingham Canal used like that again?

Nearby is a virgin but now threatened eco-system on Kaattupalli Island. Here, scrub forest, backwaters and huge sand dunes are an inviting setting for the eco-tourist. But the whole area is threatened by the power plant, the newly developed Ennore Port – the city's second major harbour – and a private harbour facility built and managed by Larsen & Toubro. All of which is leading to the industrialisation of the hinterland.

Down by the Riverside

"*The Cooum River has been presenting a problem of great difficulty owing to its having become narrowed and silted up in the course of its channel and sand-barred at its mouth. The Buckingham Canal and this river emit an evil odour, especially in the hot season when the water level is very low. Some years ago a scheme was tried for pumping sea water into the river and thus enabling its level to rise and the volume of its flow to become large enough to burst the bar at the mouth whereby the sea water could rush in and carry back the dirty water of the channel. The Adyar presents very much the same appearance as the Cooum and has formed lagoons at its mouth...*"

These may well have been words spoken, by one of the more polite speakers, at seminars on the Cooum in the 1980s and 1990s. In fact, they were written nearly EIGHTY years earlier. Nothing changes in Madras, a city of tradition, it's always been said!

The problem of the Cooum everyone is agreed on. How to cut the sand bar and keep open an exit to the ocean all the year round is only one of the problems. The others rise from as traditional reasons.

In the years just before World War I, when J W Madeley, the Corporation Engineer, was developing the City's water drainage system, sewage water was let out through the sewers; stormwater drains carried only excess rainwater into the Otteri Nullah, Buckingham Canal and the Cooum. No wonder they all stank! And they could only stink the more in later years when untreated sewage has also been draining into all three, with sewage facilities proving inadequate for a city exploding with people.

That population explosion is an intrinsic part of the Cooum problem. To add to the sewage from the drains, there is the daily output from the use of the river and its banks as an enormous outdoor lavatory by the shanty towns that have sprung up on its banks. But there is nothing new about such slums in Madras either.

Writing in 1939, on the 300th anniversary of the city, the same author quoted above, C S Srinivasachari, said, "One peculiar feature of Madras that has been found difficult of eradication, is the existence of numerous plots of ground known as hutting spaces, wherein one-room dwellings of mud and thatch rise up in hundreds. Some of these hutting grounds are the sites of early villages. They are generally kept in a very insanitary condition and are easily subject to fire. In 1871 ... there were 10,752 huts of this type... A Special Housing Committee of the Corporation, appointed in 1933... estimated the slum huts at 15,942 and the total population living in them about a lakh (15% of the total population)."[1]

This is nothing to be surprised about. From the very beginning, Madras has been a trading centre, the entrepreneurs dependent on a migrant population to serve their needs. Francis Day and Beri Thimmappa brought in cloth-makers in 1639 when they founded the city and dumped them by the Elambore River (now the Buckingham Canal and its Washermenpet reaches) and let them fend for themselves. Ever since, traders, merchants and industrialists have been doing the same. Business and industry set up in Madras need the shanty-dweller to run it – and the entrepreneur doesn't care where the employee lives or what facilities he has. The result is the Cooum situation – not yesterday and today, but from the beginning of Our Towne.

Certainly there must have been a time when the Cooum was not all that hopeless. But there is very little record of that – though it is there by implication.

Madras today is divided into three by the west-to-east flowing Adyar and Cooum and into two from north to south by the Buckingham Canal, but in its earliest days Madras was bounded by only the Cooum and the Elambore River.[2] The Cooum or, as it was first known, the Poonamallee, has been a river associated with the development of Madras from the

---

[1] Chennai city, today, has a slum population of about 700,000 in 1,300-plus slums. A further 250,000 dwell in 400-plus slums in the suburbs, making a total of about a million in Greater Madras's 7 million.

[2] North River.

very earliest days. Dividing Chetput and Nungambakkam, Egmore and Chintadripet, creating The Island, it was a river that provided welcome coolness to the early British settlers. Governor Thomas Pitt made The Island a park for his constitutionals. And, later, the great 'garden houses' came up on the Choultry Plain, on the south bank of the Cooum, and across it in Egmore and Chetput. Making homes away from home almost on the banks of the river does not indicate a malodorous river in the 17th, 18th and 19th Centuries. In fact, the scene painted of those times is positively idyllic. Early in the 19th Century, Lord Valentia, a visitor wrote:

"In appearance, Madras differs widely from Calcutta, having no European town, except a few houses, which are chiefly used as warehouses in the Fort. The gentlemen of the settlement live entirely in their garden-houses, as they very properly call them; for these are all surrounded by gardens, so closely planted, that the neighbouring houses is rarely visible. Choultry Plain .... is now covered by these peaceful habitations, which have changed a barren sand into a beautiful scene of vegetation."

In the 1820s, on the Egmore bank of the Cooum were The Pantheon, *where public balls, dinners and other "amusements" were held by, and for, Madras Society, and the College of Fort St George, where the Presidency's Civilians were trained in the local languages and the art of administration. The College is now the Director of Public Instruction's campus, but, by the riverside here, there remains one of the most magnificent archways in the city. Such a splendid gateway could only have been meant for ceremonial entrances, and, indeed, the Governors and their ilk travelled by boat from the Fort to the College on formal occasions, such as convocations, and made grand entrances through this gateway.*

Of the 65 km long Cooum, 18 km are in the city. Not only was this stretch navigable, but it might even have been considered sacred. Across the Harris Bridge (1855, now Adithan Bridge) from Mount Road is Komaleswaranpet, a part of Pudupet. And here, in great simplicity, lived, on the banks of the river, that leading dubash *and great philanthropist Pachaiyappa Mudaliar. Several other eminent Indians were his neighbours. One of them was W S Swamy Naick (Samy Nayak), who was put in charge of introducing vaccination in Madras – and the*

Presidency. He rose from "native dresser" to Chief Medical Practitioner, Department of Vaccination, in the early 19th Century. There is in the vicinity of his house on Harris Road a small park named after him and a plaque to his memory. All of them, it is reported, used to bathe in the waters of the Cooum before their daily prayers. Today, we are told, the hardiest fish will not survive more than 30 hours in the river!

Even as late as 1907-8, the Cooum apparently was pleasing. Sir Ralph Benson, of the Madras High Court, used to live in those days in Doveton House, *now part of Women's Christian College. House guests of his appear to have written home about the placid, silvery Cooum nearby and all the trees that shaded it!*

But for all these kind references, there were indications that all was not well with the river. Grant-Duff, on a visit to Madras in 1876, before he became Governor, wrote that he drove through the city, "admiring the brilliant yellow flowers of the Thespesia populnea, *which is planted in avenues, and crossing two rivers – one of which, the Adiar, is rather pretty." Obviously, the other wasn't. It could only have been the Cooum.*

Over a century and a half earlier began the 'deprettying' process, a process that has been commonplace throughout the history of the city. In 1734, Governor Morton Pitt felt more cloth was needed for export and so he decided to build a new weavers' town. He acquired for this purpose Chief Merchant Sunka Rama's garden in the last loop of the Cooum before the river flows into the sea, the acquisition being made easier by the Chief Merchant having been dismissed and so being out of favour with the Government. Pitt now "resolved to settle several hundred families of spinners, weavers, painters, washers and dyers along with Brahmans and dancing women and other necessary attendants of the pagoda. The village was to be called 'Chintadre Pettah', the village of small looms" The commercialisation – and slumming – of the Cooum had begun. It's been going on ever since.

9

Magnificent Marina

1. Memorials on the beach

The second main road going south from Fort St George is South Beach Road, now named Kamarajar Salai. Constructed in 1846, it now runs past the Assembly Commemorative arch, George V, sculpted by Mani Nagappa's father in 1942, for which he got a Rao Bahadur title, and a handsome War Memorial built around 1919/20, a commemorative pillar encircled by an elliptical corridor. The site of the War Memorial was once known as Cupid's Bow, and once even featured a bandstand for the couples who took the air there.

The road then emerges from the now-expanded-by-duplication Napier Bridge (which in 1943 replaced the 1869 'Iron Bridge') where it crosses the southern bank of the Cooum's near-silted mouth, and runs south, die-straight 3½ km or so, to the northern bounds of historic San Thomé. To its right is the memorable Madras skyline of Indo-Saracenic palaces and educational institutions built like palaces; to its left is a splendid Italianate promenade with evergreen gardens and a stretch of sandy beach that the guide books call the second longest urban beach in the world, and which is more certainly one of the broadest and longest stretches of urban beach anywhere. All this is the Marina to the people of Madras.

The Madras beach once stretched, in all its glorious width, from the Harbour to Elliot's Beach beyond the Adyar River, ten kilometres and more. Today, much of it is built over, except the stretch by what should accurately be called 'The Marina'.

The Marina that Governor Mountstuart Elphinstone Grant-Duff (1881-86) conceived and built is really the handsome promenade that skirts the beach. Grant-Duff wasn't a great success as a Governor in the five years he spent in Madras. In fact, he has been described as having been "a failure," possibly because he was "feeble, sickly, unable to do his work himself, and wholly in the hands of the permanent officials." But he was a lover of beauty, a patron of education, science and the arts, and a man of letters. In other words, a man of some sensitivity – and there can be no better memorial to that sensitivity than The Marina.

When Grant-Duff first visited Madras in the 1870s, during a grand tour of India, he was struck by the possibilities of the city's beach. Writing about it in a memoir he recalls, "Our way lay first along the shore and made me think of the very sensible answer made to me by F-, when I was talking about going to India. 'Go,' he said, 'for God's sake. If you only spend twelve hours on the beach at Madras, it will be a great deal better than nothing.' " Impressed as he was by the beach, Grant-Duff was determined to make something more of it when he came to Madras equipped with the powers of office. For beach to be made a "lung ... for thousands ... in quest of cooling breezes from the sea," it needed beautifying. And, so, Grant-Duff ordered The Marina to be built.

Soon after he declared open The Marina, the Governor wrote in a letter home, "We have greatly benefited Madras by turning the rather dismal beach of five years ago into one of the most beautiful promenades in the world. From old Sicilian recollections, I gave in 1884 to our new creation the name of Marina; and I was not a little amused when, walking there with General Saletta, he suddenly said to me, 'On se dirai a Palerme.'" The Italian was reminded of Palermo!

What Grant-Duff began others have further contributed to over the years. Trees, gardens, ornamental flower beds, avenues close by the sands, colourful lighting are all integrated embellishments that are later additions. But encroachments too there have been. At weekends and holidays, however, the beach crowds and hordes of vendors make it a memorable and noisy experience, with the raucous cries of competing stall-holders selling a variety of 'hot-hot' snacks and every imaginable kind of trinket, the shell variety predominating, mingling with the outpourings from radios and loudspeakers. A 'Clean Marina' project that got off the beach in 2003, with a mechanical cleaner, has seen one of the two swimming pools, a couple of restaurants, and a boathouse all flattened. The pool by the central stretch of the Marina and the restaurant adjacent to it were legacies from World War II – amenities built for the

Servicemen. A dais in the section known as Triplicane Beach, which had been a renowned venue for public meetings graced by Bal GangadharTilak, Gandhiji (five times), Nehru and Subramania Bharati among others, also fell victim to the clean-up drive which banned public meetings on the beach. It was announced by freedom fighter Subramania Siva – the first political prisoner in the Madras Presidency — at a public meeting at the venue in 1908 that it would be called *Tilak Ghat (ThilakarThidal)*, but as the memory of the struggle for independence faded, it was renamed *Seerani Arangam*. Now, even that name does not exist in public memory. A campaign by one man, a Gandhian journalist P.N. Srinivasan, however, resulted in a large memorial plaque being readied in 2003 but it was only in January 2010 that the State Government permitted its installation near the spot, proclaiming it *Tilak Ghat (Thilakar Thidal)* once again. It's a slab on a stretch of lawn that's little heeded today.

The aquarium established nearby in 1909 to a plan by Governor Lord Ampthill and Museum Director Edgar Thurston – the country's first, and one which, with its 54 species of fish, came in for much praise, but which by the 1950s had become a Black Hole crying for resurrection – is no more, and, sadly, a major coastal city like Madras still does not have an aquarium that could be called a showpiece. There is, however, a small aquarium a couple of miles down the road at the Zoological Survey of India's regional office in San Thomé and there is one in Vandalur Zoo. Two dominating memorials and some amenities have been added in more recent years, at the northern end of Marina.

With an eye to blending with the surroundings, *Anna Samadhi* (the memorial to former Chief Minister Annadurai) was built in 1970 as an integral part of a lush garden and coconut grove at the northern end of the beach, just where the beach drive begins, but what could have adorned The Marina has unfortunately been marred by the dissonance of the entrance arches – the original one resembling gigantic twin tusks and the 1997 creation to the front of the tusks looking like one face of a squat, extended Arc d'Triomphe and further 'embellished' in 2012 – and crowds of hawkers to whom the grove is a shelter.

By *Anna Samadhi* there came up in 1988 the *MGR Samadhi*, another commemorative garden. This memorial honours the popular film star who became an even more popular Chief Minister in the 1980s, M G Ramachandran, and was in 1992 elaborated with a sculpted lotus and a huge entrance of hands folded in greeting ordered by the then Chief Minister Jayalalitha, an MGR film heroine, after earlier Chief Minister and rival Muthuvel Karunanidhi had erected a simpler memorial on the site where his erstwhile colleague, and then rival, MGR, was buried. In 2012, yet another entrance with political overtones – what looks like two leaves, the symbol of MGR's and Chief Minister Jayalalithaa's party, the All India Anna Dravida Munnetra Kazhagam (AIADMK), the Anna reflecting the Party's claim to be the true heirs of the Annadurai tradition – and a Pegasus-like representation between two sets of pillars have come up in front of the folded hands.

Awaited here as this edition goes to press is another memorial to yet another Chief Minister, J Jayalalithaa, who died in December 2016. She was buried in the sands behind the MGR samadhi and a tomb of sorts created. A memorial in this area has been promised, but it awaits a decision by a party unsettled by her death. Jayalalithaa died during her fourth term as Chief Minister and at the height of her popularity after a dozen or so 'Amma' schemes for the masses had enshrined her sobriquet 'Amma' (Mother) for posterity. Her rival, Mu Karunanidhi, had served as Chief Minister a record five terms.

At the southern end there is one of the newer horrors in the city – the new lighthouse. Madras's lighthouse has wandered wide from the Fort Exchange, now the Fort Museum, and has at last come to stay, from 1977, as this monstrous triangular sore thumb on the Marina. But it has became a popular attraction housing as it does a lighthouse museum and offering a climb inside its tower at the end of which are splendid overviews of Madras. With its light 185 feet above sea level, it is the only lighthouse in India with a lift. It is also the only lighthouse in India located in a city.

Between *Anna Samadhi* and the lighthouse are an array of post-Independence statues of varying degrees of artistic competence. The early ones, *Triumph of Labour* (reminiscent of the famous World War II photograph showing American Marines raising the flag on Iwo Jima) and *Homage to Gandhiji*, are striking examples of the sculptor's art. As much cannot be said for the 1968 statues that honour the literary 'greats' of Tamil: Avvaiyar, Thiruvalluvar, Kambar, Subramania Bharati, Bharathi Dasan, and European missionaries Bishop Caldwell, Pope and Fr Beschi (Veeramunivar) who made great contributions to Tamil. The statue of Kannagi, heroine of the epic *Silappathikaram* and one of this pantheon, was unceremoniously removed one night in 2003 by the then government whereupon the party at the helm of the previous government installed a similar Kannagi statue in front of its Youth League headquarters on Mount Road. When it came back to power in 2005, Kannagi was brought out of storage and back to her place on the Marina. Two other statues on this stretch have nothing to do with Tamil studies or tradition. Near the lighthouse is a statue of national political leader Kamaraj, the Congress stalwart whose name today graces the road. The statue was raised in the 1970s and shows him hand-in-hand with the children he loved, and for whom he began a free mid-day meal scheme in schools that has only been growing ever since. The other is of nationalist leader Subhas Chandra Bose, remembered here no one is quite sure why when the road named after him fronts George Town, about three kilometres away.

Both the Gandhi statue – in the 'March to Dandi' stride – and the Labour commemoration raised in 1959 are the works of the outstanding sculptor Debi Prasad Roy Chowdhury. The Gandhi statue was some years ago duplicated on the lawns of Parliament House, New Delhi, as well as in Bombay and Calcutta. Roy Chowdhury was appointed the first Indian Principal of the Madras School of Arts and Crafts when he was just 30. It is said that "the next thirty years he spent in Madras were the most fruitful period of his life as a painter and sculptor." Almost a desecration of his memory is a new neighbour, to the Labour memorial, a man-made mini-mountain which was to be bathed in waterfalls and lighting, both of which seem to be on again, off again embellishments. This jarring sight was part of a beautification-of-the-beach drive that keeps stopping-and-starting with each successive government, which ignores the basic necessity of maintaining a beach as a beach – and a clean one at that.

Across the way from these pedestalled sentinels commemorating the past is what, at Independence, must have been one of the world's most striking skylines. Over two centuries ago, that skyline probably consisted only of the two halves of Chepauk Palace (more of which anon)and its outbuildings that stretched as far as the Cooum. The splendours of the palace are now hidden by later construction, some that took their architectural cue from the Indo-Saracenic style that gave Madras a distinguished skyline which existed well into the first half of this century, and more recent ones that reflect the variable aesthetics of modern Public Works Department architecture and are incongruous.

2. Building for education

In what were once the gardens of Chepauk palace – stretching north from Wallajah Road to the Cooum – there came up the University buildings. In the southern gardens, stretching to Pycroft's Road, there was first integrated, with its original utilitarian name, a new two-storey Indo-Saracenic building of exposed brick to house the Public Works Department in 1865-67, Robert Fellowes Chisholm creating the design. Leading westward from the two ends of the main building are two long rectangular office blocks, the northern one dating to c.1871 and the southern one to 1910 when the main block was also extended southwards with a separate new block set slightly back from the frontage of the main block, but reflecting it in style and linked to it by a passage. Adjoining it, further south, in the gardens, was built, the home of South India's first tertiary education institution, Presidency College, its dignified, ageing, Italianate red-brick facaded buildings today dominated by the Fyson (a former Principal and eminent botanist) clock and dome raised in 1940 to mark the centenary of the of the institution and painted in recent years in a raucous pink that cries for redemption. The Nawab's Courts of Justice once used to be by the College site. Additions in 1874, 1897 and 1908 and that dome have rather changed the Chisholm perspective.

The Madras skyline begins across the way from Anna Memorial with the impressive Indo-Saracenic buildings of the University of Madras, which was incorporated in 1857, one of India's three oldest universities. Alexander J Arbuthnot, who as Director of Public Instruction organised the Department of Education, was "instrumental in founding the University of Madras" and in 1858 "delivered the first address to the first graduates." The first graduates were C N Thamotharanpillai, who finished first, and Caroll V Visuvanathapillai, both from Jaffna in northern Ceylon. Arbuthnot was to become Vice-Chancellor in 1871-2, but Chief Justice Sir Christopher Rawlinson of the Supreme Court (as the Madras High Court was known till 1862) was the first Vice-Chancellor of the University. Thirty years earlier, the Danes had established India's first modern university at Frederiksborg (Serampore, now Srirampur, West Bengal), albeit a religious one. Instrumental for this were the missionaries headquartered in Tranquebar, near Madras. This university survives as a unitary institution, still granting divinity degrees under the Danish Royal charter, but Madras, Bombay and Calcutta grew into the three great government initiated universities of pre-Independence India which have given birth to almost all the post-1947 universities. Madras University was, like the other two, originally solely an examining university. It became a postgraduate teaching and residential university in 1923. During the last 100 years or so, it has given birth to several other Universities in South India: Mysore (1916), Osmania (1918), Andhra (1926), Annamalai (1929), Travancore (Kerala) (1937), Sri Venkateswara (1954), and all the post-1967 universities of Tamil Nadu.

The Madras University offices, which had been in Presidency College, moved into the Indo-Saracenic-styled *Senate House* in 1879, a building built on the site of the Nawab's Artillery Park from where gun salutes were fired to greet visiting dignitaries. The library and teaching department buildings were built, in sympathetic style, in the 1930s on the site of *Marine Villa*, a part of the Chepauk Palace complex and once Nawab Wallajah's octagonal-shaped bathing pavilion by the Cooum river; indeed, it was called the *Nawab's Octagon*. Lord Clive the Younger occupied this pavilion for a time when Governor-General Wellesley stayed in *Governor's House* in the Fort while conducting the last Mysore War. The pavilion was demolished in 1930 after it. Between *Senate House* and the library block there came up the *Centenary Building* where the Vice-Chancellor and Registrar have their offices and from where some departments function. The foundation stone was laid on January 31, 1957 and the building, conforming to a prize-winning design by Prynne, Abbott and Davis, was opened for occupation in August 1961.

British architect and planning consultant Donald Insall, a staunch conservationist and a member of the Historic Buildings Council of England, on a 1980s visit to Madras was charmed by, er, Arcot Palace, as he called Chepauk, but he was positively bowled over by *Senate House*, just kitty-corner from it. "That's a work of a sheer genius. See how it harmonises with the Palace. See how it was planned to integrate!" The genius was that of long-forgotten Robert Fellowes Chisholm, to whom Madras owes much for its Neo-Indo-Saracenic architecture. And on Chisholm's work on the Marina we need to dwell.

As Presidency College expanded and the University began to consider where it should be headed, greater built-up space became the need of the early 1860s. In 1864, the Madras Government advertised an all India competition for the design of two buildings – one to house Presidency college, and the other to provide offices and an examination hall for the University of Madras.

The designs of Chisholm, a young engineer who had joined the Bengal PWD in 1859, were chosen the winners of both competitions in 1864. A 21-year old Chisholm arrived in Madras in 1865 to supervise the building of both sites. In 1872, he was appointed Consulting Architect to the Government of Madras, an appointment pushed through by Governor Lord Napier who virtually became his patron. In 1877, he was also appointed the Superintendent of the Government School of Industrial Arts (now the College of Arts and Crafts). He retired in 1889 to take up similar positions with the Gaekwad of Baroda. He left India in 1902 to practise in London. Apart from his work in Madras he was responsible for designing some of the finest 19th Century buildings in India. Amongst them are the Lakshmi Vilas Palace and the Museum in Baroda, the Napier Museum, Trivandrum, the Lawrence (Asylum) School and Town Library in Ootacamund, and the Rangoon Cathedral. He was also responsible for the restoration of the Tirumala Nayak's Palace in Madurai. During his twenty years in Madras, he not only changed the city skyline, but he spread the Indo-Saracenic architectural style he was considered master of throughout India.

Chisholm's work in Madras should have begun with Presidency College and *Senate House,* but bureaucratic delays had him starting on the new PWD building – a stand-alone structure he designed and supervised the building of – and the Revenue Board office, a transformation of the main northern building of the Palace. In 1867, Chisholm began supervising the construction of the Presidency College building, combining the Italianate with the Saracen and the Hindu. Many buildings were added later.

In 1869, he began work on the first University building across from Chepauk Palace. The building was to be called *Senate House*. The story of *Senate House* begins with a dispatch from Sir C Wood, Secretary of State for India, to the Governor, dated India Office, London, July 23, 1864. It reads, "The Senate having already expressed an opinion in conformity with that given by the Secretary of State, as to the inexpediency of combining the buildings for the University and the Presidency College in one design, the Governor in Council resolved to direct that, as suggested by the Senate in their Registrar's letter of the

January 11th last, the University shall be erected on the site adjoining Marshall's Road[1], which was recommended for the Presidency College by the Director of Public Instruction in his letter of the August 12th, 1863, and the Presidency College on the site already fixed on at Chepauk."

The suggested site of the University building provoked a controversy, which accounted for the delay in starting the work on it. Finally, the Governor, Lord Napier, in his Minute dated November 28, 1867, stated his views categorically. He wrote:

"The site on Marshall's Road stands at a great distance from the Presidency College, the College of Civil Engineers, the Medical College, the principal schools and the quarters which supply the greatest number of students and persons concerned in literary pursuits. But it is hoped that the University buildings will not be circumscribed to a mere hall or Senate House for the offering of Degrees and other rare solemnities. We expect that, eventually, University Professorships will be established and that University lectures will be delivered (*emphasis mine*). Even at the present moment it is most desirable that a University library should be founded, which would serve as the General Public library for the studious classes in the capital, a library in which the valuable Manuscripts belonging to the Government may be lodged and in which the past and current publications of the Presidency (which we are now directed to register and preserve) may be deposited and, as I trust, united with an ample collection of works useful to the general student and particularly interesting to the educated inhabitants of Southern India. If such should be the eventual character of the University buildings it is obvious that nothing is more desirable than to place them in some degree of juxtaposition with the principal haunts of education and to provide them with cheerful attractive aspects as well as a good supply of air... (*emphasis mine*).

"The proposals which I accordingly submit to Council are comprised under the following three heads:-

"(i) To affirm that the proper site for a University building is the ground between the Marine Villa and the Revenue Board office.

---

[1] Now Rukmini Lakshmipathy Road in Egmore. The site considered is the present Rajaratnam Stadium of the Police Department.

"(ii) To address the Government of India, in order to obtain their sanction for the application of a portion of the capital of the Educational Fund for this purpose.

"(iii) To call upon Mr Chisholm to attend Council, at an early date, with the designs formerly prepared for a University building with a view to the adaptation of those designs to the proposed locality and to the various objects which it is deemed expedient that such a structure should include."

The Commander-in-Chief, W A McCleverty, in his minute dated November 30, 1867 confirmed that Marshall's Road was most suitable for lodging the Infantry and not the University. A J Arbuthnot, the Director of Public Instruction, in his minute dated December 5, 1867 concurred: "In the opinion of His Excellency the Governor... the time has arrived for commencing the erection of the long projected Senate House for the University of Madras and that the site which his Lordship proposes for it, viz., the piece of ground facing the sea beach between the Marine Villa and the Revenue Board Office is in every respect the most suitable site available..."

And so it came about that R S Ellis, the Chief Secretary, issued orders dated December 17, 1867, to the Registrar: "I am directed by His Excellency the Governor in Council to inform the Vice-Chancellor and Fellows of the University that it is the intention of the Government to commence the erection of the Senate House for the University of Madras at an early date...The new building will not be limited to a large hall or Senate House for the conferring of Degrees and other rare solemnities, but that provision will be made for the University Professorships which it is hoped will eventually be established and for the University lectures which will be delivered... Between this new site, on which it is proposed to build the Senate House, and the Presidency College now under construction, three public buildings – the Revenue Board Office, the Chepauk Palace and the Public Works Department – intervene and by these the two new buildings will be completely separated, while a still further distinction may be secured by a dissimilarity of design which Mr. Chisholm, the Architect, can be instructed to observe in the Senate House..."

On March 11, 1868 it was reported that the "site for the proposed Senate House was laid before the Senate of the Madras University (and) was unanimously accepted."

The proceedings of the Madras Government, Public Works Department, in April 1868, stated, "Mr Chisholm having laid before Government a ground plan of his design for the new Senate House at Madras, His Excellency the Governor in Council, pending the approval of the design by the Syndicate, resolves to direct the Superintending Engineer of the 4th Division to authorise Mr Chisholm to take measures for the early commencement of the work." Chisholm, writing as "Executive Engineer, Presidency," to the Secretary to Government, Public Works Department, on April 30, 1868, stated: "I am now in a position to start the work with the view of laying the foundation stone on the 25th Proximo." Eventually, work on *Senate House* began in 1869 and was completed in 1873.

Senate House consists essentially of a cellar hall, a ground floor hall with a high ceiling (called the Great Hall), and northern and southern wings with the main entry porches. In addition, the building is adorned with minarets and has porches on the eastern and western sides.

The Madras Mail reported on the day of the inauguration of *Senate House*:

"The Senate House is in the Hindoo-Saracenic style of architecture. It is built of red hand-pressed brick with white gneiss dressings, and consists of a Convocation Hall, in the centre, 150 feet in length, 60 feet in width, and 50 feet in height, from the boarded floor to the ceiling. On each side of this hall are arcaded verandahs supported by massive stone columns 3 feet in diameter, and 25 feet high, with carved capitals. The roof is covered with Broomhall's tiles, and the ceiling is panelled in 21 sections of canvas-covered panels richly painted.

"The lower portion of the hall is lighted on each side by seven large windows, 12 feet broad and 40 feet high, the upper portions being circular, and fitted with geometrical wood-work, and cathedral tinted glass. The upper portion of the hall, or clerestory, is lighted by 14 large windows in triplets fitted with stained glass, worked in a variety of patterns. The spaces between the windows are ornamented with bands of geometrical patterns; the North and South walls are diapered with a Mooresque pattern in colours. This mode of decoration, called graffito work, was lately introduced by Mr Chisholm, and is executed in Portland cement, tinted. It sets very hard, and is calculated to last a long time; it withstands the action of the sea air, which corrodes the ordinary lime plastering, and makes it crumble in a very short time. The dais at the north end of the hall is common to the Lecture Hall (behind) as well. A drop curtain will eventually divide the two, if occasion should require them to be separated, in order to make the hall as acoustically perfect as possible. The dais end is formed of a massive bell-shaped vault worked from a span of 48 feet on the face to 24 feet at the back.

"Galleries run on each side of the hall with seats for the public, a thousand for the students being ranged in the centre. Seats have been provided to-day to accommodate 1,500 persons, but almost double that number may be accommodated by a closer arrangement of the sittings. All the platforms forming the side galleries and the seats are portable, and will be removed to the cellars below the hall, when it is used for the examinations which take place annually.

"The Lecture Hall which forms the south wing of the building is 58 by 40 feet, and of the same height as the Convocation Hall. It contains a double semi-circular gallery and has 500 sittings. The upper gallery, horse-shoe in plan, is supported with cast-iron columns surmounted with railings of the same material in geometrical patterns. There are also two retiring rooms suitable fitted up. The ceiling is divided into painted panels.

"The north wing has an upper storey. The ground or basement floor contains a library on one side, and a lecture room on the other, with a central passage. The upper floor contains a Senate meeting room 58 by 25 feet, with 'robing' room and Registrar's office attached. The South Eastern tower, entered from the Registrar's room by a spiral stair, is fitted with shelves for records.

"There are four towers at the angles of the Great Hall containing staircases, the lower portions forming entrance porches. There are two porches besides, one at the north and the other at the south end. The roofs of these porches are domiform. The exterior angles of the north and south wings contain spiral stairs which reach the roof, and terminate in domed spires.

"All the furniture has been from designs by Mr Chisholm, the greater portion of it being manufactured by Messrs Deschamps & Co. The glass painting recently introduced into this country, by Mr. Chisholm, with great success, was done at the Madras School of Industrial Arts under his personal superintendence. The sections of canvas ceiling were also painted at the same institution.

"The cost of the building (which has been erected from Pagoda Funds) including the furniture and fittings is Rs 2,80,000. The whole work was executed by natives under native supervision, with Gooroosawmy Modelliar as clerk of the works. The only thing imported was the pot metal window glass."

To what *The Madras Mail* said may be added the following notes:

The arched big window on top of each door in the Greater Hall is decorated aesthetically with stained glass. Light streaming through these windows used to make Convocations of yesteryears a colourful experience;

The capitals of the 12 pillars flanking the verandahs have a strong Hindu element being carved with deities, human and animal figures and geometric designs;

Imported Marezzo marble was used for the sunken floor of the Hall;

Below the Great Hall is the Cellar Hall, its floor 9 feet below the ground level;

There are six porches, two each on the eastern and western sides of the building and one each on the northern and southern sides of the building. The porches are each 18 feet high and 25'x22' in dimension and all provide entry to the building; and

A magnificent wooden staircase coming down from the handsome Senate meeting room divides into two branches that lead to the Great Hall and then on to the Cellar Hall.

Allowed to deteriorate from the 1970s, the building was crying for restoration till, finally, in 2004 the work was initiated. The splendidly restored building was inaugurated in 2007. During the three-year restoration project, much of the original interior was discovered beneath layers of paint. *Senate House* is undoubtedly one of the most striking buildings in Madras. But restricted access to it makes its beauty blush unseen. Disuse since has also led to deterioration, money and labour wasted.

Additions homogeneously made to the building in 1884 and 1889 are models architects of today might note when building anew where the old exists side by side.

Presidency College, growing out of the first High School, was the nucleus of Madras University. Its beginnings were a preparatory school that began in 1840 in *Edinburgh House*, Egmore, possibly off Pantheon Road, before it shifted to Popham's Broadway. It became a High School (a department of the University) on April 4, 1841, when it moved into *D'Monte House,* Egmore. The building also housed the first offices of the University till Presidency College was built and provided space for them. Since the 1860s it has housed the Metropolitan Magistrate's Court. Eyre Burton Powell was the first principal. The first Proficient of the High School of the Madras University was C V Ranganatha Sastri. A linguist, he began his career as a translator and went on to become a Judge of the Small Causes Court.

In April 1853, the collegiate departments were added to the school and in 1855 the institution was named Presidency College. The College moved into its new building in 1870-71. The statue of Powell, later a Director of Public Instruction, was erected in the middle square of this building in 1882. Seven years later, women were admitted to the college. Presidency College was also 'the law college', until Law College was started in 1891-2, and the University Office, until *Senate House* was built. The High School itself was an offshoot of a school to train teachers that was part of the grand education design of Thomas Munro. It eventually closed in 1884. The first Indian Governor-General, C Rajagopalachari, and Nobel Prize winners C V Raman and Dr. S. Chandrashekhar were among the distinguished alumni of the College. The English Lecture Hall in the College, Room M-28, is today dedicated to these two Nobel Laureates who both had sat in this room for lectures during their days at Presidency. In the grounds of the College, south of the main block, are three 200-years-old tombs of members of the Arcot family. A few more are in neighbouring Wenlock Park. To the south of the College buildings are its cricket grounds, once called the Marina Grounds. Tended for years by P.R. Subramaniam, 'Subbu' to all, it was a ground with turf good enough for a Ranji Trophy match. Today, after long being reduced to an ill-kept 'lung' for children from the neighbouring slums, it has been restored to its first class status and maintained by Simpson & Co.

Starting with Presidency College, Madras University fast expanded, including in the process several other institutions that grew out of the early technical or general education schools. The Government Survey School of 1794, the first 'modern' technical training institution outside Europe, became the Engineering College; the Madras Medical School of 1835, another first in the country, became the Madras Medical College in 1851; the Scots Mission's General Assembly's School of 1837 became Madras Christian College; and Pachaiyappa's Central Institution of 1842, Pachaiyappa College. The Teachers' College was linked with the University in 1887 and Law College was established as a separate entity in 1891. The first women's college in the city, Queen Mary's College, founded in 1914, became affiliated to the University in 1916, the same year as the Government Muhammadan College (now a women's arts college) on Binny Road opened on the grounds of stately *Umda Bagh*.

Much of the development of Madras University was centred in the Chepauk educational complex on the Marina, a part of which is the corridor-linked University Library and Departments/Teaching Building. Built in a more Lutyen-ish Indo-Saracenic style, these were designed by Edward Reid and Booth. The Teaching Block, whose foundation stone was laid in 1913 after which work was long delayed, was eventually inaugurated in 1936. A wall clock tower dominates it and it is sometimes called the Clock Tower Block.

The Library was inaugurated in 1936. Attached to the library is housed the Government Oriental Manuscripts' Library (founded in 1867), now an adjunct of the Archaelogical Department of the Tamil Nadu Government. This is one of the world's largest and best manuscripts' libraries and is mainly composed of three major collections: The Col Mackenzie, the East India House (Dr John Leyden, M D) and the C P Brown. The Mackenzie Collection, "the most exclusive and most valuable collection of historical documents relative to India that ever was made by any individual in Europe or in Asia," represents 14 years of devotion on the part of Col Colin Mackenzie of the Madras Engineers and India's first Surveyor-General, who began "the favourite object of his pursuit" in 1796. After his death in 1821, Government bought and shipped to England much of the Orientalist's collection, though most of it was returned years later, a part of it to Madras. The Oriental Manuscripts' Library had as its nucleus what was left in India of Col Mackenzie's priceless Dravidian Collection. These leftovers were moved to the Madras Literary Society premises from *Landon's Gardens*, his house in Kilpauk, south of the 'garden house' Dare of Parry's lived in. They were then transferred to the Fort St George College in 1828 and to Presidency College in 1869. The Mackenzie Collection included over 1,500 manuscripts, 6,200 coins, 2,300 drawings, 150 images and 'antiquities' and hundreds of books. About 8,000 of these items eventually found their way back to Madras. The library has 50,000 palm-leaf manuscripts, 20,000 paper manuscripts and 23,000 books; several manuscripts here have still not been deciphered. Its oldest holding is a 450-year old medical manuscript inspired by Agasthiyar. Till 1997, this was a gloomy, little-used library, but since then it has been air-conditioned, made brighter and catalogued better, encouraging greater use.

Newer buildings in the University complex include the capacious Centenary Auditorium, opened in 1966 across from and to the west of *Senate House*. Near it, and facing away from *Senate House's* lecture hall, is an 1887 statue of Queen Victoria, a Queen still remembered!. The Queen Victoria bronze was a gift of the Maharani of Vizianagaram. Round the corner from the Queen's statue and facing the Marina, also with its back to *Senate House,* is the statue of S. Subramania Aiyar, the first Indian Vice-Chancellor. Not far from Subramania Aiyar's statue is one of V. Krishnaswami Aiyer.

Subramania Aiyar, who was Vice-Chancellor for only a few months in 1904, acted as Chief Justice three times. One of the 72 who founded the Indian National Congress, he was an outspoken social reformer who renounced in 1918 the knighthood he had received in 1900. Chief Justices becoming Vice-Chancellors was an early Madras University tradition. The first Indian to serve as Vice-Chancellor for some length of time was Sir P S Sivaswami Aiyar, who took charge in 1916. But the University's golden age was undoubtedly when Dr Sir A Lakshmanaswami Mudaliar served it from 1942 to 1969, a record 27 years. Sir Sivaswami Aiyar, in 1928, became the first President of the Madras Neo-Malthusian League. The League, deriving from the Hindu Malthusian League founded 1882 by Gazulu Lakshminarasu Chetty and others, had been founded by Sir Vepa Ramesam and was the first lasting movement in India to advocate "birth control".

The main buildings of the University, mentioned above, are in what is called the Chepauk campus. A neighbouring campus houses the Ramanujan Institute of Advanced Mathematical Studies. A third campus, called the Marina campus, was home to the University's Examination Hall and is now the Oriental Research Institute – for the study of the South Indian vernaculars. The main building here is another Lutyen-ish example of Indo-Saracenic styling. It is south of Presidency College and was built in 1930. The University has five other campuses: The Guindy campus adjacent to the AC College of Technology and the College of Engineering and home to the Science departments from 1944; the Taramani campus where the Dr. A.L. Mudaliar Post Graduate Institute of Basic Medical Sciences; the Chetput campus that's devoted to Physical Education and sports facilities; and, from around 1967, the Maduravoyal campus, the home, in a suburb, of the Field Research Laboratory for the Centre for Advanced Studies in Botany. These eight campuses house 17 Schools with 68 postgraduate teaching departments.

Dr.A. Lakshmanaswami Mudaliar had dreamed of a postgraduate institute of basic medical sciences during his tenure as Vice-Chancellor. But it was not to be, till he passed away in 1969. No sooner Dr.Malcolm Adiseshaiah became Vice-Chancellor, he revived the idea and appointed Dr.A.Venugopal, the illustrious doctor son of Dr. A.L. Mudaliar, and a pioneer in Urology in India, who established in 1967 the country's first dedicated Urology Department in Madras Medical College, as Honorary Director to see the project through. The Institute was inaugurated in 1969 and has not looked back since, only expanding over the years and moving into its Taramani campus as it expanded in 1976. Today it bears the name of the visionary who had wanted it established. It was under Dr.Venugopal's leadership that department after department was established in a couple of years, starting with the Department of Medical Biochemistry and followed by Departments of Endocrinology, Genetics, Microbiology, Pharmacology, Physiology, Environmental Toxicology, Anatomy, and Pathology. It is today considered one of India's leading research centres.

The University, which once granted degrees to students from all the colleges in the Madras Presidency, now confers undergraduate degrees only to students from 127 affiliated colleges in Madras and two adjacent Tamil Nadu districts. Postgraduate degrees are conferred on its own students and any from affiliated colleges that might have postgraduate departments.

A little past the Chepauk campus and before the Marina campus is tree-shaded Lady Wenlock Park, with its ancient county-style pavilion, that is the local headquarters of the Boy Scouts and Girl Guides movement. It was in the 1980s saved from some bright government spark's dream of building here another inelegant government edifice like *Ezhilagam*, which, across the way from *Senate House*, has, since the mid-1960s, blotted out Chepauk Palace.

Buckingham Canal, dug to relieve a famine disaster...now a waterway in ill-kept disuse in its urban stretch.

*Indo-Saracenic at its best...*Senate House, *once pride of a University campus where Victoria still has a place (statue, centre).*

19. *Chisholm's embellishments to Chepauk Palace... including the imperial tower he built, to join the Du* Hall, *which he transformed into the Revenue Board Building (on left), with the Palace,* Khalsa Mahal right). *The Palace's insides were gutted by a fire in 2012.*

20. Ice House *on the Marina...where ice was stored and Swami Vivekananda (statue) later slept. Now renove* as a museum in his memory.

The first Scout camp in India was held under the banyan tree in the Theosophical Society gardens in Adyar on October 1, 1916. Two scouts associations and a girl guide association emerged in the years that followed, but were merged in 1950 as the Bharat Scouts and Guides. The Lady Wenlock Park headquarters of the Bharat Scout Movement had originally been developed by Governor Wenlock in the 1890s as a park for "*Gosha* ladies" but was leased to the Boy Scouts Association in 1924 on the orders of Governor Viscount Goschen. Annie Besant, beturbanned to suit her role, played a significant part in getting Indian scouting underway. With scouting in India no longer the lively activity it was, there was a question about whether the lease would be extended in 1999, but when it was, a deteriorating campus was given a new lease of life and began refurbishing itself.

Lady Wenlock Park owes in 1890s origin to the Governor's lady of that name. She had it developed with a clubhouse and *gosha* (ladies to meet and enjoy both company, and environment in seclusion. A statue of Annie Besant was raised nearby.

Another building of an earlier age on The Marina – though now a far cry from its original shape – is *Vivekananda Illam*, once known as *Ice House*, for here, in its vaults, used to be stored ice that was imported all the way from the USA!

3. When the icemen cometh

The famous 19th Century American essayist, Henry David Thoreau, was undoubtedly being fanciful when he wrote, "The sweltering inhabitants of Charleston and New Orleans, of Madras and Bombay and Calcutta, drink at my well ... The pure Walden water is mingled with the sacred water of the Ganges..." But that Walden's waters came to India's Presidency towns in his day is no idle fancy. *Ice House* in Madras attests to the fact and is a monument to the resourcefulness of New Englanders, the original Yankees, who turned a pretty penny from frozen water.

Ice House is not a particularly attractive building. In fact, standing alongside several handsome buildings that line the Marina, it appears positively out of place. To all intents and purposes, it was built like a block of ice, topped with a curved 'tower'. It once had a flagstaff standing tall over it and from which flew the only 'Stars and Stripes' in the Madras of the day. A pillared and parapeted portico was a part of the frontage and a carriageway swept upto it. The original entrance portico was, sometime in the building's history, embellished and moved 90 degrees to its right. This repositioned portico could be seen only behind the protective walls. A renovation in 2016-17 has brought a portico back to its original sea-facing position.

During earlier reconstruction, a bulky, even more curved sea-facing side was added to the building and swept back along the sides, making it look a Victorian dowager. In the 1880s, a second curved storey was added to the bustle and the sides and opened to sun and air with scores of arches. Windows to close the arches were still later additions, when it became a widows' hostel. Whatever its appearance, *Ice House* is a memorial to a quaint little part of Madras history. When it was built, the only thing between it and the Fort, two miles away, was Chepauk Palace. And across from it was Madras's magnificent beach.

Ice House, specifically built to store ice, was the work of Major J J Underwood. He chose a Syrian-style of construction for the domed roof using earthenware cylinders instead of timber which would absorb moisture and rot. He used the same technology for the Madras Medical School (later College) building he constructed. He was also the architect of the Lodge of Perfect Unanimity's building, now the Police headquarters, on the Marina.

It was on this beach, north of where *Ice House* came up, that Admiral Mahé de la Bourdannais of France landed his Marines and marched on Fort St George in 1746. The Fort surrendered without much ado after a few shells were fired over its walls and the Admiral, after bickering with Dupleix, the Governor of French, Pondicherry made off with some ransom and booty and left Madras to its fate. Dupleix, repudiating the La Bourdonnais agreement, thereby foregoing the ransom to be paid for Madras's restoration to the English, took charge of it for France and held it for three years.

It was after the restoration of Madras to the East India Company in 1749 under the Treaty of Aix la Chapelle that its modern development began. And part of that development was the luxury of ice – to cool a drink or preserve food. That *Ice House* – meant for its storage – should have been located by the beach is understandable; the imported ice blocks – duty-free, at least in the first years of the trade – could be quickly taken from ship to warehouse given its location. The ice from the holds of the clippers would first be taken to the shore in the *masula* boats. Then the huge blocks would be carried on the heads of porters across the beach sand to *Ice House*.

The *Ice House* building seems to have been built in 1838 by public subscription and was leased by Government in 1845 to the Tudor Ice Company for its 'depot in St Thomé' that is mentioned in Higginbotham's *Madras Guide* of 1875.

Tudor's was the pioneer of the ice trade not only in India but, probably, the world over. The original lease, given to Tudor's Agent-in-charge, Andrew Bancroft, was for 20 years and was extended in 1865. Ice in those days was sold at 1¼ annas[2] a pound[3], "terms cash"!

Frederic Tudor of Boston was a 13-year-old attending a birthday party on a freezing winter's day when he was struck by a casual remark by his brother William who wondered why the ice in the ponds around Boston could not be "harvested" and sold in the West Indies. Acting on the idea, Frederic exported a shipment of 130 tons of ice to Martinique not long afterwards. But the $ 10,000 cargo melted before arrival. Refusing to give up, Tudor continued to work on establishing an ice trade that would help "render a beverage... or tepid water...palatable." He worked on getting the blocks cut into uniform size, then on preventing the blocks from melting. It was a friend, Nathaniel Jarvis Wyeth, who came up with the idea of wrapping the ice "in felt and sweet smelling pine sawdust."

The discovery that sawdust would prevent ice melting was the making of Tudor's business. Ice was harvested every winter from the frozen ponds that dotted New England. At other times, Labrador icebergs would be worked by the crews of the ships. Thoreau once described the "ice harvesters" at work at Walden Pond: "A hundred Irishmen, with Yankee overseers, came from Cambridge (Massachusetts) every day to get out the ice. They divided it into cakes...and these, being sledded to the shore, were rapidly hauled off to an ice platform, and raised by grappling iron and block and tackle, worked by horses, on to a stack... They told me that in a good day they could get out a thousand tons, which was the yield of about one acre."

---

[2] An anna in the pre-decimal era was one-sixteenth of a rupee.
[3] A pound was approximately 455 grams.

It was in 1833 that Tudor sent his first iceship to India. The clipper *Tuscany* arrived in Calcutta on September 6th, with 180 tons of ice that remained intact in blocks after the four-month journey. Tudor's partner William Rogers was permitted to land his cargo without delay and without duty. The huge profit Tudor made from the immediate sale of this consignment led to the establishment of a Tudor Ice Company branch and depot in Calcutta.

The Company opened branches in Madras and Bombay by the mid–1840s. The Calcutta address is believed to have been Hare Street, the Bombay address Marine Street and the Madras headquarters address, 30 years after Tudor's had first moved into *Ice House* and when it had become merely a depot, was Gen. Patter's Road. Ice could be obtained from here and American apples as well – "from 6 am till 9 pm and after these hours for medicinal purposes alone." Trade was busy at 4 annas (25 paise) a pound of ice.

One of the ships that brought ice to India was the 696-ton *Arabella*, one of the largest merchant vessels of the time. She made two voyages to India, carrying ice and other goods, in the 1850s. The *Arabella* was named after Arabella Rice, daughter of one of the ship's co-owners, Capt. Robert Rice of Maine. This ship was the subject of a sketch by Rosamund Tudor, grand-daughter of Frederic Tudor. Her daughter, well-known American children's book author and illustrator, Tasha Tudor, herself had done a water-colour of the 'Madras Ice House' as seen in its heyday. This sketch was based on the original which is in the Baker Library Historical Collection at Harvard University's Business School.

The Tudor Ice Company prospered in Madras for nearly 40 years. In fact, the export ice trade of the northeastern States of the US was as much as 150,000 tons of ice a year in the 1850s. But when mechanical refrigeration was invented in America in 1834, it was only a matter of time before the trade of Tudor and his ilk would be threatened.

When the Madras Ice Company and the International Ice Company were established in Madras in 1865 and 1874 respectively, "to manufacture ice by steam process", Tudor's did not feel endangered. But, in 1886, the South India Ice Company and then the Crystal Ice Company – later, the South Indian Royal Ice Company — both in the Egmore area, set up business and the death knell of the Tudor Ice Company was rung.

After *Ice House* fell on lean days with the import of ice coming to a stop, it was bought as a residence by an advocate, Bilagiri Iyengar, who named it *Castle Kernan* after a Justice of the Madras High Court who had acted as Chief Justice in 1885 (James Kernan). On his return from the West in February 1897, Swami Vivekananda stayed here for nine days and addressed crowds daily in different parts of the city. It was here that the Ramakrishna movement in South India was started by a fellow disciple, Swami Ramakrishnananda.

It was during Swami Vivekananda's visit to the city in 1892 that Alasinga Perumal, later to be a professor at Pachaiyappa's College, and his friends met the Swamiji at a meeting he was addressing at the Triplicane Literary Society and urged him to represent Hinduism at the Parliament of Religions. When Swamiji agreed, it was Alasinga Perumal and his friends who collected funds for Swami Vivekananda's travel to and, later, for his stay in the U.S. It was this group that also helped Swami Ramakrishnananda to establish the Mutt in Madras.

In 1907, *Castle Kernan* was auctioned to settle the dues of a bankrupt Bilagiri Iyengar who had died five years earlier. The Mutt perforce had to move to an outhouse and then to a house in Mylapore till it bought its present site nearby and built its permanent home. After the Marina property passed through a couple of other hands, it was acquired by Government in 1930.

Sister Subbalakshimi rented it in July 1912 as a widows' home, Sarada Ashram, and this home for child widows was there till 1928 when she handed over the ashram to the Ramakrishna Mission and they moved it out; it is now in T'Nagar. Lady Willingdon Teachers' Training College had, meanwhile, been founded next door in 1922/23 and *Ice House* became a hostel of the College from 1930 till 1941. This college was in 1988 renamed the Lady Willingdon Institute of Advanced Study in Education. *Ice House* continued as its hostel till the 1990s, its condition dilapidated, its cream paint peeling. But those who stayed there were more touched by the grace of Swami Vivekananda – whose statue nearby, inaugurated in 1964, is almost hidden – than the convivial warmth thoughts of the clinking ice might generate.

It was in 1963, at the beginning of the Swami Vivekananda Centenary, that Government ordered the building to be called *Vivekananda Illam*. And since then, on every January 12th, the Swamiji's birthday, local

Bengalis have come to pay homage in the building. In 1997, Government gifted the building to the Ramakrishna Mission which has, since then, restored the building and created a museum, art gallery, library and centre of meditation in the premises. A further restoration was done, as already mentioned, in 2016-17. But restoration or not, its ice house links are still remembered. Ice House Road, which ran adjacent to it is now Annie Besant Road and her statue adorns the junction, but old habits die hard, and road and building remain *Ice House*-linked.

Of more recent times are the workmanlike buildings of many colleges and government offices on this stretch, one or two horrific! Exceptions are the new offices of the Slum Clearance Board, whose architecture is slightly out of the PWD ordinary, and the buildings in the Queen Mary's College campus, which are of some vintage.

Queen Mary's College – the Madras College for Women when it opened in July 1914 – was the second women's college in the South and Madras's first. It became Queen Mary's College for Women in 1917 and the bust of the Queen, whom the College honoured in its name, is still prominently displayed.

It was Sir P S Sivaswami Iyer, then holding the portfolio for Education apart from several other subjects, who requested Governor Pentland to start a Government women's college and on April 5, 1913, submitted a minute to Pentland formalising his request. Sir Sivaswami Iyer also suggested that the college be named after Queen Mary – that was done only in 1917 when he was Vice Chancellor of the University of Madras (1916-18) – and that Dorothy de la Hey be appointed its Principal, an appointment that was to last till 1937 when she retired. Succeeding her was Miss Myers. Then, in 1946, Nallamuthu Ramamurthy became the College's first Indian Principal. She was the sister of Dr. Muthulakshmi Reddy.

The College has, over the years, followed the example of its founder-principal, Miss Dorothy de la Hey, and played a significant role in the emancipation of women in South India. But it beginnings were small. It opened with just 37 students in what had been known as *Capper House* Hotel. Col Francis Capper's once-beautiful isolated house, the first on the Marina, was a run-down hotel on the verge of closure when Government first rented, then, in 1915, acquired the building and its 14 acres to which 16 acres were later added and made it both college and hostel. Capper was a soldier and geographer and it is significant that QMC remains one of the few colleges in India paying more than passing attention to Geography.

Capper House, facing QMC's eastern gates, was pulled down in 2002, but the other buildings in the 17 acre campus have fortunately survived a plan in 2003 by former Chief Minister Jayalalithaa to pull them down and build a new Government Secretariat and Legislature. A sit-in protest by girls displaying the spirit of Miss de la Hey, and public interest litigation, led to the abandonment of these plans. Now there remain on the campus: *Pentland House* built in 1915, *Stone House* (1918), named after Sir Henry Stone, the Director of Public Instruction, who sanctioned it, and *Jeypore House* (1921) towards which the Maharajah of Jeypore contributed Rs.1,00,000 by Edward Elliot's Road, *Beach House*, used as staff quarters (*Beach House*, built by Justice Sir S Subramania Aiyar when he retired from the High Court, was the first private Indian residence on the Marina); and opposite it the slightly younger bungalow that belonged to Justice Sankaran Iyer.

Sir Subramania Iyer was the first to receive an honorary doctorate from the University of Madras and he was also its first Indian Vice-Chancellor, a post he resigned from. *Beach House* hosted every Saturday from 1888 to 1891 at 11 am the eponymously named Saturday Club where the leading members of the Madras Bar used to critically analyse cases where verdicts had been given.

Beach House and this bungalow were bought by the College in the 1920s, a little after most of the other buildings on the campus had been built in classical style, harmonising with *Capper House*, through the efforts of Miss de la Hey, and Lord Pentland. Both houses are under threat, to be pulled down. *Capper House* itself has been replaced with a building of indeterminate style, though vestiges of the past are discernible. This building, now 'crowned', is called *Kalai Maligai*. Named *Kalaignar Maligai* at the time of inauguration, the last four letters in the reference to the Chief Minister in whose time it was built, were removed over in the next Chief Minister's time.

The college, in 1931, built a swimming pool, the first for women in Madras. But swimming today seems an activity of the past.

4. Beyond education

At Marina's end, a little before San Thomé, are the offices of the Director General of Police, originally built as a Masonic Temple by one of the oldest English orders in India. Constructed in 1839 at a cost of nearly Rs 25,000, this handsome building, replete with Masonic symbols, was the home of the Lodge of Perfect Unanimity till 1856. Umdat-ul-Umrah, Prince of Arcot, was the first Indian to be admitted as a Mason in Madras. All the freemasons of Madras, whatever their Lodge, now meet in the Freemasons Hall off Commander-in-Chief Road (Ethiraj Salai), inaugurated in 1925 on the banks of the Cooum River. Here there is a treasure trove of Masonic memorabilia exhibited from time to time.

The Madras Police was formalised as a service in 1858 and its Headquarters moved in 1865, on rent, into what had been the Lodge. The building was acquired by the Government for Rs 20,000 in 1874. After the Criminal Investigation Department was formed in 1906, the building was extended in 1909 to house the Department and got its present elongated and pillared presence. A further sympathetic extension was added some years later. Behind this lengthy building there used to be a rifle shooting butt in the early years of the 20th Century. And before it the Mounted Police, resplendent in their uniforms, did sentry duty after the unit was formed in 1926.

Police headquarters was threatened in 1993 with demolition – and replacement with a ten-storey building – but conservationists went to court and won a stay, the first positive action by a heritage movement which began to emerge only in the 1980s. When there was a change of government, the new Government ordered the restoration and the work was completed by the Police Housing Department in 1998 at a cost of Rs 15 million. Today, it is an ornament on the Marina and is a cynosure of all eyes when lit up at night. It also was further extended with another long, pillared block in sympathy with the rest. A parallel block in the same style was built to the west of it, as promised, and inaugurated in 2012.

The last major building on the Marina before San Thomé is the All India Radio Station. The station first moved into new buildings on the Marina in 1954 and these buildings survive to the rear of the present handsome building, with its enormous doorway and tall-pillared entrance, a tribute to Chola Architecture, into which the station moved in 1963.

This construction is, perhaps, the first modern attempt in Madras at going back to traditional Indian style architecture.

The first broadcasting service in India was provided by Carnavalli V Krishnaswamy Chetty, a Manchester-trained municipal electrical engineer, and his Madras Presidency Radio Club in 1924, just four years after the Marconi Co's programmes in Europe and two years after the BBC. Generous patronage was provided by G T Boag, the Corporation's Commissioner. The Club's station was inaugurated at *Holloway's Gardens*, Egmore, on July 31st and the first radio broadcast in India made. When the Club had to wind up in 1927 due to financial difficulties, Krishnaswamy persuaded the Municipal Corporation to run Madras broadcasting as a Municipal Service. Which it did from 1929 in its 'home', *Ripon Buildings*, the transmitter located near the Zoo. The Municipal Service ran for over eight years, till All India Radio opened its Madras Station in June 1938, in Marshall's Road, Egmore. The handsome 'garden house', *East Nook*, in which a 250-watt medium wave transmitter was installed and inaugurated by Governor Lord Erskine, remained its home till 1953 but has now made way for modern highrise and the station itself is on the Marina. In 1977, the country's first ever regular FM Service was broadcast by this station. Krishnaswamy's transmitter had long before found a niche in the Madras Museum.

The Marina, across from all this development, is no longer what it was – no matter the fun-place evening crowds try to make it, particularly on holidays, with Kaanum Pongal Day, January 16th or 17th, witnessing a sea of humanity obliterating the sands. The beach atmosphere today is more mundane than what it was. The beach is dirtier and a rash of food and trinket stalls on the sands have only made the beach more fair-like and trashy, but an equanimity not found elsewhere in Madras still prevails closer the gardens and roads. Here, modern matter-of-factness today tastelessly mingles with the gracious products of a more elegant age – and, in the process, it may be, rather tragically, overwhelming the past. But there is still a peace and a quiet and stateliness about it that is hard to find anywhere else in the City. Especially in the early morning, when elderly strollers gather to reminisce about another age, ignoring more modern joggers and sportsmen in training.

Bathing in the waters lapping Marina Beach, however, is not advised at the best of times, but there is the foolhardy – or the deep paddler –

who occasionally courts danger. And danger it is that they court here, for cyclone wrecks provide lurking traps. Over the centuries, cyclones, with windspeeds of 65-125 km and more, have taken a toll of ships, but that of November 1966 was one of the worst. Four Liberty ships awaiting cargo were blown out to sea. Then one crashed on the Aga Light breakwater in Royapuram and broke in two. Another beached closed to it. A third beached opposite Fort St George and the *Stamatis* was blown aground once, then, in a second cyclone a few days later, a second time on to Marina Beach opposite the PWD offices. For several years, the *Stamatis* remained one of the sights of Madras, till the shipbreakers took over. Eventually, finding the buried keel too much for them, they left it where it was – and the whirlpools it forms still take lives on this stretch of the beach.

5. The majesty of Chepauk

Among the buildings on the Marina, the most historic and still very striking – at least that part that can be seen – is *Chepauk Palace*, which belonged to the Nawabs of the Carnatic until the Government dispossessed them of the property in 1855. Chepauk Palace and Gardens were eventually bought by the Government in auction for Rs 5,80,000 in 1859. Since then, it has mundanely housed ill-kept Government offices!

When Day acquired his Madras, all the land around his acquisition was part of the Vijayanagar Empire's Carnatic. Seven years later the Carnatic came under the sovereignty of the victorious Sultan of Golconda, who, in turn, was defeated by Aurangzeb and the Mughals. In theory, the Wazir at Hyderabad governed the South, through his *nazims*, for the paramount power in Delhi. But as the Mughal Empire disintegrated, the *nazims* of the Carnatic became a law unto themselves and the feuds between the *nazims*of the Deccan and the Carnatic (a bit more than the present Tamil Nadu) led to the Carnatic Wars, with the French and the British backing rival claimants to the Nawabi governance of the territory.

British triumph led to Muhammad Ali Wallajah becoming the Nawab of the Carnatic (1749-1795), whereupon he sought a permanent residence in Madras, preferably in Fort St. George itself. Instead, it was suggested that he build under the protective shadows of the Fort. Chepauk Palace – some say designed and built by Paul Benfield, a Company engineer always in trouble till he quit and became a building contractor, and who later acquired international notoriety as chief moneylender to the Nawab, an activity that, in retrospect, helped land the Carnatic firmly in the lap of the British and set them on the course of empire – was the outcome in 1768. By 1770, the Palace grounds were 117 acres in extent. It was this palace that undoubtedly pioneered the Indo-Saracenic architectural style, later followed by 'Mad' Mant, Robert Chisholm, Henry Irwin and others and which culminated in Lutyens' and Baker's New Delhi of the 1930s. The architectural development of the Palace is, however, one of the most intriguing mysteries of Madras, so little documentation traceable and so much guesswork being made possible.

Today, the Palace is much hidden and even less cared for. But till the 1950s, it was undoubtedly the most striking landmark in the city and would still be if all the post-1960s additions were removed and the buildings restored. What a viewer would then see would not be the original Chepauk Palace but what it had been transformed into over a hundred years by various architects and PWD engineers.

The original palace was just two buildings, the northern *Humayun Mahal* and the southern *Khalsa* (or *Khalas*) *Mahal*, the former a single-storey building with a large central Durbar Hall whose domed roof soared another storey high, the latter two-storeyed, smaller domed and built in 1764. When Government decided to use *Humayun Mahal* as the Revenue Board Offices, the PWD began haphazard work on altering it. But then came Governor Lord Francis Napier determined to create an awe-inspiring imperial vision in an Indian style and decided that Robert Chisholm was the man for it. So began the transformation of it from 1868 till 1871; the *Khalsa Mahal*, however, was little touched and remained so till fire consumed its interior in 2012. Restoration was completed in 2017 and work began on Humayun Mahal.

Khalsa Mahal, which was popularly called 'The Palace', was home from 1859 to what that year became the Civil Engineering College and then the College of Engineering and, even earlier, to the PWD, till they both got their own buildings. *Khalsa Mahal* had elaborate entrances in the west and south and Chisholm's grand entrance east of *Humayun Mahal* undoubtedly drew inspiration from them.

With the decision to leave *Khalsa Mahal* as it was, Chisholm got down to work on *Humayun Mahal* between 1865 and 1871. He brought down the roof of the Durbar Hall and added a Madras terrace-roof to the ground floor and raised a first floor following the contours of the ground floor, providing additional rooms and corridors for government offices around a courtyard that the ground floor roof provided. He then brought it all together with a palatial façade with Islamic overtones, inspired by *Khalsa Mahal*. A part of this is what is now visible from Wallajah Road. And to give the complex a more visible presence as the pride of the Marina, he built a magnificent, minareted east-facing entrance which led visitors into *Humayun Mahal* after they passed through what became known as the Records Office, a square block facaded like its neighbour and whose east face centre hosted the entrance. *Khalsa Mahal* and this grand eastern entrance were linked by an overbridge.

Sadly, what is most strikingly visible now is the 75-foot tall, square minareted and domed tower designed by Chisholm and built to link the *Humayun* and *Khalsa Mahals* as part of this transformation. It was a tower built ostensibly for the storage of records (it once did have shelves within) but in fact was meant as a symbol of post-1857 imperialism. Work on the Records Tower, as it was called as an excuse for raising it, was completed in 1870.

Over the years that followed, several other buildings came up in the campus, most of them not faithful to Lord Napier's Indianised imperial vision. But then, after the 1960s, worse was to follow; large new Government buildings (*Ezhilagam,* one of them is called) came up on the eastern and northern sides hiding the splendid entrance and much of the northern façade of the Revenue Board's Office, and another new building (for the Land Survey Department) was added in the northwest, all of them far from being in harmony with the old.

In its heyday, the grounds of Chepauk Palace stretched from what is now Bell's Road to the beach, from Pycroft's Road to the Cooum River! Indeed an area fit for the elephants once stabled within the grounds and which were bathed in a tank where the Ice House Police Station has now come up, Yanaikulam (Elephant Tank) is a name still in use in the locality. And the whole area was surrounded by a wall with the main entrance in the northwest, a massive triple-arched gateway located on Wallajah Road, near where the canal was later dug. Music once used to be played of an evening on the top storey of this *Naubat Khana*. If memory serves me right, it was standing c. 1940s – but without music playing. Since it does not figure in records of Chisholm's work, it could well have been a Benfield creation, particularly as it opened out on the Palace.

Alleged treason on the part of the Nawab Umdat-ul-Umrah, Wallajah's son and successor, who was accused of conspiring with Tippu Sultan, led to the second Lord Clive sending in the troops to occupy the palace in 1801, after the death of the Nawab. The annexation of the Carnatic (from the Nellore to the Tirunelveli Districts) followed and so did the abolition of the 'Nawabocracy'. Instead, a Titular Nawab was created, and when the last Titular Nawab, Ghulam Ghouse Khan Bahadur, died in 1855, Government made plans to make its occupancy permanent. The auction of the Chepauk property followed, Government alone being able to afford it.

The annexation of the Carnatic in 1801 – and all India followed – was a sequel of the Government undertaking to liquidate the Nawab's Carnatic Debts (Benfield was the largest creditor!) in return. Muhammad Ali's public debts were estimated at 3 million pagodas and his private liabilities at 7 million pagodas. But after the annexation, further private claims amounting to nearly £ 30½ million[4] were proffered, nearly £ 28 millions of them being thrown out as false or fraudulent!

Much of Government House Estate – which extends from the palace to the Cooum, from west of the University buildings to Round Tana – was also part of the vast Chepauk estate of the Nawabs, who were finally left with only the right, granted by the British, to be called 'Princes of Arcot'. Pensions amounting to about Rs 150,000 a year were also paid to the Prince and certain relatives from 1868. Successive governments of India to this day respect these treaty obligations. In 1870, the British decided to give the Arcot family a residence of their own. A building on Pycroft's Road built in 1798 and being used by the Royapettah Police Court at the time was sanctioned and Chisholm was asked to convert it into a palatial residence. His final design amalgamated Indo-Saracenic features with the design of *Osborne House,* Queen Victoria's Italian-style villa on the Isle of Wight, and work on it began in 1874. The Prince of Arcot lived in *Shadi Mahal* on Triplicane High Road until the move to the 14 acres of *Amir (Arcot) Mahal* in 1875.

---

[4] Pagoda about Rs 25 today; £1 about Rs 80. In those days, a pagoda and a pound were about the same, Rs 10.

The Arcot palace no longer has sentries announcing the hour while on main gate duty nor *shehnai* music entertaining passers-by of an evening, though drums are beaten on ceremonial occasions even now. Except on such occasions, it just looks deserted. But within, past a row of yesteryear artillery, there is a hive of activity in the palace and several homes in the 14-acre grounds where live the Prince of Arcot, Muhammad Abdul Ali, and 600 kin and retainers. The Durbar Hall and Banquet Hall still retain much of the grandeur of another age here, though the magnificent chandeliers are all usually wrapped in cloth to hold the cost of maintenance to Rs.100,000 a year, paid for by the Government of India which between 2009 and 2012 authorised much restoration of *Amir Mahal* and the family's private mosque.

When the Nawabs of Arcot were made the Amir-e-Arcot in 1868 by Queen Victoria they were also granted a political pension (the 'Carnatic Stipend'). That pension of Rs.14,000 a month, income tax exemption of Rs. 24,000 (both as increased in the 1920s and no doubt increased subsequently) and vehicle tax exemption, continues to this day. Protocol ranks the Prince of Arcot with a State Cabinet Minister, grants him a full police escort and allows him use of his royal crest and flag. Arcot is one of the four princely families still recognised by the Government of India with a pension and various privileges, including using their royal titles, honouring the treaties they had made with Queen Victoria, the others being Tanjore, Calicut and Oudh.

Legend has it that a tunnel used to connect *Amir Mahal* with another Arcot property in Royapettah. In this house, now garishly painted and called *Acharya Graha*, on Royapettah High Road, the Regional Provident Fund office used to function till it got its new building here. Amongst its previous owners were Justice S Subramania Aiyer, the Zamindar of Arni, and Congress associate T M Srinivasan, who entertained several Congress visitors, including Gandhiji and Tilak, here.

Neighbouring the palace, and barely recognisable now, is a tall white building on Bharati Salai called Gandhi Peak. Built in 1930 by S P Ayyaswamy Mudaliar, an erstwhile PWD engineer and a staunch Congress supporter, it hosted many a Congress leader, including Subhas Chandra Bose shortly after he founded the Forward Bloc and Rajendra Prasad. There is in the building a 1935 bust of Gandhiji unveiled by C. Rajagopalachari in 1955. A free reading room made it popular in the neighbourhood. Ayyaswamy, after retiring from government service, during which he was involved with the building of the old Adyar (Elphinstone) Bridge became a building contractor who contributed significantly to the design of the buildings he constructed in the 1930s, which included C. Rajam's India House, Curzon & Co and Chellaram's, the last two in the Round Tana area. Curzon & Co, Chellaram's and *Gandhi Peak* still stand today. Near *Gandhi Peak* was Coimbatore Krishna Iyer's famous restaurant. And in Zam Bazaar is the 125-year-old Subramania Swamy Temple.

The nearby Presentation Church, consecrated in 1848 in a 21-ground plot in Royapettah, granted by the Nawab in 1813, is sometimes called the *Wallajahpet Church*. It is, however, believed that a church, the Purification Church, existed on this site from 1769.

Also in Triplicane, off Dr Radhakrishnan Salai, is Dastagir *dargah* which, legend has it, was built by a European who became a Muslim. In fact, the tomb is that of Hazrath Shaik Maqdoom Abdul Haq Sawi, better known as Hazrath Dastagir Sahib. Descended from a Turkish family whose home was in Sawa, Hazrath Dastagir Sahib was more immediately kin of the Aadil Shahi dynasty of Bijapur, where he was born. After much travelling, he settled in Madras, but continued to travel throughout South India as a spiritual leader. He died in Hyderabad in 1752, but in time the Nawab Wallajah had his body brought to Madras for burial. And over the burial site the Nawab built a great *dargah* in 1789. Much of this holy personage's work on Sufism is preserved in the Dewan Sahib Bagh Library near the Goudia Math.

Near the Dastagir Sahib *dargah* is Sufidar, a unique temple run by the Sindhis but open to all faiths and where the prayers and practices of all religions are followed. Among those revered is Pir Dada Dastagir Badshah of Baghdad, a Sufi saint.

Not far from here is the ill-kept Lloyd's Road (Avvai Shanmugham Salai) cemetery midst slums. In it are three small enclosures, one a cemetery for the Chinese of Chennai, another the Jewish cemetery already referred to, and the third a Bahai cemetery.

6. Cricket's Madras home

Another part of the Nawab's estate is famed Chepauk (Grounds). It was once part of the gardens of the palace. With its circular boundary of tall, flowering trees, and cut off from the rest of the world by a high red brick wall, it was once one of the most beautiful cricket grounds in the world, with a sporting turf wicket. It then became a towering steel and concrete stadium, its wicket more dust than turf. But in 2010 it got another facelift and 'tents' that soared like sails gave the seating protection from the elements and gave the stadium a much more breezy and open look and the pitches began to remember their historic past. The home of the Madras Cricket Club, one of the oldest cricket clubs in India, has today become the headquarters of cricket in the State, the Club only retaining a corner and the Tamil Nadu Cricket Association looking after the rest.

Cricket came to India with the East Indiamen in the 1720s, but though Madras was the first Presidency, the game took much longer to take root here. The first cricket matches in India about which the records speak were in the 1780s, Calcutta's presently-called Eden Gardens the venue. Vansittart, a Councillor and son of an old Madras colleague of Clive the Senior, scored the first recorded century there. A Thomas Daniell painting of cricket in India done in 1792, the year he was in Madras, is possibly of The Island grounds where, it is said, the sailors introduced the game.

Alexander J Arbuthnot, a Civilian whose family played a leading part in the history of old Madras and who was to act as Governor in 1872, was the moving spirit behind the formation of the Madras Cricket Club. His memoirs state that he founded the Club in 1846. The earliest matches of the Club were played on makeshift pitches on The Island, behind where the Bodyguard Lines were, near the present Army headquarters. A tent put up for the occasion served as a pavilion, a view seen in the Daniell painting.

When the Club wanted to make its tenancy on The Island permanent in 1865, it requested Government permission to fence a piece of these grounds, 100 yards by 80. Even Alexander Arbuthnot, then the Chief Secretary, could not, as now, move the Military. Government, however, relented to a second request made by the Club Secretary, Lt J J Pennycuick[5], later the same year. Government having acquired Chepauk Palace and its vast estate, a request by the Club for a portion of these grounds was favourably viewed by the 'Governor-in-Council' who authorised the "members of the Madras Cricket Club to enclose a piece

---

[5] Pennycuick, in the 1880s, was to be responsible for what was described as "one of the greatest feats of civil engineering in India" and "the most extraordinary engineering feat ever performed," the building of the Mullai-Periyar Dam that helped irrigate what is now Southwest Tamil Nadu.

of ground on the Chepauk premises as a cricket ground..." A piece of land 150 yards by 180 was approved by the PWD Secretary and subscriptions were invited for preparing the grounds. Of the Rs 783-13- -6 raised, Rs 730 was spent by November 1865 in levelling the ground, but the scarcity of funds prevented it being fenced in. The next year, the ground was enlarged, a pavilion designed by Chisholm built from the Rs 3,700 raised by subscription, and a representative match played – against Calcutta. The first representative match the Club had played was against Bangalore in 1862 at the army grounds in Guindy.

The original Madras Cricket Club ground was more or less where the present ground is located. A history of the Club says, "The piece of ground... was bounded on the East by a road running in front of the Civil Engineering College (in the *Khalsa Mahal*), on the West by a road running parallel to this (presumably Bell's Road) and joining it a little further south, on the North by a road running from *Government House* to the Public Works and Secretariat offices (just north of what is now Wallajah Road) and on the South by a line from East to West at a distance of about 180 yards from the northern boundary..." It would appear the grounds at the time were rectangular, the longer sides to the north and south. The little red-brick, wooden-verandahed pavilion was located near the Wallajah Road-Bell's Road junction and faced east. The pitches were parallel to where Wallajah Road now is.

Despite its protests, however, the Club had to vacate these grounds in 1877 to enable the Buckingham Canal to cut through its eastern portion. Government promised that "the pond to the south of the cricket pavilion will be filled up and space will then be given for the formation of a larger cricket ground than now in use." And so, with its turf being dug up, the Club returned to The Island, where it marked time till 1879, when it moved back to Chepauk and there it has remained ever since. The new eastern boundary became Victoria Hostel Road, and the pitches till today, parallel to this road, are where the pond was. The new grounds were still rectangular, but the longer sides were now the eastern and western ones and it still retained the western half of the old rectangle where the pavilion was. The Club received a grant of Rs 2,000 from Government to level these grounds and a further Rs 2,500 to alter the pavilion. The clubhouse alterations, however, made it "absolutely unsuited for the purpose" of watching cricket, facing the southeast and the day-long glare as it did. Fortunately a cyclone wrecked this piece of folly in 1888 and it was decided to build a northfacing pavilion at a cost of around Rs 13,000.

By the end of 1891, the Henry Irwin-designed pavilion, which was in use till the 1970s, was ready for occupation, and the pavilion of 1866 was sold for Rs. 600 and demolished. With the completion of the last 'link' in the new M A Chidambaram Stadium in 1980, a similar fate befell the pavilion of 1891, kitchens replacing part of the historic old building in 1982 and badminton courts and a swimming pool the rest in 1984 and 1989, respectively. Today, only the old squash courts (c. 1899), the 'new block' for billiards (c. 1937) and a few of the old trees (particularly the one that shaded the old scoreboard) remain, the relics of a sporting past. The only other link remaining with a more leisurely age of cricket are a couple of the distinctive pillars that were part of the surrounding wall built in the 1920s. The wall was replaced by a newer one in 2012 but the few original corner pillars that survived have been retained in it. The Club, now more a social venue than a major promoter of sports, however, survives as an institution, occupying a part of a stadium and a corner of its grounds.

On Wallajah Road, between the Stadium and erstwhile Round Tana, are several buildings typical of the variety of late 19th Century and early 20th Century colonial architecture – the State Government Guesthouse, Government Estate quarters, Chellaram's, the Standard Chartered Bank's premises and Curzon's. To these have been added, since 2015, the PWD-style buildings of a medical college, hostels for medical students and nurses, on the eastern edge, huge rebuilt theatre space, Kalaivanar Arangam, more of which anon and a government VIP guesthouse that shamelessly draws inspiration from Sydney's famed Opera House.

Curzon and Co, quality furniture makers, have been at this spot on Wallajah Road since 1898, founded by Chimata Alavandan Chetty and named after a viceroy, though the present building is of the later Art Deco period. Amongst its specialities is library furniture, first built under the guidance of that grand old man of library science, the late Dr S R Ranganathan.

Of an earlier age, midst all this commercial construction, was an 1858 building, across from the Mohammedan Library, that would have been splendidly Mughal if only it had been tended at all. The little-looked-after Mohammedan Public Library was founded in 1850 as the Madras Muslim Public Library by Surgeon Edward Green Balfour, head of the

Museum and an expert in Oriental languages, and his sponsor, Nawab Ghulam Mohammed Ghouse Khan of Arcot. It had over 6,000 priceless Urdu, Arabic and Persian books and manuscripts, besides several 19th Century English publications. Despite its neglected state, its treasures drew research scholars from all over the world. Sadly, instead of renovation, the building was pulled down in 1994. It, however, got a new home on the same site which opened in 2006, but without that Islamic architectural look of yesteryear. Maintenance of the collection has now improved. Not far from here are the offices of *The Daily Mussalman,* an Urdu newspaper publishing since 1926 and still using calligraphy.

Today, though the old State Guesthouse built in the Art Deco style survives across from the Mohammedan Library, many of the other buildings in this part of Government Estate were pulled down in 2009-10 to make way for the service buildings for the new Secretariat and Assembly building raised further north on the road. But with a change of government in 2011, work that had been stalled for over a year slowly got started in January 2013 on the secretariat and assembly building, adaptive re-use as a hospital being permitted by a High Court ruling.

The hospital, a multi-speciality teaching facility is now supported by a campus of functional buildings for the medical college referred to above.

Chepauk's Lovely Cricket

Chepauk, to most citizens of Madras, not to mention all those persons in other parts of India and the world to whom first love is that game beloved of mad dogs and Englishmen, is not Palace but Cricket, 'Lovely Cricket'.

To me – and to most enthusiasts of the game as played in another, more leisurely, perhaps, even more gracious, age – cricket in Madras will for ever be associated with Chepauk's lovely sward of lush springy turf tended with infinite patience and care to billiard table smoothness by Munuswamy of old, the entire emerald oval surrounded by towering cassias and acacias, some a century old, shedding their cool shade over low, tin-roofed stands. From these stands, which did nothing to mar the English county cricket ground atmosphere of Chepauk, you could watch in stretch-legged comfort Johnstone and Ward and Nailer, Gopalan and Ram Singh and Rangachari do epic battle against each other in the annual Pongal Week 'Tests', the Presidency Match that pitted European versus Indian in many a famous contest, then team up together to do yeoman duty for Madras against the rest of India in the Ranji Trophy matches of the 1930s and 1940s. It was here that the first-ever match in India's national tournament for the Ranji Trophy was played on November 4, 1934, Madras proving victorious in a memorable 3-day game that ended in one day!

The grounds of the Madras Cricket Club in those halcyon days seemed the nearest thing this side of Suez to the cricket fields of Kent and Essex, Somerset and Sussex. Its red-washed, red-tiled pavilion with green-painted wooden trimmings, in the southwest corner of Chepauk, was the home of a club for 'Europeans only', not for Indians till 1935 when the Kumararajah of Chettinad – M A Muthiah Chettiar, at the time the first Mayor of Madras – Dr P Subbaroyan, the Yuvaraja of Pithapuram and V R Lakshmi Ratan were admitted as members, the first-named a few months before the others. It was 1947 before T Murari Naidu, an Army 'vet', who as a student got his 'Half Blue' at Oxford and played for Glamorgan, became the first Indian to play for the Club's First team. That same year, the tennis-playing Justice K P Lakshmana Rao became the first Indian elected to the committee. In 1959, A M M Arunachalam was elected the first Indian President and was faced with the challenge of a demand to government by the Madras Cricket Association for the lease of the Madras Cricket Club grounds at Chepauk. A happy resolution of the awkward situation led to the Club keeping on one lease the area around its pavilion and the Madras Cricket Association, founded in 1930 and absorbing in 1936 the Indian Cricket Federation founded in 1932, getting the rest, on another, for a stadium. The foundation stone for the stadium was laid in 1971. Till all that happened, from the 'Long Room' comfort of the Madras Cricket Club pavilion – its length measured by the long, well-patronised Bar that faced the side wide open to the pitch and its three walls faced with teak panels on which were engraved the names of European Presidency teams and those of overseas teams – members, their guests, Indian VIPs and the players watched the play in a variety of matches, from home-and-home games to Test matches. And there, too, as befitting the headquarters of Madras Cricket, many a wordy duel was fought on policy, emulating the Long Room of Lords, home of that illustrious Club, Marylebone[6], whose initials the Madras club sports. Alas, the famous clubhouse is no more, rather wantonly pulled down by a new aristocracy that should have known better but preferred other values to conservation.

Any reader seeing the painting[7] of Chepauk done by Paul Raj in 1953 for the Lord's collection of the great cricket grounds of the world may consider my word picture inadequate, but he or she will find it closer to that charming, idyllic picture than today's headquarters of Tamil Nadu cricket. But then, in those days, the grounds were, first and foremost, the home of the second oldest cricket club in India, not a business-like cricket association's.

---

[6] Pronounced 'Marleyburne'.
[7] Copies hang in the club.

As club and pavilion for the elite of Imperial Madras, these hallowed portals were not for most Madrasis; nevertheless, to that majority, Madras (or Tamil Nadu) cricket, then as now, is Chepauk and the Madras C C's "green, green grass of home". And every Madrasi's memories of cricket till the 1960s are of matches that are an inextricable part of the history of these grounds.

The first English team to visit India, G F Vernon's XI of 1889-90, was to have played here but gave Madras a miss, because of what a cyclone had done to Chepauk. It was left to a Ceylon European XI to provide the grounds its baptismal foreign presence in 1892; the Club's famed Long Room in the pavilion was also inaugurated on the occasion. But the first genuinely foreign team to, so to speak, 'open the visitors' innings' at Chepauk was Lord Hawke's side later the same year. Hawke's team was hosted by the Governor, Lord Wenlock, a past President of the Marylebone Cricket Club and still a fair club cricketer during his Madras sojourn. Wenlock and that other, more famous cricketing Governor, Bombay's Lord Harris, who made Bombay cricket what it is, opened many an innings in festive Indian cricket and demonstrated that if it were not for their status they would have been playing a more active role in first class Indian cricket of that almost all-European era.

The 'local' star of this first 'Test' at Chepauk was undoubtedly the hard-hitting E H D Sewell who represented the Presidency then and on several subsequent occasions. Sewell was later to play for Essex and still later become better known as a cricket-writer. But his most significant memory of this match was an incident involving Stanley Jackson, one of the legends of that golden age of English batting when he vied with the immortal Ranji to be called England's best batsman. Jackson, the first of the world's great players to grace Chepauk, hit a 'six' over the trees on the square leg boundary off the Presidency's star bowler. Sewell, recalling that 'six' decades later, wrote: "I have seen some 'sixers', including one over the long-leg boundary by Constantine at Lord's, but never the equal of this one for easy, effortless acquisition. The ball seemed to be persuaded over the trees, not hit." Sewell had by then perhaps forgotten his own 'sixer' on this ground, a "hit of 147 yards from hit to pitch" on a memorable February day two years after Jackson's feat. A couple of years after this 'sixer', Sewell scored 74 out of 78 in the first innings and 51 out of 56 in the second in a first class match on these grounds!

When the Oxford Authentics played at Chepauk in 1903, captaining Madras was Cantabrigian C T Studd, who had played for England in the historic Oval match against Australia that ended with an Australian victory by seven runs and the 'birth' of the Ashes (1882). Studd, in whose footsteps David Sheppard was to follow in England over half a century later, preached the Gospel in Ooty from 1900 to 1906, but could always find time for cricket. Playing for the Authentics was a remarkable all-rounder called Simpson-Hayward, who bowled underarm lobs and batted so well that his county cricket record of 3,000 runs in a season stood till 1947 when it was demolished by Denis Compton. Simpson-Hayward later played for England, but back in Madras he skittled out the Presidency twice on a rain-affected wicket.

The first team to be sent out by the MCC (London) to India was Gilligan's XI and it played on the MCC's (Madras) home ground in 1927. A 25-year-old bachelor planting in the High Range was included in the Presidency side for the one-day game against the visitors and top-scored with 48, earning an entry in Wisden, even though that venerable almanac spelt his name wrong. Right-hand bat Cowdrey was, some years later, so determined that his son should play for England that when the boy was born in Bangalore he christened him Michael Colin, thus endowing him with the initials, MCC, which the boy went on to honour! To commemorate the first visit by an MCC team, A C Hanbury gifted the Madras Cricket Club its pavilion turret clock in 1927, a landmark until the Irwin Pavilion was pulled down in 1981.

The modern era in Indian cricket commenced with the Indian team's tour of England in 1932, the same year India was admitted to the Imperial Cricket Conference. The first official tour of India by the M C C followed, Douglas Jardine's team playing a three-Test series in India in 1933-34. Their last game in India marked the debut of Chepauk as a Test centre and England celebrated the occasion with a 202-run win that gave them the rubber 2-0. Verity, with a match bag of 11 for 153, was mainly responsible for the English victory, the only Indian batsman to play him comfortably being the Yuvaraja of Patiala who top-scored with 60 in India's second innings. Amar Singh contained England's first innings with 7 for 86, but it was not enough; opening batsman Cyril Walters hit 102 in the second innings after scoring 59 in the first and Jardine got his highest score of the series with a tidy 65 in England's first innings. Even though the inventor of 'Bodyline' did not suspect it at that time, this was the last game he was to play for England; his exit from international cricket was "the price England had to pay to restore amicable relations with Australia".

Daniel Richmond, the gruff President of the Madras Cricket Club who brooked no opposition on the field or off it, was responsible for the organisation of this first-ever Test match at Chepauk in 1934, his blueprint to be followed here faithfully for the next two decades. On this first occasion, however, it was Richmond himself who was victim of his 'efficiency drive'. 'Tommies' were to do gate-duty and had been briefed by Richmond not to admit anyone without a ticket or a badge. When, on the first morning of the match, Richmond himself turned up without a badge, the 'Tommy' at the gate stood fast, despite Richmond's expostulations that he was the President of the Madras CC and of the Madras Cricket Association. Richmond had to go back home and bring his badge before he was let in – the 'Tommy' earning two bottles of beer then sent out to him by Richmond!

Jardine's easy victories in India made the MCC return to the practice of sending out only 'unofficial' sides. The last such English side to tour India before World War II was Lord Tennyson's. In the match against the Presidency, Joe Hardstaff scored 213, the highest score for Tennyson's XI during the tour. A great 98 by M J Gopalan lent respectability to the Presidency's uphill struggle in this match. But while Tennyson's team had the better of this match, they were very much at the receiving end in the 'Test' that followed, the fourth of the series. The result in this 1938 match was the first of India's several great victories on Chepauk's lively turf. Revelling in the conditions underfoot, Amar Singh for the second time in the series bagged 11 wickets, but this time it was a match-winning effort, India scoring a memorable innings victory to even the series, before losing it by 13 runs in the last 'Test'.

Soon after that Chepauk defeat, a Madras Englishman came up to Lord Tennyson in the Madras CC's 'Long Room' bar and suggested that the Englishmen had made a gift of the game to the Indians by not trying hard enough. M'Lord was furious. Later that evening, replying to the toast at the banquet held in Chesney Hall *(once upon a time in Commander-in-Chief Road), Tennyson took the opportunity to set the record straight. "India won deservedly and only 'rats' will say we did not try hard," he said, much to the discomfiture of the 'rat' who was present at the dinner!*

In this era, when Indian Cricket was still finding its feet, the 'Big Match' at Chepauk – indeed, in the whole South – was the Pongal Week Presidency Match every January 14th,15th and 16th. As far back as 1896 it was thought that it was high time a combined Indian team played a European XI to demonstrate the best cricket in the Presidency. But it was an idea more actively pursued by one of the founding fathers and captain of the Madras United Club, Buchi Babu Naidu, who negotiated the first match with P W Partridge of the Madras CC in 1908. Tragically, however, Buchi Babu did not live to lead the Indians – for, shortly before the game, he died and B S Ramulu led them. There was no follow-up thereafter and the game did not become an annual feature until 1916, when the efforts of Richmond and B S Subramaniam (Buchi Babu's trusted lieutenant) bore fruit and both led their respective teams out in what is generally accepted as the first match of a series that went on without a break till 1952. The Europeans, who were represented by players from as far as the High Range, Bangalore and Kolar, won 8 of the 33 games. The Indians, who won 15, used to occasionally field players from out of the Presidency, but with Madras connections; C K Nayudu was perhaps the best of the 'imports'.

By the 1930s, cricket in India had a sufficiently broad base to warrant a national tournament and the Ranji Trophy competition got under way in 1934, Madras playing the first match in the tournament against Mysore, naturally at Chepauk. And what a match it was, ending in an innings victory for the hosts in a single day! Madras was captained by C.P. Johnstone, of Cambridge and Kent, who won every single match he led Madras in from then till 1941 when he lost in a low-scoring game to Maharashtra. In this first game, supporting Ram Singh's devastating 11-wicket bowling, C.P. Johnstone helped bowl out Mysore on a Chepauk 'glue pot' for 48 and 50, Madras scoring 130 in between. Buchi Babu's son, C Ramaswami, top-scored for Madras with Gopalan, each getting 23. The quick result, still a record, could not have been anticipated by anyone, but Richmond was always cautious – and had insured the game for Rs 3,000! When the first day's collection was only Rs 800, the Commercial Union Assurance Company had to shell out the rest. No insurance company thereafter was willing to take the risk, and on at least two occasions thirty MCC members paid Rs 100 each to meet Ranji Trophy losses.

Ramaswami, Gopalan and Rangachari all went on to play Test Cricket, but Ram Singh's mesmerising bowling was little recognised by the Indian

Selectors, though in fairness to them it must be said that Ram Singh always played in the shadow of that other great all-rounder Vinoo Mankad. Gopalan went on to play hockey for India too.

One other foreign team played at Chepauk in this era before the War, Jack Ryder's Australians who were sponsored by the Maharaja of Patiala in 1936. In the 'Test' against them, Amar Singh hit a 'six' that landed on Bell's Road – yet his stroke was described as a "mishit"! After the War, Indian cricket took on a more professional approach – and with it, after 25 official Tests, came the country's first victory, on February 10, 1952. Hazare led India to an innings' triumph over England, a result fittingly achieved at Chepauk. Pankaj Roy and Polly Umrigar scored centuries and Mankad took 12 wickets.

Test cricket moved out of Chepauk to Park Town in 1956, as a consequence of differences between the Madras Cricket Club and the Madras Cricket Association. The big matches were thereafter played at the atmosphere-less Nehru Stadium of the Municipal Corporation of Madras on a lifeless wicket. But better wisdom soon prevailed. When the Club's 40-year lease ended in 1966, the new lease, as already narrated, was negotiated amicably by both Club and Association and Test cricket returned to Chepauk, with the West Indies playing there in 1967, towering casuarina stands coming up for the game. These temporary arrangements that enabled one of the world's most beautiful cricket grounds to remain a sylvan paradise the rest of the year were, as related, replaced by a concrete structure, with its wire fencing not very successfully 'caging' spectators unafraid of even hordes of policemen.

Forecasting such fencing indirectly, as far back as 1951, was Vijay Merchant. He was leading India against the second Commonwealth XI and had struggled to 50 in the second innings when a youngster came out to garland him. Merchant refused the garland, spoke to the boy and then asked the umpires to send the lad away. When the crowd then started barracking Merchant, he gestured to them challengingly. On second, and calmer, thought, Merchant the next day issued a statement to the Press stating such interruptions disturbed a player's concentration and that he had asked the boy to bring the garland to the dressing room after the day's play and be photographed with him. He praised the knowledgeable Madras crowd and hoped they would never have to suffer "the kind of fencing we have in Bombay to keep the crowd from encroaching on the field of play."

In the years before Independence, no one playing at Chepauk would have dreamed of playing in a fenced-in field. As C R Rangachari recalls, "No one dared to go anywhere near the boundary lines, as the European police sergeants were a terror." Just a couple of those beefy, red-faced sergeants, in their long trousers, buttoned-up tunic-coats, solar topees and umbrellas, lounging on the bottom steps or the corner chairs of each stand, were sufficient for the crowds to not only give them a wide berth but also to stay outside the boundary line. But obviously, with Independence has come a new spirit at Chepauk. And with freedom there has also come a gradual change of outlook on all matters there.

The spirit of Chepauk, however, is neither the boisterous crowds of today nor its sporting pitch, always promising a result. To most of us with memories of another day in Madras cricket, it is Rusi Modi's unsurpassed elegance while scoring 203 against the Australian Services XI in the first 'big match' at Chepauk after the War, a truly fabulous innings that would never have been if it had not been for C.P. Johnstone of Burmah Shell. It was Johnstone who was instrumental in getting down the Aussie Servicemen, led by Lindsay Hassett and marking the baptism in international cricket of Keith Miller – who will always remember Chepauk for the unforgettable catch Johnstone took off Ghulam Ahmed's bowling to get him out in the match against South India. Many still feel it is the best catch ever taken at Chepauk. That spirit is also the batting and catching of Conrad Powell Johnstone over all the years from 1934 "he bestrode Chepauk like a colossus." He played his last match in his home away from home in 1948 when he was 52, much as Richmond had done when he was 55. And that spirit is the mesmerising bowling of Ram Singh who teamed with Gopalan and Rangachari, Nailer and Ward to form under Johnstone a team that was synonymous with Chepauk and all it stood for, and who then went on to give Madras and Indian Cricket several sons, nephews and students.

The Madras Cricket Club was responsible for much of Madras's sporting beginnings. The Club not only gave Madras cricket, but it also introduced hockey to Madras in 1894 (organising the South's first hockey tournament in 1901). It also formalised squash (racquets) in 1884 (organising the first squash tournament in 1910) and tennis around the same time (organising the first tennis tournament in 1887).

R C Summerhayes of Oxford and the Madras Cricket Club hockey team may well have contributed more to international sport than the cricketers. *As the famous centre-half of the chocolate-and-golds in the late 1920s he gave Indian hockey – and the world – the push stroke, the lunged tackle and the through pass to the wing. But it was the Johnstone brigade who epitomised the spirit of Chepauk, playing a game for gentlemen and not grouches. A game to be enjoyed, not toiled at for its riches.*

There was one brief moment of that again in September 1986. Camelot returned when India picked up the Australian gauntlet and the result was only the second tie in the entire history of Test Cricket. When Australian Greg Matthew took the wicket of Maninder Singh with the scores level after five days of high scoring and only one ball left in the game, history was made once more at Chepauk, and cricket became lovely cricket again for a day.

Lovely cricket was to be seen for a day, rather, a day and a night in 1997[8] and that was when Saeed Anwar scored a world record 194 to help Pakistan beat India and take it into the Independence Cup Final. The spirit of Chepauk was once again seen in the way the visitors were cheered after their victory; Pakistan has never forgotten the applause.

Much of that has changed now. Ranji Trophy cricket draws no crowds to a modern stadium, Test matches a few more. Fifty-over internationals draw a crowd, topped a bit by 20 – over internationals but a packed screaming crowd enjoying a tamasha is only seen at T-20 professional league matches with international players participating. And if the Chennai Super Kings are playing at home, Chepauk's crowds are the largest and noisiest ever. But a betting scandal – inevitable, the way the game has been going and the many involved — knocked CSK out of the tournament in 2016 and 2017. They'll be back in 2018 to bring Chepauk alive again.

---

[8] Chepauk got its floodlights and first taste of day-night one-day cricket match excitement in 1996, during the World Cup.

10
The Town of Thomas

At the south end of Marina is San Thomé[1] (today a part of Mylapore), with its inspiring Basilica on a site where for 19 continuous centuries has stood some church or other.

Just before the Basilica on this road is the former palace of the Maharaja of Mysore, now hidden behind formidable gates. Here live the representatives in Madras of Russia. Their trade representatives too work in a palatial location – their modern, functional building having come up on the site of the Rajah of Ramnad's palace in Cenotaph Road. Russian interest in San Thomé may be minimal, but the area is a part of Madras with a fascinating story 1,900 and more years old.

San Thomé owes its name, understandably, to the Saint who was named the Apostle of India in 1972 and who, it is believed, lived in the Mylapore area for 12 years in the 1st Century CE, and was buried in the beach there. Thomas the Apostle, tradition has it, built with his own hands a little chapel on the beach here. And it was at his chapel that he daily prayed and preached, the faithful fervently believe. There is, certainly, evidence that a Monastery of St Thomas, with its own church, existed here from 390.

The Arabs knew the village as Betumah, the 'Town of Thomas', in the 8th and 9th Centuries, but it owes its present name to the Portuguese of the 'Age of Exploration'. Some time in the early 10th Century, a band of Nestorian Christians from Persia are believed to have founded a Christian village here and built a church and tomb over the burial site of

---

[1] It is locally called Santhome (as in 'home'). The Portuguese called it Sao Thomé.

St Thomas, which site was, at the time, sacred to Christians, Hindus and 'Saracens' (Muslims) as well. That site is believed to have been his chapel.

Marco Polo, who visited the village in the 13th Century, mentions the Nestorian Chapel there and the tomb of St Thomas as well as a monastery the Nestorians had built atop St Thomas' Mount. Between 1507 and 1509, two Portuguese merchants, Diogo Fernandes and Bastiao Fernandes, paid several visits to the spot to pray at an ancient church there. From then on, other Portuguese – and always Diogo Fernandes – kept calling here and between 1521 and 1524 a Portuguese settlement grew by the site. The settlers repaired the old Nestorian chapel as well as the Nestorian monastery on the Mount during these years. They also built a new church by the side of the church near the beach in 1524. The Portuguese settlement was little more than a monastic one till the 1550s, though records of the 1540s indicate that by then it was being called Sao Thomé. Francis Xavier visited Mylapore in 1544-45 to pray at the tomb of St Thomas before sailing on to the countries of the East.

Tradition has it that the tomb of St Thomas has been opened four times – the first time just a few years after Thomas' death when a pat of blood-stained earth and bloodied lance were found in it; the second, between 222 and 235 CE, when most of the saint's relics were removed for a troubled journey that finally ended in 1258 in Ortona, Italy; the third, by the Portuguese when they were rebuilding the church over the tomb in the 1520s; and the final opening in 1729, when Coja Petrus Uscan, benefactor of several Roman Catholic institutions, including the Augustinian St Rita's Church in San Thomé, was one of the witnesses.

Between 1567 and 1582, San Thomé grew as a Portuguese settlement, and, as befitting an important trading port, it got its fort as well, pushing back from shore the ancient town of Mylapore. By 1635, when its fortifications were complete, it was a rectangular fortified town of about 850 yards along the beach and about 400 yards from east to west. Between 1635 and 1660, the Portuguese added another rectangle, about 600 yards from north to south and 400 yards east to west in western San Thomé, at its north end, and built new fortifications with four gates. The enclosed area was about twice that of Fort St George at the time. And within were seven churches.

It was in January 1606 that the Diocese of San Thomé (later Mylapore, and now Madras-Mylapore) was established at the personal request of

Philip II of Portugal to Pope Paul V, with Dom Sebastiao de San Pedro arriving in 1608 to be the first Bishop. The diocese's territory in those days stretched from Cape Comorin to Bengal and thence to Pegu in Burma, taking in Bihar as well!! With the creation of a diocese, the Portuguese chapel and the old Nestorian shrine, it is believed, were pulled down, the remains of Thomas moved from the shore to an inland resting place, and a new church, to serve as the diocese's cathedral, was built over them by the Portuguese in 1610. This long, low-roofed, red-tiled cathedral was demolished in 1894, and, in 1896, a new cathedral, the towering structure of today, was consecrated. The magnificent neo-Gothic cathedral, with its awe-inspiring spire (155 feet tall) reaching to the skies, was built on the orders of Dom Henriques Joseph Reed da Silva, a Portuguese and the Bishop of Mylapore at the time.

Excavations near this site have revealed Jain and Hindu relics. A Jain temple in the locality was probably the Sri Neminathar shrine mentioned in the 12th Century. Fearing sea erosion, the idol of this shore temple was moved to Melsithamoor in South Arcot. The Portuguese, it is stated, used the deserted temple as a fortification, before destroying it and the nearby Hindu temple.

The Diocese of Madras, on the other hand, was created as a Vicariate Apostolic in 1832, though the Capuchins had established themselves in Madras (Fort St George and surrounds) nearly two centuries earlier. The Rev Daniel O'Connor was appointed, in 1834, the first permanent Vicar Apostolic. The Church of St Mary of the Angels, established by the Capuchins in Armenian Street in 1658, rebuilt in 1692 and 1775 and enlarged in 1785 and 1837, was further developed and became St Mary's Cathedral in 1886, when the Vicariate Apostolic was raised in status to an Archdiocese. When the Archdioceses of Mylapore and Madras became amalgamated as one, the Archdiocese of Madras-Mylapore, on December 12, 1952, with a new Archdiocese of Vellore being carved out separately, St Mary's became the Co-Cathedral. The first Archbishop of the new Archdiocese was the Rev. Dr. Louis Mathias, remembered in a road in Mylapore's Boat Club area. The diocese is divided by the Cooum River, San Thomé Cathedral serving the southern half and St.Mary's Cathedral the northern half.

The earliest Archbishops of Mylapore lived, first, in the Portuguese fort and then in the compound of the Madre de Deus Church till 1672, when the French gave the diocese the Portuguese Governor's house in

San Thomé as its episcopal residence. The Mylapore Catholic Institute was later developed on this site. The Archbishops lived here, except for occasional exigencies, till 1887. Bishop Dom Henriques da Silva then moved into a property where in 1947 Stella Maris College was established. Today, the Archbishop's Palace is separated only by a narrow lane from the Basilica. This property was, in its original state, bought by the Church in 1838 after it had passed through many hands from the time it was built in 1804. It was a house that had once even belonged to Thomas Parry for a while. In 1896, just before the consecration of the Basilica, Bishop da Silva made it his episcopal palace. It was renovated and considerably expanded in 1952/3 for Dr Mathias. The handsome gates were made by the Salesian Technical Institute, then at Basin Bridge. Within were several antiquities in a Museum – that more recently were moved into a Museum to the rear of the Cathedral – and a wealth of records in its Archives. Unfortunately, the latter is not particularly visitor-friendly.

San Thomé's pride, the Basilica, is the only church in India, and one of three in the world, built over the tomb of an Apostle of Christ. Where nave meets transept, the very centre of the building, there is a crypt containing the tomb of the Apostle, over which rises the cathedral's second, and smaller, spire. The crypt, during a restoration in 2004, was made accessible only from the outside of the Church, through a tunnel that cut through many relics of the past. The new crypt that the tunnel leads to has a cinematic look to it, not least in the rather unfortunate depiction of St Thomas being martyred.

The Cathedral is 199 feet long and 33 feet wide with a 104-foot-long transept. It is 43 feet at its tallest. The Basilica was designed and its construction supervised as a labour of love by Capt J A Power, who had retired from the Royal Engineers and was a parishioner of the church.

A large stained glass window in the Basilica portrays in three panels the story of 'Doubting Thomas' verifying that his Master had truly risen. The window panels were made by Franz Mayer & Co, Munich and installed in 1870. A three-foot statue in the Cathedral of Our Lady of Mylapore, the Blessed Virgin Mary, is believed to have been brought from Portugal in 1543 by that most active of all parish priests, Fr Gaspar Coelho – making it possibly the oldest Western sculpture on India's east coast. In front of it, in the Cathedral, is Father Gaspar's tomb. Next to

San Thomé Basilica...towering over where the Apostle of India was once buried.

The crypt of St Thomas...a bone and a spearhead within a tomb immemorial.

23. *Descanco Church in the restful grove of Thomas... built by the Madeiros family (of 'Maderas'?)*
24. *Luz Church in "Portuguee Town"...oldest Western architecture on the Coromandel coast?*

the Basilica, in the same compound, is the little museum, already referred to, that tells much of this story.

Preparing for the commemoration of 1,900th year of St Thomas' martyrdom held here in April 1972, the Basilica received a facelift and much renovation. More restoration work was done in 2004. Its youthful appearance today may well suit prosperous San Thomé, but many miss the splendour of the cathedral's weather-beaten patinaed appearance of yesteryear. Be that as it may, the Basilica remains the hub, as it has been for centuries, of the thriving neighbourhood of San Thomé, where the saint's revered name graces a variety of institutions.

One of these is the sparkling white Church of St Thomas-by-the-sea, now known as the St Thomas' English Church. Set in a garden location, off the main road, it is the oldest Protestant church in San Thomé. Though the Vepery Mission and other missions had been working here from 1810, it was not until the 1840s that work began on the church. It was consecrated in 1842. The Rev Robert Carver, who was responsible for concept and creation of the church, died in 1845 and was buried beneath the altar. At one time, this was the church of the Protestant elite in Madras, the residents of the garden-houses of Adyar, with the Governor having his own pew. A separate Tamil Church was established nearby in 1848. The English Church is believed to have the oldest organ in Madras. It's an 1822 organ that came to the Church after use in Britain.

San Thomé, however, is strongly Roman Catholic. Besides St Rita's Church, Armenian funded work on which began in 1729 and ended in 1740 under the supervision of Fr Gaspar dos Reis, there are several other old churches and Roman Catholic mansions – most of them with schools in them now – in coastal San Thomé. The Church of Our Lady's Nativity (Madre de Deus or Mae de Deus) was rebuilt in 1748 and renovated in 1928 but traces its beginnings to the Madeiros (or Madra) family; it is said to have been first built in 1575, consecrated in 1576 and had Jesuit connections from 1587. It is this church and this family with which are linked two theories for the name 'Madras'. Where the original shrine was, there was built a church in the French style in 1748 and it survived till 1997 in a coconut grove, later called Dhyana Ashram. Pulled down despite protests from old parishioners, all that survive today are the former entrances to the church in the north and south walls of the Ashram. A new church, however, has been built to take its place and was consecrated in 1999.

The main entrance to this campus, a spiritual retreat with every facility, is on Matha Church Road. The Church of the Holy Rosary, on Rosary Church Road, a Dominican church, dates to 1635. Descanco Church on St Mary's Road, associated with the Thoman tradition, was refurbished by the Madeiros family in 1703, the earlier church on the site being built in the 1650s. A second church, recently built right next to the ancient shrine, further diminishes the sanctity it once inspired. Lazarus Church Road derives its name from a Portuguese-built church that was in existence in San Thomé in 1582 and which was rebuilt in 1637 by the Madeiros family. Rebuilt yet again in 1928, incorporating parts of the old Portuguese church, Lazarus Church now resembles the Velankanni shrine and was renamed in 1952 the Church of Our Lady of Guidance. Amongst the other antiquities of San Thomé is a 16th Century tombstone (in the Archdiocese Museum) inscribed, "Here lies Coja Martinho with his wife Marta Toscana and their son Diogo". Could Marta Toscana have been the Maria Toscana whom Francis Xavier miraculously cured when he visited 'Meliapor' in 1545?

A church not connected with the Thoman tradition is the church of St. John, the Baptist in Mylapore that has been cared for from 1566 by the Jesuits. Amongst the Catholic schools here are St. Bede's, Montfort, Rosary Matriculation and Dominic Savio (developed on the site of famed film director K.Subrahmanyan's 10,000 sq.ft house which he built in 1937 and sold to the school when it started in 1953). A well-known CSI School here is the school established in 1912 for those with hearing disabilities. It became a Higher Secondary school in 1947.

From the 1560s, San Thomé, enjoyed immense prosperity due to the Portuguese trade monopoly. As the years passed and the politics of the Coromandel Coast waxed and waned, San Thomé passed into the hands of Golconda, the French, the Dutch and the Carnatic Nawabs, in turn. The King of Golconda occupied San Thomé in 1662, but Portuguese settlement continued. The French ousted Golconda in 1672, but remained only for two years before being ousted by Golconda again. In 1746, the French were back again. Eventually, in 1749, the British moved in after receiving the town from the French as part of the restoration of Madras, but between 1675 and 1697 what was left of the fortifications of the town had been totally demolished by the 'Moors', egged on by the Dutch. No building in the town was, however, touched. Under the British, the village gained a new lease of vitality, with many of its citizens finding employment in Fort St George as well.

So thorough was the demolition of San Thomé's walls that their exact location is not known today. But it may be inferred that the western bounds of the old Portuguese fort of San Thomé were just a little past Mylapore Bazaar Road. In fact, the western gate was very likely on Kutchery Road (so named after the courthouse Golconda had established on this road), where it meets Arundale Street. The northern bounds were probably about where San Thomé High Road falls into South Beach Road and the southern near the Foreshore Estate-Adyar backwaters junction. The northern gate is believed to have been a little to the west of San Thomé High Road. Foreshore Estate was an area known until Independence as 'Butt Medu' (Butt Mount), where soldiers practised on the shooting range. Across from Foreshore Estate is Mandaveli, where the Maharajah of Vizianagaram (not Vijayanagar as some would have it) used to live in *Admiralty House*. A large wooden coat-of-arms of the United Kingdom was part of the decoration of the house; on the Maharajah's death, it was gifted to the Madras Club where it remains to this day. The house is recorded on this site as far back as 1892, but came into the Maharajah's possession around 1914. A forgotten connection the palace has was with film-maker AV. Meiyappa Chettiar. In his initial days of film-making he had teamed with a Bangalore-based cinema theatre owner, Jayanthilal, and they formed Pragati Pictures. Pragati Pictures leased Admiralty House as its studio in the late 1930s and remained there till 1942 when the Japanese threat to Madras had AVM moving to Karaikudi. Cinema chronicler Randor Guy describes *Admiralty House* as "a palatial building with an impressive flight of steps, tall pillars and high ceilings..." When AVM took the place on long lease, the rent was only Rs.250 a month, according to Randor!

Subsequently the house was occupied by the Admiralty Hotel, then used as the SBI Training College, a wedding hall, Sun TV studios, Murray's auction house, and nurses as their quarters. The buildings have now been adapted for a school. It would be interesting to know what the school is paying as the latest lessee.

To the southeast of the Basilica, a little further south, just off San Thomé High Road, is *Leith Castle*, a grand old garden house built on the site of the ruins of the English San Thomé Redoubt. This little fort had been built for the Mylapore Garrison in 1751, two years after British occupation of San Thomé. Relics of the redoubt existed till the 1990s in the gardens of this private residence, when modern development began and not only erased the gardens but also hid the mansion.

Military Engineer Benjamin Robins built the moated[2] redoubt in 1751 around what was called *Moore's Bungalow.* The cost was almost 6,400 pagodas (Rs 450,000 today). The redoubt, with walls 15 feet high and three feet thick, went into disuse towards the end of the 18th Century and permission to build a house on the ruins was given in 1794 to Col John Braithwaite, the hero of the third fall of Pondicherry. Thomas Parry acquired the 14½ acre property in 1796, two years after he married Mary Pearce in St Mary's-in-the-Fort. He rebuilt the house and gave it the name *Parry Castle* which survived upto 1837.

To Thomas Parry goes the honour of founding the first industrial factory (on record) in Madras. In 1805, he established a tannery in San Thomé near his *Castle,* and this gradually grew into an establishment employing 300 men and exporting its products – boots and army leather-goods – to England, the US, Australia and South Africa! Parry died in 1824 and Major General James Leith, a neighbour, is believed to have then acquired the property. Leith died in 1829. Leith's purchase may even have been before Parry's death, because the Parrys fled the house, a couple of years after they had purchased it, for the "less pungent atmosphere of Nungambakkam" and what was called *Wallace Gardens.* Both properties still survive, *Leith Castle* still a threatened private home but now surrounded by new development and *Wallace Gardens,* also private property but a money-spinner as a favourite location for film-makers.

A little further south on this road, just before Adyar River, were two other famous 'castles' – *Somerford,* adopted in the 1920s into *Chettinad Palace,* a Baroque creation by an Italian architect, it is said, and *Brodie Castle* – both on Quibble Island, the peninsular sand banks formed by the Adyar River estuary as the river flows out into the sea (an earlier branch that made it an island is no more). Also on the 'island' and taking its name is an old cemetery, well maintained and shared by the Roman Catholics and Protestants. Next to the Chettinad Palace grounds is *Underwood Gardens,* a handsome 19th Century garden house that is now home to the regional managers of the State Bank of India.

Brodie Castle, an imposing, gleaming white structure, owes its existence to Company servant James Brodie who built it with twin castellated towers between 1796 and 1798 on an 11-acre grant. Brodie

---

[2] Forty feet wide, it is said.

later fell on ill-times and rented the house to various members of the Establishment; it was the house of the first Chief Justice of the Supreme Court, and occupation by other judges followed. Brodie himself was drowned in 1801 in a boating accident on the river he so loved and his family was forced to sell the *Castle*. The ill-fated Arbuthnots occupied it for a while, then it appears to have become government property. *Brodie Castle* is today the home of the Tamil Nadu Government College of Music (now a univeristy) and is called *Thenral*. The College opened in 1945 in *Rahamath Bagh,* San Thomé, under the name Government College of Carnatic Music, Prof P Sambamoorthy setting up the college with a focus on *Tamizh Isai*. In 1951 it moved to *Bridge House*, near Thiru-vi-ka Bridge and behind the Andhra Mahila Sabha. Then, in 1956, it moved to *Brodie Castle* which became *Thenral* where the College has evolved into the Tamil Nadu Government Music and Fine Arts University in 2013. The University now hosts the Tagore Film Centre, a 100-seater, state-of-the-art screening facility.

San Thomé High Road – off which most of these 'castles' are – curves right into Adyar's Greenway's Road which, running parallel to the Adyar River, reaches Cenotaph Road and Teynampet *via* Chamier's Road and the modern 'garden houses' of executives of commercial organisations in Madras.

Many of these houses, between Chamiers Road and the Adyar, have come up on the old Moubray Estate, the first garden house property to be developed on the southern boundary of Madras, the north bank of the Adyar River. *Brodie Castle* was built a few year later. The sites for these houses were carved out of *Moubray's Gardens* after John de Monte had bequeathed it to the San Thomé Diocese. *Beachborough, Adyar House*[3] and *Ben's Gardens* are some of these houses which came up after 1816. *Ben's Gardens* was, for years, a large, treeshaded garden where the executives of Parry's lived in several newer houses. Parry's moved out of the property in 1996 at the end of its 99-year-lease and the Diocese is, no doubt, looking at upmarket development of it with commercial partners, but its attempts have been stifled by parishioners taking the matter to Court and the campus is a jungle as these lines are written.

---

[3] This is the first *Adyar House*; a mansion in Kotturpuram, to be referred to later, came up a long time afterwards.

At the end of this road is the Madras Boat Club which gives its name to both road and upmarket residential area. The Boat Club is said to have started in 1867 as the Rowing Club, its first competition being against Calcutta in 1869. Record-keeping began in 1874-75 when, it was recorded, there were 32 rowing members and 24 non-rowing members, a classification that still exists. It was in 1892 that the Club moved to its present location, where F H Wilson dominated the early regattas.

The Club elected its first Indian President, M M Muthiah, in 1967 and its first Indian Captain, K Varugis, in 1957. 'Janji' Varugis was the first Indian to row for the Club. U Prabhakar Rao was the first Indian to win the Club's sculls championship (1963).

A founder-member of the Amateur Rowing Association of the East, organised in 1933, MBC teams won the fours and pairs at the inaugural meet in Pune. Neighbouring it are the Alumni Club, started by the alumni of Guindy Engineering College and whose engineering skills have been used to develop it well, and a police commando training camp and barracks in what were once the acreage of a garden house.

Chamier's Road falls into Greenway's Road and on both halves of Greenway's Road are the 'garden houses' of today – homes of Ministers of the State Government, a few of them of earlier vintage but most of them PWD architecture of the 1980s at its worst. The first house of an earlier era on the western half of Greenway's Road, near the Chamier's Road end, is *Pugh's Gardens* – on whose site has been built a shrine and meeting place for the followers of Sathya Sai Babha, an opulent structure but rather spartan within. And then there is the historic *Grange,* now used by Government as a management school but built in 1853 by John Bruce Norton, later Advocate-General of Madras and father of Eardley Norton, the leading barrister of early 20th Century Madras.

The story of The Grange begins with about 60 acres of temple land, which appears to have been from 1803 eyed by various office-bearers of the "temples of Kadari and Kumeswara". An Alanda Narayanaswami Nayak, a rich landowner, eventually laid his hands on it. But heavy losses on speculation made him bankrupt and the Court in 1827 ordered his properties to be sold to repay his creditors. A civil servant, Leveson Murray, fourth son of the Earl of Dunmore and who lived in Murray's Gate Road, Alwarpet, became the new owner. After being owned over the years by several other eminent Europeans of Madras, this property on the Adyar finally became that of John Norton in 1852 and the next year he built his home there, the building that still survives, calling it Norton's Gardens. Norton's subsequent battle to hold on to the land became a cause célébré in Madras, with several claimants taking him to court. After all matters relating to the title were sorted out, Norton's Gardens was sold in 1865 to Alexander Mackenzie of Arbuthnot &Co. and became Mackenzie's Gardens. In 1907 it was recorded for the first time as The Grange, tenanted by Sir Murray Hammick, a Civilian who was in 1912 to act as Governor of Madras. The Maharajah of Vizianagaram appears to have been one of its many owners post-1870s. Its last private owner was P.Venkatachellum, who owned over 100 houses in Madras. Government acquired it from him in 1917 for Rs.1,56,803 to use for a Rajkumars' (Princes's) College, but that never came through. Instead, it was used by Government as residence, meeting place, offices etc., till it came back to education with the establishment of the Anna Institute of Management.

Its vast gardens are now chock-a-block with more jerry-built houses for ministers, gleaming only in their newness but a sad contrast to the solid, but, till recently, badly neglected mansion of yesterday. A crashing beam fortunately did not result in a government decision to pull down the building but, instead, to a partial restoration of it.

Another of John Norton's properties was a 13-acre one in Alwarpet with a large mansion in it that was called *Baobab* because of the numerous baobabs in the acreage. The whole property was sold to Chentsal Rao Pantulu for Rs. 26,000 before Norton left for England in 1871. Pantulu divided the property and sold off the eastern portion of nine acres, after sub-dividing it. It was three acres from the eastern portion that became the site of *The Grove* owned by Sir C.P. Ramaswami Aiyar. The western four acres retained Norton's mansion, Baobab, and most of the baobab trees till sometime in the 1930s when another lawyer, Mohammed Usman, the first Indian to act as Governor of Madras, bought it in an auction. A commercial complex called *Usman Court* has come up on a portion of this site. *The Grove* remains with a great-grand-daughter of Sir CP and a portion is used for a research foundation and lecture/exhibition venue. The CP Ramaswami Aiyar Foundation hosts here a splendid but little-used library with over 50,000 books, built around 10,000 books belonging to Sir CP and his numerous files as well as the Foundation's own strong Environment collection.

The Grove is at the junction of Moubray's (TTK) Road and Eldam's Road, and across from the latter there was once another large property, *Soundaraya*, spread over 1.3 acres. Its last owner was M. Seshadri Iyengar, one of the proprietors of M. Doraisamy Iyengar and Brothers, that had its origins in 1894 and became one of the largest timber merchants in the Presidency.

But back to Adyar, between *Brodie Castle* and *The Grange* were several garden houses on the Adyar River's north bank – *Yerolyte, Bridge House, Riverside, Hovingham, Greenway, Cherwell* and *Ardmayle,* many razed in post-Independence years and converted into homes for ministers and Government officials.

On the other side of Greenway's Road was, apart from the vast acreage of *Bishop's Garden, Serle's Gardens. Bishop's Gardens* dated to 1817 and figured in a distress sale by P V Subramaniam, heir of P Venkatachellum and better known by the latter name. The sale, in 1927, saw it being parcelled out into a few separate properties. Stanley Edwards, later to be the last European Chairman of Spencer's, was gifted 2¾ acres here by his father-in-law, J O Robinson, who paid Rs 14,750 for it. On this property, the Edwards built a 7,000 sq ft mansion, *Grayshott,* and moved in in 1929-30. Thereafter, till the Edwards left in 1957, it was a place remembered for the "memorable" parties held there every weekend. When the Edwards left, Spencer's took over the property for Rs 150,000 and when Spencer's was trying to sell the property in the 1990s, the Income Tax Department bought it for Rs 191.8 million. How property value had appreciated in 70 years! The property was acquired by a private developer in auction in 2003 and made into a residential complex after pulling down *Grayshott*.

A portion of the vast Bishop's Gardens property was bought by Annie Besant and some of his followers for the philosopher-guru J Krishnamurthi in 1929. Here, the present building was designed by architect Surendranath Kar, built by D K Telange in 1935-36 and named *Vasantha Vihar.* It was home for Krishnamurthi and his annual gatherings till litigation overtook the property in 1965. The Krishnamurthi Foundation in India re-established its right to the property in 1976 and, till his death in 1986, Krishnamurthi met the faithful here annually. In the garden, where he held his discourses, is a simple memorial to him, rough-cut rock on a patch of green.

Vasantha Vihar, the abode of spring, is a splendid example of Victorian residential-colonial architecture and is sited in six acres of beautiful gardens. Now renovated, its focal point is 'The Study' on the first floor, which houses a Krishnamurthi library and audio and video cassettes of his talks and discussions. The main feature of 'The Study' is its red girders that, spoke-like, converge on a spherical dome. On the first floor is a library with a much wider collection of books on religion, philosophy, human thought, etc. Together, the two libraries of the Krishnamurthi Study Centre keep alive Krishnamurthi's wish that people look into themselves for spiritual help.

A Little Bit of France

If only Clive had not enjoyed a couple of his nine lives at besieged Arcot in 1751, succeeding beyond Governor Saunders' fondest expectation in creating the diversion so sought after by Muhammad Ali, Nawab Wallajah of Arcot....

If only Subedar Mohammed Yusuf Khan, Stringer Lawrence's "excellent partizan" who knew well the jungle trails of Tondeman country (Pudukkottai), had not in 1754 ambushed the French ambushers lying in wait, on information received, for the food convoy he was running into besieged Trichinopoly whose existence depended on it....

If only that temperamental Irishman, O'Mullally of Tullendally, better known to history as the Comte de Lally de Tollendal of France, had moved quicker in 1758, from what is now called Parry's Corner to the ramparts near the south end of today's Reserve Bank building, as he trenched his way by inches towards a final assault on Fort St George...

If only Lally's last brilliant throw as he burst out of beleaguered Pondicherry in 1760-1 had not been so fast that his right wing, which was to sweep down from the north to take Eyre Coote's besiegers in the rear, instead wound up behind his own advance guard that was patiently waiting for the sandwich to be completed ...

In only ... If only ... If only ....so many "If onlys" in those decades from 1745 to 1814 when the Wars of the Carnatic were waged and Madras and Pondicherry were alternatively besieged and destroyed. But if only ONE of the "if onlys" had come to pass, you may well be reading this piece in French! That's how close India came to being part of the French Empire instead of the British. No Empire was created more haphazardly, no Empire ever owed its existence to more fortuitous, touch-and-go victories, than the British.

On the other hand, there may never have been a British Empire if Joseph Francois Dupleix[4], who had come out to India to make money by trade, had not, through financial necessity it has been said, become territorially ambitious in order to ensure a fixed revenue for the French in India, "which could be assured only by the exercise of political power ... creating a ... colonial empire .... where we would be practically the masters under the authority, more nominal than real, of Indian princes, who would owe their thrones or their security to us." This idea, attributed by many to 'Joanna Begum', Madame Dupleix, was, according to historian Alfred Martineau, to "change the face of India and in a certain measure that of the world." For where Dupleix showed the way, Britain followed – and more successfully.

But Dupleix's dream of Empire could never have been translated into reality without the force to back it up – and that force was that of the spahis *or* sipahis *(the sepoys), Indian troops trained on European lines. It was the French who, amongst all the European powers in India, first perceived that Indian troops could be trained to French disciplinary standards and it was the French, under the brilliant Swiss engineer-officer Paradis, who, at the Battle of the Adyar in 1746, demonstrated that a few hundred French regulars and trained* sipahis *could rout an army of thousands if the latter were untrained rabble. When Paradis routed the Nawab of Carnatic's 10,000-strong army in this battle fought in the shallows of the Adyar River and on what was later to be called Quibble Island[5], he showed Europeans for generations to come how Indians could be organised to fight for foreign powers. And so was born the idea that grew into today's Indian Army, rooted in British tradition.*

Dupleix and Paradis, however, only built on a foundation laid by a man as little remembered today as Madras's Francis Day or Andrew Cogan. Francois Martin was to French India what the two British East India Company-men were to Madras and the British Indian Empire-to-be. Pondicherry is Martin's memorial – though that "little bit of France" in India today remembers only Dupleix. Martin was one of the French pioneers in East Indian waters, following in the wake of those first French

---

[4] Pronounced 'Dewplay' by the British – and, so, by most Indians – or 'Duplex' by the French – and, so, by many Pondicherrians.

[5] Once indeed an island, being one of the half a dozen islands that existed in the Adyar Estuary till landfill made them part of the mainland.

traders in India, Francois Caron and Marcara. They were the men who sailed under Louis XIV's flag and did the bidding of that great statesman Colbert, the first French leader to realise that France was losing out in the race for the "wealth of the Indies". A French historian, Henri Martin, was, years later, to wail: "Asia would have been ours if, with Dupleix and Bussy in India, we could have (had) Louis XIV and Colbert at Versailles..."

The French entered the Indian Ocean late. The Portuguese were there from 1498, then there were the British, from the 1590s, and the Dutch from the dawn of the 17th Century. The French, however, did not venture into these waters until Richelieu sent out the first men to explore what wealth Madagascar and the nearby islands could offer France. But even then the French did not venture beyond these islands. It was only after Colbert organised the French East India Company in 1664 that the French moved into India, Caron founding the Surat factory in 1667 and Marcara the Machilipatam factory in 1669 after obtaining letters of patent from the Sultan of Golconda. One of the Directors (Factors) of the Machilipatam establishment was Francois Martin.

By this time, the British were as well settled on the Coromandel Coast as the Dutch were at Castle Geldria, Pulicat. And, after Winter's coup, prospering. Francis Day, who had scoured the coast south of Pulicat three decades earlier, had preferred the site of Madras to "Pollecheere", Kunimedu thirteen miles to its north or a Portuguese welcome in San Thomé. The Portuguese anxiety to have the British as neighbours was soon understandable. San Thomé was constantly threatened by the Dutch, who encouraged the Sultan of Golconda to attack the town on several occasions. The final Golconda attack in May 1663 left the Mussalmen with the town and San Thomé remained under their control until 1672. In that year, Admiral de la Haye and his French fleet, buccaneering in the waters between Machilipatam and the Iles de France, put into San Thomé for supplies. When the Governor refused them provisions – and, no doubt, ransom – de la Haye stormed the town and took possession. Awaiting the inevitable sequel, the French strengthened the fortifications of the town and then settled back to await the besiegers, Golconda, in quest of revenge, and, in their support, the Dutch, anxious to avenge the sufferings inflicted on them at home by the soldiers of Louis XIV.

Over the next two years, the French at San Thomé faced two sieges. Fortifying Mylapore's Sri Kapaleeswarar Temple as their western outpost and Triplicane's Parthasarathy Temple as their northern bastion, setting yet another example the European powers were to follow in later years – namely, of using the solidly built, wall-encircled Hindu 'pagodas' as miniature forts – the French beat back the besiegers. But then the Dutch took a more active hand. Their fleet blockaded the sea approach left open when de la Haye fled before the 1673-74 Monsoon, while their soldiers together with Golconda's army invested the town on the landside for almost a year. The French were thus starved into surrender. On September 6, 1674, Fort San Thomé was surrendered to the Dutch by the French, and the Dutch, in turn, handed it over to Golconda – but not before allowing the French the honours of war and permitting them safe passage to France, much to the chagrin of the Sultan, who had to be content with obtaining his revenge by carrying out the British wish that what was left of Fort San Thomé, after the Dutch had done with it, be completely reduced. Dutch and British engineers and overseers worked together from 1675 to ensure destruction of the Fort.

Martin, who had been sailing home with de la Haye's fleet and who found himself unwittingly a captain during the San Thomé siege, had, towards the end of 1673, sailed south from San Thomé and obtained a grant from the Governor of Gingee, Sher Khan Lodi, representing the Sultan of Bijapur, for a strip of coast he called "Phulcheree" (Poocheri? Pudu-cheri?). Returning to San Thomé, he led a party of Frenchmen to his newly acquired village just before the Fort's surrender. And around the village he built protective walls – and so was born Pondicherry, in 1674.

Pollecheree or Pulicheri – village of tamarind trees; Phulcheree or Poocheri – village of flowers; or just plain, simple, unglamorous Puduchcheri – new village – the French bastion has remained Pondicherry to English speakers to this day. But in Tamil, ever since Madrasis can remember, it has been Puducheri – and that is what it has officially become since 2007. Could it be that Martin's land-grant was for an unnamed stretch of land where he built a new town? But could it also have been that he cultivated the land around here so well – as some records have it – that his town came to be called, by some, the town of flowers? Whatever the reasons, the earlier names seem to make much more sense than the much later 'Pondicherry' – whose meaning is obscure, but whose existence has enabled France's impress on India to remain to this day.

Once settled in Pondicherry, Martin not only tilled the fertile soil faithfully but he also traded wisely and well, causing his 'New Town' to prosper. And to protect this prosperity he soon began training Indian recruits on European military lines. In a few years, he had made Pondicherry the most important French possession in India. But in Europe, Dutch and French enmity continued and when war between them broke out there, the repercussions were felt in India. For twelve days in 1693, Martin and 36 Frenchmen, together with less than 400 sipahis they had trained, held Pondicherry against 19 blockading, block-busting Dutch ships-of-the-line and 1,500 infantrymen they had landed to invest the 'Pride of France'. The defence was conducted as gallantly as the French had fought at San Thomé but in the end the odds proved too great and Pondicherry surrendered.

In September 1697, the town was restored to the French by the Treaty of Ryswick but the Dutch did not actually leave Martin his town till 1699. In occupation again, Martin once more made Pondicherry prosper. And so well did the town do under him that, when in 1700, as a consequence of the War of Spanish Succession, the French closed down their factories in Surat, Machilipatnam and Bantam (in the East Indies), Pondicherry continued to fly the flag of France. On December 31, 1706, Martin died in the town that was his own – and Pondicherry caught the malaise of the other erstwhile French settlements. But when the French East India Company was reorganised as the 'Perpetual Company of the Indies' in June 1720, Pondicherry's situation improved. From then, until 1742, two active governors blessed with the sagacity of Martin restored Pondicherry to its earlier glory. Lenoir and Dumas not only developed their enclave in today's South Arcot District, but between 1722 and 1723 acquired Mahé (enclaved today in Kerala's Cannanore District) and Yanam (enclaved today in Andhra's East Godavari District) and, in 1739, Karaikal, enclaved today in Nagapattinam District and the last reminder of France's struggle for Tanjore and Trichinopoly.

The development of Pondicherry, the establishment of new factories by acquisition through grants, were in this period solely motivated by commerce, though Dumas, to protect France's possession, recruited and trained 3-4,000 Muslim mercenaries. The first real recruitment of Indians by European powers intent on building up an army, Dumas' troops were the embryo of the Sipahi (Sepoy) Army that was to grow into today's Indian Army. Then, along came Dupleix, the ambitious and flamboyant

Governor of Chandernagore (near Calcutta) who was asked to succeed Dumas. And, of course, Joanna Begum, the Madame Jeanne Dupleix, the San Thomé Tamil-Portuguese-French beauty with a mind Machiavellian, if you are to believe contemporary accounts. Together they viewed France's role in India in a fresh light and ruthlessly pursued a political approach that was to lead to the Carnatic Wars and, unexpectedly, the emergence of Britain as the paramount power in India.

When Dupleix, the son of a wine-merchant, took over Pondicherry from Dumas in 1742 he was fifty, with almost thirty years of service in India. Small-made, hard-working but grandeur-loving, he had entered the Company's service to make his fortune. In India, he had married the multilingual Jeanne Vincens, a widow, whose eldest of three daughters by her first marriage was Marie-Rose de Barneval, wife of a Councillor at Fort St George, a neighbour of Petrus Uscan's and a girl said to be more beautiful than her mother. It has been held by many that Jeanne Dupleix, even more ambitious and avaricious than her husband, showed him that the way to Empire lay in playing off local Nawab against local Nawab, a game the pair called "Le Grand Jeu" and in whose cause the Creole beauty did not hesitate to use her daughter's looks and charms. But that path did not need much pointing to Dupleix. He arrived in Pondicherry to succeed to the honours Dumas had earned for himself.

Dumas and Dupleix saw more clearly than other Europeans of the time that the doom of the Mughal Empire loomed large in the not too distant future. That Empire in the south was, at most, a loose federation of mainly hereditary, ever-squabbling local chiefs and governors, often threatened by independent Hindu chieftains. Dupleix saw that, if he played the political game right, untold wealth and honours awaited him. The only hindrance to his dreams he saw as the English in Madras whose masters were fighting France in Europe. In 1746, he marched into Madras and was to remain there till 1749 when, under the Treaty of Aix la Chappelle, he was forced to return not only Madras to the English but also hand over San Thomé to them. In return, the French accepted what in retrospect would appear the worse half of the bargain, Cape Breton Island of northeast Canada. But in the three years Dupleix lorded it over both Madras and Pondicherry, he was fully committed to the game that, centuries later, was to be known as 'protectionism'. Yet over the next twenty years, two of France's leaders in India, Admiral de la Bourdannais, who had captured Madras in 1746, and Lally, were to see the inside of the Bastille, and die, as a consequence, for their exploits in India. And Dupleix himself was condemned to a fate worse than death – he was discredited and IGNORED! Hating every minute of it, he lived in Paris until his death in 1763, a financially ruined man who had "given my youth, my fortune, my life to enrich my country in Asia," but who found in defeat his "services treated as fables, and I as the vilest of mankind."

The "pacifick" Godheu succeeded Dupleix; de Leyrit took over from Godheu. Then, on April 28, 1758, there arrived in Pondicherry Lally, the new Governor-General, raring to go. So began the second campaign in the Carnatic, which ended with the surrender of Pondicherry on January 16, 1761. By the Treaty of Paris in 1763, France regained Pondicherry but lost most of its Indian empire, and Britain's Indian Empire was born.

When Pondicherry was restored to the French in April 1765, the town Dupleix had so embellished that it was one of the most beautiful in all India had been razed to the ground before Eyre Coote quit it. Not only was the city destroyed but it was also ransacked and depopulated. Governor Pigot and Stringer Lawrence, commander of the British forces, justified their actions on the grounds that this was virtually what Dupleix had done to Madras in 1746, what Lally had done to Fort St. David in 1758 (when he left it "a heap of ruins"), and what he had threatened to do to Madras in 1759, should his siege have proved successful.

Jacques Law received Pondicherry from the British in 1765 and in three years rebuilt it into the glorious city of Dupleix, but no longer were the French hell-bent on expansionism – though they were ever ready to twist the Lion's tail – and so Pondicherry never again regained the status it enjoyed under Dupleix.

When in 1778 Britain and France were at war again, Hector Munro stormed the French town and accepted its surrender. Eyre Coote, returning to India as Commander-in-Chief, landed in Madras in December that year, heard the news of Munro's success and immediately ordered him to raze the city. And so Pondicherry was to be destroyed again, before being restored to France in 1785.

This was not the last time Pondicherry passed into British hands. After Cornwallis had made his peace with Tippu Sultan and left India, the British turned their attention to Pondicherry again. Col Baird, who was in command of a regiment at this siege of Pondicherry, recorded that the besiegers got news of the guillotining of Louis XIV and wadded the papers containing this information into dead shells which they lobbed over the fortifications to the defenders, hastening the surrender of the town. The town was restored to the French for the last time in 1814, by which time the French were a colonial power themselves in Africa.

With this colonial experience, the French promptly proceeded to make Pondicherry a French settlement in 1816, creating a typical French coastal colonial town of sleepy French provincialism. There came the die-straight, clean streets that criss-crossed each other, making square or rectangular blocks of the town; there was built 'Ville Blanche', gleaming white on the beach, greeting the visitor from the sea with its neat orderliness; there grew 'Ville Noire' ('Black Town') behind the 'White', with less semblance of order; and there began the recruitment of a new 'army' of French Indians to man the administrative services of France's far-flung overseas 'departments', from Martinique to Indo-China. And, in time, there arose all those monuments typical of small French towns – the statue of Jeanne d'Arc and the memorial to the poilus *who died in World War I; the statue to the town's heroes, in this case Dupleix; the towering cathedral; and the replica of the Arc d'Triomphe.*

This typically French town, where French was till the 1980s what English is to the rest of India, where almost every middle class family still has at least one member in the service of France, and whose political inheritance appeared, until recently, to remain true to its French heritage, at least in instability, was transferred to independent India on November 1, 1954, after mutual accord between France and India. Once more Pondicherry had changed hands – but it has never lost the character Francois Martin first gave it.

11

Of Peacocks and Lilies

1. A town of temples

Centuries before Madras there was Mylapore. Ptolemy the Greek, *c*.140 CE, wrote of the great port of Maillarpha (or Mylarphon). The Arabs of the 8th and 9th Centuries spoke of Maila and Meilan. The Nestorian Christians of Persia in the 10th Century talked of ancient Meliapor. A Catalan map of 1375 CE shows Mirapor. And Camoens, author of the national epic of Portugal, *The Lusiads* (1572), sang,

> *Here rose the potent city, Meliapor*
> *Named, in olden times rich, vast and grand:*
> *Her sons their olden idols did adore,*
> *As still adoreth that iniquitous band:*
> *In those past ages stood she far from shore,*
> *When, to declare glad tidings over the land,*
> *Thomé came preaching, after he had trod*
> *A thousand regions taught to know his god.*

Pushed back from shore, Mylapore became Portuguese San Thomé's 'Black Town' and the Portuguese influence is still apparent in the southern part of this area. A mile from San Thomé Basilica, near St Isabel Hospital, is Luz (today pronounced like 'buzz', but should be like 'ruse') Church, almost certainly the oldest church construction still in existence in Madras. Curiously, its was declared a shrine – the 'Shrine of Our Lady of Light'– only in 2012, long after ten other Roman Catholic churches in the city had been declared Shrines. *Kaattu Kovil* (Forest temple), as the church is known to this day in Tamil, has a romantic legend associated with its construction. It is related how some Portuguese sailors, in distress while at sea, were guided to safety by a light. They beached safely and followed the light till it disappeared. On the spot they built Luz Church, dedicated to Our Lady of Light. More prosaic though is the information found inscribed in the church – that it was built by a Franciscan monk, Friar Pedro de Atongia, in 1516. There is, however, no additional evidence of such early construction, but the Roman Catholic Church believes that this ancient inscription on black stone is the oldest European inscription on India's eastern coast. Most evidence points to a building date between 1547 and 1582 and reconstruction thereafter. Renovation has been done in the new Millennium. Less than two kilometres from Luz Church is a church that resembled it somewhat in basic form, Descanco[1] Church, but which has lost out to the glamour created for the former when it celebrated its 500th anniversary with restoration. It is also stated that some Portuguese friars, a part of a team establishing a Cochin-Malacca sea route, built a church in Pulicat in 1515 to Our Lady of Glory around a wooden statue of Mother Mary, which still remains *in situ*. It is considered the oldest church of the Madras-Mylapore Diocese.

Hundreds of years before the Portuguese, however, Mylapore was a great town, once second only to Mamallapuram (Mahabalipuram) as a Pallava port, from whence went Tamil culture to the islands of the East and the lands of the Menam and the Mekong. Today, it is best known for its ancient Hindu temple, a beautifully sculptured building with a large tank, a surrounding shopping 'arcade' on the four streets around the temple and its tank, that is ever busy, and several *mutts* (Hindu mission establishments) nearby; Luz, an enticing shopping centre; and a warren of residences of the orthodox, several of the buildings once surrounded by spaciousness, but, alas, now hemmed in by smaller houses that fill up the 'gardens'.

Not a garden house, but a historic house is *Krishna Vilas* which, now the site of a block of flats, stands on Ramakrishna Mutt Road, earlier West Mada Street, near its junction with North Mada Street, next to Alliance Publishers. It was in this house of Raghunatha Rao, a former Dewan of Indore, that "seventeen good men and true" from all the major cities in India met in 1884 and resolved that "a national movement for political ends" should be founded. It was from the seeds sown at this

---

[1] Pronounced 'Descaano' and meaning 'place of rest'.

meeting that, in the following year, the Indian National Congress was born. Raghunatha Rao did not participate in the deliberations in his house, but the Madras representatives were S Subramania Aiyer, P Rangiah Naidu and P Ananda Charlu. In later years, before P S High School moved to its own premises further down R K Mutt Road, its junior classes were held in this building. Builders bringing the building down to raise highrise obliterated all traces of the plaque that commemorated the meeting. Which is among the reasons why Madras's vital contributions to the Independence movement have now been forgotten.

Rangiah Naidu used to live in *Ranga Vilas,* now 29 Police Commissioner's Road, Egmore. In the first floor of this house there was an antique, marble-topped round table. Around this table were held several more meetings of the Mylaporeans and others among the 17 before the Congress was formed. But for all its connections with the Congress as well as the Bench and the Bar, Mylapore, a traditional home of Congress leadership, is better known for its associations with the spiritual than the temporal.

No Indian village, no Indian town is complete without a temple. And so it is not unbelievable that the Saivite temple of the 'Town of Peacocks' has a tradition more than 2,000 years old. More so since it is accepted that Tiruvalluvar, author of the immortal ethical treatise *Tirukkural,* lived for many years in Mylapore, probably in the 1st Century BCE; no doubt because it was a great cultural and religious centre. But does this tradition relate to Mylapore's Sri Kapaleeswarar Temple? Quite likely, because, of all the shrines of Mylapore, including the one dedicated to the great Tamil poet – the 16th Century Tiruvalla Nayanar temple on M K Amman Street, about a mile to the north of the Kapaleeswarar Temple, and where Tiruvalluvar is the main deity and his wife Vasukiamma is enshrined – none is more important or more sacred to the Tamils in Mylapore than this big temple with its towering *gopuram!*

There is, however, some evidence that the present temple was not the original Great Sivan Temple of Mylapore, one of the oldest temples in Tamil Nadu. The date of the building of the present temple itself is not recorded. The temple authorities themselves feel "the present temple was rebuilt about 300 years ago", but according to one school of thought this rebuilding was done by the Vijayanagar kings during the 16th Century.

Two other names are also mentioned as possible rebuilders of the temple. Nainiyappan is a name commemorated in several Madras road names. It is also a name associated with the Mylapore Temple. Muthiappan, the son of this scion of the Nattu Mudaliar family of Mylapore, is stated to be the rebuilder in the translation of an ancient *ola*[2] published in 1983. There is also mention of a Chinnayan elsewhere – in fact, he is to be found in sculpture in the Lord's shrine – as the rebuilder. But whatever the date or whoever the builders, there is agreement on the fact that the Sri Kapaleeswarar Temple was rebuilt. There are also to be found in the present shrine a few fragmentary inscriptions from the old temple as well as from, probably, the Portuguese San Thomé fort.

This old temple, it is generally agreed, was on the shore in the 15th Century, no doubt part of the great port of the Pallava Kings who bore the title *Mylai Kavalar* (Protectors of Mylapore) as well. Arunagirinathar of that age sings of the Subramania Temple on the coast; after him, the next references are only foreign mention in the 17th Century. But, did sea erosion cause the port to be abandoned and the temple to be shifted inland or was it rebuilt after being destroyed by the Portuguese? An answer would appear to depend on which date you accept for the rebuilding. But there is no doubt that the Portuguese first settled here around 1522 and by 1565 had made the coastal region their fortress-town of San Thomé de Meliapore, with Mylapore its 'Black Town', "far from shore", if you accept Camoens. The port, it is believed, was by the northern end of the present estuary with ancient Mylai spreading northwards from what is now Foreshore Estate.

It is recorded that Buddhism and Jainism also thrived in early 'Mayura Sabda Pattinam' (another name for Mylapore and another reference to the peacocks of the town). This name was given to it by the Buddhist scholar-monk Buddhaghosta who composed his *Visuddhimaya* here. There is said to have existed a shrine on the shore from at least the 12th Century dedicated to the Jain *Tirthankara* (saint) Neminathar. This shrine, it is said, was destroyed by the Portuguese. The site of this temple is said to be the present deaf and dumb school in San Thomé. There is also mention of the Jain scholar Mylainathar being from Mylapore.

The Vaishnavite tradition too is strong in the town. Peyalwar, one of the 12 Vaishnavite apostles (the Alwar), was born here, near, it is believed,

---

[2] Palm-leaf manuscript.

the Vaishnavite Madhava Perumal Temple in Arundale Street, which is dedicated to his sacred memory. Another Vaishnavite saint, Tirumangai Alwar, sang of Mylapore in his hymn to the Vaishnavite temple of Lord Parthasarathy in Tiruallikeni (Triplicane), once suburb of the great international trade emporium that was Mylapore. The Adikesava Perumal Peyalwar and Srinivasa Perumal shrines on Kesava Perumal Koil Street are also Vaishnavite. Peyalwar Street in Triplicane was well into recent times the only *agraharam* (closed Brahmin settlement) in Madras.

But it is to Saivite tradition that the Sri Kapaleeswarar Temple is most sacred. The great Saivite saints, Tirugnanasambandar and Appar, visited the temple in the 7th Century and sang of it in their hymns, these hymns the earliest positive reference now available to Mylapore. Saint Arunagirinathar sang of the temple in his *Tiruppugazh*. Vayila Nayanar, one of the 63 canonised Saivite saints, was born in Mylapore and attained salvation there. The 63 saints cast in bronze adorn the outer yard of the temple and, during the ten-day festival (March-April) that is one of the highlights of the Madras year, the *Arupathumoovar* (the 63 Nayanmar) are taken out in procession round the temple on the eighth day. During the festival, there are several concerts held in the environs of the temple as part of the festivities. The Float Festival takes place in January-February, particularly impressive if there is water in the tank. In front of the temple flagmast is the shrine of Saint Gnanasambandar and in it is commemorated the miracle he wrought when he brought back to life the Chetty girl, Poompavai.

Sekkilar's *Periya Puranam* relates that a merchant of Mylapore, Sivanesan, was so inspired by the saint of Sirkazhi that he wished to give his daughter, Poompaavai, to him in marriage. But before the boy saint Gnanasambandar, then about 14, reached Mylapore, Poompaavai was bitten by a cobra, while gathering flowers for her *pooja,* and died. Legend has it that she was cremated in the fields that were opposite where stands P S School since 1899. Sivanesan preserved the ashes of his daughter in an urn and awaited the Saint's arrival. When Gnanasambandar came to Tiruvottriyur, Sivanesan invited him to Mylapore and conducted the Saint along a route he had elaborately decorated. Outside the temple, Sivanesan placed the urn of ashes before the Saint and poured out his tale of sorrow. Gnanasambandar, moved by the story, sang a hymn to Lord Kapaleeswarar, the King of the Ascetics, and no sooner had he completed the tenth verse than Poompaavai rose from the ashes. Lost in meditation, the boy saint did not see the girl till her father offered his daughter to the Saint as his bride. Gnanasambandar declined the offer and went his way, singing the praises of the Lord. The appeal he had made to Lord Kapaleeswarar was simple; the first verse was:

Where art thou, Poompaavai?
Lord Kapaleeswarar has chosen as his seat beautiful Mylapore
Surrounded by the sweet-smelling Punnai trees.
Why hast thou gone without seeing
The legions of the Lord given their repast here?

The Punnai tree in the outer courtyard of the temple – one of the few left in Mylapore – is one of the oldest trees in Madras. And beneath it is another small shrine in which is commemorated the legend which bequeathed Mylapore its name. The sculpture in the shrine shows Goddess Uma (Parvathi), in the form of a peacock, worshipping Lord Siva, represented by the traditional *lingam*. This shrine is yet another of the many additions to the rebuilt temple. The shrine of the Divine Mother Karpagambal (Karpagavalli, She who grants all Her devotees' wishes like the celestial tree Karpagam) was one of these additions and was connected to the main shrine by the present *mandapam*.

The large temple tank, to the west of the shrine, was dug in the 18th Century, on land given by the Nawabs of the Carnatic, but its steps and parapet walls were built only early in this century, from subscriptions raised in Mylapore-Tiruallikeni. In recognition of the gift and in a splendid display of secularism, Muslims are allowed to use the tank on Muharram day, with several Hindus too participating in the mourning and the bearing of symbolic *panjas*. With no water in the tank – and no lilies either – in recent times, the tradition died out, but with restoration of the tank in the 1990s, this century-and-more old practice has had a new lease of life. The tank today has water the year round and fish thrive in it.

The temple's spectacular 120-foot tall *gopuram* was built in 1906 and the stucco figures on it narrate important Puranic legends. Like the Vignesvara shrine, it faces east, while the main shrine faces the tank to the west. Curiously, the *gopuram* over the western entrance is smaller than the eastern entrance, raising questions of which is the main entrance and why does the main temple face west, an orientation less common.

Mylapore's Muslim connection, as reflected in the temple tank tradition, dates to the 1760s when Muhammad Ali Wallajah moved from Arcot to settle in Madras where his Chepauk Palace was being built. Till the Palace was ready, he and his huge retinue settled in what is now Mandaveli, a southern suburb of Mylapore that was once farmland. But an even older Muslim location in Mylapore is the Jumma Mosque off Kutchery Road which dates to 1699.

The Sri Kapaleeswarar Temple was, in the 16th and 17th Centuries, often fortified for use by the Western powers fighting for the Coromandel Coast. The French, between 1672 and 1674, made it their western outpost in San Thomé – and when they were the attackers in 1746, sacked it twice! The loot was valued at around a million pagodas (Rs 10 million then)! North of the temple are several Chola shrines of the 11th-12th Centuries: the Valisvarar and Karnisvarar Temple in Karnisvarakovil Street, Mylapore's ancient northern boundary, and the nearby Virupakshisvarar Temple. South of the temple is the once-beautiful Chitrakulam, a man-made tank now in a state of neglect. Between this tank and temple is the Lady P S Sivaswami Girls' Higher Secondary School. The School, one of the first girls' schools in Madras, had its genesis in the Vizianagaram Maharajah's Hindu Girls' School founded by the Maharajah in 1869 in a rented building in Mylapore. The school moved into its own premises, the present East Mada Street location, in 1910. After several changes of name from 1869 onwards, it took its present name in 1946. Near it is the Sivaswami Kalalaya which houses Sir P S Sivaswami Aiyar's art collection and library which he had left to the school he had nurtured.

Near the Kapaleeswarar Temple is the Mylapore Veda Adhyayana established in 1932 by the then Senior Seer of the Kanchi Mutt to teach Veda lessons following the Gurukulam system. This is the ideal venue to see this ancient teaching system in practise.

There are several other temples in Mylapore with a hoary lineage. They include the Chengalunir Pillaiyar Temple (on the street of the same name and about 100 years old), the Ellaiamman and Peyandiamman Temples (Nochikkuppam, about 300 years), Gnanasundara Vinayakar Temple (R K Mutt-St Mary's Road, about 400 years), Varasiddhi Vinayakar Temple (Appu Mudali Street, about 300 years), Sidderi Vinayakar Temple (Kesava Perumal Koil Street, abut 300 years), Selva Vinayakar Temple (Mandaveli Street, about 300 years) and Mavadi

Kapaleeswarar Temple...an ancient temple rebuilt in the 'Port of Peacocks'.

Brodie Castle...Thenral...a 'garden house', now a music college in Adyar, on the banks of the river that claimed its builder.

27. *Parthasarathy Temple, Triplicane, that Subramania Bharati used to visit.*

28. *Triplicane's Big Mosque...200 years of Wallajah history.*

Vinayakar Temple (on the street of the same name, about 100 years). Next to the Anjaneyar Temple is where the Thannithurai Market, established in 1939, was till the official wreckers brought it down in 2012. Set up on the bank of the Buckingham Canal it used to open at 3 a.m. every day, to receive, till the 1960s, produce that came to Madras in boats plying in the Canal.

2. Of colleges and commerce

A little to the south of the temple tank, on R K Mutt Road, once Brodie's Road in its southern half (leading as it did to *Brodie's Castle*), midst all the bustle of Mylapore, is a serene oasis, the campus of the Ramakrishna Mutt, with its buildings rather more North Indian looking than others in the area, its missionaries generally Bengali and its library a treasure trove. Swami Ramakrishnananda, addressed by all as Sasi Maharaj, started the Ramakrishna *mutt* in Madras in March 1897. The *mutt* was started in a house in Mylapore, moved to *Ice House*, which Swami Vivekananda had graced on his return to India from the U S in 1897, and finally settled in its present premises in Mylapore in 1917. Next to it is a beautiful temple, a striking contrast to South Indian temples. The foundation stone for what is called the Universal Temple, with Hindu, Muslim and Christian features, was laid in 1994 and the temple was consecrated in 2001 in its sylvan setting.

Some way to the north of the *mutt* in Mylapore, the Sri Ramakrishna Mission established in 1946 its second college in the South (the first was at Belur, in 1942). Vivekananda College, with its impressive buildings and magnificent library with 80,000 books and more, has grown into one of the City's major educational institutions. The College's Chemistry Department is a recognised research centre, producing in the brief period of its existence over 75 PhDs. The College also was the first Madras University external institution offering facilities for doctoral studies in Sanskrit and Philosophy. But for all its academic record, it also has an enviable record in cricket.

Vivekananda College occupies part of an even older one-acre campus on which the permanent buildings for the Ramakrishna Mission Students' Home were built in 1921. The Students' Home, for destitute boys, was founded in 1905 by two cousins, C Ramaswamy Aiyangar and C Ramanujachari. Starting with seven boys in a South Mada Street house, the Home moved to bigger premises in 1909. The gift of a portion of a *dhobi ghat* in 1915, west of the Sanskrit College on Royapettah High Road, helped the Home get a permanent location. Splendid buildings came up here in the 1920s to house Home, High School and College.

The Sanskrit College, still partially in sloped, tiled-roofed buildings of another age with plenty of spaciousness around till recent years when ugly modern construction overwhelmed its airy surroundings, is in a campus where there are several other Sanskritic organisations founded in the first quarter of this century. Perhaps the best known of these, the Sanskrit Academy, was founded in 1927, with Prof Kuppuswamy Sastri as its President, to encourage and spread Sanskrit learning. The Kuppuswami Sastri Research Institute here, established in the 1950s, has around 50,000 books in Sanskrit and on Indology, as well as over 1000 *olas* in Grantham, Tamil and Sanskrit. In its campus is the erstwhile home of the *Madras Law Journal*, the oldest in the South. Established in a building here in 1891, it moved out only in 2006-2007 when an international publishing house acquired the title. From the heritage building, however, the descendants of the founder continue to bring out other publications. Elsewhere in Mylapore, on South Mada Street, there is still published *The Law Weekly* which first came out in 1914.

The Law Weekly was started by V C Seshachariar, the nephew of Vembakkam Sadagopacharlu, who in 1862 was the first Indian to be nominated to the Indian Legislative Council. Seshachariar, a lawyer, started the journal in his home on South Mada Street because he felt the law journals started earlier, the *Madras Law Journal*, the *Madras Weekly News*, and the Government-run *Indian Law Reporter*, were not paying enough attention to proceedings in the mofussil courts. But though he started with a mofussil focus, the journal gradually began to spread its wings, first looking at Madras Presidency cases and, later, the national scene. *The Law Weekly* is still run from Seshachariar's house and remains a family-owned and -edited publication.

Not far from here, next to the Vidya Mandir School – established in 1956 on the site of the first home of the Mylapore Ladies' Club which formed a society to found the school – is the Potti Sreeramulu Building commemorating the man who fasted unto death in 1952 for the carving out of a separate Telugu-speaking Andhra State. Andhra Pradesh was born in 1953 – and the formation of States on linguistic grounds became accepted Indian policy. In the building, in a memorial shrine room, is a marble slab marking the spot where there was the cot on which Potti

Sreeramulu had spent his last days. The house was bought by the Andhra Pradesh Government in 1955 to serve as a memorial to the martyr. The Club was founded by Ambujammal, the daughter of S Srinivasa Iyengar, and Sister Subbalakshmi in 1931. In turn, it founded Vidya Mandir. Ambujajammal also established, on TTK Road in neighbouring Alwarpet, the Srinivasa Gandhi Nilayam where, beneath a *tulsi* plant, a portion of the Mahatma's ashes are buried. All Gandhian anniversaries are commemorated here.

On Musiri Subramania Road (Oliver Road) not far from here was Sampradaya, a library of Carnatic Music established in 1980 by a German, Ludwig Pesch, that has 5000 hours of Carnatic Music on tape, records of interviews with Carnatic musicians, and a rich collection of literature on the subject. It is now housed in Kalakshetra, and is looked after by a committee headed by maverick vocalist T M Krishna. Near where it was, on the same road, is St Isabel Hospital, possibly the first hospital to be established by a Roman Catholic Order in the city. Named after a 14th Century Queen of Portugal who entered Holy Orders after the death of her husband, the hospital, founded by the Franciscan Hospitaller Sisters of Portugal, opened in 1949, appropriately in once-Portuguese Luz.

Nearby is *Jammi Buildings*, clinic and headquarters of Jammi Pharmaceuticals from 1949 till the 1980s. The business grew out of the clinic and pharmacy Ayurvedic doctor Jammi Venkataramanayya established in Mylapore in 1928. There he made 'Jammi Liver Cure' a household name – a reputation that has survived. In Luz is made another household name – 'Amrutanjan' – an all-purpose soothing pain balm with a history dating to an 1893 preparation in Bombay by K Nageswara Rao Pantulu. Moving to Madras not long afterwards, he established Amrutanjan Ltd in 1936, today a major ayurvedic pharma player. He is remembered in a well-kept park here that neighbours Amrutanjan's modern factory and the family's garden-house *Sri Bagh*. It was in this house that the *Sri Bagh* Agreement was signed leading to the founding of Andhra Pradesh. The 4-acre Park, established in 1940 on the site of an old tank, *Arathakuttai*, to which four other neighbours contributed land, plays host to young musical talent every Sunday morning, sponsored by TVS Finance. A plaque in Nageswara Rao Pantulu Park lists those who transformed the dry tank into one of the best and most active parks in the city. Just east of Amrutanjan is the Mylapore Club established as "A Proprietors' Club" in 1804 by the 'Mylapore Brahmins' led by V Krishnaswami Aiyer, who dominated the Law Courts. It still offers traditional vegetarian fare, considered outstanding, but Bridge and Tennis have diminished in priority.

Near the Kapaleeswarar Temple are several old commercial names of Mylapore. By the temple is Radha Silk Emporium, its famed showroom opening in 1939 across from the Sannadi Street site where they had started in 1915 as RKT (Thiruvengadam Chettiar) Bros., 'textile wholesalers'. The present showroom came up in 1969. In nearby South Mada Street is the Mylapore Hindu Permanent Fund, a mutual benefit fund started in 1871 by a lawyer, Balaji Ram, in his house in North Mada Street. As the Fund grew, it moved to bigger premises in South Mada Street where it developed its own headquarters building in 1931. Recurring deposits was one of the schemes it first introduced in Madras. Across the Tank from the temple is Alliance & Co, at this R K Mutt Road location from the 1940s, but founded in Mylapore in 1901 by V Kuppu-swami Iyer who had made a beginning of promoting Tamil literature in 1896.

Alliance has remained in its present premises, an unremarkable single-storey building out of the past, since Independence. Four generations have guided its fortune. Kuppuswami Iyer established Alliance with his brother, the firm's name a reflection of the team spirit with which the business was founded and which remains. Its first infusion of nourishment came in the 1930s when Rajaji, a close friend of 'Alliance Iyer', gave the publishing house on nominal terms the rights to his short stories and commentaries on the *Upanishads*. The second infusion came in 1995 when 'Cho' Ramaswamy gave Alliance the publishing rights for his varied writings. But while such kindness improved Alliance's fortunes, the publishing house will always be remembered for two significant contributions of its own. One was the monthly magazine, *Viveka Bodhini*, and the other was its zeal in encouraging the Tamil short story to become a significant part of Tamil Literature.

'Alliance Iyer' left a permanent memorial to this role by publishing between 1942 and 1946 four volumes comprising 255 short stories, every author someone he had published and no author figuring anywhere in the volumes twice. Alliance has published over 20,000 titles, including a few in English and other Indian languages.

Karpagam Mess across from the Kapaleeswarar Temple is another old Mylapore commercial name. Two others are Rayar Cafe, once in Kutchery Road and now in neighbouring Arundale Street, and Dubba Chetty's shop. The former, an old-fashioned home cooking-style restaurant, was started by R V Srinivasa Rao ('Rayar') in the late 1920s, a few doors down from the present premises which used to be stables. A limited menu, and limited breakfast and 'tea' service, ensures maintenance of quality. That is the same watchword at the nearby herbal drugs shop on the same road which Krishnaswami Chetty founded in 1885, the 'dubba' name deriving from giving every customer his purchase in a lidded tin container (a *dubba*).

Contributing considerably to Dubba Chetty's low-key business has been the Venkataramana Ayurvedic College and Dispensary, established down the road in 1905. Another Madras institution founded by V. Krishnaswami Aiyer, who contributed 12 grounds and Rs.15,000 towards it, it functioned for a year in East Mada Street before moving to the present premises. University affiliation first came in 1926 and upgradation in 1979. The College is now in Korattur and a modern Ayurvedic hospital is planned for the Mylapore campus. Across the road from the Ayurveda institution and neighbours of Dubba Chetty are a beautiful 'small' Jain temple (towering over its neighbours) and a century-old institution that once produced many of Madras's secretarial staff. The Shorthand School, established in 1909 by P. Srikant Aiyar in the MLA complex, moved here in 1933 and still finds a clientele, though the typewriter and shorthand have almost vanished. Another old Mylapore business is Crown Bakery, on Bazaar Road, established in 1905.

On North Mada Street and in several streets off it, are some of the best known shops specialising in 'costume' dance and temple jewellery and traditional musical instruments like the *mridangam* (drum) and *veena* (a stringed instrument). Mathala Narayanan Street here is the best known of them for South Indian musical instruments and their repair.

3. Where the lilies grew

Off South Beach Road, just before Mylapore-San Thomé, is the ancient village of Triplicane. Here, where once lived the nationalist poet Subramania Bharati and that mathematics prodigy Ramanujan – who died young, leaving posterity and his Cambridge guru, Prof Hardy, to wonder how much more he would have accomplished had he lived –

there is the striking temple dedicated to Sri Parthasarathy – Sri Krishna, as the charioteer of Arjuna. The temple dates back to at least the middle of the 8th Century, Pallava times. The earliest inscription in it is dated to 807 CE, during the reign of Nantivarma Pallava, and in it, it is indicated that the temple had long been established. The oldest shrine in the complex is that of Ranganathar. The temple tank is truly a structure of beauty, but went dry in 1969. Attempts have since been made with varying success to restore its water content. The sacred lily tank – to which the village owes its name (Tiru-Alli-Keni) – is, however, not the present tank; it is a legendary tank believed to have been sited at nearby Vedavallipuram.

Tradition has it that a king, Sumathi, wanted to have *darshan* of Lord Venkateswara of Tirupati as Lord Krishna. The Lord fulfilled his wish by appearing before him as Lord Krishna. And so He is enshrined in the temple as Lord Venkatakrishna. The Alwar saints visited here and sang in praise of the Lord. Sri Ramanuja, Swami Vivekananda and other religious leaders have also worshipped here. It is festival time at the Triplicane temple throughout the year, but the Float Festival, which draws the largest crowds is in February-March over seven days.

This temple had also been the scene of many battles, Golconda, the Dutch and the French occupying it at various times. It was renovated in 1992, 17 years after the last renovation. Near the temple is perhaps the only *agraharam* (a 'village' of Brahmins) in the city – a narrow lane with doors at either end. All around the temple are the most crowded and chaotic roads in the city today. To the free-for-all on the roads here there is an added dimension: this is perhaps the only area left within Corporation limits where leisurely wandering cattle demand their space on the road.

It was while returning home after worshipping at the Parthasarathy Temple that Subramania Bharati was knocked down by the temple elephant that he had stopped to feed. He recovered, but was never the same again and died shortly afterwards. The house where he last lived, 75 (new 67) Thulasinga Perumal Kovil Street, neighbouring the temple, is a century-old building that was unrecognisably refurbished in recent years by its latter day owner. Government acquired the property in the early 1990s, restored it rather more faithfully and converted it into a memorial museum that opened in 1993, named *Bharati Illam*. Plans to make it a vibrant, living cultural institution have, however, not really taken off, though literary programmes are held in it from time to time. Ramanujan, the great mathematician, lived in a small-house in a by-lane off South Tank Square – which is still owned by the family, who now live elsewhere and keep the empty house locked. Here is a house that deserves to be treated by Government with the same regard as Bharati's.

Another ancient temple in Triplicane is the 500-year-old Tiruvetiswarar Temple in Thiruvetiswaranpet. As in the Mylapore temple, the 63 Nayanmar are enshrined here too.

Near these temples was founded, evolving from the Sangitha Vidwan Sabha of 1896, the Sri Parthasarathy Swami Sabha in 1900, a forerunner of the City's numerous cultural groups that offer a variety of cultural entertainment almost weekly to their memberships. Founded by Manni Thirumalachariar, the Sabha had no permanent place for its programmes till it acquired a bit of property, an old cremation ground, in 1959. An open air theatre was raised by 1962, but its lease of this property ran out in the 1980s and it has been holding its programmes at different venues ever since. This uncertainty has eroded its membership, but the *sabha* struggles on in hope.

Another old *sabha* is the Rasika Ranjani Sabha, founded in 1929 in neighbouring Mylapore and offering everything from instrumental music to theatre. It moved in 1956 from a shed on its property off East Mada Street into its own *Sundreswarar Hall* raised there, on the eponymously named street. On its site has risen a handsome new hall in 2017 after years of bickering. Near here too, by the temple tank, was a run-down publishing house whose Meenakshi Ammal's *Samaithu Paar* ('Cook and See') must be since 1951 the most popular cook book in the South. Today, her family publish the book in three parts, in half a dozen languages, from Ramakrishna Mutt Road, Mylapore.

To Golconda, Triplicane owes its large Muslim community, this ancient settlement growing bigger when Chepauk became the Nawab's headquarters. Their splendid Big (Wallajah) Mosque, historic and impressive, is set in vast grounds on Triplicane High Road, but almost hidden behind new construction and entered through a gate that can almost be missed. It was built in 1795, Nawab Wallajah's family playing a major role in its construction. Built of grey granite, with no wood or steel used, the mosque is one of the most beautiful in South India. On its western wall is a chronogram engraved in stone and unique because it is perhaps the only work by a Hindu to be found in a mosque. Written in Persian, its author was Rajah Makhan Lal Khirat, Private Secretary to Nawab Wallajah and a Persian and Arabic scholar of repute.

The present Prince of Arcot and his family are still closely connected with this hallowed place of worship in whose graveyard is the tomb of Maulana Bahrul Uloom, a scholar and divine of the Wallajah era, and the tombs of the Nawabs and several other Muslim leaders of Madras. Also in Triplicane is historic Zam Bazaar Mosque, in a crowded part of the city replete with connections with the Wallajahs of Chepauk.

In the Wallajah Mosque compound is a 3-storied building that was the Ottoman Turkish consulate. The Badshah Sahib family were consular representatives from the second half of the 19th Century till the Great War.

Near the mosque is Big Street with large, 'Government red' buildings that are another landmark in the area. These buildings, dating to 1897, belong to what was called the Hindu High School since that time and the Hindu Higher Secondary School since 1978. The school had its origins in the Dravida Patasala founded in this area in 1852. In 1864, a girls' wing was added and in 1870 both Telugu-teaching schools were merged as the Anglo-Vernacular High School, a name still popular with the older residents in the area. Nobel Prize winner, the late S Chandra-sekhar, was a student of the school from 1921 to 1925. The school in its heyday was considered the feeder school to Presidency College.

Triplicane, the first suburban village acquired by the Company and, by the 1750s, a favourite residential area of Company servants, is traversed by Triplicane High Road. In those early days it was part of the main road to San Thomé from Fort St George, the latter half being what are now called Dr Natesan Road and Mylapore Bazaar Road. Between the two villages, where Krishnampet now is, were paddy fields. In Tripli-cane also is that great *dubash* Alangatha Pillai – the first Indian to serve on the Company's Council in Fort St George – remembered, in the name of an insignificant street. Also here is the *Triplicane Lodge* of the Theosophical Society, its fine Mani Aiyar (S. Subramania Aiyar) Hall, library and rooms developed between 1920 and 1928. A meeting place that had faded in recent years, it was renovated and revived in 2004.

The 'mansions' of Madras are what Triplicane is now well known for. These modest highrises have for decades been offering inexpensive sharing accommodation for single males, mainly students and low income white-collar workers. Rather handsomer than a mansion is the Sree Venkateswara Students' Hostel on Triplicane High Road. A philanthropic offering of a once well-known printer, Rao Bahadur Vemuru Ranganatham Chetty, it was opened in 1931. Built in the Indo-Saracenic style, it was one of the last buildings to be raised in this architectural idiom.

Little remembered too is the fact that Triplicane was where the Justice Party was conceived and given birth to in 1917. It paved the way for the Dravidian movement that has dominated government in the State from 1967. It was Dr. C. Natesa Mudaliar's Madras Dravidian Association that opened a non-Brahmin students' hostel in Akbar Sahib Street here and sowed the seeds for Dravidian resurgence, leading to the first non-Congress Government, formed by the Justice Party in 1920, coming to power in a province in India.

Between Triplicane and Mount Road was the Great Choultry Plain, an open expanse stretching to Mylapore. In Mylapore, till the 1930s, in and around the four temple (*mada*) streets lived the Brahmins, most of them poor but educated and often clerical; between Luz Church Road and Edward Elliot's Road, lived 19th Century Indian Society, the intellectual Madras Brahmins – most of them lawyers – in large 'compound houses'. On the Great Plain, lived British Society. Today, the Great Plain, though more crowded and almost denuded of 'garden houses', is one of the better residential localities of the City; but Mylapore is in decline, the gracious mansions of the lawyers, administrators, teachers and scholars of yesteryear, who superseded in eminence the *dubashes* of the 18th Century, becoming fewer and fewer with each passing year. The space they occupied and the plantain and betel gardens which separated them have given way to congested middle class building, highrise and shopping complexes.

The road from Mount Road to the Beach, Cathedral Road continuing as Dr Radhakrishnan Salai, once Edward Elliot's Road, however, retains a few of these homes. Among these luxurious homes of another age are Indian President Radhakrishnan's *Girija*, Amalgamations' Anantharama-krishnan's *Sudharma,* built by Sir P S Sivaswami Aiyar and now used by the closely-held Amalgamations Group as Board Room, family offices, and family entertainment space, and a couple of others. The biggest of them all was, perhaps, *Devakottai House*, belonging to the

Zamindar of Devakottai, but, alas, it is no more. Where it stood, now stands AVM Rajeswari Kalyana Mandapam. Pioneering industrialist C Rajam's *India House* was built by him across the road in the 1930s. It later became the Raja of Sivaganga's before S S Vasan bought it and renamed it *Gemini House*. It was pulled down in 2005 for IT highrise, a sad end to a house closely connected with the Tamil film industry and which, in an earlier time, had been sold by Rajam to fund his Madras Institute of Technology in suburban Chromepet. The road, and its northern extension, Nungambakkam High Road (in 1997 renamed after the Father of the Nation, Gandhiji), have been since the late 1990s a hive of dining-out and shopping activity. Not only are there a variety of hotels located on all three roads, but there is a wealth of restaurants, jewellery shops and shopping malls, making these two of the busiest roads in the City and a reflection of the City coming out of its shell of conservativeness.

On Uttamar Gandhi Salai (Nungambakkam High Road) is the Taj Coromandel, the first deluxe hotel in the South, which opened in 1974. The hotel came up on the site of a garden house called *Chipstead* and named its bar eponymously. Not far from it and leading off the opposite side of it is Khader Nawaz Khan Road, named after the descendant of a noble in the court of Nawab Umrat-Ul-Umlah. Khader Nawaz Khan became a Madras Civilian and retired as a Collector. A narrow, ill-kept road, it's chock-a-block with luxury shops and a host of restaurants serving a wide variety of Indian and international cuisine, making it one of the most crowded streets in Madras despite the priciness of its offerings. This is Madras's 'Bond Street'.

About midway on Cathedral Road is the Welcomgroup's My Fortune Hotel, which, as the Group's Chola Sheraton, was the first of the five-star hotels in 20th Century Madras. It was built on the site of a historic house, which the hotel remembers by conscientiously tending an old squat pillar on the pavement in front of it. It was in this house, Kasturi Ranga Iyengar's guest house, *Tilak Bhavan,* occupied at the time by C Rajagopalachariar, that Gandhiji was staying during a visit to Madras in 1919 when he heard the announcement of the infamous Rowlatt Bill. Gathering round him local leaders, and using Rajaji as a sounding board, he discussed the draconian Act the British Government proposed to implement and then announced, for the first time, the launching of Satyagraha in protest. It is that momentous announcement, virtually the start of the freedom struggle, that is commemorated in the pillar, *in situ* long before the hotel. Once, the My Fortune's sister hotel, the luxurious Park Sheraton is now the Crowne Plaza Adyar Gate. About a mile to the south, it is also in historic grounds. Its name, when it was started in the late 1970s, was Adyar Gate and it took it from the gates to the garden of an old 'garden house' on which site it was built. That house, a renovated neighbour, is now Hongkong Bank property.

Here and there, particularly on and off Luz Church Road, can be spotted other 19th and early 20th Century homes of Madras's Indian aristocracy. For instance, at the end of a narrow lane off Luz Church Road, was *Luz House*. Its huge portico and verandahs have been demolished, the house turned ornate and refurbished in 1998 for re-use as a hightech pre-press-facility owned by an Oxford publishing unit. To think that Ranji himself, that Prince of Cricketers, and the Nayudu brothers once played on the grounds of this mansion that belonged to the *dubash* of Parry & Co, Moddavarapu Venkataswamy Naidu. His son Buchi Babu was responsible for founding 'Indian' cricket in Madras – and the first major Indian cricket club in the city, the Madras United Club (1888). Buchi Babu's sons Bhat, Baliah and Ramaswamy and their sons and grandsons strengthened that game. Still visible is the *White House* that had earlier been the *Red House*; both names deriving from the colours the house was painted. The biggest of them all, Justice P R Sundara Iyer's *Sri Bagh* which stretched from Luz Road to the Canal, is now part of the Amrutanjan campus. Opposite it was his 'Siamese Twin', V Krishnaswami Aiyer's house, *Ashrama*.

Before the aristocratic Mylapore Brahmins of Luz settled there in the 19th Century, this "suburban village" was favoured by the Europeans almost as much as the Great Choultry Plain. James Taylor, a writer, was perhaps the first of these settlers to apply for land in "Luce" in the early 1760s. Another early resident was Dr James Dott, one of the Nawab's six surgeons. Muhammad Ali's other surgeons included a Dr Plott; imagine a medical team of Dott and Plott! Several Portuguese also lived here.

In what was "luxuriant", tree-shaded Luz of the 18th Century, the British established a military outpost for a short time. Sir John Burgoyne's 23rd Light Dragoons arrived in 1782 and were quartered here with three infantry regiments. Some of the infantry were reported to have been billeted in "ecclesiastical buildings" in San Thomé till 1786 – Hindu or Roman Catholic, it is not stated, but both would have been no surprise.

St Ebba's Girls' School, started in 1886 in northwestern Luz, now incorporates the towered and battlemented garden house of Benjamin Sulivan, Attorney General in the 1780s and later a Judge. Another eminent legal luminary, Sir P S Sivaswami Aiyar, built his mansion on the other side of what was Sulivan Garden's Road and has now, belatedly, gained recognition in the road name here; this was the striking house that Anantharamakrishnan acquired *c*. 1953 and re-named *Sudharma*. Apparently much-coveted *Sulivan's Gardens* was bought in the 1840s for Rs 20,000 by the Madras Diocesan Committee of the Society for Propagating the Gospel in Foreign Parts and converted into a kind of seminary and "quasi college". The property remained with the Church, but soon was put to better use as St. Ebba's.

Diagonally across is the home of scholar-statesman Dr. S. Radhakrishnan, who was Vice-President, then President of India. The road is now named after him; kitty corner from it is the Children's Garden School started by V N Sharma and his German wife Ellen in 1937 as one of the city's first Montessori Schools.

Luz Church Road leads across Moubray's Road to Murray's Gate Road, which led to *Dunmore House* where Leveson Keith Murray, Earl of Dunmore, lived when he was Collector of Madras between 1822 and 1831. Now Venus Colony, *Dunmore House* was where Laurence Hope (she of "Pale hands I loved by the Shalimar" fame) lived for a while before taking her life. Her husband, General Nicholson, had died a few months earlier. The Nicholsons – she was Adela Florence Nicholson but wrote as Laurence Hope, her impassioned poetry recited to music at late 19th Century, early 20th Century, tea soireés – are buried side by side in St Mary's cemetery on the Island, fitting footnote to their spring-autumn great romance that scandalised the sahibs of Victorian India. The property was later occupied, first by Eardley Norton and, then, by the Maharajah of Pithapuram, when yet another tragic death occurred in the house. It was later the home of Venus Studios. There were several other large bungalows from here to Cathedral Road, but nearby CIT Colony was paddy fields!

The peregrinating Sadr Court functioned in Triplicane and later by Murray's Gate Road, near Kasturi Ranga Iyengar Road in Alwarpet. *Sadr Gardens* still survives here, its links with the law close until former High Court Justice Basheer Ahmed Sayeed, who lived in the large mansion, died in 1985. Several High Court Justices had, in turn, lived in the property earlier. A neighbour was K Bhashyam Iyengar, a leading advocate, and their road 'double-barrels' their name and is called Bhashyam-Basheer Ahmed Road. Between this road and Cathedral Road was the Kasturi Ranga Iyengar property, now blocked out plots in which live his heirs to *The Hindu*. Midst these homes of *The Hindu* family, there is a perfect little village tank straight out of another era that helps sustain a plant nursery. Justice Basheer Ahmed contributed significantly to Muslim women's education with his South India Educational Trust which set up the first Muslim women's college in the city, SIET College, not far away.

South of Luz and west of the Mylapore temples were more paddy fields till they developed, around 1934, as Abhiramapuram.

The Universal Scientist and the Magical Genius

By awarding an honorary doctorate in 1983 to one of its most eminent sons – for whom it did not have a teaching post in 1936! – the University of Madras pre-empted the Nobel Prize Committee by a month. Like the University, the Swedish Academy of Science too took years to recognise the genius of Dr Subrahmanyan Chandrasekhar. When it eventually got around to announcing the physics award to Dr Chandrasekhar, it was the fifth Nobel Prize to be won by a person with close Indian ties. Rabindranath Tagore, Chandrasekhar V Raman, Hargobind Khorana and Mother Teresa had now been followed by the Chicago-based astrophysicist. Five awards won by Indians in the 82-year-old history of the prizes in six disciplines are not many, but two prizes to be won by one family, both in the same category, and 53 years apart, must indeed be unique. Even more curious is the fact that Dr Chandrasekhar himself believed that the Nobel Prize was awarded to him for "my work in 1930, which is related to the maximum mass of slight white dwarfs"; 1930 was the year his father's brother[3], C V Raman, was awarded the prize!

---

[3] Chandrasekhar belonged to one of India's most distinguished academic families. His great-grandfather, Ramanathan Ayyar, a middle-class landowner, had three sons and a daughter. The eldest son, Chandrasekhara Ayyar, was a professor of Mathematics and Physics in Vishakhapatnam. Chandrasekhara Ayyar had five sons and three daughters. Subrahmanya Ayyar, the oldest son, was an Accountant General of India and an authority on Carnatic Music. C V Raman was the Nobel Laureate. And Dr Ramaswamy, the youngest son, was Director-General of Observatories. Their sisters included Mangalam and Seethalakshmi.

Subrahmanya Ayyar's children included Dr Chandrasekhar, the Nobel Laureate; Dr Balakrishnan, a famous physician and writer; Vidya, a famous musicologist; and Dr Ramnath, who was Director of Evaluation and Planning, Vikram Sarabhai Space Centre. Sir C V Raman's two sons were Chandrasekharan, a leading lawyer, and Dr Radhakrishnan, Director, Raman Research Institute. Mangalam's youngest son was Dr Chandrasekhar, the internationally renowned demographer. Seethalakshmi was the mother of Dr Ramanathan, Director, Indian Institute of Science, and Dr Chandrasekhar, a Fellow of the Royal Society, London. Ramaswamy's three sons were Chandrasekhar, who was a professor of Rural Statistics; Sundar, who was a Statistician with the Indian Institute of Applied Economic Research; and Dr Rajaram, who was a physicist with the Indian Institute of Geometrics.

The then 73-year-old scientist[4], who got news of his prize as a birthday gift, became an American citizen in 1953. But his associations with India remained close. Many of his sisters – he was born in a family of six girls and four boys – as well as his wife Lalitha's sisters lived in Madras. Whenever he was in Madras he visited the family house in Teynampet (a part of ancient Mylapore) and his old college, Presidency, strolling through its gardens and corridors, stopping to chat with a student here, a professor there. And he kept in touch with several Indian scientists. About his college days in India he used to say in his last years: "In those days there was a sense of pride and self-respect among young Indians, a feeling that Indians had to be recognised by universal standards. Now it seems that feeling has gone."

Mathematician, physicist and astronomer extraordinary – though, it has been said, he is a 'pencil and paper' astronomer rather than a wielder of a telescope – Chandrasekhar was to mathematics and erudition born. Chandrasekhar, who was born in Lahore, did his senior schooling in Hindu High School, Triplicane, where his scientific bent became obvious. It was his father who persuaded him to choose Physics in preference to Mathematics at Presidency. His first research paper – on 'The Thermodynamics of the Compton Effect with Reference to Interior of the Stars' – was published in the Indian Journal of Physics *just four days before his 18th birthday; it surprised even his uncle, C V Raman. The next year he was off on a scholarship to Trinity College, Cambridge. From then on his scientific life was lived entirely abroad.*

"My loyalty," he once said, explaining his stay abroad, "is not the parochial or flag-waving type of thing. My first loyalty is to science." Not that he did not feel strongly about India. Speaking of his India of the 1920s, he once said, "We were proud of Mahatma Gandhi, of Nehru, of Tagore, of Ramanujan (whom he profoundly admired and whose memory he did much to keep alive). We were proud of the fact that anything we could do would equate to anything else in the world. I did not participate in politics, but I felt that as a person I could do the best if I could have the opportunity." Opportunity is what he felt could be found only abroad.

Sir C V Raman had never been very keen on Indian scientists – including his nephew – going abroad. He even made it the subject of a convocation address. But Chandrasekhar viewed it differently. In a letter to his father he wrote, "I was glad to read CVR's convocation address.

---

[4] Chandrasekhar passed away in August 1995.

I was in general agreement with his deprecation of the craze for foreign degrees, but I think he is overlooking the obvious when he says that those who have benefited by going abroad would have 'done infinitely better' by staying at home. I wonder how he can explain Ramanujan. After four years at Cambridge, and with Hardy, he lived to become the greatest name in Mathematics of this century. Anyone who has even a passing acquaintance with R's life will accede that he would have died unknown and unwept, if he had continued the last five precious years of his life in India. Again, in a different plane, I can assert that I could not have done 'infinitely better' had I continued in India – I am sure to have done much worse. However, with his larger thesis, that it is up to us Indians to improve our universities and centres of education in India, I entirely agree. And, for my part, I hope that one day I shall contribute my small measure to this development..."

This ambivalent attitude to India – the great future is out there, but something must be done about the conditions in India – persisted throughout Chandrasekhar's life. Years after the letter referred to, he was saying that had he lived and worked in India he might "have done less myself. But maybe, I would have created ten people and in this way perhaps I would have done much more for science than what I have done."

On other questions, however, he could be quite decisive. He felt that many scientists tended to have a closed mind once they had attained a certain eminence. "How did Einstein know that God does not play dice?" he once asked. And as for Arthur Eddington, the well-known British astronomer, "He was a great man. But he said there must be a law of nature to prevent a star from becoming a black hole. Why did he say that? Just because he thought it was bad?" wondered Chandrasekhar.

Eddington was the man who shot down Chandrasekhar's theories on stellar evolution in 1935 at a meeting of the Royal Astronomical Society. This theory of what is now called the Chandrasekhar Limit, arrived at while working at Yerkes Laboratory, Wisconsin, was only accepted by the scientific world 20 years later. At the time of its enunciation, Eddington put paid to it and Chandrasekhar ruefully later remembered, "I had gone to the meeting thinking I would be acclaimed for making a startling discovery. But Sir Arthur made a fool of me. I was distraught. I did not know whether to continue my career or not." But continue he did – and was at last proved right.

If Eddington had been less dogmatic, Chandrasekhar may have sprung to fame much earlier. On the other hand, his own character may have had something to do with honours having passed him by earlier. Unlike C V Raman, who was a flamboyant, lively, abrasive and extroverted personality who had developed the art of public relations, Chandrasekhar was a shy, reclusive introvert who looked like a retired, faded, middle-level government official. He tended to be a behind-the-scenes worker – doing a 12 hours a day stint till his death– who did not hazard fanciful opinions or seek the limelight with startling theories. His was a single-minded dedication to pure science. He likened his research in pure science to climbing a hill and perceiving the valley beyond. "The reason for pursuing pure science cannot be measured in terms of needs, though needs are relevant and important and in many instances have the first priority. But to say that human needs have the first priority is not to say that the long range needs of the human spirit can be ignored," he once said.

Chandrasekhar's retiring nature enabled him to remain wedded to a partly Madras Brahmin way of life. A vegetarian – who also liked to dabble in the cooking of such food – and a connoisseur of Carnatic music, he nevertheless acquired, together with atheism, a taste for Western classical music and Western literature. But he often regretted that "one of the unfortunate facts about the pursuit of pure science, the way I have done it, is that it has distorted my personality. I had to sacrifice other interests in life – literature, music, travelling."

Typical of the way he pursued science was to drive 80 miles each weekend from Chicago to teach two students at the Yerkes Observatory in the mid-40s. The pair, Tsung Dao Lee and Chen Ning Yang, won the Nobel Prize when they were still in their thirties! Chandrasekhar was to be suddenly remembered by the world only about four decades later.

Once asked what he would like for a gift, Chandrasekhar replied, "Pencils. They are the only things I use." A simple, sensitive man with strong family ties, Chandrasekhar always enjoyed working with the young (Alice in Wonderland *was perhaps his favourite book!*). *Often, he would say, "the oldest person I was working with was half my age." Referring to the two young prize-winning Chinese he had worked with, he once said in a manner typical of his gentle humour, "My whole class has won the Nobel Prize."*

But what would it all have been without the Eddington episode? He was to later write, "I was to be sorely tested during those years. Yet the experience had a sobering effect and it contributed in no small measure to the way I developed and matured as a scientist. I had no solace then ... Now ... I am grateful – profoundly." That is character beyond science.

* * *

Mathematicians from all over the world gathered at the University of Illinois in June 1987 to celebrate the 100th anniversary of the birth of a man described as "a magical genius". In his home environment, Tamil Nadu, that was when memories of the forgotten genius were revived and a search begun for his "lost papers".

According to an American professor, an 'ordinary' genius is one about whose work it might be said, "Oh yes, I would have thought of that if I were a hundred times brighter." But a 'magical' genius is a person of whom it would be said, "One has no idea where his results come from." When that renowned Cambridge mathematician G H Hardy, who was to rescue Srinivasa Ramanujan from the obscurity of early 20th Century Madras, first assessed the shy, retiring South Indian Brahmin's work, he said, "The man's a genius. His results have to be true; if they were not, no one would have had the imagination to invent them."

That genius, however, was not good enough to get Ramanujan into a Madras college. Indeed, he had virtually no formal education. Not even in Mathematics. Yet in that short span of 32 years that he lived, he blazed through the mathematical firmament like a meteor, leaving behind results that still dim the work of today's mathematicians. "He's our Nemesis," said another American professor. "He is for ever reaching out of the grave and snatching our neatest results." Mathematician after mathematician has found that his best ideas had already been discovered by Ramanujan, often in those days before Cambridge, when he was an impoverished clerk in Madras.

The Madras days of mathematical toil were preceded by a youth in the temple towns of the Kaveri delta south of Madras. He was born in Erode on December 22, 1887. Not long after Ramanujan's birth, the family moved to Kumbakonam, a Brahmin stronghold, when his father got a job as an accounts clerk with a cloth merchant. Middle class the family might have been, but a clerk's job around the turn of the century was only one step removed from poverty. Ramanujan, his brother and his parents had to make do with a one-room mud house and live on a meal a day.

In the local school, Ramanujan showed no signs of being anything extraordinary. He was just another smart boy who learned his lessons by rote and followed convention strictly, down to wearing his long hair in a top knot. But his whole life changed when he was 12; he happened to chance upon a senior student's Plane Trigonometry *by S L Loney. Fascinated by the world of logarithms, complex numbers, infinite products and infinite series, he read the book right through.*

Pursuing the interest Loney had created, a couple of years later he borrowed from the local library G S Carr's Synopsis of Elementary Results in Pure Mathematics. *In it he found 6,000 mathematical theorems stated but not proved. He set about proving them. And never looked into another book, mathematical or otherwise, at any time afterwards.*

With the solution of mathematical problems obsessing him, Ramanujan paid the price by failing the entrance examinations to Madras University twice. He had not studied any other subject but Mathematics. But higher education was not what he wanted; he sought time only to pursue the mysteries of Mathematics.

To Janaki, his wife, whom he married in 1909, Mathematics never meant anything, but she alway remembered how she and Ramanujan's mother, who lived with them, used to take turns to feed him so that he could continue working on his problems even during mealtimes. He barely slept; it was almost as though time was running out on him and he still had so many problems to solve.

The opportunity he needed to devote himself to Mathematics was offered him when he got a job in March 1912 as a Class III, Grade IV clerk in the newly formed Madras Port Trust through the intercession of its Deputy Chief Accountant, S Narayana Ayyar, who was also a problem-solver in Mathematics, though a lesser one. Francis Spring, its Chairman and the man who built the Madras Harbour, and Narayana Ayyar encouraged Ramanujan's single-mindedness, even if it meant that his work suffered.

The problems he had solved in 1912 and 1913 were in the thousands, but no one knew their value. Spring and Ayyar urged him to send his results to England for an opinion. His first letters to Cambridge did not even elicit replies. But a third he wrote to another Cambridge Professor, G H Hardy, on January 16, 1913, was to open the floodgates of his mathematics to the world. Helping to get Hardy's attention was an endorsement by Dr Gilbert T Walker, the Head of the Indian Meteorological Department, who had been shown Ramanujan's work by Spring.

Recognising Ramanujan's genius, Hardy invited Ramanujan to Trinity College, Cambridge, and the mathematician from Madras, having been granted a scholarship and two years' leave by the Government of Madras, on Spring acceding to Ayyar's pleas to help the young genius, arrived there in April 1914. For the next three years, Ramanujan was to amaze not only his colleagues in Cambridge, but also "the collected wisdom of Europe," according to Hardy, "with the singularity and beauty of his uncanny results."

Those same three years, however, were to see the physical decline of a mental giant who was frail of body. A strict vegetarian, as befitting an orthodox Brahmin, he found food to his liking difficult to get in wartime England. And bereft of his family, he found no one to care for his needs as he pursued his workaholic habits of problem-solving for 24 to 36 hours at a stretch.

He fell ill in May 1917 and remained sickly for the rest of his short life. Becoming progressively weaker and more depressed, he sailed for home in 1919. There were just a few months more of work left to him on a sick bed in Madras he never left. He died in April 1920. And was virtually forgotten thereafter by all but the mathematicians.

Ramanujan's legacy to the world of Mathematics is in several parts. There are three notebooks filled with 4,000 theorems stated without proofs. These were all done before he came to England. There are also the scribblings he did on brown wrapping paper while with the Port Trust; it was sixty mathematical propositions so scribbled that first impressed Hardy when he received Ramanujan's letter. There are the papers he published while in England, many of them in tandem with Hardy. And there are the results he mailed to Hardy after his return home and which, for many years, lay ignored in the Trinity College Library.

Many a Mathematics professor is convinced, however, there is still more of Ramanujan's work to be found. There is said to have been a steel trunk full of his work in the house at the time he died, most of it calculations done in that last year in Madras as tuberculosis consumed him. Janaki Ammal[5], his widow, thought a local professor had taken them from the house while Ramanujan's funeral was going on. The renowned Ramanujan Institute of Advanced Studies in Mathematics, Madras University, insists that it has no unknown papers of Ramanujan; what it does have are bound volumes of his papers that are known to mathematicians the world over. The 'Watson trunk' that an American Professor discovered in the Trinity College Library and which he called "the lost notebooks" might, however, be this treasure.

Even without this work of the last year of his life, when Ramanujan scribbled in notebooks almost incessantly, there is enough Ramanujan material available in the libraries of Madras, Cambridge and parts of the United States to keep mathematicians busy for several generations to come.

A Ramanujan scholar and mathematician,Bruce Berndt of the University of Illinois, said in the 1990s,"For ten years all I have done is to go through Ramanujan's first three notebooks trying to prove the theorems. It has been spellbinding. With the help of others, I have just finished proving everything I can make sense of in the 21 chapters in the second book. But to keep at them is to feel like Polya did when he first saw them; he was afraid if he kept at them he would never again prove any results of his own."

Mathematicians elsewhere in the world continue to find what others have already found; wherever they arrive, Ramanujan's been there first; all they have spent their years doing is verifying theorems he had propounded long before them.

The biggest problem, however, that Ramanujan has left behind and to which no answer has been found is whether Ramanujan would have been a still greater mathematical genius if he had had a more formal education. "It could have also ruined him," felt one of his professorial fans. But the debate continues, even as the search goes on for lost Ramanujan scribbles.

---

[5] Janaki Ammal died in 1992 at the age of 94.

12
The Retreats of Theosophy

1. Sanctuary and serenity

Going south from San Thomé, you travel through what was once the backwaters of the Adyar Estuary. Once, the Estuary was 100 acres and had half a dozen large islands in it. By integrating these islands into one land mass, half the Estuary has been lost. Worse, where once were only Quibble Island cemetery (an interdenominational Christian property) and a few large garden houses and *Brodie Castle,* rampant development has been permitted post-Independence, particularly in the new Millennium when huge luxury hotels, wedding halls, and towering residential and office blocks have been allowed to come up.

Past them, you curve left and reach the Adyar of post-Independence development. The curve begins with, on the right, the Andhra Mahila Sabha complex, and on the left what was M.G. Ramachandran's Sathya Studios and is now a women's college named after his wife Janaki. Nearby is a memorial built in 2017 to honour that great film star and thespian, Sivaji Ganesan. The statue of him on the Marina has been moved here, a consequence of a High Court order responding to a plea that it affected vehicular visibility on the Beach Road.

As you cross the Adyar River, over either of the new bridges — the Thiru-Vi-Ka Bridge inaugurated in 1973 and a parallel bridge opened in January 2013 – built besides the now forlorn, 18-arch Elphinstone Bridge which in 1840 replaced a causeway and was long a city landmark with its iron-girdered sides. The girders were sold some years ago and there were plans to develop the flat top as a bird-watching site, as, from it, you got to see the Adyar Estuary, with a few mangrove stands on its south shore, a paradise still not quite lost to birdwatchers. But as usual such environment friendly plans came to naught and the surface was used by the authorities to lay giant pipes on.

In an area that offers river, marsh, woods, backwaters, islets, sea and open ground, over 150 species of birds have been recorded, including flamingoes. Around 70 migratory species, several from the far north of Asia, turn up here from August till March every year. Then it is time for the Indian birds, 50 breeding species nesting here. Conservationists have failed to get the estuary declared a sanctuary, and the several species of animals – jackals, foxes, wild cats – reptiles – snakes and lizards – and birds that thrive here have not even the protection that goes with the status of a 'Reserve Forest'. Development since the latter 1990s, and particularly since the early 2000s when the conservationists lost their case in the Supreme Court, threatened to drive all fauna from the estuary and stifle much of the flora, but subsequent court orders hold out promise. The backwaters, some distance before the bridges, across the way from Chettinad Palace and next to the B R Ambedkar Memorial, a domed building inaugurated in June 2000 in a small garden reclaimed from the backwaters, have been developed into the 58-acre Adyar Eco-park, a nature study centre developed at a cost of Rs. 250 million and open from 2011, but only to schools intitially, though, more recently, to others by appointment. To create the Park, 90,000 trees and plants belonging to 172 species were planted. 85 species of birds have been seen since, and 200 species of fish, amphibians and reptiles are to be found in what is locally called the 'Adyar Poonga'. The second stage of the plan for the restoration of the Adyar Estuary and backwaters is to regenerate 300 acres by the estuary itself. But, sadly, this plan remains, for about five years now, a promise unfulfilled.

On the south bank of the estuary – and a tremendous support to its ecosystem – is the peaceful retreat that is the world headquarters of the Theosophical Society, with its splendid old headquarters building, its shrines of all faiths, the serene *Garden of Remembrance* and huge old-banyan tree, one of the world's largest trees, all set midst 270 acres of gardens and estates. In the estate can to be found 110 species of birds, 250 spices of flora, and a host of insects, reptiles and small fauna.

The Society's founders were an odd couple. She was a dumpy Russian aristocrat, with a talent for music, art and writing, a reputation for clairvoyance and a lineage that included Ivan the Terrible somewhere.

He was a tall, bushy-bearded American Civil War veteran, an officer who had investigated corruption in the Union Army, a man who had tried his hand at farming and journalism before the war and who, after it, was on the way to becoming something of a rationalist.

They met at the farmstead of a Mary Baker Eddy in Vermont, USA, in the 1870s. She was to talk on spiritualism, he was the journalist investigating the phenomenon of 'Eddy's Ghosts' and other manifestations of spiritualism. When Col Henry S Olcott lit Russian-born Helena Petrovna Blavatsky's cigarette, he was later to recall, "Our acquaintance began in smoke but it stirred up a great and permanent fire." The flame they lit has blazed as the message of Universal Brotherhood, ever since.

Seven years after they founded the Society in New York (November 17, 1875), following the signs in a vision Blavatsky had, they were in Madras, after spending three years in Bombay. In 1882 they acquired for £ 600, on the thickly wooded banks of the Adyar River, a garden house and two small houses set in a 27-acre estate of orchards and parks. There, in *Huddlestone Gardens*, they established in December 1883 the world headquarters of the spiritual movement that aims to found a "Universal Brotherhood of Humanity, without distinction of race, creed, sex, caste or colour," searches for Truth in the wisdom of all the great religions of the world, and seeks to investigate the powers latent in Man. The main house, the present headquarters building, was the home from the 1780s of John Huddlestone, Madras Civilian from 1766 and one of the three envoys sent to negotiate with Tippu Sultan in 1784. Till the turn of the 19th Century, alterations continued under Olcott's supervision to make the main mansion fit to be the headquarters of a movement that aimed to influence the entire world. The refurbished main hall of the headquarters building, with its statue and *bas reliefs*, is, today, as architecturally tasteful as it is serene. Besides *Huddlestone Gardens* there are several other interesting old homes on the campus, including the house where Col Olcott lived.

In 1905, the Theosophical Society was formally incorporated. It was during Annie Besant's presidency from 1907 that over 200 acres of neighbouring gardens and property were added. By 1910, the headquarters estate had grown to over 250 acres, much of it wooded, especially with casuarina trees. In this vast acreage, new gardens were developed – *Olcott Gardens*, *Besant Gardens*, *Blavatsky Gardens*,

Damodar Gardens, the serene *Garden of Remembrance* – and several new buildings built for others who, in the years ahead, would come to follow the founders in their search for truth, to study religion, philosophy and Man and his place in the universe.

Among these buildings are the shrines of all faiths: the Hindu temple with an oil lamp, and not an idol, the object of worship; the Buddhist *vihara* in a coconut grove, with an 800-year-old statue of Buddha within and a Bodhi tree without growing from a sapling of the Holy Tree in Bodh Gaya that President Jinarajadasa planted next to it in 1950; a mosque modelled on the famous Pearl Mosque of Agra; a chapel of St Michael and All Angels; a Zoroastrian temple with Assyrian motifs; and a *gurdwara*.

Bigger by far than all these small chapels of worship is the headquarters building, with its huge portico and the splendid, reverently silent Great Hall that leads off the portico and into the original building. *Bas reliefs* of Zarathustra, Gautama, Jesus and Krishna, a verse from the Koran as well as symbols of Moses, Lao-tse, Confucius, Nanak, Mahavir, Mithra, Orpheus and Osiris decorate the hall. Watching over those who pass through it or who tarry a while are the statues of Mme Blavatsky, erected soon after her death in 1891, and one of Col Olcott standing by her side, added shortly after his death in 1907. But what dominates, as much in the Great Hall as everywhere else in the campus, is the serenity and silence.

Elsewhere on the campus are the best-known institutions of the Society. One of them is the great banyan tree which came with Annie Besant's property acquisitions for the Society in 1908. This tree, estimated to be around 450 years old, is believed to be the second biggest in India, its sprawling branches at present shading an estimated 65,000 square feet of space. And in that shade, when it was only about 40,000 sq.ft,, have sat as many as 3,000 persons at a time in conclave or listening to Annie Besant and J Krishnamurthi and Maria Montessori. Over a thousand pillar-like root stems, small and big, enabled the tree to grow further and further, a growth which Theosophists feel best symbolises the way the Society itself has grown. It is estimated that 10,000 visitors a month stream into the Society's estate just to see this marvel of nature. Alas, its main, 40-foot tall, 30-ton trunk was uprooted in a gale in 1989. Attempts to replant the trunk have only partially succeeded and the canopy survives on a weakened trunk and the tree's myriad drop roots.

More internationally known is the Society's library that Olcott founded in 1886. The quest for Truth, the Society has always felt, should be as much through the interaction of all faiths as through a search in the manuscripts of ancient Asia and the printed words of the West. It was an appreciation of what would make this mission easier that induced Olcott to found what is now called the Adyar Library and Research Centre, which he described as "that child of my brain, that hope of my heart". It was with about 200 books in 24 languages, most of them his, and a few the Society's co-founder's, that the first President of the Theosophical Society started the library. The books ranged in subject from witchcraft to science, but included material from all religions. The first book Olcott placed in it on December 28, 1886, was *Isis Unveiled* by Mme Blavatsky.

In the years that followed, the peregrinating Col Olcott began to add to the library valuable material he collected in different parts of the world. And as he added to the Adyar Library Collections, his dream of Oriental revivalism began to take firmer shape. "The revival of oriental literature, the rehabilitation of the true Pandit in public esteem, the promotion of a higher moral sense and spiritual aspiration among Asiatic youth, and a stronger mutual regard between the learned of the East and the West" is what he intended the library to foster. As the pandits he employed began to scour the villages for forgotten *ola* (palm leaf) manuscripts in vanished tongues – most of them in Sanskrit written in the South Indian *grantha* script – that would add to the library's wealth, and as Indian and Western scholars began to delve into these riches, the library began to take on a more meaningful role in the Adyar campus. It encouraged research, it provided information, it began publishing, especially translations of the *ola* and parchment manuscripts. In fact, it became a pioneering institution in Asia for the revival and presentation of Oriental literature and a promoter of the study of comparative religion, philosophy and science.

As early as 1888, Olcott and Max Mueller were in correspondence, as a result of which Dr Otto F Schrader came out from Germany to research and publish a work on the *Upanishads* (1912). The library's earliest publications were catechisms and summarised philosophies of different religions, for which the Colonel himself was responsible. The Adyar Library's scholarly titles are now about 200 in number, all printed in the Society's own printing press on the campus which prides itself on the quality of its work. The subjects range from religious works to lexicography, from linguistics and grammar to ancient medicine and astrology. The extension of Col Olcott's dream – "with the combined labour of the Eastern and Western scholars we hope to bring to light and publish much valuable knowledge now stored away in Eastern languages or, if rendered into Asian Vernaculars, still beyond the reach of the thousands of earnest students who are only familiar with the Greek and Latin classics and their European derivatives" – has come to pass.

The Society's press, started in 1907, is called Vasantha Press, 'Vasantha' being a Sanskritised 'Besant'. Originally located just outside the campus, its growth led to it moving into spacious premises in the campus and being inaugurated in 1971.

The original location of the then small library, the East Wing of the Great Hall that Olcott built, now houses the Society's Museum. If Col Olcott were, however, to re-appear in this sylvan, tree-shaded Adyar campus, stroll past all those quiet places of meditation and wander through the new white building that came up long after his time, he would find in its air-conditioned and spacious storage facilities a wealth of works, on Eastern civilisation, the Classics, philosophy, mysticism and religion, far beyond his fondest dreams. Facing his dream project is a sculpted bust of Olcott.

2. A library and beyond

Today, the Adyar Library has one of the world's finest collections on Eastern civilisation. Its 200,000 books and nearly 20,000 palm-leaf and parchment manuscripts constitute such a magnificent repository of knowledge that the institution has not only become a major Indological centre but is also recognised by Madras University as a centre of post-graduate work in Sanskrit and Indology.

The riches of the library are inestimable. Many of them are rare records, first editions or out of print books any museum or archive in the world would be proud to possess. A 600-year-old copy of Koranic text, a 500-year-old book of rare *stotras* in Sanskrit, a 500-year-old Latin text on astronomy and geography with charts and diagrams, a 300-year-old book on embalming the dead written by a London surgeon, a 300-year-old *Biblia* – Martin Luther's German translation of *The Bible*, printed in Nuremberg and the biggest book in the library – and 800-year-old scroll pictures of the Buddha are only exemplars of the institution's priceless possessions. Other prized possessions include a

Nepalese Tantric manuscript of the *Masnavi* of Rumi and several Chinese encyclopaedias rarely seen outside China. A sheepskin manuscript and tamarind seed writing are fascinating to view. Its small art collection, of works Eastern and Western, is unique for its philosophic specialisation.

Intent on reviving the original Hindu and Buddhist traditions, Col Olcott concentrated on acquiring for his library the invaluable records of that heritage. And it is these acquisitions that are the library's finest collection. There are Tibetan xylographs on handmade bark paper that are translations of Buddhist manuscripts in Sanskrit which have been lost to the world, *Tripitakas* (Buddhist teachings) in several languages, including a Siamese set that had been gifted to the Colonel by the King of Siam, and a beautiful one on illuminated paper with gold scripting achieved by delicate Chinese brushwork. A Burmese Buddhist manuscript has been beautifully ornamented with lacquerwork in red, gold and black. A set of Pali manuscripts commemorate the Colonel's contribution to the Buddhist revival in Ceylon in the mid-1880s. And the list can go on and on.

There are religious and philosophic texts in almost all the major languages of the world, Classical, Eastern and Western. The Bible is to be found in several languages and sizes; one miniature Bible is smaller than a thumbnail, yet is in seven languages, all clearly readable when viewed through a special magnifying glass! The Lord's Prayer in about 200 languages is one of the library's prize collections.

While the philosophic and religious are the library's strength, the humanities are not completely ignored. There is a good collection of books on art and architecture and a lot of non-Theosophical archival material. There is even a collection of detective novels that had been gifted by a former President, G S Arundale!

Dr Annie Besant's political library, her press clippings, pamphlets and other Home Rule material, the complete sets of the daily *New India* and weekly *Commonwealth* she edited – they all constitute an excellent record of an important part of India's freedom struggle. Col Olcott's 30-volume diaries, Mme Blavatsky's scrapbooks and some of their personal belongings – including her mini-diary and the pencil she used to make notes in it – all give an insight into another world. And there is a treasure house of Theosophical Society history and the stories and beliefs of the men and women who created it.

It is a world where Edwin Arnold can gift to Olcott the first draft of his epic, *Light of Asia*, and where Olcott could take pleasure from simple little things. He notes in his diary on Tuesday, December 19, 1882: "Reached Madras early in the morning. Met at Station by about 50 fellows, including the leading ones...a lot of them escorted us to Adyar. Our beautiful home seemed a fairy place to us. Happy days are in store for us here."

The happy days have become a legend now and the library he left behind a monument to happiness. Much of the happiness is in giving, its wealth swelling as friends gift it hundreds of invaluable literary treasures. The treasures await readers, researchers and translators in numbers far more than at present. A 'book hospital' that is a model for the country preserves these treasures.

A brief experiment in national education was also conducted on this campus, with the founding of a National University that had Tagore as its Chancellor and Sir S Subramania Aiyar, a justice of the Madras High Court and first Indian Vice-Chancellor of the University of Madras, as its first Pro-Chancellor. The first college of this independent university – now no more – opened in 1918 in the *Damodar Gardens*. At the *Blavatsky Bungalow*, near the banyan tree, scholars now find a quiet retreat to work in. It was in this bungalow that Rabindranath Tagore lived in 1934.

Today, the Society has 1,200 branches in 60 countries. The headquarters campus has 80 buildings. And the publication work is on the increase. Watching over it all is the statue of Mme Blavatsky, beneath which a portion of her ashes are interred. The fire she lit burns as strong as ever worldwide, even today. But it was that rebellious Irishwoman, Annie Besant, who made sure the Society sank its roots deep and permanently in India.

With Mme Blavatsky more at home in London and Col Olcott turning towards Ceylon and Buddhism, Annie Besant, who joined the Society in 1889, arrived in India in 1893 and became the Society's President in 1907. The Central Hindu School and College she founded in Varanasi was to be the nucleus of the Benares Hindu University. Gradually, she became the moving spirit of the Theosophical Society which she allied to the Hindu revivalist movement even as she herself turned more and more towards the Indian National Congress and the politics of Independence. It was under the shade of the famed banyan tree that she and her associates first discussed Home Rule. After Besant passed away in 1933, the Society turned once more towards a universal religious philosophy and slowly cut itself off from the mainstream of Indian life.

The Indian National Congress, with which Besant was closely associated, was founded and held its first sessions in 1885 in Bombay. One of its founders – described by many as its 'father' – was a former British Civil Servant, Alan Octavian Hume, a staunch Theosophist. It was he who had first mooted the idea of the Congress at that discussion under the banyan tree, which took a hard look at the suggestions of the 'Mylapore 17'. Hume was elected general secretary of the Congress at its first session and remained so till his return to England in 1898. The first resolution moved at that session was by G Subramania Aiyer, Founder Editor of *The Hindu*.

The first sessions of Congress to be held in Madras were in 1887 when Lord Connemara was Governor. Among the Madras leaders who participated were the Maharajah of Vizianagaram and those founding stalwarts of *The Hindu*, Veeraraghavachariar and Subramania Aiyer. Lord Connemara on this occasion even invited the Congress delegates to a garden-party at *Government House!* This Government attitude changed – even as early as the second sessions to be held in Madras – seven years later. Yet, in 1914, the 29th sessions (held in Madras once again, this time in the *Doveton House* grounds) was visited – and acclaimed – by Governor Lord Pentland, the first visit ever paid to a Congress Sessions by a representative of the Crown. At the 23rd gathering held in Madras in 1908, Annie Besant was instrumental in reunifying Congress which had split at the Surat Sessions the previous year.

On the beach south of the Adyar River, by Theosophical Society property, J Krishnamurthi is remembered in a memorial pillar, 25 feet tall and with his words engraved on it. It was Annie Besant who had proclaimed the boy Krishnamurthi a messiah, a World Teacher. An older Krishnamurthi became a revered guru, but disassociated himself with the roles in which he had been cast as a boy.

The Theosophists played a significant role in several aspects of Indian life. As far back as 1879, Col Olcott organised the first Swadeshi Exhibition in Bombay. In 1917, Annie Besant, Margaret Cousins and Dorothy Jinarajadasa organised the Indian Women's Association, on which foundation the women's movement developed in this country. Dorothy Jinarajadasa was married to a Sinhalese Theosophist who took the words of Theosophy to the world, succeeding Olcott in this mission. The Scout movement was started under the banyan tree when Annie Besant organised a rally after Baden-Powell had refused permission for an Indian Scout Movement. Rukmini Devi Arundale's institution devoted to the classical South Indian dance, music, and arts and crafts, Kalakshetra, was founded in 1936 in the Theosophical Society's *Besant Gardens*, during the tenure of the dancer's husband as the Society's President.

Between Kalakshetra and the Theosophical Society and bordering Besant Nagar, is Elliot's Beach, Madras's favourite bathing beach for the Europeans till the early 1960s, with, at one time, weekend cottages built by some of the British business houses and a special one for the Governor that was resurrected *c*.2008. Recent residential development, larger crowds and the Indian lack of interest in swimming has made the beach a second Marina, a place to 'pass-time'. On the beach is a memorial to a young Danish shipping executive with the East Asiatic Company, Kaj Schmidt, who was drowned in the surf while trying to rescue an English girl on December 30th morning, 1930. The next evening, the girl arrived at a grand ball being held in the city, as though nothing had happened. But when she was presented to the Governor, he pointedly ignored her. The Schmidt memorial came up soon after. Restoration of the memorial and revival of 'Bessie (Besant) Beach' – to give it its popular name – were done in 2008, but the memorial is back to a sad state – almost even endangered – as these lines are written.

In spacious Adyar too are some of the oldest British houses still surviving in the city – 'castles' built on land first owned by employees of the East India Company. A splendid example near Adyar junction is the former Maharajah of Travancore's 'garden house' – *Ramalayam* – with resounding silence in its empty halls and corridors and school-children's loud cries in its gardens. Before *Ramalayam* was built, the Maharajah from time to time used to stay as a guest near Pachaiyappa's College in Kilpauk, in what was known as *Kushaldoss Gardens*. For a while, till around the early 1990s, handsome *Kushaldoss Gardens,* with black granite pillars and left-over cannon as decoration inside, and ornate half-pillars right round, was used as the local NCC headquarters. Thereafter, it was let out for a variety of activities, including film shooting, but in 2006 it was pulled down to make way for highrise.

But Adyar has an even older historic heritage than its British houses. On the banks of the river, megalithic burial urns were discovered. More modern history is the victorious battle Vijayanagar troops fought against the iconoclastic Portuguese in 1559. And then, in November 1746, during the French occupation of Madras, there was the historic Battle of the Adyar River already referred to.

This Indian defeat has been honoured with historic significance by some historians who tend to believe that the idea of empire was born in this French victory, when it was first realised that a handful of disciplined European and European-trained Indian *s(i)pahis (sepoys)* with cannon were more than a match for thousands of undisciplined, unorganised local forces.

Overlooking the Adyar River near what is now called Gandhi Nagar is St Patrick's School, the oldest school in Adyar. When a boys' orphanage founded in Armenian Street in 1840 grew into a school managed by the Patrician Brothers, it needed more space to spread itself in. And so *Elphinstone Park*, a garden house set midst 150 acres, was bought in July 1885 for Rs. 20,000 and the School moved in and sank firm roots. Today it owns a 23-acre campus. St. Patrick's was started as an industrial school and developed into a regular school. Other schools followed it in Adyar. Nearby, in once St. Patrick's land, is the St Louis Institute for the Deaf and Blind started in 1962 and a successful Higher Secondary School from 1990. The Institute is known for its much-appreciated band.

Gandhi Nagar was the first of the planned middle class housing developments in the wilderness Adyar was south of the river in the late 1940s. It was followed by Kasturba Nagar. To the south of these were later developed Indira Nagar and, to their east, Shastri Nagar and Besant Nagar. And then you are in the ancient village of Tiruvanmiyur.

3. The road to Mahabalipuram

In 1963, that 'Temple of Art', Kalakshetra, dedicated to Carnatic Music and Bharata Natyam, traditional weaving and textile-design, moved out in search of space to the coast at Tiruvanmiyur, three kilometres from its Theosophical Society home, on the road to Mahabalipuram/ Mamallapuram. Here its Crafts Research and Education Centre, founded by Rukmini Devi in 1937 to ensure that only traditional designs are used for the sarees of the dancers, continues to research and weave cotton and silk in the designs of old. And its students learn dance and music, often in the open air of its 300-acre sylvan surroundings. Its auditorium, *Koothambalam,* in the Kerala architectural style, is particularly striking. Here too, Kalakshetra tends the U V Swaminatha Iyer Library of Tamil manuscripts, U.Ve.Sa. being, perhaps, the greatest Tamil scholar in the last 130 years.

Kalakshetra, together with the Besant-Memorial School (founded in 1934 by Dr Arundale) and the G S Arundale Training Centre for teachers (founded in 1946 by his widow), whose beginnings were in the several schools Olcott started in and around the Society's gardens in 1894, for first generation learners at that time, form the Annie Besant Cultural Centre in Tiruvanmiyur. Today, the Olcott Memorial High School that has emerged from these schools still thrives as the oldest school in the area. It was in these schools that Annie Besant first introduced scouting and guiding. It was here also that the Montessori teaching method was introduced in India by her successors. Maria Montessori arrived in Madras in 1939, invited by Rukmini Arundale and her husband to train teachers and prepare study material. The War however found her (she was Italian) interned in Kodaikanal, where she wrote most of the training material that was printed at the Kalakshetra printing press set up by the Arundales.

Another educational institution on this campus is The School founded by the Jiddu Krishnamurti Foundation in India in 1973. With the expiry of its lease, the school moves out of *Damodar Gardens* in 2018. An older sister school is the Rishi Valley School near Madanapalle in Andhra Pradesh. This boarding school was founded in 1926. These schools and those on the Theosophical Society campus follow regular educational streams, but have a more 'Indianising' influence on their wards.

Beyond Elliot's Beach, Valmiki Nagar is a development of the 1990s with scores of upmarket apartment blocks. And then you are in the ancient village of Tiruvanmiyur with its 10th-11th Century Chola temple dedicated to Marundeeswarar. The *Ramayana's* author, Valmiki, is said to have worshipped here. Several Chola inscriptions dating to the 11th Century are to be found in the temple. The 63 Nayanmar and 108 *lingams* are enshrined here. Pamban Swamigal's *samadhi* is near the Valmiki shrine. The two temple tanks after years of being dry, and the main entrance *gopuram* left unfinished for years, did no justice to the beautiful temple. But when Tiruvanmiyur and the neighbouring villages began to see mushrooming residential growth by the end of the first decade of the 21st Century, the tanks were revived, the *gopuram* completed and other facilities added in the temple precincts, which now has a substantial congregation.

With rather different religious links is Sathya Nilayam on Lattice Bridge Road in Tiruvanmiyur. This Jesuit Research Centre, now in 7 acres, had its beginnings in a Jesuit Training College established in 1895 in 57 acres in Shenbaganur, Kodaikanal. In Shenbaganur on campus is an outstanding natural history museum. The research centre was moved to Tiruvanmiyur in 1980 and is affiliated to Loyola College and the University of Madras. It has an outstanding library with over 45,000 books. Fr. Ceyrac is a name long linked with both institutes.

The main road from Tiruvanmiyur to Mahabalipuram, the world heritage site that's an open air museum of sculpted rock created in the 6th and 7th Centuries, was one of the best highways built in the South, the East Coast Road (ECR), in the last 25 years. It is along it that there are numerous attractions for the tourist, weekender, and culture buff, including cuisine from several parts of the world, every mile or so, it would seem. But it is also along this road, in villages like Injambakkam, Kottivakkam and Neelankarai, that the city has begun to develop from the late 1990s with all of them becoming residential townships crowding out the luxurious farm and beach houses of the wealthy that had been built here from the 1970s. At the rate development is going on here, it will be no surprise if it reaches Mahabalipuram by 2020. But there are in 2017 ominous signs of sea erosion threatening these houses at beach-edge.

This mushrooming development, converting seaside villages into busy little towns of substantial population and virtually merging with each other, has made the highway to Pondicherry, the East Coast Road, a ribbon of shops on either side of it from Tiruvanmiyur for about ten kilometres. Beyond the toll gate, development threatens, though at the time of writing the highway is still picturesque in several stretches where the sea is visible and leaves the traveller with a picture of what it was like in the past. But even after this busy stretch, with its scores of restaurants, is passed, there are dine-outs aplenty offering a variety of cuisines and drawing the youth of the city. The increasing number of vehicles using a highway in the process of slowly being widened makes this a dangerous stretch for drivers.

On this road, not far from Tiruvanmiyur, there is in a casuarina grove the artists' village of Cholamandal, an experiment in co-operative living and work founded in 1965 by the late Dr.K C S Paniker, once Principal of the Academy-minded Government College of Arts and Crafts, but who later, with Roy Choudhury, became dedicated to Modernism and started what became known as the Madras Movement. Paniker gathered around him, on eight acres edged by the sea, some 30 artists and sculptors, most of them former students of his, and encouraged them to settle there and practise their art as they willed and work on handicrafts for a more mundane livelihood. In fact, some of the first seed money, about Rs.40,000, for Cholamandal was generated from the first batik exhibition in India held in 1965 in the Lalit Kala Akademi, a Central Government art sponsor, then housed in a three-storey house in the campus of Ewart School, Vepery, where it encouraged artists by providing them space to paint and also earn a living through their ceramic and batik creations. In charge of this was M.Vasudevan, better known as M.V. Devan, artist, writer, cultural activist and architect. His was a seminal contribution to the Madras Movement. The Government of Madras had in 1962 promoted what was called the Madras Lalit Kala Akademi, supported with funds from the Central Government's Akademi. Devan was its first Secretary. By the time he left for Kerala in 1969, he had made the Akademi a memorable institution, literally nursing the young artists and their talent he drew to it.

The Ewart School campus being not far from the School of Arts and Crafts, many a student came there, and found a father-figure in Devan, though he wasn't much older than them. In and around the Akademi were sown the seeds of community living, an artists' colony, that was to point the way to the establishing of Cholamandal Artists' Village and laying the foundation for what became the Madras Movement. The Akademi itself survived till 1976, when the Tamil Nadu Government decided to re-name it the Oviya Nunkalai Kuzhu and locate it as part of the Department of Art and Culture in the Tamil Nadu Government Music College in Adyar (now the Tamil Nadu Music and Fine Arts University) where it lost touch with most of the artists of the Madras Movement. Today, Modern Art flourishes in Cholamandal amidst sun and sand, and so, occasionally, do modern theatre and poetry – in the open air.

A modern art gallery, a museum, and performance, dining and shopping spaces have been created here in the last few years, which to a degree have reduced the rural ambience, which was a major draw for many years after the quiet start of this village of artists. The art gallery, with two exhibition spaces, *Laburnum* and *Indigo,* and the K C S Paniker Museum of the Madras Movement are in what is called the Cholamandal

Centre for Contemporary Art which was opened in February 2009. And surrounding it is an open air international sculpture park. The Museum is the only one in the country organised and run by artists. The Madras Movement, which started in the 1940s, was at its peak in the 1970s and '80s.

A little further along are: VGP Golden Beach, a local version of Disneyland with much Tamil kitsch; the city's only drive-in theatre, Prarthana; a couple of more fun-of-the-fair places; DakshinaChitra, a heritage project where the traditional homes of the four Southern States have been recreated in village clusters in which handicraft artisans often ply their crafts, traditional performances are held, and exhibitions, talks and seminars are organised; Covelong (Kovalam/Cabelon), once a Belgian trading post (1719-1751) they called Cabelon, where there is today a beach resort in the lee of an ancient Dutch fort, a church that's home to several relics associated with the early 19th Century business magnate John de Monte who built the church (it annual festival draws crowds of the faithful from the surrounding districts, many travelling by boat in the Buckingham Canal); the Coromandel Coast's first surfing and water sports centre, that has inspired several more 'metors' in the area; a camera museum with 100 cameras on display run by a Dr. Arun; and a crocodile farm whose story follows a few pages later. Then, it is the other half of the 56 km road to Mahabalipuram.

A Rebel's Legacy, 'A Cultural Empire'

Annie Besant was a 19th Century British rebel. Divorcee, suffragette and Theosophist, she became a 20th Century educationist, journalist and political leader in India, seeking Home Rule for the country she made her home and salvation for mankind through Hinduism.

At the world headquarters of the Theosophical movement in Madras, she also played controversial parent to a boy and a girl who, shaking off the scandal midst which they grew up, became internationally renowned figures in the worlds of philosophy and dance. Both died within a week of each other in February 1986 and left legions of devoted followers totally leaderless.

Jiddu Krishnamurthi, a Brahmin boy with a distaste for school, was decreed a Messiah by Besant who made herself his guardian and got fellow-Theosophist J Leadbeater to be his instructor. The legal action the boy's father brought against Besant and Leadbeater for custody of his son and the defamation case that followed, as a consequence of the allegations of "unnatural practices" made against Leadbeater, were cause célébres in Madras in the years before World War I. Eventually, Krishnamurthi broke away from the Theosophists as well as other formalised religious institutions in 1929 and spent the rest of his life as "the seer who walked alone", lecturing all around the world to all who would listen.

A tall, handsome man with a splendid mane of white hair, Krishnamurthi held audiences spell-bound with his soft-spoken words of wisdom that offered believers salvation through self-realisation. Described as "one of the most original chapters in the history of religious philosophy," Krishnamurthi is considered by many as "one of the most stimulating philosophers of the 20th Century." He was 91 when he died in Ojai, California, one of his two homes, the other being Madras to which he returned every year, almost as though in search of renewal after his long lecture tours.

Ten years younger than JK was Rukmini Devi Arundale who died just a few days short of her 82nd birthday. In her last years, she was a stern disciplinarian and as domineering as Annie Besant; in her youth, she had been as much a rebel as the Irishwoman who had treated her as a daughter. But while Besant did not live to see much of what she strived for come to pass, Rukmini Devi saw the revolution she started become an integral part of the Indian cultural scene and be described by the then Indian Vice President, R Venkataraman, as "a cultural empire".

Rukmini Nilakanta Sastri was a slip of a girl, but a beauty by any standards, when she came into the limelight. She belonged to an orthodox Brahmin family, many of whose members became ardent Theosophists shedding their orthodoxy. Her spiritual preceptors were, therefore, at the time, Annie Besant and George Sydney Arundale, an Australian who had come out as principal of the school Besant had founded on the Adyar campus of the Theosophical Society. When the 16-year-old Rukmini Sastri fell in love with the 42-year-old Arundale and Besant encouraged their spring-autumn marriage, the romance became the second sensation the Society was responsible for in less than a decade.

In an editorial titled "Adyar Ways", the conservative Hindu *thundered, "We have had our own suspicions regarding the atmosphere and surroundings of Adyar.... It is a matter of the utmost concern to the community as a whole." But neither editorial comment nor Brahmin ire could stop the marriage in 1920. It is fortunate that the protestants were not successful; it was this marriage that enabled Rukmini Devi Arundale's genius to flower.*

Rukmini Arundale had always been interested in classical South Indian (Carnatic) music and was considered a good singer. Arundale opened up a whole new world of the fine arts for her. He was constantly travelling, spreading the gospel of Theosophy. She began to accompany him. One evening in 1926, in his native Australia, they went to see Anna Pavlova dance. Rukmini Arundale was "a changed person from that moment." She too wanted to be part of the "fascinating world of movement and expression."

She studied with Pavlova and other ballet teachers whenever she got the opportunity. Then, back in India and still stirred by dance, she went one evening in 1933 to see two sisters perform in a sadir *programme. In those days, the classical* sadir *or* chinna melam *could only be danced by the* devadasis, *the handmaidens of the gods. In those days, too, many* devadasis *had become more universal courtesans and their dance to the gods mere public entertainment. The programme the Arundales watched was, fortunately, pristinely classical. And, as a friend of hers recalls, "Rukmini Devi was never the same person again."*

She had been "ushered into a new world of rhythmic beauty and meaning," she was to later say. The experience also made her determined "to find young people who would dedicate themselves, along with me, to its revival as a factor in the cultural renaissance of India." She took it as a personal challenge to disseminate knowledge of "this beautiful and profound art that had been restricted to a few specialists."

To do that, she had to learn the dance form herself. And few instructors were willing to teach a Brahmin girl a devadasi *art. But constant badgering of some of the most renowned temple tutors led to two years of hard and secret training. At the International Theosophical Conference in 1935, she unveiled what she had learnt.*

For centuries, musicians and dance gurus had stood facing their audiences and moving behind the dancer. There had never been a backdrop. And the costuming was always vulgar. Now, dancing in the open under a banyan tree, Rukmini Devi caused a revolution in an instant. The musicians were on a side, there was a bare backdrop where they used to stand, and she dominated the aesthetic experience in costuming and jewellery which went back to the ancient sculptures.

The audience at that first performance sat enthralled; a bishop of Madras who was present was quoted as saying that he felt as though he had been at a benediction ceremony. He was echoing George Arundale's introductory remarks on the dance form being a spiritual art. But few elsewhere echoed Arundale's belief that his wife's dancing in public was for the betterment of Indian culture. All Madras, nay, all India that heard about it was shocked that a Brahmin woman had publicly performed the "art of temple harlots". George Arundale, on the other hand, used to meditate in the wings whenever she danced!

*Another institution which encouraged women from non-*devadasi *backgrounds to perform in public was the Egmore Ladies' Club founded by Lady Sankaran Nair. The first of those performances was a* Harikatha *recital by that prodigy C Saraswathi Bai, a Brahmin girl, when she was 11. This was followed twenty years later by a vocal recital by another* *young Brahmin, D K Pattammal. Art was at last beginning to come out of the closet in Madras.*

Responsible for taking these first steps forward was Rukmini Devi backed by Besant and Arundale. In 1936, she established the International Centre for Arts in the Society's campus, "with no money, no land, no building and just one student under one tree that was our only classroom." It was from such beginnings that the Centre, now known as Kalakshetra (The Temple of Art), grew, and Rukmini Devi's last public appearance was at its Golden Jubilee celebrations.

Thanks to the efforts of the Music Academy, Madras, classical South Indian dance, hitherto the preserve of devadasis *and called* Sadir, *was renamed Bharata Natyam, the dance of the Sage Bharata. By urging friends and relations to join her school and emphasising the spiritual content of the dance form – by eliminating the erotic mood – Rukmini Devi made Bharata Natyam respectable. But authoritarian that she was, she institutionalised Bharata Natyam at Kalakshetra and would permit no individual interpretation. It was only after they left Kalakshetra that most of the country's finest Bharata Natyam dancers flowered. Away from her dominant personality, they got the chance to express themselves and bloom, but without her regimentation they would never have been inculcated with the discipline great dance needs, most of them readily admit. And they undoubtfully benefited from her giving Bharata Natyam a new dimension by making it the idiom of the new genre she created – dance-drama. Kalakshetra's annual dance-dramas are still one of the special features of the Madras arts scene.*

Today, Kalakshetra trains students from all over the world, with the students and gurus living on the same campus in that spartan, ancient Indian tradition of the gurukulam, *where education becomes a spiritual experience. Looking forward to becoming a university, Kalakshetra has its own 100-acre campus where classical Carnatic music as well as Bharata Natyam are taught midst this near-religious puritanism. It also has classes in painting, weaving and other ancient crafts. But its soul is the dance form that Rukmini Devi uncompromisingly "transformed into an expression of love of god." Bharata Natyam has become the best known Indian dance form throughout the country and abroad and most of its finest exponents are Kalakshetra alumnae/i. It is a far cry from those early days when George Arundale had to make an introductory speech before each Kalakshetra performance, explaining how the school was using Bharata Natyam to defeat social prejudices and restore dignity to art.*

Apart from the arts and education, it was Theosophy, animal welfare and vegetarianism that had, in a way, brought the Arundales together – and remained Rukmini Devi's life-long interests. She served two terms in India's Upper House, the Rajya Sabha, and, from there, she piloted the Prevention of Cruelty to Animals Bill in 1960. Besides Kalakshetra, she also helped establish several schools around the campus, in memory of Besant and Arundale. She also helped spread the Montessori message in India.

All this lifetime of activity made fellow-vegetarian Morarji Desai think of her for the Presidentship of India when he became the first non-Congress Prime Minister of India. But thought did not get translated into deed, when Rukmini Devi refused the offer. During her last years, however, there were several disappointments – the Theosophical Society rivalries, teachers seeking individualism leaving Kalakshetra, students starting new schools – but she carried on regardless, a serene presence in public. She may have become plump of face and bulky of body, but with her long silver hair in a tidy knot and her gentle half smile she remained a strikingly attractive woman and everyone's 'Aththai' (Aunty), the name her thousands of students called her to the end.

No one has done as much for art in the country, especially Bharata Natyam, as she had; no one will do as much as 'Aththai' in the next hundred years, says a former student who went his own way. "We might not have agreed with her rigid attitude, but without it we could not have developed into the teachers we are," he added. The stern, grandmotherly-looking aunty who appeared to be ever angry when on campus would have gently smiled if she heard this epitaph to a life's work spent on building a temple of art "where she looked upon herself not as the presiding deity but as the first devotee."

13

Where the Deer and the Black Buck Play

West of Adyar, you move into Guindy and much of what is worth seeing in modern Madras. In the Adyar-Guindy area, locked in by the Theosophical Society in Adyar, Guindy Park, and Kalakshetra in Tiruvanmiyur, are what were, till recent over-development overwhelmed parts of them, some of the city's nicest middle class residential 'colonies' – Gandhi Nagar, Kasturba Nagar, Kamaraj Nagar, Shastri Nagar, Indira Nagar, Besant Nagar, Kalakshetra Colony and the newest of the lot, Valmiki Nagar, developments that began in the late 1940s and only slowed down in the early 1980s, when the development boom a decade later led to spaciousness making way for urban congestion. Even as building was going on in Gandhi Nagar from 1948, developing Kasturba Nagar began around 1951. The 136 acres of the former, carved out of *Bishop's Gardens* which belonged to the Roman Catholic Diocese of Mylapore, and the 125 acres of the latter, which belonged to Benegal Rama Rau and his brothers, were bought by cooperative societies with the help of Municipal Commissioner C Narasimham, who was a tower of strength in their development, following the example of a predecessor, J P L Shenoy. This cooperative development was initiated by J C Ryan, Registrar of Cooperative Societies, as a pioneering venture in India. The Rs. 14.5 lakh from the sale of *Bishop's Gardens* enabled the building of the handsome Art Deco *Catholic Centre*, prime office space, in Armenian Street, George Town.

Gandhi Nagar was the dream of Daniel Thomas, Local Administration Minister in the Omandur Ramasamy Reddiar cabinet (1947-49), who wanted to help develop a big middle class housing colony in the city. By the time Narasimham's Rs.15 lakh for the Bishop's Garden property was countered by the Bishop's Rs.17 lakh and promptly accepted, Thomas had got the Gandhinagar House Building Cooperative Society registered. It arranged for teak to be delivered at the site at Rs.6 a cubic foot and bricks at Rs.19 per thousand. A maximum loan of up to Rs.40,000 per house at 5.5 per cent interest, repayable in 20 years, was sanctioned, and houseowners got a four-bedroom house in a 30 cents plot for less than Rs.60,000 with all services provided!

The rush for applications was so great that Thomas decided to develop another colony nearby. And the Society identified 130 acres opposite Gandhi Nagar belonging to the brothers Sir Benegal Rama Rau, ics, Governor of the Reserve Bank, B. Narasinga Rau, ics, Constitutional Advisor to the Constituent Assembly, and B. Shiva Rau, the well-known journalist. It didn't take Sir Rama Rau more than an hour, during a visit to Madras with his wife, to come to an agreement with the Society on the price. And plans for Kasturba Nagar got underway.

Two popular institutions in Gandhi Nagar are the eponymously named club started in 1951 and the Prof K Venkateswara Research Foundation with its Sanskrit Library and collection of ancient Indian documentation.

Besant Nagar has a new Ashtalakshmi temple (1976), a gem of modern temple art and one of only three shore temples still open for worship on the east coast; a newer Vinayagar (Ganesh) Temple; the Aarupadai Veedu temple complex; a Shrine to the Madonna of Velankanni; and Elliot's Beach, popularly called Bessie Beach. The Ashtalakshmi Temple has shrines to eight aspects of the Goddess Lakshmi in the main temple and shrines to other deities elsewhere in the complex. The Aarupadai Veedu, a one-stop venue for the pilgrimage to six Murugan abodes of the deep south, were built between 1995 and 2003, fulfilling a dream of Dr. Alagappa Alagappan, a UN official known as the American temple-builder. Muthiah Sthapathi was the architect of this all granite complex. The rajagopuram was consecrated in 2015. The neighbouring Velankanni shrine, started in a thatched hut in the 1960s, got a proper home in 1972 with a 97-feet tall belfry. It was expanded into a larger church and consecrated in 1985.

At the edge of this residential area, on the road to Guindy, are the new and old halves of the internationally renowned Muthulakshmi Reddy-inspired Cancer Institute, with many firsts to its credit. Then you move west into one of Madras's most prestigious and fascinating areas.

There is here the residential Indian Institute of Technology – one of the first of India's 23 premier institutions of engineering[1] – with its beautiful 630-acre campus of modern buildings, spacious gardens and forest. IIT-Madras, as it is known, was established in 1959, its first classes being held in A.C. Tech and two rooms in the Central Leather Research Institute serving as office. In 1960 it moved into its own campus where the self-contained community that grew over the next few years is testimonial to successful Indo-German collaboration. It was the IIT's first Director, Dr B B Sengupta, who was responsible for ensuring the sylvan atmosphere here, fighting to save every tree that the builders wanted to fell in what was an extension of the Reserve Forest that was part of the Governor's estate till 1958. More recent Directors have not been so tree-friendly and have added new buildings at the cost of trees. Of particular interest here is the Institute's Heritage Centre inaugurated in 2006 with a permanent pictorial record and holding a wealth of documents recording the history of the Institute.

No less impressive is the Central Institute of Technology campus behind IIT's, with its numerous vocation-oriented training institutes, ranging from catering to printing. The country's first Regional School of Printing (now Institute of Printing Technology) – part of this campus from 1968 when it moved from the Madras Trades School (founded in 1916) premises at the end of Broadway, where now there is a women's educational institution – is a reminder that Madras was India's first State to start a diploma course in printing. Its Catering Institute (now Institute of Hotel Management and Catering Technology) and Women's Polytechnic are also among the first established in the country.

Across from IIT-M is the pioneering College of Engineering, now part of Anna University, which, in turn, in 1982, became the first institution in the country to start a degree course in printing. The Central Leather Research Institute, also opposite IIT, is one of the nation's finest research institutions and the ILO-backed Regional Labour Institute, just by IIT, is internationally known. The CLRI owes much to its first director, Dr B M Das, who scoured the country for talent to make possible this research institute which, in its first days, was woefully short of staff.

---

[1] From the first one established in Kharagpur, near Calcutta, in 1951, till 1994, there were only five IITs.

Later, Dr Nayuduamma made it internationally renowned. Heading southward from the CLRI, past the CIT institutions, is the Old Mahabalipuram Road (OMR), developed in 2006/7 as a major highway of international standard, popularly called the IT Highway – but officially named the Rajiv Gandhi Highway – reflecting the construction boom taking place here to accommodate a part of India's biggest success story since Independence, the Information Technology Industry. Madras is one of the top three IT destinations in the country and all along road, starting with huge TIDEL Park, are coming up the tall, architecturally modern towers of every major Indian and foreign player in the industry. When complete, this development, with hotels, foodcourts, shopping malls and huge gated communities with the most modern accommodation, is expected to extend over a 35-km stretch leading to Siruseri. Near here is Semmancheri with an 800-year-old banyan tree smack in the middle of the RG highway and protected from uprooting by the local citizenry.

Rajiv Gandhi Salai starts with the Madhya Kailash temple, one of the city's post-Independence shrines, and the Voluntary Health Services Hospital, a Society-run institution that has served the less privileged in exemplary fashion and has the city's best blood bank. Conceived in 1958 by Dr. R.S. Sanjivi, it was granted 25 acres of scrubland by Government and began functioning in 1961 even as its first building was being raised on donations. Today, with over 450 beds, it's the largest hospital in Adyar. Then comes the CIT campus stretching to TIDEL Park and, just before the latter, the huge Ramanujan Technopark being developed by Government and Tata's, the site of this park being a major part of once the sprawling M G R Film City whose numerous sets were meant to be both shooting sets as well as a tourist attraction but failed on both counts. Nearby is Government's M G R Film and Television Institute that has made a significant manpower contribution to the film industry.

To this campus has been added in the last few decades some of the country's most prestigious institutions. The M S Swaminathan Research Institute, founded by Dr M S Swaminathan, one of the fathers of the Green Revolution that made India self-sufficient in foodgrain, focuses on agricultural research and improving rural lives. The Roja Muthiah Research Library holds 250,000 items, mainly of Tamil printed material ranging from the late 18th Century till today, with its best holdings being in the fields of Tamil (classical and folk), Bhakti (devotional), indigenous medicine, and film and popular culture literature. Then there's the Research Institute for Newspaper Development, which also hosts the Indian Press Institute, and the Asian College of Journalism which has links with *The Hindu* and the BBC. Nearby is the International Institute of Tamil Studies, started in 1970. Once visited only by scholars, it opened a museum in 2017 to highlight the achievements of the Tamil people from ancient times and drew to it a wider audience.

West of TIDEL Park and south of the IIT campus are several major educational facilities – the University of Madras's new science research campus and its Dr A L Mudaliar Postgraduate Institute of Basic Medical Sciences opened in 1975, a National Institute of Fashion Technology branch, and the US-sponsored International School, among others. Linking the area, Taramani, with the city, or Beach Station, is the Mass Rapid Transit System (MRTS) – a surface and elevated commuter railway service that's taken ten years in the building but which only from 2007 began getting into its stride. It is still far from close to full utilisation as these lines are written, but has reached Velachery and is heading for St. Thomas' Mount. That with its huge stations the MRTS mars the city skyline and has ruined the Buckingham Canal is the price being paid for progress.

Adding to that disfigurement will be the huge station at St.Thomas' Mount which will be a crossover junction for the MRTS, Metro, Suburban and Southern Railway systems when the work on the first two named is completed, expectedly, before 2020.

In Guindy, too, is what is possibly the world's only game reserve within a city – the deer sanctuary, now a National Park – one of the last natural grazing grounds of the black buck. The only National Park in India within city limits, Guindy National Park, approximately 680 acres of deciduous scrub jungle, has about 125 species of trees and other flora. There are in it over 140 species of birds, several small animal and reptile species and its pride, large herds of spotted deer (over 2600 at last count), which were introduced here from the Government Estate gardens in the city by Governor Lord Elphinstone c.1840, and black buck. The spiral-horned, shiny coated black buck (*Antelope cervicapra*), now an endangered species but numbering over 400 here, were added to c.1950 by the Governor of Madras at the time, the Maharajah of Bhavnagar, who introduced the albino variety and the strain has survived. Today,

Raj Bhavan...*gubernatorial splendour in green-girt isolation.*
Where (the deer and) the black buck play... in the sanctuary of a city jungle.

29. *The World Headquarters of Theosophy...serenity surrounding* Huddlestone Gardens.

30. *What's left of the 400-year-old banyan tree...Theosophical symbol in the Society's* Garden of Remembrance.

these antelopes haunt the open spaces of the park – what was the Governor's polo ground and the space by the *Raj Bhavan* quarters. The Park, part of the Governor's 1300-acre country retreat from 1821, came under Forest Department supervision in 1910 when it was declared a Reserve Forest. When the Governor's mansion became *Raj Bhavan* in 1948, the first Indian Governor, Maharaja Sri Krishna Kumarasinji Bhavsinji, handed over about 1,000 acres to the Government, leaving his estate 156 acres in extent. In 1958, the forest was formally handed over to the Forest Department. A Children's Park was developed in a corner of the forest at Prime Minister Nehru's request, together with a child-friendly mini-zoo and deer park. With land in the forest reserve being handed over for various memorials, educational institutions and hospitals between 1954 and 1977 – most of these were raised in forest clearings and retain much of the natural surroundings – the Forest Reserve dwindled to about 680 acres and this area was declared a National Park in 1978.

In Guindy Park has been established a unique snake park and reptilium. The Snake Park, founded in the early 1970s by an American settled in India, Romulus Whitaker, has been widely copied in several other parts of India, where his ideas on venom extraction are also being profitably put to use. He also helped the Irulas, tribesmen who earned a livelihood by catching snakes and rats, to found a snake-catchers' cooperative that now thrives on venom extraction. Whitaker later moved from snakes to crocodiles and founded the country's first crocodile bank a little outside Madras, on the Mamallapuram road. The hatcheries here were intended to help restock the crocodile-depleted estuaries of India and, like the Snake Park, were emulated elsewhere in the country. But the estuaries lost interest in crocodiles when people complained about their unfriendliness. The hatcheries as a consequence hold unmanageable stocks which no one knows what to do with. Whitaker's pioneering Crocodile Bank has around 20 species of crocodiles comprising over 5,000 muggers and gharials, as well as other reptilian species. Migrant birds too come visiting here. Meanwhile, the Snake Park is run by a Trust, exhibits several snake species, has an excellent interactive museum since 2014, and publishes several books on snakes.

Next door to the small parks in Guindy Park are several other enclaves, officially sanctioned 'encroachments' on reserved forest land. Octagonal Rajaji Memorial (1974) commemorates India's first Indian Governor-

General, that most astute of all Madras politicians, C Rajagopalachari. The building's crowning 32-foot tall *gopuram* was conceived by a Chief Minister of the 1970s, Mu Karunanidhi, to evoke memories of Lord Rama, hero of the *Ramayana*, whom 'C R' immortalised in his English version of the classic. Further on is stately Gandhi Mandapam (1954), Madras's memorial to the Father of the Nation, and another (1975) to one of his most ardent followers, Congress stalwart Kamaraj, a revered name in Tamil Nadu politics. In the Gandhi Mandapam campus there was raised in 1998 another memorial, to the last Congress Chief Minister of the State, M Bhaktavatsalam (1963-67). During the first decade of the 21st Century, three more memorials have been built midst these, making it quite possible for this edge of Guindy National Park to be called 'Memorial Park'!

The new memorials commemorate Rettamalai Srinivasan, a Dalit leader from Tamil Nadu who was a close associate of Gandhi, the Tamil freedom-fighters who gave their lives (*Thiyagigal*) during the struggle for Independence (this memorial also hosts the oil extractor V O Chidambaram Pillai, who challenged British Shipping, was made to push in prison), and those who were martyred during the anti-Hindi agitations (*Mozhipor Thiyagigal*) in 1965. All this – and *Raj Bhavan* too! – were part of what was once an enormous Governor's Estate, through which the deer and the black buck still wander. In 1977/78, the large new block of the Cancer Institute, an institute of excellence established in 1954 (by the canal in Gandhi Nagar), was added to the architectural clutter here. At the other end of the estate, land was given in 1970 for the Guru Nanak College, founded by the Punjabis of Madras, an institution which has one of Madras's two gurdwaras.

Across the way from this Estate are some of the finest educational centres in the country. Amongst these institutions is the College of Engineering, its roots in the oldest technical institution outside Europe. Its Indo-Saracenic E-shaped building is particularly handsome. The college, popularly called Guindy Engineering, grew out of the Government Survey School which was founded on May 17, 1794, in Fort St George with eight students from the Military Orphan Asylum and headed by Michael Topping, who was succeeded by John Goldingham. This was the same year that the world's very first technical school was founded in Paris. Several 'graduates' of this school went on to be the pioneer surveyors who worked with William Lambton on the

Great Trigonometrical Survey of India that he started from a St. Thomas' Mount–Observatory pillar (today) baseline in 1802/3. The commencement of that great effort and the naming of the granite found here as 'Charnockite' in 1893 are both commemorated on the Mount.

The Fort St George survey school, after being closed from 1810 to 1819, re-opened in the Observatory in Nungambakkam, then moved to the PWD-occupied *Khalsa Mahal* building in Chepauk in 1859, the year after it took on a new name: the Civil Engineering School.[2]

A Major Maitland played a significant role in the School in those early days. He was the Superintendent of the Gun Carriage Factory on Poonamallee High Road, kitty-corner from St.Andrew's Kirk. In 1842 he set up a school on his own to train ordinance artificers and apprentices.

Offering as it did sound training in mechanical skills, it was felt in 1849 that it would well-serve the Survey School if they were amalgamated. Major Maitland agreed, but not the Military Board. It urged that a technical college be started. The Public Works Commissioners endorsed this view and a Civil Engineering College was proposed.

Nothing, however, happened till 1855 when Director of Public Instruction Alexander Arbuthnot – to whom Madras owes much — presented a proposal to establish an engineering school or college with three departments and a workshop. The Government approved the proposal in 1856 but insisted that every student had to master one trade or craft in Major Maitland's School – where, in fact, many a student had on his own gone for training in one skill or another.

In 1857, Lt.George Winscom was appointed Principal of the Survey School which, after the changes he wrought, was named the Civil Engineering School in October 1858. In September 1859 it was renamed the Civil Engineering College and, later that year, the Engineering College. It became a college of the University of Madras in 1861. The subjects taught were: Surveying, Plotting, Planning and Estimation, Costume Engineering, Mechanical Engineering, Hydraulics, Elementary Mathematics, Tamil, and Telugu. Significantly, for practical training in Mechanical Engineering, the students continued to go to Major

---

[2] Pigot could will be considered the man responsible for sowing the seeds of the British Empire; he helped raise the Indian Army; he defeated the French; and he enabled Clive's victory at Plassey. He also established the seniority of the Civil **over** the military leadership.

Maitland's School. They also went to the Grand Arsenal (in Fort St. George) for practical training, presumably in the kind of strength walls had to have to withstand different kinds of ammunition, military engineering being the focus of the institution from the first.

Indeed, till 1894 when the College became the first in India to offer a Mechanical Engineering stream for a degree, Maitland's School was the only school training students in mechanical skills. Maitland's School for Carnatic Ordinance Artificers and Apprentices therefore had not only a signal role in supplementing the knowledge of the students of the Civil Engineering School/College for over 50 years but also sowed the seeds for the Mechanical Engineering degree in India. It was also, I would like to think, the forerunner of today's ITIs.

The first set of students to receive the BCE degree did so in 1864. The first degree was awarded to S Subbarayachariar, who in 1872 became the first Indian to be made an Assistant Engineer in the Presidency. The first person to get the Mechanical Engineering degree was Devaisikhamani Pillai in 1896. Diwan Bahadur A V Ramalinga Iyer, an old student, became in 1923 the Presidency's first Indian Chief Engineer and, two years later, Rao Bahadur G Nagarathnam Ayyar became the College's first Indian principal. Nagarathnam Ayyar is remembered in a bust in the Alumni Club (a neighbour of the Boat Club), whose members are mainly from the College of Engineering. The first girl student was admitted by the College in 1940.

She was A Lalitha, who took Electrical Engineering and she was followed in Civil Engineering that year by Leelamma George and P.K. Thressia. All three graduated in 1943 and went to work as engineers, pioneers in the country. Thressia became the first woman Chief Engineer in a State in India, rising to the position in Kerala. Then, in 1948, Rajyalakshmi graduated as the first woman Telecommunications engineer in India. A contemporary Civil Engineering woman graduate, May George, became the first woman Chief Engineer in Tamil Nadu.

When the school developed into a college, it got more buildings in Chepauk, near the Victoria Students' Hostel of today. Chepauk's southern car park and tennis courts were its sports grounds. Still surviving near this first campus of the Madras Engineering College are several fine old residential buildings, among them one occupied by the Warden of the Victoria Hostel, but neither the hostel nor the other buildings are in the best of condition. The bungalow occupied by the Warden of Victoria Hostel was once the home of now-forgotten principals, Col Henry Davison Love, who famously wrote *Vestiges of Old Madras* which was published in 1913, one of them. The three volumes of this classic are the most complete history of Madras from its founding to 1800. A President of the Madras Club, he also wrote a historical note on the Club's first seventy years.

The Hostel itself, once used by the Engineering College's students amongst others, was built by Thaticonda Namberumal Chetty, who established his contracting, building and engineering business in 1880. At the opening of the Hostel in January 1900, Governor Sir Arthur Havelock said, "Mr Namberumal Chetty will have his name recorded in Madras in connection with many large and beautiful buildings in stone, brick and mortar. It should be a proud remembrance for him and his descendants that he has had so much to do with the beautifying of the city." Alas, the Dewan Bahadur, whose memory will be resurrected many times in the pages that follow in connection with the many magnificent buildings he gave the city, was not remembered at all for decades in Madras. But then, in 1998, a hospital in his memory was opened in Egmore in the Red Cross Society's campus to help the slum-dwellers of the city. In the Namberumal Chetty Day Hospital now hangs a portrait of the man who had built so much of the lasting grandeur of Madras. There also hangs here a painting of Namberumal Chetty and his wife.

In 1920, the College moved into its new Guindy building set in a spacious 200-acre campus. The oldest technical institution in Asia, rooted as it is in the Survey School, 'Guindy Engineering' has several firsts to its credit; the degree course in Mechanical Engineering (1894), Electrical Engineering (1930), Telecommunication and Highways (1945), and Printing Technology (1982). This institution, together with the neighbouring Alagappa Chettiar College of Technology, the Madras School of Architecture and Town Planning, and the Madras Institute of Technology in Chromepet, formed in 1978 the Anna University of Technology, one of the finest engineering universities in the country. To it, in an on again, off again exercise have been affiliated some or all the engineering colleges in Tamil Nadu, around 626 in number, most of these colleges sorely affecting the University's overall quality and standing. Its main administrative building is one of the new additions to this campus.

AC College, with its emphasis on textile and leather technology, was founded in 1944 through the munificence of the philanthropist Rm Alagappa Chettiar, after whom a University is named in his native Chettinad. The Madras Institute of Technology, founded in 1949 by industrialist C Rajam, with such specialities as aeronautical and automobile engineering, is another splendid example of private endowment. MIT's most famous graduate is A P J Abdul Kalam, father of India's space programme and from 2003 to 2007 the President of India. The School of Architecture, founded in 1957 as part of AC College, became a separate unit in 1963 and is now known as the School of Architecture and Town Planning.

Behind these campuses, in the vast College of Engineering grounds, is what is perhaps one of the best-looking modern buildings in the city, the well-equipped Anna Centenary Library inaugurated in 2010, in this biggest hub in the city of some of the country's leading educational and research institutions. The Library boasts a 1300-seat auditorium and two well-equipped conference halls. This nine-storey building was raised on a site by a Government whose predecessor wanted to build a new Legislature and Secretariat here and even laid the foundation stone for it. Now that the latter's in power, as these lines are written, it reluctantly supports the Library with its 1.2 million books only because of Court insistence.

Between Guindy Engineering and the CLRI campus are two additions of the 1980s to the Madras scene. One is the country's fifth B M Birla planetarium; it was opened in 1985. The planetarium is a part of the second and bigger addition, the Tamil Nadu Science and Technology Centre, a museum where science and technology have been simplified and made interesting to create popular interest and awareness.

Beyond *Raj Bhavan Estate,* Sardar Vallabhbhai Patel Road (the old Elliot's Beach Road) joins Mount Road heading south. Near the bridge into bustling Guindy and hidden by newer construction is the King Institute of Preventive Medicine, opened in 1899 to supply vaccine lymph to the entire Presidency, and, since 1948, functioning in expanded capacity. Its main Indo-Saracenic block (1905) and the cottage where it began are heritage landmarks in the campus. Founded to manufacture smallpox vaccine, it began the manufacture of cholera and typhoid vaccine too in the 1920s. Its first Indian Director was Dr M Kesava Pai (c.1918), a tuberculosis specialist. But its best-known scientist was Dr. K .V. Venkatraman whose work on cholera is internationally recognised.

Across from the King Institute campus is the main building of the MGR Medical University, opened in 1998 to affiliate all the medical colleges in the State. Its polished granite reflects the favoured style of embellishment in PWD architecture of the 1990s, while the building strives for the Chola palatial look favoured by Government. Near here are two of the newest luxury hotels in the city. The Welcomgroup's Grand Chola, next to the Medical University, is the closest thing to the vision today of Chola grandeur, but its spaciousness is rather overwhelming and its size rather daunting. Nevertheless, it is one of Madras's new landmarks. Quite a contrast is the Park Hyatt, just behind the Grand Chola, its interiors a vision in modern design and minimalism. The city, enjoying a luxury hotel boom in the second decade of the 21st Century, hosts, besides these two and older ones mentioned elsewhere, an opulent Leela Palace, a Hilton, the Hyatt Regency, the Taj Club House, Marriotts, The Park, the Meridien, a Holiday Inn, a Westin and a couple of Radissons among others.

Not far from the Medical University is the racecourse, a once glorious complex worthy of the first centre in India to take to its heart the 'Sport of Kings". The first race meet in the country was held around 1760 on the Island Grounds. But the sport moved to Guindy in 1777 when land was granted to it by Government for a racecourse. The Madras Race Club was founded in 1837, but did not really take off and faded out in 1875. It, however, was revived in 1887 and has continued ever since, despite numerous ups and downs. Its first stands were built in 1920, thanks to the munificence of two Indian princes. Near the racecourse was a forlorn building that, not so long ago, dated racing in Madras. This building, set in spacious open surroundings, was the centre of attention in one of that famous series of paintings Thomas Daniell and his nephew William did of 18th Century India. The painting, done in 1792, was titled *The Assembly Rooms on the Race Ground, near Madras*. The Daniells noted that the race ground was to the left of the *Assembly Rooms* – which would place it just about where it is now – and added, "The amusement (racing) takes place in the cool season, when the ladies of the settlement are invited to a splendid ball" (in the *Assembly Rooms*, no doubt). Once a large Palladian building with a fine flight of steps that divided the building into two, it was, in the 1980s, a decrepit shell of a much abbreviated building. It was eventually pulled down in 1985, despite the pleas of conservationists.

Racing in its early years featured only Gentlemen Riders and began at six in the morning in order to finish early enough to allow enthusiasts to get to work by 10 a.m. The gallop back from Guindy would often be as thrilling as the action on the track. The track dates to 1777 when Government granted 81 cannies to the informal club and added 35 cannies c. 1860. Racing, it is believed, had a setback during the Mysore Wars and was revived in 1804. A more formal club was formed in 1837 and survived till 1875. But it faded from the scene again, only to be revived in 1887 as the Madras Race Club with 50 members. This time it stayed and, in 1896, the Madras Race Club was reconstituted by members of the Madras Club whose members had formed the earlier club. Since then, Madras has enjoyed almost continuous racing, though, for one reason or another, there have been breaks. Now the sport enjoys a November-March season where it began in India and Madras is considered one of the major racing centres in the country. The club was gifted its first grandstand by the Rajahs of Bobbili and Venkatagiri in 1920 and in 1931 Guindy Lodge was built as a home for a full time secretary.

It was at the *Assembly Rooms* too that the Madras Hunt assembled twice a week to run to ground the jackal and, occasionally, the smaller Indian silver fox. There are references to a Madras Hunting Society as far back as 1776, which would make the Madras Hunt the oldest in India. The country hunted was to the south and west of Madras and in this terrain and climate the 'jacks' proved hardier, usually surviving a season (though it be a 'cold weather' season only) better than the hounds. The sport in Madras appears to have died out before World War I.

Across from the racecourse is the sprawling 450-acre campus of the Thiru Vi Ka Industrial Estate in Guindy, named after a pioneering labour leader. It was the first Government-sponsored scheme to provide integrated amenities for small-scale industry in India. Starting with 30 sheds in 1958, the brainchild of State Industries Minister R Venkataraman who went on to become the President of India in the late 1980s, there were at its peak over 400 units here with a turnover of over Rs.1,000 million a year. New industrialisation all around the city has had a rather depressing effect on this pioneering industrial estate, but it received a new lease of life in the early 2000s with the IT industry moving in and modern highrise coming up as small-scale engineering industries close down and offer space at a price.

The city ends just past the estate, with a colossal new clover-leaf flyover, said to be largest in Asia, at Kathipara Junction where huge, sweeping highrise roads herald the New Madras, appropriately as you enter the city. These merge it with St Thomas' Mount and link Mount Road and the new Ring Road with the highways to Cape Comorin and Bangalore. Jawaharlal Nehru, by Mani Nagappa, is honoured in glittering bronze at the roundabout. Around the junction, now a hive of new building activity, were, until the 1980s, several crumbling old residences of the British. Was one where Stringer Lawrence used to enjoy his R & R? Was another where Governor George Pigot[3] was kept prisoner by his kidnappers? These residences were built along a road between the steps to the Mount and the road south. Lawrence's was said to be the closest to the main road – which might place it on the site where that college of engineering, H I E T, has come up.

Nearby Velachery is an ancient village, its Selliamman and Dandisvarar Temples, both of Chola construction, possessing inscriptions dating to the 10th Century. Velachery, with much agricultural land till the 1980s, has become, from the early 2000s, one of the fastest developing areas of the city with its main road a veritable shopping mall befitting all the highrise coming up in the area to serve a burgeoning population living in a maze of hastily ill-laid out streets.

Between Velachery and Tambaram is the Nanmangalam Reserve Forest with a host of small fauna and bird life. But it is nearby Pallikarnai marsh that is yet another of Madras's bird-watchers' paradises. Once 5000 ha of swamp and grassland which acted as a sink for rainwater and provided migrant birds a welcome resting place, it has been progressively degraded through construction and dumping of waste. In 2012, citizens' pleas were at last heeded – after a Court ruling – and 750 ha have been declared 'protected'. About 110 species of birds, 45 species of fish and 20 species of reptiles, besides a host of insects and small fauna, have been identified as using the marsh, either as seasonal visitors or permanent residents. All around is urban development and congestion.

Printing Comes to India

The Chinese, it is generally accepted, invented a form of printing, using engraved wooden blocks, and this art, called xylography, is believed to have spread to parts of the sub-Himalayan regions of India through Tibet and Nepal. But it was left to the Germanic central Europeans to invent printing with movable type in the mid-15th Century. For the next hundred years or so, printing by this means spread only through Europe; it was the mid-16th Century before the craft moved out of there. The Spaniards took it to Mexico and, a few years later, the Portuguese brought it to Goa, India thus becoming the first Asian recipient of the new European craft. The first printing press in India was set up by the Portuguese Jesuits in 1556, commandeering a printing press and its printer bound for their Mission in Ethiopia, the opportunity coming their way when the Abyssinian-bound vessel put into Goa for victualling. The press was set up in the College of St Paul, where a seminary still functions.

The first printing material turned out by this press was, naturally, Christian literature, all of it in Latin. In 1575, however, the Visitor-General of the Goa Jesuit congregation ordered that such literature also be printed in Konkani and Tamil (called Malabar by the Portuguese). The preparation of work in Tamil was entrusted to Henrique Henriques, the Jesuit Superior in Punnaikayal on the southernmost Fisheries Coast (the Tuticorin coast) and the recognised European scholar in the language at the time.

Henriques sent Pedro Luis, a member of his Tamil flock, to Goa to help a Portuguese blacksmith, Joao Goncalves, design and cut the first fount of Tamil types. Goncalves succeeded in casting the new type in 1577. Specimens of this fount were reproduced in the first book ever to be printed in Tamil – the translation by Henriques of the catechism

Doctrina Christam. *The small booklet was printed in October 1578 at Coulam (Quilon) by Joao de Faria, an architect-cum-printer, who used Tamil fount he had designed and, to display its superiority, also printed in a spirit of one-upmanship a few pages with Goncalves' first type! This was the first book printed in an Indian language. When Portuguese policy changed, emphasising the use of Latin again in worship, printing, which never really caught on in India, died out.*

Despite its 16th Century beginnings on the Konkan and Malabar Coasts, printing did not reach the Coromandel Coast till King Frederick IV of Denmark sent out, in 1706, Bartholomaeus Ziegenbalg, a German Lutheran from Halle, to establish in Danish Tranquebar (Tarangambadi) the first Protestant mission in India. Ziegenbalg was a scholar and so was his fellow-missionary Heinrich Plütschau. Together they learned Tamil – from an unskilled teacher called Ellappar, who taught them the alphabet in the ancient Tamil way, by getting them to trace the letters in the sand. Ziegenbalg, who headed the Danish Halle Mission, was to set an example for his fellow Pietists who followed him to India over the next hundred years by focussing on the study of Indian religions, Indian scientific knowledge, and Indian languages. What they left to the Francke Foundation in Halle in Germany was a pioneering tradition of Indology.

By 1711, Ziegenbalg and Plütschau had completed translating the New Testament *– but had to wait till 1715 for it to be printed. This delay in printing was due to the non-availability of a printing press. The press meant for the mission was shipped out of London in 1711 by the Society for Promoting Christian Knowledge (SPCK), who had been persuaded to do so when Ziegenbalg had visited England during 'home leave'. But the French captured the East Indiaman carrying the press and its printer, Jonas Finck, and released the vessel only after ransom was paid. The ship eventually reached Madras in June 1712 – but without Finck, who had fallen overboard! The missionaries, however, found a soldier in Madras to work the press, and both printer and press left for Tranquebar, where, by the end of the year, a few small publications were printed in Portuguese, the lingua franca of both coasts at the time. This was the first printing to be done outside the Malabar Coast, and marked the revival of printing in India.*

The Tranquebar Mission Press was strengthened in 1713 by three German printers who brought with them Tamil types cut in Halle. In October that year, the first publication of the press in Tamil was brought out, but the large Halle types ate up paper! Johann Gottlieb Adler, one of the printers, then set to work designing and casting smaller type – from, legend has it, the lead covers of tins of Cheshire cheese sent out by the SPCK! With the first type of the Tranquebar Foundry, Adler printed a Tamil hymnal, followed by, in July 1715, Ziegenbalg and Grundler's New Testament, *the first such translation to be printed in any Indian language. Ziegenbalg, who was only 36 when he died in 1719, also had several children's primers printed at the press in King Street – the first books published for schoolchildren in India. In 1716, there was issued from here the first work in English to be printed in India:* A Guide to the English Tongue *by Thomas Dyche. And that same year, the enterprising Adler set up just outside Tranquebar a paper-mill that was, however, not to prove successful and an ink factory that was more successful. Before coming to Madras, as the first Protestant missionary to work there, Benjamin Schultze completed Ziegenbalg's* magnum opus, *the Tamil translation of the* Old Testament, *which was published by the press in four volumes between 1723 and 1728.*

It was long after the heyday of the Tranquebar Mission Press that printing came to Madras. Crotchety old General Eyre Coote acquired, during the loot of Pondicherry in 1761, "a hand-press and some cases of type and other equipment" that were in the Governor's mansion. This equipment had been brought to Pondicherry in 1758 by the debonair Comte de Lally, the Irish rebel who led a Brigade of his fellow-Irishmen for France. But Lally had little chance to put the press to use – other than to print notes of credit – for he spent most of his command at Pondicherry besieged by the tenacious Coote. Johannes P Fabricius, a German missionary and a scholar, was at the time in charge of the Mission (that in 1798 developed into the SPCK's) at Vepery and he made a request to Governor Pigot for this booty. The Madras Government handed over the press to the Mission on the understanding that Government printing should take priority over the Mission's work. Fabricius, who became manager of the press known both as the East India Company's Press and the Vepery Press, remained in charge from 1761 until 1769.

In 1766, Fabricius expanded the press with the acquisition of another printing machine (from Tranquebar?), Tamil type cast in Halle and a Tamil printer, Thomas, from Tranquebar. It was this new wing of the Vepery Press that was to develop as the famous SPCK Press – and grow into the CLS, or Diocesan, Press of today – after the Company's 'share' was transferred from Vepery to Fort St George to eventually become the Government Press. The main building of the CLS Press, going back to the 19th Century, was sold after the press moved to smaller premises on the same campus and was pulled down by the developers in 1998.

The first publication in Tamil issued by the SPCK Press was a catechism by Fabricius, printed in 1766, but the first major work of the press was Fabricius' revised version of the Malabar New Testament, *completed in 1772 and a copy of which is still available. That same year, the Armenian Jacob Shameer established in Armenian Street a second press in Madras and printed* Hordorak, *a reader for Armenian schoolchildren. Shameer's press continued until 1788. In 1779, the Vepery Press issued its greatest publication, the* Malabar (Tamil) – English Dictionary, *Fabricius and Breithaupt following up this joint venture with a second part in 1786. The Catholic Mission in Madurai had, much earlier, done considerable pioneering work in basic Tamil. Roberto de Nobili, who, it is said, combined "the sanctity of the Sanyasi with the erudition of the Pundit" and Constantius Beschi (1680-1747) – Veeramunivar – a great scholar and poet in Tamil, were two Italian Jesuits to whom Tamil owes much. Some of Beschi's work was printed at Tranquebar, but most of it survives through efforts of the College of Fort St George, which was founded in 1812, with press, book depots and library attached.*

Though originally established to teach civilians the languages of the Presidency, the College in Nungambakkam took upon itself considerable research and publishing in these languages. Beschi's 'Low Tamil' Grammar *and* A Brief Exposition of Tamil *by Chidambara Pandaram, head Tamil Master of the College, were amongst the College's first publications.* Andhra Dipika, *a dictionary by Mammudi Venkayya of Machilipatnam, was the first copyright acquired (for 1,000 pagodas) by the College in the Telugu language.* A Grammar of Teloogoo Language Commonly Termed the Gentoo *by A D Campbell was printed by the College Press in 1816, its second Telugu acquisition. John McKerell's* 'Kanarese' Grammar *was the first acquisition in that language, being bought and published in 1820. Rev C M Whish's* Malayalam Grammar and Dictionary *was the first work in Malayalam.*

Older than the College Press, however, was the press attached to the Male Orphan Asylum. This orphanage printed the Government Gazette *for many years. It also published the* Madras Male Asylum Almanac *which, later, until World War II, was issued as the* Lawrence Asylum Press Almanac. *The Lawrence Asylum Press was situated in Mount Road, near Higginbotham's, in premises now occupied by a part of the Government Press.* The Government Gazette *in its earliest years was a weekly newspaper; it did not take on its official character until the Government Press set up shop in Fort St George in 1831 (with its share of the Vepery Press), the first official* Government Gazette *being issued on January 4, 1832. But even before Government Press moved into the Fort, there is reported to have been a Government Lithographic Press there from 1828 which even produced Hindu religious pictures in 1850! Government Press moved to its present location at the end of Mint Street in George Town in 1888, by which time Madras had a well-established printing industry.*

Pioneers of that industry in the private sector included Hoe & Co of Stringer Street (1886); the Guardian Press (1850); V Ramaswami Sastrulu & Co (1851), specialists in Telugu printing and a major contributor to Telugu publishing; Payne & Co (1869) on Francis Joseph Street; Addison & Co (1873), now connected with printing only though Associated Printers who are a part of the same Amalgamations Group; Thompson Press (1879); The Huxley Press; Solden & Co of Triplicane, started in 1909; and the Law Printing House also dating to 1909 and which has grown into the Madras Law Journal Press. The Vavilla Ramaswami Sastrulu Press is specially noteworthy for republishing in 1910 at Bangalore Nagarathnammal's request, Radhika Santwanamu *by Muddu Palani, a courtesan. Following protests against its "obscenity", the Government in 1911 banned the book, the first ban of a book in Madras on grounds of obscenity.*

In the first third of the 20th Century, Hoe & Co, the M L J Press, the Caxton Press, Associated Printers and the Madras Publishing House on Mount Road were the big printing houses in Madras and it was in these presses, and the Government and Southern Railway Presses, that there apprenticed the first students in India to receive formal training in printing.

The Madras Government in 1916 started the Madras Trades School with part-time apprentices. It was intended to supply the Presidency with skilled mechanics, electricians, draughtsmen and plumbers. Evening classes in printing were added in 1926 and the first-ever organised course in printing in India was started at this school the next year when a four-year, part-time certificate course was introduced for employees and apprentices working in the city's printing presses. The Madras Trades School in those years was located in a building at the end of Broadway. As the institution grew, it became the School of Technology (1938) and then the Central Polytechnic (1946).

In 1937, a third-year student, Chandy Kurien, led a deputation to meet C Rajagopalachari, then Premier of the Presidency's first popular Government. They requested that the Printing Certificate course be changed into a Diploma course, as in the case of Engineering disciplines. Government, after due consideration, agreed to make the course a 5-year Diploma one and, in 1938, the first Diploma examination was held, after the students' committee had suggested various titles – M P (Master Printer), L P (Licentiate in Printing), D G A (Diploma in Graphic Arts) etc. – to be awarded since there was no precedent even in Britain. Eventually, Government added the T to L P and the first Licentiates in Printing Technology in India passed out of the institution – R Venkateswaran, doyen of the Madras printing industry and an all-India figure in printing circles till his death in 1998; R Ramaswamy, who ran the Government of India Press and the Dewas Bank Note Press, a pioneering venture in the country; N Palanivelu, who worked with the Southern Railways' printing unit; and R Ramakrishnan, who was with the Government Press, Nagpur.

In August 1955, the Printing Section of the Central Polytechnic was inaugurated as the country's first Regional School of Printing, one of the four suggested by the Council for Technical Education. When the Central Polytechnic moved to its new campus in Adyar in 1958, the Broadway building was handed over to the Regional School of Printing. Later, a new home for the former was built at the Central Institute of Technology (that the Polytechnic has become) *campus, Adyar, to which Rs 10-lakh building the School moved in July 1968. Soon afterwards, it became the Regional Institute of Printing Technology it is today. And then, in 1982, the Guindy Engineering College, a neighbour, introduced the first degree course in printing technology in the country.*

14
Bhavans of the Raj

Raj Bhavan, the residence of the Governor of the State, and its estate in Guindy, like most of modern Madras, date back to Britain's most glorious era, the Age of Empire. Once Madras got a Governor, it was inevitable that it should also *get a Government House.* And, so, it has been that in the centuries since George Foxcroft, the first Governor (1668), Madras has had its fair share of Governor's mansions.

The first Governors lived in the 'Factory House' in the centre of Fort St George, where they shared a common table with all the employees of the Company, down to the juniormost writer. But from the latter half of the 18th Century, the Governor began dining separately at a Governor's Table, as the Common Table always lacked decorum, arrack and punch flowing too freely. "Indecencys and disorders" were so frequent at table that, on occasion, "files of musqueteers" had to be sent for to "keep the peace at dinner time"! And so, in 1772, the Common Table was abolished.

With the Common Table situation being like this from the very beginning, no wonder Presidents and Governors felt the need not only for separate accommodation but also garden space for recreation for the Company's complement. The first garden was the old 'Guava Garden', about eight acres in extent and located, with its small pavilion, where the Law College now is. But with 'Black Town' encroaching, Governor Streynsham Master, around 1680, developed a new garden in which he built himself a 'garden house'. It was located along the Cooum River, having a landing site for boat traffic, where the Medical College is now situated, across from The Island. This house was used by successive Governors for uninhibited R & R, as later Americans would term it, and not so much for residence! The French used the site for gun emplacements in 1746, when they besieged Madras, and levelled it when they withdrew. So when the City was rendered to the British, the first thing the British did was to begin looking for a suitable garden house for the Governor. The house they finally acquired belonged to Mrs Antonia de Madeiros, one of the Company's most loyal friends in Madras and widow of the seafaring Luis de Madeiros (or Luis Madra) of San Thomé.

The Company was indebted to the wealthy Mrs Madeiros for the large sums of money she had lent it whenever the Council was financially prostrate – and that appears to have been quite often! Her 'garden house' to the southwest of the Cooum had been acquired by Luis de Madeiros from an unknown owner several years before the French attack on Madras. La Bourdannais' advance guard plundered the house and left it a shell. But after the French withdrew in 1749, leaving a shattered town, even a shell was good enough for a Governor without a 'garden house'. And so Mrs Madeiros' house was rented in 1752. In October that year, a two-day storm damaged the house further. Taking advantage of the 'as is, where is' offer of the house, Governor Thomas Saunders acquired it for 3,500 pagodas (about Rs 1,00,000 today) on August 28, 1753, though the house was "esteem'd worth more than the Sum 'tis offered at." This is the house that was the nucleus of the main mansion that was developed as *Government House* in what is known as *Government Estate,* near Round Tana. In 1756, more land was added to the Estate, which was again occupied by the French during Lally's 67-day siege of Fort St George (1758-59)! This town estate was further extended in 1855 with the addition of parts of the Nawab of Carnatic's estate. The entire estate, then called Chepauk Park, was one of the most beautiful open spaces in Madras after an intense tree-planting (over 50 species), gardening and pond-construction programme was carried out from 1883. Alas, much of this green cover has been neglected or cut down in recent years and a variety of highrise government accommodations was raised in the 1990s vitiating the park atmosphere.

That most notorious of 'Nabobs', Thomas Rumbold (1778-80), and Edward, Lord Clive the Second (1798-1803), considerably expanded the house and brought it to what it looked like in its last years in the early 21st Century, though the third storey was added only in 1860. The

Fort St George authorities wanted to create a building that could stand unashamed beside the magnificence of neighbouring Chepauk Palace. Part of this grand scheme was the building of the stately *Banqueting Hall* (now *Rajaji Hall*) with rows of Doric, Ionic and Corinthian columns within and without, and handsome pediments at the ends. Built in the form of a Greek temple, by Company astronomer and engineer Goldingham, it was completed in 1802, and inaugurated with a grand ball. Goldingham, who was partly Danish, had started his career in Madras in 1786, assisting at the private Observatory. He was a friend of Edward Clive and had been entrusted, in 1800, with the extensions to the main building and its remodelling. He was then given the assignment of building a commemoration hall worthy of British achievements at arms in India and to integrate it harmoniously with the Classically impressive *Government House* he had created. The Hall was inaugurated with a grand ball in 1802. Much remodelling of the Hall was done from 1875 till the terrace was enclosed by the arcaded verandah in 1895.

The Hall's superb flights of steps, the original narrow flight being widened, and its open terraces enclosed by rows of arches linked by columns and low walls, are all part of the later expansions, but remain architectural additions to be appreciated. The only major change in the Hall since then is that the giant portraits of great Anglo-Indians, by George Chinnery, Thomas Hickey, Robert Home, Tilly Kettle and others, have been replaced by even bigger ones of leaders, lay and royal, who have graced Tamil history. And, of course, Governors no longer give here those spectacular banquets of more leisured years, nor are stately functions held beneath the chandeliers of yesteryear. Its steps now seem to be more used to display in state the remains of Chief Ministers before they begin their last journeys accompanied by the wails of the masses.

Behind *Government House* there was a building opened in 1952 for the assembly, built when it was seen that the House of the composite Madras State would, after the first General Elections (held in January 1952), have 375 members and the existing Legislative Council would not have the space for them without considerative alteration. The last British Governor, Sir Archibald Nye, offered this space to the Assembly in 1947 to raise the building and work on it began in 1950. The State Assembly, as already related, met in this functional building till it was again moved.

The main mansion, used by successive Governors as their residence until Independence, was used in the years after Independence as a Legislators' Hostel until other accommodation for the legislators was built in the Estate. The mansion was left a mess when it was vacated and with disuse became almost a derelict. When Police Headquarters in 1993/94 needed temporary accommodation, because its own building on the Marina, one of similar lineage, was being restored, *Government House* was spruced up for the purpose. When the police moved back again in 1998, they didn't want to give up this building that was handsome even after only partial restoration! So other police offices moved in. Both hall and mansion warranted faithful restoration, the surroundings a wooded garden, even an abbreviated one, and litterless environs. The conservationists' hopes that it would happen came to nought. And to that we'll come in a moment.

Facing the Cooum River was another less splendid residence, *Cooum House* which, at Independence, was planned to be the official residence of the Chief Minister. T Prakasam, however, was the only one to occupy it. Later, it became the official residence of the Speakers of the Tamil Nadu Legislative Assembly but, in more recent times, was put to less distinguished public use till, with the Chennai Metro passing through its front garden, it was no longer considered a part of history. It was demolished to build the Assembly-cum-Secretariat. Not far from *Cooum House* was *Gandhi Illam* – a permanent exhibition in memory of the 'Father of the Nation'. It was opened in 1969 near Government Estate's main north gates. In its building there was also from 1979 the Jawahar Bal Bhavan which trained children in the arts and culture of Tamil Nadu. The school has now moved to the premises of the Tamil Nadu Government Music College by the Adyar River.

In recent times, the fire- and rain-damaged *Gandhi Illam* building too was allowed to languish. So too a memorial to the quest for Independence: an oil-press pulled by Swadeshi-championing V O Chidambaram, while he was imprisoned by the British in Coimbatore jail. This was sited in the yard of *Gandhi Illam* till it was moved to the 'memorial park' in Guindy where, in Gandhi Mandapam, it was joined by other exhibits from the exhibition. Gandhi Illam itself was pulled down to make way for new construction to be detailed anon.

And in the southwest corner of the Estate there was the building that was readied by May 1952 for the 375-member Assembly but which was transformed after its Assembly days into what was called Children's Theatre and inaugurated in 1957 by Prime Minister Nehru. This theatre underwent another makeover and opened in 1974 as a 1000-seat auditorium called *Kalaivanar Arangam* (Artists' Theatre). It was later renamed the Kalaivanar N S Krishnan Auditorium, recalling a DMK stalwart and the leading comedian of the Tamil cinema from the 1940s to the 1960s. 'Kalaivanar' ('Great Actor') was a title bestowed on him by the public by then.

Also once part of *Government Estate* was the office of the Madras Public Service Commission, the first recruiter to Provincial Government Service established in the country. Set up in 1929, it has moved elsewhere in the area and is now known as the Tamil Nadu Public Service Commission.

Starting with historic *Government House*, where 200 years of South Indian and much of Indian history was written, all these buildings, including *Kalaivanar Arangam* which was initially not scheduled for the wreckers' hammers, came tumbling down in 2008-9 despite heritage-lovers' pleas as the contractors got to work preparing the ground for a new Secretariat and Legislature. Chief Minister M Karunanidhi, in a record fifth term at the helm, decided in 2007 that he had no wish to hold office in a "colonial" building – where he had happily spent four earlier terms – and decided to build a new Secretariat and Legislature on the rubble of *Government House* and its neighbouring buildings.

With the Chief Minister in the past favouring what was his vision of Chola architecture, palatial buildings in that style were anticipated. But he turned to German architects and surprised everyone by approving a massive Teutonic structure that, for all the glib talk about incorporating various traditional Indian philosophical concepts, looks like a towering rock as you approach it from Mount Road and like three huge oil storage tanks when you approach it from the Fort. As for the park-like atmosphere, that's all vanished. The new building, considerable parts of it, including its crowning dome, unfinished, was inaugurated on March 13, 2010, with Chief Minister M Karunanidhi anxious to celebrate his 50 years as a legislator and fifth term as a Chief Minister in this memorial that was being built at a cost of Rs.4000 million. East Coast Construction, who built the Anna Flyover at Gemini Circle, were contracted to build the seven-storey high (198 ft.), 920,000 sq. ft. building and adjuncts set in 26 acres of space that was denuded of trees. The building when inaugurated was described as the "World's First 'Green' Legislative Assembly Building".

When Chief Minister J Jayalalithaa returned to power in 2011 (her third stint), she was determined to literally keep her promise to "return to Fort St. George". The Legislature and Secretariat (six of whose thirty departments had been shifted) were moved back to where they had been, in different forms and shapes, for over 300 years and Karunanidhi's dream project was left a shell, with other phases of it not even begun. She then decided to convert the building and much of this historic acreage into a medical centre of excellence to rival the All-India Institute of Medical Sciences, Delhi, the country's premier medical institution. The High Court threw out all challenges to this plan and stated that work on a super-speciality hospital and teaching institution could begin. And it did in early 2013. Much work still has to be done to make it a full-fledged hospital, but it has been functioning from 2014. Meanwhile, the Legislature has returned to where it has long been, displacing the Central Institute of Classical Tamil whose 20,000-books-strong library and office Chief Minister Karunanidhi had ordered be located in the 4000 sq. ft. Assembly Hall and its two balconies of 1000 sq.ft. each when he moved into the new complex.

Dwarfed behind the forbidding-looking dark building that was inaugurated in 2010 is *Rajaji Hall* crying for re-use. The old north gates still open on to what was once a magnificent sweeping driveway leading to this hall when it was *Banqueting Hall* and past it to *Government House,* with newly built multi-storey apartment blocks for legislators and government officials, raised in their vicinity to contrast incongruously with the old. Flanking the stately silver-painted iron gates was the shelters for the Governor's mounted bodyguard, the most colourful and handsomest body of troops in a forgotten era. The 'Changing of the Guard' during that era was every bit as impressive as what still takes place at Buckingham Palace in London. The barren stalls for the brilliantly uniformed guards were not so long ago demolished during the construction of what was meant to be the new Assembly complex.

On the southern side of Government Estate there still remain the Triplicane Police Station from 1890, in a heritage building (between 1825 and 1855 the home of the *langarkhana* – poor feeding centre – established by Nawab Wallajah in the grounds of his palace), the State

Tourism Centre, the Press Club, and two old Art Deco style State Guest Houses. Their neighbours in the space between them and the Madras version of 'Rock Fort', are characterless multistorey blocks to house the medical college, students, and nurses. Rather a contrast to them, is the new, handsome *Kalaivanar Arangam*, a striking conference and performance centre. Completed in 2016 at a cost of Rs.63 crore and functional from 2017, the fully air-conditioned auditorium and conference halls have seats for 1,100 persons in the second-floor auditorium and about 1,300 persons in the third-floor multi-purpose hall. The structure has about 50,000 square feet of space on each of four floors – the ground floor housing administration offices etc, the first floor serving as a large lobby, the second as a fully-equipped auditorium with a large lobby, and the third a multi-purpose hall and lobby. A mini-hall for training programmes is in each of the second and third floors. The magnificent Corinthian columns on the frontage and the imposing sheet glass covering the combined height of three floors form a graceful totality that deserves floodlighting to show off what governmental architecture could be.

A long, long time before these additions to *Government Estate*, Governors in an expanding city, where they used the Fort House for official business and lived in what they began to consider a "Town House", felt the need for a country house. And so the house in Guindy was acquired.

The present *Raj Bhavan* – or *Guindy Lodge*, as the building was once known – belonged in the 1680s to Chinna Venkatadri, the youngest brother of Beri Thimmappa. Chinna Venkatadri, it is believed, acquired the house and surrounding estate from his friend and benefactor Sir William Langhorne, a fairly successful Governor. It was sometime during his tenure that Langhorne built *Guindy Lodge* and carved from the forest the necessary garden that gave it the status of a 'garden house'. Before sailing back to England in January 1678, Langhorne sold *Guindy Lodge* and its environs to Chinna Venkatadri. But Chinna Venkatadri and his family soon had problems with the Company. And to mollify the Council, they virtually gifted their recently acquired *Guindy Lodge* to it. Since the Company found that the location and the house offered "a very commodious pleasant place for sickly people to recover their healths at," a mutually profitable deal was stuck.

Track of the house is, more or less, lost after that, but presumably the trouble with the French and Mysore had something to do with the

Government relinquishing its possession of *Guindy Lodge* to private ownership, the house becoming one more 'garden house' in the area that was then popularly known as St Thomas' Mount. *Guindy Lodge* is again heard of in 1813 in connection with a loan sought by a Gilbert Ricketts against the mortgage of the house. When Ricketts died intestate in 1817, the Government bank took over the property at 'Guindy Mode' (presumably, Guindy *Medu* – Guindy Mount) only to find that the impecunious Ricketts, who had died insolvent as well, had mortgaged the property a second time to a Griffiths! The legal tangle was eventually resolved in favour of the bank, and, in 1821, the bank offered the Government the property as well as a neighbouring one that had been mortgaged to it by the Armenian Joseph Nazar Shawmier. Government took over the two properties for Rs 35,000 and Rs 8,750 respectively.

The acquisition was facilitated by Governor Thomas Munro recording the necessity he felt for a country house "where he can transact public business uninterruptedly." At the time, Sir Thomas had two official residences, the traditional one in the Fort – which was in the process of being given up, "with the exception of the Council Chamber, as Offices to the Secretaries to Government" – and the one considered the country house or 'Government Garden' in Chepauk, but which had, in fact, become, "from the accumulation of buildings in its vicinity", a 'Town House'. It was Munro who suggested the practice of the government moving to Ooty for the summer.

Between 1821 and 1824, Government, with another land purchase, linked *Guindy Lodge* to Shawmier-land and the present *Raj Bhavan* was developed. When the scholarly Lord Elphinstone governed Madras between 1837 and 1842, one of his pet projects was the development of *Guindy Lodge*, and the additions and alterations he and Governors Marquis of Tweeddale, Sir Henry Pottinger, Lord Harris and Sir Henry Ward initiated have made it what it is today. But looking back on it all, the greatest contribution to the Guindy mansion may be said to be Elphinstone's, a road that leads directly to the main gates from Mount Road, beyond Marmalong Bridge – Taluk Office Road – on which is a striking, solitary old world building that gave it its name. This building, also once used by the Collector of Chingleput on his visits to the area, is now both government office and courthouse. A contrast near this is a business-like but striking modern building that is Church and offices of the Mormons, a new entry on the Madras Christian scene.

It was also Elphinstone who first regularised the custom of Government moving its southern seat up to the Nilgiris for the summer. He introduced the practice in 1840 and it went on till shortly before Independence. Governors and officialdom moved up for at least four months in a year to Ooty, where Governors had a magnificent mansion developed by Lord Elphinstone and improved by later Governors!

In more recent times, Taluk Office Road was broadened and beautified to make it a fit ceremonial drive for a Governor (though Governors shun ceremony now and only petitioning processionists use it). But it was Elphinstone who first saw the possibilities of such a road and had it built by cutting away the rock of a spur of Little Mount, creating a road handsome even for the 1840s! Traffic in the 2000s has, however, made Taluk Office Road anything but an avenue of beauty; near gridlock and traffic barriers have made it a maze.

Government House, Chepauk, was, eventually, vacated by Governors in 1948, when the new Governors of Independent India felt their now limited powers did not make it necessary for them to stay close to the Fort, the seat of Government. But in fact, from the 1820s till the 1920s, there was a prolonged debate whether Governors should give up the Chepauk property and move permanently into the Guindy house to which considerable improvements had been made, the primary one being a corridor linking three buildings to form one huge mansion. The first block was the Governor's residence (on the first floor) office and reception rooms, the second his banqueting hall and the third a guesthouse. Further improvements have been a large Durbar Hall for banquets, functions etc. coming up in 2001 some distance from the main block. Between them there was opened in 2008 a handsome Presidential Block for VVIP's. Both new buildings harmonise to a great extent with the Governor's mansion.

The Dalliance of Miss Mansell

"There's no such thing as rape, 'cos Woman can run faster with skirts up than Man can with pants down," quaintly philosophised what undoubtedly must have been a male chauvinist pig of many aeons ago. But in his wildest dreams he would not have dreamt that the substance of this little bit of alleged Confucian wit would confound a solemn 18th Century Madras President and his Council, called in session to decide on what really happened between Captain Cummings and Miss Mansell.

Governor Richard Benyon had other things on his mind, especially the invasion of the Carnatic by the Marathas, when *"the Hon'ble Company's ship* Caesar, *Captain Robert Cummings, from England"* arrived in Madras Roads on the evening of Monday, February 2, 1741.

The first official inkling that the Caesar had brought Fort St George something more than the packet of orders from London, military reinforcements, fiscal aid and supplies, was when Benyon called the Board to an extraordinary 'Consultation' on February 27th, Augustus Burton, Export Warehousekeeper and Third in Council not participating. Miss Elizabeth Mansell, Burton's niece, who had come out in the Caesar to stay with her uncle (and, no doubt, look for a husband, as was common custom at the time), had, it appeared, sworn out a complaint of rape against Captain Cummings. Import Warehousekeeper William Monson, Fifth in Council and one of the Justices of the Peace of Madraspatnam, had interrogated Miss Mansell earlier the same day and recorded the complaint he then presented to the Council.

Elizabeth Mansell had complained that between nine and ten on the night of July 24th, the Captain came out from the round house to the balcony where she was standing and, *"by force and violence"*, threw her on the floor. To prevent her crying out, Robert Cummings *"did stop her mouth in such a manner as she could not speak or scarcely breathe," she complained, before going on to the crux of her accusation: "He....did then and there ravish and carnally know (me) without (my) free consent or will."*

As far as is traceable Miss Mansell's charges gave Madras its first rape hearing. But even before the case could get started, the legal wrangling began – and there was almost no hearing! The Council sessions of the 27th were stormy, the arguments raging over questions of jurisdiction. Since the alleged offence was committed on the high seas and since His Majesty's Charter limited the cognisance of the 'Commissioners of Oyer and Terminer' to Fort St George "and ten miles around", the Council decided it had no powers to try the case. 'The Commission of Pyracy', which gave the Council authority to sit as a Court of Admiralty "to robberies committed upon the high seas", was then examined. Some felt the word 'felonies' covered the present case; others argued that the word related only to crimes that threatened the "general safety of trade and navigation" and that "single crimes which affected only individuals" should be referred to "courts at home". The Council eventually agreed that it had "no power to examine this matter in our judicial capacities" but resolved to examine it as President and Council.

Elizabeth Mansell and Robert Cummings were called in and she affirmed her accusations, whereas he denied "the fact and every circumstance of it". A fuller examination of all the facts now being found necessary, the sessions were adjourned for the morrow, with Captain Cummings being remanded into the custody of the Captain of the Guard.

The next day, sensational evidence was forthcoming, but unfortunately there was no audience to be titillated or to appreciate Cummings' skilful and incisive defence of himself. All the evidence soon leaked out – then, as now, nothing was really secret in Madraspatnam – and the town had a whale of a time discussing all the allegations and insinuations. But no one ever did get to the bottom of the matter. The Council, "Mr Burton sitting by", however, tried.

Miss Mansell was called in first, then questioned under oath. How had the rape taken place? Where had it taken place? Where were the two young women, her fellow passengers, at the time? Why hadn't she called out to them? She told the Council that the two women were in the round house, whereas she was on the balcony; that the Captain "stopped her mouth with his hand", thereby preventing her from calling for assistance. But then, under cross-examination, she confessed that at the

Cape she had consented to go to bed with the Captain. However, she swore, "the former time he knew her against her will" and since then had "beat her, pulled her by the hair of her head, and called her 'whore' and several other names."

Cummings – faced with a charge that was a capital offence – was no gentleman. He said that Elizabeth Mansell had shown a "fondness for him even at Portsmouth" to such a degree that Mrs Cummings had been so upset she had burst into tears, which he had only "overcome by promises of a prudent behaviour." Thereafter, for two full months, he had "withstood dayly repeated importunities", but at last Miss Mansell "prevailed on him" and he had "lain with her" for "most of the rest of the voyage." There was never any question of rape, not with Miss Mansell! Why, during the brief passage between Gravesend and Portsmouth, she had herself a young fellow! And before that, she had been "intimate with a young man in the house with her", behaving generally "so ill that the family she lived with were resolved to get rid of her at any rate"!!

Faced with conflicting stories, the Council summoned witnesses. First, naturally, were the Mistresses Mary and Martha Coales, who had shared the round house. They both averred that they had often seen Elizabeth crying – "on Christmas day last she (was in) a flood of tears" – and attributed the tears to quarrels she had had with the Captain. However, neither of them had heard any noises from the balcony, though they were both in the round house, within hearing distance, and had never suspected rape – the word being mentioned to them only after they came ashore, Mr Burton first speaking of it. Mary Coales coyly simpered that she had suspected "an intimacy" between Elizabeth and Capt Cummings because Elizabeth "was often in a passion if the Captain happened to take any notice of herself (Mrs Coales)." And Martha Coales added that one day, when she was in the Great Cabin with Elizabeth, the Captain "said or did something that provoked Miss Mansell," who angrily retorted, calling him "villain and rogue and other names, adding that he had taken away her character." This evidence was corroborated by Surgeon's Mate John Pope and a passenger, John Legg, who had been talking together on the other side of a partition separating them from the cabin. They also "thought they heard the word ravish" uttered by her. Another passenger, John Clause, testified that he had heard the Captain and Miss Mansell quarrelling, about four to six weeks before arrival in Madraspatnam, but he had not taken notice of the words. The three men, asked whether they had ever suspected that Miss Mansell had been raped by the Captain, agreed that "no body ever suspected rape", but that there had been familiarity they were fairly certain; "it was the general opinion of everybody that they (Miss Mansell and the Captain) were great together."

Robert Cummings now summoned his witnesses. Both William Fern, Chief Mate, and Charles Bateman agreed that they did not suspect rape but they also agreed that Miss Mansell called the Captain "many names", used "very high words" on him and accused him of ruining her and implied that he had "debauched her." The Captain's steward, Antony Wood, however, spoke up well and true for his master. He had seen Miss Mansell – apparently a kittenish type whom he'd noticed "playing at Tagg with a couple of footmen" at Portsmouth – make her bid for the Captain at Portsmouth itself, and Mrs Cummings, who'd also seen it all, was "uneasy she was to go in the ship." But of rape or quarrels he knew nothing.

Now followed evidence that was to be grist for the scandal mill of Madraspatnam for months to come. Mark Romney deposed that there was great intimacy and familiarity between Miss Mansell and Captain Cummings, Elizabeth flying "into a passion" if the Captain showed even "any civility" to the other ladies. At the Cape, he tattled, "she went so publicly to the Captain's chamber and came from it" that it was common talk in the lodging house where they stayed, one of the other lodgers even speaking to him about it. And, snickering, he narrated how aboard ship, at about 11 o'clock one night, he saw the Captain and Miss Mansell sitting in two chairs on the poop, "the Captain's leg in her lap, and she with her arm around the Captain's neck." He heard her call Cummings "Dear Captain" and saw her kiss him. He related how he pointed out this delightful interlude to his companion "who bid him make no noise least they should be heard." Romney then "beckoned to a midshipman who was a small distance off, to come and look", but the middy "put his finger to his nose, but would not come."

Elizabeth Mansell was now recalled and asked why she had remained quiet so long and why, when she had resolved on board to prosecute the Captain, she had sent letters ashore by the catamarans, giving him a good character. She replied that she had acted under duress; that he had dictated the letters she had written and had made her swear "never to disclose what had passed between them just before they got in here."

Captain Cummings replied that it is true he wrote the letter "foul but he did not dictate it." Indeed, she wanted him to put in a lot more "in his commendation" but he convinced her, with a great deal of difficulty, that it would lead to people being suspicious of her feelings towards him. In fact, the oath he asked her to take was "not for fear of being accused of rape, but because knowing the impetuosity of her temper and her furious passions, he feared she would by word or action betray herself and therefore hoped the type of an oath might check her and save her from ruining herself in the manner she has done." He was convinced that she was put up to making these charges, because she had been in touch with him many times since coming ashore, telling him "secrets of the family" and complaining of "unfair usage she fancied she had received" from them.

On Miss Mansell confessing to this latter correspondence and exchange of confidences, the Council agreed that there "did not appear sufficient cause to say a rape", so they discharged the Captain. But to indicate their solidarity with fellow Councillor Burton, they told Cummings that his "conduct with relation to this young woman would be a perpetual blot on him, since she was under his care and protection." No gentleman to the end, Captain Cummings answered this stricture by insinuating that "she was loose before she came on board." The Council promptly shut him up, and asked him to withdraw. Miss Mansell got off without even a reprimand.

The Cummings Affair, however, would not just lie down and die. On March 12th, a harassed Council received a petition from the officers of the Caesar, *complaining of ill-treatment by the Captain. But it took a few months for the Council to inspect the* Caesar. *They found the ship in "very good condition" but the Chief Mate and another member of the crew no longer alive, two midshipmen and a sailor missing, reported as deserters, and the surgeon and purser not on board. But on June 27th at Consultation, it was reported that Cummings and his officers had come to an agreement and that the petitions of March 12th were being withdrawn "by mutual consent by both parties."*

On September 28th, the Caesar, *in the company of the* Prince of Wales *and* Nottingham, *sailed for England. Aboard the* Prince of Wales *was Elizabeth Mansell who had decided just three days earlier that Madras was too hot for her.*

15
The Road North

1. The pillars of commerce

Heading north from Fort St George, you move into areas where modern Madras's commercial history had its beginnings. Here, in George Town[1] and areas further north, Parry's and Binny's and Arbuthnot's, all firms with late 18th Century backgrounds, once dominated the South Indian commercial scene. They were fine examples of establishments founded by British businessmen who "not only advanced their own interests but also contributed... to the...prosperity of...South India...(and the) commercial and social and agricultural development" of this part of the country. Of them, Parry's alone, now Indianised survives and flourishes. Binny's, also Indianised, is no longer in commerce, effectively having become an owner of large real estate. As for Arburthnot's, it's a sad story that we will come to before long, but all that's left of it for now is a name in the branch office of a Calcutta offshoot, Gillanders, Arbuthnot.

Parry's, the oldest British mercantile name surviving in Madras, and the second oldest in India, the Forbes name in Bombay a couple of years older, can trace its history to Chase and Parry in 1790. The Parry in question, Thomas Parry, arrived in Madras in 1788 and was licensed as a free merchant. Parry's sustained occupancy of the site has made the

---

[1] The suggestion that it should be called V O Chidambaram Nagar, commemorating a great Tamil patriot, who challenged British maritime power with a small merchant fleet of his own during the heyday of Empire and paid a martyr's price for it, has never really found general acceptance.

name a part of Madras geography, the junction here known as Parry's Corner (though now also commemorating C Rajagopalachari). Here stands *Dare House*, the Company's present art deco headquarters, built in the late 1930s on the site of old buildings (including the landmark *Lawyers' Buildings*), occupied in 1940 and named after a dynamic partner J W Dare, who joined in 1819. This Corner was site of Lally's battery that almost battered Fort St George into submission in 1758-9. But being as strategically located for trade as for war, a 182 foot by 72 foot corner plot here, stretching north to south, was purchased in 1803 by Parry, in whose days the sea washed against the walls of the buildings that were already there (they belonged to a Nawab of the Carnatic and were occupied by one of his Begums). Parry, embroiled in the resolution of the Nawab of the Carnatic's tangle of debts, was soon afterwards banished from Madras, moved to Colombo, but returned to Madras before long.

Parry died in 1824, near Cuddalore, where the Company's fortress-like offices, now little used, still tower over neighbouring buildings. He was buried in Christ Church, next door. Dare then took charge – and Parry's began growing again. Parry's is now part of the Murugappa Group and is the second major – and long-established – British organisation in South India to have forward-looking Nattukkottai Chettiar businessmen take an interest in; the first was Harvey Mills in Madurai – now an abbreviated Madura Coats – where the Rajah of Chettinad's family once played a significant role. Parry's may have grown manifold today as a Murugappa Group company, but, as in the early days of its growth, it is still in sugar and distilling. 'Manure', another of its old businesses, is now, fertilisers as part of another major Murugappa business. But the 'jars' (ceramics) business has been sold off, though Parryware still exists as a brand.

The Binnys were in Madras even earlier than Parry, there being a Binny here as early as 1682. Charles Binny, who came to India without licence in 1769, was the first of the family to enter Carnatic service, serving as secretary to Nawab Wallajah. But the firm owes its foundations to John 'Deaf' Binny, who arrived in Madras in 1797 and who, like earlier members of his family, joined the Nawab's service. John Binny lived until 1821 in a house and grounds on which Spencer and Co and its Connemara Hotel now stand – the short stretch of road which the Connemara fronts still being called Binny Road.

Binny founded Binny and Dennison's in 1799, a firm which moved to its Armenian Street address in 1812 and became Binny and Co in 1814. Between 1804 and 1869, Binny's bought, at different times, four plots of land for a total price of around Rs. 75,000/- from various Armenians. Maclean Street, Armenian Street and Errabalu Chetty Street framed on three sides the land which may have stretched on the fourth to Sembudoss Street. The existing buildings here were its first offices and the firm developed these in the 1930s to give itself a classic Art Deco headquarters. In 2017, this George Town landmark was razed for new development by the most recent successors to the Inchcape Group, who had taken the firm over after the Arbuthnot crash (that had badly affected Binny's) and who had sold it to Indian interests in 1981-82.

Binny's, traders, bankers, managing agents and agents of the British India Steam Navigation Co from its first days, became a leading industrial organisation when it took over some of the country's first textile mills. The Buckingham Mills in North Madras was founded in 1877 and spinning began the next year, with weaving commencing in 1893. The Carnatic Mills was founded in 1882 and spinning and weaving began in 1884. Both mills, neighbours, were amalgamated in 1920, with Binny's managing the group, 14,000 workers strong. Binny's, in the years since, made Buckingham and Carnatic khaki and drill household names in many parts of the world, and its Bangalore Woollen, Cotton & Silk Mills, founded in 1884, will be remembered by the British and Indian Armies for the blankets it supplied the troops, the horses and the mules. But all the mills saw troubled times from the mid-1970s, lack of modernisation being one cause, flood damage another. Only governmental pressure kept the mills struggling on in a part of Madras whose entire development and economy have been due to them. Some of the senior executives' houses here were a conservationist's delight – but both the mill area and the houses began at this time to be seen more in terms of their real estate than as production centres. And so the mills, fallen on bad times, closed in the mid-1990s, the executives' houses have been pulled down, and developed and, as these lines are written, the whole 70-acre mill is under development as a giant 1000 + outlets 'market' and a self-sufficient gated community.

Madras's only other textile mills were the Bombay-owned Madras United Spinning & Weaving Mills, better known as the Choolai Mills, on D'Mellow's Road, across from the Railways goods station, Salt

Cotaurs. These early 20th Century Mills were taken over by Delhi interests in 1939, then sold to the Edward Textile Mills, Bombay – but even that did not improve their fortunes. Today, its buildings are Food Corporation of India godowns.

It was in the B & C Mills that the trade union movement was born in South India, indeed India, G. Selvapathy Chettiar, whose father ran a small bangle factory, championing the cause of the workers from 1915. Selvapathy's father ran in that area a *sabha* that Selvapathy renamed the Venkatesa Gunamirthavarshini Sabha where religious discourses and *bhajan* singing were held. When Selvapathy took over the *sabha* in 1908 at *Ramanujam Nilayam,* 52, DeMellow's Road, he introduced lectures by eminent speakers whose audience at the venue was mainly workers from the B&C and Choolai Mills. After the meetings, the workers used to narrate their problems to Selvapathy. Teaming with a friend G. Ramanujalu Naidu in 1915, he began sending petitions to the management seeking redressal of these grievances of the workers. But when management responses were generally negative, he organised, under the auspices of the *sabha*, a public meeting on March 2, 1918 where Thiru Vi Kalyanasundaram, writer and journalist, urged the workers to form a union. On April 27, 1918, at a meeting presided over by B.P. Wadia, Annie Besant's cohort, the Madras Labour Union was formed, the country's first. Wadia was elected the first President and Selvapathy and Ramanujalu Joint Secretaries. Tiru Vi Ka was elected one of the Vice Presidents. In September 1931, the Union got its own headquarters building, the *Selvapathy-Ramanujalu Building*, for which the foundation stone was laid in 1927 by Gandhiji and Kasturba Gandhi. Near the union building is a Perumal temple into which Gandhi led Harijans during that trip, breaking a local taboo. The first strikes, however, were in the Perambur Railway Workshops (1905, 1911), long before the Madras Railway Union was formed in 1919.

It was at Selvapathy Chettiar's urgings that May Day was first celebrated in Madras and B.P. Wadia, of Annie Besant's New India, got interested in the labour movement and became a part of it. Thereafter, together with Tiru Vi Ka, they organised workers in almost every industry and profession – including policemen and barbers – in Madras and secured for many of them an 8-hour day instead of the 12-hour one which was the norm of the times. Today, all three are forgotten leaders, but the independent MLU tradition still continues in the city though in diminished form, with every political party having started its own trade union.

The third surviving 18th Century commercial name in Madras is Gillanders, Arbuthnot, neighbours of Parry's. This Calcutta-based company has connections with Madras history going back to the Arbuthnot name that commemorates one of its promoters, who, in the early 19th Century, lent his name to scores of businesses in India. George Arbuthnot in 1800 joined in partnership with a Francis Latour, who arrived in Madras in 1777 and was listed as a free merchant in 1780. Latour and Co, after John de Monte succeeded Latour, eventually developed into Arbuthnot and Co, Madras's leading merchant house in the 19th Century till it crashed midst scandal in the worst financial disaster ever to hit Madras. By then, various Arbuthnots had teamed with others elsewhere in India and linked new names with the Arbuthnot name – like Gillanders, Arbuthnot, which G C Arbuthnot helped to found.

A direct descendant and successor of George Arbuthnot, J A Arbuthnot, was the first president of the Madras Chamber of Commerce which was founded in 1836 on the initiative of Binny's, Dare and Arbuthnot, and was located in *Dare House* for several years. This fount of British commerce had only two 'native' members in the next 100 years. A M M Murugappa Chettiar in 1965 became the Chamber's first Indian President.

Twenty years after the Chamber was founded, the traders of Madras formed the Madras Trades Association.[2] Never quite as powerful as the Chamber, the Trades Association nevertheless played a major role in developing Madras as a city of commerce. Spencer's, Oakes, Addison's were all major players in the 1856 association that today survives as a shadow of itself.

To the rear of Parry's was founded, in 1920, on Second Line Beach, the Madras Stock Exchange. Its first president was Chandulal Motilal Kothari, who had been the driving force behind the founding of the Exchange. He later went on to establish a planting and industrial conglomerate and was the first Indian to represent the planting interests in the Madras Legislature. His son, D C Kothari, was elected the first Indian Chairman of the United Planters' Association of Southern India in 1951.

Madras's stock exchange was founded with about 100 firms on its rolls, though only a quarter of them were major players, with Huson &

---

[2] There was a social difference between those in the merchant houses (the upper class) and the traders/retailers (the lower class).

Tod leading the pack. But with the Great Depression, all the firms began to suffer. By 1926, only two were still in business, Huson & Tod, in the old Chartered Bank building (now renovated on NSC Bose Road) and Kothari & Sons in a building now occupied by the Central Bank on Broadway.

By the early 1930s, the Great Depression, overtrading and speculation affected the market severely and Huson, Tod & Co found itself in trouble and closed down in 1935. R.C. Paterson, an assistant in the firm, for which he had worked from the time of his arrival in Madras in 1926, took over the business with the backing of the Chartered Bank and established in September 1935 Paterson & Co, a firm which to this day is one of the leading stock broking institutions in South India. When the Madras Stock Exchange was registered on August 12, 1937, Paterson's, Kothari's and three others were the founding fathers. Eightyfour companies were listed on the Exchange, besides Government and other securities, when trading began. In 2009, the Hinduja Bank (Switzerland) took a controlling interest in Paterson's.

Gordon Woodroffe's, founded in 1868 headquartered in its original premises, still survives as a name in Madras, now Gordon Woodroffe Logistics, the Madras branch of a Bombay head quartered firm. Best & Crompton (founded in 1879) and T A Taylor's, another firm of the same period, also continued in business in the area till the 1970s/80s, but today, operating from elsewhere in the city, they are but shadows of their former selves. Woodroffe's used to be big in palmyrah fibre in the early days but later moved into leather. Besides its imports and exports, Woodroffe's was in shipping, insurance and managing agents businesses that were strictly separated though in one and the same building. The Best story is related a little further on.

Hoe & Co, the 'Premier Press' (1886), and Thompson and Co established in 1879 by O Candasamy Mudaliar, the former in Stringer Street and the latter on Broadway, both printing presses among the pioneer mechanised ventures in the City, are also early George Town commercial names that survived here well into the 1980s. Hoe & Co and its magnificent premises, a landmark in the area, belonged to V Perumal Chetty, who started in 1840 what was to become the city's leading wholesale and retail stationers. The Perumal Chetty family, another old Madras name, were railway *dubashes* and the first auctioneers in the city, concentrating on railway scrap. Legend has it that the Hoe name is a legacy from bailing out in 1886 a railway printer named Hoe, a Chinese – or was he British – whose press was opposite their stationery store in Stringer Street. Much old printing equipment of another age could be seen in the press until it closed down in 1986 and the company began to take a second look at where it should head. The massive property with its Gothic and Saracenic arches, broad verandahs and wooden floors was sold to developers and duly demolished. Hoe & Co's diary was an annual feature in Madras from 1912 till the 1990s, treasured by those who wanted information about the sun, the moon and the stars. Also with the Perumal Chetty group was the Madras Pencil Factory, one of the City's earliest industries, acquired from the Government in 1919 and also now no more.

Broadway, till the 20th Century, was where most of the British shops and trade establishments were located, Mount Road becoming popular only in the 20th Century. Several firms were, however, founded in the Mount Road area in the 19th Century and are still going strong, now fully Indianised.

Madras, founded for trade, has remained a city sought by traders, even as it has grown into one of the major industrial centres of the country. A region which in 1639 was developed for its textile skills is still today the country's largest handloom exporter and is capital of a State that is a major centre of the textile industry. Then as now its coir cordage was the best in the East, 'Madras cables' long sought after by the East Indiamen. Its hides and skins export has grown into a major leather industry. And the Jews and the Armenians, who exported Golconda's diamonds and imported coral and silver in return, fostered a jewellery market which thrives to this day in the hands of merchants from Gujarat and Kerala.

2. The towers of justice

Across from Parry's Corner is the High Court-Law College campus. This campus was previously the Esplanade, created when 'Old Black Town', the first Indian settlement developed by Fort St George – for the weavers and dyers it brought from the Nellore and Machilipatnam areas in what is now Andhra Pradesh – was finally and totally demolished in 1760, completing a French-interrupted task that had begun in 1756. By then, Muthialpet-Peddanaickenpet to the north of the Esplanade had become 'New Black Town'. The French had, during the 1746-49

Parry's Corner... Dare House... marking the beginning of North Beach commerce... and one of the pillars marking the bounds of what was the Fort Esplanade (encircled).

The towers of justice (on the site of the first 'Black Town'). Inset: A plaque on its sea-facing wall commemorating the shelling by the Emden.

DURING THE BOMBARDMENT OF MADRAS
BY THE GERMAN CRUISER *Emden* ON
THE NIGHT OF THE 22ND SEPTEMBER 1914
A SHELL STRUCK THIS SPOT AND CARRIED
AWAY A PORTION OF THE COMPOUND WALL

35. *Anderson's Church steeple in isolated splendour... memorial to Christian education.*
36. *Pachaiyappa's Athenian splendour...a hall on the edge of an esplanade that's now no stroller's wa*

occupation, razed all of 'Old Black Town' to an extent of 400 yards from the Fort's north wall, for defence purposes, making a new Black Town necessary. The British completed what the French had begun when the latter, during their 1759 siege of the Fort, used what was left as a protective shield.

The High Court's imposing, labyrinthine Indo-Saracenic buildings, with long corridors, high ceilings, much ornamental tiling, carving and iron-work, beautiful stained glass arches and a portrait gallery, are one of the City's landmarks. These buildings, for which the foundation stone was laid in 1889, were declared open for occupation on July 12, 1892, Sir Arthur Collins, the first Chief Justice to sit in it. They had taken four years to build and had cost Rs 13 lakh. J N Brassington was the original designer, Henry Irwin developed those designs, and Engineer J H Stephen supervised the construction and made modifications to the design. New buildings, such as the Small Causes Court (1931), were added in the same style. And even newer buildings in the 1990s have, to some extent, followed an integrating style.

On the tallest minaret of the High Court building, 175 feet tall, was established in 1894 the third Madras lighthouse. Using kerosene to produce 18,000 candles intensity of flashing light, till electricity, arrived, it functioned until the late 1970s when the one on Marina was built. A curiosity here is the rows of stylised cobras that surround the bases of the main dome and the surmounting dome. The High Court lighthouse replaced the 1844 Esplanade lighthouse designed by Captain Thomas John Smith, work on which began in 1838. This lighthouse, after being dismantled, remains in the High Court grounds as an ornamental 125 feet tall Doric column that also serves as a Standard Bench Mark for Madras.

The Doric column lighthouse cost about Rs. 75,000, almost Rs. 50,000 of this for the Pallavaram granite cladding. The 84-foot hollow shaft with stairway inside tapered from a base diameter of 16 feet to 11 feet by the light which was at 117 feet height. The light had a range of 20 miles. The heavy expense on granite was necessitated by the need " to save (the column) from the salt breeze…" This lighthouse, as a part of the commemoration of the High Court building's 125th birthday, has handsomely been observed by the lighthouse authorities with a dummy light chamber in the base, the High Court Heritage Committee has installed an attractive exhibition of 'Madras Firsts' and 'Judicial History'.

The High Court lighthouse which replaced the Doric column lighthouse was built atop the largest dome over the tallest minaret. The lantern room was 8 ½ feet in diameter and when it was in place, with ornamentation above it, the total height of the minaret was 190 feet. Restoration tower as well as the light chamber is planned.

It may or may not have been the High Court lighthouse, its beam sweeping out to sea 19 nautical miles, that attracted the marauding German cruiser, the *Emden*, in 1914, but that raider's shelling of the City on September 22nd is commemorated in a plaque set in the eastern wall of the Court compound which it had smashed – a plaque that usually has to be searched for beneath all the posters pasted over it. The *Emden's* shells succeeded in setting the Burmah-Shell's oil tanks on fire and damaged the Yacht Club. More visible are the bits and pieces of the *Emden's* shells recovered in Madras; these are preserved in the Fort Museum to commemorate a daring and fearless raider whose name has been absorbed into the Tamil language to describe a brave and strong bruiser. The *Emden* was eventually sunk off the Cocos Islands by the Australian cruiser *Sydney*. The Kaiser, honouring the *Emden's* crew, permitted all of them and their descendants to add to their names the word 'Emden'. Thus, her skipper is remembered as Müller-Emden.

Almost from the very beginnings of the Madras settlement, courts of one sort or another functioned, bringing the rule of Western law to the new territory. There were first the Choultry Courts (today's magistrate's courts) where 'native judges' dispensed justice to the Indian citizenry. In 1678, there came the Superior Court or Court of Judicature (High Court), presided over by the Governor. This appeal court was founded by Governor Streynsham Master. The first trial by jury in India took place in this court on April 10, 1678, Henry Law being sentenced to be burnt in the hand. Soon there followed a Court of Admiralty, then a Mayor's Court, a Court of Small Causes and, in 1796, the Recorder's Court. Not long after the abolition of the Court of Judicature in 1796, the Supreme Court of Madras was established.

It was on December 26, 1800, that the Supreme Court began functioning in the Fort in what was called Choultry Gate Street. Then, after one more shift, it moved, in 1817, to *Bentinck's Building,* on North Beach Road, which had originally been built as office space for the merchants. Sir Thomas Strange was the first Chief Justice and Sir Colley

Scotland the last. The Supreme Court, in effect, was a fusion of the Court of Admiralty and the Recorder's Court of 1796.

After the events of 1857, the Company gave way to the Sarkar of the Raj and, in 1862, a High Court was established for the Madras Presidency, taking over from the Supreme Court and the Company's Sadr Court. Sir Colley Scotland became the first Chief Justice of the new High Court. The very first case to be argued here was by John D Mayne, an authority on Hindu Law. Appointed as Acting Judge of the Madras High Court in 1878 and confirmed in 1883 as a Puisne Justice was the first Indian to hold those offices, the socratic Sir Tiruvarur Muthuswami Aiyer, that great legal luminary whose statue to this day adorns the High Court buildings. Sir Muthuswami Aiyer also acted as Chief Justice in 1891, the first Indian to do so. The first Indian to be confirmed as Chief Justice of the Madras High Court was Dr P V Rajamannar in 1948. The first Indian to ever act as Advocate General was V Bashyam Iyengar, in 1897.

The Madras Advocates' Association was founded as the Vakils' Association in March 1889 at the urging of P Ananda Charlu, with stormy petrel V Krishnaswami Aiyer (commemorated in a statue near *Senate House*) as its Secretary. Vakils were allowed to wear their robes in Court like the barristers – only after Sir Arthur Collins recognised their equality.

The Association's premises are in the High Court, and in its Library are over 60,000 volumes of books and records. Opposite its building is the statue of Bashyam Iyengar raised in 1927. In a north-eastern corner of the High Court campus is a statue of C. Rajagopalachari, who was, besides his other accomplishments, a successful lawyer. And in the southwest corner a statue remembers another eminent lawyer, T. Prakasam, the first Chief Minister of Andhra Pradesh after serving as a Chief Minister of Madras. Both gave up the Law for politics and statesmanship.

Three new High Court buildings which were opened in 1991 have added 15,000 square metres of floor space at a cost of Rs 45 million, to what's considered the second largest judicial employer in the world. In raising these buildings, the PWD engineers have made some effort to integrate the modern with the century-old main buildings in architectural style and construction material. But they lost sight of the height needed to keep them cool. Air-conditioning has, therefore, become necessary and has followed elsewhere, even where it was not needed; the air-conditioning of Court No.1, the Chief Justice's and other chambers in the old building is a modernisation not strictly called for, given the Court's traditional comfort, and has led to huge ducts disfiguring stately corridors. Hopefully, in the restoration underway as these lines are written, things get hidden.

In the High Court premises, there was created in 2005 a museum which is proving an attraction for the heritage lover. A feature of it is a re-created court room, said to be the room where one of the most famous murder trials in Madras history, the Lakshmikanthan Murder Case, was tried. As part of the 125th anniversary celebrations of the High Court building, a more accessible home for the museum was built in 2014. To the west of the Court are the Indo-Saracenic buildings of the Law College, designed by Henry Irwin, built by Namberumal Chetty and opened in 1899 on the site of 'White Town's' first burial grounds in the 'Guava Garden' which had become a cattle pound by then. The cost of the completed building was a little over Rs 340,000. The College, however, had opened in May 1891 with Reginald Nelson as its first principal, functioning in Presidency College where Law classes had been started in 1855, with John Bruce Norton as the first Professor of Law. The first woman graduate was B. Ananda Bai who was enrolled in the Madras High Court in 1929 as the first locally qualified woman advocate in the Madras Presidency. Seetha Devadoss, a London qualified barrister, was enrolled a little earlier.

A few desecrated masonry relics, from time to time cleaned up, once stood in the Law College's campus attesting to the use to which these grounds used to be put. This was the site of the first English cemetery in Madras. Among them is the Hynmer's Obelisk, an arched pedestal with an obelisk above being the memorial Elihu Yale built to commemorate his son David and friend Joseph Hynmer, who were buried next to each other. Yale married Hynmer's widow and their son David died when he was four. Nearby was the Powney vault of another old Madras British family. The Powneys were associated with Madras from 1703. Capt. John Powney was a mariner turned businessman who became the 'First and modern Mayor of Madraspatnam' on August 17, 1727. He died in 1740 and was buried besides three children who had predeceased him. He had willed that a vault be built over them with a 30-foot tall monument atop it – and this was duly done. Joining them in the vault in 1780 was

John Powney's widow Mary, who was very likely Madras's first European centenarian. Of the monument and vault there is no trace today, a sudden disappearance.

The Hynmer's Obelisk was refurbished in 1987 through the efforts of the Indo-American Society and the Archaeological Survey of India and is now a recognisable monument in the Law College campus, entry to it best being from the Rajah Annamalai Hall side. But from time to time it keeps falling into a state of neglect and a 'jungle' hides it.

Just across from Law College, on the Muthialpet side to the north, are the Jaipur-Jaina-style sandstone-faced buildings of the YMCA, built with some of the earliest American 'aid' to this part of the world. The YMCA established itself in Madras when David McConaughy from the US was sent out on the request of the Indian YMCA for an organiser. He arrived in January 1890 and in February got the Madras YMCA underway. A go-getter, General Secretary McConaughy planned for a major YMCA presence in Madras from the first. A year after his arrival, McConaughy helped found in Madras the National Council of YMCAs in India. It was in 1933 that the 'Y' got its first Indian General Secretary, G Solomon, grandfather of P H Pandian who, some years ago, was a controversial Speaker of the Tamil Nadu Legislative Assembly.

The original site of YMCA activity in Madras, the Church of England's Temperance Institute, was acquired and the foundation for the new building was laid there in 1895, and work was completed in 1900. Government Architect G S T Harris, constantly advised on Indian architectural style by Governor Arthur Havelock, designed the building and who else but Namberumal Chetty should build it, the first Madras public building with sandstone-facing. Governor Havelock inaugurated it in 1900, the long delay in its completion being due to lack of funds – which only became available when the Postmaster General of the US, John Wanamaker, donated $ 40,000.

To the east of the YMCA building is Anderson Church and to its east, adjoining it, were the handsome former buildings of the Madras Christian College, hardly any vestiges of them now surviving. There remained but one building, in Linghi Chetty Street, its shingled tower replicating Anderson Church's. Split into tiny offices by its present owners, the Life Insurance Corporation of India, it was tenanted by lawyers, but this too has given way to new construction. The College succeeded John

Anderson's General Assembly's School. Anderson, who headed the School till his death in 1855, was obsessed with spreading education and even founded a Muslim girls' school near Bell's Road, Triplicane. He also founded St. Columba's in Chingleput and the Anderson School in Kanchipuram. The Rev Anderson and his wife are buried in the little-known London Mission Cemetery on Tana Road (off Purasawalkam High Road), a notified heritage precinct.

Anderson's pioneering school first met in 1835 and grew into the more formal Free Church of Scotland's Central Institution in 1845. College classes began in 1866/7 and students were sent up for the degree in 1868/69. The Institution was one of the first to adopt Dr Bell's 'monitorial system' of education.

First located in what today has become the Ophthalmic Hospital premises, Egmore, the Institution then moved to Armenian Street. There was another move, to Errabalu Chetty Street, before the Institution acquired a former sailors' home on the Esplanade and moved there in 1846. There was considerable addition to this building, from the time the Institution was christened Madras Christian School and College in 1876/7, till the turn of the century. Additional buildings were raised in the 1880s and further extensions, including the labs and equipment, were done in 1909-11 by T Batchacharry, whose prosperous carpentry business had by them spread into construction contracting. The last association of the College with these premises that remain in George Town today is Anderson's Church, with its unique, slim, towering steeple.

The College and the School were once associated with four stately buildings just to the west of Parry's. The earliest one to come up, and the furthest west, was the *Evangelistic Hall,* built by the Free Church of Scotland Mission, work on it beginning in 1857 and completed in 1859. Work started immediately after that, and just to the east of it, on the College Chapel, which was consecrated in 1862. After Miller took over, he switched the roles of the two buildings – *Evangelistic Hall* was reconstructed in 1893 as Anderson Church and the Chapel was transformed into the *College (Assembly) Hall* with a dome dominating the skyline when work was completed in 1895.

Meanwhile, the sailors' home Anderson acquired for the School immediately to the west of Parry's and as a home for him and his Swiss wife Margaret was reconstructed as *College House,* the hostel with a corner for the Andersons and a small girls' school that she ran till the Millers moved it to Royapuram as Northwick. To the west of it came up what was known as the College, the classrooms block.

Of this row of handsome buildings and a couple of other buildings behind them that the College built, only Anderson Church remains, its interior rather cinematically restored in 2011. In place of the other three buildings, there came up in the 1950s tall (for the time) Art Deco-style office buildings. The Madras Provincial Cooperative Bank in 1936 took over *College House* and then in 1970 pulled it down and built a six-storeyed Modernist building that in 1974 was occupied by what had become known as the Tamil Nadu State Cooperative Bank. The College block was bought c.1937 by the Bombay Mutual Insurance Co. which moved into in 1955 with Art Deco highrise that it replaced the old building with. And in 1957, the State Bank of Mysore moved into a new building that it replaced *College Hall* with after acquiring the property in 1937. Together with Parry's, this is today an outstanding stretch of Art Deco office architecture.

Associated from the beginning with the Church of Scotland, the School and College had a number of outstanding Scottish missionary teachers over the years. It was under Dr William Miller, who came out in 1862 as the School's principal, that the institution really began to grow and it was he who made it a college. He also founded the country's first alumni association here in 1891 – and today it has over 20 chapters, including several abroad. Miller, who became Vice-Chancellor of Madras University, is remembered in a statue that once was on the College's George Town site, then across from it by the High Court campus and is now in the School's Chetput campus.

The College's first Indian professor was Prof J B Raju, appointed Professor of Philosophy in 1916. The first Indian Principal, Dr Chandran Devanesan, took charge in 1963. And the first women students were admitted in 1939, with women being accepted on the teaching staff from 1940. The first Indian headmaster of the School was appointed in 1931; Kuruvilla Jacob became a legend.

Between the two Christian institutions is the Young Men's Indian Association, started on Armenian Street in 1914. Its founder was the indefatigable Annie Besant, who bore the cost of constructing the Association's handsome home with its splendidly-built hall which opened in 1915. Today, *Gokhale Hall* in the YMIA building, named after Gopal Krishna Gokhale, founder of the Servants of India Society, is better remembered for its illustrious history than the Association.

Magnificently pillared and handsomely domed *Gokhale Hall* has been described as having been "a centre for public life" in Madras. It was here that Annie Besant delivered her clarion call, the 'Wake Up India' lectures, founded in 1916 the 'Home Rule League' and, later, the '1919 Club' to study the reforms introduced by the Government that year. It was also a famed platform for outstanding speakers as well as scene of the once-famed 'YMIA Parliament' debates. Here too was drafted the Commonwealth of India Bill introduced in the British Parliament in 1926. Its main hall was a centre of culture in the 1940s and 1950s. The Indian Fine Arts Society and several other cultural organisations staged their programmes here before the bigger *sabhas* built their own auditoria. The complex also provided inexpensive accommodation, simple food, gymnasium and indoor sports facilities, and a reading room.

All this was threatened as the first decade of the 21st Century came to an end and demolition work in the main hall began. A court order, in response to the plea of heritage lovers, has stopped demolition, but a final decision on restoration is awaited as these lines are written.

In the neighbouring building, 49 Moor Street (2nd Line Beach), the *YMIA* Building, is now a statue of Annie Besant and a bust of 'Sir William Wedderburn, Bart.', both moved from Gokhale Hall. Annie Besant is a part of Modern Indian history, but Wedderburn?

Wedderburn arrived in India in 1860, a member of the Indian Civil Service. He retired in 1887 as Chief Secretary, Bombay Presidency. His years in rural India led him to a sympathetic understanding of the Indian villager and this drew him to the Indian National Congress. After his retirement he became virtually a Congressman. His crusade against a bureaucracy indifferent to the peasant had him being described as a 'traitor' by many in officialdom

In 1893, Sir William became a Liberal Member of Parliament. Taking off from where he left off when he chaired the Fourth Sessions of the Indian National Congress, held in Bombay in 1889, he formed, no sooner he entered Parliament, the Indian Parliamentary Committee, which he chaired from 1893 to 1900. An active member of several Royal Commissions and Committees concerned with Indian affairs, he was also Chairman of the British Committee of the Congress from 1889 until his death in 1918.

This chairmanship led him to being invited to the 20th Session of the Congress, held in Bombay and chaired by another from Britain, Sir Henry Cotton. Five years later, Sir William presided over the Silver Jubilee Sessions of the Congress held in Allahabad. Self-Government for India is something he firmly believed in, and said so at the YMIA which he had addressed on occasion.

To the west of the YMCA is Pachaiyappa's Hall, modelled on the Athenian Temple of Theseus with its tall Doric columns. Designed by a Capt. Ludlow, it was opened in 1850, work having begun on it in 1846. It was here that the Madras (later, Jubilee) Gayana Samaj was started in 1883 with an Indian and European membership, its aim being to get the latter to appreciate Carnatic music. Chief Justice Sir Charles Turner and Justice Muthuswami Aiyer were the leading lights of the organisation. The Hall, almost opposite *Telephone House*, fronts the buildings that housed the original preparatory school and then, in 1850, Pachaiyappa's High School. Pachaiyappa's Central Institution, the preparatory school, was the pioneer non-missionary, non-British-financed Hindu educational institution in the City and offered poor Hindus free education. It was opened on January 1, 1842, the beneficiary of the major share of a lakh of pagodas (Rs 7 lakh) from all that Pachaiyappa Mudaliar had bequeathed for charities when he died young (40) in 1794.

One of the first Indians to leave a will, Pachaiyappa's bequests became cause for a 47-year-long dispute. The courts finally ordered Rs 4.5 lakh (Rs. 450,000) of what he had provided for charities be spent on religious institutions and the rest on providing Hindu youth with an English education. The Trust, to be administered by a court-appointed Board of Trustees, according to a scheme formulated by the Supreme Court in 1909, was said to be worth over Rs 200 million as the new Millennium dawned. One of the biggest Trusts in India – some say South and Southeast Asia – it now administers religious charities from Varanasi to Kanniyakumari, six colleges, a polytechnic and 16 schools in Tamil Nadu as well as several medical facilities and scores of other properties in the State.

Pachaiyappa's preparatory school, first located in Popham's Broadway with G T McNamee as headmaster in 1842, acted as a feeder to the

Presidency High School established in Egmore. In 1846, the foundation stone was laid for its present home and the school opened there in 1850, Basil Lovery its first Principal. After becoming a high school in its own right and sending up students for the entrance exam to the University in 1858, Pachaiyappa's also developed as a second grade college in 1880 in the same premises. This became a first grade college in 1889. Housed in the Pachaiyappa's School buildings is another old Madras institution, the Govinda Naicker School, founded in 1865.

Pachaiyappa Mudaliar, who was born in 1754 in a destitute rural family in Periyapalayam, made a fortune by the time he was 21, a *dubash*ship being secured for him while he was still in his teens by *dubash* 'Powney' Narayana Pillai, who became the patron of the family. Today, the only monument in Madras to this pious man, who has been described as "the greatest contributor to charity Madras has ever known", stands in the new campus of the college in Chetput. This green-rich residential campus was opened in 1940. The statue appropriately depicts Pachaiyappa Mudaliar benignly blessing a young Hindu student. Till 1947, the College admitted and employed only Hindus.

Across Esplanade Road from Law College are, to the west, some sturdy, post-1940s buildings. The South India Chamber of Commerce's fourth home was in *The United India Life Building*, built c.1940 and now occupied by State insurance. The Chamber, founded by Sir P Theagaroya Chetty as the first body in the city to represent the interests of the Indian-owned mercantile firms, was established in 1910 in the *Ramakoti Building* in Rattan Bazaar where the Indian Bank located the same year after it moved out of its first offices in Parry's buildings. After two other hops, including a building of its own inaugurated in 1913, and which it vacated to move into the United India building while its own was being re-developed, the Chamber moved in 1956 into the handsomer premises it had raised on the Esplanade, on Government land that its 1945 President, Rm Alagappa Chettiar, had persuaded the Governor to grant it that year. In the late 1980s it moved into a more modern building it built nearby for its Platinum Jubilee. Next door is the building that was the southern headquarters of the Burmah Shell Company, which established itself in the city in 1928.

Best & Co was the first to market kerosene oil in bulk in Madras, introducing the product in 1889, though Hajee Ismail Sait's English Warehouse had been importing American kerosene in tins from the early

1880s and retailing it through Spencer's. In 1903, the first tanker discharged its cargo into the oil installation opened in Royapuram that year by Shell. Arbuthnot's and Binny's also entered the oil business before World War I. Till Burmah Shell was established to tend the interests of all the oil companies represented by these old Madras firms, Binny's looked after its interests from 1903.

Not far away is ornate *Raja Annamalai Chettiar Hall,* the Tamil Isai Sangam's auditorium that opened in 1953 with a 20,000 sq. ft ground floor. It also houses a mini-museum of South Indian musical instruments. *Raja Annamalai Chettiar Hall,* like many other cultural institutions in Madras, owes its genesis to the Chettinad family whose major contribution to the State and Tamil culture is Annamalai University in Chidambaram. The Sangam was started in Chettinad in 1940 and moved to Madras in 1943. Its aim was to popularise the use of Tamil in Carnatic Classical music and dance accompaniment, which the Music Academy, the city's leading Carnatic music and Classical dance patron at the time, was not exactly enthusiastic about. Its concerts and conferences were held in the St. Mary's Co-Cathedral Parish Hall till the Sangam built its own auditorium designed by S L Chitale and its construction supervised by M A Chidambaram, the Raja's youngest son.

The Sangam started an evening school in 1944 to teach Tamil music and this in 1995 began functioning as the Tamil Music college.

The Music Academy, not far from St George's Cathedral in the Mylapore-Teynampet area, is the City's foremost cultural centre. Its T T Krishnamachari Auditorium and the *Rajah Annamalai Chettiar Hall* were the major venues of classical concerts and dance recitals till other halls, like the Narada Gana Sabha's hall near the Academy, the Thyaga Brahma Gana Sabha's *Vani Mahal* in T'Nagar, (a 1945 hall built by V Ganapathy Iyer and now redeveloped) and the Kalakshetra auditorium in Tiruvanmiyur, besides several smaller halls, were added from the 1940s onwards and have in more recent years been renovated or rebuilt. These halls are today year-round 'temples' of culture in a city whose December-January 'Festival' is a 'must' for lovers of South Indian classical music and dance. The annual Music Festival is from December 15th to the 30th, following an old tradition that made fullest use of the bagful of holidays that marked the Christmas season in British times. It began in 1927 with the first All India Music Conference ever held in Madras; the Conference was organised to coincide with the Indian

National Congress session that year. The first music performance organised by the Conference Committee was held on December 24, 1927 at the Museum Theatre. Concerts on the next two days were in a *pandal* erected on the dry bed of Spur Tank. The Conference developed as the Music Academy, which was formally inaugurated in 1928 in the YMCA Hall in George Town, and in 1930 the Academy organised its own Conference and the first 'Season'.

In 1931, E Krishna Iyer brought the dance of the *devadasis, sadir,* to the Music Academy stage with the Kalyani Daughters. An ancient devotional dance form that the handmaidens of the Gods performed for the deities had by then fallen into disrepute, though the art form itself thrived. And it was as an art form, the Music Academy felt, *sadir* should be brought centre stage. Which it did – and then named it Bharata Natyam in 1932. Ever since, it has not only flourished in South India but also internationally, wherever South Indians have settled. Today, to dance in the Academy's *T.T. Krishnamachari Auditorium* is the aspiration of every budding dancer, but only the best are called. The auditorium commemorates a music-loving Minister who guided India's financial and industrial renaissance in Nehru's day and who had helped marshal resources for the hall; it was Nehru who laid the foundation stone for this hall in 1955. The hall was inaugurated in 1962, funding delaying its completion.

While the Academy, with its music, song and dance recitals and lecture series, is undoubtedly the most sought after society by artistes wishing distinguished blessing, other societies have also now begun to attract almost as much attention. The emergence of the Indian Fine Arts Society, four years younger, and the Tamil Isai Sangam, 16 years younger and focussed on Tamil rather than Telugu in its interpretation of Carnatic music, resulted in differences with the Music Academy in 1942 and in a section breaking away, but all of them, along with several other societies, now make the December-January Season a winter festival of dance and drama, music and song to remember. Enthusiasts come from all over the world to enjoy this great cultural experience when the classicists are honoured by societies and fans.

Today, over 30 major organisations and almost the same number of smaller *sabhas,* over 70 in all, make the Season a bonanza for music and dance lovers. What was once a 15-day season now lasts nearly four months and features well over 3000 programmes in nearly 60 venues, driving the *rasikas* (fans) crazy as they try to choose between conflicting top-of-the-marque offerings. The bulk of this programme is, however, a part of the main December-January Season, though quantity is tending to prevail over quality.

The societies (or *sabhas*), it must be recorded, don't hibernate after the Season; they provide fare year-round for their membership and guests. This fare, three or four programmes a month, ranges from dance and music to theatre and cinema. It is this system of *sabha* membership, with an activity almost every week, that's kept culture alive and thriving in Madras. But during the Season it seems to be a bit much even for the *rasikas* who in at least a dozen *sabhas* are offered four programmes a day, including lecture demonstrations. They, however, have the opportunity of taking a break in the temporary 'canteens' established in the *sabhas* by the city's leading vegetarian caterers whose fare always seem better during the Season. The 'canteen' was first introduced in 1939 by the Music Academy.

The Music Academy's Teachers' Training College of Music was opened in October 1931. It started functioning in Dr. U. Rama Rau's house, *Gana Mandir*, in Thambu Chetty Street with 'Tiger' Varadachariar as its first Principal. It is this institution, offering a three-year course, that has nurtured the teachers of Carnatic music in the city and enabled the spread of classical music education. Varadachariar in 1933 became the first head of the Madras University's Department of Music. To provide support to its College, the Academy has one of the best libraries on dance and music in the country, with a collection of rare books and manuscripts on music as well as CDs that are of great help to research students. Its music collection is now digitised in its entirety. Both College and library as well as a mini-hall are located in the Academy's spacious premises on Cathedral Road. The pioneer in formal music education, however, was Queen Mary's College. In 1927, it became the first college in the country to offer Music as an optional subject for the B.A. degree.

Associated with the activities of all the *sabhas* is the Sri Thiagaraja SangeethaVidwath Samajam, an organisation started and run by musicians to care for their interests. Conceived in 1929, it was registered in 1931 and enrolled members in those days on a subscription of 8 annas (50 paise) for the *sa* category and 4 annas (25 paise) for the *pa* category.

3. A challenge in the face of nature

Madras really began to grow in the last years of the 18th Century, after the defeat of Tippu Sultan. The British began moving out of the Fort, their safety assured by the beginnings of Empire. The 'garden houses' of southwest Madras were built and the major business houses were established on First Line Beach. North Beach Road – as First Line Beach later came to be known – was constructed in 1814 on reclaimed land, paralleled to its west by Second Line Beach. On those two roads the British established the great merchant houses and banking institutions that made Madras a major commercial city, as well as several government offices. On virtually just two roads, betwixt city and surf, the British built the institutions that were to provide them over the next 150 years much of their financial foundation in India's South. Behind these two roads, to the west, on the land side, is Muthialpet, the eastern half of George Town. On the sea side is the harbour.

Why Francis Day enthused over the desolate sandy strip of land he was granted in 1639 we will never know. It was an open beach, little more than a sandbank, with no harbour at all. This surf-lashed, exposed spit from which Madras grew may have been a narrow peninsula well protected on two sides by rivers and on the third by the sea, where a wall in the north would ensure safety, but ships could not visit it during the monsoon months, and at other times of the year they had to anchor far from shore. The annual monsoons, the major one during October to December and the milder one in May-June, virtually closed the roadstead, for winds of cyclone force could ravage the shipping. The first cyclone that is mentioned in the records as having devastated shipping in Madras Roads after Fort St George was founded occurred in May 1662, nine ships being destroyed!

Even in the dry season, ships had to lie at anchor outside the surf opposite the Fort, in the open roadstead, and land passengers and goods in local boats. On this cyclone-wracked coast – the records show that cyclones have struck Madras in every month of the year – the sea was always more a menace than a protection, the passage from ship to shore in the angry surf being anything but pacific even in fair weather.

Founded with not a thought of safe anchorage, Day's defence-oriented Madras condemned ships calling at it to this open roadstead, treacherous winds, unpredictable currents and towering waves. Able to brave these were only the frail *kattumaram* (logs lashed together temporarily with rope) and *masula* (planks sewn together with rope) boats that rode the waves and provided a two-mile ferry service from ship to shore: "....The boatmen waited for a big wave, came in on the crest of it till it was spent, paddled hard to get past the breaking place of the next wave so as to be carried by it right up the beach. And as they waited outside the surf for a good wave they bargained with their passengers...".

The daring boatmen, who struck a hard bargain for risking their lives, would bring back from the East Indiamen goods and passengers to be "piled anyhow on the sand in front of the sea gate at the Fort, where the road now runs." North Beach Road was really the line of the beach well into the 19th Century.

In 1796, 191 three-masted ships, 46 two-masted ships and 707 one-masted *dhonis*, sloops etc. of net tonnage 150,000 had entered Madras Roads. The tonnage during the next few years kept increasing. Robert Clive's son, the second Lord Clive, was the Governor who in 1798 made the far-sighted decision to move the godowns and the 'Sea Customer' (Collectorate of Customs, we would call it today) out of the Fort, where they had been by the Sea Gate – goods being landed on the beach in front of this gate – to the paddy godowns (used by the French as a prison) on the open northeast beach, on which site stands *Customs House* today. Thus, from the end of the 18th Century, goods were landed on this northern beach – what later generations were to call First Line Beach! This led to the growth of First Line Beach as the mercantile centre of the city. But until 1809, there was still commercial occupation of Fort St George's godowns. It was only in that year that the public offices alone were left concentrated in the Fort.

In those days, First Line Beach was indeed beach, and up to what is now Parry's Corner, was the 'Marina' for 'Black Town' dwellers, who thronged it every evening. But with Lord Clive's decision, 'Black Town', over the decades that followed, lost a 'lung' and acquired a handsome commercial skyline. However, till the harbour began reclaiming much of this beach for its wharfs, North Beach remained an open, unprotected stretch of sand on which, near the present main gates of the harbour, was located the main embarkation and disembarkation point from which the frail *masula* boats and *kattumaram* plied to the East Indiamen, ferrying goods and fearful passengers.

Without the doughty boatmen who rode the angry waves there could have been no ship-to-shore link in the first 250 years of Madras! But the factors and traders felt that the hardy *masula* boatmen were making too huge a profit out of their monopoly, that the losses in transit of goods were excessive: damage, pilferage and the losses from boats that capsized – often, it has been said, on purpose, the goods being recovered later by skilled swimmers – were all affecting the profitability of the Company's operations. "The loss in this way between ship and shore was estimated at 90% of the loss on the whole voyage, and at 20% of trade profit," according to one writer. And, so, the Chamber of Commerce, in 1868, began to press for some sort of safer anchorage.

A scheme for a harbour was first mooted in 1845, to overcome the drawbacks of the surf. This plan called for a 1,100-ft screw pier to be pushed out into the surf; goods were to be landed on it from the ferrying boats. The plan was approved in 1857, work commenced in 1859 and, after a rash of troubles, the mole was opened in 1861. In 1868, it was damaged by one storm and, three years later, put out of commission by another. So arose the necessity for another plan, one approved in 1873 by Governor Lord Vere Hobart and which called for a breakwater and a closed harbour. This was the plan of a Mr Parkes "who had been very successful in Karachi but had not at that time even seen Madras"!

As far back as 1770, a pier projecting beyond the surf had been recommended by Second Member and Export Warehouse-Keeper Warren Hastings, who sought plans from England for such a scheme based on the Margate Pier, but no enthusiasm was shown for it and the boatmen continued to enjoy a monopoly. Others suggested similar action in 1786 and 1798, but the boatmen's monopoly first became threatened only when the 1861 screw pier was built and virtually ended when, in 1876, work began on the first harbour of Madras according to the vision of William Parkes. Pushing it through was the Madras Chamber of Commerce, particularly G G Arbuthnot and Patrick Macfadyen, two men who were to die in disgrace years later for their dubious business practices. Parkes' plan entailed twin parallel masonry breakwaters, each 3,000 feet long and 3,000 feet apart, to be built on either side of an iron pier. The breakwaters were then to turn in towards each other to form a 515-foot east-facing entrance. Within these two breakwaters there would be shelter for nine ships, each of 3,000-7,000 tonnage. By 1881, the work was more or less complete and it was recorded that Madras had at last got a harbour. But the harbour was almost completely destroyed in November that year and had to be rebuilt from scratch.

The cyclone of 1881, one of the worst in the history of Madras, "washed away half a mile of the breakwaters, threw the two top courses of concrete blocks into the harbour, hurled over two of the Titan cranes used on the works, lowered and spread out the rubble base of the breakwater and washed away one and a half miles of construction railway." Two small ships in harbour were also sunk! All of which was only to be expected as the walls were only 2½ feet above sea level at the best of times! But Government promptly took up the entire project exactly as originally planned, refused to listen to experts advising modifications, and completed it in 1896 with two "jaws of pincers running out into the sea" and leaving between them a 515-feet-wide entrance still facing east!

A writer of the time describes the harbour as a basin a thousand yards square, "enclosed within masonry groynes running out into the sea from North and South of the pier which turning to each other leave an opening in the centre of the basin... for entrance and exit. These groynes are formed of concrete blocks, of certain proportions of granite and cement moulded together, which dovetail together."

Another reporter says the 1876 harbour was "just two walls, shaped like the jaws of a pincers, running out into the sea. Ships entered straight from the East through the opening of the jaws and anchored in a basin within. Boats conveyed the passengers to an old pier of wood and iron which jutted out from the shore. Merchandise was unloaded from ships to lighters, to be unloaded again on the shore."

But the first commentator took a dim view of the entire proceedings. "The harbour from its position, can never be a harbour of refuge and all that these costly works will secure is immunity for landing and operations from the November surf which is so general along the whole of the Coromandel Shipping Coast." Nevertheless, by 1900, a harbour of sorts was complete. But surf-driven sand silting up the entrance made this harbour dangerous for navigation.

In charge of the Harbour was a Madras Harbour Board established in 1886. This was to become the Madras Port Trust in 1905. Its first Chairman was Sir Francis Spring, who had earlier served the Indian government for 33 years and had lastly retired as Secretary of the Madras Government's Railways Department. He arrived on the scene in 1904 and found the harbour "arrangements were about as bad they could possibly be!" By the time he left in 1919, few could deny that he was the 'maker of the Madras Port' we know today. He's remembered in the main building of the harbour, a wharf and the road leading to the wharf. On Springhaven Road were several spacious bungalows of World War I vintage, which used to be occupied by senior officers of the Port Trust. They have all been pulled down in the 2000s by those enamoured of multistorey construction.

On Springhaven Wharf is a tiny 'private' harbour and a clubhouse, the home of the Royal Madras Yacht Club founded by Sir Francis in 1911 on separation from the rowing-oriented Boat Club. The 'harbour' is the erstwhile Timber Pond where logs of wood were stored. Yachting had been popular in several coastal and inland venues in and round Madras from 1855 but was formalised only when Sir Francis acted. The 'Royal' prefix was conferred on the Club in 1926 by King George V and it remains one of the few institutions in India to retain the honorific. The 'Europeans Only' club got its first Indian Commodore in 1966, L M Krishnan, who was the first member of the Club to win a national title. That was at the first Yachting Association of India championships which were held in 1960. A new clubhouse was inaugurated in 1987 – rather a contrast to the old in its modern-looks, but with traces of the past in its wood-embellished interiors.

After acquiring its separate identity, the Club not only spent more time training young yachtsmen but it also began organising more regattas. The first major one was in 1924 when the Madras Sailing Club met the Royal Colombo Yacht Club. This remained an annual exchange between the two clubs till the ethnic conflict in the Island put an end to it.

Across from the club is the Tamil Nadu Sailing Association's clubhouse. The Association, formed in 2002 with the focus on training youth, is a major visible competitor in national competitions. Near the Club, there informally functions the Madras Anglers' Club, its beginnings said to be in the 1940s though angling has been a sport in Madras from the City's earliest days.

Spring, when he got down to work, created a new entrance in the northeastern corner of the harbour and closed the eastern entrance. To protect this new entrance, a new breakwater was built projecting into the sea north of it. This artificial harbour, that retained its shape well into the years after Independence, encompassed "200 acres, with an entrance, 400 feet wide, on the northeastern corner (opened in 1909), protected by an outer sheltering arm, 1,791 feet in length. The depth of water at the entrance is about 37 feet at high water and about 34 feet at low water and the normal daily tidal variation is 2½ feet. Vessels can enter and leave the harbour at all states of the tide and at all times of day or night and lie in smooth water in all weathers. During the cyclone season (April-June and October-November), however, steamers may very occasionally have to leave the harbour and proceed to sea, on account of heavy rage inside the harbour when a cyclone passes over or is near the port."

The first Port Trust office was built in stages between 1908 and 1916, a splendid stone-faced, two-floor building with a central clock tower. This was replaced by a soul-less transit shed in 1964. The new Port Trust office, with its echoes of Art Deco, was constructed away from the wharves between 1957 and 1960. Additions to the Port's facilities are still being made as they have been over the years from Spring's time – making it today one of the largest man-made ports in Asia.

Madras grew in its first hundred years from Day's sliver of sand into a Presidency capital that sent forth empire-builders and from a textile centre into one of the inspirations for the Industrial Revolution. But when Kipling saw the town in 1896, he ruefully sang:

Clive kissed me on the mouth and eyes and brow,
Wonderful kisses, so that I became
Crowned above queens;
A withered beldame now,
Brooding on ancient fame.

Sir Francis Spring, founder of the Madras Port Trust of 1905, was convinced that a harbour would give new life to the withered beldame. And so he worked unremittingly on seeing that money was spent on this "challenge flaunted in the face of nature." By the time he left in 1919, "just at the beginning of the great boom, when the trade and prosperity of the city leapt up", Madras had a harbour worthy of the first, and still growing, Presidency. He was, unfortunately, not around to see the results of the boom and the subsequent growth of Madras. But before he had left Madras he had stated his conviction that Madras harbour would have to grow in the next 20, 30 or 50 years. And grow it did, till no more addition of facilities was possible. A satellite harbour was seen as the solution in the 1990s and work began on it in 1997.

The Ennore satellite port, originally mainly for coal, oil, gas and other fuel, was completed in 2001 near the 'island' formed by the entrances to the Ennore and Pulicat backwaters, the sea and the Buckingham Canal (once the Elambore River). A long, 125 sq km island of giant futuristic sand dunes, Kaattupalli, this is where the North Chennai Thermal Power Station has come up, replacing the one north of Royapuram in Basin Bridge. Nearby, there has been developed a smaller port, built by Larsen & Toubro and Government in a private-public sector partnership. The two-berth, deep sea harbour and shipyard were formally inaugurated in January 2013, but received its first ship only in April 2013. Further industrialisation of the island is forecast, threatening the three villages that exist on it and the avifauna and the aquatic wealth of the backwaters. The Pulicat backwaters and the lake form one of the most inviting flamingo havens in the country and are a bird-watchers' paradise from November to March when the migrants arrive from winter climes in northern Asia. Pulicat, once a Dutch settlement and rich in heritage, and its rich environment are themselves threatened by all this development, its potential as a significant recreational destination now unlikely to materialise.

4. Betwixt city and surf

With the growth of the Harbour there also grew the mercantile importance of North Beach Road alongside it. On this road, betwixt George Town and surf, there are, today, some of the finest buildings in the city. A once-stately pillared and pedimented quasi-Classical building, now Royapuram's suburban railway station, marks the end of this road. When inaugurated in 1856, it had been the main terminus of the Madras Railways, the Presidency's first. A neighbouring building of the same period, the headquarters building, was pulled down some years ago, but the station has precariously survived, commemorating the opening of the railway in the South. It had been inaugurated by Lord Harris, the Governor, before an elite gathering whose attire and gaiety befitted a ball. His Lordship mentioned in his speech that the 65 miles of track from Royapuram to Arcot had taken three years to lay and had cost £5,500 a mile. This Ionic-pillared building, looking for all the world like a memory of a Regency mansion, was restored in 2006 – but painted a ghastly red, forgetting that Raj era buildings in Classical style always had white exteriors.

Not so fortunate has been *Bentinck's Building*, south of Customs House, which, despite all the efforts of the conservationists, was pulled down in 1991-92, over a year being necessary for the wreckers' hammers to complete their task, so solid was its construction. The building was named after Lord William Bentinck, Governor of Madras (1803-1807) and, later, a reformist Governor-General who abolished *sati*, took on the thuggis and introduced, for better or worse, on Macaulay's recommendations, the pattern of education and jurisprudence still in existence in India, work on which Macaulay began in Ooty.

The merchants of Fort St George, under increasing pressure to leave it and set up business outside, began work in 1793 on the site of the old Marine Yard on what was to be their new Business Exchange – to be named Bentinck's Building. Customs House was built next to it, from 1798 onwards. Adjacent to this new 'home' of the merchants was built a stationery store, which still survives as the Government Stationery Depot. All the grain godowns were close by and these gave their names to neighbouring streets, such as Godown Street and Bunder Street. These godowns were once called 'bankshalls' (named no doubt due to the goods in the warehouses being pledged to banks).

By 1817, the merchants were becoming bigger than the facilities that Bentinck's Building could provide. They began building headquarters for themselves on the same stretch. Whereupon, into Bentinck's Building moved the Supreme Court of Madras in 1862 when it became the High Court. The Court stayed there till 1892 when it moved into its handsome new premises. Bentinck's Building then became the Collectorate of Madras. It was demolished in the 1990s and new, rather tasteless multi-storey PWD construction was raised and named Singaravelar Maligai. It houses the Collectorate and Special Courts. Outside it stands a rather incongruous relic of the past, the cupola that once housed the statue of Lord Cornwallis.

Bentinck's Building was built with its ground floor and first floor each of about 27,000 sq foot extent. With its Burma teak rafters, heavy iron windows and liberal use of cut stone, it had cost Rs 370,000. The large stationery store to the south was added in 1817, its 34,000 sq feet costing about Rs 320,000. Several smaller buildings, including a 'jail', were also later added. So were a few naval offices, now no more.

A much newer building a little south is what was the headquarters building of the Indian Bank till a few years ago. Incorporated in 1907, one of the first Indian-owned banks in the country and the first Madras headquartered one, it was born out of the collapse of Arbuthnot & Co in 1906 (more of which anon). The widespread misery caused to Indian depositors by the failure of the leading British company in India made men like V Krishnaswami Aiyer determined to establish a bank owned and managed by Indians. Nattukkottai Chettiar funding enabled the bank to prosper from its earliest years. In 1909, the Bank acquired for Rs 135,000 the *Arbuthnot Building* separated from the *Bentinck's Building* campus by Arbuthnot Street. Moving from Rattan Bazaar in July 1910, the Indian Bank established its headquarters here and, in 1970, built on the same site in place of the stately old building a characterless multistorey building. Arbuthnot Street by the side of the Indian Bank headquarters commemorates in its name a sad chapter in Madras banking history and the birth of a new chapter in development. The Indian Bank itself has moved its headquarters again, this time to a sleek, glass-dominated 21st Century building opened in January 2012 on Lloyd's Road, near the Music Academy.

Still further south is the Art Deco Mercantile Bank building (1923). While *Bentinck's Building* reflects British Colonial Old and the Mercantile Bank, now the Hongkong & Shanghai Bank, building is Colonial New, the magnificent red-painted 55,000 square foot General Post Office building might be described as a Victorian County-Colonial or Victorian Gothic-Colonial overlay on Indo-Saracenic. This building, yet another Chisholm design, 350 feet long, 160 feet broad and with 125-foot-tall twin towers, was built on the site of the Abercrombie Battery. These towers once sported the Kerala roof-influenced 'caps' Chisholm favoured atop towers, after his building assignments in Travancore, but are now 'capless', the four-sided, sharply-sloping 'caps' having been removed after a storm in the mid-20th Century. The smaller towers still sport the 'caps'. Construction of the building started in 1874 and occupation from early 1884, with the GPO finally shifting from Popham's Broadway to open its doors here on April 26, 1884, after Rs.6.8 lakh that had been hard to find had been spent on it, a considerable part of it contributed by the Madras Chamber of Commerce. Besides a high-ceilinged central hall, the ground floor provided space for stores, kitchen, servants etc. The first floor was used for offices, initially manned by one Writer (clerk), five sorters, a head peon and ten postmen. The second floor served as residence for the Presidency Postmaster General. He moved in on March 1, 1884 from space he was occupying in the

Mercantile Bank further down the road. The Broadway staff began functioning here from April 26th. The building's interior was gutted by fire in 2000, after which the interior was redesigned and made functional again while maintaining the building's façade, but a glorious opportunity for model restoration was lost. It would have also prevented some damage during the Monsoon of 2011.

It was Governor Harrison (1711-1717) who in 1712 first started a Company Postal Service in Madras – to carry mail to Bengal by *dak*-runner. By 1736, a postal system of sorts, with a somewhat greater vision, was in place. In 1774, a beginning was made on charging postage on private letters. It was, however, only after two Civilians, John P Burlton and Thomas Lewin, suggested to Government in 1785 and 1786 that it was necessary to lay down postal rules, draw up a postal network and establish a postal authority that the first Madras Post Office, with fixed postal rates, was established by Governor Sir Archibold Cambell. It was called the General Post Office, Madras, and was opened for business on June 1, 1786, just outside the Sea Gate, in what was called Fort St George Square, with A M Campbell, a kingsman of the Governor as Postmaster-General. The Company over-ruled Campbell's appointment and, eventually, Oliver Colt was appointed the first Postmaster-General of Madras. It moved into the Fort, into the old Bank building, near the North Gate, in 1837. By then (in 1834) two 'receiving' post offices – Vepery and Royapettah – had been established. Over the next few years, a few other such offices was established. It was a while before full-fledged offices with delivery service were started. The move to *Garden House*, Broadway, came in 1856, a year after the first letter-box had appeared in the city (at Moubray's Road) and two years after a Post Office Act came into force, an organised postal system established and stamps first introduced. The postal service grew when railway connections were established with the other Presidencies in 1871. By 1874, there were nine post offices in the city. The internal carriage of mail in Madras was by horse cart (*jutkas*) till 1918, though a beginning with motorised transport was made in 1915. The telegraph came to Madras in 1853 but was made available to the public only from February 1, 1855, when 41 offices covering a distance of 3,000 miles could be reached.

The old State Bank of India building, next to the GPO and a little newer, truly attesting to its Imperial (Bank) heritage, is yet another splendid example of Madras's best known architectural form –

Indo-Saracenic – and the building skills of Thatikonda Namberumal Chetty. Col Samuel Jacob, who did St Stephen's College in Delhi, is mentioned in connection with the initial design of this building, but it was Henry Irwin who was appointed the architect and Namberumal Chetty who was awarded the Rs 3 lakh building contract. The site had been bought from Government in 1895 for Rs 1 lakh and work commenced on it the next year.

Built as the headquarters of the Bank of Madras, which had moved from the Fort to Popham's Broadway, it had a magnificent marble-floored banking hall on the first floor, with ornate woodwork and beautiful stained glass in its lofty, vaulted ceiling, much of it still visible. Also visible are the Bank of Madras's insignia (BM) on the glass-panelled doors leading to the Banking Hall. On the second floor, where once were both quarters and offices, there are today offices still with the heavy ornamented doors of yesteryear and scores of richly embellished wooden, brick and granite arches. There are said to be 1,200 stained glass panels in the building. A particularly striking one is the panel with hooded serpents and a two-headed bird. As many as six colours are used in the mosaic of the smaller panels that combine to make the whole. The building now houses the main Madras branch of the SBI.

As early as 1682/3 there was a bank established by Governor Gifford and his council, the Madras or Government Bank, but the first formal bank, incorporated as a joint stock company, was the Carnatic Bank, established in Fort St George in 1788. This was followed by the British Bank of Madras in 1795 and the Asiatic Bank in 1804. The first issues of banknotes in Madras were from the Carnatic Bank (1788), the Government Bank (1806) and the Bank of Madras (1843). The last-named's notes featured erstwhile Madras Governor Thomas Munro. The representation recalled his 1839 statue on the Island Grounds. The era of individual banks issuing notes came to an end in 1861 when the Government of India began issuing them.

The Madras banks amalgamated and there was established in the Fort Exchange a joint stock bank, the Bank of Madras, with a capital of Rs 3 million in 1843. Government held shares in this Presidency bank until 1876. In 1921, it merged with the Bombay and Bengal Banks to become the Imperial Bank – since 1955, the State Bank of India, branch-wise the world's largest bank. The Bank of Madras's headquarters then became the SBI's Madras Presidency headquarters. When the Reserve Bank of

Built as the Bank of Madras's headquarters, this splendid pile of Indo-Saracenic has one of the most ornate commercial interiors in Madras. Now the home of the State Bank of India's main branch.

The embellished facade of a Magistrate's Court on left and the General Post Office – its 'Kerala caps' no more – on right... all part of North Beach's former glory.

39. *Now Government Press...but once site of a gunpowder factory, then the Mint.*
40. *The road for which a tax was sought...Wall Tax Road, its walls, on the left, once the city's western lim*

India was formed in 1935 to transact government business, issue curency notes and "monitor the fiscal health of the economy", taking over what the Imperial Bank had been additionally doing, the RBI's regional office shared the SBI's Presidency headquarters building till it built its own building further south, where North and South Beach Roads meet, and moved in, in 1961. Tarapore & Co were the builders of the RBI Building, the new Customs House, the A C College of Technology, and the Meenambakkam Airport, among others, in a grand building spree. This Madras-based company, a partnership between (C. S. Loganathan Mudaliar and J.H. Tarapore from 1936, was one of the leading building contractors in the country in the 1950s and 1960s. As one of the largest engineering contractors in India in the early years after Independence, the firm also handled many major contracts outside the State. These included major contributions to the Farakka Barrage in West Bengal, Hirakud Dam, the Rourkela Steel Plant, the Indian Aluminium plant in Orissa, the Sharavathi Hydroelectric Project in Mysore, the Travancore Cements and Rayons factories in Kerala, the aerodome in Trivandrum, and the Trivandrum-Nagercoil concrete road.

Of the exchange banks, the Standard Chartered Bank, established in Britain in 1853 without the 'Standard' prefix, opened a branch in Madras in 1900 in a building it had built in 1871, opposite the High Court, at the Armenian Street junction. The main Madras branch remains on the site, but the old building, with its church-like interior, has regrettably given way to a new commercial look that has made even the exterior unrecognisable. The new regional headquarters of the Standard Chartered is an even more modern complex in a large, well-greened campus on College Road which also houses many of its international bank offices.

The National Bank, absorbed by A N Z Grindlays which in turn has been absorbed by Standard Chartered, opened in North Beach Road in 1877 and moved into new premises built by Namberumal Chetty further up the road, and closer to the High Court, in 1915. This handsome example of Indo-Saracenic – complete with cupolas, Italian marble, rosewood and red Porbander granite – was hit by an *Emden* shell in 1914, while construction was going on, but suffered little damage. It had an 150-foot frontage, a width of 30 feet and a height of 60 feet with its domed, Irwinesque towers rising 95 feet. Grindlay's, originally represented in Madras by Binny's, opened its first branch in South India in 1877 in Armenian Street. Its modernised regional headquarters came up on the National Bank site – the heritage building demolished without a word of protest, as 'heritage' was a word hardly known in Madras at the time – and was occupied in 1981, one of the first post-Independence buildings in Madras to use polished black gneiss imaginatively. The neighbouring *Circle Top House* of the State Bank of India is now the SBI's regional headquarters. Raised in the space where *The Madras Mail* had been and in the stableyard, then car shed, of the old headquarters building, it is another new granite and glass building that uses polished black gneiss well, making it too one of the better examples of modern architecture. It was opened for occupation in 1977.

In 1854, there opened in Moor Street in 'Black Town' a new banking institution, the Chartered Mercantile Bank of India, London and China. In 1893, it was reconstituted as the Mercantile Bank of India Ltd, but by then it had moved to Maclean Street and, then, to First Line Beach. Now absorbed by the Hongkong & Shanghai Banking Corporation, its home since 1923 has been refurbished, but still houses the building traditions of the days of the mercantile Raj. These premises were, in the years before World War II, one of the most impressive buildings on First Line Beach, the front an English-style Renaissance block dominated by two towers each 90-foot-tall. The exterior was renewed and the interior imaginatively redesigned after the Hongkong & Shanghai moved in in the mid-1990s. The first Madras-based Indian bank was, as already related, the Indian Bank. The Indian Overseas Bank was the second major Madras Indian bank, which was established to focus more on overseas business than was the practice at the time.

Between Standard Chartered, Grindlays and *Circle Top House* is a quaint building reflecting, in outward appearance, a gentler, more gracious and punctilious age. This is the Gothic-windowed building that housed a part of the operations of Thomas Cook's, those venerable travel agents who pioneered world travel. Past it and the State Bank buildings and the GPO is another bit of quaintness, a red and colourfully ornamented building designed by Henry Irwin and inaugurated in 1892, the Metropolitan Magistrate's Court, popularly called the George Town Court, which echoes vaguely the High Court if it had no towers, but is nowhere near as well kept. Restoration of the cramped building with its six courts has been sanctioned as these lines are written. And then comes one of Madras's first modern highrises, and the first on First Line Beach, *TIAM House,* built as the headquarters of the TI Group. *TIAM House* came up on the site of a handsome Regency style three-storied building, pillared, verandahed and pedimented, that Best & Co (1872) built around 1900 and to which it added a smaller building in 1923. Best's sold its big building to the Khaleelis around 1925 and they in turn sold it to the Tube Investments Group, as the Murugappa Group was then known, in 1956. TI's, not as conscious then of heritage conservation as the Group now is, pulled down the handsome building of Best's heyday and inaugurated its new highrise in 1960. As in the case of the LIC tower, British architects and engineers had worked on this one too. Best's meanwhile moved into its smaller building and remained there till 1983 when it sold the building to the Unit Trust of India who pulled it down in 1987 and built its own building for occupation by 1990. Its architect is undoubtedly alone in thinking it reflects the old in the new. In 2006, *TIAM House* was sold by the Murugappa Group to a religious organisation and it consolidated its headquarters in *Dare House*, Parry & Co now being part of the Group.

Across the road from these buildings, starting to the east of Parry's Corner and stretching to Beach Station are a row of shops known as 'Burma Bazaar'. The shops, once a treasure trove of mysteriously 'imported' luxury items, are generally believed to be run by Indian refugees from Burma who returned to the country in the last few decades. But in practice the antecedents of the shopkeepers are as mysterious as their sources of supply of genuine and spurious foreign goods. Behind this row of shops, to the east, is Railway and Port Trust property – built on reclaimed land! A subway was opened in 1967, linking South Beach Road with North Beach Road just before Parry's Corner. During excavation work for this subway, part of the Great Bulwark, the stone sea wall built by de Havilland to protect the Fort and its neighbourhood from the angry surf, was revealed. In 1978, when the Beach Station subway was being dug, more bits of this wall were found.

Beyond Burma Bazaar is the Anchor Gate, the new entrance to the Harbour. North Beach Road then leads on to Clive Battery. Edward Clive, the son of Robert, lent his name to the fortification built in his time – around 1800 – at the sea end of the 'Black Town' rampart walls, but battery there was none in the 20th Century, only homes of another age where lived Port Trust officers. Now, even the roadside walls and entrance, which served as a reminder of the Battery's heritage, are no more. They have been pulled down for an overbridge built to quicker link the busy 'villages' of Royapuram and Tondiarpet with North Beach Road. Thereafter, the fast-eroding road leads on to the historic village of Tiruvottriyur, followed by Manali and Ennore, some of the most industrialised areas of modern Madras.

Across from the harbour gates are the homes of old shipping companies. Biggest of them is what was the Classical home of Gordon Woodroffe's, which has been on this site since the founding of the Company in 1868. On either side of it are, southward, N Selvaradjalou Chetty & Co, on this site from around 1914, and to the north of it J M Baxi. Still further north is the rather run down Mariners' Club, with a history dating to the early 20th Century. In better shape is the Seafarers' Club at the opposite end of North Beach Road. Opened in 1964, in 39 grounds of spaciousness, the Seafarers' Club is a home away from home for merchant mariners.

5. The villages in the north

Royapuram, historically, in latter-day British times, was a 'village' associated with the Railways and goods storage. The associations still remain in an area where you can still see some of the City's earliest Railway buildings and yards. Royapuram's Anglo-Indian population (only a fraction of what it once was) is yet another reminder of the area's links with the railways, whose backbone before Independence was the Anglo-Indian community.

Royapuram is the spiritual home of the Parsis of Madras. The first Parsis, seven of them, including two priests, arrived in Madras in 1795. As Madras prospered, the community too began to grow. To meet the needs of the community, the Madras Parsi Panchayat, formed in 1876, began collecting monthly contributions from members for a Mobed (priest) Fund from 1887; the fund was intended as much for maintaining a priest as for eventually establishing a place of worship. A significant contribution was made by Sir Dinshaw Petit of Bombay in 1896 and this enabled the purchase of a plot of land in Royapuram where the community had established itself. However, plans to build a temple were slow in taking off.

In February 1906, the small community lost 13-year-old Jal Phiroj Clubwala. His father, Phiroj Muncherji Clubwala, decided to create a corpus that would enable Madras to avail the services of a *mobed* who could conduct all obligatory ceremonies. The first *mobed* was Ervad *Dosabhai Pavri*.

The next year, Phiroj Muncherji Clubwala, decided to gift the Madras Parsi Zarthosti Anjuman (the successor of the Panchayat) land on West Madha Church Street in Royapuram, near the earlier earmarked site, and build a fully equipped *agiari* on it, provided the community raised Rs.30,000 to maintain the temple. With the community raising the money, Clubwala built the temple and the Anjuman decided to name it the Jal Phiroj Clubwala Dar-e-Meher in memory of the donor's son.

The foundation stone was laid for the *agiari* on February 9, 1909 by Hormusji Nowroji, the President of the Anjuman (Panchayat). Nowroji, a civil engineer, designed the temple and supervised its building. And on August 7, 1910 the temple was consecrated. Shortly before the consecration, Dosabhai Pavri had retired and Ervad Hormasji Adarji Gai was appointed priest in his place. With the consecration of the temple, he became its first *pathank* (priest-in-charge). For the priests to live in, Phiroj Muncherji Clubwala gifted the Anjuman a block of land adjacent to the temple and raised, in what is also called Anjuman Bagh, a house for their accommodation in 1908. This was remodeled in 1985 to sympathise in style with the dar-e-meher. The Parsi cemetery is also in the Bagh and the oldest tombstone in it dates to 1878.

The community next got together not long after Phiroj Muncherji Clubwala passed away in August 1927 to take steps to honour his memory. The Phiroj Clubwala Memorial Hall, further down the road, which could, as already mentioned, be called 'The Road of Perfect Harmony', was declared open by his widow Srinibai on August 14, 1930. The hall was renovated and air-conditioned in 2010/11.

An ancient church in Royapuram is St Peter's built in its original form in 1824 by the Roman Catholic boat-owners of Royapuram, who had migrated from Chepauk in the 1790s. There were several disputes over ownership between the boat-owners, fishermen and the ecclesiastical authorities, before the latter were given the church in 1867 by the Madras High Court. The church was thereafter developed to its present form, but the tradition of no pews has been preserved. Rayappan is the Tamil equivalent of Peter and Royapuram derives its name from this equation (Rayappar-*puram* = Town of Peter).

In Royapuram too is found reflected, in the Ramanujan Museum close to the Police Station, one man's admiration for another's genius. What government has failed to do, a retired mathematics school teacher,

P K Srinivasan, did with the help of a few wellwishers: he has developed a museum to remember Ramanujan, the mathematics genius, and in it attempted to portray Ramanujan through letters, notes, cuttings and photographs. The labour of love, established in 1992 as part of the Avvai Kalai Kazhagam which offers a library, auditorium and crafts training, may be in an obscure corner of the City but deserves far greater attention and support than what it receives.

Another labour of love here is the Christina Rainy Hospital, named after its chief benefactor, a Scottish educationist who raised funds for it in Scotland. This hospital, now called the CSI Rainy Multi Specialty Hospital and modernised with multistorey buildings, matching facilities and 250 beds, goes back to when there were almost no medicare facilities in the Washermenpet-Royapuram area of the early 19th Century till Dr John Scudder of the American Mission (whose name should be writ large in the annals of Education and Medicine in Jaffna and Tamil Nadu) began in 1830 to go to Royapuram to conduct a roadside clinic. In 1856, he was succeeded by Scottish medical missionaries. In 1888, one of these doctors, Matilda (I've found the name Alexandrina too!) Macphail, made the visiting facility a permanent dispensary. This facility in time added a few beds and that was what Christina Rainy, a Scottish educationist, saw when she visited Madras towards the end of the 19th Century. Back in Scotland, Rainy raised funds for a full-fledged mission hospital in Royapuram and its main block was inaugurated in 1914. This block still stands, but in sorry shape, towered over by new buildings.

Off Tiruvottriyur High Road, in Tondiarpet, Vavilla Ramaswami Sastrulu & Sons, the pioneers of Telugu publishing, put down roots in 1851. The firm not only published Telugu and Sanskrit classics, the latter in Telugu letters, but the founder himself was responsible for several Telugu types that are in use to this day. The first publication of the Adi Saraswathi Nilaya Press was in 1854. Shortly after the founder's death, the press took his name and from 1906 was known as the Vavilla Ramaswami Sastrulu Press. When Vavilla Ramaswami Sastrulu and Sons in 1910 published Radhika Santwanamu by Muddu Palani, a courtesan at the court of Tanjore's Maratha ruler Pratapasimha (1739-1763), at the behest of Nagarathnamma, that latter-day courtesan and feminist, it was publishing what, almost certainly, was the first erotic work by a woman in South India. The publication was immediately banned by the Government of Madras on grounds of obscenity.

The publisher's offices were raided and nine titles (including the Santwanamu) were seized in May 1911. When it was found that one of the seized titles had been published with support from the Raja of Venkatagiri, the Government decided to soft pedal the whole issue. Eventually, the Chief Presidency Magistrate decided that only the Santwanamu needed to be banned and every copy of it destroyed. It was the first obscenity-in-print case in Madras. No sooner Premier Prakasam lifted the ban in 1947, the Nagarathnamma edition was re-issued by Vavilla in 1952.

After Independence, Andhra Pradesh, the homeland of the Telugus, became the centre of Telugu publishing – but Ramaswami Sastrulu's remained till the new Millenium, when it closed down, an important centre of Telugu knowledge in a city whose origins have the closest links with the Telugus. Near here is the 200-year old Arunachaleswar Temple.

Between Tondiarpet and Tiruvottriyur is the former village of weavers and 'painters', Colletpetta – named after Governor Collet – corrupted to Kaladipetta (which, unfortunately, means loafers' village). Collet, who was Governor from 1717-20, seized Tiruvottriyur by force and, in 1719, a little south of it, founded his weavers' village. It wasn't long before he also built the Kalyana Varadaraja Perumal Temple here as a conciliatory gesture.

One of his Indian assistants, it is related, used to go to Kanchipuram every morning to worship at the Varadaraja Perumal Temple there before returning to go to work. This long journey daily delayed his reporting for duty. An enraged Governor one day berated him when he heard that it was worship that made the devotee late every day. "If your relationship with your God is so close, tell me what he is doing at this moment?" the Governor challenged. The Indian assistant replied, "He is in a chariot that has been stopped by an accident," and went on to describe the scene as he saw it in his vision. When the vision proved true on verification, Governor Collet had the temple in Colletpetta built – to permit his devotee to pray in Madras instead of making the long journey to Kanchipuram. He also endowed it lavishly – and regularly – from his export earnings, and also made Viraraghavan, the devotee, the shrine's first trustee. The daily visit to Kanchipuram in the age of the bullock cart must remain in the realm of story-telling, but Viraraghava's family remain associated with the temple.

The Tiruvottriyur Saivite shrine, the Padampakkanathar Temple, pre-dating the 8th Century, is associated with the great philosopher-saint Sankaracharya as well as the saints Gnanasambandar and Pattinathar, the latter attaining salvation here. Pattinathar's *samadhi* on the shore may be a hallowed spot, but it was little tended till recently, when a Pattinathar temple was built here. It is believed that a college for higher Vedic studies was attached to the Tiruvottriyur temple as far back as the 9th Century. Rajendra Chola I (11th Century) is believed to have built another temple was built, the Aadipureswarar Temple. To the rear of this temple is the Thyagarajaswami shrine, with the 63 Nayanmar in bronze. Durga Devi in the main shrine is associated with Kannagi, the heroine of the *Silappathikaram,* and a 15-day festival is celebrated in her honour.

Beyond Tiruvottriyur are Ennore, Sathangadu and Pulicat. In Sathangadu, an iron and steel wholesale market was opened around 2002 to move the trade from congested George Town. The developments on the island near Ennore have already been referred to. These developments began with the new thermal power station, which has the tallest chimney in the country.

Past industrialised Tondiarpet and Tiruvottriyur are Manali and Madhavaram. Manali is another major industrial centre while Madhavaram is home to the huge Aavin milk-conversion centre and the Tamil Nadu University of Veterinary and Animal Sciences. Manali and Madhavaram also once had considerable acres of swampland – called *jheels* – which were a bird-watcher's paradise. Sadly, much of the area has been built over, but there are still patches of swamp and grassfields where migrant birds regularly nest.

In Madhavaram are the 7th Century Kailasanathar and Kalivaradaraja Perumal Temples. The former claims to have the biggest lingam in Tamil Nadu, the latter has a 21-foot tall Anjaneyar statue all in white.

Between Sembiam and Madhavaram is Micetich Colony developed for Anglo-Indians by a Croatian sailor who had arrived here during World War I and then worked in the harbour as a diver. He settled in Madras after marrying an Anglo-Indian and building a home around which he plotted the 'Colony'. In more recent times, Madhavaram has become a favoured area for re-settlement by Anglo-Indians.

6. Northwest passage to industry

To the west of the northern villages, in northwest Madras, are Perambur and Vyasarpadi with the huge Railway Colony, the massive

Integral Coach Factory, the Sembiam factories of the Amalgamations group by the Northern Trunk Road, and, once, the gigantic Buckingham and Carnatic Mills of Binny's.

The Integral Coach Factory (ICF) near Villivakkam, established in 1953, originally with Swiss collaboration, and the Buckingham and Carnatic Mills, now closed after a struggle to survive, are two of the biggest factories of their type in the world. Of the mills much has already been said. ICF, a unit of Indian Railways, was founded with technical inputs from the Swiss Car & Elevator Manufacturing Corporation. Production started in 1955 and in 1956 the first indigenous coach rolled out. With expansion of facilities, the first fully furnished coach was produced in 1961. Today, ICF is the main supplier of coaches to Indian Railways. Near this railway hub is the headquarters building of the Southern Railway Employees Sangh, its roots in one of the country's first trade unions, a union formed by the employees of the M&SM Railway. The foundation stone for the building was laid by Gandhiji in 1927. Also in Perambur is the Madras home of V.O. Chidambaram Pillai, who, as we've seen, challenged British shipping interests.

Near here, in Agaram GKM Nagar, Perambur, is a unique, but now desultorily cared for shrine. The first temple built to deify a lay personality, the enshrined deity here is the late M G Ramachandran, former Chief Minister of Tamil Nadu and the people's hero. Built in 1990 by local loyalists, *pujas* used to be regularly performed here until party factionalism rent the neighbourhood and the temple got neglected.

Perambur, which once was home to the M&SM Railway workshop (now called the Loco Work Shops), one of the first major industrial units in early 20th Century Madras, still has a significant Anglo-Indian presence. Associated with the European and Anglo-Indian railway settlement in the area and neighbouring areas is the Smith Field Bakery established in 1885 by Sadras P. Ponnusamy Naidu and still going strong baking bread and cakes in the old-fashioned wood-fire way and running out of stock before the day is out. The bakery was named after Conran Smith, the first ICS Commissioner of the Corporation. A significant part of life here since 1891 is what is known as the Railway Mixed Higher Secondary School started by Anglo-Indian families as a primary school and then run by the Madras Railway for children of its employees. Later it was run by the Madras & Southern Mahratta Railway and is now run by Southern Railway which has five other schools in Tamil Nadu. Its striking building dates to its earliest days. Also a vintage railway institution here is the Railway Institute in *Marlboro House*, now called *New Hall*, dating to 1900, memories of Anglo-Indian dances long forgotten.

Another Perambur landmark is the Baptist Church established in 1886 by the Rev. Norman Mather Waterbury, an American, who, sadly, died on the day it was consecrated in 1886. This was the first Telugu church to be founded in Madras. A place of worship in Perambur better known is the Shrine of Our Lady of Lourdes, a church replicating in form the famous church in France. It was designed by a "Chevalier (J.R.) Davis, who designed the Catholic Centre in George Town." He also did the shrine in Kilpauk.

While the plans for building the Perambur shrine date to the 1940s, the Church's history goes back to 1879 when Fr. H.E. Hennessey from Vepery built a chapel in Perambur near where the Presentation Convent was later established. The next year he dedicated the chapel to 'Our Lady of Lourdes'. It was to be 1935 when the sixth parish priest, Fr. Michael Murray, began to think of developing the chapel into something like the Basilica at Lourdes. He launched a collection drive – including collecting the cost of a brick or that of a bag of cement – that got a tremendous response, continuing through the early 1940s. The Archbishop of Madras, the Most Rev Dr. Louis Mathias, then invited Davis to design the shrine to resemble the one in France.

It was to be January 1951, however, before Dr.Mathias laid the foundation stone and February 22, 1953 when he consecrated the lower church of the Shrine. In March 1958, the foundation stone was laid for the upper church and, after another fund-raising drive, the work was completed in 1960. Archbishop Mathias, who had seen the work from conception to completion, was there to consecrate the upper church on February 11, 1960. Today, services are held in Tamil in one church and in English in the other. But in the early years, the congregation was mainly Anglo-Indian, drawn from two institutions which helped the chapel to grow, the B & C Mills and the Railway Workshops.

J R Davis was a partner of the then leading firm of Madras architects, Prynne, Abbott and Davis, which developed out of Jackson and Barker and grew into Pithavadian and Partners. Davis was responsible for the second Madras Club in Branson Bagh, the Centenary and Library buildings of the University of Madras, *Catholic Centre,* and buildings at Sri Venkateswara University. Working with the firm when Davis was the only partner left was Australian Kiffen-Peterson who had a hand in designing the IOB building on Mount Road.

In nearby Ayyanavaram, is Tawker's Choultry, the Sri Kasi Viswanathar Temple (1805) and other charities endowed by a trust set up in 1804 by two women of the Gujarati Tawker family. The Tawkers first settled in Madras in the early 18th Century, their business officially opening here in 1761. At one time they were the leading jewellers and gem merchants of Madras. The choultry is now an *agraharam*. The Tirupati umbrellas taken to the Seven Hills from Madras are traditionally kept in the Kasi Viswanathar Temple for a night, before they are taken onwards. The Tawkers' family mansion was in a 12-acre campus on Mount Road. After the family declared bankruptcy, mainly due to debts, both *Tawker Gardens* and *Tawker Building* were sold. Government brought the latter, then sold it to the Maharajah of Limbdi who sold it to a Muslim Educational Trust that established New College here on a campus which today sports some splendid modern Islamic architecture.

On Konnur High Road in Ayyanavaram is the Madras Pinjrapole, opened in 1906 as an old age home for cattle. Built on 12 acres gifted by Govindoss Chatoorbhoojadoss and with contributions from other Gujaratis and the Maharajah of Vizianagaram, remembered in a gateway, the Pinjrapole in 1937 began to take in stray cattle and dry cows as well. Today, in expanded surroundings, it also runs a dairy farm.

The Sembiam site of the Amalgamations group's factories is called *Huzur Gardens*. A palm grove and an unused cemetery that was *Huzur* (Government) land was acquired in 1947 by the Group and, in the 1950s, converted into one of the most beautiful factory sites in the world. Over 10,000 trees, all numbered, two lily ponds, several well laid-out gardens and a marsh make a verdant setting for the eight factories here and an undeclared sanctuary for ornithologists. Nearly a hundred bird species have been recorded in the garden and the heronry has periods when over 5,000 birds, mostly migratory, are in residence. About 20,000 birds make *Huzur Gardens* their home at different times of the year. The lily pond is a breeding site for about 2,000 pairs of birds. Until not so long ago, the factories here used to have snake-catchers on their rolls – and they were necessary, remember old-timers! Some spotted deer are now being bred in fenced-in open-space.

Merchant Princes at North Beach

To India's cyclone-wracked, surf-pounded East Coast they came, to the fabled sands of the Coromandel, hard-headed traders from Ancient Greece and Rome, shrewd merchants from Araby and old Cathay. And from these shores of Cholamandalam there went the culture of once-proud empires to the islands of the East and the lands of the Menam and the Mekong. And produce, always produce.

For centuries, the shores of Coromandel have been a trader's paradise. The Arabs and the Romans were followed by the Portuguese. And then came the Dutch, the Danes, the English and the French. Even the Americans, Belgians and Swedes. They all came in search of gold and diamonds, spices and salt petre. But, above all, they came for the sheerest muslins, the softest chintzes, the most exquisite Daccas, the brightest calicos painted with the finest dyes known to the world and a variety of cottons unknown elsewhere.

In search of this wealth came the British 400 years ago. They first came to the West Coast, to the great Mughal port of Surat. But proximity to the disturbing Dutch and the petulant Portuguese and dissatisfaction with the quality of cloth available induced them to look for a new base for trading operations. Scouring the East Coast of India, 'Honourable John Company' discovered Machilipatnam (now in Andhra Pradesh), 250 miles north of modern Madras. Behind it was the hinterland of legendary Golconda and south of it the finest textile weavers and dyers in all India.

By 1639, however, Machilipatnam was unprosperous, Armagon south of it hopeless, so the never-say-die Factor of Armagon, Francis Day, went exploring. He came to what was virtually only a sandbank, near a fishing village north of San Thomé, and was granted this strip of land on such terms and "extraordinary favour" that to turn it down would have been to look a gift horse in the mouth.

From these beginnings grew the Madras of today, a city of millions, spreading itself out spaciously, a gracious city of traditions. True to those traditions, it is also still a trading city, though it has now emerged with a flourish into the new ages of Indian Industrialism and Consumerism. The traditions of courtesy and courtliness, one's word of honour being one's bond, of moving slowly but steadily and surely, of service and concern for others, of shrewd trading and fair practice... they have all, however, still not been hustled out of Madras by modernisation. And in this city remain names of long dead merchant princes whose businesses survive in others' hands.

* * *

Thomas Parry belonged to that social class which provided the East India Company with most of its civilian and military employees. But he began his career in India as a free merchant, not as a Writer or Cadet. In hindsight it may be said that he did not suffer much because of this, though he did have his share of troubles. But, in his time, it was, if not exactly a disgrace, at least a somewhat dubious social status.

Despite the Company's disapproval of the breed, the free merchants, for all practical purposes, except that of trade, moved on equal social terms with the privileged official classes. There were too few Europeans in Madras at the time to permit any social or business distinctions, except, and here the Company was inflexible, in trade with Britain and China.

The Parrys were 'carriage gentry'; that is, people with means enough to maintain that symbol of status, a horse carriage. They even claimed some royal blood. Parry's great-great-grandfather Richard, who was appointed Burgess of Welshpool around 1690, recorded that the family was directly descended from the rulers of Powys in mid-Wales whose line continued through the Welsh hero of the 10th Century, Elystan Glodrydd. This founder of the Fifth Royal Tribe of Wales is said to have been buried in Trelystan, not far from where Thomas Parry was born.

The Parrys, who claim one of the most ancient surnames in Wales, and whose name derives from 'Ap-Harry', 'son of Harry', owned many acres of land at Disserth in Radnorshire. The flat fertile land here is ideal for farming. The Parrys are also credited with having introduced the famed black Anglesey cattle to this part of Wales.

Richard Parry's two grandsons, David and Edward, farmed in the area of Llanerchydol, on the outskirts of the market town of Welshpool, in the early part of the 18th Century. Edward Parry, Thomas's grandfather, owned a large farm called The Dairy. *He married an Anne Pryce and had a large family, Edward, John, Richard, Anne, Elizabeth, David, Sarah, Mary and Martha. The younger Edward followed his father into farming and also married an Anne, Anne Vaughan of Trelystan. They had eight children, Mary (1748), Jane (1752), Ann (1754), Elizabeth (1759), Edward (1762), John (1764), Thomas (1768) and David (1770). Thomas Parry was baptised in Trelystan Church on May 15, 1768, and was therefore probably born in early April that year. In time, he was to become the second distinguished Welshman to be associated with Madras; the first was Elihu Yale, Governor from 1687 to 1692.*

Edward Parry's prosperity brought him social position as well and he was recognised as the local squire. He is described in the official record as "an hereditary burgess sworn". To suit his position, he leased Leighton Hall *from the Corbet family around 1750. The Corbets go back to the Domesday Book of 1086 and the first Hall is said to have been built some time before that. With the last of the Corbet squires non-resident, the Hall was leased out from about 1700.*

The estate was enormous and the vast grounds suited the Parrys, by all accounts a lively family, as well as being a very close one, like most large families are. Ann Parry, for instance, married a Thomas Pugh in 1773, when she was 19 years old, and produced a family of 16 children, including David and Joseph Pugh who later had much to do with Parry's of Madras. This was a runaway match and instead of going to her wedding in a coach, she went to church on a horse ridden by the chief witness, a Mr Smith.

The Parrys also lived in some state. Many an old inhabitant of the area in the 1780s has recalled the marvellous days they spent as children at Leighton Hall, *enjoying the squire's wonderful hospitality. Christmas Day, for instance, was a very special one with the doors of the Hall open to all.*

Edward Parry died in 1774, but when Anne Parry died seems to be a mystery. There is a letter written by Thomas Parry in 1808 requesting a friend to forward a portrait of himself to his mother. It is possible she married again.

Edward, Thomas's eldest brother, appears to have taken over the Hall and was still living there in 1818, when he and his younger brother David settled in nearby Severn Cottage *by the banks of the famous river, both eventually dying unmarried.*

How long the Parry family lived on in Leighton Hall *is not known. The first public census taken in early 1841 shows Robert Parry, farmer and nephew of Thomas, living there. But by the 1851 census the Hall was empty. By all accounts, the Hall had been sold by a Panton Corbet to a gentleman who had given it to his nephew as a wedding present with £ 100,000 for modernising it. It had been rebuilt completely and embellished, with landscaped gardens, when the Naylor family sold it in 1934.* Leighton Hall *still stands today, the main structure much the same as in Parry's day.*

Edward Parry died when Thomas was six years old. Details of Thomas Parry's life in Wales (to which he was never to return) are scanty. But it may be surmised that, born in such a family as he was, he must have not only received an adequate education but might also have served an apprenticeship in a business house. This, however, is only conjecture, based on the unlikelihood of a youth of twenty venturing on a commercial career in a country six thousand miles away without any preparation for it.

It is likely that with his affluent background Parry would have at an early age had a tutor or governess, then, when old enough, would have attended the local school for boys and girls at the Episcopal Chapel in Trelystan. He would have only spoken and written in Welsh, his mother tongue, but, living by the English border, he probably picked up more English than most boys living further inland. At the age of 14, he probably went on to a public school near the market town of Welshpool. While it is true that there is no record of him attending university, one thing cannot be disputed. He must have been an educated young man to have held official posts in Madras at a time when English was only his second language.

A boy from such a background might perhaps have aspired to a career in Britain itself. Why Thomas sought a life abroad is not very clear. Whatever the reason, he was only 20 years old when he set sail for

India. The Company's Writers and Cadets, it should be said, were often younger. John Company's presence in India was, it would seem, sustained by juveniles in the early stages.

Thomas Parry, it is obvious, was exceptional in many respects. He established a company that was to survive two centuries. He preserved his integrity and honesty in the welter of corruption and disorder that existed in the Madras of his time. He never descended to anything mean or despicable. And he was a firm and determined friend, never deserting colleagues in their hour of need, often acting with passionate partisanship on their behalf.

But all this was in the future of the youth who sailed from England in 1788. The ship he made the voyage in made one of the fastest sailings to India upto that time, arriving in Madras Roads on July 14, 1788. And the Manship's *log records showed that on Thursday, July 17, 1788, there were "Run from the ship Thomas Parry and James Dixon, Seamen."*

Thomas Parry, however, was no deserter, as that statement might imply. According to Young's Nautical Dictionary *(1846), 'run' is an old seafarers' term deriving from "to run ashore" and meaning the departure from the ship of a person who had signed on with the intention of leaving the vessel at a certain port of call. Parry's destination was obviously Madras and that's where he signed off, collecting £ 3 12s 8d for the work he had put in during his three months and 19 days as a seaman on board the* Manship.

The payment Thomas Parry received is recorded in a paymaster's account book that states Thomas Parry boarded the Manship *– a troopship and not an East Indiaman, this probably explaining the exceptionally fast, nonstop voyage and Parry's curious passage – at Gravesend on March 28, 1788. His wages were reckoned from that date. Judging from the record, the normal wage for a 'seaman' in those days was £ 2 12s a month. But Parry worked for £1 a month. It would seem then that he signed on as a supernumerary and worked his passage to India on a nominal wage, probably because there was no accommodation aboard a troopship for a civilian. If that were indeed the case, it would seem to indicate that Parry's sponsors had influence where it counted most.*

Parry left Wales for London in 1787 and served an apprenticeship with the East India Company. Shortly thereafter began the journey to India, a voyage that was, from all accounts, not without incident. The

Manship*'s log book provides a description of a voyage that had its moments of excitement.*

That log records that the Manship, *a vessel of 812 tons, was skippered by Captain Charles Gregoric and that, like all ships belonging to the East India Company, it began its voyage from the docks at Deptford on the south bank of the river Thames in London. Here the main cargo, 320 tons of copper, was loaded from December 24, 1787, despite the heavy snow. The ship then sailed for Gravesend with a skeleton crew and its full complement of officers.*

The Manship *arrived in Gravesend on January 9, 1788, and began taking on 213 "chests of Arms" and groceries. In March it "received" 117 of "the Companies recruits" and five women, probably the wives of some of the recruits. Then, on March 27th, there occurred the first of the mishaps that dogged the* Manship *on this voyage: one of the recruits fell overboard and was drowned.*

The Manship *eventually sailed for Madras on All Fool's Day and dropped its pilot off Dover on April 4th. The captain soon afterwards recorded more problems: trouble amongst the recruits, William Gorden, "a young black boy", and John Bell apparently the chief culprits. These ructions were followed by heavy gales at the end of May. Then, on June 17th, a John Sutton attacked seaman John Miles with a knife, wounding him, and received "3 dozen lashes" for his transgressions. Six days later, Noah Caplan, another recruit, was lost overboard.*

Thereafter the voyage was uneventful. "The Land of Ceylon" was sighted on July 10th and on the 14th Fort St George greeted the Manship *with a 9-gun salute, "which was returned by the same number." Over the next couple of days the troopship took on board 16 butts of water and nine boatloads of red wood. Then, on July 17th, after Parry and Dixon had been 'run from the ship', Captain Gregoric came aboard at 10 a.m. and the ship weighed anchor at 11 a.m. As it left Madras Roads, it saluted the fort with 11 guns, "which was returned." And so sailed the* Manship *for Bengal, leaving Parry behind in Madras.*

Thomas Parry landed in a city that had grown substantially from the time Fort St George was built in the previous century. Besides the British, there were Portuguese, French and Dutch in Parry's Madras. There were also Armenians and Jews.

It is almost certain that what brought Parry to Madras was the recommendation of his brother-in-law, Gilbert Ross, who had married his cousin and Parry's fourth sister, Elizabeth. Ross had a local representative in Fort St George, Thomas Chase, and an influential relative, Captain Patrick Ross, the Chief Engineer who had much to do with rebuilding the Fort. With their help, and the "Governor's Permission", Parry obtained his licence to trade as a free merchant. His status is confirmed in a Fort St George register, the entry dated February 12, 1789.

Parry traded without any partner during his first months in Madras, but in 1789 Chase took him as a partner and the firm of Chase and Parry was founded. Chase was a civil servant, and had been one since 1782, but that was no bar to his trading privately; it was not till 1800 that civil servants were prohibited from private trading.

Chase was "Senior Merchant, Clerk of Justice, Clerk to the Commissioner of Stores, Coroner and French Translator," all in one, besides representing Ross's firm. Parry too conducted business on his own account; "he had two strings to his bow." All this might appear confusing, but that was the way of Madras business two centuries ago.

The first Parry firm did a varied business as a general agency and trading company. It acted as real estate agents, sold "a quantity of Madeira Wine of superior quality, upwards of two years old", acted as administrators of estates of deceased persons, even sold Bengal lottery tickets, discounted Navy bills, sold passages in Europe-bound ships and also distributed books "newly published." All was grist that came to its mill. But its principal business was banking, then and for long after.

The company which Parry established the same year he arrived in Madras is the second oldest British-founded business house in India still surviving. Such commercial longevity is rare. The trade cycles of 'boom' and 'slump' have destroyed many a company in every part of the world. But Parry's (as the firm is best known, even if its full name today is E I D Parry (India) Ltd.) has survived two hundred years, though sometimes not without great struggle. Whatever the problems, Parry's endured, overcoming the difficulties with vitality and confidence. In the process, it has written a glorious chapter in Indian commercial history.

* * *

Among other upholders of the city's traditions was Best & Crompton Engineering Ltd, who, as Best & Co, was a member of the 'second generation' of British traders in the city. Of the 'first generation' of British-founded firms, only Parry's and the vestiges of Binny's remain. Of the Victorian age is the 'second generation'. But there were Bests associated with India ever since the first British merchantmen came to the country.

There was, in the early 1600s, a Captain Thomas Best with William Hawkins in Surat, the bravest of the brave sea-captains who took on the Portuguese fleets. In later years, the Bests were particularly associated with the South. There was James Kershaw Best, a lay preacher in the Tirunelveli District, whose son became a Madras civil servant in the mid-19th Century. About the same period was Captain Samuel Best, "the first to carry out a comprehensive scheme of roads for the Madras Presidency." And, of course, there was Andrew Vans Dunlop Best. Andrew Best's picture in Best & Co's portrait gallery was dated 1867-1894 – the dates presumably being for the period he served as the head of Best & Co. These dates rather shroud Best & Co's beginnings in mystery, since the generally accepted version does not explain the dates, especially the 1867 one.

"The best businessman is he who can put up a sound proposal on grounds of public utility while perfecting his own plans for a move which will give him a lead over his competitors," cynically wrote a latter-day Englishman reviewing the 'Cochin Saga'. He was undoubtedly thinking of J H Aspinwall, the President of the British Cochin Chamber of Commerce in 1870 and the leading trader on the southwest coast. The "sound proposal" was a dream Aspinwall had for years. With the opening of Suez in 1869 and with no port worth its name all the way round the Indian coast from Bombay to Calcutta, he dreamt of Cochin becoming "the gateway of South India." The proposed development of Madras harbour he dismissed as "a small and hazardous experiment."

Nevertheless, Aspinwall, possibly with the idea of having a second string to his bow, had opened a Madras branch – in 1867, it would seem. However, it wasn't long before he was obsessed with his dream and spent all his time in Cochin, to judge by the brass plaque in St Francis' Church there which today commemorates his regard for that town. Paying as he did scant attention to Madras, once he got involved in the affairs of Cochin, it was inevitable that Aspinwall's Madras office would become more associated with his representative than with him. That agent appears to have been a Scotsman, Andrew Vans Dunlop Best, with, very likely, some Dutch antecedents. When and how Aspinwall became Best is not clear, but the Madras Chamber of Commerce lists Best & Co as a member in 1872. And there is also a popular local tradition that Best acquired the firm by "marrying the boss's daughter."

More substantial is the fact that Andrew Best and a John McLintock, probably another Aspinwall employee, "entered into partnership in 1879, taking over (the Madras branch) and continuing the business connections of Aspinwall & Co."

Also a fact and a great tradition was the Aspinwall-Best agreement not to operate on each other's coast, the Malabar coast in the west Aspinwall's, the Coromandel Best's. It was an article of faith that was surviving even in the 1940s, when the gentleman's agreement was once again demonstrated, 'permission' being sought from Aspinwall & Co for Crompton Engineering Co (Madras) Ltd, an associate of Best's (before their merger), to open a Calicut branch on the west coast.

Aspinwall's dream for Cochin had to wait many years. The shifting sands of Cochin needed the dredging technique of harbour building, still many years away. In the second half of the 19th Century, concrete blocks sunk into the sea, to make a sea-wall and breakwater, was still the accepted technique. So Madras got its harbour over 50 years before Cochin and 'built' its prosperity. "It was a trading settlement that Francis Day founded.... When in the nineteenth century her trade declined, her importance sank to nothing. As efforts were made to improve her shipping accommodation, her trade began to return.... The more the Harbour grew, the more trade and prosperity returned...." And Madras grew.

Sir Thomas Ainscough, the British Trade Commissioner for India and Ceylon, wrote in 1936, "The remarkable commercial, industrial and agricultural development of the Presidency is attributable in a marked degree to the courage, foresight and imaginative energy of three generations of members (of the Madras Chamber of Commerce which celebrated its Centenary that year). While regulating their business activities on sound lines, they have not only advanced their own interests but also have contributed in a generous measure to the welfare and prosperity of the people of South India."

One of those referred to is undoubtedly Andrew Best, who first tied his fortunes to the city at an ebb point but soared with the next wave. Best's decision to take over Aspinwall's Madras operation was based on a firm conviction that Madras would get its harbour come what may and become one of the great trading cities of the East. It was a faith that has been justified.

When Best and McLintock began business, they took over what was basically a shipping and trading firm. As agents for charterers, it was their business to see that chartered ships sailed back to England with full holds.

The earliest exports from the Presidency were block-printed chintzes, white calicos and blue morree cotton cloth (denims). Spices, raw cotton, indigo, groundnut and the mineral wealth of Golconda were other exports from the Coromandel Coast. But when the bottom fell out of textiles and minerals, the emphasis shifted to imports rather than exports. Best's benefited with the growing shipping business and import of piecegoods.

As best can be established, Best & Co began business on August 9, 1879 with an Indian staff of five, supplementing, presumably, Best himself and McLintock. This staff was to rapidly increase within just a few years.

By 1885, McLintock appeared to be out of the picture and Best was thinking of going back to England (which he did, it would seem, in 1894) – though he retained his association with the company till at least 1911. As partners came in Robert James Black (later Chairman of the Mercantile Bank and elevated to the peerage, an association which was to help Best & Co considerably over the years) and Charles Slater. Robert Black's association with Best and his business appears to have been from 1878 and lasted, in India, till 1898. During this period, Black was responsible for transforming the slow, sleepy shipping and trading firm into one of South India's leading business houses, a dynamic organisation.

He did it with kerosene. Best's was only the second firm to import kerosene into South India. But it was the first to do it on a large scale, as an organised business, not concentrating on the small retail sales of the first importer.

In 1889, Best's was appointed the agents of Samuel & Co, the 'ancestors' of the Burmah-Shell Oil Storage & Distribution Co Ltd, and *it started marketing kerosene in Madras. In 1893, Shell Transport and Trading Co Ltd built its own storage installations at Royapuram, but Best's association with the new firm, the successors to Samuel's, continued. The first kerosene tanker arrived in Madras the same year.*

For an unbroken period of forty years, Best's was known as the "kerosene people" of Madras and really "oiled the wheels of existence." Up until 1938, Burmah Shell had its offices in the main Best & Co building on First Line Beach.

Robert Black guided the fortunes of the growing firm through the last years of the 19th Century. From essentially a shipping and insurance firm, dabbling in some banking and trade, Best's became, under his guidance, an eminent trading organisation. It had begun to spread its wings.

For years, Best's provided local assistance to the company which ran the Kolar Gold Fields, a relationship that made Best's 'solid gold'.

In the 1970s, Best's became Best & Crompton when it merged with it the old electrical engineering company, Crompton Engineering, in Madras from 1890. In the 1990s, Best & Crompton became a part of a conglomerate which included another old George Town neighbour, McDowell's, established in Madras in 1825 by an Angus McDowell. Founded as wine merchants, McDowell's is still going strong in the liquor business. It had passed through various hands and was incorporated as McDowell & Co in 1898, with A M Hooper, G D Coleman and G N Ruppell as the principal shareholders of its Rs 8 lakh capital. McDowell's in its time was famed for the cigars it manufactured, upto 100,000 handmade ones in its factory in Madras. In 1904, 24 years after it had gone into cigars, McDowell's also went into cigarette manufacture, 500,000 a day made with the latest machinery of the times. Cigars and cigarettes are now forgotten lines, as is tea – particularly McDowell's 'Miss India Tea', – but liquor manufacture is big business. In 1998, the Bangalore-based UB (United Breweries) conglomerate sold off a fading Best & Crompton and now focusses on its core liquor business, with McDowell's one of its successes. Best & Crompton, may not be in the front ranks of Madras business, its various divisions and subsidiaries each under different ownership, but it is a name that is remembered.

16

The City Within

1. Minting wealth

Turning left at now non-existent Clive Battery, where a flyover has come up, and heading along Old Jail Road, you are close to Seven Wells (almost opposite Stanley Hospital), up till the 19th Century the City's primary source of water supply. Seven Wells Government Waterworks, a scheme executed in 1772, was the City's first organised water supply, though initially it was meant only for the Fort. The wells, ten, not seven, in number supplied 140,000 gallons a day and showed no signs of exhaustion even a century later when Red Hills reservoir became the City's main source of water supply. The wells, however, do not exist today, but the site retains its connection with civic amenities, being the home of a pumping station! Sylvester Nicholas, a retired soldier, was put in charge of the Wells in 1799, in perpetuity, as reward for distinguished service, and, in hereditary fashion, one Nicholas family member after another was in charge here over the next 125 years. And many of their descendants who are still in Madras remember that past. Most of them worshipped at St Roque's Church in Washermenpet, just north of Seven Wells, a church well over 100 years old. Most of the Nicholases were also buried in its cemetery.

Near here was the Manonmani Vilasam Press till it moved to Purasawalkam and in 1947 to Kondithope from where it still publishes the Pambu Panchangam (almanac) started in 1884 and an essential annual reference for thousands of Hindu homes in Madras.

Washermenpet derives its name from the early days of Madras when bleaching ('washing') and dyeing of cloth were done in the nearby river. A footnote to this history is the Washermenpet Police Station, a heritage building if ever there is one, dating to 1898, which has two historical plaques embedded in its wall. One dates the police station, the other talks of being the first stone marking a boundary of an esplanade dating to 1822. Madras's less-known esplanade dates to 1783 when Chief Engineer Ross reported, "The Environs of the Black Town Wall to the Westward (where People's Park was later developed) are nearly cleared to the extent of six hundred yards... and to the Northward (too), except the (Monegar) Choultry, which contains sick charity poor, and three others situated near the extremity of the prescribed distance... One of them, the Company's Washing Choultry, now contains that part of the Body Guard stationed for the protection of the washing town (very possibly where the police station came up)." In Ravenshaw's map of 1822, five obelisks are shown on an esplanade north of the Black Town Wall, between Royapuram and Monegar Choultry, and that depiction is perhaps what led to the remembrance in the police station.

In Washermenpet is Robinson Park (now called Aringnar Anna Park), established as a private botanical garden and fernery in the early 19th Century by A.Arumugam Mudaliar, a leading citizen of the area. It was handed over to the Corporation in 1899 and then named after the first Inspector General of Police of Madras – and the first IGP in India – W. Robinson.

Governor Lord Harris (1854-1859) teamed with Robinson, a Civilian, to draw up a plan that would set up a formal police force for the entire Presidency. In 1857, one of the last acts of the East India Company was to approve the plan and, in May 1858, Robinson was named Chief of the Madras Presidency Police. The Harris-Robinson plan became the basis of the Madras District Police Act XXIV of 1859 after it was passed on September 6th that year. When the Crown took over from the Company, one of its first acts was to promulgate the Act. Madras, thus, became the first Presidency/Province in British India to establish "an integrated system of provincial policing." Under the Act, the head of the Presidency Police was to be an Inspector General of Police and Robinson was the first.

It was in that Park that C.N. Annadurai announced to the public on September 18, 1949, a decision taken the previous day, at 7 Coral Merchant Street, a house that's now an apartment complex, namely, the breaking away from Periyar's Dravida Kazhagam (DK) and the forming of the Dravida Munnetra Kazhagam (DMK), the Dravidian Progressive

Party, an event that was to transform Tamil Nadu (then, Madras) politics. When Annadurai led the party to victory in the 1967 elections, Dravidian political rule had virtually come to stay in the State. The DMK has since given birth to over a score of Dravidian splinter groups, the chief one being the All India Anna DMK founded by M.G. Ramachandran and, till her death in 2016, led by J. Jayalalithaa, but plagued for a while by power struggles thereafter.

Another political leader – of an earlier age – who lived in this area was Sir Pitti Theagaroya Chetty, whose house and his brother's neighbouring one were connected in 1922 by a bridge over street level, still a curiosity. Theagaroya Chetty was one of the founders of the Justice Party in 1915. It was this Party which gave birth to the Dravidian movement as a counter to the then Brahmin domination in politics and governance.

Before Seven Wells, drinking water for the Fort was carted in from other wells in this part of Peddanaickenpet. But what was particularly relished was 'mountain water' from St. Thomas' Mount. Once Seven Wells was unable to cope, the Red Hills (not hills but an elevated laterite area) water supply scheme was conceived and implemented from May 1872, making use of the water of the Kortalayar River twenty miles from Madras. Water from the Red Hills Reservoir was delivered to the Madras Municipal City Waterworks – its buildings in Kilpauk, near the ICF end, inaugurated in 1914 and still impressively Indo-Saracenic – which then distributed the water to the city. Substantial extensions were carried out between 1907 and 1924, but by 1914 it could truly be said that a city water supply scheme was in place, J.M. Madeley responsible for having planned it. He was also responsible for the city's sewage system which was inaugurated in 1907. In the 1910s, another Corporation Commissioner, J. Chartres Molony, was in office when the first water under the Red Hills scheme was delivered to the city. The brown coloured water was soon dubbed 'Molony's Mixture'. First chlorinated water was supplied from 1927. The Kilpauk Water Works campus is home to several heritage structures. Like a 177 ft. tall chimney in use from 1914 till 1955, a 6.8 million litre capacity storage tank that has been replaced only in the new Millennium, and the first treatment plant. From handling 80 mld of water a day in the early days, the plant now handles 270 mld.

The Red Hills reservoir is now a favourite picnic spot. Jones Tower, built in 1881 at one end of the Red Hills lake, is the principal conduit of water supply to Madras. With the City dependent on the monsoons (particularly the Northeast in October/November) for its water, Jones Tower is, in many a year, more tower than conduit, sticking out of the low-level water as high as it does. Near here, at Puzhal, is the new 154-acre prison complex planned with a considerable degree of comfort for the inmates. It replaced in 2007 Park Town's Central Jail, once known as the Madras Penitentiary, built on 13 acres in 1837 and renamed Central Jail in 1855. The Central Jail's shell has been converted into a modernised extension of Madras Medical College and was inaugurated in 2013.

Back in the Seven Wells area you are near the Old Jail, the Mint and the 'basin' Trevelyan planned, in 1854, to store fresh drinking water for the city. The Old Jail dates to 1804 when it was located near one of the bastions of the North Wall, which ran along what are now Ebrahim Sahib Street, Old Jail Road and Basin Bridge Road. In parts of this stretch of road, there are remnants of the massive protective wall, the most noticeable stretch a protected monument atop which was developed a park in 1957, *Maadi Poonga*. Both protective wall and park were allowed to deteriorate for long, till post-Millennium restoration made them look like a cinema set. In these walls were magazines for arms, all these storage spaces now blocked up. North Wall Street still commemorates the old wall.

The Old Jail traces its beginnings to a debtors' jail established in the vicinity in 1692. This was later called the Civil Jail and moved to the corner of what became Popham's Broadway and Old Jail Road. It was better developed in the late 18th Century, with Sheriff Edward Atkinson making the greatest contribution in 1793. Many of the buildings of this era still remain – but for different use.

Shortly after Independence, the jail was cleared of prisoners and its buildings were used by the Congress Prachar Sabha as a cottage industries training centre. After Chief Minister Kamaraj stepped down in 1963, this training venture gradually faded out and in 1964 the Government took over the complex to lodge the expanding Central Polytechnic Institute and a new Arts College for Women. When the Polytechnic's last constituent, the Regional School of Printing, moved to Adyar in 1968, the women's college expanded, named itself the Bharati Women's College and flourished here in the rather dilapidated buildings in which could be recognised the vestiges of the Old (Civil) Jail. It then got new buildings on the campus and most of the jail buildings were left to the elements.

The Mint goes back to 1640, when it functioned in the Fort, and coined Madras pagodas, fanams (36 to the pagoda), cash (80 to the fanam) and doodoos (ten to the cash). It was 1692 before the Mughals authorised the East India Company to mint gold *mohurs* and silver rupees to their standards in the Company's Mint. In 1742, by the new Nawab's *firman*, the Poonamallee Mint was shifted to Chintadripet, where Linghi Chetty, the contractor of the Fort Mint, now struck Arcot rupees as well as star pagodas and gold *mohurs*. Rupees (replacing star pagodas valued at Rs 3½ each), annas and pies currency was introduced by the British in 1816 and the Mint began functioning from 1841 in a building erected on the site where, in 1804, had stood a powder mill. This move took the two Madras mints to the buildings that are at the north end of what is called Mint Street today, the longest street in North Madras, 4 km long and extending over three pincodes. The move took years. After the powder mill was moved to The Island, work began on building the new mint. The buildings were ready by 1807, but the machinery was not perfect. It was only towards the end of 1841 that perfection could be achieved and the move of the Mint finalised. But to what use? With minting no more in Madras, the Mint buildings are today only part of the huge Government Press.

At 300 Mint Street was the Navalar Vidyanupalana Press started by Jaffna's renowned scholar, famed Arumuga Navalar, who had worked with the Rev P Percival on a Tamil *Bible* published in 1850 and who had come to Madras in 1846 to finish the work. It is now run by the Navalar Trust and sells the titles it once published in Madras and Chidambaram. It also runs the Navalar High School in Chidambaram.

With most of the City's commercial activities concentrated in this congested area, between 4 km long Mint Street with its three pin codes and North Beach Road, George Town is to Madras what 'The City' is to London and Lower Manhattan in the Wall Street area is to New York. Development to this stage, however, took over 150 years. In the earliest years of 'Black Town', there was a spaciousness about even this part of Madras. Thomas Salmon, writing in 1699, stated that 'Black Town', "where the Portuguese, Indians, Armenians and a great variety of other people inhabit... is built in the form of a square...better than a mile and a half in circumference; being surrounded with a brick wall seventeen feet thick... The streets of the Black Town are wide, and trees planted in some of them; and having the sea on one side and a river on the other, there are few towns so pleasantly situated or better supplied; but except some few brick houses the rest are miserable cottages, built with clay and thatched and not so much as a window to be seen on the outside... but I must say, not withstanding all this appearance of poverty, I never was in a place where wealth abounded more, or where ready money was more plentiful about twenty years ago.... Beyond the Black Town are gardens for half a mile together planted with mangoes, coconuts, guavoes, oranges... where every body has the liberty of walking and may purchase the most delicious fruits for a trifle..."

Salmon's 'Black Town' was the settlement that grew out of John Company's need for the cloths made in India. The first settlers of 'Black Town' were the weavers and dyers that the *dubashes* brought in from present-day Andhra. While traders and middlemen settled in the northern shadow of the Fort, the cloth-makers worked closer to the Elambore (Elumbur) River (that is now part of the Buckingham Canal), in Comerpet (later known as Peddanaickenpet). Many of the streets in this area once had names that reflected the major industry of Comerpet. In Pitt's map of 1709, Mint Street was called Washers' Street – the street of calico washers and 'bleeders' (bleachers) – Nainiappa Naicken Street was called Weavers' Street (Yale had first settled 50 families of weavers here) and China Bazaar was River Street. In the area north of Old Jail Road, the name Washermenpet lingers to this day.

In the police station here from 1898 is a plaque stating that it commemorates the northern boundary of Madras in 1822. This boundary was marked by several 15-ft tall obelicks that have now vanished.

With washers and bleachers and 'bleeders', weavers and 'painters' (dyers) having for decades made their homes in northern and southern Peddanaickenpet near the river, central Peddanaickenpet and Muthialpet developed as areas where lived the merchants, traders and financiers who did business with the cloth-makers. This business community from earliest times was a cosmopolitan one. A congested area to the west of central Mint Street is still called Sowcarpet and is the home of Gujaratis ('Saurashtras' whose association with the Indian cloth trade is historic; the 'Guzeratis' of Madras are referred to by Ananda Ranga Pillai,

Dupleix's *dubash*, in his famous diaries of 1746), Marwaris from Rajasthan and other North Indian merchants and bankers, many of whom belong to families that have lived here for generations. In this area are several Jain temples where these settlers worship. Armenian Street got its name from the many Armenians who lived and worshipped there, only a privileged few being permitted residence in the Fort. And in North Muthialpet is Coral Merchants Street which, as already related, owes its name to the trade of the small Jewish community that once lived in it. When Golconda yielded no more, the community left for pastures new.

In Muthialpet is one of the oldest schools in George Town, the Muthialpet School established in 1847. In and off Mint Street are the Thondamandalam Thruva Vellalar School (1854), the Hindu Theological School (1889) and the Madras Progressive Union School (1888). Indeed, by the end of the 19th Century, Madras had a fair scattering of schools following Western syllabi.

The Hindu Theological School in Mint Street will ever be associated with the legendary Balakrishna Joshi, who may have looked old school in his attire, but on English, History and Moral Science/Theology he was a remarkable communicator in a fast-changing world. Honoured with the title Kulapthi by the Jagadguru Sankaracharya, Joshi was as much a nationally renowned teacher as he was a much-listened-to mentor of the South Indian Teachers' Union and the Madras Teachers' Guild.

Born into a Gujarati family that had connections with Madras from the early 17th Century, Balakrishna Joshi followed his father and grandfather into the portals of the Hindu Theological School. His grandfather must have been amongst the first pupils of the School founded by Sivasankara Pandyaji. Joshi himself, schooling and college finished, joined his alma mater as a teacher when he was just 19 and was assigned the SSLC class, teaching students as old or older than him. He found himself in rather a similar position when, in 1944, as a 34-year old, he was elected by the staff, most of them older than him and many who had taught him, as Headmaster of the School. He was to serve as Headmaster till the rules forced him to retire in 1970. He had been associated with the school for 55 years. The day after he retired, Balakrishna Joshi took over as the Founder Principal of DAV School and within five years made it one of the leading secondary educational institutions in Madras. In 1975, he retired from DAV and within months became Founder Principal of the Sindhi Model School. When he finally retired in 1978, he had actively served education for 50 years and thereafter continued to serve it as an advisor to many an institution till he passed away in 1992.

2. Bazaars and broadways

Back at Parry's Corner, if you turn west, you are headed towards the busy market places of the city – Evening Bazaar, Rattan (Cane) Bazaar, Mat Bazaar, Fruit Market, Flower Bazaar, even what may be called a new China Bazaar, a stretch between Evening and Rattan Bazaars that was home till recently of many Chinese dentists and shoemakers and what have you! With the young seeking pastures new, only a couple of Chinese establishments remain here today. Curiously, the old 'Buzzar' under the Fort's north walls was called China Bazaar in the records of 1758 – for what reason, it is not clear, though it is known that John Company traded with China and chinaware was popular with both the English and the Mughals. After Lally's siege, the 'Buzzar' had to move – and it moved west, and developed along with newer bazaars and became the broad road between Esplanade/High Court and New Black Town that in time was called Esplanade Road and is now known as Netaji Subhas Chandra Bose Road. Among all these popular shopping stretches, Evening Bazaar is where the Europeans of the time found shopping made easy in the cool of the evening. Little is left of all these bazaars but occasionally remembered names.

The Rattan Bazaar stretch is today home of the bullion market, some of the City's leading jewellery and handloom houses and, since 1905 (at its present site since 1918), Joonus Sait & Sons, founded by Yunus Sait from Kachchh. The city's largest stockists of woollen clothes from its early years, Sait's was most popular with the 'Home'-going British, the Plantation gentry, and those living or holidaying in the hills. Its famed tailoring department specialised (and still does) not only in woollens but in judges' robes and, till a couple of decades ago when the office was abolished, in Sheriffs' as well.

Another Kachchhi name in Rattan Bazaar was Mohamed Ebrahim Sait who in 1926 opened 'Gramophone House', offering records and HMV records. Now with a Mount Road address and known as the MECO group, the family are into electronic goods manufacture and consumer durables distribution.

Also from Gujarat – Saurashtra, specifically – and now on Mount Road is Poppat Jamal who in 1901 opened a crockery and glassware business in Broadway. In 1930, the company opened the city's first glass factory – to manufacture 'Stag' chimneys – in Tondiarpet. Today, retailing and distribution of its original lines are its main business. But it has added 'pop' music too. Most of the jewellery and silverware shops long rooted here, now led by a forward-looking younger generation, have opened fashion-oriented showrooms in the T'Nagar, Nungambakkam and Cathedral Road areas.

Another Western Indian name here for a hundred years and a bit is Ebrahim Currim and Sons. They are the makers and sellers of umbrellas that are a household name in Madras. Stag's the brand.

In Flower Bazaar, next to Fruit Market, is the 1925 *Telephone House*, home of Madras Telephones, now a Central Government institution but which had its beginnings in 1881 in the Oriental Telephone and Electric Co Ltd, incorporated in England to operate the Madras, Bombay and Calcutta telephone systems, just five years after Alexander Graham Bell had invented the telephone, and managed in Madras by Arbuthnot's. The first telephone exchange was opened at 37 Errabalu Chetty Street on January 28, 1882 and served 25 subscribers with 40 lines. The second was commissioned at Blacker's Road soon after. A trunk exchange came into operation in 1906. Orient's first telephone directory was published, in 1893 and listed 75 lines, including a record three for Parry's. By 1910 there were 350 lines.

Orient Telephones was taken over in 1923 by The Madras Telephones Company, another private company, and an automatic system was introduced with the opening of the present headquarters in 1925. The man responsible for popularising the telephone during this period was Director and General Manager G W Bromhead. In 1934, the Company took over the Government's private Mount Road Exchange, but the next year it was still looking for more business – it was offering Rs 5 for every phone connection canvassed and promising special rates to subscribers! The Company was nationalised in 1943 when there were three exchanges, Central, Mambalam and Mount Road, and 3200 lines!

Little known, however, is the fact that long before all this, sometime in 1877, a successful telephone connection was tried out by G.K. Winter, the Telegraph Engineer of the Madras Railway Company. His trial was conducted one night, using the Railways' telegraph lines between Madras and Arakonam, a distance of 42 miles. *The Madras Mail* of December 18, 1877 reported that its correspondent had the opportunity shortly before the trial to examine "this wonderful speaking instrument" and that Winter had made his instruments based on the descriptions given in a couple of scientific journals.

Once the connection was tested, the *The Madras Mail*'s correspondent was given an opportunity to test the telephone and was so delighted with the results of the conversation that he burst into song on the line. So, do we take Winter's experiment as the first use of the telephone in South India?

As for electricity, it was first publicly demonstrated in People's Park in 1879 by a Frenchman, Amedee Verne. His apparatus was bought by the Corporation, but public supply in Madras took time, being first effected only in 1906 by a private company, the Madras Electricity Supply Corporation (MESC). Binny's mills, in the private sector, and the Mount Road Post Office were, it is believed, the first institutions to receive electricity from the Corporation.

Trams, plying in Madras from 1895, received electricity from a small thermal power station established at Basin Bridge by the MESC. These trams belonged to the Madras Tramways Corporation (MTC), founded in London in 1892 by Hutchinson & Co. The MTC was sold to the Madras Electric Tramways (1904) Limited (MET), a company founded in London. The MET was established with an authorised share capital of £1, 100,000, much of it paid up, mainly by German investors. Its Madras office was at 1 Rundall's Road, Vepery.

Having as it did a contract to supply electricity in perpetuity to the Madras Electric Tramways (1904) Ltd., the MESC held in 1935 all the Ordinary shares of the tramways company. It also supplied electricity to the South Indian Railways' suburban electric service.

Madras got its trams, a full six years before any other Indian city – or, for that matter, London – only ten years after they were first introduced in America. Madras Tramways continued until 1953, when trams finally disappeared from the Madras scene following a labour dispute. At the time MET wound up operations, it plied six routes, 17 miles in all, linking Mylapore, Purasawalkam, Washermenpet and areas in between, expansions having taken place in 1905, 1911 and 1919. It had 110 single-deck tramcars, a daily car mileage of about 7,500 miles and a daily passenger load of about 175,000 persons. Its main shed was off Poonamallee High Road. On Edward Eliott's Road (Dr Radhakrishnan Salai), in the heart of town, is a vast campus of Madras Electricity Supply offices. These were in the days of the tram part of another large tram shed.

Street lighting became electrified in 1920. Street lights had increased from 15 in 1914 to 8300 by 1924, with all kerosene lights having been replaced. By around then, there were a few electrical contractors and engineers in the city. Namely, English Electric Co. Ltd., Oriental Telephone and Electric Corporation Ltd., Crompton Engineering Works (Madras) Ltd. (1918), and Roche & Sundaram Ltd. (1922). Around this time, electricity tariffs were 8 annas per unit for lighting, 5 annas per unit for lighting and fans on the combined circuit, and Rs.8 per KW of maximum demand plus one anna per unit consumed for industrial power.

Northwards from NSC Bose Road is a maze of narrow, busy streets, named after prominent Indian businessmen (most of them *dubashes*) of another age. Once this was 'New Black Town', but now this is George Town, a warren of trade and trading families, a congested, overpopulated area of about 850 acres, bounded today by Rajaji Salai on the east, NSC Bose Road on the south, Wall Tax Road and Buckingham Canal on the west and Basin Bridge Road, Old Jail Road and Ebrahim Sahib Street on the north. However, over the years, the more open area to the south of NSC Bose Road, the eastern half of which was occupied by the earliest 'Black Town', has also been considered part of George Town, so that its generally accepted southern boundary today is Rasappa Chetty Street-Fraser Bridge Road, making the area slightly more rectangular. (And I also tend to incorporate Park Town – contiguous with this rectangle and stretching to the Cooum – into what I visualise as George Town.)

The 'New Black Town' was originally made up of Muthialpet and Peddanaickenpet, two unequal halves of a square – Muthialpet, by and large, the village of the Left Hand Castes (those without social privileges, the traders and artisans, oil-mongers, weavers, leather-workers, etc.) and Peddanaickenpet, 'home' of the Right Hand Castes (those with social privileges, the landowners, accountants, etc., and in the early days most of the Company's brokers and merchants). The Left Hand Castes were also permitted to live in what is today called Park Town. This was a separation that became more permanent after the Great Castes Dispute of 1707, when 'Pirate' Pitt laid down the law with a heavy hand. Cutting across these general caste barriers there were other caste- and language-based geographical considerations in those early days. For instance, the Arya Vaisyas and Beri Chetties, Telugu-speaking, generally lived west of Broadway, while the Tamil-speaking Senguntha Mudaliars used to live east of Broadway.

(Curiously, people of the same caste could belong to the Left Hand or Right Hand caste, presumably based on social status or occupation).

Between the two *pettais* and north of them were gardens and paddy fields in the early years, much of northwest Peddanaickenpet remaining cultivable land till as late as 1755. Southern Peddanaickenpet ceased to be a fashionable European residential quarter about 1700, but Europeans, like assistants in the 'English' stores and artisans, continued to live there till almost the 20th Century. In 1726, a revenue survey noted 26 gardens north of Muthialpet, that is, beyond where the Town Wall would, in time, come up. Among them were the big *Company's Gardens*, where French commander Lally quartered his Kaffir (African) Regiment during the siege of 1758-9, *Maria Pois Gardens*, *Kama Chetti's Gardens*, *Chinna Mutha's Gardens* and upto *Narayan's Gardens* and *Addison's Gardens*, owned by Sunku Rama Chetty, on the Pulicat Road.

Vertically separating the two *pettais* in halves is Popham's Broadway, the Popham now forgotten and the rest of the name a joke. But eccentric Stephen Popham was no joke. A leading solicitor of 18th Century Madras (1778-95), Popham was responsible for much of the development of 'New Black Town' as well as many of Madras's civic facilities, not the least of which was a police force to take over from the Pedda Nayak and his 'peons', the hereditary law-enforcers of 'Black Town'. The Pedda Nayak (which office lent its name to Peddanaickenpet) was the Chief Poligar who, from the time of the Vijayanagar Kingdom, employed the town watchmen in the Madras region. This hereditary office was recognised by John Company as far back as 1659. The first talk of establishing a 'Board of Police' took place in Governor Du Pre's Council in 1770. But constant differences of opinion between Town and Fort on the role of the Pedda Nayak led nowhere, until Popham submitted a scheme in 1782 for the establishment of a police force that would also have municipal and judicial functions. This scheme was tried out between 1786 and 1791, then dropped. But in 1797 another plan for a police force was implemented, the force thus organised having its hand strengthened when the Pedda Nayak's office was abolished in 1806. The Mounted Police was formed in 1928. When police reformation was instituted in 1858, the present police force was born. W Robinson, a Civilian, was the first Inspector General of Police and Lt Col J C Boulderson the first Commissioner of Police, Madras. Boulderson appointed two Deputy Commissioners, a European and an Indian. T Ramachendra Row was the Indian and, thus, became the first Indian to hold a senior appointment in the Police. C K Vijayaraghavan, a Civilian, in 1947 became the first Indian to head the Police. When P Parangusam Naidu was appointed as an interim Commissioner in 1919, the first Indian to be in charge of the City Police, it was recognition of the sterling contribution he had made over seven years while in charge of North Madras and, simultaneously, the newly set up Harbour Police. In 1947, A V Patro became the first Indian to be formally designated Commissioner.

Popham, who had once been an MP for County Mayo (Ireland) in Westminster, decided his fortune lay in India and arrived in Calcutta in the 1770s. In 1778, he quit the Advocate-General's office in Calcutta for advocacy and do-gooding in Madras and, thereafter, spent much of his years here drawing up civic plans for the improvement of 'Black Town'. He viewed his policemen as registrars of Madras addresses, vehicles and carriage animals, arbiters of wage disputes between servants and employers, regulators of prices in the markets, and supervisors of the town's cleanliness, in addition to preserving law and order. This police was supervised by the short-lived Committee of Regulation, whose Secretary was, naturally, Popham, who had also advocated the construction of main and cross drains in 'Black Town' to carry away stagnant water, the naming and lighting of streets, the registration of births and deaths, the licensing of liquor shops of all varieties, the cultivation of a protective bound hedge to the north of the town, the "extirpation of *Dubashism*" and construction of a navigable canal from the Ennore backwaters to The Island to bring in produce and fish from the north (this canal eventually being built as the Cochrane Canal).

The tireless lawyer was also actively concerned with the development of Attapallam (a name now in disuse and meaning *atta* = deep and *pallam* = depression = deep channel), levelling of Hog Hill and the commencement of the main market. Hog Hill was raised ground in the southeast corner of Peddanaickenpet (the area now taking in Park Town

Post Office, the MUC grounds and the hospital complex), which had once been considered the site for a new fort, if the original fort were washed away by the sea! But with Fort St George secure, Hog Hill became a fashionable residential quarter, one of its best-known residents being Nicolo Manucci, a Venetian physician who lived in India half a century and acquired a rare reputation as an honest diplomat, Mughal courtier and a historian known as 'The Pepys of Mughal India'.

Manucci had from the late 1690s to 1709 lived in a "palatial" house in St. Thomas' Mount, thought to be "palatial" because he had hosted Daud Khan of the Carnatic there. The house had two gardens, in one of which Manucci grew herbs and plants for his ayurvedic-allopathic medical practice. After he sold this house to a Frenchman in July 1709, Manucci moved to Pondicherry till his wife was granted a house by the East India Company in Madras in 1712 for services her first husband had rendered.

The house in Black Town he inherited from his wife Elizabeth, the widow of Thomas Clarke, the first European known to have lived outside Fort St.George, was on the seaward side of Broadway where it now meets NSC Bose Road. This was granted to him on perpetual lease by the Council of Madras and he lived there till at least 1719.

Manucci is remembered internationally by those interested in Mughal history. His Storia do Mogor is considered a classic for Mughal studies, as it was a first-hand account of life in Aurangzeb's court in and around which he spent 30 years from 1656 till he arrived in Madras. The entire book was written during the years Manucci spent in Madras.

When Commander-in-Chief Eyre Coote wanted the high ground levelled to ensure the safety of the Fort, Popham drew up a plan for bungalow-owners of Hog Hill to be compensated with money for homes destroyed and land elsewhere for new building. Despite initial difficulties, the residents eventually agreed to move and Hog Hill was levelled in 1781. Manucci's erstwhile home was among those razed.

Popham, for all his civic consciousness, appears never to have suggested anything if there wasn't something in it for him. The levelling of Hog Hill enabled him to get earth to fill low-lying Attapallam, much of which he owned. Attapallam was wasteland that separated Peddanaickenpet and Muthialpet and through it ran the drainage channel from north to south, emptying itself into what was the Elambore River.

Popham, who had acquired parts of this land, now suggested that it be reclaimed for expansion of 'Black Town' which was becoming overcrowded. Hog Hill residue was used to raise the level of Attapallam (at least one street and part of this area has acquired the name of Mannady – in Tamil = mud foundations), the drainage channel was made more effective and running beside it was built the main north-south road of George Town, Popham's Broadway.

Popham's other activities included rearing silkworms and cultivating cotton, when he wasn't busy planning 'Black Town'. The "perpetual projectour" died in 1795, following injuries suffered when he fell from his two-wheeled, two-horsed curricle. He was only 53.

Before Broadway as a descriptive name became a joke, it was 19th Century Madras's main commercial thoroughfare. Amongst the many businesses here was John Gantz's lithographic press. It is to John and his son Justinian's talent that we owe many water colours, aquantints, etc. of old Madras buildings, private and public. Mrs. Klug's pioneering *Bioscope* was on this road and the building in which it was, still survives, now home to the Sukrutha Lakshmi Vilasa Sabha founded in 1900 and in these premises from 1944. The Sabha is a social and recreational club with a special interest in theatre.

Two of the best-known commercial names on 18th Century Broadway no longer survive here, but they still survive in Madras with differing degrees of recognition. P Venkatachellum's is, today, little more than a minor player, but Harrison's is still very much into hospitality.

It was in 1860 that P Venkatachellum started a condiment business in Kutchery Road, Mylapore. Soon business grew and P Venkatachellum's moved to Broadway, its factory located behind it, in Umpherson Street. In 1871, Venkatachellum's condiments, chutneys and pickles were shipped to London for the first time – and before long it was the only recognised name in "curry circles" in London, a reputation that lasted till the 1960s when what it had started began a "curry wave" that's made curry Britain's favourite food since the 1990s.

Subramaniam Pillai, Venkatachellum's son but better known as 'P Venkatachellum', joined the business in 1875 and made it a major industry after his father's death in 1867. Two years later he acquired the South India Ice Factory in Periamet and modernised it, providing it with a store-room that could hold 80,000 lbs of ice blocks! When factory-made ice went out of vogue, it became yet another Venkatachellum condiments factory.

As Subramaniam Pillai built up the P Venkatachellum empire, he became one of the city's major landlords. At one time, among the 75 residential properties he owned in Madras, were almost all the major garden houses in the city – *Brodie Castle* and *Somerford* in Adyar, *Morison's Gardens* and *Graeme's Gardens* in the Nungambakkam area, and *The Grange* and *Bishop's Gardens* off Greenway's Road among them, all tenanted by some of the leading British citizens of Madras. But to all of them he remained P Venkatachellum!

In the 1930s, when Venkatachellum's international reputation was at its peak, the third generation mechanised the factories and concentrated on increasing exports – long before 'liberalisation'. But in more recent times, P Venkatachellum's has not been able to keep the competition at bay and has virtually returned to where it started – making condiments of quality in a small way, for export only.

A neighbour on Broadway used to be Harrison's, founded in 1891 by G Varadharajulu Chetty and which was a name to reckon with in catering circles in the city. Harrison's of Broadway in the early 20th Century was a two-storey building with the confectionery shop on the ground floor and a restaurant on the first floor renowned for its 'Officers' lunches' and its string band. After Varadharajulu Chetty, Harrison's was run by a Trust, but survived due to the excellence of catering-in-charge Kanniappa Naicker. In 1939, P Nammalwar Naidu acquired the business and it remains, though expanded and partitioned, in the family. The Harrison name's visual presence now is a boutique hotel of the same name that was opened in 2004 on Nungambakkam High Road.

It was in Broadway that the first private hospital in Madras was opened. Dr T A Sankaranarayanan, heir to the Zamindari of Kulatur (Tirunelveli), an E N T Specialist, established this speciality hospital with 24 beds in 1914, in a handsome 3-storey building. Nearby is the large Wesley Church, dedicated in 1822. It owes its genesis to the first Methodist missionary to arrive in Madras, the Rev James Lynch, who came from Ireland in 1817 and began his mission, first, in a stable, then, in a godown in Black Town.

Off Broadway, where Loane Square now is, was developed Madras's first organised market in the 1780s. This General Market was built in 1789 with funds borrowed from local Europeans, Popham at the time remarking that the scheme was neither better nor worse for his being "the Proprietor of that Central Spot of Ground which must be the site of the Public Market"! Popham's Market remained on this site till it was condemned in 1865 as being insanitary. It was to get away from the growing crush of this area that Moore Market was developed.

Before Popham's Market was built, there was little organisation in the town's several small bazaars. In 1777, a *Kotwal* (overseer) of Markets was appointed. In 1780, he was superseded by a Superintendent of Police who was not only Inspector of Markets but also the regulator of prices in the various bazaars. But it was not till Popham's Market grew that the institution of the *Kotwal* regained its importance. *Kothawal Chavadi* (the *Kotwal's* market), the main wholesale vegetable and condiments market of Madras till 1996, was developed in 1803-4 a stone's throw from the city's earliest organised market. Its 50-acre premises were owned by a private trust, the Sri Kannikaparameswari Devasthanam Charities.

The Kannikaparameswari temple was built in 1769 and its market was developed on the site of the vegetable garden – Kooragayala or Komatla Thota – donated by its owner to the temple in the late 18th Century for charitable purpose. The Trust is now managed by a committee of Vysyas. Till the market was made to close down by Government as an answer to congestion, it awoke to activity around 3 a.m. every day and more than 5,000 people hustled and bustled to get its stalls ready for the morning sales. But though some of this still continues in the area, the bulk of the market's activity – as well as much else of George Town's wholesale trade activity – has moved to a location outside Madras, Koyambedu, in the western outskirts. The move to the large, spacious, modern market in Koyambedu by the Ring Road, off Anna Nagar, was made in 1996. The new Koyambedu Wholesale Market Complex, developed on what was once marsh and reed beds, has over 450 flower shops, 400 fruit shops and 1,400 vegetable shops. This complex, together with its support facilities, was built at a cost of approximately Rs.375 million in a 295-acre campus.Wholesale foodgrains and textile markets are scheduled to be built in the same campus. A huge bus terminus, for vehicles from the districts, the largest in Asia, was opened here in 2003 and a lorry terminus is planned. A wholesale iron and steel market has also opened, in Sathangadu in North Madras. With the completion of these facilities it is hoped to decongest George Town.

Kothawal Chavadi is just one aspect of the bustling activity that typifies George Town, the commercial core of Madras that, according to one description, is "characterised by high density of population, intensive development, mixed land use, exorbitant land values, narrow streets and excessive traffic, concentrations of financial and banking institutions and commercial establishments..." Through its 100-acre core there used to move till not so long ago an estimated 12,000 trucks and 15,000 hand-pushed vehicles daily! The numbers have not changed much. As for people, it was 'standing room only'!! Curiously, this bustle, here and elsewhere in George Town, is only during the day. George Town is virtually 'dead' soon after dark falls, the North Indian settlers who dominate the trade here retiring to their opulent homes fitted with every convenience above the rickety, dirty and crowded stores and offices below.

3. A tax for a wall

Broadway continues as Monegar Choultry Road in Royapuram. The Choultry – refuge, asylum, resthouse – dates back to the worst-ever famine in Madras history, the famine of 1781 that followed Hyder Ali's raids. What was perhaps the first-ever organised charity in the South, if not India, it was launched by Government and St Mary's Church in 1782, with a building just outside the north wall being rented by the Famine Relief Fund Committee as a gruel centre. The poor-feeding centre was developed as an old age home for the destitute, primarily for women, but later with accommodation for men. The unnamed choultry continued as a paupers' refuge even after conditions improved in 1784. Today, it has around 60 residents, most of them women. And it is the women who virtually run the place, cooking and serving quality food, keeping the premises clean, and looking after the cubicles. The Monegar and Rajah of Venkatagiri Choultries, as it is now known and run as one, also has an ancient Amman Shrine under an old tree in its garden that is tended by the male residents.

How the Choultry got the name Monegar has never been properly explained, but it is related that a village headman, a *Manugakkaran* (Monegar), used to run a gruel centre nearby. Perhaps that explains the government order sparing only one building – was it the Monegar's Choultry? – outside 'Black Town's' walls when it cleared a field of fire in the 1780s. This was, perhaps, the building the Famine Relief Fund took over. Whatever the reason for the name, the choultry developed

Once-spacious 'Black Town', now congested George Town...
...where Man and Beast and Machine jostle for space.

43. *The Monegar's Choultry is only a name and a plaque now... newer buildings have taken the place of old.*

44. *Bits of the Old Town Wall before unimaginative restoration. Once the northern boundary... its rooms rent are now no more.*

மாடிப் பூங்கா

into something more, especially after Government took over its entire management in 1808 from the Committee.

A hospital, the 'Native Infirmary', was founded in these premises in 1799 by Company Surgeon John Underwood and was developed by Government in 1809 as the main refuge for sick Indians in North Madras, amalgamating it with a Native Hospital that had existed in Purasawalkam. The Monegar Choultry Hospital was taken over by Government in 1910 and became Royapuram Hospital. The Choultry moved to adjoining premises by which came up the Rajah of Venkatagiri's Choultry. Around 1990, several old buildings of both choultries were pulled down, replaced by long overdue new premises and integrated. One of its rules is that when a resident dies, his or her body should be given to the neibouring Stanley Medical College.

The Auxiliary Royapuram Medical School had been established in 1877. It was renamed Stanley Medical School in 1933. When it was merged in 1938 with the Lady Willingdon Medical School for Women, started in 1923, the new medical college and hospital took the name of Governor George Stanley.

It was in this area that the British began to build a wall from 1770 to protect the northern and western boundaries of 'Black Town'. This protective wall – most of it built by engineer-contractor Paul Benfield for over a million pagodas! – was a consequence of Hyder Ali's forays that devastated several suburban villages. Work on the walls commenced in 1764 but desultorily proceeded until 1769 when the tempo picked up – only after Hyder Ali had twice proved the efficiency of his plundering irregular cavalry. The city had little protection during Hyder Ali's raids in 1767 and 1769 – the first led by his young son Tippu Sultan threatening even *Government House*, the second led by Hyder Ali himself resulting in the plunder of St Thomas' Mount, San Thomé and neighbouring villages.

When the work on the western and northern sections of the wall were finally completed in 1772, the wall ran a length of 3½ miles and had 17 bastions and seven gateways. In the lay-out of today, this wall would be located between the Clive Battery flyover and Basin Bridge railway station in the north and from that station to the Central Station junction at Poonamallee High Road in the west. Pully Gate at the end of Thambu Chetty Street, Tiruvottriyur (Monegar Choultry) Gate at the end of Broadway, Ennore Gate near the north end of Mint Street, Elephant Gate at the end of the street named after it, Chuckler's Gate at the Rasappa Chetty Street end, and Hospital Gate near the present General Hospital were the main gateways in the fortifications. The west wall ran close to the Elambore River. Outside it, the land was cleared to a distance of 600 yards, creating esplanades that provided clear fields of fire. The southwest esplanade was converted into People's Park in 1859 by Governor Charles Trevelyan. The northwest esplanade became Salt Cotaurs, where once salt was manufactured. The area was later converted into a railways goods yard. Most of the fortifications were pulled down about the same time, though stretches of wall exist here and there.

But when the walls existed, a 50-foot wide cleared space was created within, with a good road running by it, for easy communication inside the wall-enclosed area. Originally it was intended that this road-making should be funded by a tax – but legal complications as much as citizens' protests floored the proposal and it was only many years later that Wall Tax Road, now known for bamboo-ware, was built, its name a reminder of an ill-fated tax proposal. The fact that the arches in the rampart could be occupied by Indians on payment of rent, lent added substance to the name. Bastions in the northwest angle of the walls – at the Basin Bridge-Wall Tax Road junction – were used to house debtor-prisoners.

On Wall Tax Road is Schultze's 1729 church, now known as Trinity Church. This area is today known for its wholesale dry fish market, Moolagothram.

4. Amenities for the people

Mint Street runs straight to the southern third of George Town – in reality Park Town, an area that no doubt took its name from the park developed near here by Governor Trevelyan. This busy area of public institutions is between the Canal on the west and the Fort in the southeast, the Cooum River in the south and Rasappa Chetty Street-Fraser Bridge Road in the north. At Mint Street's southern end is General Hospital Road, that leads into Poonamallee High Road – now named E V R Periyar Salai after the Tamil rationalist who founded the Dravidian political philosophy that has dominated governance in the State since 1968. This road is yet another axial thoroughfare leading out of the Fort and, like Mount Road, military in origin, leading 23 km from the Fort to Poonamallee (Poo-manatha-malli = the waft of jasmines), generally called Poonthamallee. Poonamallee was Madras's western outpost in 1750 (when it was granted to the English by Nawab Muhammad Ali) and, earlier still, Damarla Ayyappa Nayak's citadel when he made the land grant to Francis Day.

The short stretch of G H Road is flanked by the General Hospital's sprawling buildings and Medical College; the striking red buildings of Central Railway Station and the impressive grey stone-cladded head offices of the Southern Railway built on the site of the old park, Jamburathottam; and Memorial Hall, built at the Mint Street corner as thanksgiving by English residents of the city for being "spared from the horrors of the Indian Mutiny," and now a part of the almost equally architecturally quaint Christian Literature Society complex of buildings – indeed, a historic stretch of amenities for the people. The Hall, built on a raised platform and possessing a fine Ionic portico, was designed by Col George Winscom and later built, with modifications, by Col Horsley. Work which began in 1858 appears to have gone on for a few years, but from the first the intent appeared to be to link the activities of the Hall with those of such missionary organisations as the Bible Society.

The country's first hospital – in the Western sense – was established in Fort St George in 1664. This hospital was in a Cogan-owned house, which had been rented for the purpose by Agent Edward Winter. A further step forward was taken between 1679 and 1688 when 838 pagodas (Rs 3,000) were raised by public subscription and spent on building a two-storey hospital near St Mary's, to be administered by the Church and Vestry. Yale's Council acquired this building and built, by 1690, at a cost of 2,500 pagodas, a new hospital in James Street, near the north end of the barracks and, like them, a handsome Tuscan style building. Here the hospital stayed put for the next half century or so.

During the wars with the French – that uncertain period in Madras history which lasted from 1746 to 1759 – the hospital kept moving in and out of the Fort, from its own buildings to rented ones, 12 Portuguese-owned houses near what is now the Madras United Club, close to the present site of the hospital, being used as far back as 1753. In 1759, the hospital was moved, for the ninth time, to the cemetery site later occupied by the Armenian and Capuchin churches in Armenian Street and stayed there for 13 years, until the building of the new church and Cathedral got underway. The decision to shift to the present site – once part of the lower slopes of Hog's Hill and where the Company's 'Garden House' had stood in the 1680s – was taken in 1762, Armenian Street, with its cemeteries, being found "unhealthy". But for all Chief Engineer Call's diligence, work began only in 1771, by which time Col Patrick Ross was in charge. By October 15, 1772, 42,000 pagodas later, the new hospital was ready, built by John Sulivan, who had quoted lower than Paul Benfield, Ross' choice till the Council intervened. The Sulivan building was expanded into two large blocks with additions in 1859 and 1893 and survived till 2002 when they were pulled down and a new two-block main building built. Several other hospital buildings were added between 1928 and 1934 and much reconstruction was also done. To the east of these building are the Medical College buildings – among the oldest in the campus. The oldest datable building is a handsomely pillared one that was restored in haphazard fashion, a few years ago. This 'Seminar Hall' is dated to 1835. To its east is the main medical college administrative block with its twin wings, their fronts curved , one of the wings called "Zero Hall" by students. Still further east is the campus's more recognisable building, Indo-Saracenic in style, painted in red and with stepped classrooms reaching to the ceilings. Called by students the 'Red Fort', this building, the anatomy block, dates to 1897 – and so does its furniture. Medical College in 2013 moved into newly raised buildings where the Central Jail was and plans were been announced to convert the 'Red Fort' into a major medical museum – the extra space allowing the present museum established on the campus in 1928 to be considerably expanded.

Near here, on Muthuswami Aiyar Bridge, between Fort and Park Town railway station, is Zero Point for NH 45 to Trichy, NH4 to Bangalore and NH5 to Calcutta.

Across from the 'Red Fort' on what was the west glacis of the Fort there is a little noticed tombstone and memorial to a Dr Edward Bulkley. Appointed the head of the 'Government Hospital' in 1692, he on August 23, 1693 performed the first medico-legal autopsy in India. That same year, he issued India's first leave certificate for "absence on medical grounds" and two years later he issued the first injury certificate. He went on to become a well-considered citizen of Madras. Less remembered than Bulkley were Company surgeons John Waldo and Bezaliel Sherman who in 1678 for the first time in India certified a custodial death. Thomas Savage, a drunken soldier, had died – due to the manner in which the Guard had bound him, feet to neck.

A medallion found on a wall of office space in General Hospital reads "Hospital founded 1753" and rather confuses the issue, though it might refer to the date the hospital was moved to the northwest esplanade. The hospital, however, became truly general, open to Indians as well, only after 1842, and it was 1899 before it became a purely civilian institution.

Another commemorative plaque in the hospital, now sadly missing after the main blocks were pulled down, remembered Col C Donovan who in 1903 made the hospital's most famous discovery – the organism that causes Kala-Azar. Donovan was at the time working in the Hospital and was a professor at MMC. The news took three months to reach London, by which time Leishman had also made the same discovery. So the organism was called *Leishmania donovani*, transit time of the news resulting in Donovan getting only secondary billing. Col Donovan was later the first Superintendent of the Royapettah Branch of General Hospital (opened in 1912). In the hospital, still preserved under glass, are the drawings on a blackboard Donovan did of the Kala Azar organism.

Yet another plaque in the hospital – this one still in place – is in the room where Dr Md Habibulla, who was in charge of Administration, was murdered by a hospital employee in 1947.

The Medical College began functioning in 1835 as the Madras Medical School, taking its present name on October 1, 1850, after it got its full complement of staff. The first woman student was admitted in 1876; Mary Ann Dacomb Scharleib, who was British, passed out in 1878. Mary Dacomb Bird was 20 when she married William Scharleib, who was practising law in Madras, and she came out in 1866. In Madras she helped her husband bring out two monthly law journals, one the *Madras Jurist*, till she saw that Indian women needed women doctors more than the law. And so she sought enrolment in medical college – setting an example that still continues in Madras of young married girls continuing their education after marriage. Dr Branfoot, surgeon at the women's and children's hospital, angrily told her at the time, "I cannot prevent you walking round the wards, but I will not teach you."

Mary Scharleib, however, prevailed. After graduating, she returned to London and studied further. In 1882, she graduated from the Royal London School of Medicine as its first woman doctor, and then worked there till she returned to Madras in 1883. Here she founded in 1884 / 85 the Royal Victoria Hospital for Caste and Gosha Women, now the

Kasturba Gandhi Hospital for Women, and lectured at Madras Medical College. She returned to Britain in 1887, but never quite lost touch with India; in 1916, she helped establish the Women's Medical Service, India. The first woman MD of London University in 1888, and the first woman consultant to its teaching hospital, she was made a Dame of the British Empire in 1926.

Scharleib's admission to MMC opened the doors for women and in 1876 three young Anglo-Indian women, the Misses White, Beale and Mitchell, were admitted. White topped the LMP Class of 1878, with Scharleib ranking second and Beale also getting a first class. The next batch of women students, ten in number, passed out in 1887 and included a Burgher from Ceylon, Mrs A M Van Ingen, who became the first woman to graduate in medicine from the University of Madras. The first non-Anglo-Indian Indian woman to enter MMC was Kirupabhai Sathianadhan, who topped her first year. But ill-health forced her to discontinue her studies. Three Indian Christians, Abala Das, Rose Govindurajulu and Gurdial Singh, were in the class of 1887 and were the first non-Anglo-Indian Indians to study for the LMP. Govindurajulu and Singh joined the Mysore Medical Services. The first Indian woman to get a medical degree from the University of Madras was Dr. Muthulakshmi Reddy, now remembered in a small park in Adyar for her extraordinary contributions to medicine, social service and legislation in the Presidency. She graduated in 1912 and, in time, became the first woman house surgeon in the Government Maternity Hospital and the Government Ophthalmic Hospital. Dr Reddy, whose sister died of cancer, fought a never-say-die battle from 1928 till she got the support needed for the city's first cancer hospital, which she conceived in 1949 and founded in Adyar in 1954. The Cancer Institute is now a research centre as well.

The first woman to become the Deputy President of any Legislative Council in India, Dr Reddy fought in the Madras Council for passage of the law to abolish the *devadasi* system, the Immoral Traffic Control Act, and the Act to prevent cruelty to children. When the *devadasi* ban was passed, the temple dancers sought new homes in the women's hostels of Madras and were refused. And, so, Dr Reddy founded the *Avvai Home* in Adyar in 1930 for destitute women and children. She was truly an indomitable woman.

The Home was started in her own house, *Shanti*, built in 1930 and where she lived till 1968. The Home moved in 1936 to a nearby Adyar location and here new space was built for them in 2014.

The first Indian principal of the Medical College was Dr A Lakshmanaswami Mudaliar, appointed in 1939 and in charge till he was made Vice-Chancellor of Madras University in 1942. An eminent gynaecologist and a gifted teacher, Dr Mudaliar's teaching method, in his own words, was "to leave students to stew in their own juice of ignorance... To put a knife and a part of a cadaver in the hands of the student and leave him to it."

A statue dominating the hospital entrance is of Dr S Rangachari, a surgeon whose contribution to the hospital was legendary. His only extravagance was a Rolls Royce that was recognisable all over Madras. Other owner-drivers of Rolls Royces in the 1920s and 1930s included M Ct Chidambaram Chettyar, Thiruvengadathan Chetty of the Perumal Chetty family who had two of them, the Rajah of Ramnad, and C Rangaswami Iyengar, Deputy Commissioner of Police and from a wealthy family. Another statue in the General Hospital campus is opposite the Medical College; it is of the dedicated doctor and teacher Dr M R Guruswami Mudaliar.

Two significant bits of Madras medical history relate to Radiology and TB. Such pioneering work laid the foundation for Madras in the new Millennium becoming the medicare capital of India.

Radiology came to Madras in 1900, when the General Hospital got an X-ray unit only five years after W.C. Roentgen's discovery and before such facilities, it is claimed, were established in much of Europe and the rest of the world. Captain T.W.Barnard was appointed in 1920 to organise a radiological service. Two years later he was appointed the Radiologist for the Madras Presidency, then, Director, Government X-ray Institute, Madras. In 1933, the building that still houses the Institute was raised and on March 26, 1934 it was inaugurated as the Barnard Institute of Radiology. In 1956, it was upgraded as an all-India postgraduate and research institute.

Barnard, who was Director of the Institute till 1940, and was described as the 'Father of Radiology in South India', used the 400KV X-ray unit installed in 1934 for the first time in India on his wife's hand, much as Roentgen had done the first X-ray ever on his wife's hand.

The second pioneering institution, one whose work is recognised worldwide, the Tuberculosis Research Centre, on Spur Tank Road in Chetput, is now known as the National Institute for Research in Tuberculosis. Its neighbour is the State's Tuberculosis Research Centre. Both are memorials to Dr.Wallace Fox, who was in charge of the Madras Tuberculosis Experiment.

It was during international discussions on the common problems in handling Tuberculosis in all developing countries that the World Health Organisation agreed to study it. With the Indian Council for Medical Research (ICMR) offering to host the study and the British Medical Research Council willing to send out a team of specialists, WHO launched the project. The Madras Government, which had a long history of anti-tuberculosis work, agreed to have the study conducted in the State. And in 1956 it welcomed the team led by Wallace Fox.

Over the next five years, supervising strictly controlled trials and carefully monitoring statistics, Fox and his team found that tuberculosis patients treated with a strictly supervised medication regime (which included a cocktail of drugs), even in the overcrowded homes of the poor where diets were not nutritious, did as well as patients in well-run sanatoria that provided good food and comfortable facilities for rest. The research team also found that in the case of home treatment, the disease was not communicated to anyone in the house. The report of Fox's team made world headlines, reducing as it did the need for sanatoria.

Another significant contribution to medicine in India is the Department of Neurosurgery that Dr B Ramamurti started at the General Hospital in 1950 with the country's first head injury ward beings established there.

A Naval Hospital shared space in Fort St George with the Garrison Hospital, established in 1664 and a facility that evolved into the Government General Hospital of today as well as the Military Hospital at St Thomas' Mount.

In 1745, the Naval Hospital got its own premises, just outside the Fort and by the beach. By the 1780s, the hospital building was in sad shape and Government ordered it to move into a new building to be built further inland. A site was acquired in 1784 but no further action was taken. By 1790, the Naval Hospital was in such a sorry state that the sick from the fleet were tended to in the Garrison Hospital inside the Fort. Then, in 1808, the new Naval Hospital was built on the very site chosen for it nearly 25 years earlier. Here, at the junction of Poonamallee High Road and what became known as Naval Hospital Road – which it still is today – the hospital was to remain till 1831. The decision to hand over the naval hospital buildings for a gun-carriage factory, which incorporated the one set up in Srirangapatnam in 1820, was taken that year as the number of sailors needing medical attention had dwindled with fewer naval vessels calling at Madras. It was felt that the General Hospital had enough beds for the naval sick too. Later, when there was no use for a gun carriage factory, its buildings were handed over to the Medical Stores Department. In its gun carriage days, Major Maitland, as we've already seen, trained in it, apprentices in aspects of mechanical engineering.

The present buildings probably include a core of Dr. Lucas' mansion that Admiral Peter Rainier bought in 1797 "to separate the Naval from the Military Hospital." Naval Hospital Road is in an area once called New Town (now a part of Periamet), which was strongly Anglo-Indian middle class, most of its residents working in the Government facilities in the area like the railways and hospitals. The best-known Anglo-Indian in the South, David S. White, founded the Anglo-Indian Association for Southern India in 1879 at a meeting held in the Prayer Hall in New Town. Later, White Memorial Hall was raised to his memory in Egmore, just across the railway tracks from New Town. It was located where the Hotel Ramada Chennai now is, just behind where the Chennai Metropolitan Development Authority's (CMDA) stainless steel-pillared tower blocks came up. The Hall and its acreage, but for a small corner, were sold in the 1970s and a small building was raised in that corner to house the Association's office.

The CMDA's headquarters was named the Thalamuthu-Natarajan Building when its was opened in 1989, remembering two who died in the first anti-Hindi agitation which took place in 1937-39.

Other government medical institutions include the Ophthalmic Hospital, founded in 1819 in Royapettah and now called the Regional Ophthalmic Institute; the Leprosy Hospital founded in 1816 opposite the Monegar Choultry in Washermenpet and moved out of the city in 1920; the 700-bed Government Women and Children's Hospital founded in 1844 as the country's first Government Lying-in Hospital, by the Egmore railway line and facing the Cooum river, next to where the *White Memorial Hall* came up, and which moved to its present Pantheon Road site in 1882 as the Government Maternity Hospital; the neighbouring Institute of Child Health, the biggest in India; the Royal Victoria Hospital for Caste and Gosha Women (now the Kasturba Gandhi Hospital for Women) founded in 1885 on its present site in Triplicane to the south of Chepauk, the Rajahs of Venkatagiri and Vizianagaram contributing considerably towards the building expenses; the Isolation Hospitals founded in the 1850s in Krishnampet and Royapuram, which merged with the Isolation Hospital in Tondiarpet, founded in 1924, and became the Infectious Diseases Hospital in the 1940s. The Mental Hospital was founded in 1794 in Purasawalkam (a name very likely from the *purasu* tree) by Assistant Surgeon Valentus Connolly, as a private 'home'. The School of Indian Medicine was established in 1925. The Tuberculosis Sanatorium at Tambaram and the splendid Railway Hospital established in 1928 in Perambur are two of the best run medical institutions in the country, the latter producing several of the country's best heart surgeons.

The Women and Children's Hospital, now the Institute of Obstetrics and Gynaecology and Child Health, was headed by Dr A Lakshmanaswami Mudaliar from 1938 and in his day was considered the best maternity hospital east of Suez. It today is a major teaching centre for South Asia. The Gosha Hospital's Beadon Ward was named after its first Superintendent, Dr Mary Beadon (1921-27), and its Lazarus Ward after its first Indian Superintendent, Dr Hilda Lazarus (1927-40).

The internationally renowned Regional Ophthalmic Institute is the second oldest specialist eye hospital in the world and the oldest in Asia. It was founded in 1819 as the Madras Eye Infirmary (MEI), modelled on Moorfields in London, which, just one year older, is the oldest eye hospital in the world.

The MEI was set up by R. Richardson, an eye surgeon, sent out by the East India Company. He established it in Royapettah, somewhere behind what is the 'Express Avenue' mall today. But within a year the number of patients had increased so much that Richardson had to look for new premises which he found near what is now Periyar Thidal after having once served as the major tram shed of the city. And still the number of patients grew, so land was acquired at the Institute's present Marshall's Road site in Egmore in 1884 and three blocks were built as well as an out-patient dispensary facility. These buildings were inaugurated in 1888 as the Government Ophthalmic Hospital, the driving force behind it Dr. E.F. Drake Brockman (Superintendent, 1873-94).

Substantial expansion of the hospital took place after Lt. Col. R.H. Elliott I.M.S. took over as Superintendent in 1904. Before he left in 1913 he had set in motion plans for the establishment of a School of Ophthalmology. The building for the School was completed by year-end 1919. Honouring his contributions, the School was named 'The Elliott School of Ophthalmology' when it was inaugurated in the new building on February 7, 1920. The plans of Elliott for further enlarging the School, the Hospital and getting both institutions the latest equipment were implemented over the 25 years that followed his departure. Serving for 18 years through this period, the longest anyone has headed the Hospital, was Lt. Col. R.E. Wright, I.M.S. It was during Wright's tenure that he conceived and implemented the establishment of a museum in the Elliott School. The Elliott Museum acquired a world reputation, which it still has even though it could do with a little more attention and maintenance, just like the other striking heritage building in the campus. Its holdings include an 1829 painting of an affected eye, 19th Century case registers, 19th Century specimens of affected eyes, and century-and-more-old instruments.

Dewan Bahadur Koman Nayar was appointed Superintendent in December 1940, the first Indian to be selected for the post. Dr.R.E.S. Muthayya, who was appointed Superintendent in 1947, was the first and only head of the Hospital to have a Doctorate in Ophthalmology (from Oxford). During his nine-year tenure, he established the first Eye Bank in India, a Master's degree in Ophthalmology, and laid the foundation for the acquisition of Shawfield Gardens, across the way from the College. When the garden house and its considerable acreage were taken over in 1960, nurses' quarters and a School for Optometry, also named after Elliot, were built there, the School opening in 1962. In 1969, a new building was raised in the Shawfield campus to host an Outpatients Block and an Administration Block. And the hospital has continued to grow ever since, befitting an institution with a significant international reputation.

As for Connolly's Asylum, it began in 1794 in 45 acres of space with "16 airy apartments" and continued after Connolly's time to be run by James Dalton and his heirs at the site that was to be in the 1930s developed as *College Park,* the Medical College's hostels near Kelly's (Kiliyur = (T) village (*oor*) of parrots (*kili*)?). Dalton and his successor

James Lauder established here a separate facility that in 1840 was named the Mental Leper Hospital.

When Government moved the mental asylum in 1871 into new buildings, the present ones on Medavakkam Tank Road, Kilpauk, just 1 ½ km to the northwest of the very first *Locock's Garden* location, the Connolly-Dalton property was used to house the Madras Medical College's Principal and Staff. Still in use at the Mental Hospital are several wards, all separate buildings favouring verandahs and arches, and the lovely old Superintendent's Bungalow, all the "new buildings of 1871" .

With superintendents not staying on campus in more recent years, the bungalow has become the superintendent's office. The old 'lock up' confinement cells are no longer used, but remain as mute witnesses to another age of medicare. Of comparatively newer vintage are the airy, tiled criminal wards reflecting a rural architectural style.

Special features of what is now called the Institute of Mental Health are the bakery, where the inmates make their own bread and bread for nearby Stanley Hospital, the kitchen where they cook their meals, the clothing unit where they spin, weave and tailor their own clothes, a carpentry unit and a smithy which serve the institute, an animal farm and a vegetable garden where they grow much of what their kitchen needs. Confidence-building is what the institute aims at.

This long, proud reputation of Madras for medical facilities continues to this day, with private medicare playing a dominant role. Dewan Bahadur N. Subrahmanyam, the first Indian Official Trustee and Administrator-General of Madras, donated to the Wesleyan Mission in 1902 a hospital for women and children. When he was named for the AG post, it was reported that there were less than half a dozen Indian Christians in all India who had been appointed to such high office till then. In 1911, he requested that it be named Kalyani Hospital after his mother, who had never forgiven him for becoming a Christian, died. It is today called the CSI Kalyani Multispeciality Hospital. Scottish missionaries, working in medicare from 1856, set up the Christina Rainy Hospital in Tondiarpet in 1914, which proved a boon to North Madras. St. Isabel's in Luz started as a maternity home in 1949. In 1954, Prof H Viswanathan, the 'Father of Diabetology' in India, founded the M V Hospital for Diabetes in Royapuram. And the Cancer Institute followed.

The first of the polyclinics was H M Hospital which Dr H Mehta opened in 1967/8 on St Mary's Road. The first major multispeciality hospital followed not long after, the Vijaya Hospital started in 1972 by B M Nagi Reddy in Vadapalani. Then, in 1983, the giant Apollo Hospital was established off Graeme's Road, bringing the concept of corporate medicare to India. Since then, there's been a rash of private hospitals coming up in the city, many of them of outstanding merit – like the Madras Medical Mission, which got underway in 1987 and is now in an architecturally interesting building opened in 1996 in Mogappair, specialising in heartcare, the Sri Ramachandra Hospital Medical College and Research Institute, its beginning in 1985 with its all-purpose hospital established in Porur in 1988, and the Sankara Nethralaya eye hospital established in 1978 in Nungambakkam. With institutions like these and many more, Madras has been acquiring the reputation of being the "Medicare Capital of India" and is sought by many from West, South and Southeast Asia, East Africa and Eastern India.

Another significant amenity has been the railways. The first rail track in India was laid for demonstration purposes near Chintadripet Bridge in 1836. This was followed the next year by a track that A. P. Cotton, a PWD engineer, laid from Red Hills to the stone quarries near St. Thomas' Mount. The Red Hills Railway, like its predecessor, depended on wind power and manpower to function. The first to look at steam locomotion in India, Madras specifically, was a group of businessmen in London in 1832. Their ideas, however, only took off with the Madras Railway Company, founded in England in 1845, and succeeded by a new company in 1849, which laid the first line in the South in 1853, linking Arcot (then titular capital of the Nawabs of the Carnatic and today Wallajahpet, near Ranipet), to the west, with Royapuram on the north Madras coast. The line was extended east and south to the beach, just south of the harbour. The 67-mile line was opened for steam locomotion traffic on July 1, 1856, three years after India's first line (Bori Bunder – Bombay V T – Thane). The carriages for that historic journey were built by Simpson's, the coach-builders.

Royapuram's handsome quasi-classical buildings remained the main terminal station of Madras until 1907, when further route extensions made Madras Central the city's premier station. The original Central Station – a smaller one with only four platforms – was opened to the public in 1873 when the Vyasarpadi-Madras line was inaugurated, but work went on, on George Harding's design, till 1878. Improvements to the buildings were later made by Chisholm. The present striking building, with its dominating 135-ft tall clock tower – its Gillett and Bland clock from London dating to 1874 – was finally completed in 1900. Further additions were made in 1938, 1959 and 1981. And now it has further spread westwards, with its platforms 12 in number – and a duplication of the main building built in 1998.

In 1908, the Madras and Southern Mahratta Railway Co (M & SM) was formed by the merger of several regional companies (including the parent Madras Railway Company and the Southern Mahratta Railway Company) and operated from headquarters in Royapuram until it moved, in 1922, into the magnificent buildings in General Hospital Road that are now the headquarters of the Southern Railway. At the time it was formed it had about 3,150 miles of track in the northern Madras Presidency. Its Royapuram headquarters building, complementing the Royapuram station, was razed in the 1980s.

The Great Southern Indian Railway Co, founded in 1853 in England, began line construction in the southern reaches of the Presidency in 1859 and opened its tracks for traffic in 1861. But it was only after the Great Southern India and the Carnatic Railway Company were merged as the South Indian Railway (SIR) in 1874, that the lines were pushed southwards faster, Trichinopoly-Tuticorin opening in 1876. The South Indian Railway Company was registered only in 1890 in London and Trichinopoly became its Indian headquarters. At that time, it had nearly 1,850 miles of track in the southern reaches of the Madras Presidency – south, say, of an arbitrary line between Mangalore on the west coast and Madras. The suburban electric train service of this company, 29 km from Tambaram to Madras Beach, was conceived in 1923, work began on it in 1926 and it was inaugurated in April 1931 with 13 stations between Beach and Tambaram and three more later. In time, it offered a service of 100 trains a day. This metre gauge commuter service which switched to AC in 1962 came to an end in July 2005, a broad gauge service taking its place. The Electric Multiple Units (EMUs), which carried three million passengers a year when the service started, carried about 250 million commuters annually in the 2000s. The SIR, M & SM and Mysore Railways merged on April 1, 1951 as the first nationalised unit of the Indian Railways, the Southern Railway which would serve 6,000 miles. Nationalisation of the other zones went on till the mid-

1950s. At the time nationalisation began, there were 21 railways in the country. Railway electrification began in 1962 and broad gauging of almost all lines in the new Millennium.

The new M&SM headquarters, across from Central Station, was the work of T Samynada Pillai, a leading building contractor in Bangalore from 1879. Samynada Pillai, whose best-known Bangalore work was the Seshadri Iyer Memorial Hall in Cubbon Park, moved his activities, to what is now Tamil Nadu, when he undertook major SIR work in Trichinopoly (SIR headquarters) and Madurai. This work led to his being given the contract for the SIR's main station building in Egmore. That handsome building was built on the site of a small existing station and took three years to build at a cost of over Rs.17 lakh. Designed by Henry Irwin and its construction supervised by E.C. Bird, it opened in 1908 in a 3.5 acre site, most of the land being acquired from the Dr. Pulney Andy family. Successful completion of this contract by Samynada Pillai led to an even bigger contract, of nearly Rs.30 lakh, to build the M&SM headquarters, whose granite looks (it is really granite cladded) echo the Mysore Palace's. N Grayson of Railways, who obviously was inspired by Henry Irwin who had done the palace, designed what has now become the Southern Railway Headquarters and which, in turn, has been echoed by Bangalore's Legislature and Secretariat, the *Vidhana Soudha*. The foundations of the railway building are unique, being the first in India laid in reinforced concrete.

Central Station and the Railway headquarters, which was inaugurated in 1922, came up in an open area that had once been called John Pereira's Gardens. Fallen into disuse, it had become a gaming den, cock-fighting, watched by the soldiers from the Fort, the favourite sport. The founding of Trinity chapel in 1831 near here helped make the area less boisterous and the railways finally replaced one form of activity with a more industrious bustle.

It was Madras Tramways which, from 1925 to 1928, operated the first organised bus system in the city, but it had to wind up this operation which, with 50 motor buses, provided an excellent link with the suburbs. The unorganised sector proved too much for it. Organised bus transport then came back to Madras only in 1933, with 'The Red Ladies', red and yellow buses, but as far back as 1910 Simpson's was selling buses to owners who ran disorganised services both in the City and Mofussil. Presidency Transport, with its red buses, and City Motor Service, with its blue ones, long dominated this transport service. By July 1948, the entire bus system was nationalised.

Roads were little developed in the whole of South India during the first 200 years of Madras. An 1856 report says there were only 3,400 miles of road in the Presidency – an area 2½ times England and Wales and with a population 25 per cent more numerous – and the greater part of these 'made roads' had not been made at all!! A Trunk Road Department was first formed in 1845. The first automatic traffic signal was installed at the Hall's Road Junction just before Egmore Railway Station in 1962.

5. The city within today

Between General Hospital in the south and the remains of the great wall in the north lies the George Town of today – busy public institutions in the south and east, a hive of trading activity in the centre and a crowded residential quarter in the north, where the roadside homes are today much as they were in 1699 when Ensign Thomas Salmon was stationed here and recorded, on his return to England, "...brick houses...of the better sort...are of the same materials and built usually in one Form, that is with a little square in the middle from which they receive all their light..." And in these homes, the 'Gentus' and 'Malabarrs' – the Telugus and Tamils of George Town today – live life very much as it must have been in 1674, when there were only 75 houses in 'Black Town' or in 1750 when there were 8,700. In 1855, a *Gazetteer* recorded, "The minor streets...are numerous...extremely narrow... The form of the house (here) resembles... a hollow square, the rooms opening into a courtyard in the centre, which is entered by one door, from the street. This effectually secures the privacy so much desiderated by the Natives, but at the same time prevents proper ventilation, and is the source of many diseases. The streets, with few exceptions, have drains on both sides which are deep and narrow..."

Little changes in George Town, it just keeps getting more and more congested. In the northern half, there still remain the country-tiled houses as described above, with pillared verandahs, short and heavy doors inches thick and with 'caste marks' at the entrance. The southern half of the 'the city within', mainly in Peddanaickenpet, is Madras's wholesale market, street after street, narrow and crowded, specialising on street level in particular goods, with palatially-equipped homes often occupying the upper reaches of the same dingy buildings.

Here, paper is the main stock-in-trade of Anderson Street and a couple of streets on either side of it. Audiappa Naicken Street is where the grain merchants are. In Badrian Chetty Street are to be found the fireworks shops and flower shops. Bunder Street is where the fruit-vendors get their stock, and Malayaperumal Street is where the vegetable sellers get their vegetables. Devaraja Mudali Street specialises in turmeric and *kumkum*, silk thread for charms, false hair, glass and mica. Godown Street, Nainiappan Naicken Street, Govindappa Naicken Street are the domain of textile wholesalers – the latter having their share of jewellery shops as well – while Elephant Gate Street is full of cut-piece (remnant) shops. In the Nainiappa Naicken Street-NSC Bose Road area are several old names associated with the best in jewellery and diamonds. Gujarati settlers in Madras for over 100 years, Bapalal's, Surajmal's, Veecumsees – who later built the Sapphire Theatre complex – all still have shops here though they have also established plush showrooms on Cathedral Road, closer to the more modern heart of the city, Mount Road, from the 1980s. Lungi shops are to be found in their numbers in Angappa Naicken Street, Thambu Chetty Street, Armenian Street and Mannady Street. Kasi Chetty Street and Narayana Mudali Street are lined with shops selling plasticware and 'fancy goods', the former also specialising in pens and rivalling Burma Bazaar in its range of 'foreign' goods. Hardware and steel goods, steel trunks shops as well as glass and plywood shops occupy much of Nainiappa Naicken Street, Devaraja Mudali Street, Sembudoss Street, Rasappa Chetty Street, Errabalu Chetty Street, Jones Street, Post Office Road, Mooker Nallamuthu Street, Venkatachala Mudali Street and Mannady Street. Engineering equipment in all its variety is to be found in Angappa Naicken, Linghi Chetty, Thambu Chetty, Errabalu Chetty and Mannady Streets. On Nainiappa Naicken Street and Govindappa Naicken Street are wholesale dealers in bulk chemicals and surgical equipment, the former also offering a wide range of perfumes, while on Venkatachala Mudali Street it is paint. On Narayanappa Naicken Street is an antique market of sorts – the left-overs from old buildings pulled down are displayed for sale here. Between Armenian Street and Linghi Chetty Street, there are lorry booking offices by the score. And on Broadway are a host of optical goods and bicycle shops. Also near Broadway, on McClean Street, is Thomas Rodrigo & Sons, dating to around 1880, a one-stop shop for all religious and decorative material for Christian worship and celebration. There are said to be 300 shops in George Town selling temple requisites.

In many of these streets are also found old Madras institutions, often run by migrants from the North who have become an integral part of the City. For instance, in Govindappa Naicken Street is Arya Bhavan which, in 1915, introduced Madras to Gujarati sweets and savouries, *pooris* and potatoes. Today, the much-remodelled restaurant, run by founder M B Sharma's grandsons, offers South Indian cuisine as well as its traditional North Indian specialities. But Arya Bhavan sweets and *halwas* are still a name to reckon with. Then, in Nainiappa Naicken Street, there has been from 1930 Dadha & Co, once the city's leading name in pharmaceutical retailing and distribution. The Rajasthani family founded its business in Genguamman Street in 1914 and today has moved into pharmaceutical manufacturing, but the retail outlet still exists, run by a family charitable trust. Also on this street is the Chennapura Aradhana Samajam, established in 1890 by Moogalur Cunniah Chetty and moving into its own building in 1895. It pioneered a mid-day meal scheme with 13 students and still continues with the scheme for several more students. In Rasappa Chetty Street from 1825 is 'Perungayam' Ramanujam Chetty's, a tiny shop with oil lamps that till the Millennium shunned electricity. Started to sell herbal medicines, it built its reputation on its asafoetida and betelnut powder, both still specialities. The shop is now looked after by the sixth generation who rent the premises from a fourth generation owner! Rather different from the rest of George Town, it maintains strict – and early – office hours and lunch breaks!

On NSC Bose Road, opposite the High Court, Smith Stocking & Co still does business, now the oldest pharmacy in George Town, having been established in 1913. Established even earlier is a pharmacy that was a neighbour, Appah & Co (1894), but it is no longer in business, though descendants of the family run a pharmacy elsewhere in Anna Nagar.

6. Temples in 'Thimmappa-town'

Madras and its suburbs have over 600 Hindu temples, many of them historic shrines of ancient villages that, in time, were swallowed by the growing metropolis. The temples of George Town, however, are unique because they were the first temples to be built in the new settlement of Madras that was to grow into the city of today.

The Patnam Perumal Temple that Beri Thimmappa built, also known as the Chennakesava Perumal Temple, was the 'Town Temple' from the day it was consecrated, a day un-recorded though the existence of the temple is noted in the records of 1648. Describing the temple in 1673, Dr Fryer wrote: "Madras...enjoys... one PAGOD, contained in a square stone-wall, wherein are a number of Chappels...not under one Roof, but distinctly separate, though altogether, they bear the name of one intire PAGODA. The work is inimitably durable but admitting neither light nor air...On the walls of good sculpture were obscene images, where ARETINE might have furnished his fancy for Bawdy Postures...The Floor is stoned...Their outside show workmanship and cost enough, wrought around with monstrous Effigies; so that OLEUM and OPERAM PERDERE, Pains and Cost to no purpose may not improperly be applied to them. Their gates are commonly the highest of the work..." In this house of worship, town meetings were often held and, at them, excitement, it is recorded, often ran high! But this was the one temple that never caused a caste dispute.

Both Thimmappa and Nagabattan are referred to, in a law suit nearly two centuries after their death, as having endowed this 'Great Town Pagoda', the latter's endowment even being referred to as being in 1646. It is quite possible that Nagabattan endowed and built a small temple which Thimmappa two years later enlarged into the 'Great Town Pagoda', or it could be the other way round; Fryer certainly refers to it as towering over the buildings that surrounded it. There is also a tradition that the Kesava Perumal Temple was first built and that, later, the Chenna Mallikeswarar temple was added to it, this perhaps explaining the Thimappa – Nagabattan controversy.

This temple, which is clearly indicated in Pitt's map of 1709 as a 90-yard square, and occupying the spot where the High Court has now risen, survived the ravages of the French but was pulled down in 1757 by the British – the bricks and stones being used in the building of the Fort's new north wall! As compensation for this destruction, the Company in February 1762 offered the Hindus of Chennapatnam 565½ pagodas (to pay for the houses pulled down) and an area in Gengu Ramiah Street, by Devaraja Mudali Street, equal to that occupied by the century-old shrine (23,944 sq ft). And it is on this site that there arose the twin-temples, the Vaishnava Chenna Kesava Perumal and Saivite Chenna

Mallikeswarar, which survive in Flower Bazaar to this day, but now well hidden by police station, vehicles and trees, and almost forgotten as well. Governor Pigot's *dubash* and the last Chief Merchant of the Company, Manali Muthukrishna Mudaliar, opened a subscription list in 1762 to build this new 'Town Temple', himself subscribing 5,202 pagodas and the Government contributing a further 1,173 pagodas. A total of 15,652 pagodas was subscribed, work began on the temple and it was consecrated in 1766, though work continued until 1780.

Beri Thimmappa (Thimmanna, as most records call him, but who, his descendants[7] insist, was Thimmappa), negotiator for Day and temple builder, was instrumental in creating the first 'Black Town' to the north of the factory, bringing in settlers from many parts of the surrounding country, but especially from his Nellore area. He, like Day and Cogan, is scarcely remembered today. Kasi Viranna, Sunku Rama Chetty and Thambu Chetty were Thimmappa's aides – and are remembered in road names today. But not Thimmappa! Thimmappa, who, it is stated, had a seat in Council and was entitled to a five-gun salute, died in 1678. Kasi Viranna succeeded Thimmappa as Chief Merchant and when he died in 1680 he received a 30-gun salute! When Viranna's wife was to be cremated with his body, the Governor prohibited it, the earliest ban on *sati* by Government. Viranna was succeeded as Chief Merchant by Pedda Venkatadri, Thimmappa's brother, who, in turn, was succeeded in 1689 by Alangatha Pillai, the most outstanding of the early *dubashes*.

Though public recognition there is little, the Thimmappa connection with Madras survives to this day, a fact which captured the limelight briefly during a couple of the celebrations that marked the 350th year of the city and has appeared to have faded from memory thereafter. It was revealed at that time that a firm of commission agents and grain and spice merchants, Appah & Co, had been founded in Madras in 1894 by descendants of Beri Thimmappa. In 1913, the shop was in Audiappa Naicken Street, next to the family home, and its partners were Ketty Thimmappa Bhashyam Naidu and Ketty Narayanappa Naidu, who received temple honours from the 'Town Temple' built by their ancestors. It developed as one of the city's leading pharmacies from 1928 but closed down in the 1960s. Amongst the descendants of Appah & Co's partners are the proprietors of Narayanappah & Co, pharmacists now in Anna Nagar. Another descendant is a young doctor who, heritage unknown to the organisers or the contestants, was quite coincidentally one of the

45. *The Chenna Kesavaperumal Temple, one of the twin temples of George Town...the 'new' city's first, rebuilt after the wars with the French.*

46. *One of the* mandirs *of Sowcarpet...where the North worships in the South.*

47. *Memories of the Armenian nation...in a garden church behind high walls.*

48. *St Mary's Co-Cathedral...where the Fort's first church is remembered.*

quizmasters at the commemorative quiz contest that was one of the few celebrations that marked the little-remembered 350th anniversary of Madras. A distinguished guest at the prize distribution was Alavandar Naidu, than the oldest surviving descendant of Beri Thimmappa.

Alavandar Naidu, who in an interview at the time recalled the heyday of Appah & Co, when it held national agencies for several pharmaceuticals, also recalled his brother K Venkataswamy Naidu who was Mayor of Madras and a Minister in Rajaji's Cabinet. *Appah Gardens*, Kilpauk, on Appah Gardens Road near Taylor's Road, was then the garden house of the family. And in Bhashyam Naidu Park nearby there is a bust of their father, great-great-great-great grandson of Beri Thimmappa, one of the founders of the city. This 'First Family of Madras' descends through Beri Thimmappa's only child, a daughter, who married into the Ketty family, which still calls Madras home.

While Thimmappa's descendants are still associated with the temples their ancestors built in George Town, so are those of other 'first families'. Almost all the historic temples of George Town are the outcome of the generosity of former Chief Merchants and *dubashes*. Nearly as old as the first Town Temple is 'Mally Carjun's Old Pagoda'. This temple, Mallikeswara, at the northern end of Linghi Chetty Street, is historically documented as far back as 1652. Rebuilding took place between 1897 and 1925. In the temple are the statues of the 63 Nayanmar. Lally quartered the regiment named after him here during his siege of Madras. Built not far from it, and at about the same time, when the outer walls of the Fort were being completed, was the Kalahastiswarar Temple in the heart of Coral Merchants' Street. Alangatha Pillai in the 1680s built what is now the heart of the Sri Ekambareswarar Temple in south Mint Street. This Saiva temple, known in the official records as 'Allingall's Pagoda' and marked in Pitt's map, was at first used by both the Right Hand and Left Hand Castes, but was later recognised as belonging to the former. A statue of a devotee is in the temple; it is that of Ve Mu - Appukutti Chettiar who built the *gopuram* (tower). Curiously, Alangatha Pillai is commemorated quite some distance from the temple – in a street name in Triplicane!

The Ekambareswar Temple became the chief temple of the Gujarati Saurashtrian weavers who had first settled around Madurai and Tirunelveli in the 11th Century and some of whom, in the 17th Century, moved to the growing entrepot of Madras. They were followed in the late 18th Century by the diamond and silk merchants and the Kachchhi traders, who gave Sowcarpet its name. In the 18th and 19th Centuries came more Gujarati traders, including the Gujarat Parsis who made Royapuram their home. Today, there are around 50,000 Gujaratis in the city, many of whose roots here go back over 300 years.

The 18th Century temples of George Town include Muthialpet's Chintadri Pillaiyar Kovil, in Devaraja Mudali Street, built in 1717 near the Mallikeswara Temple and over which arose a Komatti Chetty-Beri Chetty dispute. The Government had to arbitrate, before the temple, which was closed, reopened. Armenian Street's Kachchaleswarar Temple was built around 1725, perhaps by *dubash* Kalvai Chetty but certainly on his land. The 'Great Kachali Pagoda' gave the street its original name, 'Katchala Pagoda Street', and it is recorded that dancing girls once used to live on this street. These "singing women", the records state, were "part of the equipage of a great man when he goes abroad," preceding him in the procession. This temple of the Left Hand Caste was the cause of one of 'Black Town's' first bitter caste disputes. Government arbitration led to a new approach to the temple being built, one that did not encroach on Right Hand Caste property. Also as part of the settlement, the dancing girls, in residence here from about 1700, were permitted to remain in the houses from which they had been evicted during the dispute, when the houses were handed over to Brahmin families.

The Krishnaswami Temple in Muthialpet, built around 1787, was focal point of another major caste dispute. When the Right Hand Caste hoisted their flag in place of the Left Hand Caste's in 1790, a riot ensued, Government arbitration leading to the hoisting of the ensign of St George as a compromise! In this area too is the Bairagimadam Temple built by Ketti Narayanan, the son-in-law of Beri Thimmappa. This temple, once known as Lorraine's (Narayan's) Pagoda, is dedicated to Lord Sri Ventakeswara and is situated between Mint Street and China Bazaar. The Beri Chetties built one of the finest temples in George Town in the 1670s, the Kandaswami Temple in Rasappa Chetty Street, near the south end of Mint Street. This shrine, with an idol from Tirupporur, is richly endowed, was renovated in the 1930s and has an annual festival of significance in Madras. Here, too, the famed social reformer Ramalinga Swamigal sang the immortal *Deivamanimaalai*. It was at the Kalikambal Kameswarar Temple in Thambu Chetty Street that the Emperor Shivaji is said to have worshipped in October 1677. Centuries later, Subramania

Bharati used to worship there. A new 10-m high *rajagopuram* was added to this temple in the late 1980s. Near here is the Sri Krishna Temple, perhaps the oldest Krishna temple in the city. It has a 15-foot tall *stambh* (pillar), unique because it is a single piece of granite.

Other old temples include the Adikesava Perumal Temple in Acharappan Street and the Chandraprabhu Bhagwan Jain Swetambar Temple in Mint Street, looking for all the world like a residence on the ground floor, but developed in North Indian shrine-style on the upper floors. Nearby, on Mint Street was constructed in 1994 the Chandraprabhu Naya Jain Mandir, built in the beautiful, sculpted marble style of the Mt Abu Jain temples. This shrine was built on the site of the 90-year-old Swetambar Jain Temple. On Chandrappa Mudali Street was consecrated in 1978 the Sri Mahavir Swamy Digambar Jain Temple, reflecting Jaipuri construction here and there. Since the 1980s, several other Jain temples – all in the Mt Abu style – have been built in different parts of the City.

Though there were caste riots in the earliest Company times – the first dispute recorded in 1652 – there do not seem to have been religious riots from the earliest days of Madras. Places of worship of all religions stood cheek by jowl in George Town! The Company records mention two mosques in 'Black Town', the older one reported to have been due east of the first 'Town Temple', which would put it by the present subway location, and the second one in Muthialpet, built in Governor Yale's day. But there seems to be some confusion about this second mosque. For it is also recorded that the earliest mosque in this area was built by that redoubtable successor of Thimmappa, Kasi Viranna, a Chief Merchant so close to the Golconda Sultanate and its several representatives that he even had a Muslim name, Hasan Khan. Kasi Viranna's mosque is stated to have been completed just before he died in 1680, in what later became known – and is still better known – as Moor Street (and NOT Moore), where some of the best residences of the 'Moors' of early Madras were situated. The main Bohra mosque, the Saifee mosque, is on this street too. The Muslim settlements in Triplicane also first date back to the time the Company let out the village of Triplicane to Kasi Viranna. It was Kasi Viranna who established, in the 1670s, the first joint stock company in India, what the records call 'Cassa Verona and Company'.

A newer mosque in Muthialpet is the Masjid Mamoor, built in the 18th Century and rebuilt by the Nawab of Arcot's family in granite over a hundred years ago. It is located in Angappa Naicken Street, the northern part of which is a Muslim locality. More recent additions to the mosque are architecturally unique, the vast main hall supported by only the outer walls and two pillars. There is space here for over 5,000 worshippers at a time.

With the Portuguese settlement at San Thomé much older than Day's Madras, Catholicism was already well established in the region when Fort St George was built. When the Company found that the Portuguese and the *topasses* (=wearers of *topees*/hats, therefore *mestizos*, Portuguese-Indians) were well-acquainted with the languages, customs and manners of the region, it promptly employed them in subordinate positions, recruited them for the gendarmerie and encouraged them as tradesmen. Thus, in its first years, Fort St George had a much larger Catholic population than a Protestant one and the first priest in the Fort, Fr Ephraim de Nevers, a Frenchman, served it, though it was of the Italian Capuchin Order. With a growing Portuguese and *mestizo* population from San Thomé serving Fort George, and many setting just to the north of it, the Catholics built a church at one end of the British settlement – the Church of the Assumption of Our Lady – a tablet in the Church reading "built in 1640? Extended in 1857". This church, now rebuilt, survives in Portuguese Church Street in northern George Town (an area once called 'The Great Paracheri' – the village of those of low caste), but unrecognised as being of historic importance despite being one of the oldest surviving churches built in what might be called British India. The Assumption Church, an unprotected monument, was without warning pulled down in the early 1990s and a new church, with none of the weathered charm of the old, consecrated in 1994. The only memory of the old building is a painting of it in the new, on the inside, above the front entrance, that worshippers are unlikely to even glance at as they leave.

That query alone after the '1640' has, over the years, had many wondering whether it did indeed pre-date Fr De Nevers' St Andrew's Church in the Fort which was destroyed by the British after the French quit Madras, and the priests externed from the Fort because the Company felt that Madras had "suffered greatly by the number of priests and popish inhabitants...who have acted a very treacherous part to us continually in that place..." But as the power of the French declined in the region, the

Government permitted the development of de Nevers' church in Armenian Street, his second, that has grown today into the Cathedral of St Mary of the Angels. This has been, from 1886, the Cathedral of Madras; San Thomé was the Cathedral of Mylapore. The two dioceses, separated by the Cooum River, are now the diocese of Madras-Mylapore.

The origins of the Cathedral go back to 1658 when Fr de Nevers was granted the ground here by government to build a second church for his flock. The records state he put up the 'open pandall chappell' on this site that year. This structure, decaying in the 1690s, was rebuilt in 1692. Damaged during the second French siege, it was rebuilt in 1775 and enlarged in 1785. The Capuchins had inscribed on its gates the date 1642, the year of their first church in Madras, and that date has been preserved at the Cathedral's entrance, despite all the improvements that have taken place over the years and the attainment of Apostolic status in 1834 and Cathedral status in 1886. It is, however, contended by many that the 1642 date refers to the establishment of a cemetery here. The church was reconstructed in 1837, altered in 1857 and further improvements went on till 1931, when the last major work was done. In the Cathedral are some beautiful old oils of the Crucifixion and Mary Magdalene. Attached to the Cathedral is the Moorat Chapel, last resting place of that eminent Armenian family. In the Cathedral too are other Armenian tombstones. A niche for St Anthony in the Cathedral draws thousands of all faiths on Tuesdays. The niche was created long after some Portuguese sailors had gifted the statue of the saint to the Church in 1929.

In the Cathedral's campus was established in 1839 the first Catholic School in Madras, St Mary's Seminary; the school started by the Rt Rev Joseph Carew, still survives in Armenian Street, but with no seminary to its name. The seeds for this institution were, however, sown when Father de Nevers started his school in the Church in Fort St. George in 1642. It taught the three R's in English and Portuguese to British, Portuguese, and Indian students whose fathers worked in the Fort. When the Church was razed in 1753 by the British, the school moved to its new location in New Black Town. And there it developed as the Seminary.

St. Mary's Seminary became a second grade college of the University of Madras in 1882 and was re-named St. Mary's College. Under subsequent regulations, it became St Mary's European High School in 1906. After Independence, the 'European' became 'Anglo Indian' in the name of the School and, in 1985, higher secondary classes were added. It is today called St. Mary's Anglo-Indian Higher Secondary School. It wouldn't be too far off the mark if the School claimed to be the oldest English language Roman Catholic school in the country, even Asia, given its seeding in 1642. St Andrew's, sadly destroyed by the British in 1752, was resurrected when a new St Andrew's was built in Vepery in 1830. Around this time, the Capuchins put down further roots in North Madras, spreading from St Mary's.

Next door to the Cathedral, hidden behind yellow walls and massive 10-foot-high black wooden doors, silver studded but always open during the day, is the Armenian Church, built in 1772 on the site of the old Armenian cemetery. A new cemetery was established on The Island, opposite the St. Mary's Cemetery, many years later, but is in total neglect today and with slums all around completely hiding it. Beyond the doors of the church is a simple but spotlessly clean haven of peace where the plumeria blooms rich in the courtyard-garden paved with red brick and elaborately decorated and inscribed gravestones. In the church are gleaming pews and an all-wood altar built in 1712 and brought here from the first Armenian church. In the belfry are the biggest bells in Madras. And the Church's proudest possession is a block-printed Armenian Bible dating to 1686. This church of the Armenian Orthodoxy, who began to settle in Madras in the 1660s, displays a plaque reading '1712'. That date commemorates the building of the first Armenian church in 'Old Black Town', a timber edifice that was not far from the 'Town Temple' and which suffered the same fate. From the time the Rev D H Davathian, last officiating priest, died in 1963, the Armenian Church of St Mary was lovingly tended by George Gregorian and his wife, who moved here from Calcutta in 1964. In 1997, they were succeeded by a young Armenian caretaker whose home was Bangalore. He too has moved – to Calcutta – and a local caretaker tends the church where restoration began in 2007 and has resulted in a beautiful campus of well-maintained buildings, where an ambience of quietude and serenity reigns midst the bustle of George Town. In the street behind the Armenian Church is St Columban's School, established in 1841.

Not far from the Armenian church there was built the first church by a Protestant missionary, Benjamin Schultze of the German Lutheran Mission (operating out of Tranquebar). He arrived in Madras in 1726, the first Protestant missionary to make Madras his home.

While the Company encouraged French Roman Catholics and German Lutherans, it steadfastly refused to admit into Madras British Protestant missionaries, fearing Church interference and even competition! Thus, while St Mary's in the Fort was built as a Company Church, and the Lutherans built their church about 50 years later outside the Fort, the first British mission church was not built till 1810. This was the London Missionary Society Church in Davidson Street, 'Black Town', built by William C Loveless, the first L M S Missionary, who had arrived in Madras in 1805 and founded the Bible Society. Once called the Loveless Church, someone in recent years woke up to the unfortunate implication of the name and, so, it is the William Charles Church now. The Church Missionary Society was not slow in following Loveless' lead and the first church for "the Native Protestants" was opened in Popham's Broadway on October 11, 1820, the Rev Dr Rottler preaching in Tamil to an overflowing congregation in the church now known as Tucker's Church. This church taking the name of the second CMS Missionary in Madras, Rev. John Tucker, was built after Government had, in 1817, stopped the CMS building its church near the Mint following protests from the Hindu residents of the area. It was consecrated in 1820. Rottler was another of the Germans from the Tranquebar Mission; for many years pastors from this mission served the CMS. On the same road as Tucker's Church is the 'English Church' of the L M S, whose traditions were developed by the Methodist missionary, James Lynch, and the L M S's Loveless and Traveller. Lynch established the Wesley Methodist Mission in 1819 in a church built in Royapettah that year. This first church of the Mission was rebuilt in 1853 and was consecrated as Wesley Church. It is the main Methodist Church in Madras. Next to it was founded the Meston Teachers' Training College in 1937. Lynch founded the Broadway Wesley Church in 1822 and it evolved as the Broadway Tamil Wesley Church in 1861. The Scots arrived in 1837, John Anderson the first in a long line of Highland missionaries. And he immediately got down to starting the school that today is Madras Christian.

Anderson's name survives in church and in Anderson Day School (1875), one of the three schools started in George Town by Rev P Rajah Gopaul (Rajagopal), the first Indian Christian to take Holy Orders. The others are CSI Rajagopal (1874) and Mint Middle (1885). Other old Protestant schools in the city are Wesley (1851) and Monahan Girls' School (1858) in Royapettah and St Ebba's (1886) in Mylapore. It was in Royapettah that Lynch bought a house for himself in 1818 and built his methodist church. Lynch is a name no longer remembered in any institution, but other early missionary names are still remembered in schools named after them. Fabricius (1849) in Vepery, Kellett (1889) in Triplicane, and Northwick (1852) in Royapuram. The Rev Miller of Madras Christian College and his sister Elizabeth were the founders of Northwick, which had its roots in a girls' school Anderson had got his associate John Braidwood's wife Isabella to start.

An English Failure, An Indian Success

In the last quarter of 1906, Madras was hit by the worst financial crisis the city was ever to suffer. Of the three best known British commercial names in 19th Century Madras, one crashed, a second had to be resurrected by a distress sale and the third had to be bailed out by a benevolent benefactor! It was out of this financial shambles that the Indian Bank rose after a circular issued on November 2, 1906 had stated: "The failure of Arbuthnot's and Binny's has set many people thinking as to whether an Indian bank on a financially sound basis should not now be established."

The agency house to close shop was considered the soundest of the three. In Madras today, Gillanders, Arbuthnot survives as the branch office of a Calcutta firm, but in the 19th Century Arbuthnot's was the Madras-based company that spawned the Calcutta firm and many others in India and Britain. Parry's may have been the earliest of these three British firms and Binny's may have had the oldest associations with Madras, but it was Arbuthnot & Co that was the city's strongest commercial organisation in the 19th Century.

George Arbuthnot, an Aberdeenshire Scot, came out to Madras as a free merchant in 1800 and joined the firm of Francis Latour & Co, a company founded by a veteran British naval officer who arrived in Madras with Admiral Harland's fleet in 1777 and found trading with the Royal Navy more profitable than serving with it. His first business was with the fleet and the Hanoverian Regiments. His position in the Madras scene of the time may be judged from the fact that he was married in Government House *in 1780. Arbuthnot and John de Monte took over the firm in 1810 and it became Arbuthnot, de Monte & Co, before finally becoming Arbuthnot & Co, presumably on John de Monte's death in 1821, without an heir to succeed him. This company was sponsor of some of the earliest industry in India; it established the Madras Portland Cement Works, the Bangalore Bricks & Tiles Works, the Reliance Engineering Works, the Chittalvasal Jute Mills and several other factories. In its century of existence, several persons who were kin of the Arbuthnots who ran the company, or who were kin of theirs, became men of substance and power in England and in India. Amongst them were an acting Governor of the Madras Presidency, a Governor of the Bank of England, a Madras Civilian and several senior army officers. One of the military branch was Field Marshal Viscount Gough whose daughter married Archibald Arbuthnot, a nephew of the founder of the Company. Their son, Sir George Gough Arbuthnot, was the head of Arbuthnot & Co at the time of the crash. He was a member of the Madras Legislative Council and a prominent figure in Madras society at the time.*

Sir George's social eminence had not a little to do with the travails of the firm. He used the deposits those in his social circle made for speculation and personal advantage. Much money was also spent on searching for gold in the Nilgiris and the Anamalais, on investment in South American railway projects, on new South African gold fields and in the plantation crops of the West Indies. Arbuthnot & Co was drained dry. When P Macfadyen, senior partner of P Macfadyen & Co, London, Arbuthnot's correspondent and associate in England, and an old Madras Arbuthnot hand, committed suicide on October 20, 1906, the crisis broke. Both firms petitioned the courts on the 22nd to be declared insolvent. The auditors appointed by the Official Assignee estimated Arbuthnot & Co's liabilities at Rs 27 million and its assets at only Rs 7½ million! The firm had 2,300 operating accounts in India with balances of Rs 2.75 million and about 4,000 fixed deposits with claims amounting to over Rs 25 million. With the assets being described as being only on paper and "beyond all belief, worthless, which crumble to dust when touched," there was no way to meet the claims of the depositors, who were almost any and everyone in Madras who had savings or some money to invest.

Describing the scene at Arbuthnot's when it put up a notice announcing suspension of all payments, The Hindu *of the day wrote, "Since Saturday last there has been a great commotion in Madras. The anguish of the disappointed creditors can be more imagined than described. A regular panic had taken hold of them and a rush was made to the High Court where it was understood that an application would be made for the taking of insolvency proceedings."*

The paper went on to say, "The consequences of this sudden and disastrous failure...will... mean the ruin of many hundreds of families in Southern India. The firm was the most popular one in Madras until the new firm, Arbuthnot Industries, was started. At this time there was a shrewd suspicion in the minds of some that all was not as it should be. But the public confidence in the integrity of the firm was so great that its transactions did not in any way suffer. An enormous business was being done and vast sums of money belonging to Maharajas, Rajas, and Zamindars, the well-to-do official classes, the Governments of native states, public charitable endowments and private trusts, mutual benefit funds and Nidhis, besides the small hard earned investments of the earning classes were all there... To the vast majority of the investors who with their helpless dependants can be counted by the thousands in Southern India, the insolvency of the firm is a calamity which might well nigh mean their ruin. At present the feeling is one of general consternation in the city and as the news spread over the Presidency, the extent of suffering can be realised. It will be years before the large body of our countrymen who have been affected by the sudden blow can hope to recover from its effects. To the confiding public it had seemed that the solvency of Arbuthnot & Co was almost as stable as the British Government itself. It cannot be gainsaid that the prestige of the British capitalist and his reputation for integrity and right dealing had been associated in men's minds with the long established name of Arbuthnot and Co in Madras."

When The Hindu *announced on October 23rd the death of Macfadyen, it thundered, "The public will be shocked to hear that a man who was at the head of a firm of merchants who enjoyed for such a long period and in such abundant measure their wholehearted confidence and respect should not only have caused the wreck of so many homes and unspeakable anguish in many households but has closed his inglorious career by an act of supreme selfishness and cowardice... It will be true to say that it is sufficient to blast for a long time to come the reputation of Englishmen for probity and righteousness."*

In the aftermath of the crash several things happened. Sir Arthur Lawley, Governor of Madras and himself a victim of the bankrupt company, launched a public fund to raise money to help the weaker sections who had lost everything in Arbuthnot's. Amongst the scores of letters in The Hindu *on the scandal, there was one that suggested the starting of an Indian bank "now that European integrity and honesty (have come) under a cloud." Sir George was tried on eleven counts which could generally be summed up as "maintaining false accounts and diverting credits to his personal accounts" and those of his family. After he had been sentenced to 18 months R I,* The Hindu *wrote, "For a dozen years now, the business of Messrs Arbuthnot & Co has been a swindle of the vilest description. The firm has kept on a banking business under false pretences, decoying innumerable innocent men and women into investing in its rapacious maw all their hard earned savings and earnings, moneys which the members of the firm could have had no reasonable prospect of repaying in full. How many widows, orphans, old pensioners, Government officials and others have been lured into the net of the pretended pompousness of this firm to deposit their moneys in, not knowing that Messrs Arbuthnot & Co was but a white sepulchre?"*

Parry's and Binny's too had their problems. The former owed about Rs 2.5 million to the public and the latter about Rs 4 million. Parry's managed to raise a quick loan from a benefactor in London to withstand the run, but Binny's couldn't raise the money. And so Binny's passed out of the hands of the Binny family, Sir James Mackay, later to become the Earl of Inchcape, purchasing the firm and settling all creditors by December 1908.

Eventually, the most constructive thing to come out of the 1906 scandal was the Indian Bank. A young vakil, V Krishnaswami Aiyer, later to become an eminent lawyer and High Court Judge but at the time just making his way up, was then active on behalf of several Arbuthnot creditors. Taking his cue from the letter that appeared in The Hindu, *he set out with a will to promote an Indian bank. He got together eight other prominent citizens of Madras who also felt, in the words of the historian of the Bank, R K Seshadri, "that a bank which depended on the savings of those in the South had to be incorporated locally and managed by Indians who were locally known and respected."*

Joint stock banking as such was not unknown in Madras. As early as 1682 there is mention of banking activity in Fort St George, the Council accepting deposits. Then, from the late 18th Century, British joint stock banks were founded, as we have already seen, and from the late 19th Century other British banks began establishing branch offices in Madras. Several Indian banks were also founded in the Presidency; the Tanjore Permanent Fund that was to grow into the Thanjavur Bank was started in 1901; the South Indian Bank, Tinnevelly, in 1903; the predecessor of the present Kumbakonam City Union Bank in 1904; the Canara Banking Corporation, Udipi, now the Corporation Bank, and the Canara Hindu Permanent Fund, Mangalore, now the Canara Bank, both in 1906. But none of these Indian banks operated in Madras nor were they Madras-founded. The capital of the Presidency, the chief city of the South, sorely lacked an Indian bank.

It was to remedy this that Krishnaswami Aiyer and his co-promoters sent out their first circular on November 2, 1906, inviting the public's views on the possibility of starting "a Native Bank in Madras." The encouraging response they received prompted them to call a meeting that was attended by 28 citizens. At this meeting it was decided to go ahead with plans to establish an Indian bank. What resulted from these plans was The Indian Bank Limited, which was registered on March 5, 1907 and opened its doors for business on August 15th.

From their very first circular it was clear that the promoters were relying on "the indigenous bankers" of South India, the Nattukkottai Chettiars, for finance and the business acumen to found the bank and make a success of it. In the event, though only three Chettiars attended the historic meeting at the Mahajana Sabha Hall, the community rallied around its leaders and helped finance the bank and run it successfully till nationalisation changed bank administration. In the process, the Bank did much to help Chettiar business between the two World Wars.

From these beginnings, the Bank, for all its conservative traditions, has grown into one of the Big Twelve. But long before that it had continued traditions established centuries before joint stock banking came to India. It was an English banker who wrote in 1926. "It may be accepted that a system of banking, eminently suited to India's then requirements was in force in that country many centuries before the science of banking became an accomplished fact in England. It is true that the methods of old in force in India were vastly different from the European idea of banking today and partook more of money lending, money changing and later of the hundi business; nevertheless, as applied to the conditions then existing in India, they admirably acted their part and must be recognised as having rendered immense services to the country as a whole, particularly when we keep in view the enormous agricultural interest of India." The Indian Bank has helped keep that tradition alive.

17

The Road to Poonamallee

1. The civic tradition

Ancient salt pans, now the Salt Cotaurs railway goods yards, 45 acres in extent and established in 1859, were just north of that part of Vepery – an ancient village (Veppore or Vepamaree – *veppam = neem*, therefore *neem*-town or trees?) once known for its palmyrah and coconut gardens – which lies in the right angle formed by the railway line south and the line north. To the north of Poonamallee High Road, just before Vepery, are Victoria Public Hall, what's left of Ashok Vihar (the pillar is there but not the garden restaurant), My Ladye's Garden, the former pavilion of the Ashley Biggs Railway Institute, the Corporation's Nehru and Indoor Stadiums – all in what was once People's Park – stately *Ripon Building*, home of the Corporation of Madras that is now Chennai, and the new buildings of the expanding Central railway station.

People's Park was 116 acres in extent when created in 1859/60 on the wide, open esplanade that remained outside the west town wall after that wall had been demolished; now it has shrunk considerably. An ancient potter's village – documented in 1769 – existed on this site. Once, a fine garden with ornamental palms and well-laid-out walks and flower-beds, this brainchild of Sir Charles Trevelyan was then the City's largest lung. Today, little survives, not even the name, the Park being overrun with 'improvements' and intrusions.

Sir Charles, who married Macaulay's sister Hannah More when Macaulay and he were John Company men in the 1820s, was a man of the utmost integrity. His brief spell as Governor of the Presidency, from early 1859 until his recall in mid-1860, was marked as much by tremendous civic activity as the creation of a tempest in the Governor-General's comfortable teapot. For bluntly minuting his disagreement with the Government of India's budget and its proposed taxation policy, it was considered that the Governor of Madras was guilty of "palpable and plain insubordination" and he was recalled to England. Two years later, the brilliant Trevelyan was back in India, the Central Government's Financial Member of Council, "his financial views that he had so unwisely made public" now having been found "just".

Charles Trevelyan, little remembered in Madras for the People's Park he created and only slightly better remembered for his efforts to provide the City with adequate drinking water – Trevelyan Basin near Elephant Gate was part of that effort – is the man many more recognise as the creator of the high traditions of the once-famed Indian Civil Service, whose seeds he sowed while in England betwixt the Madras and Calcutta appointments. But Madras remembers the man's contributions to India, and to the city, in the most insignificant way possible – a small, unused fountain in the area, with his head in bas *relief* on one side of it. This now little-noticed memorial, by the side of Victoria Public Hall, was restored in 1993 together with one room of what was better known as the Town Hall, but as these lines are written the long-prolonged restoration of what was once Madras's best theatre is nearing completion.

People's Park had, in its heyday, 11 ponds (it now has four), 5 ½ miles of road, a bandstand, a public bath, two tennis courts and the nucleus of a zoo. The main entrance to the park was from Poonamallee High Road, near where Moore Market later came up. One of the first attempts to develop People's Park into something more interesting than an airy 'lung', albeit a beautiful bit of open space, was the decision to move to its northern end the zoo that had been founded in 1855 in the gardens of the Museum in Pantheon Road.

It was Trevelyan who approved the People's Park plan, staked out the ground and turned the first sod before his recall to the UK. His successor, Sir William Denison, showed "a hearty approval of an undertaking so intimately connected with the health and pleasure of the middle-class population" and ensured the Park was completed by 1861. It was managed by a Committee of Management. The earliest record of the Park traceable, dated 1863, lists Col. W.P. Macdonald as the President of the Committee, Surgeon Major J.W. Mudge as Secretary, and, amongst its six other members, the Hon'ble Alexander J. Arbuthnot that

significant contributor to Madras over the years. The Superintendent of
the Park was D. Riordan and his house was in the Park.

Amongst the Park's ponds was Victoria Lake, in which two boats
plied for pleasure boating. Its roads included a metalled one on the eastern
verge of the Park called 'The Equestrians' Ride'. And it had two masonry
basins with fountains, a bandstand that was the centre of the Park, and
an aviary. Hundreds of trees were planted along the sides of some
stretches of road, creating avenues, and, elsewhere, trees were planted
to create small groves. To make the Park self-supporting in some
measure, hay was successfully cultivated and fetched Rs.41 a tonne!

The nucleus of its zoo was tigers, a cheetah, bears and various deer
and monkey species. Lions from South Africa and elephants were awaited
at the time of the report. The Zoo was the first 'victim' of the planned
destruction of the eastern half of this park to make way for the tracks
and buildings of the suburban terminal of the Southern Railway's northern
commuter service to Gummidipoondi and the further expansion of Central
Station.

All that's left of the park here is My Ladye's Garden where on January
1, 1933, the Kalyani Daughters gave the first public performance of
Bharata Natyam. It is still an ornamental park of sorts but no longer the
venue of an annual flower show that had been held for over a hundred
years or of other entertainments. Badly tended till 2007, this once
beautiful little garden used to be rich with fountains and ornamental
sculpture created by what is now the College of Fine Arts. Much of the
latter lay broken on the grass or stood victims of vandals; nor did the
fountains work. But restoration in 2007 has re-created enough to make
recall of My Ladye's youthful beauty now possible. The Ashoka Pillar is
now its focal point, especially for practitioners of yoga. Another institution
with the Ashoka name – Ashoka Vihar – has, however, vanished. A
health centre set up by the Corporation, it was very popular as a place
where whole families could receive advice on health. The Zoo, however,
was several years earlier re-established well outside Madras in the
southern suburb of Vandalur, 40 kilometres south of Fort St George, as
the Aringnar Anna Zoological Park but popularly called the Vandalur
Zoo. Here, a vast open-air 'green' zoo has been carved out of the forest
and developed over 600 hectare.

Opened to the public from 1985, this zoo is one of South Asia's
finest and India's largest. It hosts over 1500 fauna, including about 50

species of mammals, 60 species of birds and 30 species of reptiles. Its pride is a collection of over a dozen White Tigers, many bred in-house. Despite its distance from the city, it attracts over 2 million visitors a year. One of the showpieces of Madras, and one of the best zoos in the country, it has a very successful breeding programme and a lot of scientific animal knowhow.

The second institution threatened in this area was Moore Market and the threat to it in the early 1980s caused the first great uproar amongst Madras conservationists. The conservationists appeared to have won the battle when, suddenly, the market, a veritable shopping institution in Madras, most mysteriously went up in flames in 1985. The Railways, to whom the area was promised, could still have saved the facade and amalgamated it into a new building, but all that government authority seemed to be in was a hurry to pull this Madras landmark down as quickly as possible. A new, tasteless bit of highrise, serving as railway reservation offices and reservation centre, has risen in its place. And in the parking lot, hardly visible, is Moore Market memorialised in miniature. To its west is Town Hall and then *Ripon Building*.

When it was decided to honour Queen Victoria on her Golden Jubilee in 1887, it was agreed that two buildings be constructed in her name. One was intended to accommodate the Victoria Technical Institute founded that year; this slow-to-get-off-the-ground building on Pantheon Road, after serving for several years the purpose for which it was built, was handed over to the Museum. The other was *Victoria Public Hall,* a civic token of regard to be built by public subscription. Architects selected to construct both buildings naturally chose the characteristic Indo-Saracenic style favoured in the official Madras of the day and the buildings are splendid examples of that school of architecture. The builder of both was Namberumal Chetty.

The *Victoria Public Hall* owes its existence to the drive of Sir A T Arundel, President of the Corporation at the time and later a member of the Viceroy's Council. Arundel, who conceived this form of affirmation of loyalty to the Crown on Queen Victoria's Jubilee, ensured that adequate funds were raised and saw to it that the Hall was opened in 1887 by Lord Connemara, the Governor, who celebrated his new barony simultaneously. But Arundel's work would have been the harder if it had not been for the generosity and enthusiasm of Rajah Sir Ananda Gajapati,

49. *The* Victoria Public Hall *(left)...relic of the gaslight era, under renewal for a new beginning in 2014.*

50. *Trevelyan's services to Madras citizenry remembered... and forgotten.*

51. *Different times, different Railway styles. Central Station on right and its extension to its left and, extreme left, new railway highrise where Moore Market once was.*

52. *A vision in white...Ripon Building...the City Corporation's headquarters.*

the Maharajah of Vizianagaram. To build the Hall, 3½ acres (57 grounds) from People's Park acreage were granted to a Board of Trustees on a 99-year-lease at 8 annas (50 paise) a ground per year!

Chisholm is said to have been responsible for the Hall which, till recently managed by a Board of Trustees, though at odds with the lessor, the Corporation of Madras, was once rented out for public and private meetings, public lectures, stage performances theatrical and otherwise, balls at a time when ballroom dancing was popular, and other entertainments. It was also meant for "many other purposes conducing to the moral, social and intellectual welfare, or rational recreation of the public of Madras."

It was also here that on December 5, 1896, there was the first screening of films in Madras. Madras owed this novelty to T Stevenson of the Madras Photographic Store. All this led to the Hall becoming better known as *The Town Hall*. The interior of the Hall is decidedly gaslight Victorian and in its run-down condition it did indeed seem like "a sleazy strip-joint", as a 'Magazine of Madras' described it in the 1980s. As we entered the new Millennium it began to look even more decrepit, despite being presided over from on high by Queen Victoria's stage presence. The lessees eventually handed over the theatre to the Corporation around 2009 and not long afterwards restoration work began, giving it reason to dream of possible glory again as a badly-needed theatre in North Madras. But work has dragged on, though an end appears to be in sight as these lines are written. Once, it seated 600 in the lower hall, 600 in the upper hall and 200 in the balcony. Rentals in the early 1900s ranged from Rs.3-8-0 to Rs.40 per night depending on room and usage.

Succeeding to occupancy of VPH in 1939 after the Suguna Vilasa Sabha, founded in 1891 by Pammal Sambanda Mudaliar as a pioneer of modern Tamil theatre, moved to Mount Road was the Chennapuri Andhra Mahasabha, founded in George Town in 1914 by Sir P Theagaroya Chetty. Its aim was to promote Telugu culture and literature, which it successfully did in the 30-odd years it was in *The Town Hall*. But it also did much for Billiards, Chess and Table Tennis in the city and between 1948 and 1952 helped found the District Associations for these games in its premises. In 1966, it moved to its own premises built in *VPH* property and neighbouring the Hall. The Mahasabha's place was occupied by the South Indian Athletic Assoication after it vacated its nearby Moore Pavilion, but this historic sporting association has moved out and hopes it can renew its past glory in its new home.

Between the *VPH* and erstwhile Moore Market was an area that was once known as *Guzili Bazaar*, where the old and the worn-out, the stolen and the second-hand from the City's homes could be bought for a song. In more recent times, you paid fancy prices for similar 'bargains' in the row of shops to the east of Moore Market and the barrow-shops that, from the 1970s, took over all space around the market, virtually hiding it and strangling its life within. The Market in its heyday consisted of the main Indo-Saracenic block – where 'fancy-goods emporia' around a courtyard did brisk business, mainly with visitors from neighbouring States and abroad – and the poultry, meat, pets and vegetable and fruit bazaars behind, more frequented by the local populace. A large number of shops in the Market also specialised in second-hand books – frequented as much by students in search of bargains as by those in search of rare books.

In pre-War years, the main shopping market of the City's middle and upper classes, and until the 1970s the premier municipal market, Moore Market was conceived by Lt Col Sir George Moore, President of the then municipality. The foundation stone for the quadrangular, corner-turreted building was, appropriately, laid by him in August 1898. When the building was opened for business in November 1900 by Governor Arthur Havelock, it offered more comfortable shopping than what prevailed in the insanitary conditions found in the markets off Popham's Broadway. The move from Broadway was the brainchild of Moore who planned on transforming the *Guzili Bazaar* area into a modern 40,000 sq ft market for 'English goods', the new building to blend harmoniously with the hybrid stylings of the *VPH* and Central Station. Go-getter Moore selected R E Ellis as architect for this work, awarded the contract to A Subramania Aiyer and got the wo rk done in record time. *Guzili Bazaar* was formalised in 1910 when it moved to its new permanent premises east of the main market. As this market, named after Moore, developed, it became part of the very ethos of Madras and no visitor to Madras between the Wars would have been given the opportunity by his or her hosts to leave the city without visiting Moore Market.

In an attempt to re-create this ethos, a new 12,500 sq ft market complex, built in a vaguely 'copycat' fashion at a cost of about Rs 65 million, was opened in fast-diminishing People's Park in late 1991. Set in 1½ acres on the site of what was once the beautiful Lily Pond of People's Park, the Moore Market rubble used to fill it, the 857-shop market, popularly called the Lily Pond Complex, has since its opening been a victim of traders and the municipal authorities warring with each other on the terms of occupancy and maintenance. The result has been few occupants and the vandalising of the greater part of the complex that remained vacant, till several law courts took them over while their heritage premises were being renovated. Some business, however, still goes on inside and outside the other part of the premises, which is still the best place in Madras for book bargains.

Behind the Market were the grounds acquired by the Railways from the South India Athletic Association, which was founded in 1901. The Association, which did much to foster sporting talent in the City, and on whose track many national record-breakers (as well as light racing horse carts – *reklas*) went through their paces, was best known for its contribution to boxing; it has often been described as "the birthplace of boxing in India" (1903). From the Association's inception, the SIAA successfully ran the Park Fair and Carnival of Sport (particularly *rekla*-racing) every Christmas, another of the seasonal highlights, particularly in the years between the two Wars. In the years after Independence, all the fun of the Fair diminished till, in 1977, it was finally extinguished. When its lease ended, the SIAA began functioning from *Victoria Public Hall*, a shadow of its former self, with no grounds for its Fair. Before the Association was invited to run the Fair, a citizens' committee convened by the Corporation ran it. On December 31, 1886, a major fire, the city's biggest till then, devastated the Fair. But, Phoenix-like, it rose again and continued as an annual Madras event for nearly a hundred years.

The Sir Ashley Biggs Institute, which nurtured much railways sporting – not to mention music and dance – talent in the past, took over in 1978 the Moore Pavilion that was once the SIAA's pride. The two-storeyed Moore Pavilion, whose foundation stone was laid in 1902 by Municipal Commissioner Sir George Moore, is a charming old-world building with a sloping, tiled roof. Viewing for the members and VIPs was from the first floor, above a pillared verandah, and overlooked what used to be terraced stands and a tidy lawn. It is now completely cut off from access and is hardly maintained.

Apart from boxing in its early years, the SIAA was particularly known for its contribution to football (1902) , billiards (1903) and tennis (1906). Cricket was a major sport from 1909 till the 1930s. The Association's first President was Col Sir George Moore and its first Indian President was Sir C P Ramaswami Aiyar, elected in 1924. Its first Indian office-bearer was V Bodhaguruswami Pillai, elected to office in 1913. Indians, however, were committee members from the inception of the Association.

Between the Lily Pond Complex and the Moore Pavilion have come up the massive Jawaharlal Nehru Stadium, mainly for Football and Athletics, and a well-equipped Indoor Stadium. Unfortunately, both stadiums tend to get used as much for non-sporting activities as for sport, though Football is beginning to make greater use of it, and drawing large crowds, as the game gets professionalised in the city.

When J P L Shenoy I.C.S. became Municipal Commissioner in 1944, one of his priorities was to develop a large sports stadium in what had been People's Park. This he achieved in 1946, the Stadium's facilities focused on Football and Athletics but later used for Cricket Tests too. In 1962, the facility was improved and named the Nehru Stadium. In 1993, it was further improved with covered stands for 40,000 and to international football standards, C R Viswanathan of the Madras Football Association playing a major advisory role. It was named the Jawaharlal Nehru Stadium. It was further improved in 2012-2013. When Shenoy built the open-air stadium, he simultaneously had built nearby a stadium for tennis, which has been much improved to international standards since!

Ending this stretch of striking public buildings on Poonamallee High Road – now renamed to commemorate Periyar Ramaswamy, the rationalist and Dravidian movement leader – is the Corporation of Madras's splendid headquarters building, a mansion of gleaming white, that hides the Lily Pond Complex and stadiums from being seen from the arterial road. Company 'Chairman' Josiah Child was responsible for conceiving the Corporation which owns most of the property in this area. The Corporation, the first in British Asia, was created by a Royal Charter issued by King James II in December 1687. It, however, began to function as a cohesive unit only after the clear delineation of its duties in 1856. In 1919, the Corporation Commissioners were designated Councillors and P Theagaroya Chetty elected the first Indian President of the Council. The Office of Mayor was re-created in 1933, Kumararajah

M A Muthiah Chettiar, of the Chettinad family, being the last President and first new Mayor. In 1957 Tara Cherian was to become India's first woman Mayor.

The Corporation grew out of the early Company administration of Fort and Town. The Company Agent, at the beginning of the latter half of the 17th Century, was assisted in ministering to the needs of the 7,000-strong population of the town by the Adhikari (Administrator), Kanakkapulle (Accountant) and Pedda Nayak (Law Enforcer). The Governor, assisted by the Kanakkapulle, sat as Justice of Peace in a building at the junction of Market and Choultry Streets in the Fort. Streynsham Master made the system more sophisticated and also introduced taxes and licence fees. Complications arising out of these taxes and growing expenses demanded a more formal body. Sir Josiah's plans were implemented, rather reluctantly, by Governor Elihu Yale, who saw in them an erosion of his authority. Three Indians – Chinna Venkatadri (younger brother of Beri Thimmappa), Mudda Viranna and Alangatha Pillai – were among its first twelve aldermen. The City was divided into eight wards, and the Charter, issued on December 30, 1687, came into force on September 29, 1688. The Corporation first met in what was called the *Town Hall* in Fort St George, a long building south of St Mary's Church and now the Army's main office in the Fort.

Shenoy, shortly after he was appointed Municipal Commissioner of Madras, urged Mayor Dr. Syed Niyamatuallah to celebrate September 29th (the day the Corporation was found in 1688) as Inauguration Day. And what a celebration it was, with all past mayors, commissioners and councillors participating in it together with members of the Government and other eminent citizens. At the hugely attended public meeting at My Ladye's Garden, speaker after speaker exhorted the citizenry "to feel proud of their great city, cooperate with the Corporation in its achievements and help achieve the ideal of the 'City Beautiful'." Obviously the concepts of 'Singara Chennai' and 'Ezhilmigu Chennai' long pre-date today's exhortations.

September 29, 1944 concluded with a grand banquet on the terrace of Ripon Building, replete with music, a fireworks display and a determination to celebrate September 29 as Inauguration Day annually. The celebrations continued for several years into Independence, but were not heard of till 2017 when revival was promised.

Shenoy was only 2 ½ years in office before he retired, but during that time he made an immense contribution to the city. Madras had only shortly before his assumption of office expanded by about 20 square miles (about 50 sq.km) and received an additional population of 110,000 by including within its bounds the Saidapet Municipality (which comprised Saidapet, Mambalam, Kodambakkam, Adyar, Alandur etc.), and Sembiam, Aminjikarai and Velacheri Panchayats as well as 14 villages administered by the 'Chingleput District Board'. Shenoy ensured that these areas got, in the quickest possible time, all the same amenities the rest of the city had. Then, to administer what had become a 49.7 sq. mile (appx.130 sq km) city, he implemented decentralisation, establishing a Division Office in each of the 40 divisions to respond to the needs of the citizens of the division.

Ripon Building, a fine attempt at fusing the Neo-Classical with elements of the Indo-Saracenic, is the present headquarters of the Corporation, to which the move from Errabalu Chetty Street was made in 1913. A magnificent white building, it was designed by G S T Harris and built by P Loganatha Mudaliar who received Rs 5.5 lakhfor his share of the Rs.7.5 lakh work. Four years under construction, *Ripon Building* is 252 feet long and 126 feet wide. Its tower is 132 feet tall and features a clock eight feet in diameter, supplied by Oakes in 1913. The first of its three floors has a 25,000 sq ft area. It was declared open at a function attended by over 3,000 of the city's elite. Lord Ripon, Viceroy from 1880-1884, during which period he introduced government reforms, is remembered in statue and name here. As these lines are written, the restoration of *Ripon Building* is nearing completion after six years of work. It is expected that while the Mayor's chamber and Council chamber will remain in the building, the rest of the building will be turned into a museum on the history of Madras. Behind *Ripon Building*, a building in vaguely sympathetic style has been raised to accommodate all the offices that were in *Ripon Building* before restoration.

Called *Amma Maligai*, this 150, 000 sq.ft annexe was built at a cost of Rs. 230 million and opened in 2015. Its pillars alone reflect Tamil architecture.

Across the road from *Ripon Building* are the minareted choultries for travellers built by Raja Sir Ramaswami Mudaliar in 1884 and Abdul

Hakim Sahib, both 19th Century merchant princes. The latter's minareted contribution, completed in 1920, is called *Siddique Serai*. Ramaswami Mudaliar, appointed in 1887 the first Indian Sheriff of Madras, made his fortune as the *dubash* of Dymes & Co, which became the Bombay Company. Apart from the choultry, his charity extended to building in 1880 the R S R M Lying-in Hospital, now part of Stanley Hospital in Washermenpet, and maternity hospitals in Cuddalore and Kanchipuram, and water and feed troughs for animals in several points in these towns. He was awarded the title Rajah by the British government in 1891. Among the vast properties he owned was what is now Kilpauk Garden Colony (in a corner of which the family burial ground remains), *Serle's Garden*, by the Adyar River, obtained from the man after whom the road on which it is is named – Edward Croft Greenway, a Civilian who became a Puisne Judge – and property all along Flower's Road, where he lived. As these lines are written, the Serai still welcomes travelers and offers them inexpensive resting facilities, but the choultry remains unused and untended, its fate in the hands of the Metro. So are the gardens of Ripon Building and the Town Hall. The Metro promises their restoration, but how will the Metro affect the view of all these heritage buildings?

North of where the Zoo was, are Elephant Gate (commemorating, it is stated, 'elephant gardens' that were north of here in the 17th Century) and Salt Cotaurs. Beyond is Basin Bridge, by which, once, were the city's first thermal power station and, opposite it, Charles Trevelyan's 'basin' – three in number and used for purifying water. Both are no longer in operation. The ruins of the power station's three stacks and the basins were imploded in 1996. Moving northwest you approach the Buckingham and Carnatic Mills, Vyasarpadi, Perambur and Ayyanavaram – the last two areas a giant railway colony.

Between this now industrialised area and Poonamallee High Road to the south are, from east to west, the old villages of Vepery, Purasawalkam, Kilpauk (all once extensive paddy fields but gradually developed as residential areas of the gentry) and the new residential colonies of Shenoy Nagar and Anna Nagar, a part of the latter on the Neduvakkarai site of an international trade fair held in 1967. Vepery, Purasawalkam and Egmore (*Elambore* – Tamil = Seventh village, or *Elumbur*) were all the first residential areas popular with those 18th Century Europeans who moved out of the Fort and could afford 'garden houses'. Through this area runs unhealthy Otteri Nullah, a rivulet joining the Buckingham Canal just north of Basin Bridge and serving as an open drain for this part of the city.

The first 'garden houses' in Egmore, Richard Horden's and Thomas Theobald's, were built around 1715. Soon afterwards, further grants for 'garden houses' were opposed by the 'Renters of Egmore' complaining of the loss of agricultural lands, but they were ignored and, from 1720 onwards, the 'garden houses' of Egmore came up. Roads like Casa Major Road, Marshall's Road, Lang's Garden Road, Hall's Road and Montieth Road all date to between 1720 and 1820. They got their names from senior Civilians or army officers who built their garden homes here during that period. Basil Cochrane, the canal builder, who had two houses where Montieth later built one, is, however, forgotten in the commemorative road-naming!

The century-and-more-old Ladies Recreation Club is on a campus called Willingdon Estate, just off Marshall's Road (now called Rukmini Lakshmipathy Salai). It owes it beginnings to a spark lit by Mrs. Madeley, the wife of the Chief Engineer, Mrs.Seethamma Tiruvenkatachariar, daughter of Justice Sir V Bashyam Iyengar and wife of C.R. Tiruvenkatachariar the well-known lawyer, and Mrs. R S Subramaniam who met on August 21, 1911 at Sylvan Lodge, Mylapore, the home of Lady Masilmoney Chellammal Devadoss, wife of Justice Sir David M. Devadoss, and decided to found a ladies' club. Its objects were "to promote social and friendly intercourse between European and Indian ladies, and between Indian ladies of all classes and creeds; also to provide healthy recreation suitable to members of the club." That recreation, the members decided, would be badminton and croquet. Lady Carmichael, wife of the Governor of Madras, was elected the first President, a practice that was to continue for a long time. Lady Atkins was elected the first Chairman and three European and three Indian members were elected to share the duties of Vice-President, Honorary Secretary and Honorary Treasurer.

By the end of the first year, membership had so grown, the Club was looking for premises of its own. In 1912, the club moved into Luz House, in Mylapore, and formally named itself The Ladies Recreation Club. It also introduced tennis.

In 1920, Lady Willingdon took over the presidency of the Club and breathed action into the institution. A club needs a permanent home, she announced, and set about collecting the Rs.2,50,000 necessary to buy the building on Marshall's Road that was for decades to remain the Club's home. Rs.2 lakh of the donation came from S.Rm.M. Annamalai Chettiar (later to become Rajah Sir) who appended a request that the building be named after the Willingdons. So Willingdon it became.

A Trust, headed by the Governor, was formed and it nominated a Council to manage the property. Recreational activities increased with the spaciousness available and table tennis, indoor badminton, billiards, carrom and auction bridge all swelled the Club's programme. Lady Willingdon herself was one of the most active participants in many of these games.

When the men's clubs began opening their doors to women in the 1960s, many of the activities in Willingdon, the heart of Willingdon Estate, began fading and, before long, all outdoor activities came to a stop. With the Club losing its dynamism, the whole property passed into the hands of the Chettinad family and its Annamalai University. But in the first and second floor of a ladies' hostel here, the Club survives, with rummy its main activity and the occasional 'Tea'. In its heyday, it was the premier and, possibly, first women's club in South India.

Off Hall's Road in Kilpauk is the Kilpauk Votive shrine and the neighbouring Mercy Home for aged women, both built on the site of Edgar Raphael Prudhomme's erstwhile home, *Fonteroy*, he gifted the Roman Catholic Church. They were both inaugurated in 1957.

2. Spreading knowledge

In Vepery is the City's oldest press, the CLS Press, founded in 1761 as the SPCK Press[1]. Its first manager, as already related, was the missionary Fabricius, who was in charge of the mission of the Society for Promoting Christian Knowledge, which was founded in Vepery in 1716 by Johann Grundler, the third member of the team that established the Tranquebar Mission. From 1815, the press was known as the Diocesan Press, taking its name from a Diocesan Committee that was set up at the time to run it. The Committee sold the press to the American Mission Board around 1850 but reacquired it in 1866 and has run it – and the Christian Literature Society – ever since. It was the American Mission Press that printed Miron Winslow's Tamil-English dictionary.

---

[1] It is also the oldest surviving printing press in the country.

The printing owed much to another American missionary, Phineas R Hunt, who designed and cut the type for it. This was a type design that existed well into the 1940s, even migrating into mechanical typesetting.

In 1991, the press changed its name again and became the CLS Press. The historical main building of the press, dating to the early days of the Diocesan Press, was pulled down in 1998 after being sold to highrise developers. The abbreviated press now functions in a small new building on the same campus. Not far from this press there used to be – till it moved to Purasawalkam – the Tranquebar Printing & Publishing House, all that was left of Tranquebar's signal contribution to printing, publishing and education in India! Even that no longer survives.

Near the CLS Press are several historic churches associated with the German missionaries from Halle, by way of Tranquebar, who were the only Protestant missionaries permitted by the East India Company to work in Madras till the early 1800s. With the Company chary of what influence British missionaries would have with the Government at home, they encouraged the Germans who, in turn, became the local representatives of the British SPCK. Schultze (1726), Fabricius (1742), Gericke (1788) and Rottler (1808) (who has a street named after him in Vepery) – their's was a distinguished line of scholars whose contribution to education in Madras and Tamil has been immense. The dates in brackets are when these scholars became head of the Vepery (SPCK) Mission. Schultze, it must be recorded, walked all the way from Tranquebar in 1726. From 1716 till 1836, these German missionaries played a major role not only in the life of Vepery but in education and influencing the Madras Government as well. St Paul's, Vepery, was the first missionary-founded school in India. Its beginnings were in a Portuguese school and a Tamil school (known as the Malabar Charity School) Johann Grundler established in 1716 as charity institutions. These developed into the Vepery High School in 1862 and became St Paul's in 1912. Later, Schultze established in this area the first English school.

What the records say about the schools is that Bartholomaeus Ziegenbalg, head of the Danish Tranquebar Mission, visited Madras in 1716 and agreed to set up two charity schools there – one for the Portuguese in Fort St George and one for the Malabars (Tamils) in Black Town. Ziegenbalg was apparently accompanied by Johann Grundler, who stayed behind to set up the schools for the Society for

Tranquebar's legacy to Indian printing...the CLS Press in Vepery, oldest in the country...but now this, its main block, is no more and even the Press survives only on miniscule scale.

St Matthias' Church...raised where Fabricius took over Coja Petrus Uscan's chapel (but not his tombstone).

55. *Beneath the dome of St Andrew's Kirk...stars in the Scottish sky.*

56. *Red-brick for schooling... at St George's in Kilpauk, descended from India's first Western-style school.*

Promoting Christian Knowledge. Geister, who came with them, was left to run the two schools. Neither school was very successful and missionary education really got started only with Benjamin Schultze combining the two schools in 1726 in Vepery as the Anglo Vernacular School. St. Paul's, Vepery, however, claims to descend from the 1716 Tamil school, rather confusing the issue. The house of the Principal of St. Paul's is rather fancifully classified as being associated with Robert Clive. In Robert Clive's day, the English had not moved out of Fort St. George, so probably an occupant of the house from time to time was very likely his son Edward who hosted entertainments all around town.

Grundler arrived in Tranquebar in 1709 and died there in 1720. Grundler was a teacher in Halle before he decided to become a cleric and was sent out as the third missionary of the Danish Mission, after Ziegenbalg and Plutschau. On arrival, Grundler virtually fell in love with Tamizhagam. So, more than the schools, he gave greater attention to the study of Tamil knowledge, particularly Siddha medicine and tropical herbology. A decade of research led to a treatise titled *Malabar Medicus* (Tamil Doctor). Details of diagnoses, dosages etc were all noted by him.

Johann Fabricius, who served in Madras from 1742 till he died in 1791, and after whom a school established on Purasawalkam High Road in 1849 was named in 1898, founded the first Protestant church in Vepery in 1750. On its site was consecrated in 1858 the Gothic-style St Paul's Church for the benefit of the Tamil-speaking congregation. Not far from St Paul's there had been consecrated, in 1823, the new Vepery Mission Church, St Matthias'. Dr Johann Rottler was its inspiration and John Law designed it in Gothic style; the site was Coja Petrus Uscan's private chapel that the Government, irked with the Catholics, had taken over. The oldest tombstone in Anglican St Matthias' cemetery is that of the Armenian Roman Catholic Petrus Uscan who was John Company's "most loyal friend" and who died in 1757. Other tombstones here are of German missionaries from Tranquebar who served the SPCK, like Rottler, Gericke, and Breithaupt. In the case of Fabricius, however, it is not certain he lies beneath his tombstone. Several accounts of his life refer to his pauper's grave and his burial expenses being met only by passing the hat around. The tombstone therefore could well be a later addition when the SPCK was more affluent. Fabricius, however, is remembered in the name of a school in Vepery, the E.L.M. (Evangelical

Lutheran Mission) Fabricius School founded in 1849 as the Lutheran School. It took its present name in 1893 and moved to the present address in 1894. The original building was considerably renovated in the new Millennium. This was a school that R K Narayan, the famous author, attended. Five other tombstones here are of, perhaps, the only Dutch from Pulicat to be buried in Madras. The one in the best condition is that of Martinus Stoffenberg, Chief at Pulicat, who was buried here on August 9, 1789.

The Roman Catholic educational presence in Vepery was established in 1875 and the school grew into St Joseph's in 1883 and Presentation Convent in 1884. St Aloysius' was founded in 1889. Very much older, however, are schools of other denominations, the oldest being Lady Bentinck's Higher Secondary School. Founded in Purasawalkam as Mrs Drew's Orphanage in 1838, it moved to its present Vepery site in 1852 as Miss Porter's School. It later was known as the London Mission Female School. In 1915, it became Lady Bentinck's School. Anna Drew, wife of the Rev William Drew of the Missionary Chapel and who had started the Orphanage, had been an Anna Sheridan and was a cousin of the dramatist R B Sheridan.

Other old schools in the area are Doveton Corrie (1855/56), its history already narrated, Government-run Presidency Girls' School in Egmore (1870, and at its present site since 1883), which has done yeoman service for women's education in Malayalam, Tamil, Telugu and English, and the first schools to be run in the area by a Hindu charitable trust, the M Ct M Schools in Purasawalkam (1891).

The first school for Anglo-Indians was established in Vepery in 1784; this has developed, through various mergers, into Doveton Corrie School, Vepery, today. The Doveton part of the name comes from the bequest of Capt John Doveton of the Nizam's Army, an alumnus of the Madras Male Military Asylum, who died in 1853 in London. The bequests resulted in the Doveton College for Boys (1855) and a Doveton for girls in 1856. The Parental Academy, a school started near Tucker's Church in 1836, was named Bishop Corrie School after Corrie was crowned the first Anglican Bishop of Madras in 1835. The high school of this institution was amalgamated in 1929 with the Doveton schools, and the Vepery schools became Doveton Corrie. They remain two Doveton Corries, but on one Vepery campus. Meanwhile, what was left of Bishop Corrie's

Parental Academy became the Madras Grammar School and, in 1896, the Bishop Corrie School. But it was 1959 before it became a George Town high school again! The earliest private schools were John Holmes' Madras Academy, established in 1790, and Mrs Murray's Female Boarding School, established in 1791, both in 'Black Town'.

Dobbin Hall – a forgotten name even in this area – was the residence of Lt Col Dobbin and it was here that the pioneering veterinary education institution in India began with 20 students in 1903. The first veterinary college in India to get affiliation to a university (1936), the Madras Veterinary College, has grown into the Tamil Nadu University of Veterinary and Animal Sciences, established in 1989 as India's first such university in six acres in Madhavaram, but the College and some departments still function from the same handsome Indo-Saracenic premises and hospital of the College at Vepery High Road, almost across the road from *Ripon Building's* west face. The main building, which rose on the site of *Dobbin Hall*, was built by Masilamony Mudaliar to a Henry Irwin design and opened for use in 1904. Major Gunn was the first principal; V Krishnamurthi Ayyar became the first Indian principal in 1929. N. Kalyani and P. Sakkurai graduated from here as India's first women vets in 1952.

Opposite the Veterinary College is the Indo-Saracenic building of the SPCA, its main block raised in 1898. A proposal for a society was first discussed in 1877 by some of the leading Europeans of Madras, but it was established as the SPCA only in 1880/1, with the Governor, the Duke of Buckingham and Chandos, its first Patron and Bishop Frederick Gell its first President. It had in its first years an entirely European membership, Indians showing little interest in its activities which focused on preventing the cruelty to animals and improving the conditions under which they were maintained.

One person who later took a great deal of interest in the Society was Justice Hungerford Tudor Boddam of the Madras High Court (1896-1908). It was Boddam's efforts that led to Indians joining the Society from 1903. By then Boddam had got Raja Venugopala Mudaliar of Venkatagiri to fund the Hospital for Animals that stands in the Society's 17-ground premises in Vepery that were acquired in 1898. The hospital was inaugurated in 1900. Boddam is one of the few judges in the Madras High Court to have a statue raised for him. He was a mediocre judge of humans, but his concept for animals has him remembered by a statue. The hospital was used to train the Veterinary College students when the latter institution first started and was later gifted to the College.

The SPCA had no plenary powers during the first years of its existence. In 1894, the SPCA was granted police powers to charge persons ill-treating animals. Starting with action it took when, in 1936, 23 goats were slaughtered in a *mutt* in Kumbakonam to the chanting of mantras and the flesh offered to the deities, it did much to bring down animal sacrifice in the State.

Boddam was also responsible for persuading the local citizenry to found a pinjrapole. The same citizenry, mainly the Gujaratis of Madras, were those whose "subscriptions" made possible the statue for Boddam in 1911. The statue was first raised near the Willingdon (now Periyar) Bridge on Mount Road but was later moved to Napier Park from where it's gone into seclusion till the Metro authorities keep their promise and return it to Napier Park once their work in finished.

Round the corner from the SPCA and the College, on Sydenham's Road, is the Periamet Lebbai Mosque, one of the city's biggest. First built in 1838, and reconstructed twice since Independence (in 1950-52 and 1968-71), it is an offering to the Muslims of the area from the wealthy Muslim traders in skins and hides and jaggery whose businesses are still here. Now, its echo-less, pillarless main hall, a unique architectural construction, can accommodate 5,000 persons. Its minarets are 75 feet tall. Jammal Moideen Saib& Sons and Roshan N M A Carim Oomar& Co were pioneers here in the hides and skins trade. Between mosque and veterinary hospital is the Baynes Baptist Church, established here in 1847.

Sydenham's Road was once popularly called "Armoury Road", as shops on it, alongside the mosque, specialised in arms, ammunition, and military wear. Many of these shops have now moved elsewhere in the neighbourhood.

Also in this area, where Purasawalkam High Road meets Perambur Barracks Road, is where *Maskelyne Thottam Paracheri* used to be. Once it was a famed house and garden, first built on ground granted by government and occupied in 1753 - 61 by Capt. Edward Maskelyne whose sister Robert Clive married. It was here that Nawab Wallajah stayed during his first visit to Madras in 1756. When Maskelyne left in 1762, it was bought by the Nawab who improved it and, by 1798, made its gardens an ornamental park. A map of 1798 shows the property replete with walks, trees and ornamental ponds. By 1816, it had disappeared off the map. It had also then become a "parachery" – what we'd call a Dalit slum today. Judging from a recent map of Madras, *Maskelyne Thottam* would have been an area in Purasawalkam now bounded by Purasawalkam High Road, Mookathal Street, Bishop Lane and Perambur Barracks Road, where the Mekala Theatre, till demolished, was the main landmark.

In street-criss-crossed former *Maskelyne Gardens* is the Purasawalkam Missionary Chapel which opened for worship in December 1819. When the Rev Richard Knill laid the foundation stone for it on June 12, 1819, it was the first step taken in Madras by the London Missionary Society.

On the south side of Poonamallee High Road are the old Hindu and Muslim choultries already mentioned and the Friend-in-Need Society, an old-age home with church charity beginnings and now host mainly to poor Anglo-Indians. Behind the choultries used to be the Central Jail, already referred to. East of it is Stanley Viaduct, now in quite different shape to accommodate the Metro, but built in the 1930s to link George Town and Park Town with The Island and, thence, Mount Road.

Further down Poonamallee High Road, by the now-expanded Gandhi-Irwin overbridge, is the Government College of Arts and Crafts, a rather tradition-bound institution with its output suited to its Chisholm-designed Gothic-style home till the last few decades. Its 4.5-acre campus is graced by two heritage buildings of note. The 'White Building' that is the Principal's office, once his home too, with a permanent exhibition gallery in place now, and the adjoining museum block, the 'Red Building', which housed the library too. Both present a striking Gothic roadside façade. The College's permanent collection has what could be an interesting exhibit of artefacts, paintings and old photographs, if only attention was paid to it and the public could view it.

Robert Fellowes Chisholm, the Consulting Architect at the time, was additionally appointed Superintendent (Principal) of the Government School of Industrial Arts in 1877. He succeeded the founder, Dr Alexander Hunter, a military surgeon, who started the Madras School of Arts as a private institution in Popham's Broadway in May 1850. The School was taken over by the Government in 1852 and Dr Hunter was given the task of reorganising the curriculum. His eight-member committee reconstituted the Madras School of Arts and renamed it the Government School of Industrial Arts, with two departments, the Artistic and the Industrial, the latter concentrating on building materials and accessories, the former on drawing, engraving and pottery. Hunter was officially put in charge of the School, as its first Superintendent, in 1855, and that was when he decided to introduce Photography in it. He was determined to develop the School along the lines of the South Kensington Institute, transforming what till then had been a drawing and painting academy. The College still has a fine collection of 19th Century photography focussed on South India – including a good Capt. Linnaeus Tripe and Capt. Lyons trove – all squirreled away. Hunter also aimed at nullifying "the injurious influence which the large importations of European manufacturers of the worst possible designs have had on native handicrafts and also to train students for engraving and other useful occupations." Dr. Hunter, who was also the founder in 1857 of the Madras Photographic Society, which still thrives, retired in 1868 and was replaced by Chisholm, who did not get an official designation till 1877. Around this time, E E Howell introduced wood carving and carpentry, which was to be followed by metal-work.

Some of the portraits Chisholm (1840-1915), a Gothicist, painted hang in Madras's Gallery of Contemporary Art. The School's first Indian principal, the legendary Debi Prasad Roy Chowdhury, hunter, wrestler, painter and sculptor, perhaps the best-known contemporary Indian artist of the 1940s and 1950s, was appointed in 1929. He attracted talent from all over the country and produced some of the most important artists of the decades that followed.

One of the School's most significant achievements was the introduction in India in 1898 of working with aluminium. This work of the School's Metal Working Department led to leading barrister Eardley Norton founding in 1900 the Indian Aluminium Company to develop the work done by the School. In 1903, the Company took over the business developed at the School and began introducing aluminium goods into the Indian market.

To the west of the College is St Andrew's Kirk. The church, one of the finest examples of Georgian architecture in Asia, was consecrated in 1821 on the site of an old Freemasons' Lodge, where its foundation of wells, a traditional Indian style of foundation-laying in moist soil areas, had been sunk in 1818 to a depth of 23 feet. Described as "the noblest edifice in Hindustan", the church was built with several modifications by Major de Havilland on a design originally made by a Lt Grant. The church is basically circular, 83 feet in diameter, and has a splendid dome that is unique. This 51½ feet diameter dome of pure masonry rests on 16 finely polished Ionic pillars. The golden stars that twinkle in the blue of its painted interior are said to represent the position of the stars in Scottish skies. The spire's weathercock is 170 feet above ground level, the steeple 12 feet taller than St Martin's-in-the-Fields which it draws architectural inspiration from. Its floor is of black and white marble, its bells, alas no longer *in situ*, were the largest ever cast in Madras. A church of beauty, St Andrew's is one of the architectural marvels of 19th Century Madras. St Andrew's Parochial School, next door to the church, has been located here since 1811. What is now called Madras Christian College Higher Secondary School was founded by John Anderson in the St Andrew's Kirk campus in 1835 with 56 students.

Across Poonamallee High Road from the Kirk was the Police Traffic Commissioner's Office, once a spacious garden house and yet another owned by the P Venkatachellum family. Once, all drivers' licences were issued from there and the ample grounds provided ideal space for testing drivers. A traffic park to help children develop road sense was maintained in these grounds, but with time became less popular. In 2007, all that vanished and in 2013 Police highrise was inaugurated for Madras's Commissioner of Police. To the west of the Police Traffic Commissioner's Office were the main sheds of the Madras Tramways. After the Tramways closed, the site was sold in four plots and became Periyar Thidal, offices of the *Dina Thanthi*, and land for two garden houses. The garden house closer to the road became the Police Traffic Commissioner's office, replaced in 2013 by new Police highrise. The Former Police Commissioner's office on lower Pantheon Road was developed from an Arumugam Mudaliar's property bought by him in 1842. The property was bought by the Police in 1857 after renting it in 1842. Sprawling *Periyar Thidal* is the grounds, offices and study centre of the anti-Brahmin, anti-religious party, Dravida Kazhagam, that 'Periyar' E V Ramasamy Naicker founded initiating the Dravidian movement.

Further west on Poonamallee High Road, opposite the YWCA, are railway quarters on the site of what was first a choultry, then developed in 1703 by Governor Thomas Pitt as a small fortification. By 1713, it had been enlarged into the Egmore Redoubt, a small fort. In time it became a military convalescence home, then, from 1754, a powder mill as well. The mill was making gun-powder when the French unsuccessfully besieged Fort St George in 1758. But the occupants were successful in blowing up the mill, which returned to business only in 1762. Whether the redoubt thereafter existed side by side with the mill or whether the mill gave way to a fort again is not very clear, but it has been said that its guns had fired at the horsemen of Hyder Ali and Tippu Sultan when they raided Madras in 1767and 1769. It survived various other vicissitudes until 1793, when it was handed over to the Madras Male Asylum Orphanage; from 1800 the Government Press functioned from here, using the Asylum's wards as apprentices. In 1900, the property, to the rear of the Egmore station complex, was sold to the South Indian Railway who converted it into residential accommodation by raising a second floor on the fort's walls which remained clearly visible in the adaptation. The building survived till the nationalisation of railways; it was pulled down some years later and new railway quarters built.

Mahfuz Khan, the eldest son of the Nawab of the Carnatic, who lost the historic battle of the Adyar to the French, first regrouped at the Redoubt after he lost the Battle of Seven Wells. Then he moved on to San Thomé, before joining battle at the Adyar. While this, and most of the other history of the Redoubt mentioned above, is recorded, there appears to be considerable doubt about the little fort's exact location. One school of thought locates the Redoubt on the land where Egmore Railway Station came up. But the station is just south of the area mentioned here and probably the entire area, from the road to Poonamallee to the station front, was occupied by the 100 yards' square fort and its environs. Another school of thought has its location on the site of the present parcel godown. Gandhi-Irwin Road used to be Redoubt Road. Name changes became a habit long before Independence! Fortunately Mahfuz Khan's name remains in Street and Garden in George Town as a reminder of historical events.

On Poonamallee High Road, across from the Railways' Egmore Redoubt property, is the Young Women's Christian Association's Madras chapter, spread out in nine acres of gardens in Vepery. Once, this property was known as *Clive Gardens*, after Governor Edward Clive, the second Lord Clive, had authorised purchase in 1803 of the large house and grounds that had been leased by the East India Company from 1779 for the Redoubt Officers' Mess. That 'message' is the charming old office building, now renovated, of the YWCA; tradition had it that Lord Clive whiled away many an hour here between 1799 and 1803, often staying for several days at a time.

The YWCA, established in Madras in 1892, seventeen years after the first YWCA had opened in India in Bombay, purchased the property from the Chatoorbhoojadoss Kushaldoss family in 1906, getting the acreage and three buildings. In the 1920s and thereafter, much new building has gone on, but without affecting the garden ambience or even the small lake, now called 'Mermaid Pond', in the campus. The YWCA Madras was founded by the visiting Kinnaird sisters, who got two rival European women's associations to get together as one and open their doors to all. The new YWCA owed its fabulous growth in its early years to its first secretary, Agnes Hill, who located it in Rundall's Road and then negotiated the move to Poonamallee High Road spaciousness. The YMCA's International Guest House here, built in the late 1990s, is a well-kept, reasonably-priced home-away-from-home for budget travellers looking for mod-cons.

Between Vepery and Kilpauk and to their rear is Purasawalkam. In Kelly's here is Gurukul, the Lutheran Theological College and Research Institute founded in the 1950s and linked to the 18th Century Serampore Theological College near Calcutta – which still grants degrees on the strength of a Royal Danish charter. Its library has a good collection, theological and otherwise, particularly of archival material from the Francke Foundation, Halle, Germany, with which the Tranquebar Mission was closely associated.

Near Gurukul is the century and more old Adaikalanathar Lutheran Church named after the first Indian Lutheran priest and consecrated in 1848. In it is another of Madras's half a dozen hundred-years-and-more-old organs (40 years), this one by W E Richardson of London, coming from the Egmore Wesley Church.

Moving westwards, Poonamallee High Road takes on an aspect of being the Harley Street of Madras, with almost every nameboard a doctor's or a nursing home's. Believed to be the first nursing home here is Dr. Pandalai's, established in 1932. Then comes Kilpauk Medical College (KMC) and, further west still, Pachaiyappa's College, another institution run by the Pachaiyappa Trust. Pachaiyappa's moved to

Poonamallee High Road from George Town in the 1940s and on its campus is *Dare Bungalow*, probably once the property of Williams Dare, a legendary partner of Parry & Co *c*. 1820. Also on the campus are hostel facilities dating to 1914.

KMC has been functioning in varying forms from 1953 in the premises that had been occupied by the Government School of Indian Medicine (the Ayurvedic College). from its inception in 1925. The School was upgraded to a college in 1957, then wound up in 1960. It, however, reopened in Anna Nagar in the late 1970s as the College of Indian Medicine. And here, there functions a significant service – a whole-time department to translate into Tamil all Ayurvedic material available in the Sanskrit. Some significant publication has been done here. The School's first principal was Dr G Srinivasa Murti, an ardent Theosophist and an allopathic doctor and professor who "drank deep of the cup of the Ayurvedic system of medicine." Captain Srinivasa Murti, so called after his service in the Indian Medical Service in World War I, was the Secretary of the 1921 Usman Committee on Indian Medicine which recommended the establishment of the School. Later, Captain Srinivasa Murti founded the Indian Medical Practitioners' Co-operative Society, now on Lattice Bridge Road in Adyar, where it continues to formulate Ayurvedic medicines and tonics. Captain Srinivasa Murti is remembered on the Kilpauk campus in a statue to the west of the main building. The whole campus was once called *Hyde Park Gardens* and was owned by the Rajah of Panagal.[2] The Rajah was Prime Minister of Madras between 1921 and 1926 and not only blessed the founding of the School but also gave it his name.

Kilpauk Medical College and Hospital today straddle Poonamallee High Road, the Hospital on the Chetput side, the College on the Kilpauk side – but the entire campus, when granted to a British official in the 19th Century was one property called *Hyde Park Gardens*. KMC's origins were in the reorganisation of the School of Indian Medicine in 1953 and its being renamed the College of Integrated Medicine. The College next became, in 1965, the Woman's Medical College, but when the all-girls student body demanded a co-educational campus, the College in 1967 became Kilpauk Medical College.

---

[2] Pronounced 'Paanagal'.

To the rear of the College's hospital is a tank, Spur Tank, till recently dry most of the time, though it once held enough water and fish the year round for the Madras Anglers' Club to have a clubhouse on the tank's Poonamallee High Road bank.

In 2016, the lake was restored as Chetput Eco Park and is proving one of the more popular attractions in the city – not only in appearance but in facilities as well. The Tamil Nadu Fisheries Department Corporation has developed and showcased the park over an expanse of 16 acres, the water spread being nine acres and the land seven. A brick field had existed here prior to the 1930s, and after soil was excavated for making bricks a natural basin for rainwater to collect had formed. The deepest point of the lake was 18 feet. The Fisheries Department was given the land in 1932 and, in 1947, launched inland fisheries culture. In 1952 the mosquito fish, or Gambusia, which feeds on mosquito larvae was reared in the water. A Madras Angling Park was started here in 1962. Prior to 2014, apart from the Fisheries Research Station, the area was an uncared for no-man's land. The transformation to what it's at present has cost Rs 42 crore. The Park today offers boating in one lake, angling from the grassy embankments of a neighbouring smaller lake, a kilometre-and-half walkway around the two water bodies, watching ducks glide in the waters or waddle along the paths, or the opportunity to simply enjoy unhindered space where you can just sit and stare, away from the mayhem of a city. An aquarium and an underwater viewing facility are promised.

Behind the tank was a *Dhobi Khana* (a manual laundry run by a cooperative of dhobis) established in 1902 during Municipal Commissioner Moore's time. Today, the dhobis here find the middle class habit of giving clothes to the dhobi for laundering is slowly dying out, but there's business enough to eke out a living. Other dhobi khanas are at Washermenpet, started in 1937, and government monitors from 1979, and at Saidapet from before Independence but regularised in the 1960s.

Breaking the dominance of medicine on this stretch are striking buildings of another age which deserve greater attention than is paid to them. The Egmore Benefit Society is more interested in its featureless new block than its heritage buildings which it built as its prosperity grew. The Egmore Benefit Fund (renamed Society in 1872) was started on January 1, 1870. In 1919, it built the first of the buildings referred to, on Flower Road, adopting a pillared and pedimented Regency Style. As business grew, it extended it into an 'L'-shaped complex by adding a multipillared '*mandapam*' parallel to Flower Road. In 1971, it moved into its new centenary block, built 90 degrees to the *mandapam* and parallel to the first building which was rented to the postal authorities for the Flower Road Post Office. This heritage building partially collapsed in 2012.

Kilpauk, north of the road, is almost the furthest western locality the British built their 'garden houses' in. Road names here recall several of these houses and eminent occupants. By Landon's Road were two old 'garden houses' that were occupied by men to whom Madras owes much. One was the house Dare of Parry's acquired in 1822, twelve years after he arrived in Madras. The other, also taken over the same year by Col Colin Mackenzie, was *Landon's Gardens*. It was here that much of his studies in Indology were conducted. Gajapati Road in Kilpauk is named after the Maharajah of Parlakimedi, who represented for many years the Madras Presidency's Oriya connection, Ganjam then being part of the Presidency. When Orissa became a separate province in 1930, he became its first Premier, but never broke his residential connection with the Orme's Road area of Kilpauk. In this area too the first wealthy Nattukottai Chettiars to move to Madras bought large properties, the first of them P M A Muthiah Chettiar. Of these houses only the M Ct family's *Bedford House* bought in 1915 and Rm Alagappa Chettiar's on Poonamallee High Road are still owned by the respective families. The latter's first house, *Krishna Vilas*, which he gifted to the Ramanujan Institute of Mathematical Science, is now used by Government. Here too is a small park, the Bashyam Naidu park, the city's only link with its founder, Beri Thimmappa, whole descendent was Ketti Bashyam Naidu, a prominent public figure in 19th Century Madras whom, we've already met.

All the western end almost opposite Pachaiyappa's, are the red-brick buildings of St George's School and Orphanage, an institution descending from St Mary's Charity School in the Fort and two orphanages, the Male and Female Military Asylums. They were built in property donated by Brig T H S Conway, remembered for it in marble in St Mary's Church. The 115-year-old *Conway House*, where the school started, is still part of the campus, serving for long as a school dormitory, it now serves as an old persons' home.

The Male Military Asylum, founded in 1789, was preceded in Madras by the Female Military Asylum, set up by the German missionary Gericke in 1787. The boys from the male asylum and the girls from their asylum with a military lineage were moved to the Lawrence Military Asylum in Lovedale, Ooty, in 1871 and 1902, respectively to firm up the numbers at Lawrence and reduce the cost for the military.

The Male Asylum Orphanage will ever be remembered for it was its first Superintendent, Dr Andrew Bell, who initially introduced to Western education in 1789 the monitorial system of education that in Britain came to be known as the Madras system of education. The system, based on the ancient *gurukulam* pattern, permitted older boys to act as teachers' aides, both in instruction as well as in disciplinary matters.

Dr Bell, faced with poor pay saddling him with too few teachers and only inefficient ones at that, one day got his brightest eight-year-old to teach the alphabet to the lower classes. The experiment was a success – and "the system of mutual instruction" was born. When Dr Bell left Madras in 1796, he was determined to "repeat Madras" at home. He introduced the system at a charity school in Aldgate, then at some industrial schools in Kendall. Eventually, with church backing, he was able to introduce the 'Madras System' in over 12,000 elementary schools in Britain, but he failed to get Europe interested in it. Britain, however, has continued to use this monitorial system, in modified form, in its public schools – and some other schools – till today. Bell himself founded the Madras College in St. Andrew's, Scotland, which still thrives. Dr Richard Kerr, Bell's predecessor, had introduced vocational education in the orphanage, and the printing industry not only in Madras but also in Australia was the beneficiary..

St Mary's Charity School, founded in St Mary's in the Fort, was the first Western-style school established in India. It had its beginnings in Fort St George when Preacher Pringle in 1673 established a Portuguese and English language free school for English, Portuguese, Eurasian and Indian children resident in the Fort. In 1678, this school was more formally recognised by the Council of Fort St George with the appointment of Ralph Orde as 'Schoolmaster'. Arithmetic, 'Merchant's Accounts' and Tamil were introduced in the curriculum. It was this school that St Mary's in the Fort took over and, under the stewardship of its chaplain, the Rev William Stevenson, ran from 1715 as St. Mary's Charity School. It moved to the Island soon after and remained there till

1872 when it merged with those still left from the Military Male Orphan Asylums, and the full strength of the Military Female Asylum, (most of whom were also later moved to Lovedale) both located at the Egmore Redoubt from 1787. It now became known as the Civil Orphans' Asylum. The Civil Asylum moved to its present Poonamallee High Road site, *Conway's Gardens*, in Kilpauk in 1904. In 1954, the Asylum took the name St George's School and Orphanage – and, given its roots, is the oldest Western-style school in Asia.

The School's choirs have sung over the last 300 years in St Mary's in the Fort, a unique achievement. In the grounds of what was known in the neighbourhood as 'Conway School' is a little church that is straight out of a picture postcard scene of a rural English chapel. Now the school chapel, it was built in 1885.

The Asylum's most famous teacher was Michael Madhusudan Dutt(a) who taught there from 1848 after having to leave Calcutta. He was one of the first teachers in the High School (which became Presidency College and was the nucleus of Madras University) when he joined it in 1852. In 1855, he joined one of Madras's first newspapers, *The Spectator,* but the next year he returned to Calcutta where he was to attain fame as one of the greatest poets in Bengali.

Near St George's, at Poonamallee High Road's junction with the road leading to the new industrial suburbs of Ambattur (where there is a huge, ill-maintained industrial estate, the city's second) and Avadi (where there are military heavy vehicle, tank and ordnance factories), is a quaint "memorial", a house built by a building contractor in Regency style in 1989 and called 'Madras 350 Years'. The house that Joss Fernandez built is the only commemoration in the city of its 350th anniversary.

Just after St George's is the ancient village of Aminjikarai. The Ekambareswar Temple here is 150 years old and the Prasanna Varadaraja Perumal Temple is about a hundred years old. In Aminjikarai is a block of small residences that are accessible only through 29 walking passages criss-crossing the block.

To the rear of Aminjikarai is Shenoy Nagar. J P L Shenoy, whom we have met in these pages before, was responsible for the start of planned urban development in Madras. He was instrumental in mooting the idea in 1944 of a City Improvement Trust Act and it was enacted in July 1945. The first CIT Board was chaired by M.B. Chablani, a town planning expert. Besides offering the fullest support of the Corporation to the CIT, Shenoy conceived the idea of developing a major middle class housing scheme to meet the growing housing needs of the city. The development got underway in 1947 and was completed by his successor, C. Narasimham, whom he had had installed as the city's first Deputy Municipal Commissioner. Shenoy's contribution to the city and the new layout were recognised by the new 'colony' being named Shenoy Nagar when it was inaugurated in 1949.

Shenoy also straightened out the Cooum, constructed walls on both sides of it, ensured the pumping of sea water into the river regularly, and provided toilet facilities for slums along the bank in a determined effort to clean up the Cooum. They needed to be done regularly, he had pronounced. But that is another bit of forgotten advice, the Cooum remaining a problem for Madras.

Another name associated with CIT Development was another Municipal Commissioner, Capt. Joseph Dinakar Gnanaolivu, who in early 1954 was to transform a government cattle farm into Nandanam Extension. Why this was not named a nagar (township) and remains a mere extension has never been explained.

A little beyond is the turn to a major residential development, work on which started in 1969. In Anna Nagar is a 16-acre park named after Visweswarayya, that Mysore genius who showed the South the way to industrialisation by Indians. The choice of name was a consequence of the major industrial exhibition inspired by him and held on this site in 1968 before residential development. The centrepiece of the Park is a striking modern tower called the Panchsheel Tower (that is better known as the Visveswaraya or Anna Tower) which was built for the exhibition. All that is left of the exhibition is the Kerala Pavilion which has been converted into the Anna Nagar Club.

Anna Nagar has grown much since its development first began. Today, it has three Metro rail stations, Anna Nagar East, Anna Nagar Tower and Tirumangalam, and three postal zones, Anna Nagar East (Chennai 102), Anna Nagar West (Chennai 40) and Anna Nagar Western Extension (Chennai 101). Its blocks are named after all the letters from A to Z. It shares borders with Shenoy Nagar, Aminjikarai and Kilpauk and on its outskirts are ICF, Koyambedu, Mogappair and Padi.

Beyond Anna Nagar, and off Poonamallee High Road, is Koyambedu whose wholesale markets and transport terminals have already been referred to. And then there's the Ambattur-Avadi industrial belt. Avadi, as the Allies during World War II planned their counter-offensive against the Japanese, was home of the biggest military base in Asia. Post-war it has become host to several defence industries.

The Ambattur industrial estate – now providing space for modern highrise to meet the IT industry's insatiable demands, like the pioneering Guindy industrial estate – and the Murugappa Group's factories – including the country's first major bicycle-manufacturing facilities – are among the numerous industrial units located here. Elsewhere in the city, being produced around the same time at opposite ends of it, were the Enfield Bullet (made in northern Tiruvottriyur), the first motorcycle manufactured in the country, and the Standard (made in southern Perungalathur), its Vanguard the first car to be manufactured in India. The city's only camping grounds, Camp Tonakela, are in 15 wooded acres in Avadi. It was established by Wallace Forgie, a YMCA-associated Canadian who arrived in Madras in 1927.

Fifteen acres were acquired in 1938 by the Camp Tonakela Association, a recognised charitable institution that Forgie formed, and the Camp was born, 4 km from Ambattur and 20 km from Fort St. George. The Camp's objectives were "to provide a well-equipped campsite for groups of Madras boys and girls under suitable leadership, and to conduct training in camping and in the leadership of every form of character-building activity." Forgie also envisaged the camp as a training and support centre that would enhance their gardening, agricultural, cottage industry and handicrafts skills in nearby villages.

Forgie, outdoorsman if ever there was one, founded his camping site amidst trees and shrubs, near a large lake that offered good fishing. In the middle of the site is a small pond and a swimming pool was added. The camp's 24 tents can house 200 children. Apart from the tents and sanitary facilities, the camp has a kitchen and utensils for campers to use. It hosts about 50 camps a year with over 6,000 campers as well as over 10,000 day-picnickers.

The name Tonakela has intrigued many. Forgie chose it from a Canadian Indian tongue in which it meant 'Not for self'. Even more intriguing is the fact that the same meaning is conveyed in Tamil with the similar sounding *Thanakku illa*. Now, there's a linguistic conundrum for you.

Poonamallee High Road further west – a road laid out over a century ago by that great engineer, Sir Arthur Cotton, who was responsible for the great irrigation barrages north and south of Madras – is a historic road leading to the old village of Poonamallee, in later times a sanatorium and a cantonment for the British with a redoubt dating to the days of Edward Clive. The old barracks here later became home to the Victoria School for the Blind and the Deaf. And there is an ill-kept but historic British cemetery across from it. Beyond, the road leads to even more historic locations, ancient Indian towns and villages, like Puzhal, and whose chieftains were the lords supreme of all the land up to the coast, Tondaimandalam, including where Madras developed. Puzhal, 45km from Madras, is the new home, since 2006, of the city's Central Prison. The biggest and best maintained correctional facility in the country, it houses 3000 prisoners midst 200 acres of space, and has fine gardening and cottage industry programmes.

The Splendour that Still is Indo-Saracenic

'Mad' Mant, it is generally acknowledged, was responsible for popularising that hybrid Anglo-Indian architectural form known as Indo-Saracenic. His vision, of what has been described as a third culture's view of how the building achievements of two other cultures could be blended into a unique architectural form, resulted in 80 glorious years of stately, almost palatial, building throughout India. From the first years after the Sepoy Rebellion of 1857 until World War II, Indo-Saracenic was the preferred style for official, regal and even some private construction. Today, there is no place in India where such architecture can be better appreciated than Madras. For here, the airy spaciousness of a city that has still not crowded out the sky permits several of the best – and some of the earliest – examples of Indo-Saracenic to dominate the landscape, even if they are not looked after as well as they should.

That Madras offers the casual visitor the best overview of this school of building is, perhaps, only fitting, for it was here that what may be considered the first attempt was made by a British engineer, most likely Paul Benfield, to build something that was recognised as Indo-Saracenic only after Mant. It was also in Madras that, long years after Benfield, those who took Mant's dreams furthest lived and worked.

The Anglo-French Carnatic Wars of the 18th Century saw the East India Company emerge as the major power in South India. John Company's protégé, Muhammad Ali Wallajah, was rewarded for his loyalty by being recognised as the Nawab of the Carnatic. It was perhaps natural that, in those troubled times, the new Nawab would wish to stay as close to his benefactors as possible. But when he sought permission to build a palace in Fort St George the British hemmed and hawed their way out of a hasty promise. Eventually, Nawab Wallajah built his palace under the protection of the guns of the Fort, about two miles to its south, near the beach. The man who had drawn up the plans for the palace in the Fort was Company Engineer Benfield. By the time Chepauk Palace was built in 1768, he was a building contractor. It is believed that he adapted his original plans for the new building, which must perhaps be the earliest attempt to integrate the domes, arches, and inlay fretwork of the Mughals with the pillared spaciousness and sculptured decorativeness of the Indian and the Classical features of the Gothic or the Regency. For nearly a century, Chepauk Palace and Fort St George were the dominant features of the Madras skyline. During the first quarter of that century, Benfield made his fortune by lending money to the Nawab! In later years, when Benfield bought himself a parliamentary seat in England, the scandal of the Nawab's debts became a cause célèbre and the Company took over the whole Carnatic, ostensibly to free the Nawab of his financial worries!! The last word to this sorry story was written when the British in 1855 ousted Wallajah's successors from Chepauk Palace. Within a decade of the takeover, work had started on changing the very face of the building, Robert Fellowes Chisholm, who followed in Mant's footsteps, responsible for much of the reconstruction and new construction, but keeping in mind what was being recognised as Indo-Saracenic.

'Mad' Mant arrived in India in 1859. Not long afterwards, Major Charles Mant of the Royal Engineers got down to designing government buildings that looked like an Englishman's version of oriental palaces. So successful were his buildings that the local potentates fell over each other seeking Mant's vision for their new palaces. In the event, Cooch Behar felt Mant was too costly, but Kolhapur, Dharbanga and Baroda commissioned him. Mant planned all three palaces but did not complete any of them! When all three were a little past the foundation stage, he began to worry himself sick that he might have "done the sums wrong" and the buildings would collapse!! He fretted so much that he broke down and died tragically while yet in his forties. Others took over his work – and didn't have to change a thing to finish it. All Mant's palaces stand to this day!

Chisholm, Consulting Architect to the Government of Madras, completed the Laxmi Vilas Palace, *Baroda, in 1890, 12 years after Mant began it. From 1865, Chisholm had built Madras a skyline whose elegance is still unsurpassed: domes and towers and arches combining with Gothic and Indian ornamentation, red-brick facades lending them the distinctive touch of colour characteristic of Madras Indo-Saracenic.*

What Chisholm started continued well into the 1930s. The last of these splendid Chepauk buildings came up to the north of Senate House *when the University's new administration building and library were Indo-Saracenically integrated with the Chisholm masterpiece. Curiously, an occasional 21st Century architect has begun to reflect the style in shopping malls and apartment blocks!*

Two other superb examples of latter-day Indo-Saracenic adaptations are the headquarters of the City Corporation and the Southern Railway, both exceptions to the red rage of Indo-Saracenic. Ripon Building *is a vision in immaculate white and Railway headquarters, reminiscent of the palaces of Mysore, cladded in pale grey stone. Between the two, the red of the more traditional school demands recognition in Victoria Public Hall – an "affirmation of loyalty to the crown" that Chisholm wrought. The Railway headquarters belongs to a later age, after Henry Irwin had built Mysore's spectacular* Amba Vilas Palace *that is possibly the truest amalgam of Hindu sculptural heritage with Muslim curveate form.*

Irwin is recalled in Madras in the Connemara Public Library whose main building he designed, its main reading hall grandiosely ornamented. The Connemara Library developed as part of a cultural complex that grew in the grounds of what was once called The Pantheon. *The original Museum here is fronted by a semi-circular theatre that is itself a museumpiece, and which would undoubtedly have delighted the Elizabethans! And next door is the National Art Gallery that would have been the Victoria Memorial if it had not taken so long to build. Together these buildings reflect an architectural unity that demonstrates the various stages of Indo-Saracenic development, from Gothic-Byzantine to Rajput-Mughal and Southern Hindu-Deccani.*

Of about the same age as The Pantheon *complex are the High Court and Law College buildings. Their rich red walls, towering ornamented domes, exquisitely sculpted pillars and arches, and the intricate workmanship found throughout the maze of interminable cavernous corridors, make them among the finest examples of Indo-Saracenic to be found anywhere in India. To the north of the Courts are a former southern headquarters of the State Bank of India and the General Post Office, Chisholm in the latter being influenced by his Travancore period. Elsewhere in Madras, there are several other splendid buildings belonging* *to the Mant School – Egmore Railway Station and the Madras Literary Society building, for instance – but for sheer elegance, and blatant competitiveness in striving to catch the viewer's eye, the **two** stretches of beach road are unsurpassed.*

Less eye-catching, but every bit as refined in a quieter way, are the 'garden houses' of yesteryear. These owe little to the Oriental but much to the builders' love of spaciousness. Western Classical, Renaissance, Restoration or Georgian in concept, these mansion-homes, built in the luxuriousness of garden space, were the chosen form of private building by the eminent in 18th and 19th Century Madras.For their public face, Indo-Saracenic was created, as splendid a form of architecture as any India has produced, but also in the vision of Governor Lord Napier an awe-inspiring symbol to the subjects of what for nearly a century was the world's greatest imperial power ever.

18

In the Curves of the Cooum

1. Pantheonic splendour

With Egmore Bridge dating to 1700, the whole area south of Poonamallee High Road, nestling in the double curves of the Cooum – Egmore and Chetput with the Spur Tank of earlier years wedged between – started becoming a popular area for 'garden houses' soon after. But the British influx really began in 1774 with the allocation to Europeans of 6-15 acre plots on nominal rents. Large homes and gardens began taking over from the lush paddy fields and, even in this Millennium, an occasional 'garden house' 200 years old and more is still to be found. But Egmore itself, an 18th Century sanatorium, is an ancient village, dating to long before British times, epigraphical mention of it to be found in material as far back as the 11th Century CE.

To the west of Egmore, the origins of whose name has already been referred to, is Chetput. 'Chetty *Pettai*' is, however, a generally accepted explanation for the name, which makes it a 19th Century one, for that is when the more prosperous from among the different groups of Chetties began to buy large garden houses here from the departing British. One of the Chetties who lived here on Harrington Road was that great builder of 19th Century Madras, T Namberumal Chetty. His house, *Crynant*, still survives in the family here. In fact, at one time he owned over 2,000 grounds[1], mainly in this area, including 99 houses (he wouldn't buy the 100th stating it would bring ill-luck). There is also a view that

---

[1] 18 grounds to an acre.

Namberumal Chetty's move to the area and his houses here led to the name 'Chetty *Pettai*'. In 1905 he had decided to move from his ancestral home in George Town, which became *Anand Bhavan* (now *Mysore Cafe*), to *Jarryd Gardens* where stood *Crynant*, built by a British officer in 1858 in 64 grounds. Namberumal Chetty was a great benefactor of Ramanujan the mathematician and treated him as his third son. Ramanujan's last years were spent first in *Crynant*, then in *Gometra*, a house near *Crynant*, which his benefactor made available to the ailing mathematician. Rajaji also lived here at the same time. *Gometra* is now no more, having made way for highrise. Near here are the Madras Christian College School, the Mar Thoma Syrian Christian Church and, across from them, one of the best performance spaces in the city, the Lady Andal Hall. Lady Andal Venkatasubbarao started the Madras Seva Sadan (MSS) in 1928 to help women and children in adverse circumstances. The MSS moved into its own premises in *Shenstone Park* here in 1930. The Hall, one of the city's major schools, and over a dozen other activities are run in the campus by the MSS, which also has half a dozen other projects elsewhere in the city. Near here is the Chinmaya Heritage Centre, another large complex inaugurated in 1995 with a magnificent hall and several rooms for meditation and lectures. The Chinmaya Mission started in 1953. Near here is the Malayalee club, its origin dating to 1897, and since 2016 in a new Travancore-influenced clubhouse.

Harrington Road, one of the better kept roads in Madras, leads eastwards into Spur Tank Road where the University of Madras's sports facilities are. And then you are in Egmore. The most interesting road in Egmore is undoubtedly Pantheon Road, taking its name from what was called *The Pantheon* – or 'Public Assembly Rooms'.

The Pantheon traces its history back to August 1778 when the Governor granted 43 acres for an estate to a civil servant, who, subsequently, in 1793, assigned the grounds to a committee of 24 which regulated the public amusements in the city at the time. Lord Cornwallis was entertained here in 1793 after his success against Tippu Sultan. Arthur Wellesley was also feted here – in 1805, after he won at Assaye with Madras troops charging the guns – and opened the ball with Lady William Bentinck. In 1821, the committee sold the main house and central garden space to E S Moorat, the Armenian merchant, who, in turn, sold it back to Government in 1830. Government first used the buildings and the grounds as the Collector's 'Cutcherry', then for the 'Central Museum', many additions to the original building being constructed between 1864 and 1890. The core of the old museum building includes the only surviving remnants of *The Pantheon*, identified from the broad steps leading into it when viewed from the north.

Amongst these buildings is a noble structure with stained glass windows, ornate woodwork and elaborate stucco decorations, the Connemara Public Library. The building is yet another Namberumal Chetty triumph. But the interior flourishes, so reminiscent of the Bank of Madras's (SBI's), are Henry Irwin's and that would appear reason enough to link his name even more categorically with the Bank's design. Its magnificent reading room with a rich wooden ceiling between two curved rows of stained glass, supported by ornate pillars and arches embellished with sculpted acanthus leaves, its teakwood furniture of another age, its marbled floor and its decorative windows all contribute to making it a thing of beauty that has been restored in 2004-7, but to which, unfortunately, access is not permitted. The building now houses the Old Collection (pre-1930), which is for reference only – books brought out to the reader on request. Its oldest possession is a 1608 *Bible*. It also has an Arabic-Latin Koran dating to 1698 and one of the Tranquebar Mission Press's first Tamil titles, published in 1781. The 'new' books are now in newer, connected buildings of undistinguished PWD architecture and opened in 1974, but this National Library, expected to receive every book published in India, retains the Connemara name.

The library was formally opened in 1896 and named after its progenitor. Not so long ago, a rather puritanical letter-writer wondered whether Connemara deserved remembering. A brother of Viceroy Lord Mayo (who was stabbed while visiting the Andamans in 1872), he was married to former Governor-General Lord Dalhousie's daughter Susan. "Connemara was divorced by Susan for adultery while in office," wrote the angry letter writer; Connemara apparently had "a weakness for young girls" and Lady Connemara had, after yet another incident, flounced out of *Government House* to stay at the Albany Hotel till her ship sailed for home. That must have stirred 19th Century Madras, but is unlikely to worry the 21st Century's. Legend, however, has it that that incident led to the Albany being re-christened the Connemara when Oakshott of Spencer's took it over six or seven years later! But that's sheer storytelling; the Connemara was indeed named after M'Lord.

Both the Museum and the Library benefitted greatly from the effects of the Madras Literary Society, the Oriental Manuscripts Library and the Records Office. The Library's beginnings go back to 1861, when hundreds of books found surplus in the libraries of Haileybury College (where Civilians for India were trained in England) and the India Office were sent out to the Madras Government. Government handed them over to the Museum which established a separate library section. The Madras Literary Society functioned here till it moved into its own premises in 1906, where it still survives in a building where some restoration has been done but the holdings cry for considerable attention. The Madras University Library was located here till it moved into its own handsome premises on the Marina in 1928. The Library and Museum staff were separated in 1930 and the Library made a separate institution in 1939. It became the State Central Library in 1950, a National Library five years later.

The beginnings of the library organisation in Madras may be traced to 1662 when a bale of calico from Madras was exchanged for books in London. This and a second consignment of books were maintained as a 'standing library' in the original *Fort House* and kept in the charge of Chaplain William Whitefield who had first suggested the need for a library. The chaplains of St Mary's continued to be in charge of the Fort St George Library for over a century. The first Catalogue of the first library was prepared in 1716 and accepted, after alteration, in 1720.

The Madras Museum complex, next door to the Connemara Library and set midst over 500 trees, is one of the finest in the country in terms of holdings. It houses a wealth of variety as well as a 19th Century theatre, delightfully Olde English both inside and out, with the 'pit' meant for those who can afford more and seating for the rest of the audience in tiered seats arranged in a semi-circle around the pit. Restoration to mark the 150th anniversary of the Museum introduced airconditioning in the place of 25 fans[2] hanging from the high ceiling, but the restorers have succeded in retaining the ambience of the past. The Madras Dramatic Society had first claim on the theatre during all the years the Society existed. The most striking building in these gardens, however, is what was built as the Victoria Memorial Hall and Technical Institute

---

[2] Francis Reid, a British theatre critic, commented in 1986, "Somehow all these fans seem appropriate to the architectural ambience of turn-of-the-century Raj when the London West End was brought to humid Madras with not one collar unstarched."

but which, in 1951, became one of the country's four National Art Galleries, home of a part of the National collection.

After the establishment of the Victoria Technical Institute in 1887, as a commemoration of Queen Victoria's Golden Jubilee, Government support began to falter. But when Queen Victoria died, a memorial fund was launched in 1901 to build a magnificent memorial which the VTI, founded to promote the local arts and crafts, could also use in some way. A grand exhibition hall was decided on and the foundation stone was laid in 1906. The building, declared open in 1909, was designed by Irwin in ornate Jaipuri-Mughal style, with characteristic pink sandstone facing and sculpture, and was built by Namberumal Chetty. Inside, Madras polished plaster and marble flooring dominated. The main entrance – to the large hall – is a gateway that resembles that of Akbar's dream palace at Fatehpur Sikri. The building, closed for some years now and badly in need of restoration, has, as these lines are written, been given a lifeline with Government sanctioning handsome funding for restoration. But even as that is awaited, the building still presents a striking appearance.

The VTI moved in even as the building was under completion and was a commercial success from the start. When Government took over the VTI Hall during the War, the Institute moved to a Mount Road location and in 1952 bought the site, which it developed by 1956 and has remained there since.

A new addition to the Museum complex in 1984 was another of those buildings that may be described as 'PWD Modern'. Located next to the Jaipuri fantasy, in it is housed a collection of contemporary Indian art that is, for the most part, as unIndian as the building it inspired. This collection was started in 1898. A second addition here is a slightly more tasteful attempt at 'Jaipuri remembered'. These new galleries now exhibit the Museum's fine collection of 9th-13th Century bronzes, 16th-18th Century Rajput and Mughal paintings, 17th Century Deccani paintings, 11th-12th Century handicrafts and, last but not least, some superb Ravi Varmas, whose gods and goddesses 'live' on almost every wall in India, now converted to calendar art.

Madras's renowned Museum has a lot more to offer than this Collection which is but a sampling. Its wealth had its genesis in a gift, of its fine collection of 1,100 geological specimens, by the Madras Literary Society to the Government in 1851. The Museum, the first Government-sponsored one in the country, opened the same year on the first floor of

The Pantheon complex...Jaipuri-Jaina architecture, in the National Art Gallery...
...and Victorian theatre-in-the-semi-round at the Museum.

59. *Jaipuri-Jaina again...in a little-used repository of learning, the Madras Literary Society.*

60. *The stacks of ages... a treasure-trove in these State Archives, hidden behind Egmore greenery.*

the College of Fort St George, adjacent to the Literary Society in Nungambakkam, with an exhibit of nearly 20,000 freely gifted specimens ranging from rocks to books. These gifts were in response to a public invitation that did not have a cut-off date. When the mounting collection of geological specimens threatened the stability of this first floor, the Museum's first Officer-in-Charge, Surgeon Edward Balfour, at the time President of the Literary Society and serving the Museum in an honorary capacity, advocated moving to a new building. The move was made in 1854 to *The Pantheon*, at the time partially occupied by the Cutcherry of the Collectorate. A library and a reading room were provided for the public in 1859. And in 1864 an upper storey was added to *The Pantheon* in sympathetic style, giving the Museum more elbow room. The library got a new block in the northwest corner of *The Pantheon* in 1876, with a lecture hall provided for. That building is now, after restoration, the Centenary Exhibition Hall of the Museum. By 1896 there had been built new buildings for the Museum (where the anthropological and arms galleries now are), the Connemara Library and the Museum Theatre.

Another unique construction here survived not more than a year. It was a tower designed by Henry Irwin, to be very much part of what was called the Connemara Victoria Public Library & Museum Section. A traveller of the time, Eustace Alfred Reynolds-Ball, says it was inspired by the Palazzo Vecchio of Florence. But it was very likely Irwin trying to do something one better than Chisholm's Chepauk tower.

The tower was completed in 1897 by J H Stephen, Chief Engineer, PWD, Madras Presidency. Governor Sir Arthur Havelock inaugurated it in the presence of G S T Harris who had succeeded Irwin as Consulting Architect. Shortly afterwards, for reasons unknown, Harris began instigating a whole heap of rumours that the tower was not stable. He also persuaded the Governor that the library-museum complex would be better off without the tower. Stephen tried his best to keep the building in place, but the Governor decided the tower should be pulled down, though there was much public opposition to it. Sometime in 1898 the tower ceased to exist. But the Museum website recalls it as being 200 feet tall. All this, happened during the tenure of Thurston as Director. He was preceded by two other equally dedicated directors.

Edward Balfour's successor, Capt Jesse Mitchell, Commandant of the Madras Mounted Police, not only added, between 1859 and 1872, over 72,000 specimens, mainly zoological, to the thousands, mainly geological, Balfour had left behind, but he was also instrumental in establishing the public library that was to grow into the Connemara Public Library. One of the specimens that Mitchell added to the Zoology Gallery was the skeleton of a rearing horse, that was his when he was with the Madras Horse Artillery. But perhaps the most significant thing he did was write to the Government in 1860 urging it to fund a library: "A few hundred rupees, judiciously expended every year, would place before the public a library of reference that would in the course of time be an honour to the Government." His wish was fulfilled in 1862, when Government funding enabled the opening of a small library in June that year. This library evolved into the Connemara Library. Initially the library was supervised by the Museum, but in 1939 Dr F H Gravely, the last British Superintendent of the Museum, had the Library separated from the Museum, each with its own head. Surgeon George Bidie enriched the Museum's botanical collection[3] during his stewardship (1872-1885). He also grew medicinal plants and exotic trees in the Museum grounds. Antiquities, too, began to be collected with enthusiasm from 1872. The focus of the Museum changed to the Madras Presidency [4] under Dr Edgar Thurston, the great surgeon-anthropologist, who headed the 'Settha College' (College of the Dead) between 1885 and 1908. Anthropology, pre-history, ethnography, marine fauna and numismatics were what he concentrated on during a splendid tenure.

Balfour established the first zoo in Madras in 1855 in the Museum grounds with a nucleus of animals gifted by the Prince of Arcot. And a year later it had over 300 animals, birds and reptiles. This zoo was made a separate institution and shifted to People's Park in 1863 where it remained, not growing very much, till its move to Vandalur. Balfour, commenting on his work, pointed out that the British Museum was visited by 347,683 persons in 1855 as against the 368,873 persons who visited the Madras Museum in 1855-56. Yet the British Museum spent around £ 85,000 a year at the time, whereas the Madras Museum spent only £ 1,000 (Rs 10,000)!

Today, the Museum is housed in five buildings and has an internationally known, well-housed bronze collection as well as excellent numismatic, philatelic, musical instruments and arms collections. Its

---

[3] Including the famous Beddome Collection.
[4] A policy followed to this day, with allowances made for changing political geography.

pre-history gallery has the first Indian Palaeolithic stone tools – acquiring as it did in 1904 most of Bruce Foote's finds from Pallavaram. Its 3400-piece South Indian enthnographic exhibit is magnificent. And it probably holds the best collection of Roman artifacts in India, obtained from treasure troves in the South. But more entertaining from the casual visitor's point of view is the collection of animals, lizards and reptiles that attests to the skills of unsung taxidermists[5], and some superb sculpture that is housed in the old (rear) building, whose nucleus was *The Pantheon.* Two of the Museum's most interesting zoological exhibits are the 60-foot whale skeleton acquired from Mangalore in 1874, at a time when there were only two such specimens in all the museums of Europe, and the skeleton of the great Chengam elephant (height 10½ feet), acquired in 1887 when it was described as "the largest elephant ever killed in India." Rather incongruously, two pre-historic monsters rear up on their hind legs by the new Children's Museum, indeed looking like the toys they are! And inside is a working model to thrill the young.

The Museum's 1,700 bronzes, constituting the finest bronze collection in the world, and its 1,500 Buddhist antiquities – the largest collection in the world of the wealth of Amaravathi (200 BCE-300 CE) and first displayed here in 1878 – are its most prized possessions. Auguste Rodin was so taken up with the bronzes during a visit to Madras that he spent hours staring at them – and then wrote a monograph on them. These have recently been paid almost as much attention to by the Museum's caretakers. Over a thousand wood carvings, 800 stone sculptures – many of them in the 'Sculpture Garden' – 500 copper plate grants and 500 miscellaneous antiquities...all this and more in addition to the bronzes and Amaravathi art make the Madras Museum second only to the National Museum in Delhi as a repository of the art, culture and history of India.

In a Raj era building in the museum complex since 1990 is the Cauvery Technical Cell that deals with the river dispute with Karnataka. Of note here is the Col W M Eliss bust, remembering the man who conceived the Mettur Dam in 1910 and supervised its building between 1925 and 1934.

Pantheon Road crosses the Cooum over Anderson Bridge. Just before the bridge, on the north flank of *Pantheon Gardens*, is the headquarters

---

[5] One of the earliest was Anthony Pillay, who in the 1880s won several awards at exhibitions in England and was recognised internationally, in consequence, as one of the best taxidermists of the day.

of the Tamil Nadu Handloom Textiles Co-operative movement, whose looms turn out the finest silks and cottons in the country and whose export record is enviable, besides maintaining Madras's reputation for textiles. In the grounds of these headquarters – now embellished by a 'saree museum' – there used to be held a handloom textile exhibition and sale that was a major event in the Madras calendar every year, but has sadly not been held for some years now. But an alley nearby is 'Cotton Row' where hawkers offer an enormous range of cotton goods, made and unmade.

Across Anderson Bridge to the right are *Anderson Gardens,* blending buildings of another age with those of the more recent past to form the well-maintained State Bank of India's officers' quarters. On the left are the art galleries of the Lalit Kala Akademi, the Central Government organisation promoting Art. Year round, exhibitions are held in this campus developed in 1978. In between them used to be Tulloch's Gardens in the 19th Century, a part of which became *Cochin House,* the Madras home of the Maharajah of Cochin in the 20th Century. In 1966, Cochin House was gifted as the home to the newly founded Asan Memorial School.

A little to the northeast of Pantheon Road are the striking Indo-Saracenic buildings of Egmore Railway Station, terminus for all trains from the South (the old South Indian Railway). Inaugurated in 1908 on a site acquired in 1900, the Station's buildings were expanded in the 1930s and additions were made in the 1980s to blend harmoniously. Through all the more recent changes, the SIR has remained emblazoned on its *bas relief* crest, though the 'I' was painted out in recent years.

The land on which Egmore Station (then of the South Indian Railway) was built had belonged to Dr. Pulney Andy and he sold the 1.83 acres and several buildings on it to the SIR in 1904. It wasn't a particularly happy sale. It was his attachment to those buildings that were the cause for the reluctance of 'S.Pulney Andy, M.D., M.R.C.S. (ENG.), F.L.S.', the first Indian not an Anglo-Indian to qualify in England as a doctor.

In a letter to the Deputy Collector he stated his objection to the sale and wound up with his most significant argument: "After retiring from Government service, I have turned my mind to the remodeling of the Indian Christian Church and am the founder and the President of the National Church of India. My residence in Egmore is the Head Quarters of the movement and I have utilised a building here for the purpose of worship and there have been already two ordinations of Ministers during the past year. It was also my intention to erect a substantial building as a Temple for public worship by members of the Christian Community on the land... (which) is centrally located." Pulney Andy, however, concluded his letter:

"But should it be considered that my property is absolutely required for the purpose of Railway construction and should Government desire to compel me to part with it, under the provisions of the Act, I beg to state that I may be granted a compensation of not less than one hundred thousand rupees (Rs.100,000) for it and sufficient time should be given me for removal." His request was met with alacrity but not generosity, the 'not less' ignored. The station flagged out its first train, the Boat Mail, on June 11, 1908.

Not far from the Station, a latter-day Imperial Hotel is ensconced in the gardens of what was *Waverley House* and closer to the Museum the vegetarian Ashoka Hotel has come up in the *Munagala House* gardens, property of the Zamindar of Munagala.

2. Keeping the record straight

Almost across the road from the Egmore Station, in a red-brick building with green-painted woodwork, part of a campus that strikes the viewer as more befitting a colonial club, are the State Archives that claim to be the largest in South and Southeast Asia. Located behind the hockey stadium, nestling in its own garden and hidden by tall trees, is this haven of quiet and occasional scholarly research. In these Archives, possibly the oldest in Asia and among the oldest in the world, are the records of Madras and its districts going back over three hundred years. Since record-keeping is an activity associated with centuries more recent, the Tamil Nadu institution must be a pioneering one, world-wide!

The Archives has records in English from 1670, Dutch records from 1657, Danish records from 1777 and Persian records from 1670. It also has a fine collection of old books and maps on Madras and old Madras newspapers – including the very first issue of the *Madras Courier*, 1795.

It is to Sir William Langhorne, who arrived in Madras in 1671 to adjudicate a gubernatorial dispute, that Madras owes its meticulous record-keeping. The inquiring commissioner, a well-travelled, wealthy merchant of considerable ability, not only recorded the proceedings of his Commission in Madras, but also settled all issues pertaining to it so tactfully that in January 1672 he was appointed to succeed Foxcroft as Governor. No sooner he became Governor, William Langhorne insisted that all Madras Government records be systematically filed and maintained. The Public Consultations, the Public Letters to England and other records date from the beginning of Langhorne's governance. But the Archives' oldest records of the John Company era are the Despatches of the Court of Directors of the East India Company that were sent out from England in 1670.

Langhorne, who sought and obtained – mainly as part of his passion for records – confirmation of the Company's title to Madras, also officially acquired the village of Triplicane for the Company. He also negotiated with the Company for suitable grades, salaries and designations for its employees and, in early 1676, announced that order, at least a pecking order, had emerged from the chaos that had prevailed till then. By this order, an apprentice from England had to serve seven years before he became a Writer. Thereafter Writers became Factors, then Junior Merchants and, finally, Senior Merchants. It was only from among the Senior Merchants that the Council of the Presidency was chosen, the Governor being first in Council, the other Councillors in descending order being Book-Keeper, Warehouse-Keeper, the Customer (Customs and Revenue Collector), the Rental-General and Scavenger (who was responsible for collecting a house tax to be used for conservancy of the streets). From time to time there were also Mint-Masters and Pay-Masters (in charge of stores and what would amount to PWD work today, though usually these functions were merged with what the designation literally promised).

In Langhorne's time, and thereafter, the accumulating records were stored in the Council Room of *Fort House*. But as the accumulation increased, record-keeping also began to get out of hand. In 1803, Lord William Cavendish Bentinck arrived in Madras to succeed the second Lord Clive (Edward) as Governor. And 33 years before the Home Government passed an Act to preserve the Public Records and established the Public Records Office, London, Bentinck, on November 18, 1805, minuted as follows: "The consequence of preserving the records of this Government which are now become exceedingly voluminous and the convenience which every member of Government in general upon his appointment a perfect stranger to the details of former transactions would derive from having a regular index to each volume induce me to recommend that a Record Keeper should be appointed... obvious that the person to be selected should be a Native, conversant with the business of the Officers and likely to remain in the situation..." And so was born the first Records Office in India, headed by one Mootiah, "the Principal Native Servant in the Political and Military Department... who has engaged the respect of every Government."

Mootiah is now forgotten, but it is recorded his salary was augmented to 80 pagodas a month "in consideration of the increased duty which will be entrusted him." Mootiah's offices were located in rooms altered for the purpose in a building to the north of Fort Square (the Parade Ground of today), quite possibly one of the two buildings razed to make way for the new multi-storey structure that today dominates the Fort. In 1823 the Records Office was moved back to the main *Fort House*, then, two years later, it moved out to the 'Pillar Godown' where it remained, in varying degrees of occupancy, till it moved to its own buildings in Egmore in 1909.

Opposite Egmore railway station, early this century, stood a stately Government-owned house called *Grassmere*. It was proposed to build various medical and sanitary offices on this site, but the sewage farm to the south of it (now Mayor Radhakrishnan Stadium, Madras's hockey stadium and the only ground in Madras with Astroturf) and the noise of the railway station were considered reasons why these offices should not be built there. This debate lasted two years and, at the end of it, it was decided these objections did not hold for construction of a suitable Records Office. P Loganatha Mudaliar, who had earlier built St Mark's Church in Bangalore and the Medical Students' Hostel in Royapuram, was entrusted with the work. And so, after Rs 2.20 lakh were spent on the building and Rs 1.17 lakh on stacks and furniture, the new Madras Records Office opened in October 1909, with C M Schmidt, Registrar of the Secretariat, temporarily in charge. On April 15, 1911, Henry Dodwell ies, Additional Professor of English, Presidency College, and Acting Vice-Principal, Teachers' College, Saidapet, was appointed Curator, the first of an illustrious line. Printing of records had commenced in 1856, but never was printing activity as prolific as in Dodwell's dozen years. The first Indian to be appointed full-time Curator was V Sekhara Menon, in 1925. In 1935, the first trained archivist in India, Dr B S Baliga, took charge of the Archives and his next 23 years were the Archives' finest.

3. Villages for weaving

Between Commander-in-Chief Road, Pantheon Road and the Cooum is South Egmore, consisting of Pudupet and Komaleswaranpet, the latter getting its name from a temple said to ante-date Fort St George. This was an area inhabited by Indians of substance in Company days – Pachaiyappa Mudaliar used to live on Harris Road (then known as Pagoda Street) and his house, No 26 Pagoda Street, built around 1790, was a centre of Hindu religious discourses. His neighbours included a *dubash* to three governors and the first Indian employee of the Medical Department. The attraction to settle here was the cool of the riverside! Pachaiyappa Mudaliar, who built his house just a few years before he died, suffered from partial paralysis throughout those last years. In the latter part of his life, Pachaiyappa Mudaliar divided his time between Madras and the Court of Thanjavur, breaking journey regularly in Chidambaram during his travels. He died in 1794, aged 40, in Tiruvaiyyaru to where he had hastened when he fell ill in Kumbakonam. He was cremated in Tiruvaiyyaru. Of his will, mention has already been made.

Harris Road is reached from Mount Road by crossing Harris Bridge, which was built in a year, 1854-55! Governor Harris was kin of a later Lord Harris, Governor of Bombay, who formalised cricket competition in India in the 1920s. Across from Harris Bridge, towards Mount Road, there are now new multi-storey buildings belonging to the Postmaster General. In the large old mansion on this site that the Postal Department occupied till it was pulled down to make way for the new, there used to be a corner-stone with an inscription dated 1790. The building, the inscription indicated, was built by Nawab Wallajah. It was later occupied by Lewis Milner & Co, Spencer & Co and the Madras Survey before, an addition to the inscription informed the visitor, it had "lately been converted to the use of the Post-Master General."

The eastern half of this area has now fallen on lean times. Commander-in-Chief Road, in the western half, of course, gets its name from C-in-Cs who used to live in a 'garden house' here. In this area there were till the 1990s some of the best examples of 'garden houses' in the City. Some of these were on Victoria Crescent, near which was the Ethiraj mansion, across the road from Ethiraj College and derelict from 1985 till it was pulled down in the new Millennium. The City's first Victoria Hotel also used to be on the crescent. Not far from here are the Freemasons' Hall – in striking Ionic-pillared Regency architecture now renovated – some postal buildings of another era that would be striking, if only they were renovated and not hidden by the wild growth that now surrounds them, and the Presidency Club's 'garden house', hidden behind high battlemented walls and in its new, 1990s incarnation straight out of Imperium's first architectural age. The Hall and the Club still seem monuments to the era when they were the retreats of the *Sarkar's* elite.

Meticulously prepared, a gentleman with the judges, juries and the opposite side, always with a smile and ever ready to concede a point, Vellore Lakshmanasamy Ethiraj, a London-qualified barrister, had a manner that ensured a meteorically successful career. In 1937, he was made the Public Prosecutor of Madras Presidency, the first Indian appointed to the post. During the 13 years he served as Prosecutor – till his retirement at 60 – he adopted an attitude towards the defence that said "I am the prosecutor, not the persecutor." If ever there was a walking example of fair play in the Courts, it was Ethiraj. After retirement, he resumed private practice and became known as "the greatest criminal lawyer in India". His record included appearing in 44 cases on a single day in different courts and in an eight-minute defence obtaining an acquittal after days of evidence had been presented against his client!

Concerned about the state of Indian women, whom he thought were "depressed, oppressed, and suppressed," he felt that priority should be given to improving their lot. A good friend, R. M. Statham, Director of Public Instruction, suggested that, if helping women is what Ethiraj wanted to do, he should start a women's college. So was born an idea in 1944 and on July 2, 1948 it materialised as the Ethiraj College for Women, starting with 96 girls in premises leased from Hobart School, Royapettah. Ethiraj had donated Rs.5 lakh to start the institution. Subur Parthasarathi, acting Principal and Professor of English, Queen Mary's College, was permitted by Government to join as the first Principal.

When the Government sanctioned on 99-year lease the land where the College now is, 3½ acres on which then stood a palatial building housing the Public Service Commission, the College moved in there in July 1951. To this Ethiraj added 5½ acres of his property, valued at Rs.5 lakh, which abutted the Government grant. On his death in 1960, his will placed much of the proceeds of his estate with the official trustee of the High Court (about Rs.10 lakh) to be earmarked for the grant of scholarships to the needy. Today, Ethiraj College has a strength of 7000 students.

The Freemasons' Hall welcomes visitors – with permission – to view its splendidly embellished meeting halls from another era. An administrator's cottage in the spacious campus has been transformed into an inviting modern mini-theatre, with a part of it housing a small Masonic museum. The Presidency Club was founded in June 1929, when 25 "ornaments of administration and officialdom" found the Cosmopolitan Club too elite even for them. M A Candeth and M Rathnaswamy called for "real clubbable people" to join "a centre of social life free from prejudice and immune against fads." The Club was originally located in Spur Tank Road. Then, in 1932, it moved to Montieth Road and, finally, in 1937 acquired its present premises, *Fairlawns*, for Rs 75,000 from Dr P Subbaroyan, Zamindar of Kumaramangalam. A substantial portion of this property was sold in 1967 to MICO, in whose premises the German Consulate General was located till development changed the MICO (now Bosch) campus in 2006. Uniquely, the Club's constitution did not provide for a President till change was brought about in 1983, when M A M Ramaswamy was elected President. Till then, the Secretary had functioned as the Chief Executive, Ramaswamy revived the Club and restored its buildings, then moved on to do the same in the late 1990s to the Suguna Vilasa Sabha, which had given up Theatre it was once acclaimed for, when its home was the Town Hall, and put down roots in Mount Road as a social club.

Pantheon Road, running east, crosses the Cooum (possibly a contraction of Komalam or Komaleswaram) and enters a now-congested broad tongue of land that nestles in the river bend, between Egmore and The Island. This is Chintadripet, founded in 1734 by Governor George Morton Pitt, who was born in Fort St George in 1693. The village was founded as a weavers' settlement, taking its name from *chinna tari peta* (village of small looms), and 230 families were settled here by 1737.

The founding of such a village by the Company – like Collettpettah earlier – was found necessary, for it was getting increasingly difficult to obtain good cloth for export from the city as well as the mofussil. Spinners, weavers, 'painters', dyers and washers were settled here on land which belonged to a dismissed Company *dubash*, Sunku Rama. The *dubash* protested vehemently, but Pitt had the last word – fraudulent though it may have been. Audiappa (Vennala) Narayana Chetty, another Company *dubash*, built a temple here dedicated to Audi Kesava Perumal, and Audi Pureswarar, a twin shrine similar to the "Town Temple'. He also built a mosque. Audiappa Narayana Chetty and Chinnatambi Mudaliar were authorised by the Governing Council to receive loans from the Company and to be responsible for the disbursement of the money to weavers whom they were to attract to the new village with cash and loans for moving and building expenses.

Chintadripet figures prominently in the French wars, as a base camp for the besiegers of Fort St George. A beautiful new Jain shrine built in marble was consecrated here in 1985. It is dedicated to Acharya Shri Vijay Shantisuriswarji. In nearby Komaleswaranpet is the over 300-year-old Komaleswarar Temple. And a little to the north of it, in Lakshmi Narayana Perumal Street, Egmore, is the 150-year-old Srinivasa Perumal Temple. The quaintly styled Zion Church on Arunachala Naicken Street in Chintadripet, an extension of Pantheon Road, had its beginnings in 1847 with Dr. John Scudder and Dr Miron Winslow of the American Madras Mission established in the 1830s. It ws the first American Church in Madras, but, in the 1860s was sold to the Christian Missionary Society, London. It has been tended for several generations by pastors from the same family. The Church, which went through expansions in 1880 and 1912, is abutted by the Sathianathan Memorial Parish Hall dating to 1895 and built in the same style. W T Sathianathan was, in 1862, the first of five generations of the Sathianathan-Clarke family to preach here; over 135 years, son has followed father in the pulpit here, an extraordinary heritage. Across from it, and looking not unlike it, is the Lady Goschen Library founded in 1927. The Library, work on whose building started in 1926, owes its genesis to a leading citizen of the locality, Vijayaraghavalu Chitty, who wanted it built as a space for a library as well as a meeting hall. The library once had about 50,000 books; today it is an ill-kept reading room. Not far from both is Napier Park, now called May Day Park and, ironically, tended by an industrial giant, Simpson's. As these lines are written, this 1950s creation has fallen prey to the Metro which has promised to restore it when its tracks are up and its trains running.

Hidden in a corner of it is the statue of Justice H T Boddam – who could hardly have been remembered for his judicial acumen or his racial tolerance. It was raised because he was good to animals as we have already seen.

A Winter's Tale

The Agent and his son were in their Chamber,
Totting up their woes,
The Ex and present Second waited with a friend,
Behind closed doors.
When two Councillors said,
New Foxcroft they would follow,
The Captain and his Guard cried,
"Old Winter is our fellow!"

And so was launched Our Towne's first coup. But the surprising thing is that Madras had survived its first thirty years without someone taking the law into his own hands. For the city, from the very beginning, survived in a stormy atmosphere.

Andrew Cogan arrived on the Coromandel Coast in 1639 and, while deciding whether Francis Day should go ahead with his plans for Madraspatnam, quarrelled with Thomas Ivie over who should be Chief of John Company's Agency in these parts. For almost the next 150 years the pattern was set for Agents and Presidents and Governors to quarrel with their subordinates in Council. But only twice did this unsavoury, bitter bickering get out of hand in that first half of the City's history. And the first occasion was Winter's Coup, which might be described as the first coup d'etat in Modern India.

In Battersea Parish Church in England, there is, in the South Gallery, a monument to Edward Winter who died in 1686 and was buried there. Beneath the bust, of a truculent-looking man used to having his own way, is inscribed a eulogy which, in part, reads:

Nor less in Martial Honour was his name,
Witness his actions of Immortal fame:
Alone, unarm'd, a tygre He opprest,
And Crusht to death the Monster of a Beast.
Thrice-twenty mounted Moors he overthrew
Singly on foot, some wounded, some he slew;
Dispers'd the rest; what more cou'd Sampson do?
True to his friends, a terrour to his foes,
Here, now, in peace his honour'd bones repose

There appears to be little confirmation of this Samson's monster-slaying ability, but that he was aggressive and strong-willed there seems little doubt. He was just eight when he shipped out in 1630 with his older brother Tom, bound for the Coromandel Agency where Tom Winter was fellow-Councilman and crony of free-trading, roistering Francis Day who took the boy under his wing at Armagon. During Day's last years at Armagon, whenever he left the dilapidated factory to prospect for a new settlement between Pulicat and Pondicherry or to spend time with his lady-love at San Thomé or to attend Council meetings at Machilipatnam, factory steward Edward Winter, still far from being out of his teens, virtually ran the place. It is no wonder that he soon became a full-fledged employee of the Company which, when selecting an employee, insisted that the first qualification for employment was the person's ability to look after himself. The founder of Madras had indeed trained his protégé well in this and in such supporting qualifications as indulging in private trade, looking after your friends too well, looking after yourself even better and enjoying life to the full. But when Edward bought a Nawab's 'junk' that had been 'captured' in dubious circumstances by the British and proceeded to use it as a private yacht, he caught a crab: his activities proved too much for both the Nawab as well as for many of his fellow-factors and his services were dispensed with in 1659.

Winter went back to England in January 1660 to plead his case and he pleaded it so well, ingratiating himself with Charles II at the same time, that two years later he was knighted and asked to take over the Madras Agency. And so Sir Edward Winter returned in 1662 to the scenes of his early triumphs, styling himself "Knt. and Bart.", the Baronetcy however in doubt, at least one doubter testifying that in one document "the word Barronett was interlined above the line, and as plainely appeared to bee done with another inke."

For the next three years, Winter governed the Agency with a mailed fist. He survived an assassination attempt, carrying for the rest of his life a scar on his face from one of the wounds. He may have himself been involved in the murder of a Mr Court. And he had erected just outside the main gate of the Fort a gibbet, a standing threat for many years to those who did not get along with Authority, fair or unfair. As befitting a friend of Charles II, the Merry Monarch, Winter enjoyed a life of great extravagance in Madras and his private trade paid for it all. But helping himself and helping his friends was bound to have inevitable consequences, especially as his Council included some disgruntled elements who described the 'Winter Gang' as being composed of "not a few Rogues." And so, despite all Winter's protestations, the Company decided to supersede him – but at the same time gave him permission not only to continue as Second-in-Council till his three-year term was up but also to stay on in Madras, as long as he wanted, to wind up his private business.

The man John Company sent out to oust Edward Winter was George Foxcroft, an elderly London businessman with no experience of India at all. Then, compounding their folly in sending out such an inexperienced man, the Directors sent out his son Nathaniel as well with him – for what reason no one knows. And to crown their foolishness they sent out in George Foxcroft a man who had been described as "sober and God-fearing" and who might well have been a Cromwellian Puritan. Such a Roundhead must have been like a red rag to the Cavalier-spirited bully who'd governed Madras till then! Promptly on arrival, Foxcroft launched an investigation into Winter's accounts and then began asking a lot of awkward questions. He even 'raided' Winter's house – finding a cache of arms. The new Agent was, in the jargon, simply asking for it. And for an ardent Royalist, surrounded by those who liked the good life, to find a pretext that would enable him to turn the tables on a Cromwellian sympathiser was not likely to be difficult in the politically-charged atmosphere of the age.

The opportunity came one day at the General Table of Fort St George at which all employees of the Company dined and where the conversation inevitably turned to politics. The Chaplain, Simon Smythes, kinsman of Winter by recent marriage and a well-known soak who was once "drunke" for "six dayes together, the Lords day being one of them," got talking with Nathaniel Foxcroft and the conversation progressed to heated argument during which the Agent's son is alleged to have stated that he would always maintain his private interest before the King's and that he would obey and serve his monarch only as long as that King could offer him protection. Agent Foxcroft could have called both quarrellers to order, but, instead, got unwisely embroiled in their dispute himself and, stating that the only claim the King had to England's Crown was that of conquest, challenged Smythes to prove that "any King in Christendom had title to his crown by means other than conquest"!

The slanging match was all that Winter needed to, as he sanctimoniously expressed it, "show himself very chearfull and ready to assert His Majesties interest with what hazard of his owne person or estate soever." Winter's method of asserting His Majesty's interest was to go to the corps du guard with his witnesses and impeach Foxcroft before them.

Foxcroft was later to opine that Winter could never have made the treason charge stick because his two witnesses were of such "debauched" character. Smythes apparently spent much of his time playing "nynepins" and "disordering himself with drinck with the most debauched of the soldiery." As for "his other works of darkness," Foxcroft related that before the Chaplain's marriage "he was allwaies the latest that came into the Forte at night; insomuch that I was very often raised out of my bed to deliver the keyes of the Forte, that so he might be lett in...." Farley, the other witness, had come out as Foxcroft's own servant but proved to be a lewd, impudent and obnoxious young fellow whom Winter once threatened with "the correction of a boy with his breeches downe," which Foxcroft said "he would have made no difficulty to have done, being knowne to be a man of valour...." In time, however, Winter found "this saucy young varlet to be for his turne...made him his friend and companion, and further countenanced and debauched him; and by his guifts and flatteries and greate promises easily persuaded him his instrument to debauch and seduce some of the soldiers...."

But at this moment, when Winter demanded the assistance of the soldiers to seize the 'traitors', the guard stood fast and would not follow him. This, however, did not stop Winter, according to Foxcroft. Armed with six pistols, sword, dagger and buckler, and accompanied by an almost equally well-armed (four pistols!) Farley as well as Chaplain Smythes and "a crew of his servants and black attendants armed also," the fiery ex-Agent burst into Foxcroft's chamber early on the morning of September 14th. But all that transpired there was an exchange of hot words after which Winter stormed out with his forces. Before they could leave the Fort, however, Foxcroft ordered the gates closed. Then, pondering over tales he'd heard of Winter plotting mutiny – to take over the Fort himself or to hand it over to the Dutch, it was not clear, but certainly it would have been to safeguard his own interests – Foxcroft decided he must act fast and he ordered a reluctant Lieutenant Chuseman, the Captain of the Guard, to disarm Winter and his men and take them into custody, "which after long demurr was done."

Within 48 hours, however, Winter had the impecunious Chuseman eating out of his hand, promising him better prospects. Wavering Chuseman's wife too played her part in his conversion, thus obliging Winter who had given her – one is intrigued why – "fyne guifts and large promises...other cyvilities and good turnes more than ordinary." Proby, the senior Councillor and in whose chamber Winter was confined, also now threw in his lot with his ex-Chief, and the revolution was launched.

On that still dawn of September 16, 1665, while Winter patiently awaited in Proby's room, Chuseman, with about twenty men – the only ones who had agreed to follow him – stormed noisily up the stairs of Fort House. *Hearing the commotion – and, according to Foxcroft "supposing that Sir Edward might be making some attempt to make an escape" – Foxcroft and his son and Councillors Sambrooke and Dawes who were conferring with them, rushed out with arms drawn, only to find Chuseman brandishing his sword over his head and the soldiers with him shouting "For the King" one moment and "Knock them down" another. Who fired the first shot is not clear. There is more charge and counter-charge at this point in the narrative than at any other time, but the casualty list is undisputed: Dawes was fatally wounded and died some time later, Foxcroft Senior and Sambrooke were wounded in several places during the initial moments of the clash, and Nathaniel Foxcroft, who ran back for his pistols when he saw the action, was injured in a later melée with the soldiers. Foxcroft Junior, his father later related, discharged both his pistols at the Lieutenant when he returned to the fray, "but neither took fire (whether by some legerdemaine or by the moistness of the powder, he having beene twoe days before abroad in the wett...) by which meanes the Leiftenant, by all likelihood, escaped a passport out of this world (reserved to another reward)." The Agent's* son then closed with Chuseman and almost threw him into a deep well in the courtyard, but the Lieutenant was rescued by his soldiers and the younger Foxcroft knocked down and wounded. Foxcroft claimed that the shot which accounted for Dawes had been aimed not at the victim but at him, had burned the clothes and skin on his left side and had sped on to hit poor Dawes in the stomach and pass right through. Foxcroft added that two other shots just missed him while he was on the ground!

While all this activity was going on, Winter remained "like an innocent good man in Mr Proby's chamber, as if he had no hand in it nor knowledge of it." He claimed it was all "the Captaines doing" – the Lieutenant being so styled by virtue of being the Captain of the Fort's soldiery. But no sooner Winter heard "that I was fallen, he springs out of Mr Probys chamber into the Court, frisking and leaping with great joy (with sword and buckler in his hands), crying out, it is done, it is done; and how he came by sword and buckler in Mr Probys chamber you may easely ymagin," Foxcroft later narrated.

Meanwhile, the four prisoners had been bundled "into several rooms apart" and sentinels (teams of both English and Indian guards) were mounted over the rooms to keep them in and their friends out. "Thus," said Foxcroft, "they became possessed of the Fort by rebellion, blood and murder." And Winter took over, reporting to London that the "factorys, servants, etc., officers of the Honourable East India Company in Fort St George" had "unanimously agreed.... that Edward Winter, Knight and Barronett, late Agent for the aforesaid Honourable Company...be requested...to accept and take into his care the management of their affaires...." Winter's Council, of course, included Chuseman and Smythes.

By all accounts, Winter's subsequent rule was tyrannical, merchants, soldiers and sailors thought to be sympathetic to Foxcroft being imprisoned in chains and often branded. An attempt by the crew of the Indiaman Greyhound to recapture the Fort was foiled and the would-be rescuers were imprisoned. Our Towne had become Winter's Towne.

Foxcroft and his son were to remain in prison till August 1668 – when he emerged as Our Towne's first Governor, released by the arrival in Madras of the Royal Commission for the deposition of Winter and restoration of Foxcroft. The news of the revolution reached England only in January 1667 and it took till December that year for the

Commission to be announced. But even when the Commissioner arrived from England, Winter would not yield HIS fort easily. He drove a hard bargain, ensuring the safety of his person and property before surrendering Foxcroft and the Fort to the Honourable Company once again. And then continued in the city for four more years – till he settled his private estates and recouped the money he had spent on years of lavish living! Foxcroft too left Madras a few days after him.

19

The Great Choultry Plain

1. Shrines of all faiths

On either side of Mount Road, from the Island right up to Cenotaph Road, was what the British called the Great Choultry Plain, encompassing today's Nungambakkam, Teynampet and Royapettah. It is a name first mentioned in the records in 1721 and appears to have derived from the *Woodundy Choultry* that existed at the junction of White's Road and Mount Road, opposite *Mackay's Garden*. It was this area, between Triplicane High Road, then a major thoroughfare, and the 'Long Tank'– the Mylapore and Nungambakkam Tanks that were alongside the northern edge of Mount Road – 70 acres filled up in 1923 as Theagaroyanagar, and a part of Nungambakkam, that hosted the second stage of building 'garden houses' – those huge, airy mansions, with wide, colonnaded verandahs, situated in extensive compounds that each today holds scores of houses or a couple of highrise complexes. These houses freed those early Britons from restrictions that living in the Fort entailed.

The first 'garden house' on the Plain was built by an erstwhile Mayor, George Mackay, in 1785; *Mackay's Garden* was a well-known locality opposite Thousand Lights Mosque until not so long ago. The name persisted even though the property was acquired from the Mackay family by the Nawab Wallajah and, around 1798, was known as *Azim Bagh,* Azim being Wallajah's grandson. It was in *Mackay's Garden* that the Indian National Congress held its third annual conference, the first in the city where the idea of the Congress was born.

Mackay's Garden was about midway in the Plain, in a village acquired by the Company in 1744 and named Pudupakkam. Across from it to the south was *The Mansion*, another famous 'garden house', that belonged to another once and former member of the Governor's Council, Henry Sullivan Graeme. His name, commemorated in Graeme's Road today, is now spelt in a variety of ways, but rarely in the Scottish original. This road, separating *The Mansion* and *Mackay's Garden*, which were bounded by Mount Road, is only one of several roads with names commemorating old British residents of the Plain whose residences rather than contribution led to their names being left to posterity[1].

The Plain is south of Egmore, a triangle formed by the Cooum, Royapettah-Moubray's Road, and a line linking the Moubray's Road-Adyar River junction with the Nungambakkam High Road-Cooum junction. It is bisected by Mount Road, which was widened in 1796 and landscaped at the time with avenue trees three deep on either side.

For the benefit of British residents of this Great Plain, Col James Lillyman Caldwell, Madras Engineers, planned, and Maj Thomas de Havilland, executed in 1814-15, at a cost of Rs 207,000, the Anglican church now known as St George's Cathedral. The church was consecrated in 1816 by the first Anglican Bishop of India, Thomas Middleton, and was considered at the time the finest outside London. The Cathedral's spire is 140 feet tall and is identical in design to that of the Baroque St Giles-in-the-Fields, London. A noble portico and side porches, all pedimented and supported on handsome Ionic columns, provide entrance to an impressive nave, 100 ft long, 27 ft wide and 33 ft high. The belfry was completed in 1832.

The church and its cemetery are redolent with Madras imperial history in statuary and tombs, a treasurehouse of monuments. Prominent among those remembered here is Bishop Reginald Heber who sang of "Greenland's icy mountains" and India's "coral strand" and who, while on a visit to South India, drowned in his bath in Trichinopoly. The Anglican Bishops of Madras, from 1835, when the Church became the Cathedral of Madras, used to live in nearby *Pugh's Gardens* which everyone seems to call 'Pois or Poes Gardens'. The first of them, Rev Dr Daniel Corrie, and a successor, Bishop Caldwell, a Tamil scholar, are both remembered in the Cathedral. Amongst other monuments in the church are those to the memory of Thomas Parry and John Binny –

---

[1] More often than not, a road was named after the owner of the garden house to which the road led.

merchant chiefs whose business houses are still in business under new ownership, the former booming, the latter shrunk to almost a memory; to Company servant James Brodie of *Brodie Castle*; to church-and-bridge-builder de Havilland; to Presidency road-builder Samuel Best; to James Anderson – the famous doctor who introduced silk manufacture and many other natural wonders in the Presidency; to Dr William Griffith, eminent scientist, doctor and, above all, botanist; to the Nortons and Popham (of Broadway!) of legal fame; and to eminent astronomer Norman Pogson, who discovered twenty new variable stars and ten new minor planets, six of the latter while he was Government Astronomer, Madras!

Besides the Flaxman and Chantrey monuments in the church, the attached cemetery too is redolent with history. The first burial here, in 1818, was of Elizabeth de Havilland, wife of the Church's builder. Mary Patterson, who died in 1838 aged 105, is the oldest person buried here. Entry to the cemetery is through an impressive arched gateway, with a chapel beside it, both built in 1832. Enclosing the cemetery are railings made from hundreds of muskets and pistol barrels, bayonets and pikes – booty from 'Seringapatam' or war surplus, no one is quite certain.

Considerable additions were made to the Cathedral in Daniel Corrie's time. And improvements continued over the years. On September 27, 1947, the Church of South India was inaugurated here, unifying the major Protestant denominations in South India as the CSI. The CNI, the Church of North India, was to be formed many years later, in 1970. In 1955, Rev David Chellappa was installed here as the first Indian Bishop of Madras.

Not far from the Cathedral and in the Great Choultry Plain lived two bitter rivals who had governed Tamil Nadu between them for nearly 50 years. The senior in politics, Mu Karunanidhi, now in his 90s and still keeping a father's eye on his Dravida Munretra Kazhagam (the DMK Party), lives in Gopalapuram, to the rear of the Cathedral. To the south of it and not far from the Gopalapuram address, lived, till she passed away in 2017, J.Jayalalithaa who took over, after the death of her mentor, M.G. Ramachandran, who had led a breakaway group from the DMK and called it the All India Anna DMK (AIADMK). In and out of power, Jayalalithaa, who was for electoral and other reasons sworn in six times as Chief Minister, had made her 'Pois Gardens' address a household name in Madras. The one thing the rival Chief Ministers achieved was ensuring that only a Dravidian party was likely to be dominant in Tamil Nadu for a long time to come.

Amongst the historical buildings on the Great Plain, adjoining *Mackay's Garden* to its east, was *Amir Bagh*, built some time before 1798 by Nawab Wallajah. Many years later, in 1909, it became Spencer's Chairman Eugene Oakshott's property. It was once the Victoria Family, then the Elphinstone, Hotel for long-term residents, then, from 1910, the 35-room Spencer's Hotel before being run as the Ambassador Hotel from 1950 to the early 1960s. When Oakshott died in 1911 and his family lost interest in the property, Spencer's bought the hotel and grounds in 1913. Spencer's sold the property in 1944, but continued to run the hotel till 1950. This imperial building, located behind the Indian Overseas Bank headquarters, is seen in old pictures as having a magnificent approach road lined on either side with towering, ramrod straight Royal Palms and canna beds; it was in this garden that the IOB headquarters building rose after the property had been bought by the M Ct M family in the late 1950s. Before the historic building was pulled down in 1987-8, the Bank ran a training school in it. But where trainee bankers walked, there had once dined and danced the cream of Madras Society, for in Nawabi times *Amir Bagh* was often lent to the governors – including Lord Clive the Second – for their official entertainments.

Owning it as the Ambassador Hotel, with a popular restaurant called Rosemont, was C.G. Krishnaswami Naidu, who later had a friend, 'Karuppu' Srinivasan, run the hotel. The hotel was host for years to Ellis Dungan, an American who made Tamil films and whom we shall meet a few pages along.

Amir Bagh is believed to have been one of the 37 'palaces' Muhammad Ali owned in Madras in the late 18th Century. After its heyday, it was the office of the Sadr Adalat (the Nawab's high court). In 1802, it was sold to Francis Latour & Co. It later was occupied by the Agra Bank before it became a hotel. Its splendid 12-pillared, 40 feet high portico was built to allow the Nawab's howdahed elephants through. Inside was a superb ballroom, with a canopied ceiling and wooden balcony.

Next door to *Amir Bagh* was John Binny's house, which he bought from his firm in 1815 and on which site is the Connemara Hotel, the first Oakshott hotel property and the main Spencer's hotel of the late 19th Century. In 1875, there were three hotels near here. The Elphinstone was one, the Imperial gave its address as 153 Mount Road (where Binny's house had been) and the Royal is stated to have occupied what had been the Commander-in-Chief's house in the 18th Century, encircled by a crescent-shaped road. The Royal was owned for a while, around 1798, by Col Caldwell, the engineer. In the early 20th Century, it became known as the Victoria and the road too probably honoured the Queen after her death; certainly it remained Victoria Crescent till recent years, when it became Cherian Crescent, honouring the first woman Mayor of Madras. Next door was the Elphinstone Branch, which became the Royal when the latter became the Victoria. Both were on that Ethiraj College stretch, it would seem.

The Imperial Hotel (founded in 1854) took over the Binny property in 1867 and was in business till 1886 when it was succeeded by the Albany Hotel, which under new ownership became the Connemara Hotel in 1890. Eugene Oakshott took the 31-room Connemara over in 1891. As in the case of Spencer's Hotel, Eugene Oakshott's sons sold the Connemara to Spencer & Co in 1913 and it became the Company's flagship hotel. The hotel was remodelled in 1901 by Eugene Oakshott's partner James Stiven who was manager of the Hotel. Work at giving the Hotel a newer Art Deco look began in 1934 and was completed in 1937, looking as its main block does today from the outside. Sadly, the name Connemara has in the last couple of years virtually vanished, along lease arrangement with the Taj Group giving it the name Vivanta by Taj, whatever that means. As these lines are being written, the hotel is being renovated and refurbished and, perhaps by 2018, the Connemera will have its iconic name and heritage emphasised again.

Binny Road, on which the Connemara is sited, had come into existence around 1798, when it was laid to link the newly straightened Mount Road with C-in-C Road. Binny Road was joined to C-in-C Road by, first a causeway and then a bridge built in 1825 that had to be doubled in width only as late as 1994. In the years between the Wars, the Connemara came to be known as the best hotel in South India. Spencer's, in the early years of the 20th century, owned, besides its two Madras hotels, the West End in Bangalore (a hotel established in 1897 and acquired by Spencer's in 1911), and managed Brind's Hotel in Madras and Cubbon Hotel in Bangalore. It took over the Savoy Hotel in Ooty (whose beginnings were in 1841) in 1943. The Connemara, the West End and the Savoy are all on long lease to the Taj Group, Bombay, India's leading hoteliers.

Guides of the latter half of the 19th Century say the better hotels in Madras were on Mount Road. Others included English Family/Dent's Garden, Mount Road Family (*Mackay's Garden*), and Royal, Buckingham, and Branson's Garden (all on Mount Road). 'Black Town's' 'middle class' hotels were Belgravia and Harbour (2nd Line Beach), Malac (Esplanade), Esplanade (Broadway) and Napier (22 First Line Beach, also at one time in Armenian Street). Capper House was on South Beach, the Clarendon was in Mclean Street and Central in Rundall's Road, Vepery. It has been stated that Madras had no hotel accommodation before the 1750s, European visitors living with friends or in guest houses or taverns which had one or two rooms.

Across the road from the Connemara was *Umda Bagh*, built some time before 1798 and on whose site today is the Umda Bagh hostel of the Quaid-e-Millat Government College for Women – a gradual development from 1894 when plans were mooted to take over the rented premises of what was the Clothing Board for the chief Islamic school in the South, the Madrasa-I-Azam, established in 1849. The school had been founded in the late 18th Century by the Nawab Wallajah as the Madrasa-e-Aalia in his Chepauk Palace campus. Its first principal was Moulana Abdul Ali Bahrululoom of Lucknow. A Government Muhammadan College was also established in the *madrasa* until it got its own buildings on this campus in 1934. In 1948, it became a men's arts college. This college moved to Nandanam in 1972, making way for the city's fourth women's college, which was established here in 1974. The *madrasa* has continued through the years in the same compound and is now a high school, the state of its building suggesting closure one day in the not too distant future unless much restoration is done.

Umda Bagh, sometime after Nawab Umdat-ul-Umrah's death in 1801, was owned by Kola Singanna Chetty. After 1822, there lived in it Samuel Moorat and, then, in the latter part of the 19th Century, the Begum Sahiba Azum Unissa, wife of the last titular Nawab of Carnatic, a lady of legendary generosity and hospitality; the *madrasa* bears her husband's name, Ghulam Mohammed Ghouse (1825-1855).

At the Binny Road-Mount Road junction there used to be the statue of General James Neill. When Madras got its first Congress Ministry in 1937, Prime Minister[2] C Rajagopalachari had the bronze moved to the

---

[2] As Chief Ministers were then known.

Museum, one of the very few statues of the British Madras has removed from public view. Neill, of the Madras Army, was the man who marched from Allahabad to 'Cawnpore' during the 1857 Rebellion ensuring that "hardly a tree (on the 100-mile march) remained by the roadside which had not been converted into a gibbet." The hangman's statue probably deserved a worse fate, but C R always had a sense of history! An identical statue of Neill graces to this day the main square in Ayer, Scotland, his home town. Near here now is the Mani Nagappa bronze of MGR – M G Ramachandran – the film 'Robin Hood' who switched from being Douglas Fairbanks to becoming one of Tamil Nadu's most popular Chief Ministers.

Another part of the erstwhile Plain that retains associations with the Nawabs of the Carnatic is Thousand Lights where a historical mosque is sited in the angle formed by Mount Road and Peter's Road. The name of this area – which abounds with streets and houses associated with members of Nawab Wallajah's family – is believed to have derived from the tradition of using one thousand oil-lamps to light the triangular wedge of an Assembly Hall, constructed here about 1810 by a scion of the Arcot family, for Shias assembling during Muharram. A mosque was built c.1820 at a cost of about Rs 100,000, facing the hall. Renovation of the hall, the mosque and a contribution of 80 grounds were all donations by Ghulam Azadullah Doula, another member of the Wallajah family. This mosque was rebuilt around 1900 and then renovated, in 1936, by the Khaleeli Shirazi family. In 1981, a stylised new mosque, with two 64-feet-tall minarets and one large 30-feet-high dome and four small inward-curving domes showing modern Abu Dhabi influenced, was built next to the old mosque. It was designed by K M Asadullah Basha. Uniquely, it has a separate entrance leading to a mezzanine floor meant for women who wish to pray. The Thousand Lights mosque is one of the major mosques in the city. A special feature of it are the green ceramic tiles with Koranic verses baked into them that embellish the interior and exterior walls. In the campus are, besides the mosques, a library, a burial ground and a guest house.

Between Thousand Lights and what was one end of the Plain, Cenotaph Road (so named for being the original site of the peregrinating Cornwallis Cenotaph, and where it stayed for just a few years surrounded by a park), is Teynampet, abounding in old British Madras names. The Cenotaph was a meeting place for the gentry of Madras, who rode out or took their coaches out to it of an evening, met each other for a while, listened to the band in the park and then returned home. But as a way of spending an evening it soon palled and the Cenotaph soon fell out of favour – perhaps accounting for its move to the Parade Ground.

About where Teynampet begins is stately St George's Cathedral. And almost cheek by jowl are more modern but almost as noteworthy institutions and construction of more recent times – the city's first gurudwara, the Sri Guru Nanak Sat Sangh Gurudwara, with a new building raised here in the new Millennium, was developed handsomely here by the Sangh from small beginnings in 1949, Col. Gurdial Singh playing a leading role; the School for the Blind and the Deaf; Bala Mandir, a child care institution for under 5-year-olds promoted by Kamaraj, the one-time Chief Minister, and freedom fighter turned social worker Manjubhashini; the Anna Flyover; the American Consul-General's offices; memories in the city's first boutique hotel, The Park, a 2002 offering, of Gemini Studios, one of the earliest and finest in India, which gave its name to the 'Circle' here; and, till the early 2000s, wooded Woodlands Drive-in Restaurant, which we have already met in pages past. The Safire film theatre complex (the city's first multi-theatre complex, the names of the theatres reflecting the Veecumsee family's primary business (jewellery), and the South India Film Chamber buildings were two other well-known sites near here.

The Safire Theatre complex, which came up in a roadside quadrant of the Madras Club's *Branson Bagh* property, became one of the victims of television's success not long after the Millennium dawned. It then remained a shell for some years, till the wreckers' hammers went to work and has been replaced by a modern highrise office complex. Vecumsee's had bought the property for the theatre-complex from the Khivrajs the same day the latter had taken over the whole of *Branson Bagh* from the Madras Club.

Across from the Safire was another theatre, put up by the South Indian Film Chamber of Commerce founded in 1939. The Film Chamber's offices were in an old garden house next door that was associated with HMV occupancy and recordings from 1939. This charming old world building, once Khaleeli-owned, and now no more, was also once the Film Institute. The theatre was also a casualty of 21st Century development. But both theatre and chamber offices will soon have new replacement buildings to occupy.

To the west of the Cathedral, on both sides of the road, used to be the splendid gardens of the Agri-Horticultural Society which was founded in 1835. Of the 22 acres, only the nursery gardens remain, next to the Cathedral, and here the annual flower show, more than a century and a quarter old, used to be held till recent times. The larger part of the garden, across the road from the nursery, was where Woodlands Drive-in, an extremely popular restaurant on leased grounds, was till Government took over the property c.2008 and developed a botanical park midst the trees and made it a popular destination again. Robert Wight, botanist and author of *Icones Plantarum Indiae Orientalis*, was one of the enthusiastic promoters of the Madras Horticultural Society, which changed its name to its present form in 1860. The Horticulture Society's colonial cottage-like headquarters, a heritage building if ever there was one, was pulled down in 2003 and, curiously, rebuilt in the same style in 2004.

Wight was one of a long line of botanists from 1727 to 1867 who left an indelible record of flora of South India. Others associated with this recording were Patrick Russell, better-known William Roxburgh described as the Father of Indian Botany, Francis Buchanan-Hamilton, Walter Elliot and Hugh Francis Cleghorn, who in time became India's first Conservator of Forests after he had introduced an afforestation policy in the Madras Presidency. Their detailed notes were accompanied by some of the most meticulous drawings in the world, like those made by Wight's artists Rungia and Govindoo, many of which are in the Edinburgh Botanical Gardens collection today.

Patrick Russell, another Edinburgh surgeon, came to India in 1781 and in 1785 was appointed the Government of Madras's first 'Botanist and Naturalist'. His study of snakes made him 'The Father of Indian Ophiology' and the Russell's Viper is named after him. He was also the first naturalist to study the fish of the Coromandel Coast and the common Scorpion Fish was named after him, *Pterois Russelli*. Buchanan-Hamilton was responsible for the first Botanical and Zoological surveys and Elliot is better remembered for the Amaravathi finds, the Elliot Marbles, than his botanical work.

Teynampet, from Gemini Circle to Cenotaph Road, was farmland before 1800. In fact, in the 1980s, the verdict in a law suit declared a plot here as farm land! Behind erstwhile Gemini Studios (the City's biggest, and established in 1941 by that great film-maker K

Subrahmanyam as 'Movieland'; after being taken over by S S Vasan, it had an American manager to whom it owed much), and to the west of Mount Road is (East) Mambalam – now Theagaroyanagar (T'Nagar) or East Mambalam, which was developed on the site of the old Mylapore Tank and its extension, the Nungambakkam Tank. The decision to drain the tanks was taken in 1923 and work started in 1924 to reclaim 600 acres of land. In the heart of Greater Mambalam was created its focus, the 4½ acre *Panagal Park,* which was inaugurated in November 1928, T' Nagar roads radiating from it like the rays of the Sun. Many of the road names and locality names here are those of Justice Party leaders, one of them Dr. Natesan remembered in a Park developed in 1938 and then re-developed in 1950. The other half of Greater Mambalam is crowded West Mambalam, an ancient settlement. Still further west are newer developments, Kodambakkam and Vadapalani, and their contiguous residential 'nagars'.

T'Nagar has many well known temples. Among them is the 17th Century Kasi Viswanathar Temple, in Kuppiah Chetty Street, which, tradition has it, was built on this spot when it was called Mahavilva Kshetra, the contraction of which name is said to be the present-day 'Mambalam'. The Sankara Mutt of the great Saint is in Eswaran Kovil Street; the Mariamman Temple in Lake View Road has a *peepul* tree twined around the *neem* tree in its precincts; and the Kothandaramaswami Temple, near the Sankara Mutt and built in 1971, on the site of the old Pattabhiramar Temple, is famed for its exquisitely carved temple car, best seen at festival time in May. In West Mambalam is one of the earliest temples built in Madras in a style different from the traditional Dravidian. This is the Kali Bari Temple which echoes the Dakshineshwar Temple in Calcutta. It was dedicated in February 1981.

One of the City's newest temples, a creation in dazzling white so different from the multi-hued or rock dominated *gopurams* of the South, was consecrated on G N Chetty Road in Theagaroyanagar in 1979. To reach its elevated *sanctum,* high above the ground, there is a magnificent flight of steps. Its sacred pennant, fluttering high over the complex, is seen from afar. This two-tiered, 70-foot high Jain Temple, built with lime-and-soapstone from Porbandar and marble from Rajasthan, was the first of its kind in the South, it was stated at the time.

George Town has always had its share of Jain Temples. But the City had never seen such a splendid example of North Indian temple architecture as this. The construction, an immense task, only emphasised the growing cosmopolitan nature of Madras. This temple of the Swetambar sect of Jains, which took more than ten years to build, started with a dream of three men and an initial contribution of Rs 11,111 from each of them. Their dream, and contributions big and small from Jains in Madras as well as from faraway places, helped the project get started in 1968. Since then several other such Jain temples have come up in different parts of the city, like one in cramped surroundings on Cutcherry Road near the Kapaleeswarar Temple in Mylapore and others in Vepery and George Town.

The T'Nagar temple has been dedicated to Lord Shanthinath, the 16th *Thirthankara* (omniscient teacher), who has been sculpted seated, as an ikon a metre tall. The three other idols of *Tirthankaras* in this temple include one of Lord Parasnath, the 23rd *Tirthankara*, and one of Lord Mahavira, the last Great Teacher, who lived in the 6th Century BCE. All the idols are of white marble and have been sculpted by master craftsmen from various parts of the North. The temple, built after the earth was dug till the water gushed, purifying the precincts, has a large prayer hall adjacent to the *sanctum*. The Shree Shanthinath Jain Mandir is a place of worship for all, none forbidden; but the *sanctum* is only for those who bathe in the temple premises before entering.

G N Chetty Road runs on past the temple and reaches Panagal Park, a 'lung' that has many associations with 20th Century Madras political history. This is the 'heart' of Mambalam, the busiest shopping centre in the city. To the south and west of the Park are a score of shops that offer the finest selections of South Indian silks. Parallel to the Park on its west are North and South Usman Roads. The latter is a veritable gold jewellery bazaar in its northern stretch and white goods stores in its southern stretch. Off South Usman Road, leading west from it, is Ranganathan Street, a veritable mega-bazaar crowded day and night and offering every home need. Leading off the park are some of the few roads in the city that still have the giant shade trees of the past. One of these, virtually a shopping mall and a hawkers' paradise, is popularly called Pondy Bazaar, a name whose origin has been surrounded in mystery till the Government, in one of its periodic name-changing operations, stated it was restoring its original uncontracted name – Soundarapandia Bazaar. W.P.A. Soundarapandian was a leader of the Self-Respect Movement in the 1920s. On this stretch was started in

1955 Sri Muniyandi Vilas Military Hotel, the 'Military' meaning non-vegetarian fare was its speciality and 'hotel' an Indianism for a restaurant. Its success with the masses led to a rush of such 'military hotels', with over 150 of them being in place by the 1970s when slightly more upmarket 'Chettinad hotels' began replacing the majority of them. But Ponnusamy's in Royapettah and Velu Military in Nungambakkam maintain the cuisine's reputation.

Also in T'Nagar are two museums in residences, one in former Chief Minister M.G. Ramachandran's home (in Arcot Road), and the other in the home on Tirumalai Pillai Road of a former Congress Chief Minister, K Kamaraj, who went on to become a power in the Congress on the national scene. The museums feature documents, photographs, mementoes etc. Also in T'Nagar on Bazullah Road is a home of Madras's first Prime Minister and India's first Indian Governor-General, C Rajagopalachari, Rajaji to all. Rajaji was one of the few leaders in the then Madras Province who favoured Hindi being taught in its schools. But the seeds for Hindi in the South were sown in 1918 when Gandhiji sent his son Devdas Gandhi to take classes here. The classes, inaugurated by Annie Besant, were held in the Young Men's Indian Association's *Gokhale Hall* in George Town. These classes developed as the Hindi Sahitya Sammelan and, in 1927, as the Dakshina Bharat Hindi Prachar Sabha, which, moving from George Town to Mylapore to Triplicane, finally settled in its own 5-acre site in Thanikachalam Road, T'Nagar. Its splendid headquarters building was declared open in 1936 by Jawaharlal Nehru, as the home of "an Institution of National Importance". *Gandhi Nivas,* a building on the campus, was home to Gandhiji for a few days when he once visited the Sabha. Its library has over 100,000 Hindi books. And over 300,000 students in the Southern States take its exams every six months. Devadas Gandhi, incidentally, married Rajaji's daughter Lakshmi.

Another institution associated with Gandhiji in T'Nagar, not far from the Hindi Prachar Sabha, is the Thakkar Baba Vidyalaya, a skills training institution for Harijan and other underprivileged children started in 1933 in Kodambakkam by a group of Gandhians. The school was moved to its present site in Venkatanarayana Road in T' Nagar in 1947. Gandhiji, when laying the foundation stone for its main building in 1946, asked that the institution, The Harijan Industrial School, be named after A.V. Thakkar, who had long campaigned for the uplift of the Harijans. The green campus, with several buildings for classes, now also hosts a gallery of historical pictures of the Mahatma and a library whose pride is Gandhiji's works. A significant contributor to the institution was Rm. Alagappa Chettiar.

2. Repositories of learning

Northwest of Gemini Studios is Nungambakkam, up to the 19th Century much of it tanks and cultivated land, with records indicating existence as an independent village as far back as the 11th Century. In North Nungambakkam, on the south bank of the Cooum, at the bend it takes where Chetput joins Egmore on its north bank, is the site of the 'Old College' that gives a road its name. Today, the college campus houses the Department of Public Instruction, but its name is derived from early British days when it was the College of Fort St George, where junior Civilians trained for two years in two of the four main South Indian languages – and not from Women's Christian College which is on the same road.

The 'Old College' was started in 1812 and abolished in 1854, when a Board of Examiners took its place. The College and library were run by a Board which was also charged with "the pursuit in depth" of Dravidian language studies and, consequently, did considerable and invaluable publishing in this field on its own as well as by subsidising scholars.

Responsible for the genesis of the College was Francis Whyte Ellis of the Madras Civil Service. Ellis is better known for his translation of the *Tirukkural* and his identification of the Dravidian languages as a distinct language stream. Less known is the fact that he sank 27 wells in Triplicane during a drought in 1818. One of them hosted a tablet with a quotation from the *Tirukkural*; the plaque is now in the Madurai museum.

It was here that men like Charles Philip Brown, the civilian who became a Telugu scholar after his three years in the College got him fascinated with the language, made their great contributions to the South Indian languages. Published from here was C Beschi's Tamil grammar, Miron Winslow's Tamil dictionary on which the American missionary worked with Arumuga Navalar in Jaffna in its early days, A D Campbell's Telugu grammar and T C Morris' Telugu dictionary, John McKerrell's Kanarese grammar and Reeve's Kannada dictionary, and C M Whish's Malayalam grammar and dictionary.

Old *College House* was built by Samuel Moorat in 1826 and sold to Government the next year. Moorat's building was part of what was known as the *Doveton House* compound. *Doveton House* survives as the main office building of Women's Christian College, a joint European-American missionary project. Though the college planned to pull it down in the early 1980s, conservationists persuaded the authorities otherwise, and *Doveton House* continues reasonably well preserved. But the conservationists didn't stand a chance when the Tamilnad Textbook Society – a government body – decided to emulate what Government had done in the Fort and built in these sylvan surroundings yet another towering concrete monstrosity. Fortunately, two imposing arched gateways of another age survive in the campus, both of which could be better tended, one on College Road, and the more impressive one facing the river and indicative of a river landing place at which the Governor would arrive in state to review the progress of the student-Civilians.

Lt Gen John Doveton, who first arrived in Madras in 1783 and died in 1847, was the soldier who looked after Tippu Sultan's two sons when they were held hostage by Cornwallis in Madras. It was the beginning of the close regard for him Tippu had. Doveton, who got on well with Indians, is said to have surrounded himself with a colony of Brahmins when he lived here. *Doveton House*, the second European house midst the paddy fields of Nungambakkam, was built before 1798, probably by a Benjamin Roebuck; it still has the city's tallest porch! Doveton, who died in it, acquired the house around 1837 from a Linghi Chetty. He left it to one of his Brahmin families who took the name Doveton as part of their name. In 1875, the then Gaekwad of Baroda was interned in this house for his role in the attempt on the life of the British Resident in his State; he built himself an airy room on the top, which still survives, and a bandstand and monkey house which don't. The house reverted to Government occupancy after this episode and, in 1893, it became the home of Sir Ralph Benson, a judge of the High Court. He left Madras in 1913. In 1914, the Indian National Congress sessions were held in the compound. And then it was a hostel for a while.

Women's Christian College, with 41 students and seven lecturers, moved into *Doveton House* in May 1916, the building and 11-acre campus having been bought for Rs. 76,000, Rs 63,000 of it a Rockefeller contribution. The College had been founded in 1915 and spent a year in

Hyde Park Gardens, Kilpauk, where a part of the Kilpauk Medical College now is. Its Principal for the first 22 years, Dr. Eleanor McDougall, a Scot, was the first woman to deliver a Convocation Address of the University of Madras. That was in 1931. Her brother, Charles, gifted the College its huge clock in 1937.

Other buildings in *Doveton Gardens* that WCC absorbed were *Hanson's Gardens* in 1920 and *Riverlands,* giving the College a 20-acre campus. Striking features on the campus today are the Assembly Hall, where, in 1947, the birth of the Church of South India was planned at a Bishop's Retreat, the Science Building, built in classical style in 1925, and the unusual looking College chapel, designed by Quaker architects, Reginald Dann and Guy Jackson, and built in 1923 with a cross within designed by the Madras School of Arts and Crafts. The church was made possible following a $10,000 gift from 'an American friend'.

Founded on the same campus in 1923 was St Christopher's Training School (now St Christopher's College of Education) with a sister of British parliamentarian Fenner Brockway as its first Principal. Kathleen Brockway moved the School to Kilpauk in 1927 and then to Vepery in 1932 when Lady Bentinck's School, founded a hundred years earlier, became its training school. The School became recognised by the University of Madras as St. Christopher's College in 1944. In 1953 Getsie Rathnabai Samuel became the first Indian Principal of the College.

Hidden by the Text Book Society's desecrating tower block in what was once General Doveton's huge compound is a splendid, old red brick building which a few years ago housed the CARE offices and now houses other offices. This was very probably *College House*, of the College of Fort St George. Some way from it in the same compound and, in isolated splendour, is a stately red sandstone building that looks like a mausoleum built in that favoured hybrid Jaipuri style. The perpetually shuttered appearance of this building, the gloom you perceive through the sole open doorway, and its solitary setting, well apart from the rest of the busy office complex here, all tend to reinforce the view that here indeed is a stately mausoleum. And in describing this edifice as such, you wouldn't be far wrong, for entombed here is a veritable treasure – 85,000 books and more, all in various stages of disrepair or just plain disuse, mouldy or brittle. Over 1,000 of them are priceless, belonging to between the 16th and 19th Centuries. But its strength is over 30,000 19th Century editions.

This is the library, perhaps the oldest subscription library east of Suez, that belongs to the Madras Literary Society and Auxiliary of the Royal Asiatic Society. Established in 1812 as the Asiatic Society of Madras, it was closely associated with the nearby Civilians' College. The Society was reconstituted in 1829 as the Madras Literary Society, under the chairmanship of Chief Justice Sir John Henry Newbolt, and registered in 1887. Its first Indian member was Kavali Venkata Lakshmiah, who is listed among the members for 1831.

The College of Fort St George's library and museum were the Society's nucleus. Its oldest possession was once reported as being a Latin edition of Cicero's work dated 1565. The oldest book it now has dates to 1619, Aristotle's *Opera Omnia* in Greek and Latin. The report also stated that it had an Arabic grammar dated 1656 apart from several other original editions. Listed amongst these prized possessions were the *Elliot Marbles*, Sir Walter Eliot's reports on his excavations in Amaravathi, and Robert Southey's *The Curse of Kehama* (some of it set in Mamallapuram), bearing Col Colin Mackenzie's signature and the seal of the College of Fort St George. It also was reported as having a fine collection of 19th Century photographs of Madras.

From the beginning of the 21st Century, an effort has been made to revive the library. But whereas some of its valuable holdings are receiving greater protection and its building underwent restoration in 2008, it still remains an institution lacking the vibrancy of the past. But as these lines are written, youthful volunteers are trying to put new life into it and also restore some of its valuable old books.

Nearby is an old Observatory which grew into the Indian Institute of Astrophysics, by whose erstwhile premises is now the Regional Meteorological Centre. At this *Nakshathira Bangala* (Star Bungalow), where a white hemispherical dome housed the telescope, several notable discoveries were made over the years. Among them was the first modern astronomic discovery by an Indian – the discovery of the variable star named *R Reticuli* by Chinthamani Ragoonatha Chary in 1887. The Observatory's brightest era was undoubtedly that period, 1861-1891, when Chary worked with Astronomer Norman Robert Pogson, whose Scale of Magnitude to measure the brightness of stars only added lustre to all the minor planets and variable stars he discovered. Chary's contributions here were numerous and included his attempts to wed Indian and Western Astronomy and his work on the Transit of Venus.

The first modern discoveries by an Indian astronomer are attributed to Chary. Another illustrious incumbent here was Thomas Glanville Taylor (1831-43), whose Madras Catalogue, the first southern hemisphere catalogue, listed the positions of 11,015 stars and formed the basis of the British catalogue. But long before Taylor and Pogson and Chary and Evershed there had begun a pioneering venture that was recognised the world over.

It was in the garden of his nearby Egmore house that William Petrie, a Company servant from 1765, pursued his hobby of gazing at the stars, using a brass Dollond telescope. It was only after he gifted his private collection of astronomical instruments to the Company in 1789, when he was leaving Madras, that a modern observatory was established. The first modern astronomical records in India, however, date to December 5, 1786 and refer to the longitude of Machilipatnam. Petrie's private observatory had provided a reference meridian for Michael Topping's coastal survey and led to these historic jottings. Incidentally, one of Petrie's instruments, a pendulum clock "made by John Shelton... probably...in the 1760s and... identical to the one used by Captain James Cook in his famous voyages" was – according to R K Kochhar, an Observatory historian – long used at the Kodaikanal Solar Physics Observatory.

The date commemorated in the Nungambakkam centre is 1792. This date marks the move from Petrie's house to these premises – and the establishing of the first official observatory in modern India. In the garden is a 10-ton, 15-foot tall commemorative granite pillar. The name on this pillar, unveiled by Governor Sir Charles Oakeley in 1792, is, however, not Petrie's but Topping's.

Topping, the Chief Marine Surveyor and described as "the first fulltime modern professional surveyor in India", had arrived in Madras in 1785 and, from the first, worked with Petrie's instruments. He persuaded his friend Petrie to make a gift of the equipment to the Company before he left Madras. He also had to persuade the Government to accept the gift. And Government was willing to accept it only if Topping would additionally (he was already Chief Marine Surveyor and was to also become Superintendent of the Survey School which the Observatory tended from 1794 to 1801) officiate as Company's Astronomer. Topping allowed himself to be persuaded and then got Government to do his bidding. It acquired in 1791 Edward Garrow's 'garden house' – the first European dwelling in Nungambakkam – and let Topping move in. In the grounds of this new residence-cum-office of his, Topping built the Observatory the way he wanted it. And the Observatory was ready to go to work in 1792, the commemorated date. *Garrow's Gardens* has a new name now, but it is as the Observatory, and its successor, the RMC, that it is best known.

Multi-talented John Goldingham, who had served as Petrie's assistant, succeeded multi-talented Topping in 1796 and was designated the first official Astronomer. He determined the latitudes and longitudes of several Indian locations, including the first assessment of the longitude of Madras (80° 18'30"E). William Lambton, who in 1802 started his Great Trigonometrical Survey of India from St Thomas' Mount, linked his 7½ mile baseline with this location, which is considered the secondary meridian, the meridian that can be substituted for the prime meridian that is Greenwich. When George Everest completed the survey of India in 1845, the great meridianal arc of India had moved across 56,997 square miles of area from Lambton's start from the St Thomas' Mount-Madras Observatory pillar baseline.

The giant pillar, on which there was once a 12-inch altitude and azimuth instrument, believed to have been Petrie's and the first in India, has an inscription on it confirming it as the oldest benchmark in Asia. The inscription in English (and Tamil, Telugu, Urdu and Latin as well) reads: "(1) The Geoditic position (Lat 13° 4'3" 0.5 N, Long 80° 14'54"·20E) of Col William Lambton is primary original of the Survey of India. Fixed by him in 1802, it was at a point 6 feet to the south and 1 foot to the west of the centre of this pillar. (2) The centre of the meridian circle of the Madras Observatory was at a point 12 feet to the east of the centre of this pillar." This inscription is believed to have been cut after Astronomer Michie-Smith had made the final longitudinal determination of Madras in 1892.

In the RMC campus are four other granite pillars, one dating to 1792 and three to 1860. These pillars were meant for transits and standard clocks. In its early years, the Madras Observatory set the standard time for all India. There are residents of Madras who still remember that a time-gun used to be fired at 4 p.m. daily from Fort St George. This gun was directly connected to the standard clock in the Observatory. And this clock gave India its Standard Time. But while the clock remained, the Observatory moved. A more permanent Observatory was built here in 1845, but after Pogson's death in 1891 the decision was taken to move the Observatory to Kodaikanal .Work on buildings in Kodai began in 1895 and the move was made in 1899, but the Madras Observatory continued functioning till 1931. The Nungambakkam site was then left to meteorology, whose work had begun here in 1875. The Meteorological Department was in charge of the Observatory till the Indian Institute of Astrophysics was inaugurated in 1976. The Regional Meteorological Centre, Madras, was established on April 1, 1945 and got its own building c. 1960.

The Kodaikanal Solar Physics Observatory became a part of the new Institute, which established its headquarters in Bangalore in 1976. The Institute's main observational facility is, however, at Kavalur in the Javadi Hills, Tamil Nadu, and was set up in 1968. It is named the Vainu Bappu Observatory. Bappu, perhaps the best known name in 20th Century Indian astronomy and responsible for Kavalur, was Director of the Observatory for 22 years. But the first Indian director was A L Narayanan.

It is this history which has led to the Institute of Astrophysics being described as the first modern public Observatory outside Western Europe and the first modern research institute in India. This growth, however, has led to a forgetting of those 19th Century words of Sir Charles Markham, "The Madras Observatory is the sole permanent point for Observatory work in India and the only successor of the establishments founded by Jai Singh. It has produced results which entitle it to take rank with the observatories of Europe."

Not far from here, near the Central Government offices housed in *Shastri Bhavan*, is *Anderson's Gardens* mentioned earlier. These 'gardens' were, in the late 18th Century, a famous botanical gardens maintained by that silk-worm rearing, cotton-growing Physician General, Dr James Anderson, of Saidapet Nopalry fame. When the Nopalry was closed in 1800, many of its exotic plants were removed to Lal Bagh in Bangalore.

Anderson, surgeon and physician extraordinary, arrived in Madras in the 1760s, but received a permanent posting here only in 1771 when he was appointed Presidency Surgeon. He lived in a house in these 'gardens' from some time after 1778 till he died in 1809. The house was later, for a while, the offices of the College of Fort St George. Chief Secretary Thomas Pycroft appears to have then acquired the 'gardens' in 1827 and lent his name to the nearby neighbourhood where the Willingdon Hospital came up in 1947 and Apollo Hospital in the 1980s.

The Lady Ampthill Nursing Institute founded in 1904 by a few European nurses, was amalgamated in 1920 with the South India Nursing Association founded by Lady Willingdon. Governor Willingdon's Lady next raised funds to take over Sir Gordon Fraser's Hyde Park Nursing Home and amalgated the Association with the nursing facility. She moved the nurses and nursing home to the *Western Castlet*, off Mount Road, where, supported by European business houses, it thrived and took on the name Lady Willingdon Nursing Home. In 1953, it moved to its new premises in Pycroft's Garden Road and became the Lady Willingdon Hospital. Modernisation and expansion in the 1990s found it struggling for finance and, in 1998, Sankara Nethralaya a leading eye hospital, took it over. The Chennai Willingdon Corporate Foundation, which ran the eponymous hospital, has since supported medical research, heritage projects and numerous non-governmental organisations. To the rear of *Pycroft's Garden* is another old 'garden house', the Cochin Maharaja's palace, now hidden by the tall blocks of the school, Asan Memorial, that it has become. In its extensive grounds have also sprung up police flats. And the Kerala Government plans to establish a Kerala Centre in another corner.

Anderson's botanical gardens, started in 1778, and spreading to 110 acres by 1792, appears to have been bounded by College Road, Graeme's Road, Mount Road, Nungambakkam High Road and Haddow's Road. Recently-restored *Cottingley*, a handsome garden house over a hundred years old, is the residence-cum-office of the British Deputy High Commissioner. It was built in the 1880s in one of the large 'blocks' *Anderson's Gardens* was divided into. In another, where Anderson's own house still precariously survives, a heritage building much to the dismay of its owners (the SBI), were developed mansions for the Bank of Madras officers. Most of these homes remained into the 1980s, owned by the successor State Bank of India. *Red Craig* was the last survivor of these homes, but like the rest has begun to give way to flats. Another garden house developed in *Anderson's Gardens* was *Morison's Gardens*, which became the property of Grindlay's Bank and which, after Grindlay's was taken over by Standard Chartered, has now been transformed into a sprawling, tree-shaded modern complex of quarters, international training centre, huge back office for the Bank's worldwide operations, and banking facility.

61. St George's Cathedral...with monuments to the 'Coral Strand'...

62. *Gleaming white, pristine pure...a Jain shrine in T'Nagar to the glory of Saint Shanthinath.*

63. *Down by the riverside...imperial splendour in the Cooum gateway to the erstwhile College of Fort St George.*

64. Valluvar Kottam, *giant hall of stone... reviving the Tamil sculptor's skill of ages.*

Off Graeme's Road is Apollo Hospital, the pioneer of corporate medicare in the country. A huge medical facility, it attracts patients from all over India and South Asia to its numerous specialist facilities. Apollo, established in 1983, showed the way to Madras becoming the medicare capital of India. In nearby College Road is one indicator of this – Sankara Nethralaya, said to be the country's most sought after ophthalmic hospital since its establishment in 1978.

On Graeme's Road is a new landmark, the first of the buildings in modernist style to be raised in Madras. Designed by Charles Correa, a renowned 20th Century Indian architect, it houses the headquarters of MRF Ltd., one of the largest tyre manufacturers in South Asia and a firm which grew out of Mammen Mapillai's home-based balloon manufactory.

Between Nungambakkam and Kodambakkam is what was meant to be the City's biggest Tamil cultural centre, *Valluvar Kottam,* dedicated to the memory of the Tamil sage, saint and poet Tiruvalluvar, whose immortal work, the *Tirukkural*, philosophises on righteousness, wealth and love in its 1,330 stanzas. All the stanzas are scribed on the polished granite pillars of the gallery that surrounds the main auditorium. Conceived by the then Chief Minister Mu Karunanidhi, it was designed and its construction supervised by leading sculptor and stonework builder V. Ganapathi Sthapathi, it was inaugurated in 1976. The site of the huge structure is said to have been the deepest point in the old Nungambakkam Lake. The central auditorium, 220 feet by 100 feet and said to be Asia's biggest at the time of construction, can seat 4,000 persons. On its roof is a terraced garden with two large pools. Reflected in both pools is the towering dome of the 101-feet-tall chariot (*ratham*) in which is seated the life-size statue of Saint Tiruvalluvar. This 2,700-tonne granite chariot, a spectacular piece of sculpture that is a replica of the famed temple chariot of Tiruvarur, dominates the landscape in this part of Madras. The bottom portion of the chariot is sculpted in *bas relief* and depicts the 133 chapters of the sacred *Kural*. Over 3,000 blocks of granite from Tiruvannamalai have been used in the building, the largest weighing 40 tonnes. Here is a rather striking modern look back at the past that has, unfortunately, got politicised, resulting in care, or lack of it, being bestowed on the construction only on the whims and fancies of the party in power.

Elsewhere in Nungambakkam, many of the 'garden houses' of yesterday have given way to restricted highrise offices and residential complexes. Nungambakkam High Road now, with highrise lining it on both sides, is the closest Madras has come to being like modern Bombay. Multistorey buildings, garish lighting, 'pop' shopping complexes, a plethora of restaurants, and a never-ending stream of traffic have made this one of the most congested areas in the city and an object lesson on the pitfalls of modern urbanisation. Nearby is Khader Nawaz Khan Road, taking its name from a former Madras Civil Servant, who had been a Deputy Collector around 1881 and who retired as a District Collector. He was a descendant of Muhammad Abara Khan, one of Wallajah's commanders who had served as a Governor of Madurai.

This narrow, ill-kept road is perhaps the city's 'moddest' shopping and dining area, if you exclude the malls, it's a veritable 'Bond Street'. But here and there in Nungambakkam – as in threatened railway bungalows and the old Sterling Club building on the road of the same name – the old world continues to survive precariously. Nearby Harrison's Hotel on Nungambakkam High Road, once a part of that world of yesterday, has now became a modern boutique hotel. As Queen's Hotel, it had for its main building, the palace of the Maharani of Vizianagaram, a princess from Himachal.

At the end of Sterling Road is the City's leading Roman Catholic educational institution, the Jesuits' Loyola College, considered with Madras Christian College one of the Top Ten Colleges in the country in the Humanities, Sciences, Commerce and Business Management. The now-autonomous College opened in 1925, 33 years after it was first suggested by the Apostolic Delegate to the East Indies who pointed out that Madras lacked what Bombay and Calcutta had: an excellent Catholic college. Fr Bertram, the first principal, supervised the growth of a 54-acre campus that had been reclaimed from a part of Nungambakkam's 'Long Tank'. The College opened with 75 students, but by 1928 the University Commission was describing its progress as "spectacular". In 1933 there was consecrated a College and Nungambakkam landmark, the Gothic-styled Church of Christ the King – with its impressive nearly 160-feet tall spire – designed by an experienced *maistry*, not an engineer or architect, S A Gnanapragasam Pillai who designed many another buildings on the campus.

Pere Francois Bertrand, better known as Fr.Francis Bertram, the founding father of Loyola, was French-born but there were many who took him to be English, as much for his speech as his knowledge of English Literature. This love of English and his skills as a Mathematics teacher he acquired at St.Joseph's College, Trichinopoly, the first Roman Catholic College in the South (1844), to which the Jesuit Order in India sent him in 1896. By the time he left in 1925 he was its Rector and Principal.

Fr. Bertram's stewardship of St.Joseph's came soon after the announcement in 1904 of University reforms. He not only implemented these reforms but ensured that St.Joseph's provided a steady stream of teachers of science, history and economics for all the colleges of the Presidency and for many beyond. Then came the mission to start a college in Madras.

Loyola was first conceived as an idea in 1895, more seriously taken up in 1907, and made a commitment only in the first years after the Great War. Then began search for land. When the Nawab's Gardens, 16 acres at the end of Sterling Road with a large mansion in it, was offered, it was felt that the area was too small for all the buildings planned. Eventually, what is recorded as Puliyur land, across from the Nungambakkam tank, where the College now is, was agreed on. Then began the search for funds to raise the buildings.

Fr. Bertram sailed for Europe in 1920 and was disappointed in his attempts to raise the funds there. As a last try, he went to Rome and rather diffidently requested an audience with the Pope, who said, "They who want the end, they must find the means to pay." But then added, "The Pope must set the example." And he gave his visitor a hundred 1000 lire notes amounting to about Rs.27,000, a little more than a quarter of the budget Fr.Bertram had shown him. That gift from the Pope was the first for the raising of Loyola College.

Lord Willingdon, the Governor, laid the foundation stone for the first building on March 10, 1924. On May 1925 Fr.Bertram was officially named the Principal of Loyola. And on July 6 he registered the first 40 students. Over the next few days 38 more were registered.

Fr. Bertram's loyalty to Loyola was such that he turned down offers of the Vice Chancellorship of Madras and Annamalai Universities, though he did serve Madras as acting Vice Chancellor on several occasions.

But the University never responded with a doctorate. Fr. Bertram, suffering from ill-health all his life, passed away in 1936,still a young 65.

Loyola was followed in 1926 by the founding in the area of the first Corporation High School in Madras.

Leading off Nungambakkam High Road is the road to Kodambakkam, Vadapalani – with its renowned Vada Palani Andavar temple built 125 years ago – and Saligramam, an area that was the Madras 'Hollywood', popularly known as Kollywood (deriving from Kodambakkam). In its several studios – once there were here almost all of the city's 28, with nearly 100 shooting floors, now there are Madras's only two, AVM, its beginnings in 1945 but rooted here from 1949, and Prasad — were 'shot' the largest number of feature films in any city in the world. The first film-maker in the City – and South India – set up his studio, Srinivasa Cinetone (Sound City), in 1934, on Poonamallee High Road, near the present Flower Road Police Station. He was A Narayanan, who pioneered a craze that has not ended. The first to establish a studio in Kodambakkam was A Ramiah, whose Star Combines opened in 1906. In 1994, there was established in Taramani, near the Film Institute, the sprawling Rs.210 million MGR Film City on an 86 acre campus. Meant to provide all the 'sets' Kodambakkam could want, it has, like much else with Government patronage, become a victim of inter-party rivalry and, after being allowed to deteriorate, closed down and is being converted into a 25-acre IT and biotech park by the Tata's, who have named the 7.5 million sq.ft development as Ramanujan City. Neighbouring it is Tidel Park that got the IT highway started in 2000.

Kodambakkam, it is said, derives from *Goda Bagh* (horse garden) in the Hindustani. The Arcot Nawabs apparently once had stables here! But now, on either side of the main road, have sprung up the city's newest residential colonies – Ashok Nagar, K K Nagar, Gill Nagar, Mahalingapuram. Gill Nagar is named after a Sikh Inspector General of Prisons, Col. Gurdial Singh Gill, who made Madras his home, brought down to settle here 5000 Sikh and Sindhi refugees from the North after Partition, and blessed the city with Punjabi benevolence in the field of education. In Mahalingapuram is another Ayyappa temple of recent vintage, bringing more Kerala temple architecture to the city. Reflecting its splendid woodwork is its magnificently sculpted wooden chariot. Further on in Kodambakkam, besides the country's most modern studios,

L V Prasad's, in whose labs the largest number of films in the country are processed, there are the sprawling Vijaya Hospital and Health Centre on both sides of the road and, till recently, two palatial *mahals,* splendid wedding halls that were almost 'filmi' in their opulence, but which have now given way to a mall and an upmarket hotel, all parts of the legendary Nagi Reddy's erstwhile Vijaya-Vauhini film studio and printing complex, the printing unit, pioneers in offset printing in India, being the biggest in South Asia in its time. In Kodambakkam too is the 500-year-old Bharadwajeswarar Temple. Kodambakkam High Road leads on into Arcot Road and Porur from where Poonamallee is a right turn, by way of the Sri Ramachandra Hospital, Medical College and Research Centre, and St Thomas' Mount is a left turn.

Before the Hospital is the huge campus in Manapakkam of Larsen & Toubro's Engineering Construction and Contracts Division which as L & T's subsidiary Engineering Construction Corporation (ECC) established in 1944 built up an enviable repulation for construction in Asia. In its sprawling campus, are some of the most spectacular modern constructions in India, three of them international prizewinners. The latest, of futuristic design, built to commemorate the Diamond Jubilee of the firm, is the Henning Holck-Larsen Centre of Excellence and is a museum and archive of ECC's history. Larsen and Soren Kristian Toubro, two Danish engineers, founded L & T in 1937 in Bombay; today, it is the biggest engineering company in South Asia, mainly due to ECC's contribution.

The Tamil Dream-Makers

Not long after the first cinematography show was held in Paris by the Lumiére Brothers in 1895, the silent film came to India. Madras saw its first 'moving pictures' in 1898 at the Victoria Public Hall, courtesy of T Stevenson of the Madras Photographic Store. The mofussil benefitted a few years later from Swamikannu Vincent, a Trichy railwayman, who established Edison's Cinematography, a travelling cinema, in 1905. Then came Cohen's Lyric Theatre in Madras, screening occasional bits of film from 1907 and as a more permanent venue called the Empire Theatre screening films from 1913. This became the Madans' Elphinstone Theatre from 1915, the first in the city with a balcony. Meanwhile, R Venkiah founded a touring cinema in 1909 and took it around India, Burma and Ceylon. And in 1911, Mrs Klug established on Broadway, the Bioscope, the city's first cinema-focused theatre, but it closed down in six months. It was 1913 before Madras got its first commercial film shows at the Electric. The commercial success of the venture induced Venkiah to follow its example. He founded the South's first theatre chain, the Gaiety, Crown and Globe (later Roxy).

Bombay had screened its first silent films a year before Madras; it also started commercial film production earlier. Bombay's example stirred R Nataraja Mudaliyar, a Madras motor spare-parts dealer, into action. Taught to crank a camera by an Englishman in Poona, Stewart Smith, Mudaliyar returned to Madras and in 1916 founded the India Film Company with a friend, S M Dharmalingam Mudaliyar. They set up South India's first film studio on Miller's Road, Kilpauk, and established a processing laboratory in Bangalore for climatic reasons. Then, with Nataraja Mudaliyar cranking, directing, editing and supervising

Narayanaswami Achari's processing of film over the weekends, IFC made Keechaka Vatham *within 35 days of the founding of the Company, this* Mahabharata-*based mythological being the first South Indian film.*

Nataraja Mudaliyar's lead was followed by Raghupathy Prakash, Venkiah's son, who was trained in England, T H Huffton and A Narayanan. Narayanan's General Pictures Corporation, founded in August 1929, produced the largest number of South Indian silent films, established the first major distribution and exhibition network, and served as the school where later film-makers of the South learnt their first lessons. His wife Meenakshi became his sound recordist and was the first woman film technician in India. Narayanan's efforts on behalf of southern film production were supplemented by R Padmanabhan of Associated Films (1928), who encouraged K Subrahmanyam and Raja Sandow, leading film-makers of another day.

This was a director's era in film-making. Actors were only necessary adjuncts, receiving little publicity and being expected to serve as odd-job-men, though stunt men like Battling Mani and Stunt Raja were popular figures. Actresses were hard to come by; an Englishwoman played Draupadi for Nataraja Mudaliyar. Marion Hall (Vilochana), who became the highest paid actress, and Mrs Aellkot, both Anglo-Indians, were the first actresses to regularly appear in Madras-made films. Soon, the danseuses, who danced in the theatres as an added attraction at film shows, took to the screen and were then followed by the stage actresses, T P Rajalakshmi and K T Rukmani. Rajalakshmi eventually directed a few films, the first South Indian woman director. Most stage artistes of this period, however, preferred to stay where they were, as work and pay in the new medium were uncertain, and also because as trained singers or orators they had little scope in a silent medium.

The brevity of the early films as well as their erratic supply meant that most public performances took on the appearance of variety shows. There would be three or four 'shorts', the main feature, a few dance items during intervals, a short skit or two, and sometimes even stunt shows by the legendary Gunboat Jack, a Black boxer and daredevil, and others like him. An orchestra would accompany the main feature from the pit and, especially in rural areas where few could read sub-titles, there was a narrator who gave a running commentary or spoke the lines, often vying with the actors for the audience's attention. With shows drawn out in this manner – very similar to the interpolated dramas and the traditional itinerant performances they were used to – audiences were assured of their money's worth. Later, Tamil audiences, brought up on this style of public presentation, compelled the talkie to adopt the same melody-and-comedy routine that dragged out the film to a length acceptable to audiences. In a poverty-stricken country, every paisa had to be assured adequate screen time for villagers to feel their expedition to a cinema worthwhile. Indian thinking on this subject, even among the educated, has not changed very much even today.

The "mannered gestures and exaggerated pantomime" so necessary for the silent film were not new inventions, but a continuation of the traditional Tamil stage repertoire. The flamboyant and melodramatic style of the Tamil movies, which survived until recently and which Westernised critics often found in bad taste, is a natural and inevitable extension of the Tamil folk tradition. Whatever else you may say of Tamil films till the 1960s, you could not say that they were not authentically Tamil.

American films, Bombay films and South Indian mythologicals and stunt films were the staple fare of the silent era in the Madras Presidency. But by 1929 an attempt was being made to introduce social content into films. Narayanan's Dharmapathini *first introduced temperance propaganda, and the theme was subsequently repeated in many other productions. (Repeating a popular theme ad nauseam in film after film, by director after director, has become a Tamil film tradition.) Untouchability* (Nandanar – 1930 – for which Sundarambal became the first star to be paid Rs. 100,000) *and women's rights* (Anadhai Penn – 1931) *were other social issues touched on. They could not, however, wean the masses away from the epics and escapist fare. A vigorous British censorship policy also encouraged such fare, film-makers preferring to avoid socially committed films that might fall foul of the authorities.*

Unable to combat the challenge posed by the Hollywood, British and North Indian films, the Southern silent film studios began running into rough weather by 1927. Studio after studio folded and, by 1932, the silent era was over, H R Desai's Bhagya Chakra *made that year, being the last of the line. The coming of the talkie to Madras in 1931 had only hastened the end.*

Imperial Film's Alam Ara, *the first full-length Indian talkie, released in March 1931, reached Madras in June and was screened at Kinema*

Central and Murugan Talkies. Before the year was out, Madras was seeing and hearing Korathi Songs and Dances, *a 4-reeler, and* Kalidas, *a full-length film, both made in Bombay.* Kalidas, *also made by Imperial, featured the Tamil-speaking Rajalakshmi and a Telugu-speaking hero and, so, was a bilingual film. The Indian film capital and Calcutta continued to supply Tamil talkies for the next few years. Then, in 1934, Narayanan of GPC set up the first sound studio in Madras, Srinivasa Cinetone, which was located on Poonamallee High Road and was popularly called 'Sound City'.* Srinivasa Kalyanam *was produced here in Tamil the same year, the first talkie produced in the South. Within the next 12 months, 36 talkies were produced in Madras. The Southern cinema boom was on.*

Vel Picture Studio, in what had been the house of the Raja of Pithapuram at Murray's Gate – later Venus Studios – and Minakshi Cinetone in Adyar followed Srinivasa Cinetone. By 1937, there was Rs 17 crore invested in the cinema industry in Madras Presidency, which by then had nine studios in the capital, two in Coimbatore and one in Salem. Then came World War II, and during its first two years Chettiar capital from Burma and Southeast Asia began to flow into film-making, and the industry grew. The stage actors, song-writers and set decorators, who had enabled the stage to run a parallel course to the silent film, now flocked to the new medium, taking with them the pit orchestras.

The first four years of the Tamil talkie saw producers continue to churn out more of the formula films. The era of myth and melodrama dragged on, with song and dance enlivening the 15,000-20,000 footage films. Western Oriental Gentlemen and (Gentlewomen) have always sniggered at the formula and carped at the lack of artistry in most Indian film-making, but as noted film writer Devyani Chaubal says, they are a minority of 1% while Indian films, whatever the language, are made for the 99% who "just love them." The vast majority, much of it with roots in rural areas or still living in the countryside, has its entertainment values firmly entrenched in the past when song, dance and stylised acting were the stock-in-trade of the wandering minstrels and peregrinating dramas. While retaining the style, film-makers could have changed the content. But the great Indian majority is also fervently religious and whole-heartedly believes that prayer can achieve wonders and gods and saints can perform miracles to order. So mythologicals continued to thrive.

And so did romances. "We sell dreams," candidly confessed Raj Kapoor. Be it urban society or rural, Indian society is starved of premarital romance; inevitably, romantic movies became the staple diet of the average Indian film-goer, enabling him to escape into a fantasy world from the drab realities of his life. Thus was perfected the formula of the successful Indian film, with love, mythological, sublime or carnal, as its chief ingredient.

To this tested recipe the Tamil film added the stylised acting of the street theatre and the Elizabethan oratory that is as much beloved by the fans of the Tamil stage as it is by its politicians. But whereas almost all other cinema in India only briefly flirted with politics, Tamil cinema alone exploited the political potential of the medium.

From the earliest days of the Tamil film, those connected with the industry had been politicised. The political process had begun on the stage and in the songs. When the stage stars moved into films after the birth of the talkie, they did little for the medium, cinematically speaking, but they flavoured it with the spice of politics.

This development owed almost everything to a Congress leader now virtually forgotten in Tamil Nadu, the eloquent Satyamurti. He carried his enthusiasm for amateur acting into whole-hearted support for the performing arts. He was convinced these arts could be used for political purposes, though in his day what he meant by politicising theatre was to make it an integral part of the nationalist movement. "We will sing our way to freedom," he would state, urging artistes to play a major role on the political stage too. Over the years, the artistes' alliance with Congress grew. When the talkie came, Satyamurti became its most enthusiastic patron, recognising the potential it had for political propaganda. Satyamurti firmly believed that, in an illiterate country like India, only such an entertainment form could tackle the sociopolitical questions of the age. He envisioned that the talkie could play this vital role for at least three decades to come and spoke and wrote prolifically to propagate this view among the educated elite who looked down upon the popular arts.

Satyamurti's task was made easier by Narayanan, an ardent Congressman, who is generally considered the 'Father of the Tamil Cinema' and who was as enthusiastic an advocate of political propaganda through films as Satyamurti. Another dedicated supporter of Satyamurti was the singer Sundarambal who accompanied him on election tours, warming up the audience with passionately sung patriotic songs and then leaving it to be hypnotised by Satyamurti's silver tongue.

At the same time as the Civil Disobedience Movement was growing in the early 1930s, the Self-Respect Movement was gaining ground, as were Nehru's socialist theories. Temperance, Untouchability, Temple Entry, Women's Rights, Dowry, Child Marriage all became fair grist for film discussion. When strict censorship put a stop to much nationalist propaganda in the films, the social reformers got the chance to project their views on film. Out of this opportunity grew the power of, first, the Dravida Kazhagam and, later, the Dravida Munnetra Kazhagam, a united whole then, but a divided polity since the 1970s though one or the other of its major players has been in power in Tamil Nadu since 1967.

The first Tamil 'social' (meaning contemporary film) was Dumbachari, *an anti-prostitution film released in 1935. This was followed the same year by* Menaka, *a women's rights film that for the first time introduced a Bharati song on the screen.* Sathi Leelavathi *(1936) focussed on the tragedy of labour in Ceylon's tea estates and, appropriately, considering his Ceylon hill-country background, introduced in a small role to Tamil film audiences. M G Ramachandran, who grew into an adored film hero and then became a Chief Minister. K Subrahmanyam's* Bala Yogini, *"the most significant film of this period", was released in 1937. It attacked the caste system, the treatment of widows and the priesthood. The film was made for the Madras United Artistes' Corporation that Subrahmanyam, perhaps the greatest director of the pre-War Tamil talkie, formed; the Corporation was later sold to S S Vasan who named it Gemini and continued from where Subrahmanyam had left off.*

The 'social' did not do away with the classical sagas, celestially-inspired saints and contemporary stunts. Films on such popular fare continued to be the major offerings till well into the 1960s, but many such films had political overtones as well. When C Rajagopalachari formed the Madras Government in 1937 and censorship was relaxed, film-makers were released from bondage and, for 2½ years, till World War II, the social film enjoyed its heyday. The best of these films was again by Subrahmanyam; his Thyaga Bhoomi *released in 1939 advocated Gandhiism, Harijan uplift and a new role for women in a society in transition. Its political slant, however, led to it being the first Tamil film to be banned – long after its release. Subrahmanyam, a Congressman and a Brahmin who waged war on the priesthood and casteism, is another forgotten figure in Tamil Nadu. Many in power today owe much to Satyamurti and Subrahmanyam, two men who helped found the South Indian Film Chamber of Commerce, who fought for better financing facilities for the medium, who sought a school for acting (Satyamurti even wanted film-making introduced in the University curriculum) and who, above all, made the cinema respectable. Not only did the conservative publications begin to take note of the Tamil Cinema as a result of the efforts of these two – Satyamurti even wrote film reviews – but classical singers and dancers also began to take part in films; Subrahmanyam introduced S D Subbulakshmi to film audiences in* Bala Yogini.

*That great singer M.S. Subbulakshmi made just four films, Seva Sadanam, Sakunthalai, Savithri and Meera, and the two that Ellis Dungan (*Sakunthalai *and* Meera) *directed turned out to be Indian film classics. That a black and white film could be made "visually opulent" was entirely due to the technical brilliance of Dungan (an excellent cameraman in his own right) and his cinematographer, Jiten Banerjee. They created what has been described as Meera's "ethereal, angelic beauty." Dungan, an Irish-American, made between 1936 and 1950, a string of Tamil hits without knowing a word of Tamil. He did not know Hindi either, but made* Meera *in Hindi too. Before he left India, he contributed several classics to the Tamil film besides many new techniques in film-making.*

Dungan, who stumbled into Tamil films by sheer chance, Michael Ormalov and Mani Lal Tandon were classmates and friends at the University of Southern California, studying the then new medium, Film. Tandon, whose family was thinking of establishing a studio and producing films in Bombay, persuaded his friends to return with him to work in India. The Tandon family's plans, however, fell through and Ormalov went back, but Dungan stayed on to watch Tandon direct a Tamil film, Nandanar, in Calcutta. When Tandon was invited to do another Tamil film, this time in Coimbatore, he said he was busy, but recommended his friend "from Hollywood". And Dungan found himself making Sathi Leelavathi.

During most of his stay in India, Dungan stayed at the Spencer Hotel that was to become the Ambassador. There, Dungan would read, in verbatim translation in English, every instruction and every word written and spoken and sung in Tamil, in whatever film he was making, in order to keep firm control of what finally emerged. He even vetted the brilliant script Mu. Karunanidhi wrote for Manthri Kumari *in 1949. Having watched its success, Dungan returned to the U.S. for personal reasons, keeping himself busy thereafter advising film-makers shooting films in India and making historical documentaries himself almost till his last days.*

World War II saw the resignation of the C Rajagopalachari ministry and the renewal of censorship. The British Government encouraged war films, banned nationalist films and permitted frothy social films. It was time for Thyagaraja Bhagavathar, N S Krishnan and T A Mathuram to have a ball. Then the Tamil film suffered its greatest blow. With the death of Satyamurti in 1943, the Tamil cinema lost its contact with Indian political leaders and the intelligentsia. But Satyamurti's death did not seem to matter much at the time, as, with Independence, there was no more need to revert to nationalist themes. Instead, in the euphoria of independence, entertainment became the sole objective of Tamil cinema and, as the woes of a workaday world caught up with viewers, cinema, which for a few years had promised to stir the masses, began pandering to them. It was at this time that the DMK stalwarts, who had learnt well the propaganda lessons of Satyamurti and Subrahmanyam, entered the Tamil film world.

The late 1930s and the 1940s were the years when the big studios of Tamil Nadu – that had made Madras the leading film-making city in the country till the 1980s – were founded and they, in turn, began the era of big budget entertainers. T R Sundaram founded Modern Theatres in Salem in 1937, gave Karunanidhi and Kannadasan their start, and demonstrated that a film did not need to be 20,000 feet long to be successful but could be made a crowd-pleaser in half that length. Vasan's Gemini, founded in 1941, was spending as much as Rs 35 lakh back in 1948 to produce the fabulous Chandralekha *in Tamil and Hindi! A V Meiyappan, who led Chettiar money and some talent into the film business, specialised in making such tear-jerkers as* Sri Valli *at AVM Studios and thrived on experimenting with novelty;* Andha Naal *proved that a song-and-danceless film could also be a hit. Nagi Reddi, his commodity exports and imports affected when the Japanese overran Southeast Asia in 1941, set up with his brother a small printing press in Madras. When a film studio, Vauhini, belonging to a friend who had teamed with his brother B.N. Reddi, needed money, Nagi Reddi lent it what little he could and, when the studio's owner died in 1961 the debt unpaid, found himself owning the business. Thus was launched what was once India's largest studio, Vijaya Vauhini, spread over 40 acres.*

These were the studios that churned out entertainers by the hundreds till the 1960s. They also made stars of two actors – Puratchi Nadigar *(the revolutionary actor) M G Ramachandran and* Nadigar Thilagam *(the gem among actors) Sivaji Ganesan – who survived several generations of heroines and still did not lose their appeal! And they also gave the late C N Annadurai, fellow script-writers, directors, and several actors and actresses the chance to use the medium for political ends. Propaganda through films accounted in great measure for the DMK sweeping to power in 1967.*

The 1940s were a traumatic period for the Tamil film. The scandalous disclosures in yellow film journals like Cinema Thoothu *and* Indu Nesan *took the lid off a debauch-ridden film world. Murder was perhaps inevitable; editor Lakshmikantan was killed in broad daylight and top film stars M K Thyagaraja Bhagavathar and N S Krishnan were implicated (they were freed only on appeal to the Privy Council). A shaken film world, many of whose citizens were politically conscious, righteous Dravida Kazhagam members, was further shattered when their idol was deemed to have feet of clay. When their beloved leader and elder, Periyar (E V R Ramaswamy) in 1949 married "an unequal partner", a girl some 40 years younger than he, thereby committing sacrilege in the view of some of his followers, Annadurai led a revolt. The breakaway group, unlike Periyar, was almost entirely stage and screen oriented. K R Ramaswamy, not Sivaji Ganesan, who was Periyar's protégé, led the actors' revolt. N S Krishnan, the leading comedian of his day, played benevolent elder to the newly formed DMK which by adding 'Munnetram' to 'Dravida Kazhagam', was intended to be forward-looking. And a young script writer, Mu Karunanidhi, was encouraged by Krishnan to write scripts that took off from where Annadurai had left off.*

Anna (Elder Brother *to* Thanthai *Periyar's 'Great Father' image), who was as convinced of the potency of the arts as Satyamurti, had been a popular playwright. He had written the play* Vélaikkari *(Maidservant) that in its 1949 film version brought propaganda back to the screen and launched Karunanidhi and his Tamil version of Robin Hood, MGR, on the road to success. With Vélaikkari, a new era in Tamil films was launched. The films, with a tart political flavour, were often provocative. Fans were encouraged to actively participate, boo the villains, cheer the heroes and applaud not only DMK ideas but even DMK names when they appeared among the credits. Out of this audience participation were born the fan clubs* (rasigar manrams) *that till the 1980s had so much to do with mobilising votes for the parties at election time. Now they only offer adulations to the actors of the day, Rajinikanth and Kamal Hassan.*

With the message creators and bearers in power in 1967, the emphasis on spreading the DMK gospel through the film medium decreased. Moreover, educated urban audiences were getting restless. So the DMK gradually slipped out of the film world to concentrate on politics. When Annadurai died, three years of political infighting followed. The sequel was the emergence of MGR as a political rival to Karunanidhi. When the Sherwood Forest years paid off in 1976 and the film star became Chief Minister, a trend, that was to be followed a decade later in several other parts of the country, was established. But MGR's exit from films was to have another result. The last vestiges of political propaganda virtually faded out of the Tamil film.

The Tamil film of the mid-1970s and thereafter became more cinema oriented in its search for a new angle. There was a more literate audience now, an audience that was more knowledgeable about what the world had to offer, and was receptive to some change. And a new wave of film-makers, less repressed and working in a more open society, were prepared to offer the change. Entertainment remains the first priority of the film-makers, but as Director Bharati Raja says, entertainment "should not block the audience's thinking, catering only to sensory responses." Acting suited to the stage was done away with, realism was introduced, subtle characterisation took the place of stereotypes, and emphasis was placed on visual techniques to express emotions. Song and dance had to stay, but some attempt was made to integrate them with the whole, occasionally quite realistically.

It was with Sridhar that the new wave began in the Tamil film in the 1960s. Cinematography began to become more important than the spoken word. He also read the new audience right. He took the risks and found that people would now accept the experimental and the off-beat. But actor-director Bhagyaraj also perceptively noted in the 1970s that the "oldies are still running house full; regional hero-dominated

*movies still succeed." It would seem that audiences were divided 50-50.
And it was to cater to this mixed audience that entertainment was still
emphasised in even the better films. Sridhar held that the producers
were the ultimate chefs of this 'masala'. "The producers, ranging from
millowners to shopkeepers, have their eyes only on the coffers. That is
why there is so much junk in films," explains Sridhar.*

*But none of these directors has a valid reason to explain why junk
could not be made slickly and entertainment sleek.* Udhiripookkal,
Azhiyatha Kolangal, Pasi, Oru Thalai Raagam, Thanneer Thanneer,
Moondram Pirai *were successes that were part of a new Tamil cinematic
experience. Most of them had unknown stars; much of their respective
stories were plausible; in some, the script was biting and the social
comment significant; there was a great deal of sensitive understanding
of the afflicted or of suffering humanity; comedy became an integral
part of the film and not an added attraction; and both camera and
technique caught up with a more modern world. But none of these films
were compact or tightly edited, all of them were lush with colour and
had their full quota of song and dance – much of it irrelevant – and
plenty of extraneous prurient interest. The Tamil Cinema, it would seem,
was still making sure of box office success by seeing that its audience
get its money's worth of time and entertainment. The Time Machine was
the winner; the progress of the 1970s took the Tamil Cinema back to the
pre-message days of escapism. And a youthful audience, harried in its
workaday world, found satisfaction in the things it only dreamt of and
could never touch. Mani Ratnam and Kamal and Rajinikanth were the
new leaders.*

20

The Gracious City

Everywhere in Madras, its history is written in neighbourhood names – if only you would tarry awhile and quest about. Part of the charm of this far-spread city that still clings to the 'compounds' of a decreasing number of 'garden houses', a city that is still open to the skies, even as steel and concrete and glass towers and concrete pillars keep rising at an ever increasing rate, even as underground burrowing goes on apace, a city that in some ways seems a rural town but which on every road reflects its committed consumerism, is its very history that is cloaked with an aura of romanticism and grandeur.

Madras still remains a green and airy city that is beloved of those who love the slower tempo of the life of the world of yesterday. It is a city of courtesy, charm and culture, where values of another day, another age, are still cherished amidst all the ever-increasing bustle of humdrum modern living. In Madras, the past, the present and the future, tradition and the status quo and progress, exist side by side in an atmosphere of charming tolerance and cherished understanding. Greed and road rage have in no way diminished it. As Diwan Bahadur S E Runganadhan, president of the Madras Tercentenary Celebration Committee, wrote in 1939,

"The scenes around the city's temple tanks and squares are still the same as those witnessed in distant days, the crowds which chatter in the Kotwal and Triplicane Bazaars are little different from their predecessors in earlier years, and the Madras fisherman still goes out in his frail craft to earn a hazardous and precarious living from the sea exactly as his forefathers did many centuries ago."

It is still true today, nearly 80 years later!

The Changing City

A visitor from England in 1879 described Madras as an overlapping of "five or six overgrown villages,"... "hardly a town." She noted that Madras was: Fort St George, with its "primeval government offices; Black Town, or Madras proper; a commercial quarter (this is North Beach Road and the area behind it); Mount Road, a district containing the principal European shops (as distinct from mercantile institutions), is at least 3 miles distant; and beyond this again are Nungambakkam and Adyar consisting of villas, the residences of many of the high temples. Besides these suburbs there are Mylapore and Triplicane, the latter inhabited chiefly by a Mussulman population; and San Thomé, an old Portuguese settlement; further again is St Thomas' Mount."

To see Madras aright one should approach it by sea, wrote an early Civil Servant a few years later. Around the turn of the century, as today, Madras beach was divided in two by Fort St George, the Beach Road north of it being the busiest part of the city. At the time this Civilian looked across this road from the sea, he saw facing him a row of impressive buildings: Bentinck's Building; *Parry and Co, near the High Court;* Arbuthnot and Co near the mole; the Mercantile Bank; Best & Co's handsome spread; the General Post Office; the Bank of Madras (later to be the Imperial Bank, forerunner of the State Bank of India) and a couple of others.

Writing of this time, Furneaux said in 1895, "Seen from the roadstead, the fort, a row of merchant's buildings...a few spires and public buildings are all that strike the traveller...(and) it is difficult to realise that this is one of the largest cities in India." In this "city of great distances," the merchant princes enjoyed a "stately semi-suburban life." Life was "very pleasant and passably healthy," with a sufficient number of social institutions "to oil the wheels of existence."

"Excellent houses (large comfortable mansions) in the pleasant residential suburbs"... (enable people) "to get as far as possible from their workaday surroundings. Huge compounds surround each house and separate it from the others and from the road. Some compounds were of a size where golf links may be laid. One is in a park of 43 acres, another in the centre of the ground which is half a mile from one boundary to the other." The roads had a "quiet beauty" about them, lined with large trees.

It was this city that was described in 1900 as a "very charming old lady, gowned in old silks and laces. She had, perhaps, known richer, more exciting days but she was neither physically decrepit nor financially pinched."

The commercial fortunes of Madras have changed approximately every hundred years with major events. From 1639 to about 1739 the advance of general trading prosperity was very rapid. Over the next century it had slowed appreciably. The first half of the third hundred-year period saw the slowing down process that began with the Industrial Revolution – and the consequent drop in the Madras textile export market – continue, but by the turn of the century commerce began to gather momentum. And from 1939, there has been a steady build-up on the solid foundations that were laid in the last years of the previous century. Since Independence the city has burgeoned. And since the 1990s, industry, undreamed of service and information technology sectors, education, consumerisum and entertainment facilities have all mushroomed in a geometrical progression of growth. Today Madras that is Chennai is indeed one of the boom cities of the world, its new symbol, the IT Highway (named Rajiv Gandhi Salai), has transformed the old Mahabalipuram road into one of the best roads in India with steel-and-glass highrise, as much as greenery, lining it and providing space and entertainment for thousands of the young working in IT, call centres and back offices serving the world.

But the founders are forgotten. There's not even a plaque anywhere in the city commemorating Francis Day and Beri Thimmappa, Andrew Cogan and Nagabattan, who together in 1639 built a small fort and never dreamed it would be anything more.

To this day, Fort St George, that fort built on a narrow spit of desolate sand on the surf-pounded, cyclone-prone Coromandel Coast, is not only the centre from which the main radial roads of Madras spread and lead on to the rest of India, but it is also the heart of the government of the State which the city is capital of. That is appropriate. For before Fort St George there was no Madras. And after it, the city that grew in and about it became the seed from which sprouted the history of a new India, the India of today.

In and around that fort that grew into a citadel and then the seat of governments, there lived, studied and worked generations of men who forged a nation from which grew an empire, but who, when the sun set on the empire, left behind the nation they had created. Clive and Charnock, Wellington and Hastings, Malcolm and Munro, Trevelyan and Bentinck, Lawrence and Rennell, Mackenzie and Cotton, Buchanan and Lambton, the roll call is unending of those whose first steps towards empire-building were taken here. And when their successors left, there was left the India we know but which generations past had known only in isolated fragments.

Mine is not a popular view of history. Perhaps it is because of the popular view that so little of that epic past is left. But what is left, can still stir those with a sense of history. Wander round the city and the ghosts of history are almost tangible, their presence a reminder of things past that created our present.

If Cogan and Day did not dream of a metropolis, neither did their successors. In fact, ~~70~~ 75 years ago no one seemed to either. My earliest memories, dating back then, are of a spread-out town of wide tree-lined roads, large 'garden houses', few people and a leisurely but gracious lifestyle where the chief entertainment was the beach. Certainly it had none of the aura associated with its Tamil name, Pattnam, used freely in its great rural hinterland; this was no bustling entrepôt, no major port-city; it may have been the capital of a vast Presidency that was nearly a quarter of the subcontinent, but nevertheless it was a place where everyone appeared to know everyone else.

Madras today, to the surprise of the generation of the 1930s, has grown into a metropolis, but it has still not been able to shake off its small town atmosphere. Life is still, for the most part, leisurely, gracious and gentle, even if industry and commerce have brought greater hustle and bustle. The saree and plaited, beflowered hair are still parts of the city scene, dhotis are still seen outside the workaday world. The symbols of religions are as much evident on persons as in buildings; nowhere is a place of worship more than a few minutes' walk away. The battle to keep a bit of greenery thriving in decreasing garden space is still valiantly fought. The beach is still a favourite outing and Test cricket with its leisured tempo is as much appreciated as the instant variety **that** *the Chennai Super Kings provided.*

So much is passing, so much changing in the present. But for all that, Madras continues to retain its eternal charm. Perhaps it is the lack of hurry, the absence of a feeling of harried competitiveness. Perhaps it is the intense feeling of religiosity that permeates the city and makes people gentler. Or perhaps it is just a passionate attachment to old world courtesies and traditions. Nothing symbolises the charm of Madras more than the marriage season, when the marriage halls are full of families in a rainbow of Kancheepuram silk finery; their faces and hands glittering with gold, diamonds and rubies; all participating in ancient rituals to the throb of drums and trill of wind instruments while the aroma of incense and camphor in woodfires mingles with that of a score of vegetable and sweet delicacies on plantain leaves in the neighbouring dining hall. And at the end of it all, the bridegroom in a new suit and his bride with a beauty salon look and in a traditional saree worn in more fashionable style greet the guests. Like them, Madras is the past that's also catching up with the present, where the Bharata Natyam dancer is as much at home on the Music Academy's stage as she is in the discos that are an established part of today's entertainment scene or the sambhar *and curd rice connoisseur at home is the gourmand in fine dining spaces that offer a plethora of international cuisine. But for all the change, the traditions of a conservative past and memories of glorious yesterdays remain an intrinsic part of the fabric of a city of today drawing up great plans for tomorrow.*

A Chronological
History of Madras

1522	Portuguese arrive on Coromandel Coast and seeds sown for ancient Mylapore to be pushed from shore and Fort San Thomé created by them over the next fifty years.
1547c	Luz Church built. Bleeding Cross discovered at St Thomas' Mount.
1611	English establish factory in Machilipatam.
1626	Armagon factory established by English.
1630s	Rule of Venkatapathi Raya of Chandragiri, the last capital of Vijayanagar. His governors of different parts of Tondaimandalam were the Damarla Nayaks – Venkatappa (Venkatadri), Ayyappa and Anka Bhupala, all brothers.
1639	Francis Day receives for English East India Company grant of 3 sq miles of land two miles north of San Thomé from Venkatadri Nayak after negotiations by Beri Thimmappa.
1640	Day arrives in Madras to establish settlement. Agency of Andrew Cogan begins. The factory in Madras named Fort St. George. Beri Thimmappa and colleagues establish 'Black Town' and the name Chennapatnam is first used there.
1642	Accession of Sriranga Raya in Chandragiri as Rajah of Vijayanagar.
–	Capuchins build in British territory the first church, St. Andrew's. (Had been allowed to conduct worship in the Fort from 1640.) Church of the Assumption of Our Lady (Portuguese Church) built in Black Town about the same time. First church established in Company 'territory' outside Fort St George.
1645	Henry Greenhill visits the Raya and obtains his *cowle*, confirming the Nayak's grant.

1646/1648	Earliest recorded gifts made to the Madras Town Temple by Nagabattan and Beri Thimmappa.
1652	The first caste dispute.
1662-72	San Thomé occupied by Golconda.
1664	First hospital established in the Fort. Was to grow into today's General Hospital.
1665	The first 'coup' in Madras. Governor Foxcroft deposed by Edward Winter.
1670s	Joint stock company of Indian merchants organised by Kasi Viranna, India's first.
1672	Governor Langhorne orders the systematic filing and maintenance of the Madras records. Develops into the State Archives.
	– San Thomé under French occupation until 1674.
1674	Dutch take over and deliver San Thomé to Golconda.
1675	Golconda destroys San Thomé's fortifications and Portuguese resettlement begins under Golconda dominion.
1676	English acquire Triplicane from Golconda.
1678	Governor Streynsham Master establishes the Court of Judicature.
	– Starts to build St Mary's Church in the Fort.
1680	St Mary's in the Fort consecrated.
1682	Embassy of Elihu Yale to Gingee secures Maratha permission for English settlements in Porto Novo and Cuddalore.
1682/3	Bank created in Madras by the Governor and Council to receive deposits. India's first 'modern' bank.
1686/87	Court of Admiralty established in Madras.
1687	Governorship of Elihu Yale begins. He hoists the flag of England, St George's Cross, on the main Fort bastion, replacing the Company flag. Ship's mast that was used as flagpole stood till 1994 when new metal mast was raised. Creates The Island.

1688	Inauguration of the Corporation of Madras; Nathaniel Higginson the first Mayor. Mayor's Court established, the oldest Municipal Corporation in British Commonwealth, outside Britain.
1689	Indian 'peons' of Madras organised into militia companies.
1692	English get the right to coin rupees in their mint from Prince Kam Baksh.
1693	Acquisition of Egmore, Purasawalkam and Tondiarpet.
1694/95	New *Fort House* built by Nathaniel Higginson in place of the inner citadel, which is then demolished. This remains the core of the Secretariat building in the Fort.
1697	Complete demolition of San Thomé's fortifications by Golconda.
1698	Thomas 'Pirate' Pitt made Governor. Develops The Island. Has drawn c. 1708 first official map of Madras. Ends Left Hand-Right Hand caste disputes.
1708	Acquisition of Tiruvottriyur, Nungambakkam, Vyasarpadi, Kattiwakam and Sattangadu.
1712	First Armenian church built in Old Black Town.
1713/14	Egmore Redoubt constructed.
1715	First *pucca* bridge from the Fort to The Island built.
	– St Mary's Charity School (nucleus of what is now known as St George's) founded, the first Western style school established in English territory in India.
1716	Society for Promoting Christian Knowledge set up in Vepery by Johann Grundler and looked after by Halle (Tranquebar) missionaries till 1836. First Protestant missionary activity in Madras.
1717	Governor Collet seizes Tiruvottriyur by force.
1720	Actual taking over of the administration of Egmore, Purasawalkam and Tondiarpet by the Council.
1726	Marmalong Bridge over the Adyar built by the Armenian merchant Coja Petrus Uscan.
1729	Opening of the grave of St Thomas on the beach at San Thomé.

1733	Preparation of a map of Madras and its surrounding villages by order of Governor Morton Pitt.
1734	Chintadripet (Weavers' Village) founded.
1742	Grant of Vepery, Perambur, Pudupakkam, Ernavore (Ennore) and Sadayankuppam to the English.
1746	Capitulation of English Madras to the French. Fort St David, Cuddalore, becomes the seat of the Presidency and seeds are sown for the Indian Army with the raising of the Carnatic and Circars Infantry (later the Madras Regiment). Battle of the Adyar River near San Thomé, with the Nawab of the Carnatic's troops heading to re-capture the Fort being routed by the French and their *sipahis*. French then occupy San Thomé.
1749	Rendition of Madras to the English under the Treaty of Aix la Chapelle. English also take over French-occupied San Thomé, which they had coveted from the 1680s.
1751	Clive returns to Madras from successful defence of besieged Arcot and becomes the Steward of Fort St George.
1752	Madras again becomes the seat of the Presidency.
1755	A survey map of Madras drawn by Conradi.
1757-83	Further strengthening and re-forming of Fort St George into its present shape.
1758	Siege of Fort St George by Comte de Lally.
1759	French abandon siege.
1760	Demolition of tombs in the old English burial ground. 'Old Black Town' razed. Esplanade created.
–	First major renovation of the Fort begins.
1761	The S P C K establishes the first printing press in Madras.
1766	New Town Temple consecrated in Peddanaickenpet.
1768c	Construction of *Chepauk Palace*.
1770	'New Black Town' walls completed.
1777	Vira Perumal Pillai appointed first Kotwal of markets.
1779	The first botanical garden developed by Dr James Anderson.

1780	Demolition of the houses and levelling of Hog Hill on the bank of North River opposite the Fort. Demolition also of parts of 'Old Black Town'.
1781c	Popham's Broadway developed.
	– Last vestiges of Hog Hill removed and the western esplanade of the Fort formed.
1786	A Medical Department under a Physician General established.
	– The Madras Post Office started and a postal service begins.
	– Formal Police force begins functioning.
1787	Dr Andrew Bell takes over the Charity School, where Dr Richard Kerr later introduced vocational education, and introduces the monitorial system of education.
1790	Fort Exchange opened. In time, to host on its roof Madras's first lighthouse.
1792	Madras Observatory established, first in British territory.
1794	Madras Survey School opens, the first modern technical school outside Europe. In time, it grows into College of Engineering, Guindy.
	– The Madras Lunatic Asylum founded.
1796	Recorder's Court created.
1800	First Anglican church outside the Fort established by the community, led by Dr. Kerr.
1802	*Banqueting Hall* (now *Rajaji Hall*) built.
1812	College of Fort St George founded.
1814-16	St George's Cathedral built.
1818-21	St Andrew's Kirk constructed.
1819	Ophthalmic Hospital founded. Becomes in time Regional Institute of Ophthalmology.
1826	Committee of Public Instruction instituted.
1829	Asiatic Society (1812) reconstituted as the Madras Literary Society.

1832	Madras Club founded.
	– Madras Railway mooted.
1835	Madras Medical School (subsequently Madras Medical College) established.
	– Agri-Horticultural Society founded.
1836	The Madras Chamber of Commerce established.
1837	John Anderson opens the General Assembly's School (subsequently Madras Christian College School).
1840	Ootacamund becomes the summer resort of the British and seat of the Governor. The practice ends shortly before Independence.
1841	The High School (subsequently Presidency College) opened.
1842	Pachaiyappa's Central Institution (subsequently Pachaiyappa's College) is started.
	– The University Board founded.
1843	Oakes & Co, the pioneering 'department store', starts business.
1844	Women and Children's Hospital opens. (Now the Institute of Obstetrics and Gynaecology and Child Health.)
	– The second lighthouse of Madras begins operation near the start of North Beach Road.
1846	Madras Cricket Club puts down roots.
1851	Government Museum started.
1855	Titular Nawabship of the Carnatic abolished and *Chepauk Palace* acquired by Government.
	– Department of Public Instruction created.
	– Public telegraph service started.
	– First zoo established in Madras in the Museum grounds.
1856	First railway line opened, from Madras (Royapuram) to Arcot.
	– Madras Trades Association formed.

1857	University of Madras is incorporated.
1858	The Madras Police is formalised as a service. W Robinson, of the Civil Service, becomes Inspector General of Police, the first in India.
1859	People's Park seeded by Governor Charles Trevelyan and developed by Governor William Denison.

-    Government Survey School (later College of Engineering) upgraded as Civil Engineering School.
-    Publishing of the first Carnatic music book, *Sangeetha Sarvartha Sara Sangrahamu*.

1861	A screw pile pier built for the harbour.

-    Civil Engineering School becomes College of Engineering.
-    The beginnings of a public library.

1862	V Sadagopacharlu, first Indian to be appointed to the Legislative Council of Madras.

-    First charter of the Madras High Court.

1866	Robert Chisholm begins work on new Public Works Department building.
1867	Oriental Manuscripts Library founded.
1868	*The Madras Mail* starts publication.
1869-73	Madras University's *Senate House* built.
1871	First Census of Madras.
1872	Protected water-supply for Madras.
1873	Cosmopolitan Club founded.

-    Central Station opened.

1876	Construction of the Buckingham Canal through Madras.

-    Construction of Madras Harbour started.

1877	The Royapuram Auxiliary Medical School – to grow into Stanley Medical College and Hospital – opened.

-    The Buckingham Mills established.

1878	*The Hindu* begins publication.

1882	The *Swadesamitran* (Tamil) starts publication. Soon becomes first Tamil daily newspaper.
	– The Carnatic Mills founded. (Amalgamated with Buckingham Mills in 1920.)
	– The first Telephone Exchange opens with 25 subscribers.
1883	Theosophical Society Headquarters established at *Huddlestone Gardens*.
1885	The Madras Gymkhana Club founded.
1887	The Indian National Congress meets in Madras for the first time.
	– Establishment of the first Carnatic music *sabha* – The Madras Jubilee Gayan Samaj.
1888	Madras United Club, first Indian club in Madras to play cricket, founded.
1889	Construction of the High Court buildings starts.
	– The Madras Advocates' Association is founded as the Vakils' Association, the first in India.
1892	High Court buildings inaugurated. Third lighthouse in dome atop its tallest tower (1894).
1895	First tramway in the city, India's first, inaugurated, continues till 1953.
1896	Connemara Public Library opens.
	– India's first Agricultural College opens in Saidapet. In time becomes Tamil Nadu Agricultural University based in Coimbatore.
1897	W E Smith & Co's *Kardyl Building* opens for business.
	– Sri Ramakrishna Mission Mutt started.
1898	Spencer's, with beginnings in 1864, becomes a public company. Spencer & Co in time becomes Asia's biggest department store chain, catering operation and hotelier, a status it enjoyed till Independence.

1900	Moore Market opened.
	– The oldest surviving music *sabha* – Sri Parthasarathy Swami Sabha – is founded.
1901	South India Athletic Association formed.
1905	Madras Port Trust created.
1907	Work on main sewerage system begins.
	– Indian Bank founded after the Arbuthnot & Co crash in 1906.
1910	Commencement of electric street lighting.
1911	Madras' first bioscope started in Popham's Broadway by Mrs Klug.
1913	Electric Theatre, City's first permanent cinema theatre, established on Mount Road.
	– *Ripon Building* opened as the Corporation's home.
1914	*Emden* shells Madras.
	– Queen Mary's College for Women, first women's college in Madras, opens.
1915	Women's Christian College started.
1924	The first radio broadcast.
1925	School of Indian Medicine established.
	– Loyola College opens.
1927	The tradition of the December Music Festival begins. First programme in conjunction with the All India Congress Session.
1928	The Music Academy is founded.
1932	Music Academy revives *Sadir* as Bharata Natyam.
1933	Mayoralty of Madras revived.
1936	Victory Memorial opened.
	– New University buildings completed.
	– Establishment of the International Centre for Arts, later to become Kalakshetra.

1937	Madras Christian College shifted to Tambaram.
1938	E V Ramaswami Naicker sows the seeds for Dravida Kazhagam (DK, 1944)
1939	Tercentenary of the founding of Madras City celebrated.
1947	A British-founded city becomes Indian.
1948	Fort Museum opened.
1949	Dravida Munnetra Kazhagam (DMK) formed after breaking with DK.
1958	Establishment of the first Industrial Estate in the country, at Guindy.
1967	C N Annadurai leads Dravida Munnetra Kazhagam to power and ushers in a new era of Tamil consciousness.
1969	Madras State is renamed Tamil Nadu.
1972	All India Anna DMK formed after breaking from DMK.
1977	First film star to head a government anywhere, M G Ramachandran, sworn in.
1988	Janaki Ramachandran becomes first woman Chief Minister of Tamil Nadu.
1996	Madras officially named Chennai.
	– Koyambedu Wholesale Market Complex opened and traditional Kothawal Chavadi in George Town closes down.
1997	Dr Ambedkar Law University inaugurated
	– Work starts on elevated Mass Rapid Transit System.
1998	MGR Medical University started.
2006	Mu Karunanidhi (DMK) becomes Chief Minister of Tamil Nadu for a record fifth time.
2009	Construction begins on Chennai Metro Rail.
2010	A new Secretariat and Legislature building is inaugurated to mark Mu Karunanidhi's 50 years of continuous service as a Legislator.

2011   J. Jayalalithaa (AIADMK), a Chief Minister for the
             fourth time, decides to move Secretariat and Legislature
             back to Fort St George and orders the new Secretariat
             building and campus to be developed as a hospital,
             medical complex and centre for the performing arts.

2013   The new Secretariat building inaugurated as a hospital.

2017   Kalaivanar Arangam, a centre for performing arts, gets
             its new home. Nearby, a VVIP guest house is built
             inspired by Sydney's *Opera House*.

2017   J. Jayalalithaa dies and her party is thrown into turmoil
             over a successor. Solution found considered temporary.

2018   Chennai Metropolitan area extended to become country's
             second biggest urban agglomeration.

Bibliography

Arulappa, R: *History of the Archdiocese of Madras and Mylapore*. The Archbishop, San Thomé, Madras, 1986.

Asylum Press: *Almanac & Directory*. Lawrence Asylum Press, 166 Mount Road, Madras, 1800-1920.

Baskaran, Theodore: *The Message Bearers*. Cre-A, Madras, 1982.

Bhandari, R.R.: *Southern Railway (1852-2003)*. Southern Railway, Chennai, 2003.

Chaudhary, Major R K (Ed.): *The Golden Milestone*. Isis Lifestyle, Delhi/Officers' Training Academy, Chennai, 2013.

Davies, Philip: *Splendours of the Raj*. John Murray, London, 1985.

Davies, Philip: *The Penguin Guide to Monuments of India*, Viking, London, 1989.

de Souza, F: *The House of Binny*, Binny Limited, 1959.

Foster, William: *The English Factories in the India 1634-36, 1637-41*. Oxford, 1911, 1912.

Guy, Randor: *History of Tamil Cinema*. Government of Tamil Nadu, Madras, 1991.

Guy, Randor: *Starlight, Starbright: The early Tamil Cinema*. Amra Publishers, Madras, 1997.

Hosten, s j, Rev H: *Antiquities from San Thomé and Mylapore*. The Diocese of Mylapore, Madras, 1936.

Higginbotham's: *Guide to the City of Madras*. Higginbotham's, Madras, 1903.

Kalpana, K and Schiffer, Frank: *Madras – The Architectural Heritage*. INTACH (Tamil Nadu Chapter), Madras, 2003.

Keay, John: *India Discovered*, Rupa, New Delhi, 1989.

Krishna, Nanditha & Doshi, Tishani: *Madras Then, Chennai Now*. Roli Books, New Delhi. 2013.

Lawson, C: *Memories of Madras*, Swan Sonneschein & Co., London, 1905.

Leighten, David: *Vicissitudes of Fort St George*. A J Cambridge & Co, Madras, 1902.

Love, Henry Davison: *Vestiges of Old Madras*. John Murray, London-Govt. of India, 1913.

Luker, Tom: *Some Records, 1857-1925*. Addison & Co Ltd., Madras, 1928.

Madras Tercentenary Celebration Committee: *The Madras Tercentenary Commemoration Volume*. Oxford, India, 1939.

M Ct M Chidambaram Trust: *The Unfinished Journey*. The M.Ct.M.C. Trust, Madras, 2004.

Metcalf, Thomas R: *An Imperial Vision: Indian Architecture and Britain's Raj*. University of California, Berkley, U.S.A., 1989.

Molony, J. Chartres: *A Book of South-India*. Asian Educational Services (Reprint), New Delhi, 2004.

Munro, W T: *Madrasiana*. Caleb Foster, Madras, 1868.

Muthiah, S: *Parrys 200* – With N.S. Ramaswami (EID Parry & Co, 1988), *Getting India on the Move* (Simpson & Co, 1990), *A Planting Century* (UPASI, 1993), *The Spencer Legend* (Spencer & Co, 1997), *The Spirit of Chepauk* (Madras Cricket Club, 1998), and *Looking Back from Moulmein* (East-West Books (Madras), Chennai, 2000). Also *The Ace of Clubs,* (The Madras Club, 2002), *150 Years of Excellence* and *A Work of Excellence* (University of Madras, 2006), *Overcoming Challenge* (Chennai Port Trust, 2007), *The Raj Bhavans of Tamil Nadu* (South Zone Cultural Centre, Thanjavur, 2009) and *Down by the Adyar* (Madras Boat Club, 2010).

Muthiah, S: *Madras – The Gracious City* (A pictorial documentation). Murugappa Group-Affiliated East-West Books, Madras, 1989.

Muthiah, S (Ed.): *Madras/Chennai: A 400-year record of the First City of Modern India* (Volume I: The Law, The People and Their Governance). Palaniappa Brothers, Chennai, 2008.

Muthiah, S: *Madras – Its Past and its Present* (Revised). Murugappa Group- East-West Books, Chennai, 2011.

Muthiah, S: *A Madras Miscellany: A Decade of People, Places and Potpourri*. East-West Books, Chennai, 2011.

Muthiah, S (Ed.): *Madras/Chennai: A 400-year record of the First City of Modern India* (Volume II: Services, Education & The Economy). Palaniappa Brothers, Chennai, 2012.

Muthiah, S : *Tales of Old and New Madras* (Revised). East West, Chennai 2014

Muthiah, S (Ed.): *Madras/Chennai: A 400-year record of the First City of Modern India* (Volume III: Communication, Culture & Entertainment). Palaniappa Brothers, Chennai, 2017.

Narasiah, K R A: *Madraspattinam* (Tamil). Palaniappa Brothers, Chennai, 2006.

Narasimhan, C: *Me and My Times*. Distributed by Radna Corporation, Hyderabad, 1986.

Narasimhan, K L: *Madras City – A History*. Rachana, Madras, 1968.

Nirmal, C J: *Madras Perspectives*. The Institute of Indian and International Studies, Madras, 1992.

Parthasarathy, R: *A Hundred Years of The Hindu*. Kasturi & Sons, Madras, 1978.

Penny, Mrs Frank: *Fort St George*. Swan Sonneschein & Co Ltd, London, 1900.

Penny, Rev Frank: *The Church in Madras* (3 vols.), Smith Elder & Co, London, 1904 & 1912 and John Murray, London, 1922.

Playne, Someret: *Southern India*. The Foreign and Colonial Compiling and Publishing Co, London, 1915.

Rajah, N L: *The Madras High Court – A 100-year Journey from a Crown Court to a People's Court*. C. Sitaram & Co., Chennai. 2012.

Rajaraman, D: *Chennai through the Ages*. Poompozhil Publishers, Chennai, 1997.

Raman, K.V.: *The Early History of the Madras Region*. The C.P. Ramaswami Aiyar Foundation, Chennai, 1959 (Reprint 2008).

Ramaswami, N S: *The Founding of Madras*. Orient Longman, Madras, 1977.

Samy, A. Ma.: *History of Tamil Journals (19th Century)* (Tamil). Navamani Pathippakam, Chennai 2000.

Sathasivam, Kumaran: *Campaghines – IIT (M) through IITian Eyes*. Indian Institute of Technology (Madras), Chennai. 2011.

Seshadri, R K: *A Swadeshi Bank from South India 1907-1962*. Indian Bank, Madras, 1982.

Spear, T G P: *The Nabobs*. Humphrey Milford, Oxford, 1932.

Srinivasachariar, C S: *Madras 1639-1939*. P Varadachary & Co, Madras, 1939.

Sriram, V: *Carnatic Summer, Lives of Twenty Two Exponents*. East-West Books (Madras), Chennai, 2004.

Sriram, V: *The Devadasi and the Saint: the Life and Times of Bangalore Nagarathnamma*. East-West Books (Madras), Chennai, 2007.

Sriram, V: *Historic Residences of Chennai*. Kalamkriya, Chennai, 2008.

Sriram, V: *Four Score and More: A History of the Music Academy, Madras*. The Music Academy, Chennai, 2009.

Sriram, V: *Championing Enterprise: 175 years of the Madras Chamber of Commerce and Industry*. MCCI, Chennai, 2011.

Sriram, V; *The Rane Story: A Journey in Excellence*. The Rane Group of Companies, Chennai, 2011.

Swami Raghaveshananda: *Temples of Madras City*. Sri Ramakrishna Mutt, Madras, 1990.

The Hindu, for whom Kamala Ramakrishnan took a long look at the Old Madras landscape and to whose database S Muthiah's columns 'Madras Miscellany' and 'Madrascapes' and Sriram V's contributions added much, *The Madras Times, The (Madras) Mail,* the *Indian Review,* to which R A Padmanabhan made many noteworthy contributions on Madras, *The Indian Express,* Madras, for whom N S Ramaswami long followed the fortunes of Madras and Cricket and Harry Miller took a second look at the city, *Madras Musings,* which keeps looking nostalgically at The Old and also features The New, and numerous privately published biographies and commemorative volumes.

Varma, Amit: *The Pioneer Peacekeepers: The Tamil Nadu Police – 150 years*. Tamil Nadu Police, Chennai, 2009.

Wheeler, J Talboys: *Madras in the Olden Time*. Higginbotham's, Madras, 1882.

Index

www.ingramcontent.com/pod-product-compliance
Lightning Source LLC
Chambersburg PA
CBHW021208130626
46554CB00004B/1128